THE
SAMMY DAVIS, JR.,
READER

THE

SAMMY

DAVIS, JR.,

READER

EDITED AND WITH AN INTRODUCTION BY

GERALD EARLY

FARRAR, STRAUS AND GIROUX

NEW YORK

Farrar, Straus and Giroux
19 Union Square West, New York 10003

Copyright © 2001 by Gerald Early
All rights reserved
Distributed in Canada by Douglas & McIntyre Ltd.
Printed in the United States of America
First edition, 2001

Library of Congress Cataloging-in-Publication Data
The Sammy Davis, Jr., reader / edited and with an introduction
by Gerald Early.
p. cm.
ISBN 0-374-25383-8 (alk. paper)
1. Davis, Sammy, 1925–90. I. Early, Gerald Lyn.

PN2287.D322 S25 2001
792.7'028'092—dc21

00-049515

Special thanks to my research assistants, Autumn Modest and Jason Vest.

Designed by Jonathan D. Lippincott

To Ida,

a dancer of many dances

and a singer of many songs

CONTENTS

SAMMY DAVIS, JR.

○

I

RAGGED DICK AND FAUST

The thing to do is to exploit the meaning of the life you have.
—Ralph Ellison in *Conversations with Ralph Ellison*, 1960

Why must I always keep proving myself? . . . Why must I always prove
what I'm not before I can prove what I am?
—Sammy Davis, Jr., *Yes I Can*

When Sammy Davis, Jr.'s, oldest and only biological child,
Tracey, turned five, he promised her that he would be home in
time for her birthday party. Hours passed by, the partygoers
came and went, Davis did not show up. In fact, his daughter did
not see him until the next day, when he apologized for failing to
appear. He handed her an envelope that contained her birthday
gift. Later, Davis and his wife, Swedish actress May Britt, had a
heated exchange about his broken promise to his daughter. Britt
was especially annoyed that Davis did not come to his daughter's
birthday party because he was carousing with his Rat Pack buddies. Davis himself shrugged it off, saying that Tracey "would
have other birthdays." When she opened the envelope that her
father had given her, she found one hundred dollars. "He
couldn't even go out and buy something special for his daughter," Tracey wrote in her autobiography, *Sammy Davis, Jr.: My
Father*, "or even ask one of his assistants to select a gift . . . And
so he reached into his pocket and pulled out a $100 bill."[1]

A $100 bill is a strange gift, even for a neglectful father, to give a five-year-old child. What could she possibly do with it? But when Davis was five years old, he was already performing with his father and Will Mastin; his relationship with money and his understanding of it were formed in an entertainer's world of boom and bust times. Davis's mother, Elvera Sanchez—a Puerto Rican dancer—was also a member of the Will Mastin Gang, although she did not participate in the rearing of Davis. She and Sam Davis, Sr., broke up two years later after having a second child, a daughter named Ramona who was not reared with Davis, Jr. "I was in show business by the time I was two years old . . . Most kids have a choice of what they want to be—I guess you could call it a misery of choice. Not me. No chance to be bricklayer or dentist, dockworker or preacher—I guess I was meant for show business even before I was born," he said in an interview with Roy Newquist.[2] One is struck here not simply by Davis's sense of predestination but by his comfort with his fate. Show business makes him a different order of being from people with more mundane occupations. Even as a kid, Davis liked to throw money around, the few times he had any. He describes such an instance in Yes I Can, his first autobiography, when he tried to impress a group of unfriendly neighborhood boys by buying several dollars' worth of baseball cards, then proceeded to humiliate himself by trading away the most valuable ones. (Davis knew nothing about baseball or any sport as a child or as an adult.)[3]

What killed Davis's highly publicized marriage to Britt—according to his account in his second autobiography, Why Me?, and according to his daughter's book—was that she wanted a conventional bourgeois life and he had no fundamental understanding or appreciation of what that was. He could collect, but he could not save; he enjoyed instant gratification and found bourgeois morality hypocritical and unrewarding. He could be extraordinarily generous with his time and his money but he could only really give himself in the context of a stage act, in relation to an audience. Everything else provided sensation, varying jolts to the nervous system; nothing but the act provided meaning. Shirley MacLaine was right when she wrote about Davis: "He had been cultivated and nourished in the spotlight since he was three years old. He was only at home when the spotlight was on. So his sense of his life was BIG and theatrical, because that's what was real to him."[4]

On the one hand, we might dismiss the entire story of the missed birthday as typical of an overly hardworking father who had little interest in filling his leisure time with domestic activities. On the other hand, the incident reflects Davis's twin passions: his candid, tense passion about his work and his career, and his equally tense but exquisitely wrought fixation on himself as the only important person to himself. In a 1966 interview, Davis said, "I'm not Sammy Glick [the cruel and unscrupulous anti-hero of Budd Schulberg's 1941 bestselling novel, *What Makes Sammy Run*], stepping on people, destroying people. Why should you be put down because you're ambitious, because you want to succeed—so long as you're not hurting anybody? Jesus! Is it criminal to have drive?"[5] It is true that malice never seemed to form a part of Davis's character. His climb to the top was relentless, not brutal; obsessive, not pathological; self-inventive, not power hungry.[6] Clearly, Tracey found her father's drive the most dominant facet of his personality: "It would be easy to dismiss Dad as merely a workaholic. But he was more than that. He couldn't just be good; he had to be great. He couldn't just fulfill a contract; he had to give 300 percent. And each success just made him crave more . . . Dad was so focused on making it and staying on top that he had no idea about half the things that were going on in his life. By the time he was able to look up, everything he had truly loved—besides entertainment—had changed or was harmed in some way."[7] This, too, was true.

The obvious question to ask about Sammy Davis, Jr., is what made Sammy run. It is, alas, too obvious, and several journalists have asked the question in just that way over the years, describing Davis as a variant of that familiar mid-century type: the salesman sweating to get a promotion, the hustler ingratiating himself with the boss while cutting his colleagues. Yet Sammy Davis is right. He was never Sammy Glick. His insecurity and ambition transcended the rise of the salesman, the exertions of the hustler, to make Davis a profound symbol of the complexities of American success and American liberalism. What made him interesting, aside from his enormous talent— which, much to his chagrin, was probably not enough by itself to make him interesting for as long as he was interesting to the American public—was that he was so publicly desperate as a Negro. This desperation, so naked, so dramatic, so often self-serving, made his Jewish conversion seem understandable, even appropriate, to many people. There are two things that frighten the gentile about the Jew: that the Jew wishes to be Jewish and alien, and, more chillingly, that the Jew does not wish to be Jewish and does not wish to be alien but to be absorbed. For many people, it made perfect sense for him to identify with another group that was often despised for its desperateness to fit in, to erase itself, to assimilate.

By becoming a Jew, Davis came to personify the crisis of postwar American liberalism in its quest to sanctify equality and merit, difference and assimilation, rebellion and conformity, all as expressions of democratic values. As both a Jew and a black, Davis represented the two groups that were fighting the hardest for liberalism in postwar America, or, rather, were fighting hardest for their own version of the liberal state. When this uneasy coalition, with its myth of cross-cultural cooperation, failed to make a liberal state that would suit the ends of both groups, some liberal Jews then insisted that only a color-blind state could support true liberalism, while some liberal blacks took up the quasi-nationalist or quasi-deconstructionist position that only a state that continued to acknowledge the political significance of the absurd color code it created could support true liberalism. This difference was inevitable since, after all, most American Jews were white and very few American blacks were Jews. Davis never thought about these questions in such an abstract way; he spent his life torn by what Jews had and by what blacks wanted.

To many, Davis's public desperation for acceptance, for success, appeared unseemly, tasteless, and cowardly underneath its guise of defiance. For instance, Sammy Davis, Jr., as a Jew (a conversion that some thought he made simply because he hung around so many Jews in the show business world and wanted to penetrate what seemed a powerful and influential clique that had transformed stigma into exclusivity) showed, to some minds, that only a Negro could be *that* desperate not to be a Negro. A preoccupation with racial self-hatred appears repeatedly in Davis's interviews of the 1950s and 1960s, and suffuses *Yes I Can*. On the other hand, it is worth noting that Ian Fleming, the creator of James Bond and a man who had some considerably racist notions, wished to return to this world as Sammy Davis, Jr. ("He's the most incredibly gifted man I've ever seen . . . ," Fleming said.)[8] As a public figure, Sammy Davis, Jr., was a puzzle to himself; people loved him unconditionally and despised him violently. But this was only a reflection of how he felt about himself.

The question—what made Sammy run?—remains, even today, a real question about an inescapably real man, who seemed both larger than life and not large enough for the life he wanted or perhaps for the life he deserved—if it is possible to speak in any useful way about people deserving a particular life. At the height of his career, he was arguably the most famous black man in the United States, his only possible rivals being Martin Luther King and Muhammad Ali. By the mid-1960s, Davis was a Broadway star (having headlined in *Mr. Wonderful* and *Golden Boy*, unmemorable shows with respectable runs); a successful recording artist, with signature tunes like "The Birth of the Blues" and "Who Can I Turn To (When Nobody Needs Me)"; a movie and television actor so big and so widely accepted that he could appear, for instance, on *The Patty Duke Show* playing himself, something that no other black actor, no matter how accomplished or famous, could do at the time; the host of his own television variety show; one of the biggest nightclub acts in history, earning more money than any other black act in the country, almost as much as Sinatra; a bestselling autobiographer, whose book, *Yes I Can*, was one of the most widely read of its time, read by far more people than the autobiography of any other black person except possibly that of Malcolm X; an ardent civil rights activist who attended the March on Washington and the second Selma march, and did innumerable benefits for the cause. (In the mid-1960s, Davis was donating over $100,000 annually to various civil rights and charitable causes, and performed in so many benefits that he collapsed from nervous exhaustion.)[9] Despite these considerable achievements, instead of being loved by blacks, many of whom weigh the achievements of their heroes by quantity or the shrillness of their racial rhetoric rather than by importance, he was largely despised as an Uncle Tom and a sellout. He was the butt of jokes, an object of blatant disrespect. Davis never stopped trying to gain acceptance from African Americans; yet, as he wrote in *Why Me?*: "I was a member of the black race but not the black community."[10] In his 1966 *Playboy* interview, Davis said, fervently: "I would voluntarily *die* to have my own people love me as much as they love some of those goddamn phonies they think are doing so much fighting for civil rights!"[11] Yet Davis at times seemed willing, even grateful, to define himself as an outsider, more fixated on himself than his group, as when he said in *Yes I Can*: "I wish I could say I live my life as a crusade, it would be nice to get medals like 'He's a champion of his people.' But, what I do is for me. Emotionally, I'm still hungry and let's face it, paupers can't be philanthropists. I can't do anybody else much good until I get *me* straightened out."[12] This was a crucial contradiction but far from the only significant one that defined the man.

Davis was clearly disciplined and dedicated to his craft, yet he was subject to bouts of debauchery and dissipation that nearly wrecked his life and threatened to compromise his career. For instance, he spent periods of his life hanging out with the denizens of the hard-core porn industry and with practitioners of Satanism. He even suggested marriage to porn star Linda Lovelace when she was at the height of her career, cruising Hollywood and Las Vegas as a sex toy for the rich and famous. By Lovelace's account, Davis was not deterred by the fact that he was married to Altovise Gore at the time or that Lovelace was married to Chuck Traynor,[13] or by how scandalous it would be, how much of a joke he would become before his public, how much he would embarrass his family, by marrying a woman he later described as "telling stories that were obviously the product of a tortured mind that has been pushed, as I understand she admits, across the boundaries of fantasy by a life of abuse and humiliation."[14] Davis, according to Lovelace, performed the act of fellatio on Traynor, much to the latter's discomfort, to see how it felt to "deep throat" someone, and, predictably, faced public humiliation when Lovelace told all in her controversial autobiography. He was the subject of another tell-all graphic sex article by Kathy McKee that appeared in *Penthouse* in September 1991. Davis had died a year earlier, so was spared further embarrassment.

He was addicted to tobacco and alcohol, each of which handicapped him onstage and caused severe health problems. And for a considerable time in his middle age, he was a regular user of cocaine, a habit that his good friend Frank Sinatra found so unspeakably déclassé that Sinatra refused to talk to him for several years:

" . . . I was into other shit that was destructive, like coke. Now, Frank, he never did drugs. Frank's drug was wild women. Safer but no less dangerous, I used to tell him."

In the next three years, Frank and Sammy only saw each other occasionally at cocktail parties, and even then it was just a curt hello and goodbye between them. "I missed my friend," said Sammy. "But I'd just go home, do some more coke, and be fine. I'd said, 'Yeah, well screw Sinatra, if he can't let me live my own life. Least I got my cocaine.' "[15]

Davis wrote in *Why Me?*: "That he [Sinatra] was disappointed in me was an ache around my heart."[16]

On the other hand, unlike certain jazzers like Charlie Parker and Billie Holiday or any number of rock musicians, Davis never allowed his dissipation to prevent him from performing, although it often threatened to do so. In his professional life, despite an almost inhumanly grueling schedule, he hardly ever missed a show. Yet his drug use and debauchery often made his performing life more difficult, sometimes an embarrassment, as when once Davis, at the O'Keefe Center in Toronto, high on inadvertently eating some marijuana-laced brownies given to him by some drugged-out kids he was hanging around with, came out and sang one song, thought he had done an entire show, said good night to the audience, and walked off the stage.[17] He was too embarrassed to return once he realized what he had done. As Davis got further into the drug scene, he became more and more uneasy about being surrounded by strangers. Davis wrote in *Hollywood in a Suitcase*: "I woke up one morning and discovered the house full of people I hardly knew. I was disgusted with myself and with them. People were flocking to the house for a free turn-on. I would go off to do a show, feeling awful, and come back to find them all still there."[18] Yet as Davis said in an interview, ". . . I was afraid to be alone with me, because *I didn't like me. I never liked me offstage, man.*"[19] It is, of course, the curse of a star to be surrounded by strangers who give the appearance of being friends because they are so willing to provide the most intimate favors. All his life, Davis had difficulty distinguishing between healthy curiosity and perverse license. And like most show business people, he simply did not care to distinguish, much of the time, between who was really his friend and who was using him. Like most show business stars, Davis alternated between feeling that it was a perquisite of his stardom to use the people around him and feeling a cynical paranoia toward everyone outside his inner circle.

Davis embodied, quite consciously, a kind of Faustian typology—seeking knowledge and experience at whatever cost—because he had decided in his youth that life was the intense accumulation of moments when one felt most alive or when one was most flouting convention and safety. In this way, life—drug-taking, sex, partying, performance—was a series of sensations that continued until he became either numbed or bored by them. This Faustian consciousness was inseparable from his sense of himself as a Horatio Alger archetype—a poor boy who has achieved, through his own dogged efforts of work and accommodation, great success—for he constantly excused his Faustian excesses, at times by claiming the deprivations of his youth, at other times by just claiming that he earned bouts of self-indulgence because he had worked hard. "I've worked hard, baby, and I still want to enjoy the pleasures and the luxuries of life. *Nobody* enjoys luxuries more than I do," Davis said in 1966.[20]

Nothing better illustrates this need for sensation and the necessity to acknowledge hard work than Davis's attitude toward money. He made large sums of money throughout his life yet was always broke; his appetites, his need for the grand gesture, far outstripped whatever he made, whether it was $5,000 a week with the Will Mastin Trio in the early 1950s or $175,000 a week as a Las Vegas star in the 1970s. Once, in the 1970s, he bought $60,000 in furs for his mother, his mother-in-law, and his mother-in-law's friend—a woman he did not know—simply because they visited his dressing room. During one of his Vegas runs, he picked up the entire tab for his audience when he gave what he felt was a subpar performance. In 1980, he gave a $75,000 "party of the decade" for four hundred of his Hollywood chums to show the world that he wasn't broke when, in fact, he was.[21] (It is worth noting that Davis continued to divide his salary evenly with his father and Will Mastin from the late 1950s, when the trio broke up, until he reached a settlement with Mastin in the early 1970s; he continued to support his father until the latter's death in 1988. In other words, for most of his life, Davis took home just one third of what he earned.) Even his philanthropy was a form of excessive, fanciful spending: "I've never kept track of it," he said in 1980 in response to a question about his charitable giving. "I'm talking now about the legitimate bread, and also the rip-off bread—and the rip-off bread would probably equal the legitimate bread. But again, you know, it's like you do what you've got to do based on what you feel your obligation is. I've given a lot of money to the UJA [United Jewish Appeal] as well. I put up $75,000 in Vegas to bail the Indians out. Sometimes I'll pick up a paper and read something and send money to destitute people. How much does it all add up to? I don't know, but it's seven figures or more."[22] His appetite for spending was liberating in a way, adolescent in yet another way, but, finally, tragic: the poor boy, in trying to compensate for the poverty of his youth, merely enslaves himself to his own caprices and to his need to compensate. This self-indulgence produced anxiety over his failure to pay bills, forcing him to take more club dates to make money, which produced stress that could only be relieved by more whimsical self-indulgence. With his cars, clothes, jewelry, photographic equipment, and other toys of all sorts, and his expensive gifts for friends and strangers, Davis was both a product and a reflection of the popular culture of the era of his fame, the age of household gadgetry, the luxuriating playboy, and the expanding preoccupation with the self as an object and artifact of one's own desire. Because he celebrated his own conspicuous consumerism so publicly—at times, so crassly—Davis was often condemned for superficiality, for being as fake as the world he inhabited. He fought this condemnation with the twin weapons of respectability in American culture: excessive hard work and overbearing sincerity, a strategy all the more maudlin and rebellious because he was so terribly self-conscious about being a Negro, something he could no more help than any other Negro. His belief in the power of sincerity caused him to do what many other artists have done: equate emotion and reality, as James Conaway pointed out in an article about Davis in *The New York Times Magazine* in 1974.[23] Davis always thought that the more emotionally direct or honest he was, the more real he was—less defined, imprisoned, or controlled by his fame, his possessions, his needs. Like many famous people, he had a great need to be "liked for himself," as the expression goes, or to be understood on what he felt were his own terms. This is probably why he was such a confessional personality and wrote two autobiographies and gave numerous soul-baring interviews.

Davis was convinced that his looks were inadequate. They had been a source of ridicule since his early childhood, when a little girl he liked drew a picture of him with the caption UGLY. He was short (5' 3''), his nose had been broken three times in fights with racist whites, his head was slightly misshapen, and to top it all off, he lost his left eye in an automobile accident. As he wrote in *Yes I Can*: "I set a stack of my own albums on the record player. I put on a silk robe with a large 'SD Jr.' monogrammed across the breast pocket. Then I walked behind the bar and faced myself in the mirror; I ran my finger slowly along the scar which circled the bridge of my nose, I touched the eyelid that was drooping like a dope addict's. You're ugly. You've got nothing going for you except your talent and the fact that you're a star . . . Say it every day: you're *ugly*."[24] But he was, of course, vain. After all, in this confessional passage, while looking Dorian Gray–like at his own image in the mirror, he is also listening to his own records. (Incidentally, one of the first books Davis remembers reading when he began to educate himself while in the army, with the help of a sympathetic sergeant,[25] was Oscar Wilde's *The Picture of Dorian Gray*, a novel that seems to haunt Davis's first autobiography, *Yes I Can*, in its symbols and themes. In *Why Me?*, he refers to the Oscar Wilde character when talking about his involvement with Satanism: "Evil fascinated me. I felt it lying in wait for me. And I wanted to taste it. I was ready to accept the wildness, the rolling in the gutter, and having to get up the next morning and wash myself clean. Whenever I had, being a bit of Dorian Gray, I'd look at myself in the mirror and it was 'Heh-heh, I got away with that. Now, what lies ahead tomorrow?' "[26]) He was intensely proud of his slim dancer's body; he was, until he formed an alcoholic's potbelly in the seventies as a result of a damaged liver, a small, fine-boned man, lithe, nearly athletic. Still photos of him as Sportin' Life in the 1959 film version of *Porgy and Bess*, with his skintight costume (the wardrobe mistress firmly instructed him to wear no underwear[27]), reveal the quintessential Davis: the sexy, attractive, viscerally physical performer. Davis, moreover, was egotistical about being ugly. As he said in an interview: "I know I'm dreadfully ugly, one of the ugliest men you could meet, but ugliness, like beauty, is something you must learn how to use. All my life I've resisted the temptation to be a little less ugly, to have my nose fixed, for example . . . Maybe, if I'd had my nose fixed, I'd have become almost passable. But what does being passable make you? It makes you mediocre: neither ugly nor handsome. Complete ugliness, utter ugliness, like mine, though, is almost attractive. Yes, yes, I'm convinced that a really ugly man, in the end, seems attractive."[28]

The self-consciousness he felt about his looks seemed to intensify his social life, not lessen it. Inasmuch as Davis and his audience thought his ugliness a mark of perverse or negative distinction, his looks became a symbol, not just of his self-pitying victimhood but of his individuality and his rebellion. In this way, his marriage to blond actress May Britt might be seen both as the thumbing of the nose at social conventions of the day (I will marry whom I please no matter who likes it or who doesn't!) and as a desperate plea for acceptance (I can't believe the blond goddess wants to marry ugly, short, black, one-eyed me!). As with everything else Davis did, there was something at once defiant and self-loathing in his marriage to Britt. In a 1964 interview, he remarked: "And why shouldn't I have married a white woman? Because it's against the rules, obviously. What rules? *The* rules, Sammy. Rules? I've never gone by rules set by other people; I've always felt that they don't count for anything, rules, if your own conscience doesn't want to accept them." In the same interview, he continued: ". . . I said to myself no, she can't love me, there's no future in it, Sammy, don't even think about it, you're ugly, you're black, you've only got one eye, you've got a broken nose, and she looks like a fairy . . . And then I discovered that she loved me, that there was a future in it even though I was black and ugly and had only one eye and a broken nose." The interview concluded: "With my one eye I found my wife and married her. With my one eye I have made her the mother of our children: me so black, her so white, me so ugly, her so beautiful. God, isn't she extraordinary, my beautiful wife? Look, what a woman! Look! With one eye I got her, with one eye! And it doesn't matter to her at all that I only have one eye, not to her it doesn't."[29] It is hard to tell whether he married May Britt as an act of pure defiance, because he was told by society he couldn't and shouldn't, or if he married her because he saw her whiteness simply as a kind of social prize and fetish. As he said years later, after they had divorced: "I can argue with her on the telephone. I'll say, 'Will you get off my back about that?' But [May and I] never had that kind of give and take on an equal basis before because I was too busy being a martyr married to a White woman."[30]

Britt put it this way in explaining why she married Davis:

Sammy and I are complete opposites in physical build— as anyone can plainly see. But I think he's a beautiful man—that nose looks just great. It gives him character. And he's so beautiful inside. You can sit down and talk to him and he's so understanding.

He's not a saint—far from it. Sometimes he is completely impossible. But I am not out to revolutionize him.

Nor am I out to revolutionize the world. I just married the man I love.[31]

Davis was a man of no formal education.[32] Even as a child, he never attended school. Yet he was drawn to the religion of the book, Judaism. Becoming a Jew certainly did not endear him to blacks, many of whom saw his conversion as an eccentric act of assimilation. After all, he did not become a *black* Jew, did not proclaim being a Jew in some defiantly racialist and nationalist sense because the Jews were originally black people (as many black people are taught in their homemade Afrocentric centers of learning—churches, barbershops, beauty parlors, protest rallies, and the like). More than a few American blacks who have become Jews have made this claim. And since so many Jews in vaudeville, then in Hollywood, who happened also to be white, surrounded him and Jews were open to him and supportive of him, it was thought that he became a Jew merely to become more white or merely in tribute to a people who had helped him. (Davis made a point of saying in a 1960 *Ebony* article that he talked to many Jewish friends before converting: "But don't get the impression I wanted to become a Jew because these great guys who helped me were Jewish. It was just a coincidence."[33]) But if it was the case that Davis became a Jew merely for opportunistic reasons or as an expression of black self-hatred, then it would be odd to assimilate by taking on one troubled stigma, being a Jew, to erase another, being black. To be sure, he found Judaism more open to him simply because Jews themselves tended to accept him. (This would explain, in part, why Davis was never inclined, despite all the help given him by Frank Sinatra, to become Catholic in imitation of Italian Americans, who surely would not have been, as a group, as open to him.[34]) Perhaps part of what attracted Davis to Judaism was that the situation of American Jews, as a group—caught between acceptance and separation, between assimilation and a highly pronounced group consciousness, between a hunger for mainstream success and a contempt for the mainstream—mirrored with great accuracy Davis's own feelings about himself. Moreover, from Davis's own account of the considerable reading he did before his conversion, it seems safe to say that he was drawn to Judaism instead of, say, the Protestant sects to which most

African Americans have affiliation, and which value high emotion as the sign of authentic religious experience, because rational choice and intense study were the signs of Jewish conversion.

Whatever spiritual reasons compelled Davis to become a Jew, Judaism must have satisfied Davis's sense of himself as an autodidact. Because he was self-taught in so many respects or acquired his learning through copying others instead of being given formal instruction, his conversion became another exercise of self-invention, bypassing educational authority. Judaism permitted him to make up a religion (in the conversations with his rabbi that he provides in *Yes I Can*, Davis seems willfully to misread the religion) while being part of an established, ancient, religious community. As he tells one rabbi:

> I love the attitude that man is made in God's image and that he has unlimited potential, and that "In God's world all things are possible." I love the idea that we can reach for the brass ring and we can keep stretching until we're tall enough to reach it. This has been my thinking all my life and it's a joy to open a book and see that not everybody puts different people in separate cubbyholes and looks at them like "How dare they" if they try to break out. And there's none of the things I hate, like "Well, it's up to fate," and "If it's meant to be." I admire an attitude of: it is meant to be if you'll go out and get it done. I love your thinking about not waiting around for a Messiah to come and straighten everything out, that the Messiah is not an individual but mankind collectively and that it's up to them to create the kind of a world that'll be like a Kingdom of Heaven right here.[35]

Davis has created a Judaism that simply confirms what he has been thinking all his life.

Becoming a Jew intensified Davis's interest in books, and he became an inveterate reader.[36] Although he was not, by most standards, a literary man, he cultivated a taste and appreciation for film and the aesthetics of popular culture that was as rich as it was wide. At the time of his death in 1990, Davis had seen a large number of Hollywood and foreign films (he claimed to have watched at least a film a day for nearly his entire adult life; May Britt described early dates with Davis in this way: "Sammy had all his movies with him, so we stayed up every night watching them until almost dawn"[37]), including a great deal of unreleased footage, and visited hundreds of film sets, here and abroad, mainstream and pornographic—more than any film scholar can claim. He possessed a large collection of books; he knew large swaths of theatrical history, both vaudeville and Broadway; he was learned in the history of blacks and American popular entertainment. Davis could have made a living as a kind of pop culture analyst or commentator, if he had wanted to. As his book *Hollywood in a Suitcase* demonstrates, he could talk with great charm and considerable trenchant legitimacy about the arts.

Indeed, there were relatively few who could speak more authoritatively about American popular culture since World War II. Davis knew well such a variety of its major players: Frank Sinatra and Jimi Hendrix, Judy Garland and Marilyn Monroe, Humphrey Bogart and James Brown, John Wayne and Maulani Ron Karenga, Martin Luther King and Clint Eastwood, Cholly Atkins and Berry Gordy, Marlon Brando and Count Basie. And he saw so much of it unfold directly under his gaze: the rise of Las Vegas (where he was one of the first blacks to perform after World War II) and the advent of blaxploitation films (a genre in which, surprisingly, he never appeared), the demise of the old Hollywood studio and the rise of the hard-core porn industry, the emergence of Disneyland and the heyday of disco. As both observer and participant, Davis was, in many vital ways, at the center of the making of American popular culture from VJ Day to the Tet Offensive, from the Depression to Watergate, from Roosevelt to Reagan: as a performer associated with one of the biggest stars of the era (Sinatra); playing at the most expensive nightclubs; doing Broadway shows; acting in several commercially successful, if not critically acclaimed, films; appearing on dozens of television programs, from the early days of the medium in the 1950s until the year of his death, 1990. What, indeed, made Sammy run and how was he able to run so far for so long over so many obstacles, both internal and societal, to become the presence that he did? For a time Davis, even as much as Frank Sinatra and Dean Martin, personified hipness; as much as trumpeter Miles Davis or boxer Sugar Ray Robinson, he personified a kind of black cool. Davis had the clothes and the moves and the mannerisms. He was, for a time, the King of Kicks, with whiskey glass, cigarette, and garish jewelry. He never wanted to sleep and he never wanted to stop partying. As Shirley MacLaine remembered him: "Sammy tasted the feast of life as though it was his last meal. There seemed to be nothing that he left untried—booze, women, drugs, cigarettes of all kinds, impressions, instruments, voices, dance steps, drama, comedy, musicals, cars, houses, jewelry, and several religions . . . He lived completely in the present, expanding it to the fullest until it became the future."[38] Indeed, perhaps more than any of the persons most associated with the Beats and the Beat Generation, or with American existentialism—Jack Kerouac or Charlie Parker or Allen Ginsberg or William Burroughs or Timothy Leary—Davis was the ultimate hipster, who lived at both the margin and the center, who indeed brought the margin to the center of American life. What better examples of this than his highly publicized interracial marriage to May Britt in 1960, when the shadow of miscegenation fell athwart the White House itself and Jack Kennedy disinvited the couple to his inauguration, or Davis's almost single-handed conquest of white-only Las Vegas, which brought black vaudeville from the Chitlin Circuit to the most garish playground of the Western world. Davis created, like the true autodidact he was, his own meaning. Davis's interracialism, his sense of himself as an assimilated person, his insistence that he was as white as he was black, was equally threatening to the rigidity and conformity of 1950s America and to the polarized political vision of 1960s America. Davis lived on the edge, in his performances and in his personal life. Never had a public performer so stylized his desperation, his need for acceptance, as a form of self-assertion.

Davis was a pathbreaking black personality in American popular culture in three ways: first, his association with the Rat Pack, among the most insistent nonconformists of the 1950s, and his claim that he was a nonconformist, something no black in the mainstream entertainment business during the 1950s and 1960s would assert; second, his star status in Las Vegas, which gave him a far greater presence in the consciousness of middle America and a far greater association with its musical taste, which meant that he could survive despite making unsuccessful movies and having an unsuccessful television series, an accomplishment virtually unthinkable for an African American during the 1950s and 1960s; and third, the fact that while hit records helped him, he never depended on them for his career, so he never really had to be current to be hip or to keep an audience and he never became tired of himself: "Most of the trouble with most people in America who become successful is that they can really and truly get by on bullshit alone. They can survive on it. You know, you can live on a good record for months. You can live on any one thing for months if you pick and choose your spot. One good TV show can make some people last longer than they have a right to last. They milk it and get everything out of it they can without putting in a new nickel's worth . . . But I'm trying to achieve another level, and another one after that."[39] Davis combined being a performer of middle-of-the-road music with being a revolutionary black figure without most people ever truly appreciating the skill with which he reconciled this contradiction. For some it might be hard to think of Sammy Davis as the great American existentialist who, oddly, fused hipsterism—and pointless, vulgar hedonism—with the morality of race duty and the need to express gratitude. (It is perhaps what made Davis most distasteful to more militant blacks: the fact that he seemed so grateful for what he had earned, so thankful for and beholden to his audience. "If God ever took away my talent I would be a nigger again," wrote Davis in *Why Me?*[40] Or as Davis said in his 1966 *Playboy* interview, "I know the audience will courteously applaud just because I'm singing loud, but that's not what I want. I got to have them *pulling* for me: I want them feeling, 'Oh, God, if he doesn't make it, he might run off and cut his wrists.' They want me to climb that mountain. And then, 'Oh, God— he *made* it!' That's how I've got to make them feel."[41]) Sammy Davis was an American hipster, a grand Negro moralist who felt he had to be a credit to his race, even when he felt imprisoned by his race. He tried to define himself in a world that would only grudgingly permit him to do so.

II
I'M GONNA DANCE
RIGHT OUT OF MY SHOES

[Being a Negro] helped me. Enormously. It helped me in the beginning by making me mad—mad that I was colored. I saw cats around me who couldn't shine my shoes, as far as talent was concerned, getting all the breaks. This doesn't make for happiness. Then one marvelous day I woke up and said, "What the hell are you bitching about? Being colored isn't stopping you. Nothing is stopping you. Work, learn—if you want to be as good as they are learn to be as good as they are . . ."
—Sammy Davis, Jr., as quoted in *Showcase* by Roy Newquist, 1966

I've got to get so big, so powerful, so famous, that the day will come when they'll look at me and see a man—and then somewhere along the way they'll notice he's a Negro. —Sammy Davis, Jr., *Yes I Can*

Which of us has overcome his past?
—James Baldwin, "Alas, Poor Richard"

"Look, I make a lot of money," Sammy Davis, Jr., says in *Yes I Can,* "and I'm big in the business because of three things: I've got talent, I've worked hard, and every bit as important, I have let myself remain an individual."[42] In trying to understand

Sammy Davis, Jr., the man, the entertainer, and the symbol, let us take each portion of this self-evaluation in turn.

There is no question that the man often referred to as America's greatest entertainer, Mr. Entertainment, had enormous talent, probably possessing more (and more diverse) abilities than any of the other members of the Rat Pack, the group he was most famously associated with. He may, at times, have felt himself to be more gifted than the others—that he could do more on a stage than Dean Martin and Peter Lawford; that he could be funnier than Joey Bishop; that, perhaps, he could even be better than Sinatra, if he had the opportunities. He had been in show business longer than any of them and may have felt that he had paid more dues, although he made it a point in the many times he talked about Sinatra to express his admiration for how Sinatra was able to pull his career back together from its low point in the early 1950s. How Davis related to the others is a more crucial matter. He was the youngest of the principals: Bishop was seven years older, Martin eight, and Sinatra ten. Lawford was only two years older; nonetheless, despite their closeness in age, Lawford was a successful television actor who had a respectable list of movie credits to his name.[43] He was also President Kennedy's brother-in-law. Davis, who had always been starstruck, would have deferred to these men because they were older and—in the case of Martin, Sinatra, and even Lawford—for a time, more famous. Some of the degrading antics that Davis did with the others were as much the result of his relative youth (and his size) as of his race. The age difference may also explain why Sinatra played the role of older brother to Davis and why Davis, at a certain point in his life, rebelled against Sinatra's tutelage. It must be remembered that Davis had been performing with two older black men—his father and Will Mastin—all his life. He then switched, when he became a single act to the Rat Pack for several years. In short, Davis's talent has to be understood in the contexts in which he placed it. First, the shift from two black vaudeville hoofers to several white performers of varying talents, where he moved from being star with two foils from another generation to being a star performer among other stars, who despite their age differences were seen by the public *as members of the same generation.* Second, Davis shifted from performing in black vaudeville for mostly black audiences to performing in Las Vegas and expensive nightclubs for largely white audiences, where his race made him stand out as something of a novelty and served to intensify his abilities to this audience because his race intensified his presence. He was not the only black hoofer to play white venues, but he was the first to draw enormous attention to himself as a personality and the first to become a huge crossover star. And he was, more important, the only one of his era to survive the demise of the art of black hoofing and the demise of vaudeville.

Davis's range of talents made performers like Mickey Rooney, Judy Garland, and Buddy Rich his true peers: child performers who became successful as adults and who sang, danced, acted, and, in some cases, played instruments. It is no accident that Davis was good friends with all three, as close to them as he was to anyone in the Rat Pack but Sinatra. In the Rat Pack, only Shirley MacLaine, singer, dancer, actor, and multivolume autobiographer, was the same type of all-purpose performer as Davis. She was nine years younger than Davis but, in her descriptions of their relationship, often seemed to be a kind of big sister. He would have been impressed when he met MacLaine in the late 1950s not simply by her talent but by her considerable success. By the time she appeared in *Ocean's Eleven* in 1960, MacLaine had nine major film roles and an Academy Award nomination to her credit.

Davis certainly is right to claim that he worked hard. He had been a furiously physical performer, as most black hoofers were, since his early childhood, when he joined his father and Will Mastin, whom Davis, Jr., often referred to as his uncle (they were not, in fact, related), in becoming part of the Will Mastin Gang (later Trio). By the time Davis hit it big in the early 1950s, he was famous for giving everything he had onstage. Once he became a headliner, even before he was entirely freed from the Will Mastin Trio, he became noted for two- and two-and-a-half-hour performances that often left his band frazzled and bemused; club owners, interested in turning over tables, annoyed; and his audiences limp, if not a bit bewildered, by the man's remarkable need to gain their esteem. In a typical performance during his prime, Davis would dance tap, jazz, and soft-shoe; sing a dozen or more songs; do a series of comic impersonations ranging from Bogart, Cagney, and Sinatra to Jack Benny, Tony Bennett, and Louis Armstrong; play the trumpet, piano, bass fiddle, marimba, and drums; perform gun tricks; and tell jokes. Davis gave the impression throughout his act that he was ready to dance right out of his shoes, to quote a line from "The Darktown Strutters Ball," in order to please his audience, to have them know that they had experienced the "complete" Sammy Davis. He succeeded in keeping *Mr. Wonderful*, the Jule Styne–conceived musical written specifically for him, running for 383 performances, from March 22, 1956, to February 23, 1957—despite disparaging reviews—on the sheer dogged strength and vigor of his personality and animation.[44] ("Almost the entire second act [of *Mr. Wonderful*] was my nightclub act," Davis says in *Why Me?*[45]) So famous was Davis's nightclub act that his first film, *Anna Lucasta*, made in 1958 and starring Eartha Kitt, featured a montage of that act, including images of him dancing and playing the drums and the trumpet, no matter that his character, Danny, is not a nightclub performer but a sailor and cabdriver. It is an indication of his fame at that instant that the audience could be expected to recognize Davis as himself and not as a character.[46]

For a time, particularly in the 1950s and 1960s, no one in American popular culture personified energy and pizzazz, sheer endurance and willpower, more than Davis. (What else did the title of his first autobiography, *Yes I Can*, mean but that Davis felt he could successfully assert his will, his personality, his desires on the world?) Few at the time or since seem aware of how revolutionary it was for a black performer to present himself in this way, to assert so aggressively the meaning of his life as something important both to himself and to the world. It hardly made Davis a less provocative figure that he largely modeled himself after Sinatra. As he wrote in *Why Me?*: "Frank had an influence on me that no one else could have had. When I was a teenager I used to make Frank Sinatra scrapbooks. He'd always been my idol and I'd said it publicly and I'd tried to *be* him, professionally to emulate him, and personally trying to be a swinger, to do the kind of things he did: give me all that, send for this, buy all that, expensive gifts to strangers for a gesture . . . all that stuff is Sinatra. The attitude, the cockiness was Sinatra. Black people weren't cocky in those days."[47] Sinatra was older, extraordinarily successful, and had taken a protective, mentoring attitude toward Davis, so emulation was unavoidable. It unnerved many blacks and some whites that a black performer would so consciously try to imitate a famous white performer, especially because so many blacks feel that in general white performers have made it by imitating blacks. It must have been even more unnerving for many whites that a black performer would imitate a white performer who was himself such a rebellious figure. Naturally Davis wanted to be big, as Sinatra was big, an ambition partly fueled by the harsh racism Davis endured in his early career (he felt that if he could become big enough he would be immune, invulnerable to the slights and insults he endured as a Negro, that he would be free of being a Negro), partly fueled by his sense of his own myth as a performer without equal (on the Jack Eigen radio show broadcast from the Copacabana in 1959, for instance, Davis said that he thought he was bigger than Sinatra, an assertion of ego that cost him a $75,000 role in Sinatra's movie *Never So Few*).[48] Davis wanted to be loved; he believed in the power and glory of his talent; he was insecure. But he seemed, in many ways, to like his insecurities as much as he liked his talent and his feelings that he deserved to be loved. He was certainly the first black person since Jack Johnson to romanticize his insecurities, to mythologize them, so publicly— and, unlike Johnson, to meet a large degree of public tolerance, if not approval, for doing so. By living his life so publicly, by courting humiliation and scandal, Davis broke ground for the black performer as pop culture icon. And this constant public exposure, this sense of living under great pressure because of his race, because of impending scandal, because of misfortune, intensified his appearance as a hard-working performer, as someone determined to overcome adversity.

The third point of Davis's self-assessment, that he remained "an individual," is the most intriguing and the most telling. The claim sounds more than a little ironic coming from a man who was so well known for his impersonations. In 1967, Davis, in talking about his singing, once told a writer that he had "no sound." "Maybe I've been doing impressions too long. But when I'm recording, I often have trouble finding me."[49] Not surprisingly, Davis had been told earlier in his career by Sinatra that ". . . you've got to get yourself your own sound, your own style. It's okay to sound like me—if you're me. I'm only flattered that you like what I do well enough to be influenced by it, and your ear for making other people's sounds isn't helping any, but it's a dead end. No matter how good it is, no copy of anything ever sold for as high as the original."[50] This was a charge that was to dog Davis for most of his career. He was always called a great entertainer but never a great artist. Anyone who ever saw him perform conceded the magnificence of his talent, but his more discriminating audience never saw him as an original. As a singer he was often accused of sounding or phrasing like Sinatra or Mel Tormé or Billy Eckstine or Nat Cole (all singers he impersonated over the years); his acting often seemed to come from the mugging school of Mickey Rooney, his detractors said; he was a ferocious dancer and a very good one, but not an innovator, not a Fred Astaire or a Gene Kelly, among white dancers, or a John Bubbles or a Peg-leg Bates or a Bunny Briggs or a Jimmy Slyde, among black hoofers. Bill "Bojangles" Robinson, when he saw the young Davis, thought he was trying too hard. Davis played the trumpet and drums with the panache to please an audience, not to score points as a musician.

Yet the idea of his own individuality was very important to Davis. In *Yes I Can* he says: "We're all born as individuals and in a million and one little ways I've managed to remain Sammy Davis, Jr. . . . Whether the people know it or not, my individuality is part of what they're buying when they come to see me. What I'm saying is, I know I'm not perfect but whatever I am in sum total, my faults and my virtues have combined to make me one-of-a-kind, and it works for me."[51] Perhaps Davis is suggesting here that the sum total of what he offered, the entire package, was unique, even if individual aspects of this talent were not. He certainly aggressively refused to be typecast as a Negro performer from the "old school." Davis had this to say about the old black vaudeville acts he saw during his early days in show business: "I studied the acts and saw that most Negro performers work in a cubicle. They'd run on, sing twelve songs, dance, do jokes—but not to the people. The jokes weren't done like Milton Berle was doing them, to the audience, they were done between the men onstage, as if they didn't have the right to communicate with the people out front."[52] Davis broke ground as a black performer by acknowledging his white audience, by playing directly to them. He wanted to please his audience, but he felt he could make his appeal to them directly and not hide behind some sort of semi-minstrel mask. Davis had been doing impersonations of black artists like Billy Eckstine and Louis Armstrong for several years, but when he wanted to add Cagney, Bogart, and Sinatra in the late 1940s, Will Mastin was strenuously opposed, thinking a black performer mimicking white stars would offend his white audience. Davis did the white impersonations anyway and became a huge hit, once again serving as a pathbreaker for the black performer. ("Earlier in my life—despite all the barriers—it proved advantageous to be a Negro, because they hadn't ever seen a Negro doing impressions of whites, and all that jazz," said Davis in his 1966 *Playboy* interview.[53])

He became the first black actor to play a lead in a drama on an episode of *General Electric Theater* (1958) entitled "Auf

Wiedersehen," about a black soldier's attachment to a lonely boy. He fulfilled his desire to play a cowboy, something unheard of for 1950s and 1960s television, by appearing in such Westerns as *Lawman* and *The Rifleman*.[54] He also starred in an episode of *Dick Powell's Zane Grey Theater* in 1959 entitled "Mission," a Civil War drama. His turn as the tragic jazz trumpeter in the 1966 film *A Man Called Adam*, in which he played a self-absorbed, art-obsessed character, certainly added new dimensions to the characterizations that were permitted black actors at the time, particularly because he played an ambiguous black character who was not very likable.[55]

But to understand fully Davis's quest for individuality, his life must be placed in a historical context. He was born December 8, 1925, in Harlem, during the middle of the Harlem Renaissance. This was the same year that philosophy professor and Rhodes scholar Alain Locke published his famous anthology of black writing, *The New Negro*, and that poet Countee Cullen published his first volume of verse, *Color*. Langston Hughes was to publish his first volume of verse, *The Weary Blues*, the following year. Paul Robeson was appearing in Eugene O'Neill's *All God's Chillun Got Wings*. Broadway musicals such as *Shuffle Along, From Dixie to Broadway*, and *Running Wild* made black dances popular across the country and made stars of Florence Mills and Josephine Baker. W.E.B. Du Bois was the editor of the NAACP's *Crisis*; Charles S. Johnson was editing *Opportunity* for the Urban League; and Chandler Owen and A. Philip Randolph were publishing the socialist-oriented *The Messenger*. A mass migration was making the black population of the United States more urban and less southern, more industrial and less agricultural. As a result of World War I, when blacks found it difficult to get officer training or to fight in combat for the American Expeditionary Force, blacks had become more assertive, more aware of themselves as a black population in a world where dark people were colonized by Europeans, more willing to organize and use pressure tactics to defend their interests, less willing to kowtow to whites or to think whites all-powerful. The debacle of World

War I was not likely to make anyone think that white civiliza-
tion was invincible, superior, or even rational. Marcus Garvey's
Universal Negro Improvement Association, a black nationalist
movement for the physical redemption of Africa and for the
spiritual redemption of millions of African-descended peoples
around the world, had galvanized American blacks. (Garvey
also published *Negro World*, probably the most widely read of
all black newspapers of the 1920s; further, he galvanized the
West Indian communities of North America.) There were ultra-
radical black groups like the African Blood Brotherhood and
more middle-of-the-road leaders like James Weldon Johnson, of
the NAACP, who was working mightily to get Congress to pass
an antilynching bill. Jazz had become a major musical style,
both sweet and hot, attracting blacks and whites, with, on the
one hand, bands like Fletcher Henderson, the Original Dix-
ieland Jazz Band, and Duke Ellington, and, on the other, bands
like Paul Whiteman, who in 1924 commissioned George Gershwin to write the first famous jazz symphonic work, *Rhapsody
in Blue*. Great jazz soloists like Louis Armstrong, Barney Bi-
gard, Earl Hines, Frank Trumbauer, Bix Beiderbecke, Sidney
Bechet, and others were emerging. And much of this activity
was centered in New York, a good deal of it in Harlem. It was
an interesting time for Davis to enter the world, at the height of
a new wave of black assertion for political rights, social equality, and cultural parity. The black vaudeville circuit still existed
when Davis, at the age of four, joined Will Mastin and his father, Sam Davis, Sr., on the stage as a dancer. The circuit was to
exist for many years yet, and to produce a number of important
performers, among them Stepin Fetchit, Moms Mabley, Bill
Robinson, Redd Foxx, Cholly Atkins, Mantan Moreland,
Dorothy Dandridge (with whom Davis would work in the film
version of *Porgy and Bess*), and Ethel Waters, with whom
Davis appeared in the short film *Rufus Jones for President* in
1933. (Waters's polished diction and her amalgam of white and
black singing styles made her a kind of precursor to some aspects of Davis's shtick.)

Davis was born one year after another famous Harlemite,

writer James Baldwin. They were part of a new generation of blacks when they came of age in the 1940s. Just as Baldwin by the late 1940s and early 1950s was breaking down barriers in literature by writing for some of the leading intellectual journals and magazines of the day, so the Will Mastin Trio, almost solely on the strength of Davis's talent and his connections (Sinatra had taken a liking to him in the early 1940s), was breaking down barriers, professionally and personally, by playing El Rancho in Las Vegas, Ciro's in Los Angeles, the Beachcomber in Miami, and, finally, the Copacabana in New York. When Davis emerged as a star in the early 1950s, he was part of a generation of new black crossover stars who were openly rejecting segregation and the restriction of the black institutions to which they had been assigned: Jackie Robinson in baseball; Dorothy Dandridge and Sidney Poitier in film; James Baldwin, Ralph Ellison, and Gwendolyn Brooks in literature. They did not wish to be seen as black ballplayers, black actors, or black writers but as professional ballplayers, professional actors, and professional writers. Jazz musicians like Miles Davis, Charlie Parker, Thelonious Monk, Charles Mingus, Sonny Rollins, Max Roach, and others were expressly changing the public demeanor of the black jazz musician, from dance-band entertainer to serious, self-conscious artist. And jazz music, at times, became an aestheticized form of protest. Of course, what made the assertion and rebellion of these blacks especially poignant, ambivalent, and perhaps misunderstood by both blacks and whites was that it was couched in the terms of seeking the acceptance of whites, but seeking that acceptance in a new, independent, and more assertive way. These performers wanted to be accepted by whites for what they themselves thought they were and not for what whites wanted them to be. As Davis so richly expressed it in *Yes I Can*: "They'll like me even if they hate my guts!"[56] It was this drive for acceptance that motivated him during his horrendous years in the army (unlike Sinatra, Lawford, and Martin, Davis was actually in the armed services during World War II), when he was beaten, tortured, and harassed by racists.[57] He thought he could win them over with his performances in army shows. Whether he did win them over remains an open question; whether it was worth the effort is decidedly debatable. But it is clear that like many of the Harlem Renaissance intellectuals and artists, Davis thought the Negro could effect change for both himself or herself and for the group through art. This, too, is a questionable belief but not an uncommon one. As Davis wrote in *Yes I Can*: "I'd learned a lot in the army and I knew that above all things in the world I had to become so big, so strong, so important, that those [bigoted white soldiers] and their hatred could never touch me. My talent was the only thing that made me a little different from everybody else, and it was all that I could hope would shield me *because* I was different."[58] In his mind, his own fate, the war against racism, and his sense of individuality were tied together in a complex way. Acceptance as an artist had to be based on individuality, on distancing himself from blacks as a group. Many blacks, realizing this, resented him, condemned him, and finally rejected him.

To them, black individuality was even more of a threat than it was to whites. Individuality threatens racial solidarity, which the group feels is essential for its survival. As Ralph Ellison so aptly expressed in a 1945 essay on Richard Wright: "For the Negro there is relative safety as long as the impulse toward individuality is suppressed . . . This . . . gives the group its distinctive character. Which, because of Negroes' suppressed minority position, is very much in the nature of an elaborate but limited defense mechanism. Its function is dual: to protect the Negro from whirling away from the undifferentiated mass of his people into the unknown, symbolized in its most abstract form by insanity, and most concretely by lynching; and to protect him from those unknown forces *within himself* which might urge him to reach out for that social and human equality which the white South says he cannot have."[59] Davis did not want to be protected from the unknown, even if it meant courting danger by dating and bedding white women. Least of all did he want to be protected from the unknown forces within himself. Davis felt it was a sign of his liberation as a black man to explore the urges within, no matter how costly or embarrassing or destructive some of them might be.

In the 1950s, Davis was attacked by some quarters of the mainstream black press for abandoning his race, for never staying in black hotels once white hotels opened their doors to him, for having "white fever" (his partying with white chorus girls was well known). His 1958 marriage to black dancer Loray White did not help his situation.[60] He had asked her to marry him when he was drunk and under increasing pressure to discontinue his relationship with white actress Kim Novak. Everyone sensed, if not knew, that the marriage was a fraud. (Davis and White separated within weeks and divorced within months.) His marriage to May Britt in 1960 did not endear him to blacks, although portions of the black media came to his defense, probably because he was being attacked so viciously by so many whites; he was hooted from a black church in the early 1960s, unable to finish a speech for HarYouAct—a Harlem youth group—because black nationalists condemned him for having a white wife. He was still deeply bothered by black reaction to his marriage to Britt years after they divorced, as his discussion of that marriage in a 1974 *Ebony* interview reveals: "A cat on the corner would say, 'He shouldn't have married that white woman. He don't like black women.' How do you equate that? You know, it's all right to pimp off a white woman because you think she would do you a number. You can steal a little but you ain't supposed to marry and have children."[61] When he entered into what he described as an "open marriage" with black dancer Altovise Gore in 1970 one wonders if, in some measure, it was not an attempt to reconcile with blacks. As he said in his 1980 *Ebony* interview: "You see, I *love* buying my wife a $60,000 car. *Love* that. Love it all the more 'cause she's Black. I love taking her around to the shows and things. Give her a chance to shine, *because most Black women don't get a chance to shine*, not unless they are the breadwinners."[62]

His association with the white Rat Pack also did not help him in his relationship with blacks, especially as some blacks felt that he seemed to serve as the group's mascot because of portrayals like his Gunga Din–role in *Sergeants 3* and because he was the butt of several coarse, even racist jokes (despite Sinatra's staunch liberalism in the 1950s and 1960s). "At one time in my life, I was his little mascot, but I'm not his little mascot any more. But don't ask me to give up my friendship with the man. I said I was going to deal straight with you, and I'm looking you right in the eyes and telling it to you straight: I was his little mascot. But I didn't look upon myself as a mascot, not when this man was fighting for my motion picture salary, not when he was fighting to get me billings," Davis said in his 1980 *Ebony* interview.[63]

In later life, like Jackie Robinson once he left baseball and like Frank Sinatra when the Kennedys rebuffed him, Davis became a Republican, or at least he was associated with them. This, too, was to be a cause of great grief for him among blacks. Davis's political views, such as they were, would have to be characterized as strictly liberal. He believed in active government intervention to improve the lives of blacks. He was a supporter of integration and affirmative action. He was certainly no social conservative; he didn't care what people did in their bedrooms, nor did he care about prayer in public schools, and he hardly gave Communism a thought. It was unfortunate for him that he hitched his wagon to Richard Nixon, the old red-baiter and Southern strategist, instead of Nelson Rockefeller, the recognized Republican liberal, as Robinson did. But Nixon did more to expand affirmative action and government programs for blacks than any previous president had done. In this regard, Nixon was a liberal president, and it showed in his treatment of Davis. Nixon invited him to the White House, where Davis slept in the Lincoln bedroom. "Sammy and his wife spent the night with us after his performance [at the White House] and—in fulfillment of a lifelong dream—he slept in the Lincoln Bedroom," wrote Nixon in his autobiography, *RN*.[64]

Neither Kennedy (who not only kept Davis from his inauguration but pressured Sinatra not to attend Davis's wedding) nor
Johnson made such an overture to him. Davis was deeply affected by his night in the White House: "I went to sleep trying
to feel having made it on a social level with the President of the
United States, having sat up and talked to him until two in the
morning—going to bed then only because the next day we had
to be up for a ten o'clock breakfast. I could not fit into my
mind. In less than a lifetime: Mama's place in Harlem . . . Then,
somewhere along the way, without my being aware of it or
knowing when, I had escaped."[65] Moreover, Nixon, who genuinely admired Davis not only as an entertainer but as a person, listened to him. When, after a tour of Vietnam, Davis
complained about the way drug-addicted black soldiers were
treated, changes were made immediately. "It is true that a lot of
people in the black movement resented it when I hugged Nixon
on a nationwide TV show. Some of them got nasty and voluble.
The blacks stayed, mostly, lukewarm to Nixon, and very little I
said changed their minds. But I had long talks with the guy face
to face, and I must say, even now, he impressed me. He promised much more funding to black colleges and many new reforms. He had done away with the quota system, and generally
speaking, the more he said, the more I believed in him," wrote
Davis in *Hollywood in a Suitcase*.[66] The attacks made against
Davis because of his association with Nixon seem, in retrospect, to have been particularly vicious and unfair. As Davis
himself pointed out, Jesse Jackson and James Brown were also
hobnobbing with Nixon (Brown actively supported Nixon),
but they did not seem to suffer repercussions because of it.
Davis nearly had a nervous breakdown because of the black reaction to his support of Nixon, which became especially nasty
during the Watergate scandal.[67] Those who attacked Davis
failed to observe that Nixon treated Davis with far greater respect than any other political figure Davis consorted with except for Robert Kennedy. In fact, Nixon treated Davis with
more sincere respect than most white liberal politicians of the

day treated most blacks. Nixon did not patronize Davis, perhaps in part because he saw characteristics in Davis—the need to abase himself when publicly humiliated, the drive, the ambition, the need to be loved, the insecurities—that he saw in himself.

Davis was always deeply bothered that blacks rejected him. In the 1950s, he met with black publisher John H. Johnson and gave money to the NAACP. (From the 1960s on, Johnson publications gave Davis favorable coverage.) In the 1960s, he met with Maulani Ron Karenga and the Black Panthers and gave money to Chicago street gangs to run (unsuccessfully) a liquor store. He won the Spingarn Medal in 1968—the highest honor that the NAACP bestows annually on the person who did the most for civil rights and the image of blacks during his or her life. In the late 1960s and early 1970s he added more "soul" material to his act, songs for which he was totally unsuited. It didn't help him with the black masses. Davis was, perhaps, more tormented by guilt for his lack of acceptance by blacks than most other black performers.

Davis was an extraordinary survivor in many respects. He overcame racism in the army and brutal treatment in the early days of his career. He overcame the loss of his eye in a car accident in 1954. He overcame bad marriages. He overcame his sexual dissipation, the alcohol habit that scarred his liver, a hip replacement, his male menopause phase of "mod" and "disco" hip, never losing his audience or his ability to make money, never seeing his popularity wane even when his shows became gimmicky and stale, even when physical ailments prevented him from being able to perform in the manner that he liked. There were two things he could not overcome: his need to spend money at a rate faster than he earned it and his cigarette addiction, which brought on the throat cancer that finally killed him on May 16, 1990, his neck bulbous and stinking with the deadly tumor that he refused to have surgically removed for fear he would lose his voice. In the end the giant tumor, ironically, had reduced his voice to a whisper of pain and suffering. He died, as he had lived, in debt. Sammy had outrun quite a bit in his life, more than most people do, possibly because he demanded more of himself and of his life than most people do. But of course he could not outrun everything. No one can.

III
ON THE STREET OF DREAMS

Like Frank, [Sammy Davis, Jr.] believed deeply in the redemptive power of music, but where Frank thought it unseemly to do anything but *sing* a song, Sammy attacked it with his life. Audiences with whom he had nothing in common as people found themselves empathizing with his struggle and victory; to root against Sammy as he went up against a number was pure bad faith. He was a man naked against the elements with only his heart and voice to keep him alive.

—Shawn Levy, *Rat Pack Confidential*

I'm always leaving *some* place.   —Sammy Davis, Jr., *Yes I Can*

How do I remember Sammy Davis, Jr.? He was the first black entertainer I can recall who made an impression on me during my childhood; the one I saw and heard about the most; the one who, by turns, astonished and disappointed me. For me, Sammy Davis, Jr., was a man of many faces: Road Warrior, King of the Entertainers, Prince of Cool, Sage of Hipness, Knight of the Saloon, American Clotheshorse, Race Rebel, Bumbling Black Man, Establishment Toady. Sammy Davis, Jr., brought together two different eras in his very person. With the exception of the late 1960s and early 1970s, when the Black Is Beautiful craze made the bush (or natural, or Afro) popular, Davis always wore what was called a conk or a process, a demanding and, from the point of view of my generation, an unbecoming hairstyle. He said he went back to the conk after the Black Power/Black Is Beautiful period passed because he was getting a tiny bald spot on the back of his head and he felt that if he straightened his hair he would be able to cover it. There is probably some truth to this, no matter that chemically straightening one's hair is likely to make it thin out even more. Perhaps Davis simply liked having processed hair, missed wearing his hair that way, and went back to it as soon as it was politically feasible for him to do so. In any case, that hairstyle always seemed to me a throwback to another time in black American life. As a young man, I was sorry he went back to the conk. I thought he looked better without it and I wondered if he was secretly ashamed of his hair. Why else would a black man straighten his hair except to look like a white man? Perhaps wearing a conk—as with the Reverend Al Sharpton or singers James Brown, Johnny Mathis, Michael Jackson, or Prince, or boxer Sugar Ray Robinson—was simply a way of being theatrical as a black man, of being larger than life, of having style. Nearly all the black hoofers that Davis grew up with, the Nicholas Brothers, Flash McDonald, the Berry Brothers, Bunny Briggs, had straightened hair, a sign of black masculine cool. As Davis said in 1966: ". . . the only reason I leave [my hair] this way is because it's become part of my image. A show-business personality, if he's created a successful image of one kind or another, has to keep that image. Like, I don't want to see Cab Calloway with a crewcut: He's a great performer, but at this late date he'd look pretty silly with kinky hair, and so would I. Am I supposed to cut it short and let it grow in natural just to prove I'm proud to be black?"[68] Yet this is precisely what he did, although he had vehemently defended the hairstyle only a few years before. As an adolescent, I didn't quite understand that defense. It is an odd matter, and not altogether becoming, for a man to have to defend the right to be what he is or to like what he likes, and Davis, as I remember him, seemed always to be doing just that. To me his conk seemed ugly and it seemed to be saying to the world, I'm a nigger, just look at my greasy hair.

The other aspect of Davis I remember well is his speaking

voice. His diction was very good, without a trace of anything "Negro" about it. He would at times "talk colored," as he put it, during his act, especially as he began to add more racial humor and more subtle protest humor to his performances. But this was Davis adopting the mask of being African American as a performer, of making race work for him with his white audiences. The grand articulation was always there. Twice during his career he was criticized by comedians Jerry Lewis and Milton Berle for sounding stuck up, like a snob. He needed to talk more casually, less properly. How much Davis took this to heart over the course of his career, I do not know. From the many times I have seen him perform on television, I do not think he followed this advice very closely. I was glad he didn't. It meant a great deal to me to hear him talk so well on television, and I knew, as I grew older, why it meant a great deal to him as well. I don't think Lewis and Berle could fully appreciate what it meant to have unstigmatized speech, that it wouldn't do for Davis, as a black facing a white audience, to be too casual. The audience might mistake his vernacular for something else, for something from the past that should not be revisited, if a black person is to have a shred of dignity as a public person at all. "When you're around white people," my mother always told me, "don't talk like a servant or they'll treat you like one. Talk just like you're as good and as smart as they are, like they've got to respect you." And to have that dignity today it is good, ironically, for every black person to remember how long and hard it was to earn it.

As it was, Davis's voice did not have anything of the nigger in it. It was a very good speaking voice, a voice that people would respect. "People hearing me today don't think I have no education," Davis said in an interview, "I've worked hard— *hard*, man, to be able to give this impression. Blood, sweat and tears went into every combination of words that I use now. I've read, and I've remembered . . . Now, I'd be confident anywhere I was asked to speak. But I still make mistakes that infuriate me, especially when I'm corrected."[69] When I saw Davis on television in the 1950s and 1960s, with his glasses and goatee, I thought he was an intellectual. I thought the same about the other famous blacks of the era: Harry Belafonte, Sidney Poitier, Ruby Dee, Ossie Davis, Miles Davis, Oscar Brown, Jr., Nina Simone, Brock Peters, Billy Strayhorn, Sam Cooke, Ray Charles (the Genius, no less), Dionne Warwick. They seemed the smartest, the most serious, the most dignified black people in the world. "Poor, no one is poor," as the song lyric goes, and it was true for me as a boy, if one lived on the street of dreams, and in those days Davis and his peers constructed for me a street of dreams, a street of black dreams or a black street of dreams, where I could imagine being whatever I wanted to be.

When we were children, my sisters and I were often ridiculed by our black schoolmates for "talking like white people" or "sounding white." Some of this was purely in jest, some was motivated by envy and some by sheer malice and ignorance, but whatever the cause, I could never reconcile myself to it. First, I was never trying to imitate a white person's speech. At the time, the only white people I knew well were the Italians who lived in the neighborhood, and I recoiled from their ethnic expressions as much as I recoiled from "talking colored." I was imitating the speech of my black schoolteachers, of movie stars like Sidney Poitier, Harry Belafonte, Woody Strode, and James Edwards. I had heard the so-called vernacular of actors like Hattie McDaniel, Willie Best, and Stepin Fetchit, and I wanted no part of that. Indeed, I thought black vernacular was an aberration: I assumed that most black people spoke standard English or wanted to. I heard James Baldwin give an interview on the radio and he spoke standard English. So did Martin Luther King and so did Malcolm X. I once yelled at some boys who were needling me for "talking white," "I don't know any white people who talk like this." That wasn't quite true, for like all the black people around me I watched television, and like all the black children around me I read comic books, and whatever one might say about the deficiencies of the literary quality of this genre, Superman, Batman, Spiderman, and the like all spoke standard English. But what I said to those boys was very near the truth, for I was never inspired by any white person to use standard English. And I hated black vernacular speech, even though I could perfectly replicate it as a youth, when it suited my purposes to do so. I hated it because it reflected an experience that was narrow and provincial, because its vocabulary was so limited and so heavily reliant on profanity, particularly variations of the word "fuck." And, of course, the word "nigger" was used all the time by blacks, a word I utterly loathed. I hated the vernacular because it was a language with no ability to grow, a language that could not encompass what I felt, what I wanted to express, and I was as black and as poor as all the others in my neighborhood. Indeed, I was poorer than most of the black kids I grew up with. What good was this language to me, if it could not envision or accommodate my emotional or psychological existence? Here, I thought, even as a boy, was a language, this black vernacular, that was meant to be as limiting as the experiences that black people were permitted in this society, and what was even more defeating, more tragic, was that the people who spoke it exclusively had decided to accommodate themselves to those limitations. It was the language of oppression and accommodation. The vernacular could, in a meager but sometimes very affecting, even passionate way, convey anger, resentment, self-pity, the humor of cynicism, a spirituality mixed of hope and frustration, disappointment and hatred—all the emotional preoccupations of the powerless and the confined. But it could not express the ideas of power or the power of ideas, the necessity of meaning, nor could it even express the idea of itself or of the meaning of itself. I knew instinctively why Davis spoke the way he did. I knew what drove him because some variation of that drove me, too. In one very important way, I knew what it felt like to be Sammy Davis, Jr.

Davis's hair seemed a symbol of the past but his speech was the present and the future. The hair seemed some old-fashioned hip—and it *was* once hip, as I knew well—but the speech seemed a new, glorious hip. He was someone I wanted to both run away from and run toward. He was always the place I was leaving and the place I wanted to enter. He once said something that became an adage for me: "But if you can swing, if you've got the rhythm which in essence is the key to life, nothing else matters."[70] Is that what swing really is—moving between attraction and repulsion, from light to darkness and back, in a way that one can grow and disintegrate simultaneously?

Perhaps that was what the Cold War era was all about for blacks, past and present confronting each other to forge the future, and maybe Sammy Davis, Jr., symbolized that confrontation more fully and more dramatically than any other black public figure: the past of segregation and degradation and the present of integration and a new dignity, the shock of shame and the extraordinary serenity of small resistance. Davis's speech was a kind of elegance and grace, a dignity, sometimes a bit forced and self-conscious, but all the more affecting for that, that said to me as a young black kid "English is my language, too" and "I may be other things but I'm as American as anybody else." As Davis knew, despite the racism in America, where else could he have had the outsized success he did except in America. I learned from Sammy Davis, Jr., that there was nothing wrong with a black wanting to be an American, with wanting to acknowledge that, with wanting to adopt white forbears and influences as well as black ones, with seeing oneself as interracial, not simply mixing with two races but as a link to bringing two races together. So his speech was not antidemocratic but the fullest personal expression of the democracy in which he lived and for which he tried to live. His speech was, to use a popular word of today, "inclusive." His whole being was inclusive: the nigger hair and the proper voice, the white imitations and the black cool. Dancer Gregory Hines kissed Sammy Davis's feet at a 1990 tribute to Davis, a gesture of appreciation for all that Davis had taught him over the years about dancing, for his generosity. ("I was Sammy Davis, Jr., for about 4 years, between 14 and 18," said Hines in an interview. "Dressed like him. Did my hair like him. I idolized him."[71])

When I saw that I nearly cried myself and suddenly wanted

to kiss Davis's conked hair for all it symbolized as the shame and triumph of a man's life. Yes, there was about Davis a generosity that seemed a virtue whose goodness had lessons for all who saw or heard this man during the course of his life. Within that generosity—warm, humane, profound, if sometimes foolish—were good things to know. I'm very grateful to Sammy Davis, Jr., for teaching them to me.

St. Louis, Missouri
September 1, 2000

ENDNOTES

1. Tracey Davis with Dolores A. Barclay, *Sammy Davis, Jr.: My Father* (Los Angeles: General Publishing Group, 1996), p. 62.
2. Roy Newquist, "Sammy Davis, Jr.," *Showcase* (New York: William Morrow and Co., 1966), p. 81.
3. He sponsored a celebrity golf tournament for fifteen years (1973–88), the Sammy Davis, Jr., Greater Hartford Open Golf Tournament, and played the game himself, but he was not an avid golfer. Interestingly, many of the black hoofers and celebrities whom Davis knew well were passionate golfers.
4. Shirley MacLaine, *Dance While You Can* (New York: Ballantine Books, 1991), p. 280.
5. Sammy Davis, Jr., interview in *Alex Haley: The Playboy Interviews*, edited by Murray Fisher (New York: Ballantine Books, 1993), p. 217.
6. There is a wonderful scene in *Tap*, one of the last films in which Davis appeared, filmed only a year before he died, where he and several of the most famous black tap dancers of the '30s, '40s, and '50s are having a cutting contest but with real camaraderie and warmth, much as Davis probably related to these men when they were all in their prime. Davis was always held in high regard by other black hoofers, although he was not the best dancer of his generation.
7. *Sammy Davis, Jr.: My Father*, pp. 42–43.
8. Newquist, *Showcase*, p. 81.
9. An example of his enormous fund-raising abilities for civil rights organizations at this time: "Sammy Davis, Jr., Sparks Record $60,000 Take for Detroit's NAACP," in *The Pittsburgh Courier*, April 22, 1961, section 2, p. 2.
10. Sammy Davis, Jr., with Jane and Burt Boyar, *Why Me?: The Sammy Davis, Jr., Story* (New York: Farrar, Straus and Giroux, 1989), p. 214.
11. *Alex Haley: The Playboy Interviews*, p. 238.

12. Sammy Davis, Jr., with Jane and Burt Boyar, *Yes I Can: The Sammy Davis, Jr., Story* (New York: The Noonday Press, 1990), p. 380.
13. Linda Lovelace with Mike McGrady, *Ordeal: An Autobiography* (New York: Bell Publishing Co., 1980), p. 209.
14. Lerone Bennett, Jr., "Sammy Davis, Jr.," in *Ebony*, March 1980, p. 128.
15. J. Randy Taraborelli, *Sinatra: Behind the Legend* (Secaucus, New Jersey: Birch Lane Press), p. 485.
16. *Why Me?*, p. 284.
17. *Why Me?*, p. 228.
18. Sammy Davis, Jr., *Hollywood in a Suitcase* (New York: William Morrow, 1980), p. 34.
19. Bennett, *Ebony*, p. 126.
20. *Alex Haley: The Playboy Interviews*, p. 231.
21. *Why Me?*, pp. 283, 285, 298–301.
22. Bennett, *Ebony*, p. 134. Davis's contribution to black causes was international. He gave $12,500 to the British Black Power Movement, persuaded largely by Michael X, a leading militant in London in the 1960s and 1970s. See also *Hollywood in a Suitcase*, p. 260.
23. James Conaway, "Sammy Davis, Jr., Has Bought the Bus," in *The New York Times Magazine*, October 15, 1974, p. 111.
24. *Yes I Can*, p. 395.
25. *Yes I Can*, p. 63. Although Davis indicates the race of everyone else who figured largely in his army career, in *Yes I Can* and *Why Me?* he never mentions whether the sergent is black or white. Since segregation in the army during World War II almost certainly precludes the possiblity that a black sergeant would have been put in charge of a mostly white company, it may never have occurred to Davis at first that anyone would think of the sergeant as anything but white. Certainly his remarks to Alex Haley in a 1966 *Playboy* interview clearly imply that the sergeant was white. "No, there was *good* cats there [in the army], too—don't get me wrong—at least some that didn't want to get involved, or who didn't hate Negroes that bad. And I had a sergeant who was one of the finest men I'll ever meet." Later in the interview he says: "I've met too many decent white people to hold the prejudices of other whites against them—even in the Army. Like that sergeant I told you about. He's the one who got me started reading something besides comic books." (*Alex Haley: The Playboy Interviews*, pp. 222, 224.) In a lengthy article on Davis in *Ebony* in March 1974, however, the writer indicates that the sergeant was black, and in a 1976 interview with *People Weekly* Davis told Linda Witt, "A black sergeant named Williams in the Army took me aside and told me about the classics." In Davis's *New York Times* obituary, the sergeant is described as black. The inconsistency of this salient detail

raises some question as to whether the sergeant actually existed, or whether he was in fact a composite or Davis's own invention.

26. *Why Me?*, p. 208.
27. *Yes I Can*, p. 462. One wonders how Davis's willingness to accept a role in *Porgy and Bess* affected his relationship with other black actors and how much it may have spurred his civil rights charity. Harry Belafonte refused outright to take the role of Porgy when it was offered. He thought *Porgy and Bess* was degrading to blacks. (Ironically, Belafonte recorded a Porgy and Bess album in 1959 with Lena Horne. Maybe the music was all right but the story was racist.) Sidney Poitier did not want to do the role either but was pressured to do so in exchange for a role he wanted (in *The Defiant Ones*). Dorothy Dandridge was also confused about whether to appear in the film. Davis, on the other hand, campaigned for the role of Sportin' Life, which producer Sam Goldwyn wanted to give to Cab Calloway, who, incidentally, sings the role on the soundtrack album. Ira Gershwin's wife found Davis repulsive and asked Goldwyn not to give him the role. He agreed, calling Davis "a monkey." But he contracted Davis for the part when he couldn't get Calloway. The filming of the opera was tense, as many of the black actors had misgivings about being there at all, could not get along with Preminger, and were, perhaps, overpoliticizing the entire experience, but Davis, by his own account, got along well with both director Preminger and producer Goldwyn. Davis makes something of the fact that they were all Jews. Davis virtually steals the movie from the other performers and nearly earned an Oscar nomination. Various accounts of the making of the film *Porgy and Bess* can be found in Sammy Davis, Jr.'s, *Hollywood in a Suitcase* (a far fuller account than can be found in either of the autobiographies), Donald Bogle's *Dorothy Dandridge: A Biography*, Otto Preminger's *Preminger: An Autobiography*, Sidney Poitier's *This Life*, and Hollis Alpert's *The Life and Times of Porgy and Bess*.
28. Oriana Fallaci, *The Egotists: Sixteen Surprising Interviews* (Chicago: Henry Regnery Co., 1968), p. 237.
29. *The Egotists*, pp. 228, 230, 237–38.
30. Bennett, *Ebony*, p. 128.
31. May Britt, "Why I Married Sammy Davis, Jr.," in *Ebony*, January 1961, p. 102.
32. "My informal education on the road with Dad and Will was split almost evenly between what I could learn from fellow vaudeville performers and the gems I could pick up on the screen [from movies]," wrote Davis in *Hollywood in a Suitcase*, p. 39. Davis's imagination and ways of knowing were almost entirely shaped by popular culture.
33. Sammy Davis, Jr., with Trude B. Feldman, "Why I Became a Jew," in *Ebony*, February 1960, p. 68. Davis says later in the article: "I wanted to become a Jew because it gave me a great strength. I wanted

to become a Jew because I felt it gave me the answer to an inner peace in life. I wanted to become a Jew because Judaism held an honesty and spiritual peace that was lacking in my personal make-up. I wanted to become a Jew because the customs of Judaism hold a cleanliness that no other philosophy on this earth could offer. I wanted to become a Jew because it was the answer to a life filled with confusion and uncertainty. Judaism gave me security and understanding. I wanted to become a Jew because I wanted to share something with my fellow man, who has been sharing with me" (p. 69).

34. According to "Why I Became a Jew" (*Ebony*, p. 62), Davis, whose mother was Catholic, was reared a Catholic. How this was so when he was being reared largely by his father and grandmother, neither of whom were Catholic, Davis does not explain.

35. *Yes I Can*, p. 280.

36. "I have read a lot, but I am not well read," wrote Davis in *Hollywood in a Suitcase*, p. 16.

37. "[Jack Haley, Jr.] and I both have photographic memories, and out of the 10,000 movies going the rounds I reckon we could hold our own on 90 percent of them," wrote Davis in *Hollywood in a Suitcase* (p. 162). "Why I Married Sammy Davis, Jr.," in *Ebony*, p. 98.

38. *Dance While You Can*, pp. 279–80.

39. Newquist, *Showcase*, pp. 84–85.

40. *Why Me?*, p. 273.

41. *Alex Haley: The Playboy Interviews*, p. 220.

42. *Yes I Can*, p. 500.

43. Between 1957 and 1966, the height of the Rat Pack, Lawford appeared in *Never So Few, Ocean's Eleven, Exodus, Pepe, Sergeants 3, Advise and Consent, The Longest Day, Dead Ringer, Sylvia, Harlowe, The Oscar*, and *A Man Called Adam*. He also starred in the television series *The Thin Man* from 1957 to 1959. This is an impressive body of work.

44. Information on the number of performances is from the liner notes to the *Mr. Wonderful* CD.

45. *Why Me?*, p. 145.

46. This adds a note of extratextual and intertextual complexity to *Anna Lucasta*, for Davis is not exactly the star of the film. (The film is about a prostitute, Anna Lucasta, and her relationship with her family, particularly with her father, who hates her, and there are many not-so-subtle incestuous overtones. So, if anyone is the star, it would be, without question, Eartha Kitt. If anyone is remembered from this film, it is probably, without question, Sammy Davis, Jr.) He certainly does not have the biggest role. But he does sing the soundtrack song for the film and his presence seems to submerge the other actors (except Kitt), nearly all of whom were experienced black actors—Rex Ingram, Frederick O'Neal, Alvin Childress, James Edwards—many of

whom had played their roles several years earlier in the stage production.

47. *Why Me?*, p. 284.
48. Lawrence J. Quirk and William Schoell, *The Rat Pack: The Hey-Hey Days of Frank and the Boys* (Dallas: Taylor Publishing Co., 1998), p. 170; and Shawn Levy, *Rat Pack Confidential: Frank, Dean, Sammy, Peter, Joey and the Last Great Showbiz Party* (New York: Doubleday, 1998), pp. 73–74. Davis himself never admitted that this was the reason he lost the role. In his tribute to American films, *Hollywood in a Suitcase*, Davis attributes the loss of the role to creative differences with Sinatra about how the role should be played (pp. 88–89). Knowing how desperately Davis wanted to do film and television at this time (he was willing, by his admission to his agent, to appear in a Hollywood film for fifty dollars), this excuse Davis proffers for the lost role in *Never So Few* does not seem convincing.
49. Ken Barnes, liner notes for *It's All Over But the Swingin'* and *I Gotta Right to Swing* CD, MCA, 1998.
50. *Yes I Can*, p. 228.
51. *Yes I Can*, p. 500.
52. *Yes I Can*, p. 105.
53. *Alex Haley: The Playboy Interviews*, p. 237.
54. Davis, for instance, appeared in two episodes of *The Rifleman*, both times as a quick-draw sharpshooter. Obviously, producers wanted to take advantage of Davis's ability to do tricks with a gun. His first appearance, in "Two Ounces of Tin," is especially noteworthy because he plays a former Wild West performer (with Buffalo Bill) who becomes a killer. His father was murdered by a mob, when Davis's character was a youngster, with some implications about racism in the show as the sheriff does nothing to stop the mob. Davis's character now returns to the town to kill the current sheriff who happens to be the Rifleman, substituting for the real sheriff. Davis is ultimately killed in a showdown with the Rifleman but his character is generally presented sympathetically and he is certainly a more complex character morally than most black portrayals on television at the time. In a 1961 episode of *Lawman*, Davis also plays a quick-draw cowboy who kills a white man for abusing Davis's cow. In short, Davis was almost certainly the first black gunslinger on network television. This was so pathbreaking that George Lincoln Rockwell, the founder of the American Nazi Party in 1959 and a figure of some notoriety in the 1960s, mentions it in the opening chapter of his 1967 book, *White Power*: "Sammy Davis, Jr., the Negro-Jew entertainer, plays 'the fastest gun in the West' in 'The Rifleman' TV show. When this one-eyed Jewish Negro appears in the western town, we are shown all *the White men running and hiding*. Americans swallow this with-

out protest" (p. 31, emphasis Rockwell's). Davis was a particular target of Nazi protest and demonstrations when he announced his impending marriage to May Britt.

55. Davis wrote in *Hollywood in a Suitcase* about this film: "We were trying to make an 'adult' film long before the phrase was invented. It was probably before its time . . . The critics were kind to me personally, but the film itself was totally misunderstood" (p. 90). Some have always thought that *A Man Called Adam* was disguised autobiography: a car accident caused by Davis's character results in the blindness of one of the trumpeter's band members, which seems to echo the real-life car accident, where Davis was the driver, that resulted in Davis's partial blindness. Davis's character's dislike of the black old-time jazzman, played by Louis Armstrong, echoes Davis's real-life dislike of aspects of old-time black vaudeville. Davis's character's intense racial self-consciousness and hatred of discrimination clearly echo Davis's real-life feelings. Oddly, Davis had had an oral run-in in the black press with Louis Armstrong back in 1957 when Armstrong came out against President Eisenhower's reluctance to send in federal troops to protect black children integrating Central High School in Little Rock. Davis criticized Armstrong in the October 12, 1957, edition of *The Pittsburgh Courier*, one of the leading black newspapers in the country, by saying: "You cannot voice an opinion about a situation which is basically discrimination, integration, etc., and then go out and appear before segregated audiences . . . which Louis Armstrong had done for many years" (p. 22). Davis went on to criticize Armstrong for singing a song using the word "darkies." Davis is quoted as saying, quite condescendingly, it must be added: "Louis Armstrong has always been regarded—let me be as kind as I possibly can; I think Louis Armstrong first of all is a great talent—great, as much as I hate the wordage, a great credit to his race, but he has also been regarded by his race as a man who . . . well . . ." Many attacked Davis for his opinion, including jazz record producer Norman Granz (*The Pittsburgh Courier*, October 19, 1957, p. 6). Armstrong was quoted in *The Pittsburgh Courier* on March 2, 1957, a few months before the Little Rock incident, as saying, "I'll blow anywhere. The horn doesn't know anything about those 'race troubles.' " Interestingly, the black press responded very enthusiastically to Armstrong's anger over Little Rock. Both Evelyn Cunningham, the influential columnist of *The Pittsburgh Courier*, and the *Chicago Defender* editorial page suggested, a bit implausibly, that Armstrong should be awarded the NAACP's Spingarn Medal for his pronouncement about Little Rock. Perhaps by 1966, Davis and Armstrong had managed to heal the breach in order to work together on the film. It seems especially curious that Davis would attack Armstrong for being

insufficiently race conscious when he himself was being attacked by blacks at that time on the same charge. In any case, it is interesting to note that some have suggested that trumpeter Miles Davis was the model for this film because of the famed trumpeter's militant temperament and refusal to see jazz as anything but an art music, aspects that Sammy Davis's character tried to convey. Incidentally, Cicely Tyson, who was Miles Davis's girlfriend in the mid-1960s—featured on the cover of the 1967 *Sorcerer* album—and was eventually to become his fourth wife, was the female lead in *A Man Called Adam*.

56. *Yes I Can*, p. 103.

57. The army, indeed, the entire American armed services, were not integrated until the Korean War (1950–53). President Truman had issued Executive Order 9981 in 1948, which officially integrated the armed forces, but the exigencies of the war speeded up the process enormously. The army, particularly, was dragging its feet until white casualties mounted in the early days of Korea. It was always felt that all-black units were not reliable in combat and were easily demoralized, which was, to some extent, true. Blacks had a mixed record in combat in all-black units. Davis served in the army during World War II when it was still officially segregated. There was some integration in the army at that time with certain companies and regiments and Davis, obviously, had been placed in the first of these integrated units. One wonders what Davis would have felt about the army and what his experiences would have been like had he been in an all-black unit as most black soldiers were at the time. Incidentally, in an interview Davis gave *People Weekly* (August 28, 1978), he mentioned that many thought him homosexual because of his excessive jewelry. "The truth is I'm not a homosexual, but I'm not ashamed to say I had a homosexual experience . . . I was in the Army. I was 17, and I was little." One wonders how much of his army experience Davis censored for his autobiographies.

58. *Yes I Can*, p. 73.

59. Ralph Ellison, "Richard Wright's Blues," *Shadow and Act* (New York: Vintage Books, 1972), pp. 89–90.

60. The entry on Davis in *Africana: The Encyclopedia of the African and African American Experience*, edited by Kwame Anthony Appiah and Henry Louis Gates, Jr. (New York: Civitas Books, 1999), states that "[in] 1959 [Davis] married dancer Loray White but soon left her for Swedish actress May Britt . . ." This is not true. First of all, Davis married White at the beginning of 1958, not 1959. Davis and White are pictured on the front page of the January 18, 1958, issue of *The Pittsburgh Courier* as newlyweds. (The date of the marriage was January 10, 1958.) Second, Davis married White because he was being pressured (some say that he was being threatened by the Mob, but Davis has always denied this) to discontinue his affair with Kim No-

vak. Rumors of the demise of his marriage to White began to appear in the black press within a few months of his marriage, that is, in 1958. On April 25, 1958, White and Davis separated. See *The Pittsburgh Courier*, "Sammy's Bride Reported Consulting Attorney," May 31, 1958, p. 3, and "Sammy and Bride Feuding: 'She Knows How I Feel About Frankie,' " May 3, 1958. His marriage to White was legally over by early 1959, well before shooting began on *Porgy and Bess*. He had not even met Britt at this time. See *The Pittsburgh Courier*, February 14, 1959: "Seeks $2,000 Alimony from Sammy Davis, Jr.: Loray Says 'Mr. Wonderful' Is Worth a Million Bucks." Indeed, Davis had a brief engagement to another white woman, Joan Stuart, a Canadian, before the end of 1959, but her parents disapproved of the marriage. Davis did not announce the official end of this engagement until April 4, 1960. See *The Pittsburgh Courier*, April 16, 1960: "Loray Was Right; Sammy Davis, Jr., Won't Marry Joan" and *Jet*, April 21, 1960: "Joan Did the Talking, but Sammy Pulled the Strings." He first encounters Britt at the Fox commissary one month before he is scheduled to begin a movie in Las Vegas. That movie is *Ocean's Eleven*, for which shooting began in late January 1960. So he met Britt for the first time either in December 1959 or early January 1960. They announced their engagement in May 1960, one month after he officially broke off with Stuart. How much Britt may have been a rebound romance because of Davis's humiliation at the hands of Stuart is unclear, as Davis does not mention the Stuart affair in either of his autobiographies. In any case, it was Britt, not Davis, who was still married to someone else during their courtship. During Davis's marriage to White, he tried to commit suicide by running his car off a road (*Yes I Can*, p. 455). Also, the entry is incorrect when it states "[Davis and Britt] had one child, and he adopted her two children." Britt and Davis had one child and *together* they adopted two other biracial children. Britt had no children from her previous marriage, as the entry implies. Another error in this entry: "His 1965 autobiography *Yes I Can*, earned him the Spingarn Medal for the National Association for the Advancement of Colored People." He won the Spingarn Medal for the enormous amount of money he donated and raised for civil rights causes in the 1960s. Arguably, only Harry Belafonte exceeded Davis in this regard. The Spingarn Medal is a lifetime achievement award. It is not given for one accomplishment.

61. Robert A. DeLeon, "None of This Has Been Easy," in *Ebony*, March 1974, p. 44.
62. Bennett, *Ebony*, p. 128.
63. Bennett, *Ebony*, p. 132. This revelation is striking because it shows that Davis in the 1950s and 1960s was not far removed from Louis Armstrong, the old-time entertainer he had criticized in 1957. Arm-

strong always said that he had been told as a youth in New Orleans to get himself a strong white man who would put his hand "on my shoulder and say, 'That's my nigger.' " In effect, Sinatra, for a certain portion of Davis's career, had just that role.

64. Richard M. Nixon, *RN, The Memoirs of Richard Nixon* (New York: Grossett and Dunlap, 1978), p. 539.
65. *Why Me?*, p. 272.
66. *Hollywood in a Suitcase*, p. 247.
67. Ibid.
68. *Alex Haley: The Playboy Interviews*, p. 238.
69. *Alex Haley: The Playboy Interviews*, p. 225.
70. Newquist, *Showcase*, p. 89.
71. Mary Murphy, "Top Dad," in *TV Guide*, October 4–10, 1997, p. 24. The article continues: "On his deathbed in 1990, Davis comforted a grieving Hines with a prophetic gesture of kindness. 'He knew it was the last time I was going to see him, so he made a throwing motion, like picking up the ball and throwing it to me. And I caught it.' "

SAMMY DAVIS, JR., CHRONOLOGY

December 8, 1925: Born in Harlem to Sam Davis, Sr., and Elvera "Baby" Sanchez; parents' marriage lasts only two years; father and father's mother rear Davis

1927: Ramona, sister, is born; lives with mother's family

1928: Starts performing on stage regularly with father, Sam Davis, Sr., and Will Mastin as a dancer

1933: Appears with Ethel Waters in *Rufus Jones for President*; is billed as Will Mastin's Gang, featuring Little Sammy; with grandmother's help avoids attending school

1936: The act disbands as Will Mastin's Gang, a vaudeville troupe of fifteen, and becomes a dance trio, Will Mastin's Trio with Davis, Jr., as the star; they struggle for bookings through the 1930s

1941: Meets Frank Sinatra in Detroit when Sinatra is performing with the Dorsey band and the Will Mastin Trio is the opening act; the two men become friends

1943: Joins the army and is stationed at Fort Francis E. Warren in Cheyenne, Wyoming; he is harassed and severely beaten by racist white soldiers in his barracks in very early military integration (armed services were not officially integrated until 1948); goes through basic training four times; is rejected for combat duty because of an athletic heart; is assigned to Special Services and participates in stage shows for eight months

1945: Discharged from army; Will Mastin Trio travels as Mickey Rooney's opening act for six months; opens at El Rancho in segregated Las Vegas for the first time

1947: Sinatra arranges for Will Mastin Trio to open for him at the Capitol Theater in New York at $1,250 a week

1949: Signs with Capitol Records

1951: Will Mastin Trio opens for Janis Paige at Ciro's in Los Angeles and becomes a big hit; Davis, Jr., is a star

April 1953: Will Mastin Trio headlines at the Copacabana in New York

November 1954: Loses left eye in auto accident while en route to record soundtrack for Tony Curtis film *Six Bridges to Cross*; does record soundtrack after accident; signs with Decca Records, records "The Birth of the Blues"

1955: Begins investigation of Judaism, which leads eventually to conversion; roasted by the Friar's Club, first black performer so honored; begins to socialize with Humphrey Bogart's Rat Pack; releases first album, *Starring Sammy Davis, Jr.*, with hit single "That Old Black Magic"; it yields two other hits, "Hey There" and "The Birth of the Blues"

March 1956–February 1957: Stars on Broadway in *Mr. Wonderful*

1957: Bogart dies; Sinatra becomes the leader of the Rat Pack

January 1958: Marries dancer Loray White after receiving negative attention about love affair with Kim Novak; appears in *General Electric Theater* drama entitled "Auf Wiedersehen"

April 1958: Separates from Loray White

1958: Featured in *Anna Lucasta* with Eartha Kitt

December 1958: Starts divorce proceedings against Loray White

1959: Stars as Sportin' Life in *Porgy and Bess* with Sidney Poitier and Dorothy Dandridge; appears in *Dick Powell's Zane Grey Theater* Western drama entitled "Mission"

1960: *Ocean's Eleven*, first Rat Pack movie, with Davis, Frank Sinatra, Dean Martin, Peter Lawford, Joey Bishop; campaigns with Sinatra and the rest of the Rat Pack for John F. Kennedy in his Presidential bid; is booed by many delegates at the Democratic National Convention who disapprove of his impending marriage to May Britt; Davis's conversion to Judaism gains more publicity as he writes an article for the February issue of *Ebony* about his conversion to Judaism and an article about his conversion appears in *Time* (February 1) entitled "Jewish Negro"

1960: *Pepe* (cameo appearance)

November 1960: Marries Swedish actress May Britt in a Jewish ceremony; Sinatra is best man at wedding

1961: Guest appearance on television Western *Lawman*; signs with Reprise Records, Frank Sinatra's company; daughter, Tracey, is born on July 5

1962: Guest appearance on television Western *The Rifleman*; *Sergeants 3*, second Rat Pack movie with Davis; records the Newley/Bricusse songs "What Kind of Fool Am I" and "Once in a Lifetime"; both become signature tunes

1963: Guest appearance on television series *Ben Casey*; *Johnny Cool* with Henry Silva; *Threepenny Opera*

1964: *Robin and the 7 Hoods*, third Rat Pack movie with Davis, also stars Bing Crosby

1964–1966: Stars in *Golden Boy*, his second Broadway show

1965: Records the Newley/Bricusse song "Who Can I Turn To (When Nobody Needs Me)," becomes another signature tune; publishes *Yes I Can*, his first autobiography; stars in the television special *The Swinging World of Sammy Davis, Jr.*

1966: *The Sammy Davis, Jr., Show* (lasts four months); stars in *A Man Called Adam* with Louis Armstrong, Frank Sinatra, Jr., and Peter Lawford

1968: Divorces May Britt; has top-ten hit with "I've Gotta Be Me"; stars with Peter Lawford in *Salt and Pepper*; wins NAACP's Spingarn Medal

1969: Guest appearance in *Sweet Charity*, which stars Shirley MacLaine

1970: Marries dancer Altovise Gore; stars in *One More Time* with Peter Lawford, directed by Jerry Lewis, sequel to *Salt and Pepper*

1972: Records Newley/Bricusse song "The Candy Man," which hits number one on the pop chart, and Jerry Jeff Walker's

"Mr. Bojangles," which becomes another signature tune; supports Richard Nixon for re-election, is invited to perform at the White House; is booed at a PUSH convention because of his support of Nixon (chronicled in 1973 documentary, *Save the Children*); visits troops in Vietnam; wins Grammy Award for Best Male Pop Vocalist for "The Candy Man"

1975–1977: Syndicated show entitled *Sammy and Company*

1978: Stars in revival of *Stop the World, I Want to Get Off*

July 1979: Will Mastin dies

1980: Publishes *Hollywood in a Suitcase*

1981: Guest appearance in *Cannonball Run*

1983: Stops drinking alcohol when sickened by a damaged liver

1985: Has hip replacement surgery

1987: Receives Kennedy Center for the Performing Arts' Gold Medal for Lifetime Achievement from President Reagan; has second hip operation

1988: Teams up with Frank Sinatra and Dean Martin for a tour; Martin pulls out and is replaced by Liza Minnelli

May 1988: Sam Davis, Sr., dies

1989: Portrays Little Mo in *Tap*, which stars Gregory Hines, Davis's last film; publishes *Why Me?*, his second autobiography; diagnosed with throat cancer

November 1989: ABC special, *60th Anniversary Salute to Sammy Davis, Jr.*, aired February 4, 1990

May 16, 1990: Dies of throat cancer at his home in Beverly Hills, California

STAGE APPEARANCES

Mr. Wonderful, 1956–57

An Evening with Sammy Davis, Jr. (in England), 1961

Golden Boy, 1964–66

Sammy Davis . . . That's All (one-man show), Philadelphia, 1966

Sammy on Broadway, 1974

Stop the World, I Want to Get Off, 1978

FILM APPEARANCES (SIGNIFICANT ROLES)

Rufus Jones for President, 1933
Anna Lucasta, 1958
Porgy and Bess, 1959
Ocean's Eleven, 1960
Sergeants 3, 1962
Threepenny Opera, 1963
Johnny Cool, 1963
Robin and the 7 Hoods, 1964
A Man Called Adam, 1966
Salt and Pepper, 1968
Sweet Charity, 1969
One More Time, 1970
Cannonball Run, 1981
Cannonball Run II, 1983
Tap, 1989

TELEVISION SERIES (HIS OWN)

The Sammy Davis, Jr., Show, 1966
Sammy and Company, 1975–77

TELEVISION MOVIES

The Trackers, 1971
Alice in Wonderland, 1985
The Kid Who Loved Christmas, 1990

TELEVISION APPEARANCES

Davis made an extraordinary number of guest appearances on many television shows (and a bewildering variety of shows) for four decades. This list highlights only some of his noteworthy work.

General Electric Theater, 1958, 1961
Dick Powell's Zane Grey Theater, 1959
Lawman, 1961
Hennessey, 1962
The Rifleman, 1962 (two episodes)
The Andy Williams Show, 1962, 1963
Ben Casey, 1963
The Jerry Lewis Show, 1963
Burke's Law, 1963
The Danny Thomas Show, 1963
The Patty Duke Show, 1965
The Wild, Wild West, 1966
Batman, 1966
I Dream of Jeannie, 1967
The Joey Bishop Show, 1968
The Beverly Hillbillies, 1969
The Mod Squad, 1969, 1970 (three episodes)
The Flip Wilson Show, 1970
The Name of the Game, 1970
Here's Lucy, 1970
All in the Family, 1972
The Courtship of Eddie's Father, 1972
Chico and the Man, 1975
Carol Burnett Show, 1975
The Jeffersons, 1975
Charlie's Angels, 1977
One Life to Live, 1979, 1981, 1983
General Hospital, 1982
Fantasy Island, 1983
The Cosby Show, 1989

Davis made numerous appearances on *The Tonight Show* as both guest and substitute host. He also appeared many times on *The Hollywood Palace,* the *Mike Douglas Show,* the *Ed Sullivan Show, Rowan and Martin's Laugh-In,* and *Hollywood Squares.* He made appearances as well on the *Dinah Shore*

Show, the *Steve Allen Show*, the *Sonny and Cher Show*, the *Donnie and Marie Show*, the *Nat King Cole Show*, *This Is Tom Jones*, the *Eddie Cantor Show*, the *Milton Berle Show*, the *Captain and Tenille Show*, the *Dean Martin Show*, the *Dean Martin Celebrity Roast*, *Hee Haw*, the *Dick Cavett Show*, the *David Frost Show*, and the *Merv Griffin Show*. He appeared as well on *Starsky and Hutch*, *The Love Boat*, *Diff'rent Strokes*, *Gimme a Break*, *77 Sunset Strip*, *Hullabaloo*, and *Kojak*.

TELEVISION SPECIALS (HIS OWN)

The Swinging World of Sammy Davis, Jr., 1965
Sammy Davis, Jr., and the Wonderful World of Children, 1966
Sammy Davis, Jr., in Europe, 1969
60th Anniversary Salute to Sammy Davis, Jr., 1990

OTHER TELEVISION SPECIALS

The Jerry Lewis Special, 1957
Holiday in Las Vegas, 1957
The Frank Sinatra Timex Show, 1960
The Strollin' Twenties (Harry Belafonte–produced CBS special inspired by Langston Hughes's autobiography, *The Big Sea*, a tribute to Harlem of the 1920s), 1966
Danny Thomas Special, 1967
Movin' with Nancy (special hosted by Nancy Sinatra), 1967
Frank Sinatra, Jr., with Family and Friends, 1969
Rowan and Martin Bite the Hand That Feeds Them, 1970
The Bob Hope Special, 1971
Burt Bacharach Special, 1972
Duke Ellington . . . We Love You Madly, 1973
A Show Business Salute to Milton Berle, 1973
The Henry Fonda Special, 1973
Bob Hope's Bicentennial Star-Spangled Spectacular, 1976

America Salutes Richard Rodgers: The Sound of His Music,
1976

All-Star Tribute to John Wayne, 1976

*Texaco Presents Bob Hope's All-Star Comedy Spectacular from
Lake Tahoe,* 1977

*Texaco Presents Bob Hope's All-Star Tribute to the Palace The-
ater,* 1978

Steve and Eydie Celebrate Irving Berlin (Steve Lawrence and
Eydie Gorme), 1978

Celebrity Challenge of the Sexes, 1979

Circus of the Stars, 1979

The Bob Hope Special, 1979

Sinatra: The First Forty Years, 1980

*Bob Hope Presents a Celebration with Stars of Comedy and
Music,* 1981

All-Star Party for Lucille Ball, 1984

All-Star Party for Clint Eastwood, 1986

Bob Hope's High-Flying Birthday, 1986

Las Vegas: An All-Star 75th Anniversary, 1987

Bob Hope's Super Bowl Party, 1989

Frank, Liza, and Sammy: The Ultimate Event, 1989

Tappin' (behind-the-scenes look at the making of *Tap*), 1989

SELECT DISCOGRAPHY

Starring Sammy Davis, Jr., Decca, 1955

Just for Lovers, Decca, 1955

Mr. Wonderful, original cast recording, Decca, 1956

Boy Meets Girl (with Carmen McRae), Decca, 1957

Sammy Davis at Town Hall, Decca, 1959

Porgy and Bess (with Carmen McRae), Decca, 1959

I Got a Right to Swing, Decca, 1960

Wham of Sam, Reprise, 1961

What Kind of Fool Am I, Reprise, 1962

As Long As She Needs Me, Reprise, 1963

Golden Boy, original cast recording, Capitol, 1964
The Nat King Cole Songbook, Reprise, 1965
Sammy Davis, Jr., and Count Basie, Our Shining Hour, 1965, Verve
Sammy's Back on Broadway, Reprise, 1965
A Man Called Adam, soundtrack recording, Reprise, 1966
Sammy Davis, Jr., Sings, Laurindo Almeida Plays, DCC, 1966
The Sounds of '66 (with Buddy Rich), Reprise, 1966
Salt and Pepper, soundtrack recording, United Artists, 1968
Sweet Charity, soundtrack recording, Decca, 1969
I've Gotta Be Me, Reprise, 1969
Something for Everyone, Motown, 1970
Stop the World, I Want to Get Off, original cast recording, 1979
Closest of Friends, Applause, 1982

THOSE WHO KNEW
HIM

○

I realize that in those days feelings against the Negro were very high, and the Negro actor had to take what he could get. There had to be a starting place somewhere. Too many Negroes don't realize that if it hadn't been for a Hattie McDaniel, there possibly would be no Dorothy Dandridge; if there were no Stepin Fetchit, Mantan Moreland or Ben Carter, there would be no Sidney Poitier. I can understand why those Negro actors in the early days had to accept such roles as they did, but that certainly doesn't have to be done today. The Negro has proved to be the equal of any race on earth, and the producers must fall in with this line of reasoning.   —Sammy Davis, Jr., *The Pittsburgh Courier*, March 25, 1961

My people are my people, and my religion is my religion. They are not interconnected. My people are first. I happen to be a *Black* Jew. I am first Black and the religion I have chosen is Judaism. That doesn't mean that as a Black I agree with every other Black or that as a Jew I agree with every other Jew. As a Jew I would give my money to the state of Israel, and I have. I have Israel bonds, and I am committed to the independence of Israel. But there are differences of opinion in Israel and in the American Jewish community, and every Jew has a right to make up his or her mind on the issues. Now as a Jew and as a Black, I am committed to a policy of dialogue in America and in the world. As for Andrew Young, I don't know *who* was behind his forced resignation [as United States Representative to the United Nations during the Carter Administration], but as a Black I am mad as hell with *whoever* was responsible for what happened to Andrew Young.   —Sammy Davis, Jr., *Ebony*, March 1980

Sammy Davis, Jr., spoke up: "I won't be here on Monday."
"Why not?" I asked.
"It's Rosh Hashanah," he explained. "It's the Jewish New Year."
I said, "I'm Jewish too, Sammy, and I'll be here on Monday."
"There's a difference," he replied. "You're an old Jew. I'm a new Jew."
          —Otto Preminger (on the set of *Porgy and Bess*),
                    Preminger: An Autobiography

First in this section is a piece by Davis's second wife, May Britt, that appeared in *Ebony* magazine in January 1961, shortly after she married Davis, entitled "Why I Married Sammy Davis, Jr."

Next in this section is an in-depth interview with Altovise Gore that appeared in *Sepia* in 1978, where she talks honestly, though guardedly, about her then-eight-year marriage to Davis.

Sidney Poitier was a longtime close friend of Davis's. (Davis named one of his adopted sons after the famed actor.) Here, in an excerpt from *This Life*, his autobiography, Poitier describes a vacation he went on with Davis in the Bahamas where Davis tried, unsuccessfully, to make it with *Mod Squad* star Peggy Lipton, but wound up happily with Altovise Gore, a meeting that seemed to facilitate their marriage.

Linda Lovelace devotes nearly a chapter in *Ordeal* to her relationship with Davis. When the book was published, Davis countered by saying that their relationship was "casual" and suggested that she made up most of what she describes here, although he never denied that they had sex. Yet Davis, by his own admission in both *Hollywood in a Suitcase* and *Why Me?*, knew many porn stars very well and led a hedonistic life. In *Why Me?* and *Hollywood in a Suitcase*, Davis admitted to being a close friend of Chuck Traynor and Marilyn Chambers, whom Traynor married after he ditched Lovelace.

Nancy Sinatra knew Davis nearly all of her life. The excerpts from her book, *Frank Sinatra, My Father*, describe the joyous years of the Rat Pack in the early 1960s and furnish an account of Davis's disinvitation to the Kennedy Presidential inauguration.

This excerpt from Peter Harry Brown's biography, *Kim Novak: Reluctant Goddess*, provides the most detailed account of the relationship between Novak and Davis, as well as her own brief commentary about it.

Eartha Kitt describes her first encounter with Davis in the early 1950s when she was touring with a show called *New Faces of 1952*. Later, in 1958, they worked together in the film *Anna Lucasta*. Her meeting with Davis takes place after 1952 because she refers to the filming of *New Faces* being completed (it was released in 1954). But she obviously met Davis before his car accident in late 1954. In this excerpt from her autobiography, *I'm Still Here*, she claims never to have heard of Davis or the Will Mastin Trio, although Davis by this time was a major star. She mistakenly refers to the Will Mastin Trio as the "Masterson Trio."

This brief excerpt from Ava Gardner's 1990 autobiography, *Ava: My Story*, gives her account of the famous Christmas photo spread with her and Davis that appeared in *Confidential* and implied that they were lovers, an untrue allegation that deeply troubled Davis since he felt it would adversely affect his friendship with Sinatra, who had just divorced Gardner but still carried a torch.

Quincy Jones knew Davis for most of his life as a friend and sometimes collaborator. (Jones was on the vacation that Poitier describes in the excerpt from his autobiography that is used here.) This tribute, from the June 28, 1990, issue of *Rolling Stone*, remembers a man who lived hard but who opened many doors.

Kathy McKee's 1991 *Penthouse* article, "My Secret Life with Sammy Davis," confirms much of what Lovelace wrote. Once again, we have a graphic description of sex as well as some account of Davis's Satanism, which Davis himself mentioned in *Why Me?* and of which he apparently made no secret. He told his daughter, Tracey, about it as well. His cocaine use, described in this article, is also discussed frankly in *Why Me?*

Shirley MacLaine and Davis worked together in the 1969 film *Sweet Charity* and both are in *Ocean's Eleven*, although they have no scenes together. MacLaine understood Davis well, as these excerpts from two of her autobiographies demonstrate. The excerpts are from *Dance While You Can* and *My Lucky Stars: A Hollywood Memoir*.

Merle Haggard's story about how Davis stood up for him when he performed in Tahoe shows not only that Davis was Mr. Las Vegas but that he could be extraordinarily generous and kind. This excerpt is from Merle Haggard's autobiography, *My House of Memories*.

This excerpt from Cholly Atkins's autobiography, *Class Act: The Life of Choreographer Cholly Atkins* (unpublished), provides one of the best descriptions of Davis as a child performer with the Will Mastin Trio. Atkins, twelve years older, knew Davis as they both worked in the same black hoofer's milieu.

This section concludes with Tracey Davis's touching account of her reconciliation with her father after years of tension and unhappiness. This excerpt is from her book, *Sammy Davis, Jr.: My Father*.

"WHY I MARRIED SAMMY DAVIS, JR.,"
by May Britt, *Ebony*

At approximately 3:30 Sunday afternoon, November 13, 1960, I became the wife of famed entertainer Sammy Davis, Jr. It was the final act in a chain of events which, I have been assured by some, will cost me my career, friends, security and a great deal of future happiness. Why, I have been asked, would I risk all that for this one man?

The answer, to me, is very simple. I love him.

And the only reason given me why I shouldn't marry him is because of the racial difference, which seems to be a problem here in America but not in my native Sweden. Actually, the whole of Europe looks at it through different eyes than America.

I never thought about marrying a colored person before, because I never really knew any before. I don't think I even ever met any before I met Sammy.

I came to this country in 1957, and in the next three years made four motion pictures: *The Young Lions, The Hunters, Blue Angel* and *Murder, Inc.* One day last year, a girl who had worked in *Blue Angel* called me and said: "Sammy Davis, Jr., is going to have a party and wants you to come over."

I said, "I don't know Mr. Davis. If he wants me to come, tell him to call me himself."

He did. I was glad because I was waiting by the telephone. I had seen him perform about two years earlier at the Moulin Rouge in Hollywood. I didn't know it at the time, but he had seen me in *Blue Angel*, and wanted to meet me.

So I went to the party—with a date. But Sammy and I were friends from the very beginning. He invited me to Las Vegas to see his show, and I went there with my mother.

Later, a big party of us went on a boat trip to Mexico. It was an enormous boat with about ten of us on it. Sammy had all his movies with him, so we stayed up every night watching them until almost dawn.

I guess things were getting serious with us then and I knew it, but compared to the way it is now, it doesn't seem that it was so serious because the longer we know each other the closer we are.

When Sammy went to London last year, I flew there to introduce him to my father. I was a little nervous when I went to pick up my father at the airport, as I suppose every girl is at a time like that. Sammy was supposed to be busy with some rehearsals and all, so I had it all made up in my mind how I was going to tell my father about him. But when we entered the hotel, Sammy stepped off the elevator on his way out, and so they just met there in the lobby while my little speech faded into the air. After Sammy left us and we got on the elevator, my father said: "Now there's a real gentleman." He liked Sammy from the beginning.

Of course, I know now that even if my parents had been against it, I would still marry Sammy. But it is better if they are with you.

It was while in London that I got my first hate letter. It upset me, but then I realized I would keep on getting them. I know that people should have *something* better to do with their time, and if they don't—poor them.

Sammy and I have never personally run into any racial problems but people start bugging you from the outside, that's what is so ridiculous. It never happens in the entertainment business, because Sammy is very close with most of the people in it. But sometimes when we are out I see people sitting in a corner, staring us down.

This poses no real problem for me among my friends; I never had many. I very seldom went to parties, and if I were invited to dinner I could spend a whole day trying to think up excuses not to show up. Oh, I may have a few acquaintances who are shocked at the idea of Sammy and me, but that's their problem.

I never care too much what people think anyway. You can't let it ruin your life because they don't really care that deeply about you.

Besides, Sammy warned me that there would be trouble. He told me that I might lose my career and that he might lose his, too. But that if a thing were that shaky, then it wasn't worth having in the first place.

As far as my career is concerned, I'm still under contract to 20th Century-Fox. The option is up in June, 1961, and I don't know what will happen then. I would like to do one or two pictures a year because I love my work very much, but if I had to choose between it and Sammy, I would choose Sammy.

Besides, I want to raise a family. I'm 26 years old. Sammy is 34 and it's time he became a father. I think he'll make a great father, he's so wonderful with children. I guess I would like to have about 500 kids and, while everything is welcome, I think maybe I would like the first one to be a girl.

Furthermore, I am not worried about the problems my children will have being the products of a mixed marriage. I think it is up to the parents to show them more love and more security, and I don't think they can afford to hate anybody.

I guess it's hard for me to put into words all the reasons why I love the man who is going to father these children. I can't say exactly what love is, but I think that when you come across it, you know it. And I know I feel far different inside than I've ever felt before.

Sammy is very warm-hearted and sensitive and generous, qualities I admire in him. He is also very attentive to me. We like many of the same things: horseback riding, music, movies and television.

But the main thing is that we can communicate. If you can communicate with another human being, it is so much more important than whether you play golf together.

Sammy and I are the complete opposites in physical build— as anyone can plainly see. But I think he's a beautiful man— that nose looks just great. It gives him character. And he's so beautiful inside. You can sit down and talk to him and he's so understanding.

He's not a saint—far from it. Sometimes he is completely impossible. But I am not out to revolutionize him.

Nor am I out to revolutionize the world. I just married the man I love.

—*January 1961*

"MRS. SAMMY DAVIS, JR., SPEAKS OUT,"
interview with Altovise Gore, by Patrick William Salvo, *Sepia*

Q. *How does it feel to be the wife of such a great man as Sammy Davis?*

A. Well, I must tell you, it is never a dull moment. It's exciting and I love traveling around with him, as I do when he does night clubs.

Q. *So you are with him at his side constantly?*
A. Yes, quite a lot. I just started doing my own thing as far as acting again and getting into wigs and so forth. But I am usually with him as much as I can be and we always go off for the weekend or always for an opening—like Vegas, Tahoe, and those kinds of places.

Q. *Does the traveling ever get boring? Do you ever feel like part of the trappings?*
A. It's not really boring, but sometimes it's hard finding something to do in a town where there really is nothing to do. No theatre or no this or that. I don't get tired of ever seeing him perform. But I do get tired of going to a city where there is nothing constructive for me to do, except exercise, ski, or play tennis.

Q. *Was it ever brought to your attention that you would get a position in his entourage—performing or facilitating his show?*
A. When I met him originally, which was in 1969, I worked with him in London in "Golden Boy" and I played the part of his sister. After doing that at the London Palladium for about six to eight months, I went on the road with him as a lead, what they would call a soubrette—which is the lead dancer. He had five girls and we all did numbers and danced with him and so forth. So I traveled around with him then for a year. Now I don't think I would ever go back on the stage again. Especially as a singer, because I don't want to compete in singing. Besides, he says I sing off key.

Q. *So basically there is a little bit of a threat there.*
A. Well, I want to be there, be in that area. I want to pursue my career as far as acting. I don't want to sing, because I know he

sings better, although he says I'm a better dancer. But he is a better hoofer, which means a tap dancer. As a singer, I am a gypsy singer, meaning: I belt. I'm a dancer that belts loud songs and I can get that across. But the other sings his heart.

Q. They say behind every great man there is a great woman, but you are actually standing beside your man, aren't you?
A. I'm trying to be very supportive in what he does and he is being supportive in what I am doing. I guess that has come around a long time or he caught me at a good time because I feel so lucky.

Q. How do you support him?
A. By morale, by being there, by discussing things. I watched his shows and all of them are different and I have learned something from them. And he knows when I really mean it when I say "Ugh, I really didn't like this one" or "Hey, wow! That one was dynamite." He can take constructive criticism. I'm thrilled that we can be that honest. When I did a film last year, he gave me some corrective criticism.

Q. Which film was that?
A. It was with Bill Shatner and it was called "Kingdom of the Spiders." His comments were really nice—they weren't derogatory or anything. It is really helpful. We all can take it, but our egos get in the way.

Q. What advice can you give to couples who are in the same business?
A. Well, we made our eighth on May 11th. I try to remember somewhere in the back we all came from somewhere and we have to remember where we all came from and appreciate the things we have. My folks live back in New York and Sammy says, "O.K. visit your folks," and I remember that and I appreciate the things I have and try to do. I am doing a charity now called SHARE.

Q. What specific ideas can you relate to people in the same business? There is an incredible casualty rate of divorces in show business; what advice can you give to young kids?
A. My advice is to really spend the time with the people you want to spend the time with. You don't want to give up your time, because it gets so precious to people who like you for other reasons. And that takes some time to get to know who likes you for you. Once you do find that out, that is important. Sometimes you have to see certain people and you have to be at certain places, but you don't have to spend a lot of time.

Q. What do you think is the biggest thing that keeps you and Sammy together?
A. I think it's the sharing of things that we both like. He likes watching old movies and I've come to learn a lot about old movies and actresses and actors I did not know. Also he is an avid reader and I went to school and he didn't. I read because I had to, to pass; Sammy was self-taught and he has made me recognize that I can enjoy reading. So, it's good to have both common interests and interests that are not so common. Also that are separate, so you don't have to say, "What did you do today?" and say "I didn't do anything today." It's good to have different interests, even if it is just an exercise class. I think it's important to get out and have a few hours by yourself.

Q. Do you believe in giving your man "space?" And are you jealous?
A. We are both very jealous. Everybody says "space" and I guess that is an EST term. We give each other a little time and then we realize how much we really care about each other when we are together. I think for us that it is nice and it's important. I go with him for a week when he is gone for two weeks. I leave during the second week and get everything prepared at the house for him to come back and enjoy it. I think you need a couple of days away, but one always sacrifices a little bit to do something for someone else.

Q. When you are separated for those few days, do you worry a bit?
A. Oh sure. We all worry because there is always someone somewhere who is a little better at something that you do. My mother said to me, "You're not pretty, but you're not bad to look at." I mean there is always somebody somewhere that is waiting. You gotta just hang in there. Fortunately, we could always talk about it. It's hard to talk about the hurt and the pain; it's always good to talk about the good times and the fun.

Q. Were there any times where there might have been more pain?
A. Oh yeah, we had a crucial point in our marriage and we were separated for just a little time. We re-evaluated ourselves. We were apart a month and then we got together again. Marriage is a full time job and you must work at it.

Q. When you split, what was the main factor that brought you back?
A. We both decided that we would give a little leeway and try to be better in the area that bugged either one of us. We promised to do a little bit and change a little bit.

Q. Tell me about yourself and how you got into acting.
A. My mother started me dancing because I had flat feet. I used to go to dancing school on Saturday and I would spend the whole day there. Consequently, I auditioned for the High School of the Performing Arts. It was a small school where everybody knew everybody and it was terrific. After four years I knew I could be a teacher if I couldn't dance. But in my last year in high school, I did a Broadway show with Brock Peters and Sally Ann Howes. It was fun because I was the youngest member of the group. Doing shows, you do a lot of bombs as well as hits. I was in a lot of bombs. After that show, which was about 1971, I did "Mata Hari" followed by other bombs. I did have a lot of fun and met terrific people. Finally I did a

show called "High Spirits" with Bea Lillie and Tammy Grimes which I really adored. That was followed by industrial shows. Then someone asked if I wanted to go to London and be in a play with Sammy Davis, Jr., and I said, "Wow! O.K." It was great because it was a chance to act and I got a free trip to Europe and I was playing with Sammy Davis, Jr.

Q. What was your first impression on meeting "the man?" Was it love at first sight?
A. No, it wasn't love; it was respect for his talent and what he had given other people. It took five or six months to get to know the man, without all the people around. On a one-to-one basis. My first impression was, "Wow, he's really bright, and look who I am talking to. This is the greatest entertainer in the world." I was thrilled to death. He was genuine and down to earth and always loved the chorus kids. He would invite us to parties. That did it for me!

Q. How long did it take for you to realize the arrow had started hitting your heart?
A. I had been playing his sister and I looked dumpy in the clothes I was wearing. Then one night I got dressed up and he went, "This is the girl I've been waiting for!" Then one day he was co-hosting the Mike Douglas Show and he said to me, "Do you want to get married?" and I thought "Oh, come on—this is a star!" And he said, "Well, if it's not raining on Thursday, we'll get married. Because I can't play golf." We got married on Mother's Day. It was in the court house in Philadelphia. It was small. We had a couple bottles of champagne. And it's been good.

Q. Getting back to your acting, how did it start growing from there?
A. I stopped acting for a while. I decorated our house and I got into that. At first, I just traveled around with him. It was Sammy who first said I should go back into class. He said I

could really be a good actress. So I went back and it was great. I worked at the American Academy and with Lee Strasberg and that's how I got back into acting. As long as I don't work during the Christmas holidays, because we like to go away then, I do TV shows or films. I'm not opposed to reading for someone in the business, even if I know them. I like to audition and work. Recently I've done some "Charlie's Angels" and the picture with Bill Shatner. I also did a talk show here in Los Angeles that shows on the weekends. It's called "It Takes all Kinds." It's on Saturday afternoons. I really enjoy playing parts that aren't me. I played a hooker on "The Streets of San Francisco" and that was really fun. Sammy encourages me. I know he would rather have me home, but he understands and really helps me. Sometimes I get frustrated because I know I can never be as good as Sammy. To be a superstar like that is a phenomenon. I would like to just be a good, working actress. That self-satisfaction is important to me.

Q. Tell us about your wig line, the "Altovise Collection."
A. I've named the wigs after friends of mine, Susanne, Denora, Joanne, et al. The way I got started was a company approached me in Los Angeles called "Paris Associates" and they were associated with Monsanto and they asked me how would I like to be involved in wigs. I knew a lot about wigs because, when I danced in a show, I always wore one. I thought it would be fun and interesting. So I go out to the stores two or three weeks a year. This is my second year promoting the wigs. They are doing better and better. At first, they were for the black woman, but now I'm getting into blonds, grays, and strawberries. I love trying all the wigs on and fixing them. The wigs can be found in department stores. In Los Angeles they're in May Co. They're in Texas and Cleveland and all over. I love traveling all over, because I make the time for it, I'm having a lot of fun with it and I hope the wigs will get better and better.

Q. You do a lot of work with SHARE. Can you tell us about that?

A. The initials stand for "Share Happily And Reap Endlessly" and it's for mentally retarded and handicapped children. We do a show once a year which is usually in May at the Santa Monica Civic Auditorium. This year was the 25th year. It really is rewarding. Everyone comes in Western outfits. We try to get a lot of things donated. This year, because it was the 25th year, we charged $400 per couple. We have "Angels" and "Sponsors"—"Sponsors" give us $2,000 for one year and they get two free tickets, and "Angels" give us $10,000 over five years and they get two free tickets. The original ladies who started SHARE included Jeanne Martin, Janet Leigh, and Polly Bergen. And it grew and we have raised a lot of money for the children. Sometimes a parent will bring a child to the meetings and we can see the progress. The children range in ages from six to over 20. We also have the "Special Olympics" and all the children win something. Nobody really loses.

Q. At home, is Sammy ever a hard man to get along with?
A. At times, we are all hard to get along with, especially when we are working. But he is a very giving and open person.

Q. What are your signs? Are they compatible?
A. No, we are told they are not. He's a Sagittarian and I'm a Virgo. I think it is working for us. Knock on wood.

Q. What are some of Sammy's idiosyncrasies?
A. He loves to watch old movies. And he loves the news. When he is on the road, I never call him between 5:00 and 7:00 because he watches the news. He's gotta know what's happening. He's into the media and likes to give interviews. Right now, he's away doing "Stop the World, I Want to Get Off." And he is feeling and looking great. He's sounding better than ever. He sounds like Paul Robeson and Mario Lanza all together. Absolutely sensational!

Q. Would you call Sammy a chauvinist? And is he a fair man with money?

A. When I was first married, I spent money like it was water. But then I had to realize that he worked hard for this money. Now I take care of the household money, but we discuss things. He likes good things and he buys me lovely pieces of jewelry. He is very good to me. As for being a chauvinist, I guess you could have called him that in the first two or three years we were married. But we've talked about that and he's backing off with that chauvinism. As long as we respect each other and we go out and do our thing with decorum, that's the important thing. So, now, I would not say he is a chauvinist.

Q. *Are you a women's libber?*
A. No, I like the door opened for me and the cigarette lighted for me. But, there are things I would like to do for myself. I like working and I get satisfaction for myself.

Q. *Who is the accountant of the house? Do you get an allowance?*
A. Yes, I get an allowance for myself for personal things. Basically, we have a house account together to pay for household problems—things breaking down, etc.

Q. *Could you describe your home for our readers?*
A. Our home is full of things I like. For example, I like antique pieces, Fabergé boxes, 18th century, bric and brac. Sammy collects guns and buckles. We like different things, but they all work together and it is a comfortable home. It has about two acres to it and it used to be owned by Tony Newley and before him, Tony Curtis and Janet Leigh. All who owned the house have been back to see it. And they all have liked what we have done to the house. That particularly pleases us.

Q. *How many kids do you have between Sammy's marriages and yourself?*
A. The kids live with their mother, May Britt. He has three children and fortunately we all get along and we talk often. There

are two boys and a girl. They gave me a charm that said "wicked stepmother," but actually they call me "Alto," which is fine. The kids come to me when they don't want to talk to their parents. They spend the holidays with us. May is a lovely woman and she has raised the kids very well. Sometimes we all have dinner together and it is really kind of nice.

Q. What do you feel about the rumors, truths, and untruths in Sammy's life, the drugs and his affiliations with various people? A. Sammy has tried acid under a care [*sic*]. He has openly said he has done this. I have never tried it. Sammy is also a strong smoker and a drinker's drinker. Sammy doesn't smoke grass. He is not a pill-taker. Even when he is sick. But he has tried LSD and that is why some of the kids can relate to him so well. Sammy has also tried coke, but he is now into cooking and mincing and dicing and he doesn't drink any hard liquor. He has done it all and he is still here and he doesn't have to prove anything anymore.

—September 1978

"MARRIAGE,"
from *This Life,* by Sidney Poitier

In 1976, with Harry Belafonte as best man and Julie Belafonte as bridesmaid, Joanna and I got married at our home in Beverly Hills. Shortly before noon on that sunny January 23, we became husband and wife, with loads of friends and family present to share that wonderful moment. During the ceremony my mind kept flashing back to 1969—to Sammy Davis, Jr., Quincy Jones, and a wonderful adventure on the high seas around the Bahama islands, out of which, it could be said, the midday activity of January 23, 1976, very likely had its genesis.

In 1969 I invited Sammy Davis, Jr., to come down to the Bahamas for a vacation. Throughout our friendship of many years, I had always thought that Sam worked too hard and too much. From my observation, he was heading for a breakdown of some kind, or at least some serious stress-related problems. He loved his work a lot, and depended on it for more than just artistic expression or creative satisfaction; often he seemed to be depending on it for a sense of himself—almost as if without his work he didn't exist. And that, I thought, was dangerous. So as a concerned friend I decided I should speak to him about those matters, and in so doing I found myself inviting him to come away to the Caribbean for a vacation. To my delight he accepted. I then said to him, "However, you cannot come unless you leave your entourage behind—just you and a lady." "What are you trying to say, P?" "I'm saying you'll have to manage without your tape recorders, without your radio, without your telephone, and without your movies. You are going to have to deal with Sammy on a very personal and primitive level." Again to my delight he replied, "Hey, man, I'm ready for that—I'll be there, my brother. You just have some greens and hocks ready when I arrive."

Later, Joanna said to me, "Why don't we invite Ula and Quincy?" Quincy Jones and his wife, Ula, were also very good friends—in fact Ula and Joanna had worked together as models in Paris—and they were enthusiastic about coming. Our plan as we outlined it to our guests called for us to cruise the islands of the Bahamas for ten days on a private yacht. Immediately after my stint as a presenter on that year's Academy Awards show, I rushed to the L.A. airport with Joanna and the Joneses, and we all took a redeye special to New York where we rendezvoused the next morning with Sammy, his beautiful young actress friend, and two last-minute additions to the group, Terry McNeeley and his lady, Dolores.

Arriving in Nassau, Terry and I went directly to the docks to reconfirm our reservations for the use of a boat named *The Conky Joe*. Built for comfort and kept in excellent shape, that 60-foot dream of a yacht had three cabins, a lounge, two bathrooms, and an enormous deck area for dining, dancing, sunning, or whatever, but she was one cabin short of accommodating our group. Upon deciding that four couples wouldn't fit into three cabins very comfortably, I thought it best to order an additional boat—the same size, the same make, in effect a sister ship to *The Conky Joe*. When the others came down to the marina later that afternoon, they oohed and ahhed at the sight of *The Conky Joe* and became as excited as kids at Christmas when we told them that boat number two was steaming in our direction from Miami that very minute.

Everybody, that is, except Sammy's date, who seemed a bit subdued. Or is preoccupied a better word? During odd moments when she would brighten, we could see that she genuinely wanted to be with us; then without warning she would grow pensive, slip back into a haze, and stop focusing on what the group was about. Everyone noticed it, but since we didn't understand the situation, no one made any comment—we just hoped that whatever it was would work itself out so that we all could have a nice, pleasant, productive vacation. But forty-eight hours later, just as we were about to take off, she informed Sammy with many apologies that she wasn't going to go. The suggestion was that she was heading back to a long-time relationship with someone else about whom she was having an internal tug of war. Crestfallen, Mr. Davis took it as well as he could and resolved to go on without her. Sammy being Sammy, he worked feverishly to impress us that he was fine, but we knew it was bullshit and suffered with him silently. Later, as the group sat around exploring the pro and con possibilities of a ten-day trip with Sammy being the odd man out, Joanna said to Sam, "Why don't you call Altovise?" (Altovise Gore, the lead dancer on the Sammy Davis show, had an enormous affection for Sammy, and Joanna knew she had high hopes of being his number one dancer in more ways than one.) The group thought it was a great idea and Sammy agreed. He called his office in New York and told them to find Altovise and invite her to join him for our cruise. By the end of the day, Sammy's office hadn't located her, so we extended our departure time to the following morning and spent the evening close to the phone.

The next morning after breakfast, with no word of Altovise, we sailed out of Nassau harbor with Sammy leaving instructions at the airport for a private seaplane to stand by to fly her out to the boat! Late in the afternoon as we cruised through the breathtaking Exuma Keys, we got a call on the ship's phone saying that Altovise had arrived at Nassau airport and been placed on a seaplane heading toward us. About an hour later a seaplane buzzed our two boats and landed in the middle of the ocean. In the middle of the ocean—are you listening to me? When Altovise Gore stepped out of that tiny seaplane into the little dinghy we sent to pick her up, passengers and crew from both boats broke into applause. First of all, the girls were happy that Altovise, no stranger to any of them, had joined us. Quincy, Terry, and I were happy that Sammy had company. But listen to me when I tell you that Sammy Davis, Jr., was the happiest person in the fleet. Altovise Gore was a special kind of special. She made the difference, and it showed on Sammy's face. The mind-blowing image of two yachts in the ocean, the spectacular arrival of a seaplane out of which steps a black woman to enthusiastic applause *from* the world's greatest entertainer, all added up to a clear signal that a great adventure had gotten under way.

To spend the night we pulled into the protected harbor of a relatively uninhabited island called Norman's Key. The next morning the men decided to go fishing. But in order to go fishing we had to get bait, and in order to get bait we had to take a dinghy close to the shore and dive for a shellfish called conk, which gets smashed out of its shell and its meat pounded into a soft fleshy bait that Bahamian fishermen consider ideal. We kissed the girls goodby and set out to scrounge a dozen conks as a prelude to some serious deep-water fishing. While Captain Brownie and I were wading around in five feet of water looking for conk, Quincy Jones, who cannot swim, was sitting in the dinghy. Terry McNeeley, who cannot swim, was also sitting in the dinghy. Sammy Davis, Jr., bless his courageous soul, was wading in water up to his neck, right alongside Captain

Brownie and me, looking for conk. But he too cannot swim. Every now and then one of us would spot a conk lying there quietly on the bottom, and Captain Brownie or I would dive under for it. As we walked along, the floor of the sea became porous and a little rocky. Sammy, wading along enthusiastically, would cast an occasional eye of disdain at the nonswimming impotents sitting helplessly in the dinghy—Sammy who in his swimming trunks looks like a nine-year-old kid with spindly legs and a distended stomach. "Hey, Captain, there's another one," he'd shout, and Captain Brownie would dive down for the conk.

Suddenly, as the three of us are walking along, Sammy Davis disappears. We look around and there's no Sammy, only some bubbles coming up. A moment later Sammy comes popping to the surface, trying to wipe the water out of his eyes, and then he is on his way down again when Captain Brownie grabs him. Sammy says, "Captain Brownie—Captain Brownie—I, I, I stepped in that hole—I stepped in that hole or something—I can't swim, you know—I can't swim, you know???" Captain Brownie says, "I got you, Mr. Davis—I've got you—I've got you." So we climb back into the boat, Captain Brownie, Sammy, and me. We didn't want to take any more chances. I mean, that's a valuable piece of property that slipped out of sight there. You can imagine the headlines: "Sammy Davis, Jr., disappears in a hole—in five feet of water!" I thought: Jesus, how will I explain that to the Los Angeles *Times*? We sat Sammy in the boat, gave up on the conks, and just went fishing.

The next day we pull up anchor and head for Georgetown, the capital of the Exumas four hours to the east. After we explore the town—three or four small hotels, a couple of guesthouses, a supermarket, and a few bars—the girls decide to nap while we elect to have another go at fishing. This time, Captain Brownie buys our conk bait from a local fishing boat. Nonswimmer Terry McNeeley is now gun-shy. He is not about to go out in that little dinghy boat anymore, and he announces without the least shame that he intends to stay aboard one of the big boats with the girls. But when I come up on deck, there's Sammy ready in his swimming trunks—wearing Gucci slippers and carrying a Gucci bag. And in that Gucci bag he has his tape recorder, he has his cigarettes, his gold lighter, and whatever else Sammy carries in his Gucci bag. Sammy and Quincy and I climb into the dinghy with Captain Brownie and head toward the ocean to bottom-fish. After circling for about ten minutes, we find the reef the Captain's looking for, but before dropping his anchor he places a small glass-bottom bucket into the water, then looks through it to see what kind of fishlife is going on around down there. Each of us takes a look through the bucket, and the water's teeming, and I mean *teeming*—everywhere we look, nothing but fish. With rising anticipation we bait our hooks and throw our lines out. Mine doesn't get ten feet under the surface before zap! I've hooked one. Then Captain Brownie gets some action, a few moments later Quincy hooks into one, then right away Sammy connects. For Sammy and Quincy this is the first time in their lives they've had this experience, and they're going absolutely crazy. Quincy is saying, "Oh, God damn you, I've got you now, you son of a bitch." He's laying street talk on this fish in the water that's struggling for its life. "Okay, you dirty dog, come on up here. Q's got you now, you mother." Well, as soon as Quincy big fisherman Jones gets his fish in the boat he doesn't know what to do with it. He will not touch the fish. I have to put down my line or Captain Brownie has to, just to remove Quincy's fish from the hook.

Now Sammy, hooking into a fair-sized one, decides he's going to outdo Quincy in talking up to a fish. "All right, you dirty dog, I've got your tail now—you grabber, I knew I was going to get you, I just knew it—you come messing around with my bait, this is Sammy Davis, Jr., you fool! Didn't they tell you down there that this is Sammy?" Finally, he gets the fish out of the water and into the boat—a nice three-and-a-half-pounder, and it's jumping around on the line. And suddenly Sammy loses his gusto—looking at the fish, *he* doesn't know what to do with it. He says, "Captain Brownie—Captain Brownie! Will you get this thing off my line?" In the meantime, Quincy has rebaited his hook and he's back in the water with his line. In no time flat, something hits that's bigger than a three-pounder—a Margaret fish or a small gruber—something about six or seven pounds. Quincy fisherman Jones screams, "Oh, my God, I've got a whale—I've got me a whale!" and he opens up reading the riot act to the fish, challenging it to try and get away. "Ahh, you greedy son of a bitch, you just found my line was down there and you just figured old Q don't know what he's doing out here—ain't that right? Well, let me see how you gonna get off that hook! Come on in here, you dirty rat!"

At which point he's having so much fun that his foot slips on some of the shellfish slime on the floor of the dinghy and Quincy fisherman Jones falls out of the boat. Now you have got to get the picture. Quincy cannot swim, and Quincy has been talking nonstop about the dangers of sharks in those waters, because we've passed a lot of sharks just zipping around. Well, Q is now falling out of the boat, and halfway out of the boat, I can tell across Quincy's mind runs all the things we've been saying about those sharks—how vicious they are, how dangerous it would be to get into the water with one of those merciless bastards. And as the image of the sharks begins to cross Quincy's mind, something utterly, utterly miraculous happens. To this day, I think it's an impossibility, but I was there and I saw it. Quincy Jones hits the water and bounces back into the boat. Q hits the water—he's three feet from the boat when he lands in it—he hits it and bounces right back into the boat. So don't tell me that fear doesn't motivate people; fear will move many mountains, my brother. And when he gets back into the boat, Quincy Jones, a man of dark-brown complexion, is damn near as white as a sheet.

While Captain Brownie and I are trying to console Quincy, Sammy is finding the whole incident absolutely hilarious. He's beating his feet on the bottom of the boat, clapping his hands, laughing—and while he's laughing and pointing at Q, Sammy Davis, Jr., also slips on the slime covering the floor of the dinghy. But Sammy doesn't fall out of the boat. Sammy's Gucci bag falls out of the boat. And as the bag falls out of the boat, Sammy gets stone quiet. And as the Gucci bag begins to sink, all Sammy can find to say is, "Oh, Lord, my Gucci's gone—my Gucci's gone!" At that point it's my impression that Sammy and Quincy have had enough fishing for one day, so by mutual consent, we pull up anchor and head back to the big boat. There we find Terry fishing from the bow, using salami for bait. I say, "McNeeley, what are you doing?" He says, "Well, *I* eat it. I don't know why *they* don't eat it." Oh, yes—yes, indeed!

I must say about Sammy that this vacation is the most relaxed I've ever seen him. It's as if he's been wound down—he's moving differently, speaking differently, he's more fun to be with day by day, and in the end he's obviously pleased at having been able to turn "Sammy Davis, Jr.," off and just be a person.

He's not the only one affected by the trip, although the changes in the rest of us have more of a delayed bombshell effect, making big differences in the lives of each and every one of us. Quincy and Ula were soon to separate and eventually divorce. But Terry McNeeley, the bachelor of the century (in between his marriages), succumbed—Dolores caught him when his resistance was low, he said, but I think the boat trip solidified their relationship to a point where nearly all escape routes were sealed off and even Terry's legendary swiftness of foot failed him, allowing a patient, smiling Dolores to corner him, tag him, and remove him from circulation. Soon after Terry and Dolores got married, Quincy started dating the lovely young actress Sammy had originally brought along as his date—the girl who changed her mind and left before the trip got under way. Her name was Peggy Lipton. Quincy and Peggy developed a strong relationship, and soon *they* got married. Then Sammy began to realize how lucky he was to have a lovely woman like Altovise right there in his corner—someone who was really for him the person rather than him the superstar. He got wise, and he too got married.

—1980

EXCERPT FROM
Ordeal, by Linda Lovelace with Mike McGrady

Although we continued to visit [Hugh] Hefner's home, Chuck [Traynor] began to realize that the publisher was never going to be one of his pals, never going to share his wealth with him. And there had to be more to life than backgammon. It seemed a good time to accept an invitation from Sammy Davis, Jr.

As we went to Sammy's house that first night, Chuck went through the regular celebrity briefing. I was to lay down every hint I could think of and if anyone else hinted at anything, I was to pick up on it right away.

"If Sammy suggests anything—I mean anything at all—you just go along with it one-hundred percent."

Our first night at Sammy's house was a typical Hollywood social evening, dinner followed by a movie in the star's private screening room. And then the four of us—Chuck and myself, Sammy and Altovise—sat around and talked. That night the conversation remained fairly general despite Chuck's constant efforts to divert it into the gutter. Once, when Chuck was doing this, Sammy indicated surprise.

"Oh? Are you two into scenes?" he said.

To me, a "scene" was a sexual happening—an orgy, or a swap or practically anything outside the norm.

"We're into anything at all," Chuck said.

"Yeah?" Sammy seemed thoughtful. "Well, I can dig that."

Then we let it slide. I can no longer remember the first time that a scene actually came down between Sammy and myself but once it did happen, it happened almost every night. Sammy would start a movie going in the screening room and then he and I would wander off to another part of the house, leaving Chuck and Altovise together.

It wasn't all scenes with Sammy. Every night we were together, we'd spend hours just talking and sometimes we'd spend the whole night just rapping about his past. Sammy loved to remember his days as a child performer, part of a group that featured his father and his uncle. He told me about traveling across the country in those days and what would happen when their old car broke down. He talked about his marriages and kids. And he particularly loved talking about his songs. He'd play tapes of himself singing as a youngster and as a star. "Hey, listen to this," he'd say, "you'll see how my voice has changed."

Sammy never asked me much about my past, about my growing up, but that would have seemed as ordinary to him as it does to me. He was interested in now, in what I was doing with my career at the moment. For a time he seemed intrigued by the thought of my becoming part of his show, but that never came about. He did suggest that I put together a big Las Vegas act. He had advice for every part of my career except movies; he knew he wasn't the world's greatest movie actor and he wasn't getting many film roles.

Sammy looked like a savior to me. Just being in his company kept me out of other situations. And I liked him as a person. He wasn't constantly molesting me and I enjoyed just being with him, listening to his music and his words.

There were scenes with Sammy, but he wasn't beating me or hurting me. He had his own code of marital fidelity—he explained to me that he could do anything except have normal intercourse because that, the act of making love, would be cheating on his wife. What he wanted me to do, then, was to deep-throat him. Because that would not be an act of infidelity.

Chuck and Sammy seemed to have an understanding with each other. Whenever Sammy led me away for the evening, Chuck never said a word or came looking for us. This was because Chuck was sure that Sammy would do what Hefner had never done, fix him up with a lot of far-out chicks. It would have been easy for Sammy to keep Chuck happy. He would have just had to say that he was going to introduce him to a chick who liked to be whipped until she bled. If you told Chuck something like that—and you could promise it at some indefinite date—he'd do anything for you. However, Sammy never did make that effort.

While there were scenes between Chuck and Altovise, she

couldn't stand Chuck. According to Sammy, Altovise despised Chuck and wanted her husband to find someone else for her.

To this day, I have trouble understanding Altovise. If you've ever seen her, you know what a truly beautiful woman she is. And while all this was going on around her, she remained silent. She never really participated in the conversation. She was just there. I could see that Altovise wasn't into scenes any more than I was. She went along with it because it was what Sammy wanted.

I always felt a kinship with Altovise. We were alike in many ways but not alike in motivation. She did things to keep her man happy; I did things to keep my man from killing me. More than once Sammy said that he thought Altovise and I were the same kind of person; we were both "beautiful people." The one big difference, as he saw it, was that Altovise wasn't super-freaky and I was. He said that she would go along with things but she never really got into it. I, on the other hand, was really into it.

Why didn't I tell Sammy the truth? Because there was another side to him. When he was talking with me he would often describe things that he wanted to do to me. He would like to tie me down on a bed, then have other women come in and make love to me while he watched. That other side of Sammy could be scary. But even when talking about it, he would speak in a gentle voice and he never actually did anything. But I always wondered. And I was afraid that if he found out the truth, that I was not a super-freak then he'd have no more to do with me and I'd be back with Chuck all the time.

Only occasionally did Sammy's far-out ideas become reality. There were times when the two men had Altovise and myself go through a "scene" together while they watched. But I'm as sure now, as I was then, that they were the only two in the room to get any pleasure from that at all.

The four of us were always together. Every night, most of the night. And when Sammy felt like a little golfing vacation in Hawaii, we all packed up and went along. When Sammy got a suite at the Kahala Hilton, we just moved in.

During our stay in Hawaii, a change came over Sammy. One night at a private party, he and I were talking together and he said that his feelings about me were getting serious. He said that he had fought it but it was no use; he was falling in love and he wanted me with him the rest of his life. Altovise happened to overhear some of this and, naturally, she was hurt and angry. Sammy tried to calm her down but she left the party.

"She's gone back to the hotel," he said.

"I'm sorry, Sammy—you should be with her."

"No," he said. "I'm right where I should be, right where I want to be."

After that, things became even more intense. In a way, I was using him; he was the only one on earth who could prevent Chuck from doing what he wanted to do to me. But Sammy was a romantic man and the word "love" came into our conversations more and more often.

One night we were going to a nightclub opening and I decided to dress all in white: a white gown and a white fox wrap that a shop in Beverly Hills let me borrow for the evening. Sammy took one look at me, then dashed upstairs. When he came down, he was also dressed in white—a white tuxedo, white top hat, and white gloves.

He was always making romantic gestures. He put me on a pedestal and he bought me gifts, a gold bracelet, one of the early Polaroid cameras, and many trinkets. I always wondered how Altovise reacted when he catered to me. Or how she reacted when we all were out in public—Sammy and I would be creating a stir, signing autographs, while Chuck and Altovise remained in the background.

Often Sammy would talk about marriage but it was strictly what-if talk. What if I left Chuck and what if he left Altovise and what if we decided to get married and what if. . . . I didn't want him to divorce anyone to marry me. Because I didn't see where my life would get any better. What was happening between us wasn't all that terrific. All that was happening, really, was that he was keeping me out of worse scenes, away from sadism and freakishness.

Sammy Davis, Jr., gave me many gifts but the biggest present of all was one moment of revenge. I sense that this will not sound like much revenge to any reader who is aware of all that Chuck did to me. However, it was the only time I saw Chuck get a taste of his own medicine.

On this particular night Altovise had managed to find something else to do. The three of us—Chuck, Sammy, myself—were in the screening room watching a porno movie. Or, rather, the two men were watching the movie. I was on my knees in front of Sammy, deep-throating him while he watched the movie.

"I really dig that," Sammy was whispering. "I'd like to know how you do it. When are you going to teach me? When're you going to show me how you do that?"

Sammy often talked like that, asking me when I was going to teach him how to deep-throat someone. Sometimes I thought he was just joking and sometimes I wasn't so sure. On this particular night, Sammy suddenly looked over at Chuck sitting a few seats away. Chuck was staring at the movie screen.

"Hey, you think Chuck would mind?"

"Mind?" I whispered back. "No, that's the kind of thing he'd go for in a big way. But let me set it up for you."

Of course, this was definitely *not* the kind of thing Chuck would go for in a big way. In fact, that may have been his greatest fear, the one possibility he dreaded most. Whenever he was going to put down another man, he would call him "that fag."

A psychiatrist could probably explain this. All I have are suspicions. Chuck existed in a very narrow sexual area. Probably because of his experiences with his mother, he hated all women and could never just have straight sex with a woman. But he was also a former Marine and a gun nut; in that super-macho world, there was no room for gays. So where did that leave him? That left him with cruelty and animals and whatever other bizarre possibility he could dream up.

The room was pitch black except for a flickering light bouncing off a movie screen. Since Chuck was only a couple of feet away from us, he knew full well what I had just done with

Sammy. He didn't move at all—his eyes never left the movie screen—as I went over to him and reached out to unzip his trousers.

"Hey, you can't just sit there and watch," I said to Chuck. "You can't just sit there."

As I was talking to Chuck, I signaled for Sammy to come on over. Chuck grunted at me and shifted his weight, making it easier for me to do the job. He must have been really into the dirty movie because he didn't realize what was happening until it happened. I was the one who unzipped his trousers, but I wasn't the one who knelt in front of him.

A minute or two went by before Chuck realized that something was different. Then, although Chuck didn't utter a sound, his eyes were screaming for help. He looked back at me, boiling mad now, and with his right hand gestured for me to come over and free him.

I just shrugged my shoulders and laughed. Perhaps this won't seem like much revenge to the reader, but, finally, after all the awful things Chuck had done to me, I was able to put him through an ordeal, a sexual ordeal at that. You may not think he was suffering much. But that's only because you weren't there to see the agony on his face.

I was sure that Chuck would say something and end the little experiment but he didn't say a word. That was so typical. He had such unnatural respect for anyone in a position of power that he didn't dare complain. He let the scene go on and on without interrupting it.

Each time that Sammy showed signs of slowing down, I kept him going with instructional encouragement. It was, ironically enough, the same instruction that Chuck had once given me.

"No, no, Sammy," I said, "push down a little more—he'll like that. Yeah, that's right. Keep going. You're doing fine."

Chuck was glaring at me but he didn't utter a word. He would put up with anything rather than risk losing the friendship of Sammy Davis, Jr. He would rather have a heart attack than say no to a celebrity. The fact that Chuck was not responding didn't seem to bother Sammy.

"Not so fast," I said. "It's better when you do it nice and slowly. That's right, slow it down . . . yes, that's right, that's very good."

In time, Sammy finally gave up on Chuck. I knew that I'd be punished, but this time it was worth it. The expression on Chuck's face that night will be with me always.

The experience revealed something about Chuck that I hadn't known. His cowardice. There he was, in pain and scared, but unable to speak up. He didn't know how to handle it, didn't know what to do. He expected *me* to save *him*. And this was really nothing at all, nothing at all compared to the things he made me do. And he couldn't handle that. He couldn't handle the littlest thing. It was really nothing and he flipped out!

My time with Sammy was almost at an end. One night soon after, to my great surprise, he wanted normal sex with me. It was the first time we ever had intercourse; the first time he ever made love to me. In effect, he was choosing me over Altovise. However, the first time we ever made love was also the last time. In a few days I would be free of Chuck and that whole way of life would be behind me.

—1980

"THE SUMMIT,"
from *Frank Sinatra, My Father,* by Nancy Sinatra

They called themselves "the Summit." When they worked together, it was a summit meeting indeed, a gathering—within the entertainment world—of the top. Frank and Dean and Sammy. Joey Bishop. Peter Lawford. And whoever else from the upper ranks of show business—Bing Crosby, Milton Berle, Don Rickles, Judy Garland, Shirley MacLaine—happened to be around at that time and in that place.

The early sixties was their time and Las Vegas was their place. They made movies there and played nightclubs there and set a tone of arrogance and confidence, of energy and expectation that spoke to and for many of their generation.

They were in their forties, mostly—part of the generation now taking its turn at power, the generation that was forging, in politics, the New Frontier. And the man who, of course, best embodied all this was their friend.

John Kennedy had come into Dad's life some years before. Dad had met him when he was a senator, just after he married Jacqueline Bouvier. Dad remembers sitting around with some of that group during the Democratic Convention of 1956 and, the instant the '56 ticket was determined, hearing Bobby Kennedy say, "Okay. That's it. Now we go to work for the next one." For the 1960 Presidential election. Four years later. Not a minute to waste. FS was impressed.

Whenever J.F.K. or another person of prominence sat in the audience, Dad gave a colleague the honor of introducing him or her to the crowd. One time Dean Martin would do it, another time Sammy, and so on. I remember the night Dean said to a room that was full of extra excitement and some kind of tangible glow: "There's a senator here tonight and this senator is running for President or something and we play golf together, we go fishing together, and he's one of my best buddies" and he turned to FS and said, "What the hell *is* his name?" and John Kennedy started laughing . . .

It was a zany, irreverent bunch. They could say anything to each other, no offense, anything for a laugh, because they knew what was in their hearts. Billy May: "I was at Frank's house once, and Peter Lawford comes in with Pat. So, Frank—he's a gracious host—goes over to greet her. And Dean goes with him. And Sammy is across the room and he hollers at the top of his lungs: 'Get those dagos away from the President's sister.' "

Their racial and ethnic gags were awful and wonderful. No one was safe. FS said to Sammy on one occasion when the lights were low, "You better keep smiling, Smokey, so we can see where you are," but on another he forecast a future where "We're gonna' grow colored cotton and hire white pickers."

Dean: "One night Sammy came out on stage and did his dancing and he jumped on the piano and sat there. Sammy was through, but he wouldn't get off—just sat there on the piano. And Frank had to sing. So I just walked over and—Sammy only weighs about 110 pounds—I picked him up and I walked over to the mike and I said, 'I want to thank the NAACP for this wonderful trophy.' "

Poor Sammy. They had these stools they sat on up on the stage. They sawed the legs off his, made him sit on this little stool. Out on the putting green, they'd use regular golf clubs and make him use a miniature putter. Sammy: "We used to go to the steam room every day, and we all had these white robes, with our names on back. I came in one day and my robe's not there. I said, 'Where's my robe?' The attendant said, 'I'm sorry, Mr. Davis, but we had to get rid of your robe.' I said, 'Why did you get rid of my robe, man?' He said, 'Well, Mr. Sinatra told me to get you a new robe.' So he gets up and he gives me a brown robe, brown towels, and brown soap. 'Mr. Sinatra said you can't use the white soap or the white towels.' Frank comes out from behind a curtain: 'What the hell's going on out here?' I said, 'This is your idea of funny, huh?' And we all cracked up."

They were so wonderfully silly. Dad was singing the sentimental song "It Was a Very Good Year." As he sang the sweet lyric "When I was seventeen . . ." Dean Martin sang through an offstage mike, "You were a pain in the ass." Dean: "Frank broke up. Couldn't sing for two minutes." Dad quieted down, the room quieted, and everybody was back in the mood of the mellow ballad. Thirty-two bars, almost two minutes later, Dad was singing softly again, "When I was thirty-five . . ."

"You were still a pain in the ass," Dean yelled.

Jack Benny had taught Dad an important lesson. "I always open my show with three sure jokes," Jack had said. "Jokes I've used before. Sure shots. Never with untried material." Dad learned to do the same. He always opened with three sure shots—songs familiar to the audience as well as to him. This became a cardinal rule. One night, Dean came out to open one of their shows and instead of singing the songs he was supposed to do, he sang the three songs with which Sinatra planned to open. "Did them in the same key, too," he bragged later. Meanwhile, my father was in the steam room, out of earshot—as Dean knew—and when he appeared afterward to do his numbers, he sang them beautifully—but the applause was weak. Dean: "They're thinking, 'Hey, so what, not these songs again'—and Frank doesn't know what's going on." So much for cardinal rules.

That's the way it went, all the time, when they were at their summit together.

Peter Lawford: "I couldn't wait to get to work. Everybody was flowing on the same wavelength. It was so much fun. We would do two shows at night, get to bed at four-thirty or five, get up again at seven or eight, and go to work on a movie. We'd come back, go to the steam room, get something to eat, and start all over again—two shows. They were taking bets we'd all end up in a box."

Sammy: "It was like a team. The only thing missing was the marching band. You *had* to be in that steam room. Better not show up late. That was where everything began."

Dean: "We got Rickles in the steam room. He began mouthing off, abusing us. I held the door open while Frank was talking to him, and then I grabbed the towel he had around him, and Frank shoved him out. I closed the door, and there he was—outside with no clothes."

At one point, they were living in Vegas, doing two shows a night, and making a movie way out in the desert during the day. Dean: "Frank and I used to fly there in a helicopter, forty minutes. We did it two days and Frank looks at me and he says, 'This is boring.' So I said, 'What do you want me to do, throw you out?' He said, 'Something different!' I said, 'Forget about it, tomorrow it'll be different.' So I got up a little earlier than usual, I went to a gun store, I got two .22's. When we got on the helicopter—he didn't know I had them—I gave him one, a loaded .22. I said, 'Here, I guess you'll want to sit on the outside now. We can shoot some rabbits.' And time just flew by, he was shooting at anything, dust, as long as he had something to do. I started shooting across his face. He said, 'You're a little close there, dago.' Hell, I didn't want him to be bored, right?

"I mean, Frank and I are brothers, right? Blood brothers. We cut the top of our thumbs and we became brothers. He wanted to cut the wrist. I said, 'What, are you, *crazy*? No, here's good enough.' To me, he's always been my brother. We're alike."

They could kid around and call each other names in fun, but outsiders who did it with malice were in trouble. Dean: "Frank and I were at the Polo Lounge. We were with six other people, mindin' our business, and we were a little loud. When we were goin' out the door, there is a couple of guys, and one of 'em says, 'There goes the two loud dagos.' Well, Frank got there one split second ahead of me, and he hit one guy, I hit the other, picked 'em up and threw 'em against the wall. The cops came. We said we didn't know who did it and walked out."

Billy May: "Here's what Dean told the cops. Some civilian got floored and the cops were questioning Dean about what happened. 'I dunno,' says Dean. 'I just looked around and saw this guy laying there, passed out, and since that's usually *me*, I didn't pay any attention.' "

Sammy: "You've never seen such nuttiness in your life. Especially in Vegas. And it was mostly innocent fun, as compared to what people were thinking. We traveled as a group, man. And people couldn't get over it: 'Here comes Frank and Sam and Dean.' We'd go to a restaurant. Or into the lounge. And every night Frank would turn to me and say, 'We're all *men* sitting here; where are all the broads?'

"Sometimes he'd say, 'Smokey, I don't see nobody pretty here!' So one night I got dancers—chorus girls. I called up some friends and I said, 'I want ten from the Stardust.' Then, I called for ten from the Frontier. I said, 'They're all going to meet Frank Sinatra and Dean Martin.' While our show was going on, I had a big table set up in the lounge. We walked into the lounge that night, here sat all these girls, man! Oh, there must have been twenty, twenty-five. Frank said, 'You're crazy!' I said, 'Let me introduce you.'

"So all the girls were sitting around, and Frank was being Mr. Social. By four-thirty, almost everybody was gone. And I got a chick, but every time *I* tried to make a move out of there, Frank would say, 'Hey, where are you going, Smokey? Sit down! Listen—come here! You remember this story—when we—' And it was six o'clock in the morning and my girl was gone and he was still telling me stories. Just the two of us. Then, finally, we're walking back to his suite. It was broad daylight, just me and Frank and the security guys from the hotel, and walking back I said to him, 'I hope you're satisfied. There must have been twenty-five girls there.' 'Yeah,' he said, smiling. So I said, 'Then why am I alone with you?' "

Yet, for all the revelry, there was a reputation that grew beyond common sense. Few people knew the real story about most of his drinking. At a party once, he had a drink in his hand and he told me, "You take a couple of sips and you put it down in one corner and you walk away and they give you another drink and they think you're drinking a lot. It's important. They think you're as relaxed as they are, but you don't have to drink." He wasn't saying, "This is what *you* should do, Nancy." He was saying, "This is what *I* do." And I remember thinking, "Oh, is that how he does it?"

When he was in pain, or in need of comic relief, he could get good and drunk . . . usually with a couple of friends to share his misery or mirth. But socially, in that goldfish bowl, he didn't. He would never be drunk. And we're speaking of the sixties now, when the other guys could really get stoned, when the *world* was getting stoned. He could always sing well; was always alert for work. He used to have fun—but always controlled. He could keep late hours because he never slept much.

I've always felt he's had trouble sleeping because he just doesn't want to waste that precious time.

So, there was exaggeration—particularly about the drinking and the romances. Sammy: "Shirley MacLaine used to hang out with us. Crazy Shirley. She was one of the *guys*! None of us ever hit on Shirley. She said once, 'Here I was, surrounded by the most attractive men in the world, and they made me feel like a *boy*!' "

They ruled Las Vegas. Late at night, Dad and Dean and Sam used to go out in the casino and deal. The dealers would just step aside and these crazy guys would get behind the table and let everybody win. You know, turn up both their cards, so anybody would know whether to hit or not. If the dealer had twenty showing—that is, if Sinatra had twenty showing—and you had nineteen, he'd just keep hitting you until you got two aces or a deuce and then he'd take the extra cards away and say, "Okay, you've got twenty-one." And pay you with the House's money.

And, in one sense, why not? He and his friends were pulling in the people who played at the tables and the machines and put the money in the House's bank.

Grandma loved to play the slot machines. And she did *not* like to lose. So they'd rig a machine for her. Put it out of order to everyone else, then kind of dance Grandma to the right machine where she'd hit jackpot after jackpot.

"Summit" was exactly the right word, a summit of high spirits and high rolling and high living and laughter and song. When Tommy and I were married at the Sands, the bellmen kept stuffing envelopes under our door all night—gifts of money from the staff and the high rollers.

Sammy: "Oh, those were glory days. If we're together now for more than two or three hours, whatever the evening is we wind up relating some incident, something about that period. Because that Camelot time—that was a special time."

—1985

"DISCRIMINATION,"
from Frank Sinatra, My Father, by Nancy Sinatra

Sammy Davis, Jr., is part of our family. Sam and I and Frankie and Tina and Dad went to the opening of Disneyland together. Sam and I and Frankie and Tina and Dad went to Atlantic City together. A birthday in the Sinatra family, Sam was there. A wedding, Sam was there. A funeral, Sam was there.

Sammy was a part of us. The color of his skin was never an issue.

It was, though, with other people. And sometimes surprisingly so. When John Kennedy was elected President, Dad produced and starred in the Inaugural Gala. Laurence Olivier performed, and Bette Davis, Leonard Bernstein, Milton Berle, Gene Kelly, Jimmy Durante, Juliet Prowse. But although there were blacks in the show, Harry Belafonte, Sidney Poitier, Ella Fitzgerald among them, Sammy Davis was not. He was planning to marry a famous white actress and the politicians, Sam later told me, "thought that was a little too controversial for the time."

Sammy Davis, Jr.: "Peter Lawford called me on the phone. He said, 'Sam, I know you understand these things. They've got those rednecks down there and, well, The Man thinks it would just smack of . . .' 'The Man?' 'The President, yes.' I said, 'Hey, don't worry about it, man.' I never mentioned it, never brought it up with Frank."

Frank knew. He has confirmed the facts for me. He has told me it was one of the few times he ever felt at such a loss. In the past he'd always been able to help Sammy. In the years when blacks had not been allowed to live or gamble in the major Las Vegas hotels, when Sam had to stand behind a white friend who would place his bets, Dad had been able to protest, had helped bring about change. But now he could do nothing.

Sam was crushed. He adored J.F.K. Shortly after Sam received that embarrassing phone call, I had an experience that helped illuminate my own small understanding of how hurt he must have felt.

My husband Tommy and I made a trip to Nashville for a recording date. We flew there in Dad's plane. FS was always security-conscious, so to look after us he sent along his houseman, George Jacobs, a kind, friendly man.

Arriving in Nashville, we went to our hotel. We had made reservations well in advance and didn't have to wait in line. The desk clerk saw us approach and quickly welcomed us: "Mr. and Mrs. Sands, one double, and Mr. George Jacobs, one single." Tommy said the information was correct and the clerk gave him the room keys.

George was still outside, dealing with the luggage. We went to our room and waited for him. The phone rang and the desk clerk asked Tommy to come down. I went too. George was at the desk. The clerk said, "I'm sorry, but Mr. Jacobs can't stay here." I didn't know what he meant, but Tommy, who was born in Louisiana, did. So did George. I said, "Why can't he stay here?" It really didn't hit me, I swear. I was so stupid. The clerk said, "This hotel is for white people only."

I was never so shocked. The word "prejudice" had never connected before. Never gone from my head to my guts. It wasn't just the icy reality, it was the blatant disregard for another person's feelings. This sonofabitch was so matter-of-fact, so *cool* about it.

George was sweet, saying, "Don't worry, Nan, I'll stay someplace else."

"If *you* stay someplace else," I said, "*I* stay someplace else." Tommy agreed and told the bellman to take the bags and get us a taxi. Meanwhile Joe Cool, the clerk, is saying, "I don't think any of the Negro hotels will allow you to stay, Mrs. Sands."

I was determined that we would all stay in the same hotel. I called Dad from a pay phone and he told me that, since it was late, maybe we should spend the night there, let George find another place, and he would make some calls in the morning. I figured he meant to the governor of Tennessee. But I was *so mad* I would have none of it. FS said, "Okay, do what you have to do."

We went to the other side of town. The cab driver took us to what he felt was the best "Negro hotel." It was run-down, dilapidated. But we were together.

Just for a while, I had felt the effects of racial prejudice—the anger, the humiliation. I never looked at Sam the same way after that. Not because of his color but because of his *dignity* in enduring and rising above that rot.

—1985

"SCANDAL,"
from *Kim Novak: Reluctant Goddess*, by Peter Harry Brown

On a gay holiday night in late December 1957, Harry Cohn was finally the undisputed leader of Columbia Pictures. The men who had long challenged his authority had all retired and the longtime pretender to the throne, his brother Jack, was dead. So Cohn was expansive, even gracious, as he sat among his cronies at the formal New York dinner to memorialize his late brother.

The great and wealthy men gathered in a Manhattan ballroom had really come to honor Harry—Harry the survivor, Harry the omnipotent.

Never before in its history had Columbia been so prosperous. The studio had released forty-six films in 1957, among them the prestigious, Oscar-winning *Bridge on the River Kwai*. They had the most popular film star in the world, Kim Novak, whose films had helped the studio earn more than ten million dollars in clear profits during the three previous years.

Several Columbia executives remarked that they had never seen Harry so content—so at ease with himself. He even ambled about to bestow pats of encouragement for younger executives who normally cringed before him.

But then the mood at the New York gala shifted drastically. In the midst of a round of toasts, a young marketing executive slipped into the room. His face was ashen as he edged behind

Harry's chair and leaned down to whisper something in his ear. Then he ducked back out of the room, leaving a shaken Harry behind. Several executives noticed that the boss's hands were shaking as he heaved up out of his chair and lurched toward the door.

"Gotta go," he brusquely told two executives sitting next to him. He offered no further clue to the reason for his sudden departure, nor would he answer the telephone back in his suite at the Sherry Netherland Hotel. He gulped a handful of nitroglycerin pills and splashed water on his face. Then he called Evelyn Lane, his assistant in Hollywood.

"I'll be coming back tomorrow morning," he said. "Meet me at the airport."

He sank back onto the bed in exhaustion. After sleeping fitfully for two hours, he bolted awake again and grabbed for the phone. He had to tell somebody—it was too distressing a secret to keep to himself. It took several calls but he finally found Max Arnow at a party in Beverly Hills. "Max," he said, "we've got a disaster on our hands . . . you've got to help me."

Max's mind raced. He'd never heard the boss so distraught. Somebody must have died, he thought to himself fleetingly, but then he would already know about it . . .

Harry ended the suspense by breaking in: "It's Kim, Max. She's having an affair with Sammy Davis, Jr."

"Impossible, Harry," Max scoffed. "We've had private detectives on her trail for three years. I would have known."

Harry's voice became a hoarse roar. "But you didn't have her followed in Chicago, Max. You didn't have her followed when she went home."

He continued: "Believe me, Max. She's having an affair with Sammy. In fact, she took him home to meet her parents. I got it from a guy in marketing. Apparently it's been common knowledge here in New York for a couple of days. And this guy says Dorothy Kilgallen is going to print it in her column tomorrow."

"Christ, what can we do?" Max asked.

"I don't know," Harry replied. "But I'm coming back to

Hollywood immediately. Find Kim. Find Sammy. I want to be able to reach both of them the minute I get back."

Less than two hours later, the Kilgallen item was off the presses. It said, "Which top female movie star (K.N.) is seriously dating which big-name entertainer (S.D.)?" For the voracious rumor mongers of New York and Beverly Hills, however, this first item of the Kim-Sammy scandal was an anticlimax. Word had already spread from cabaret to cabaret and from martini to martini until it was the most chic spadeful of dirt during the post-Christmas season on both coasts. Truman Capote, for instance, claimed to have heard about it in New York the very same evening Kim and Sammy were having an intimate egg nog at the Novak family gathering in Aurora, Illinois.

James Bacon, the Hollywood columnist for the Associated Press, heard about it the same day on a Beverly Hills golf course. He was enjoying a clubhouse round with Jack Keller, Jerry Lewis's press agent, when Jack leaned over chummily to say: "Guess where Jerry is?" Bacon shrugged. "He just rushed to Vegas to fill in for Sammy Davis, Jr., because Sammy's flying back to seek his girl's hand in marriage."

"So?" asked a mildly interested Bacon.

"Ah," said Keller. "Guess who the girl is?"

Bacon shrugged again.

"It's Kim Novak," Keller said in a stage whisper.

"Novak?" asked Bacon. "Are you sure of that?"

"Absolutely," replied the press agent.

Bacon excused himself to rush back to the AP newsroom. He thought to himself during the drive: "This could be the biggest Hollywood scandal in twenty years."

The same morning, Harry was in the air—flying back to Hollywood. When he boarded the plane he was so weak that stewardesses had to help him to his seat. Even before the plane taxied, Harry slumped forward as if he were in a deep sleep. His hands were clamped tightly on the arm rests. But he seemed to shake it off during the first hour of flight. He drank four cups of coffee and began writing on a yellow pad.

Over the Rockies he collapsed again and moaned loudly. A stewardess ran over with water and a vial of spirits of ammonia.

"What's the matter, Mr. Cohn?" she asked.

"It's nothing . . . nothing. Don't worry about it," he groaned. She saw him gulp six or seven nitroglycerin pills and decided to inform the captain.

"We have a man who just had a heart attack. I'm sure of it," she told the captain.

He swivelled about: "How bad?"

"I think he might die."

"We'll land in Denver. Tell him," said the captain.

She rushed back to Harry and told him they were making an emergency landing.

"Wait," Cohn said with a wave of his hand. "Don't land. I'll see my own doctor in Beverly Hills." He grabbed her hand. "Don't worry, kiddo. I'll be fine."

But he wasn't fine. Tests later indicated that Harry probably suffered two mild heart attacks—one at the formal dinner just after he was informed of the pending Kilgallen column and a second in the air over Colorado.

Harry later grudgingly said that he felt "rocked by pain and dizziness while on that plane. I should have let them land, but then I thought about what it might do to Columbia stock and waved the girl off."

The minute he stepped off the plane in Los Angeles, Evelyn Lane, his aide, knew instantly that something was wrong. For one thing, Harry was always first off the plane. This time he was the last man off and had to sag against the railing to prop himself up.

Evelyn told Bob Thomas, Cohn's biographer, that she "was shocked by his appearance. I worked with him for fifteen years and had never seen him with such pallor."

The Columbia chief stumbled over to her: "Thank God you're here. I didn't think I would make it."

The chauffeur was told to push the gas on the way to Cohn's Beverly Hills home—where the doctor was already waiting. As the car sped through the streets, Harry turned to Evelyn: "Kim Novak's having an affair with Sammy Davis, Jr."

She echoed many other sentiments: "Are you sure?"

"Absolutely," he told her. "I've already checked with people in Chicago."

Then his indestructible humor took over: "I can't understand it. If she had taken up with Harry Belafonte—sure. But Sammy Davis, Jr.?"

The doctor ordered Harry into the hospital, but he refused a second time. "I can't do this to the studio. Not now. Besides, I have this crisis to handle."

"What's Columbia going to do if you die?" the physician queried.

Cohn silenced him with a frosty stare as he grabbed the phone and marshaled his public relations staff. "Find Kim, and ask her to explain this—if she can!"

Though many explanations were offered by all the principals—including several members of Kim's family—Max Arnow recalled that "none of them were really satisfactory."

Two days after Harry returned to Hollywood, the most luscious bit of gossip since Jean Harlow's death had spread through the town like wildfire. But Dorothy Kilgallen was the first to follow up her own scoop by printing: "Studio bosses now know about K.N.'s affair with S.D. and have turned *lavender* over their platinum blonde."

The following day Irving Kupcinet, the powerful columnist for the *Chicago Sun-Times*, pleaded, "C'mon Kim, give us the lowdown. Who's 'S.D.'? Who's that new man in your life, and why is your studio so angry?"

On January 3 (a day later), Walter Winchell informed his listeners that Kim was involved in an interracial romance. "But," he said, "I can't divulge the name." Across the Atlantic, the *London Daily Mirror* came right out and said it: "Kim Novak is about to become engaged to Sammy Davis, Jr." And, said the paper, "Hollywood is aghast."

By that time, Max Arnow and Harry had apparently

reached Kim in Chicago and extracted the following story from her: She had been introduced to Sammy socially at a Hollywood party given by Tony Curtis and Janet Leigh. Then, said Kim, when Sammy came to Chicago for an engagement at a local club, she was at ringside. Max Arnow paraphrased her: "She told me Sammy had called and asked her to bring her family down to the club. She also said that the black entertainer was invited to the Novak home to reciprocate for his hospitality to Joe and Blanche."

Max continued: "That was it, according to Kim. It was simple and innocent."

"Don't tell me you buy that!" Cohn said.

"Not entirely," Max answered. "I think there's a lot more to it than that."

"What can we do?" Harry asked.

"Not very damn much," Max said. "You know the press."

So Harry called in Al Horwitz and his publicity staff for a war council. "I want you to go out there and stop all this claptrap," he ordered. "And I don't care how you do it."

"Harry had become so frightened about Kim's box office power that he went quite crazy over this," Max remembered. "So he began his campaign by threatening Kim. In retrospect we should have all kept our mouths shut and allowed it to fade away."

Decades later Max Arnow was asked, "Do you think it was a harmless friendship or a serious love affair?" He thought for a few seconds before declaring, "A serious love affair."

It was already too late to gag the press corps through denials. Four of the country's top gossip columnists—Kilgallen, Kupcinet, James Bacon, and Walter Winchell—had all vowed to flush out the story no matter what. Kupcinet got to Kim first. On January 4 she called the columnist to announce: "Sammy flew here from Las Vegas to discuss a film we planned to make. . . . We are old, old friends. But I doubt that Columbia would let me make the film in any case."

Kupcinet didn't buy the story and began scouring suburban

Chicago court records hoping to unearth a marriage license. (Sources close to Kim had told Kupcinet that Kim and Sammy had already taken tentative steps toward marriage before the national furor erupted.) "There was a marriage license. I verified it," Kupcinet said in 1985. "Although everyone involved emphatically denied it, a marriage was definitely being planned."

In Hollywood, James Bacon was frustrated by his frantic search for verification of the story. "It was a page-one story, no doubt about it," he remembered. "But the AP editors told me they would only use it if I could quote Kim directly."

Bacon obtained a cross-referenced Chicago phone directory and persuaded a neighbor to give him the unlisted phone number at Kim's home on the west side of the city. He then called every half hour for two days. "Then I found out that the entire family was visiting relatives in Aurora, Illinois"—the city in which Kupcinet claimed to have discovered the marriage license application. (Since the form was never completed and returned, no records were kept by the Aurora court clerk. But a registrar for the court said, "I believe they *did* take out the application.")

On the fourth day of the scandal, and after Bacon had already missed two wire service deadlines, he finally reached Kim's dad, Joe. "She's already gone back to Hollywood," he told the reporter. "By plane?" Bacon asked hopefully. "No," said Joe, "by train—she hates to fly." Bacon took down the car and seat numbers before asking about Kim and Sammy.

"Is there any truth to the rumor that they will be married soon?" he asked. Joe coughed nervously, then started to answer but stopped himself. "You better ask Kim about that," he said. Joe admitted that Sammy had spent the holiday weekend with the family but had left several days earlier.

Bacon hung up the phone in frustration. He was on the very fringes of the story but couldn't crack it.

Then he remembered that Sammy was due to report back to the Sands in Las Vegas at nine P.M. that same night. Bacon checked and was told that Sammy was onstage for the midnight show. Kim was nowhere in sight.

Then Bacon had a hunch. Kim's train, the *City of Los Angeles*, was due to pass through Las Vegas at two A.M. What if Sammy boarded the train for a renewed rendezvous with his paramour? The reporter looked at his watch and realized he couldn't get to Vegas in time to do the sleuthing himself. So he hired a veteran tipster in the gambling capital. "Trail him," Bacon said. "Let me know if Sammy gets on that train."

At 2:15 A.M. the tipster called back. "Sammy's on the train."

Bacon's story was in the bag. He would catch the lovers as they exited the train at Los Angeles's Union Station.

Bacon conferred with editors at the Associated Press, who sternly repeated that they would only run the story if Kim herself confirmed it. "Had I been a gossip columnist, the item would have been the lead in a column, especially since I was the only reporter in town with a handle on the story."

He arrived on the train platform in time to see a somber, sulking delegation from Columbia: Muriel Roberts; Norma Kasell, Kim's business manager; and two unidentified executives. Bacon slipped into a magazine stand to escape detection and then tailed them guardedly out onto the platform.

Standing near a large column, Bacon was able to watch Kim's disembarkation undetected. Kim was agitated as she stepped from the car. Her eyes were shadowed; her face was white and she seemed to have lost a lot of weight. She turned her head continually, checking for reporters. Then, thinking it safe, she walked right into Jim Bacon's path.

"Where's Sammy?" Bacon asked.

Kim couldn't help smiling. "Sammy who?"

Bacon pressed on: "Look Kim, I know Sammy was with you and your family in Chicago. And I think he boarded this train in Las Vegas. What's the story?"

The actress stopped and turned to face him. She struggled for the right words: "Mr. Bacon, I saw Sammy in Chicago and then took my family to see him perform a benefit. That's all there was to it."

"I hear you might marry him," said Bacon.

"Marriage? Don't be ridiculous."

The actress then swept off flanked by the high-level guard of Columbia officials.

While Kim was spirited off to seclusion at a Bel Air home, a young executive used a pay phone at Union Station to alert Harry Cohn about Jim Bacon's expert sleuthing. "How much does he know?" Cohn asked. "He thinks Kim and Sammy are ready to get married, Mr. Cohn. I think he's got some evidence."

"Oh Christ," Cohn swore.

Cohn began frantically tracking the reporter with the help of the Associated Press editors. The Columbia boss finally found him having lunch at Bing Crosby's Holmby Hills home. Bacon and Crosby were huddled in the crooner's library when Bing's wife Kathryn interrupted them. "Mr. Cohn wants to talk to you," she said, obviously impressed. But Bacon found Columbia's publicity chief Al Horwitz on the phone. "The boss wants to talk to you."

Then Harry grabbed the phone and began bellowing in an angry voice, "I hear you met Kim at the train today."

"Yes, I did. But there's no story," Bacon said soothingly.

"Jesus Christ, that's good news," Harry sighed.

But the chief's desperate voice betrayed his despair over the scandal. Ever since Kilgallen broke the story, he had been bombarded by calls from Columbia's New York executives, members of the corporation board, and even stockholders. And these pressures forced Cohn to take desperate action.

Did Harry Cohn use highly placed Mafia connections to force a breakup between Kim and Sammy Davis, Jr.? There is considerable evidence that he did, and that he did it without Kim's knowledge.

Truman Capote, who interviewed twenty-five sources for an abortive book, *La Côte Basque*, claimed that Cohn *did* rely on the mob to erase Sammy from Kim's life, and that "Kim's interest in Sammy was far from platonic."

And finally, after almost thirty years of silence on the subject, Kim herself told reporters in Las Vegas two years ago that "Harry probably did employ some sort of threat against Sammy."

Al Melnick, Kim's first agent, says: "There's no doubt about it. Harry called a very highly placed attorney, a man in with the mob, and he arranged serious action against Sammy. They took him out for a 'ride' and told him he would never work again in Vegas if he even saw Kim again."

And, according to Melnick, Harry asked for something more: "He asked that Sammy be coerced into marrying a black girl as soon as possible in order to defuse the interracial bomb."

Bob Thomas, Cohn's biographer, said, "Sammy was presented with simple alternatives: end his romance with Kim or find himself denied employment by any major nightclub in America."

Sammy has always vehemently denied these claims, saying that "I was never faced with any such action. Those are all just vicious rumors."

Perhaps. But the affair followed an awfully suggestive timetable:

- On January 1, 1958, Irv Kupcinet reported the romance and hinted at an impending marriage.
- On January 3, Kim denied the romance and allegedly wrote an angry letter to Dorothy Kilgallen.
- On January 6 Sammy publicly told reporters that there was nothing to the rumors.
- On January 7 Kim arrived back in Los Angeles by train and was whisked into seclusion—not to reappear until the middle of the month.
- On January 8 Columbia director of publicity Al Horwitz issued a peculiar statement which announced

that "Kim Novak is not to be married to *any* of her beaux."

- On January 8 a scurrilous movieland trade paper, *Hollywood Closeup*, insisted that Sammy had been threatened by hoods in Vegas.
- On January 10 Sammy was suddenly married to an acquaintance, Loray White, a black chorus girl, in a makeshift ceremony in Las Vegas.
- Seven weeks later, Sammy separated from Loray and announced that "I was never threatened into marrying her. I am filing against her because Loray ran up bills of $27,000 in seven weeks and charged $6,000 during a two-week stay at the Sands."

Bill Davidson, the entertainment writer who married Kim's publicist Muriel Roberts, has indicated that there may have been a five-way conference call during the scandal between Cohn, a lawyer in Hollywood, Sammy in Las Vegas, an unidentified party in Chicago, and Frank Sinatra in Beverly Hills. (Sinatra, a close friend of Sammy as well as of Kim, allegedly told Sammy to "cool it.")

Kim didn't appear publicly again until January 12, when she told a UPI reporter that "Sammy and I are still very good friends, but we literally can't talk to each other now without people making something out of it. Cohn views me as a piece of property and has decreed that we can't see each other again— ever again."

What was the true relationship between Kim and the black entertainer? There are several versions with little in common.

First there is Kim's version, which contends that the two were acquaintances who "appreciated each other professionally and artistically."

Sammy, on the other hand, said there was "at least a hint of romance." He also claims that the two maintained a house in Malibu where they used to meet regularly and clandestinely. He once described a wild ride during which Kim hunched down on the floor of a limousine in order to sneak through the gates of the beach mansion without being seen by Cohn's detective. Sammy told a London television interviewer that "Kim continued seeing me as a sort of protest against the way Cohn and Columbia treated her. But we were never in love . . . never!"

He also denied that he boarded the train in Vegas in order to spend another stolen night with the star. "That's stupid." (James Bacon later theorized that Sammy was on the train and exited in Riverside, the last stop before the *City of Los Angeles* plunged down into the Los Angeles valley.)

Sammy also released what purported to be a conversation between the two right after the scandal erupted:

"Hi Kim, this is Sammy."

"Hi, how are you?"

"I feel horrible about the rumor going around."

"I heard it too."

"I'm sorry, Kim. I had nothing to do with it. . . . We can handle it anyway you think best—I realize the position you are in with the studio."

"But Sammy, Columbia doesn't own me."

"Well, they probably think they do."

"Don't worry about what they feel. I sure don't. Listen, I'm cooking some dinner. But I would like you to join me." (According to Sammy, he did join her.)

Dorothy Kilgallen, who started it all, wrote one more acid column on the scandal. "Kim Novak's romance, which made Columbia executives hysterical, has finally been resolved with the sudden decision of her suitor to marry another woman—a black woman."

The man most hurt by the scandal, Kim's long-suffering suitor Mac Krim, remained silent at the time but suffered many anguished nights over the dilemma. He theorized that Kilgallen manufactured the entire incident. "I remember when Kim called me about the item," he recalled. "She expressed her fury and told me she had written Dorothy an angry letter."

Mac groaned, "Oh, I wish you hadn't, Kim. That will just make her more angry. Nothing but trouble."

Still, not even Mac was convinced that the rumor was entirely groundless. "Many, many people in Hollywood really believed that Kim was heavily involved with Sammy."

One evening in late January 1958, a waiter who knew Mac called to report: "Mac, Kim and Sammy are here right now in this restaurant. I hate to be the one who tells you this, but you have a right to know."

It was a rainy night, but Mac raced across town anyway. He dashed through the front door to find an empty room. "They were here. I swear it," the waiter told him. "They scooted out of here in a hurry."

Haunted by ghost sightings of Kim and Sammy, Mac handed out twenty-dollar bills to strategic waiters in trade for future tips about his lover and Sammy. "I don't know how many times I rushed around to investigate these false sightings. But it proved fruitless each time I did it." (He estimated that he answered about twenty of the phantom calls.)

"You must remember that we were engaged to be married at this time, so the Sammy Davis, Jr., affair hurt me deeply."

One afternoon Mac received a call from a close friend. He said, "Mac, I hate to tell you this, but Kim is right here in this restaurant with Sammy."

"Oh yeah," Mac replied. "Well, I have somebody sitting right here beside me who wants to say hello." Then Mac slyly handed the phone to Kim.

Finally it became laughable. Later that spring, Mac and Kim were relaxing at a guest ranch near Santa Barbara. Mac was browsing through a Los Angeles paper when he turned to Kim and read a gossip column out loud: "This very weekend," it said, "Kim Novak and Sammy Davis, Jr., are enjoying each other's company at a secluded Palm Springs home."

Mac doubled over in laughter but noticed that Kim wasn't so jovial. "You know, Mac," she said, "there's nothing I can do. I have no way to fight back."

Last year, Kim's repressed anger about the "Sammy Davis affair" was still evident. She tremblingly told reporters in Vegas: "It was a very dangerous relationship then—a white woman and a black man, no matter his status, simply didn't mix publicly. I was suddenly in the eye of a hurricane. Harry Cohn was infuriated. My agent told me my career would be over if I continued to see Sammy. Some of my friends wouldn't even return my telephone calls."

It's clear now that Harry Cohn was the real villain. And he didn't care about the truth. He was obsessed by the rumors. Thus he was no different from most other moguls, who lived in an insulated world where gossip was far more potent than the truth.

Max Arnow explained: "Sammy was about to kill the goose that laid the golden egg. We believed he could do it. We were scared to death by it."

Kim Novak Speaks: On the Sammy Davis, Jr., Scandal

People have asked me, "How can you let rumors like this get started?" I answer, "Everything has a foundation, but it takes on a different light depending on how it's handled." I choose my friends as I see them, not as others see them. Sammy, for example, is such a nice person, and we're good friends. I always admired him as an artist. My parents and I went to see him nearly every time he performed in Chicago. The fuss all started when he came to visit me at my sister's house after Christmas 1957. He brought toys for my two nephews, and it's a shame that the whole thing was blown way out of proportion.

You want to know what brought Sammy and me together in the first place? It was our mutual deep and emotional feelings about our own families. He took me out to meet his father, and we began the friendship which was so badly misrepresented.

There was no marriage license, there was no love affair, there was no house in Malibu, and there were no secret rendezvous.

It was sad that two people couldn't share a warm friendship without having it all blown out of proportion.

—1986

I'm Still Here, by Eartha Kitt

The *New Faces* engagement at the Biltmore Theatre was over and so was my contract with the Mocombo. The film was done, as was the next album for RCA. We moved on to San Francisco for about six weeks, where we became an instant hit. Then Sammy Davis, Jr., came upon the scene. One of the girls in the show, Pat Washaver, came into the theatre one day and was standing in the stage door entrance talking to a small black boy with pressed hair. As I ran upstairs Pat said, "Kitt, this is Sammy Davis."

"Very nice to meet you," I said, "Would you please run and get me some coffee?"

Since Sammy was standing in the stage doorman's area, I took him for the errand boy. A few minutes later, Sammy Davis returned with coffee to my dressing room; he smiled as he said, "Here's your coffee." Pat Washaver laughed her head off when she explained who Sammy Davis, Jr., was and saw me crippled with embarrassment. I had never heard of the Masterson Trio, which annoyed Sammy no end when we got to know each other.

Sammy got my address and phone number from Pat. I was at the Huntington Apartments just across the street from the Fairmont Hotel where the Masterson Trio was playing. Sammy had his manager call on me to ask if I would come in to see the show. I went in for the late show and had the biggest surprise— Sammy Davis, with his dad and uncle, were about the greatest entertainers of this kind I had ever seen (except for the Nicholas Brothers, who were my favourites, along with Bill Robinson). I adored them, especially Sammy, so I accepted the invitation to visit Sammy in his hotel suite. There I found comic books on both sides of his bed piled up level with the bed; cameras of all sorts, records and record players were everywhere; his bedroom was cluttered with what to me was junk. I thought Sammy was a great entertainer but I wondered about his intelligence. What kind of mind did he have?

When the little party of the evening was over, Sammy walked me across the way to the Huntington Apartments. The next day he called me to ask if I would have dinner with him before my show. As we walked into the restaurant the maître d' said, "Miss Kitt, how nice to see you." Nothing was said to Sammy—he was not recognized. When we were seated Sammy said, "I don't get it. I have been in show business since I was four years old. You have been on the scene only a year or two and everybody knows you and they don't know me." I pretended not to hear him and went on ordering.

Sammy and I saw a lot of each other during the San Francisco run of *New Faces*. I thought Sammy was a lot of fun to be with but he was also exhausting. He gave the impression that he was looking for something but he did not know what it was. He wanted success, yes, that was understandable, but even that was haunting him. He wanted to be recognized by all and this was not yet the case; he was not yet able to achieve this on his own, though his talent was certainly obvious. Something bothered Sammy and when he was with me it seemed to bother him even more. He walked me to the theatre after dinner one evening and as we parted he said "So long." I was crossing the boulevard when I heard Sammy yelling to me through the traffic, "One of these days I'm going to be bigger than you are!" As I entered the theatre I was laughing uncontrollably at the sight of Sammy Davis, Jr., stopping the traffic with his yelling. I can still see him standing on the corner of a San Francisco street yelling, "One of these days I'm going to be bigger than you are!"

Sammy called me to ask if I would accompany him to a brunch one Sunday at a Mr. Maxwell's apartment. Mr. Maxwell owned a small museum of beautiful paintings, and his apartment was swarming with all sorts of objets d'art. After the brunch, we had a look round and discussed the art with Sammy clinging close behind, hanging onto every word. I thought it was very cute to see Sammy like this—in search of knowledge. Mr. Maxwell and I had a great time discussing the different artists. Sammy was silent but listened intently. When we left, Sammy asked, "How do you know so much about art?" I did not bother to answer because I did not take the question seriously.

The next day Sammy came to my apartment with a pile of books under his arms.

"Look! Look, Kitt! I bought all these books on painters." We investigated the artists.

"Look at this painting, isn't it great?" he asked.

"Yes, Sammy. Do you know anything about these painters?" I asked back.

"No, I just look at the pictures," he said.

"Don't you think you should read the books as well as look at the paintings, Sammy?" I asked.

"Oh, you have to read them too?" We both laughed.

I had bought a Lincoln Continental—yellow with black leather upholstery; a plaque reading "Especially Made for Eartha Kitt" was on the inside of the door. After our shows one night I drove Sammy to the top of one of the hills overlooking San Francisco and the Golden Gate Bridge in her beauty of lights. It was very romantic, but I had no romantic interest in Sammy; my desire was for Arthur Loew. Being a one-man woman no one could touch me. So there was no interest except I thought Sammy Davis was a very nice, amusing person even though he was exhausting to be with. There was always that nervous tension surrounding him, of having some place to go and not knowing how to get there. He was silent as we sat in my car looking at the beauty of San Francisco.

"I'm going to be bigger than you are one of these days," Sammy was saying softly. "I'm going to learn how to drive a car and have one of my own, one of these days. I'm going to know about paintings too, one of these days. You wait and see."

"You'll have to do more than read comic books and play with toys," I said, in the same tone he was using. I took him to the Fairmont Hotel where he sheepishly went in, turning halfway round to say, "I'm gonna be bigger than you are one of these days."

"You'll have to do more than read comic books and play with toys," I singingly repeated as I drove away.

—1989

EXCERPT FROM
Ava: My Story, by Ava Gardner

Then no sooner did I get back to New York after that tour than I got a phone call from Sammy Davis, Jr. He had stood by Frank at his darkest moments, and he had also taken the time—which I thought was terribly sweet—to have little gold loop earrings made for my wedding. They had "A.S." on them, too, for Ava Sinatra.

So when Sammy called up and asked if I would do the Christmas cover of *Ebony*, I felt I had to agree. He came in with a whole troupe of photographers, and they made an awful mess covering one whole wall of our hotel with a sheet of red paper. I found a red dress somewhere, he put on a Santa Claus beard and a red suit, and we did the cover as well as some informal shots for the inside of the magazine—Sammy sitting on the arm of my chair with his hand around the back, stuff like that.

What I hear next is that somehow these pictures have gotten into the hands of a trash publication called *Confidential*. Naturally, it was Howard Hughes who broke the news to me in his most serious voice. As a means of self-protection, he had planted spies inside the publication, and he knew exactly what was coming out in every issue.

"Ava," he said, "they are going to do a devastating piece about you and Sammy Davis, Jr., not implying but stating as truth that you and he are lovers and have been for some time. They say that red wall identifies his flat in Harlem and that you often go there and spend hours with him."

So I went to Metro and the bigwigs called a meeting the size of the League of Nations. The lawyers talked for hours about suing this and suing that, but Howard Strickling, the head of publicity, once again knew exactly what to say.

"I have to maintain," he said, very quietly, "that perhaps I am better versed in these situations than most of us sitting around the table. And really, this is my responsibility. This is a rag that is published in a cellar somewhere [I made a mental note to get him to say "sewer" next time] and has a circulation of nothing. If we sue, it's going to be front-page news in newspapers and magazines around the world, which is exactly what they want. And if you win the case, on the back page of all the newspapers there will be a little scribble that Ava Gardner won her suit. In the meantime, the story is plastered all over the world. The best thing to do is ignore it completely." Which is what we did.

What is so maddening about these things is that they take an acorn, a little kernel of truth, and build an oak tree of lies. It hurts every time it happens. You never get used to it. Never. And it hurts to have to swallow it without answering. But it's best not to.

—1990

"TRIBUTE,"
by Quincy Jones, *Rolling Stone*

Sammy Davis, Jr., was born on the road, and he lived his life on the road. He was a total entertainer, a true vaudevillian, and he made a lot of people happy.

The thing that has to be said about Sammy is that he was a groundbreaker in every way. He was one proud, fearless man. His first autobiography was called *Yes I Can*, and that really was his attitude about life. Back in the old days, black entertainers had to sit in the kitchen to eat their dinners—even when they were playing the big room. Sammy helped turn things around in terms of racial barriers. His being a member of the Rat Pack with people like Frank Sinatra and Dean Martin created a perception that friends were friends, that it didn't matter what someone's color was. Sammy could do anything that anyone else in that group could. And that was the first time you ever saw anything like that going on. Before that, you would just have Rochester hanging out with Jack Benny, or Bojangles with Shirley Temple—situations in which the black person was always in some subservient role. Sammy, on the other hand, was an equal.

I don't think a lot of young black entertainers truly appreciate all that Sammy Davis, Jr., did for them, and that's a real shame. It's so much easier for them to get ahead these days, and a lot of them assume that their success is totally the result of their own ability. But the truth of the matter is that there's a whole lot of blood on the road to their success. I know for sure that Michael Jackson knows this. Michael understands exactly how much credit someone like Sammy really deserves. He paid a great tribute to Sammy. He said, "If you weren't there, I wouldn't be here." And believe me, there are a lot of people who got places because Sammy Davis got there first.

I first met Sammy when I was twelve years old and he was twenty-one. He was in the Will Mastin Trio back then, along with his dad and his uncle. They came to Seattle, where they were making $700 a week working at the Palamar Theater. Sammy would dance and do impersonations and sing, and the others would dance with him, and sometimes they'd whistle melodies in the background. Even back then, Sammy was just an incredible performer. He really lived to be up on a stage, entertaining people.

I would take off school and go to hang out with Sammy because he had all these bebop records that I'd never heard before. The first thing I noticed about him was that he had everything he ever owned in that dressing room. And that man had *everything*. Hot plates, Sterno cans, bongos, sixteen watches, fourteen cameras, all sorts of record players. And years later, he would have even more—every videocassette ever made and 200 little suits. See, Sammy was the sort of man who never let his income get in the way of his lifestyle.

When I was playing at a place called the Washington Educational and Social Club—a real funky nightclub with strippers— Sammy would come by every night and play drums with us. We became friends all those years ago and remained friends by working on all kinds of things together: a Duke Ellington special, the album he did with Count Basie, his last television special.

Sammy managed to stay very contemporary. He was always aware of what was going on at the moment, always right in it, whether it was Miles Davis's *Birth of the Cool* or Blood Sweat and Tears or whatever was happening. In fact, a while back, when Sammy was planning to go out on the road with Dean Martin and Sinatra, I suggested that it would be hot to have the three of them rap. If anyone could have pulled off the rebelliousness of rap, it was those guys. And of course, Sammy was all for it. Man, it would have been something seeing the Rat Pack rap, wouldn't it?

He was a great person to spend time with. Just the other day, I found a tape of the time that Sammy, Sidney Poitier and I went on a vacation in the Bahamas in 1968. It must have been Sammy's first vacation, and I think it was the funniest, happiest time I ever spent. We went out on a boat, and Sammy didn't know *anything* about going near the water. We're out in a rowboat, and here's Sammy with a Gucci bag. I'll never forget the day a fish shit all over his Gucci bag. We all had the time of our lives. That's the way I want to remember Sammy, because I saw him a week before he died, and I don't want to think about that. It's too scary losing people like Sarah Vaughan and now Sammy. It's just too rough to think about losing these incredible, irreplaceable people.

I think Sammy will be remembered as one of the greatest entertainers America's ever seen. He was a man who knew how to live. He was flamboyant in every way. He was self-educated and very brilliant. He made tremendous pioneering efforts, and he made some tremendous mistakes. He did a lot of bumbling along the way, like in his association with Nixon, but Sammy always led with his heart, and you really can't blame someone for that. Sammy took a lot of flak, and he suffered every blow, because he was a very sensitive man. He wanted desperately to be loved, and he gave a lot of love. In fact, he was the most unselfish giver I ever saw in my life. If he had pneumonia, he would still perform. He always gave 100 percent. He gave every drop he had.

Toward the end, he had so much going his way. He loved his wife, Altovise, so much, and in addition to his other kids, he'd adopted a young son, Manny. And as a singer, he sounded better at the end than he had *ever* sounded. He stopped smoking, and started getting some sleep for a change, which probably shocked his body. Bill Cosby called me and said, "Let's try and find some songs for Sammy." And I'd been looking, getting a little collection together, but like everything else, you always wait until it's too late.

Sammy lived 150 years in his lifetime, because he did everything. I don't care if it was Broadway, television, records, movies—whatever you name, he could do it. Sammy Davis, Jr., did it all the way no one had done it before.

—*June 28, 1990*

"MY SECRET LIFE WITH SAMMY DAVIS,"
by Kathy McKee with Rudy Maxa, *Penthouse*

Life was never normal in the company of Sammy Davis, Jr. He partied all night and went to sleep when the sun came up. He lived in hotel suites, sometimes not knowing or caring what town he was in, as long as room service had set up the bar properly. At times he regarded his friends as sexual playthings, arranging and rearranging liaisons and generously doling out his favorite drugs, cocaine and amyl nitrite.

But things began to get too weird even for me in the late 1970s. I'd known Sammy for more than ten years. Most of that time, I'd traveled with him as a dancer and mistress of ceremonies for his nightclub act. I was also his lover. However, the events of one night at Caesar's Palace in Las Vegas convinced me that it was time to distance myself from Sammy.

The evening began as most evenings did with Sammy: After his show downstairs in the hotel, he liked to invite some of the show girls and local friends up to his suite. Room service would roll in seemingly endless trays of shrimp and caviar on ice, sandwiches, fruit, and sweets, along with buckets of champagne. The spread was for Sammy's guests—he rarely ate.

We'd watch a movie, usually a new release provided by studio friends. Finally, the party would wind down and Sammy and I would be alone. I remember that on this particular occasion, I was lying on his bed wearing a black bra, matching panties, and black panty hose. I was finishing a glass of Taittinger and waiting for Sammy, who was wandering around the suite wearing—as was his fashion—nothing at all.

Suddenly, he entered the bedroom and harshly ordered me to roll on to my stomach. This was not the voice of the Sammy Davis, Jr., I'd grown to know and love. But it was a voice I was beginning to hear more often, because during the previous months he'd discovered satanism and had become obsessed with books about devil worship. His moods had grown darker—life with Sammy was becoming like a bad Bela Lugosi movie.

I rolled over—his personality was such that everybody always did what Sammy wanted—and felt Sammy climb above me on the bed. Then I felt a sharp slash across my ass as my panty hose were shredded by what I later learned was a razor. When I tried to turn my head to look up at him, he snapped, "Don't turn over!"

I buried my face in a pillow as I felt him tearing the panty hose from my legs. I heard the sound of fabric tearing as he ripped off my panties. Then came my bra, its hooks snapping as Sammy jerked and twisted it off of me.

Then he ordered me to roll over and, much to my relief, he straddled my chest with his legs and let me take him in my mouth. I was relieved because this was the Sammy I knew, the man who was absolutely insatiable when it came to oral sex. At that moment, I knew his little experiment in sadistic lovemaking was over, that he'd pushed it as far as he would that night.

But I also knew that he was changing in ways I didn't like. Sammy was my mentor, lover, and soul mate. Over the years he'd introduced me to a wonderful life. As a dancer and entertainer, I'd blossomed with his help. In the bedroom he'd coaxed me into situations that I never thought I'd enjoy. There were instances—such as threesomes involving both me and another woman—when Sammy went too far. But he sensed it, too, and would eventually back away from his demands.

But in his suite at Caesar's Palace that night, Sammy's roughness, coupled with his new delight in the devil, was definitely not my cup of tea. During lovemaking he began to bite me hard enough to draw blood. I thought it might be about time to pack my bags.

I had dropped out of high school in Detroit at 16, leaving home to escape an unhappy home life, and to seek fame and fortune in the movies. Soon after arriving in Los Angeles, I began dating a young man who took me to Las Vegas. Ours was a brief relationship—it turned out he was a compulsive gambler, and within days after our arrival in Vegas, he ran out of money and we were locked out of our hotel room.

That same day I heard that there were auditions for dancers being held in our hotel's showroom. With no appointment or agent, and with nothing more than a talent for dancing, I walked into the auditions and did a rendition of "No more bread and butter, no more crackers and jam, I like peanut butter . . ." and was hired as an almost-nude dancer. I lied about my age.

I found out later that the man in charge felt sorry for me, but the fact that I was statuesque and had a naturally great figure didn't hurt. I also lied about my race. In 1968 a black woman couldn't get hired as a show girl in Vegas. But even though my father was a black American, my mother was a blond beauty from Finland, and I was born with light, olive skin that allowed me to pass as Mediterranean, Italian, or Jewish.

I didn't tell anyone I was 16, and I didn't try to make the history books by identifying myself as the first black show girl in Las Vegas.

You grow up real fast in this town, but before I could fall into bad company, I met Sammy Davis, Jr. Actually, I'd met him four years earlier when I was 12, in Detroit, at the home of a mutual friend. Then, while working for Minsky's burlesque review in Vegas, I ran into his father in a casino. I told him I'd met his son years earlier in Detroit, and he invited me backstage to meet Sammy.

I couldn't go that night, but a few days later I heard from Detroit that a family friend had been killed in a motorcycle accident. I knew that Sammy knew the family, so I found him at a lounge show, introduced myself, and told him the news. He was clearly affected when he heard of the death, and we wound up talking for a few minutes.

The next night, just before going onstage, I heard that Sammy was in the audience. I suspected—and hoped—that he was there to see me. When I found him in the audience later, I learned I was right. He asked me to join him for dinner, and we agreed to meet backstage in his dressing room at the Sands.

I'll never forget that first night, because I met two other members of the famous Rat Pack. When the two of us walked into Sammy's dressing room, Frank Sinatra was there. Sammy had to leave for a few minutes, and when we were alone Sinatra told me Dean Martin was due at any moment. He suggested that, as a gag, I should strip down to my underwear to greet him. I was hesitant at first, but I thought I was being put to a test to see if I could play in the big leagues. So I slipped out of my black-and-white polka-dot jumpsuit and greeted Dean Martin wearing my black bra, matching bikini panties, and white go-go boots.

"Wonderful, charming," said Martin, who told me to get dressed again "because Frank is an asshole."

Sammy returned and we joined Sinatra and his wife, Mia Farrow, for dinner. It wasn't until days later that Sammy heard about the dressing-room gag. He was furious that Sinatra had made such a demeaning suggestion.

I wasn't upset. After all, Las Vegas was a tough town, and complying with Sinatra's idea of a joke was less strenuous than facing the daily competition I felt from my fellow show girls. Many were hard, older women who, having endured face-lifts and silicone injections, resented my youth. They showed it by ripping off my jewelry or trashing my costumes.

For the next two years, Sammy included me in his life regularly. Once, he had his right-hand assistant, Murphy Bennett, invite me to a show that Sammy was putting on in Reno. A Rolls-Royce greeted me at the airport, and I was accorded the royal treatment. Sammy and I didn't date, and he never made an advance toward me. Meanwhile, I grew increasingly fond of him and eventually began to wish he *would* make a move. But I knew he had plenty of girlfriends.

In 1970, after less than two years in Las Vegas, I moved to Los Angeles, where I earned my Screen Actors Guild card by appearing in an episode of "The Bill Cosby Show," the sitcom in which Cosby played a bachelor schoolteacher. And then Sammy called to invite me to dinner with his new wife, Altovise. Nothing would ever be the same in my life again.

The new Mrs. Sammy Davis, Jr., was cool to me from the start, and I wasn't sure why. Maybe it was because of my light complexion. Maybe Altovise suspected that Sammy and I were romantically involved. Then Sammy told me why he'd asked me to visit—he wanted me to replace Altovise in his act. Maybe that accounted for her ambivalence.

I couldn't agree to Sammy's offer fast enough, and within days, I began rehearsing with the other four young women in his show in preparation for opening night at the Sands in Las Vegas. For the first few months, Sammy kept his distance from me. I heard rumors that he was having affairs with show girls from various casinos. It seemed that everyone close to him knew that he liked one or more women at a time after his shows. Why, I wondered, wasn't I one of them?

About six months into the show, he did invite me to his room. We were friends, and becoming lovers seemed effortless and natural. A few months later, Sammy dropped the other four dancers and asked me to be the mistress of ceremonies for his act. I opened the show, introduced him, and did some vaudeville bits with him onstage. When we took the show on the road, our romance really began to blossom, and only years later did I decide that Sammy kept me in his act because he wanted me around, not because he needed a pretty girl onstage.

We were inseparable while traveling. (Back home in Los Angeles, however, the rules were different—he was with Altovise and I saw anyone I wanted.) I always had my own hotel room, but I would only go to it early in the morning, after Sammy and I had had sex.

We must have made an unusual pair in bed, because Sammy was seven inches shorter than me. I think that explains why we had intercourse relatively infrequently—Sammy may have felt uncomfortable on top of me, or vice versa. But I've never met a man who so enjoyed getting head.

He had the sexual stamina of a bull. Getting three or four blowjobs a day from me was routine. I think if he hadn't had other demands on his schedule, he would have asked for twice as many. In hotel rooms, in dressing rooms, in movie theaters, backstage, in limousines, aboard airplanes, it didn't matter—if I was willing, he was ready.

Life on the road with Sammy was a separate reality. Two days before his arrival in a city, his road and production managers would precede him and set up his suite to his specifications, so that no matter where he was, he was at home. Sammy didn't just travel with routine luggage. He'd haul movies,

VCRs, television sets, and, sometimes, his own pots and pans around the country.

When Sammy would arrive at his hotel, he'd already be checked in. Bowls of cigarettes were on the coffee table, his clothes were already hung up in the closets in the usual order, and his toiletries were laid out in the bathroom. His many 35-millimeter cameras were also ready to use. He loved photography, and while he didn't always use the cameras everywhere, he liked to know they were with him in case he wanted to photograph friends.

This is not to imply that Sammy spent a lot of money traveling. His managers and assistants were very cheap. I had to wear Altovise's costumes my first year on the road, even though they were too small. Only when I protested loudly enough to Sammy did he order an assistant to spend the money to buy new outfits.

Sammy usually traveled with a couple of bodyguards, often off-duty Los Angeles policemen who were licensed to carry guns and could be waved through airport security. Ever since he learned that he had been on Charles Manson's hit list, Sammy was wary of assassins. This kind of "star treatment" was also helpful because Sammy's luggage often contained what he called his "jewels." That meant two things: his famous flashy baubles and his drugs.

He carried what looked like a woman's vanity case, inside of which was a vast amount of cocaine and amyl nitrite. I always thought this gave a new meaning to Sammy's reputation as "the Candy Man."

Sex was always preceded by cocaine. And sex without popping capsules of amyl nitrite wasn't really sex to Sammy. He luxuriated in the brief, hot, soaring high the amyl nitrite gave as I sucked him. He'd groan and clutch my head as the drug made him flush. His hips would arch upward and he'd sometimes moan, "Oh, baby, oh, baby, get it! Get it!"

I sometimes thought of Sammy as an ectomorph, a person with a very thin body but prominent features. He had long arms and legs and was very well-hung. His body was rock-hard, the body of a dancer—strong and lean. What little body hair he had was as smooth and soft as silk. He wasn't openly vain and didn't spend a lot of time fussing over his appearance like some people in show business, though before going on-stage, he'd always pop a red Life Saver in his mouth to make certain his tongue looked healthy on camera.

He loved to be surrounded by people after his shows, and he had a weak spot for pornography and the women who starred in X-rated movies. (He was best man at Marilyn [*Behind the Green Door*] Chambers's wedding.) Given his love of blowjobs, it was no surprise that Linda Lovelace, the legendary star of *Deep Throat*, became a regular guest at his parties. She quickly became—with the obvious encouragement of her then husband Chuck Traynor—Sammy's lover.

When Linda Lovelace became part of our entourage, the main event for Sammy was watching Linda swallow his cock—just as she'd done for the camera while filming *Deep Throat*.

I know that Linda later changed her lifestyle and wrote a book renouncing her years of sexual swinging. Sammy later told me that her mention of him and his wild parties in her book cost him the chance to do a commercial endorsement. But for a while during her crazy years, Linda was certainly the most fun woman at many of Sammy's parties, displaying an almost unlimited capacity for sex of every description. I must say, however, that having seen *Deep Throat* almost 100 times with Sammy, I could happily live the rest of my life without seeing it again.

Sammy liked to see how far he could take me sexually. He was thoughtful and never forced me to do anything against my will, but he began planting the idea of my making love with another woman soon after we became lovers. It wasn't something I'd ever thought about, but one night in Miami Beach, we met a beautiful blond woman, a former show girl, who Sammy knew. She was around 30 years old, and the three of us had dinner. Sammy told me she really found me attractive and wanted to have sex with me.

So that night, after our show, she came to our suite at the Deuville and I allowed her to seduce me just as if she were a man. Sammy sat back and watched for about a half hour before he joined us on the living room floor. It wasn't the sexual highlight of my life, but it wasn't unpleasant, either. And when you're 22 or 23, sometimes you're willing to try anything.

Not long after our evening with the Miami Beach blonde, Sammy asked me to drop by his suite at the Ambassador Hotel in Los Angeles, where he had reopened the showroom of what used to be the Coconut Grove.

There was another woman already in the room when Sammy greeted me at the door. Sammy's habit of walking around in the nude or wearing just a shirt was not unusual. And, of course, the evening eventually got around to taking cocaine and drinking. At one point, he asked me to come over to where he was seated.

I knew what he wanted. He wanted what he always did. As I began to go down on him, I felt the girl's hand begin to rub my back. She worked her way down to my thighs, and then I let her take over with Sammy while I returned her caresses.

It wasn't that we were particularly enjoying touching each other. We were doing it for Sammy because Sammy wanted us to. The force of his personality (as well as the inhibition-loosening effect of the champagne and cocaine) let us at least partially fulfill his fantasy. And while we didn't have oral sex, we simply kissed and stroked each other enough to entertain Sammy.

I repeated similar scenes twice more during the time I worked in Sammy's act, but he could sense that my heart wasn't in it, and he stopped forcing what could certainly have become, for him, a most dangerous liaison.

One night at the Deuville in Miami Beach, he turned off all the lights in the suite and lit some candles. "We are ancient souls who knew each other in previous lives," Sammy told me with great solemnity as we sat together—he naked, me in lingerie—on the edge of the bed. "And we will know each other again in another life."

Then he gave me a Cartier ring with three bands: one white gold, another pink gold, and the third yellow gold. He said that the ring symbolized his marriage to both Altovise and me.

I know that Altovise would have had something to say if she'd known about that, and it wouldn't have been, "Oh, how wonderful, darling." But in a way, I was the best thing to have happened to her. Yes, Sammy screwed lots of other women on the road, but I was his main lover. And unlike some of the other women, I had no interest in stealing Sammy away from Altovise. I had a boyfriend in Los Angeles and liked the relationship I had with Sammy just fine. If Altovise had to have a rival, I was the least threatening. I cared for Sammy but didn't want to marry him.

When Sammy started hanging around with the author of a book on Satan and began dabbling in the black arts, I grew wary of his personality. He had always been intense. We had no secrets. In fact, the only thing he would never discuss with me was the rumor that the Mafia had threatened to gouge out his one good eye as a warning not to marry Kim Novak when the two were lovers.

But suddenly, Sammy was reading obscure books and talking about the power of the devil. Lovemaking became a ritual tied into the worship of the occult in ways I didn't want to understand. He began watching X-rated movies with a sado-masochistic bent. His mentor, the satanic-book author, walked around Sammy's hotel suite in San Francisco wearing a black cape.

I didn't need this.

I headed back to Los Angeles. Sammy and I stayed in touch, of course, and I should have known his fascination with devil worship was simply a phase he quickly outgrew. Our friendship resumed, though we saw each other less frequently.

Did we still have sex? You couldn't be alone in a room with Sammy for five minutes without giving him a blowjob. He had always been possessive, and during our nearly ten years on the road together, I had to enjoy my affairs with other celebrities behind his back.

The one man who drove Sammy most crazy with jealousy, however, was comedian Richard Pryor, who made no secret of his desire to take me to bed. One night at Caesar's Palace, Sammy went to the trouble of hiring two prostitutes for Richard, just to stop him from hitting on me.

But I liked Richard, and we saw each other again in Los Angeles and became lovers. Once, after drinks at the Beverly Hills Hotel's Polo Lounge, Richard and I went to a jewelry store and bought a ring, visited Giorgio's and bought a $3,500 dress, and then boarded a private jet to Las Vegas. We took a suite at Caesar's and were planning to marry in one of those hokey little wedding chapels on the Strip.

Then the phone rang, and Richard excused himself. When I came back into the room, we tumbled into bed, had a great time, but never got around to getting married. Later I learned that the phone call had been from his manager, David McCoy, who advised Richard to return to Los Angeles. He thought we should sign a prenuptial agreement before we married.

I was with Richard hours before he burned himself terribly while freebasing cocaine. Earlier that evening, we had a fight. I was high on coke and booze when I walked into his bedroom and found him sitting on the bed with a girlfriend of mine.

Richard was freebasing cocaine, and while he and my friend weren't in a compromising position, I wasn't in the most rational mood. I lost my temper and stormed off. In fact, I was stopped for speeding and avoided a ticket—or worse—by telling the police officer the truth, that I was upset because of a fight with my boyfriend.

To this day I don't know if our fight disconcerted Richard so much that he was careless. All I know is that the next day, I visited him in a burn ward in Sherman Oaks.

Richard's tragedy helped me to focus on the excesses in my life. While in Los Angeles in 1985 to produce a television segment about a Tommy Hearns–Marvin Hagler roast, I met a German auto exporter who became the father of my son Khristopher. My son and I moved back to my home in Michigan, where today I teach drama and try to be the best mother in the world.

Sammy and I kept in touch sporadically, often through my younger sister Lonette, who has become a well-known movie actress. I last saw Sammy with Lonette when we visited his hotel suite in Atlantic City in 1988. Yes, we adjourned to a private room for, as Sammy put it, "old time's sake."

When he died last year, I felt a tremendous sense of loss. But then I began dreaming about him. I still do, almost nightly. I feel that his spirit is somewhere nearby, and when I listen to one of his tapes in my car, it's as if the years between us evaporate.

—*September 1991*

EXCERPT FROM
Dance While You Can, by Shirley MacLaine

When Sammy Davis, Jr., was diagnosed as having throat cancer, I gave up even the sparse social smoking I did. I never inhaled, but what difference did that make? It was his throat that was infected, not his lungs.

Sammy's sickness affected me a great deal, as it did all of his friends. Sammy tasted the feast of life as though it was his last meal. There seemed to be nothing that he left untried—booze, women, drugs, cigarettes of all kinds, impressions, instruments, voices, dance steps, drama, comedy, musicals, cars, houses, jewelry, and several religions.

I wished I had had the freedom and spontaneity to try, without concern for the future, everything he tried. He lived completely in the present, expanding it to the fullest until it became the future. It never occurred to him that he was overdoing anything. Life was to be lived, to be loved, to be laughed at.

Sammy told me he was going to recover. I had arranged for

him to undergo voice building with Gary. Gary believed that his technique could help Sammy's voice after his therapy because he had worked with radiation patients before. Sammy's attitude was optimistic, as he appeared on late-night talk shows and posed for picture magazines.

But when we sat together backstage at a benefit somewhere, his eyes warned me that death lurked behind them. He never spoke of the fear—quite the contrary—but he couldn't hide the truth. His frail body had been a wiry miracle to me, and his energy came from a source that no one else seemed able to access.

Sammy was a man who would do anything to be loved, and we all knew it. Whatever his excesses might have been, he was greedy in giving and taking.

I thought of his life as a child. He had been cultivated and nourished in the spotlight since he was three years old. He was only at home when the spotlight was on. So his sense of his life was BIG and theatrical, because that's what was real to him.

I remembered Frank Sinatra, when we were doing a picture together in the fifties, taking me to see Sammy. His show defied the logic of the saying "Jack of all trades and master of none." He was the master of everything he touched on the stage. And after the show, when we all filed into his dressing room backstage, I felt I had always known him—he had a quality of such instant, eager rapport with people because of his need to identify with others. His dressing rooms were always full of his collection of characters—some savory, some not.

In England, he'd speak with a British accent—in Paris, French . . . and so on. He was a superb imitator, because he wanted to *become* the identity of another; such was his conflict in the search for himself.

When I was making *Two Mules for Sister Sara* in Mexico, I'd go up to Mexico City and watch him perform on the weekends. We'd talk long into the night about the tricks of the trade of live performing. When we made *Sweet Charity* together, we talked long and deeply about the Rhythm of Life, inspired by the jazz gospel song he sang. Soon after that he began his search into different religions.

Sammy had a way of making show business enter your living room. Many a time he'd get me (and others) up on the stage with him, because he made performing seem so intimate. When I went into live performing for the first time, I sought the advice of Frank, Liza, and Sammy. Frank said, "Don't worry. Remember, you change the room by showing up." Liza said, "Do it because you have something to say." Sammy said, "Don't hold back; pull out all the stops."

Over a period of forty years our paths crossed many times, and each renewal was a living, continuing experience, as though no time had elapsed in between. So when Dean and Frank and Liza and I had dinner the night before Sammy's funeral, even though all of us had known the inevitable for some time, the feeling was very much that an era had ended.

We reminisced about old times (the Clan performing at the Sands in Vegas). Our bunch was never known as the Rat Pack. That was a previous group that revolved around Bogey, much earlier. The Clan came out of the film we made together called *Some Came Running*. Sammy hadn't been in that one, but he was in many subsequent films with Dean and Frank.

Over the years, our relationships have held. I'm not sure why. I think it has more to do with mutual respect for talent than anything else—plus a shared sense of irreverent humor. The practical jokes abounded. Life with Clan members was a theatrical party, where sleep and taking care of oneself were secondary to the FUN. In fact, I wondered in those days if fun wasn't more important than having discipline and caring for one's health.

Now as I sat at dinner with the Clan, reminiscing about Sammy's life, which ended at only sixty-four, my depression and ennui returned. I wondered whether the priorities of the past shouldn't have been different.

—1991

EXCERPT FROM
My Lucky Stars: A Hollywood Memoir,
by Shirley MacLaine

Sam Giancana was usually fairly nice to me, although once he gave me a glimpse of what he was capable of. It happened in Mexico City. I had a day off from the film I was making in Mexico, *Two Mules for Sister Sara* with Clint Eastwood, and had traveled to Mexico City to see Sammy Davis, Jr., perform in a club. I went backstage to congratulate Sammy, and Giancana was there. He was on the lam again, ensconced within a four-wall protected home. He greeted me (God knows Sam Giancana was not an overtly warm individual) and I shook hands with him. His grip was strong. He glared out at me from under hooded lids. His shoulders were more stooped than usual.

"Pasta?" he asked.

"No thanks, Sam," I answered. "I've had dinner."

"It's good," he continued. I sensed trouble immediately, maybe because he hadn't let go of my hand. "I want you to have some."

Much as I always do when anybody tries to force me to do anything, I balked.

"Oh yeah?" I challenged. "Well, I *don't want* to have some."

God, I was so green. I hadn't yet learned the art of feminine diplomatic compromise, in the face of possible trouble. No wonder the guys didn't think I was a girl. Well, Sam didn't either. He grabbed my arm and twisted it behind my back. It really hurt.

"Hey," I yelled, "quit that. I'm sure your pasta is numero uno, but I'm full."

He twisted harder.

Just then Sammy came out of his dressing room, jangling with gold chains and snappily dressed for the rest of the evening. He noticed my pained expression and my "disappeared" arm.

"What the hell are you doing?" Sammy asked Giancana.

I shrugged. "He wants me to eat his pasta," I explained, realizing as soon as I said it how foolish it sounded. Sammy suppressed a giggle and glanced at the pasta. He walked over to Sam.

"C'mon, Sam," he chided gently. "Let the kid go." (Everyone in our group still called me kid.) "She doesn't want any," he went on. "She's probably on a diet or something. You know how actresses can be."

Sam smiled that crooked, hooded smile of his and twisted my arm harder. I groaned.

Sammy touched his arm. "C'mon, Sam. Let go."

With that, Sam released my arm and slammed Sammy in the stomach with his fist.

"Okay"—he chuckled—"no pasta for either of you." Sammy doubled over. He had another show to do that night. I stepped back, horrified. Giancana went to the bar and made himself a drink. Sammy straightened up, took a deep breath, and said to me, "Why don't you come back later?"

I nodded and left. I wanted to deliver an exit line that would live in infamy, but I couldn't. I was confused. Sammy was in pain. My arm was wrenched. This man seemed to be a monster. Beyond those feelings I had not yet ventured.

—1995

EXCERPT FROM
My House of Memories, by Merle Haggard
with Tom Carter

I was playing Harrah's Club in Lake Tahoe, probably the most uptown venue a country star could play in the 1970s, with the exception of Carnegie Hall. I had played Carnegie Hall, also, when I was back east.

I was introduced, walked on stage, and the audience applauded as if it were asleep. I was doing an unusual show for a group of promoters, executives, and high rollers. And people like Glen Campbell, Carroll O'Connor, and Bill Cosby were in the audience, seated with these big shots that Harrah's was trying to impress. There were many other entertainers as well. I was doing my first song when someone in the crowd stopped the show.

"Hey, what is wrong with you people?" a voice yelled. I put my hand above my eyes to shield them from the spotlight. The faceless voice continued to rant.

"This is the greatest country singer since Hank Williams. You act like he's a goddamn local act. You need to be bawled out, and I'm a little short nigger son-of-a-bitch willing to do it. Now try it again, Haggard. Walk off stage, and come back and see if they can show a little respect."

I did, and the place went apeshit. They had taken orders from Sammy Davis, Jr., who was standing atop a round cocktail table.

—1999

EXCERPT FROM
Class Act: The Life of Choreographer Cholly Atkins,
by Cholly Atkins with Jacqui Malone

Will Mastin was an old vaudeville guy, a strut dancer with the straw hat and cane and so forth. A great salesman. I mean he could really do that stuff. Flash dancing was also one of his fortes, but he wasn't a real tap dancer. Sammy Davis, Jr.'s, father was a member of that trio. He did Russian steps, around the world, splits, and cartwheels. There was another guy whose name was Monty. I can't recall his last name.

Little Sammy traveled with his father and had a part in the act. Not a big part. He was like whipped cream on the jello. I first saw him when he was only seven years old, and even then he was cooking! There was a little piece of business set up to show him off after the trio finished most of the stuff they were

doing. They staged the thing so that Monty was having a dis-
agreement with Will and Sammy, Sr., about some problem, then
he says, "Well, if that's the way you guys feel about it, I quit!"
Will said, "Naw, you can't quit." Monty told him, "Oh, yes I
can. Watch me."

After he walked offstage, Sammy, Sr., looked at Will and
said, "Well, what are we gon' do now?" Will said, "Don't
worry about it." He walked over to the wings and hollered,
"Hey stage manager, wake that big boy up out there sleeping
by the radiator and send him in here." And whoever was
watching Sammy, would turn him loose and he ran out there in
a full dressed suit, with a little top hat on; the cutest thing
you've ever seen.

He'd do a little paddling and rolling. Then when he got
through doing his dance, he took his bow and the music struck
up and the three of them got together and did their exit. By the
time Monty left the group, Sammy was much older, so he took
his place. That's when he played drums and everything. He
could also play trumpet, sing, do imitations, and to top it off,
he was an excellent tap dancer. Just a well-rounded entertainer.

—2000

EXCERPT FROM
Sammy Davis, Jr.: My Father, by Tracey Davis
with Dolores A. Barclay

It was a week before my wedding and I was a little edgy. Actually, it felt as if someone had gut-punched me, I was so nervous
and keyed up. I wasn't apprehensive about my impending marriage, so that wasn't the problem.

The issue, I knew, was Dad. All these years I had carved a
monument of resentment. I disliked him for never being at
home when we were growing up, for treating us like second-
class citizens to his career, to his stardom. I had spent my entire
life fighting him. I was always challenging my father's every

move and trying to make things go wrong just to get back at him. As I was about to start a new chapter in my life, I wanted to make sure I could go forward without any unresolved concerns from the past.

Now I would have the opportunity to talk to him. Julie and I were going to Las Vegas to spend a weekend at the spa. Pop was appearing at the Desert Inn. Julie encouraged me to resolve things with him, but, oh, did I hate the idea of a confrontation with Dad. That's what was eating away at me, the realization that I would face off against Sammy Davis, Jr.

I managed to forget about the talk and have a good time with Julie and Dad. We went to his show and Pop was dynamite. Later we ran over to the Nugget to see Frank Sinatra after his show. Frank had a little party in his dressing room and toasted my marriage to Guy. When we went back to Dad's suite, Julie discreetly disappeared and left me to my destiny. This was the hardest thing I had ever done in my life. I finally worked up the nerve, swallowed hard and said, "I love you, Pop, but I've never really liked you."

I felt an enormous relief, just getting out those few words, a simple truth from my perspective. But my father pulled the rug out from under me and said, "Well, I have news for you. I've never really liked you much, either."

His words sucked the breath from me. I was struck by the realization that I had hurt him as much as he had hurt me. Fortunately, we both loved each other and that's what guided us that night. Love, and honesty. Pop poured himself a Strawberry Crush and sat down beside me on the sofa.

After all my mental agony, though, I didn't know where to begin. So I jumped on something that had happened not so long ago.

"Dad you weren't there for me. I could go back almost to the beginning of my childhood, the part I remember, anyway. But my graduation . . . let's start there. I needed you there, Pop."

He looked at me quizzically and asked, "Why didn't you tell me?"

"Because I was too scared to say anything. Because I thought you'd know that you should attend your daughter's graduation. Why did you call to find out if you should come? The question you should have asked was, 'When is the ceremony?' " I said.

Dad looked at me in a crumbled sort of way. "I screwed up, didn't I?" he admitted.

I nodded, but I didn't want to punish him. Nor did he want to punish me—that wasn't the point of our talk. "I'll be all right," I allowed. "It's not the end of the world. It was important to me that I pick up that piece of paper. But it's more important for my inner strength that I graduated. I'm happy that I completed my courses."

"Yeah," Pop laughed. "I was wondering if you were just going to switch from career to career."

"But, Dad, how could you not know that going to your daughter's graduation was a big deal?"

"Yeah, I know. I was an asshole. I knew it was important but I figured if it really meant something to you, Trace, you would have told me to come."

I guess we both were right: He should have known to be there and I should have been able to tell him how I really felt.

I thought of all my missed triumphs; certainly my college graduation was one. Dad went back to the bar, grabbed a Coke for me and poured another Strawberry Crush. He was addicted to that soft drink after giving up alcohol a few years earlier.

Dad had a liver problem caused by many years of drinking and overdrinking. He always had a drink. I never saw him drunk, but he consumed a lot of bourbon and Coke. Just thinking about it brings back that familiar, almost sweet smell of bourbon. He began to get a little beer belly and he was kind of proud of it. We would all tease him about it and he loved it. Only problem was, it wasn't a beer belly at all. His stomach had become swollen because his liver had practically shut down and was moving at a snail's pace. His doctor hospitalized him and told him if he didn't stop drinking he would be dead. So, whammo! Pop quit booze. Cold turkey, just as he had stopped using drugs years before. He still had a small glass of wine every now and then or maybe a beer, but Strawberry Crush was the definite drink of choice.

"Tell me something, Pop, did you know how much I loved basketball and how good I was?"

He shook his head. "Not really."

"I was always upset that you never witnessed all of my little accomplishments, however minuscule compared to what you had done—you never witnessed any of them. That really hurt," I said, biting my lip. Pop swallowed hard and took a swig of his drink. "I could never look up and see my dad in the stands when I was playing basketball. I'm just mad at you. That's all. I'm mad that you weren't there for me on a regular dad basis."

My voice had risen a little bit. I guess I felt on a roll and everything was tumbling out faster than I knew how to control the words.

"Well, I couldn't be a regular dad," Pop said with conviction, little puffs of smoke from his cigarette trailing his words.

"I know, Dad, but you could have tried to find out."

"You're right. You're absolutely right. I wish I would have. But one thing you should know, Trace—I always was proud of you. Your mom kept me informed about what you guys were doing. She never stopped talking about you. I was proud. And I want you to know that one reason I didn't come to any of your games was because I was worried people would be more interested in me than the team and I'd be a distraction. I didn't want to do that to you."

"Oh, bullshit," I said. "You still could have tried."

He smiled.

Despite their divorce, Mom had continued to talk to Pop about us. But she pulled more than her load and I told Dad that was very unfair of him to make her both our mother and father. He laughed a little and shook his head.

"Believe me, I feel worse about your mother than I feel about anything," he said. "That was my biggest failure. She never did anything but be a great mom and a great wife. I wasn't ready for that. I wasn't ready for your mom, the straight arrow, who didn't do drugs, who was just perfectly content with herself. I needed to run around and be crazy. So it didn't work. It had nothing to do with your mother. Today I'd marry her, because today I don't care about any of that shit that was so important then. Today, I'd be happy."

And he would have been because that was their relationship. He liked just hanging around the house, having a few friends over. Mom liked that, too. She just didn't like all the partying and the wild stuff.

"You know, Pop, when you told me you were marrying Altovise, it was very hard for me," I said.

"I understand that," he said evenly, "but you wouldn't give me an inch. You wouldn't give her an inch, either."

It was my turn to swallow. He was right. I had been totally unfair at the beginning. I always expected he would mess up again. So it became even harder for him to try with me because I was just waiting for the next disappointment, which always came.

"I liked Alto in the beginning, Dad. But once she started drinking, she was mean."

He said, "I know. I know."

"Why did you stay with her?"

"Because I didn't want another failure. I failed your mother, I failed you children. Besides, I owed Alto because she didn't leave me when I was doing drugs and maybe that's how she got started on alcohol."

I told him he could still get a divorce. He laughed and sat up straight.

"What," he almost shrieked, "and give up half of what I have? I worked too hard, too long. Who cares if she's still around? I can do whatever I damn well want to, anyway. You know what I mean?"

"Yeah," I laughed, "I sure do. You always did whatever was important for Sammy Davis, Jr. You came first, and that was that. I mean, even now, you only talk to us when we call to check in or when you see us for vacations. You never ask about our schoolwork or our friends or. . . ."

He held up his hand and stopped me. "Trace, it has always been hard for me to relate to you guys as children. Then, when you grew up, it was almost too late. I didn't know you guys then."

"Then why the hell did you ever have us?" I blurted out, tears squeezing in the corners of my eyes. He put his hand on my shoulder and kissed my forehead.

"Because I always wanted children," he said. "I wanted them for all the right reasons, but I never was sure how to go about it."

"Pop, we always felt we had to understand you, but you never had to understand us. Does that make sense to you?"

"Yeah." Dad's voice was growing raspy. I guess it was scratchy because he was trapped in the same emotional sea as I was.

"Trace, I didn't know how to be a dad," he said almost in a whisper. "I wanted to be a father, but I guess I didn't know where to begin. I just wasn't prepared. I was raising you the way my dad raised me, only I was on the road with him all the time."

What he said made sense to me and helped explain so much. It was like, "You'll see me when I'm on the road, and when I can fit you in, I'll fit you in. When I can't, play among yourselves." I'd always wished my father had been able to understand what kids wanted, what teenagers wanted. But how could he? He'd worked and worked and worked and never stopped working. Being on stage was as much his life force as a heartbeat. The only thing Granddad ever gave Pop was his love when he was growing up. They were on the road, poor and black.

There were nights when Granddad and Will Mastin drank hot water and gave my father a plate of eggs to eat, because that's all they could afford. My grandfather sacrificed for his son and raised him as best he could. Maybe that's why Dad was always showering us with money or lavish gifts, and constantly buying himself things he couldn't possibly use. That was his way of making up for all those plates of fried eggs and mugs of hot water. All I wanted was the eggs . . . and a little love.

Until that night, I had never had any philosophical or deep conversations with my father. Until then, it had been pleasantries, incidentals, idle chitchat. I got up, stretched and felt my stomach untangle for the first time in hours. I felt as though I was opening up to a stranger. It was the oddest and scariest of feelings. It also was exhilarating.

I reached for a tissue and blew my nose. "I know how difficult I was as a kid. I never made things easy for you, did I, Pop? I never went along with the program."

"Tell me about it. You remember peeing on my lap at Ciro's?" We both laughed.

"I just always felt you were screwing us over when we were little," I said. "I didn't have the guts to say it then and damn, I barely have the guts to say it now. But I just couldn't act like I was all happy and say, 'Yahoo, we're here with Sammy Davis, Jr. Isn't that wonderful?' I just didn't give a shit whether you liked it or not. That was my little bit of power as a kid."

Pop didn't say anything for a while; he was sifting through thoughts. Then he spoke: "You did everything you could to make every occasion hard or difficult. You always destroyed any good time we could have had together."

He reached over and held my hand. I started to cry. "Oh, Pop, I'm sorry. I'm so, so sorry."

He squeezed my hand a little and said, "Come on, Trace Face. Been there . . . It's over. It's all right. Listen, I always loved you, you know that."

Yes, I knew that. If the chips were down, I knew I could count on my father. I blew my nose some more and let my father continue talking.

"You know why I never worried about you, Trace?"

"Why?"

"Because you're exactly like me: You have strength, you're resilient. I never worried that you wouldn't make something out of yourself without my help. I always knew you were going to make it."

"That's why you never helped me get into the entertainment business?"

"If you had asked me, I would have used my contacts to help you."

I don't know why I had never asked. I guess that's what blind hostility does. I was so angry at Pop for so many things, I had been too stubborn to let him know that I needed him.

Early-morning sun began to filter through Dad's suite. I yawned a little bit and took another sip of Coke. Dad and I looked at each other without saying anything. He always had that ability of wordlessly communicating. Dad smiled, and I said, "I know, Pop. I love you, too." We both cried.

My father wiped his eyes and said, "You know, I never regretted having you or Mark or Jeff. I love you guys."

He put his arm around me and I settled in on his shoulder. Then I guess we were pretty much talked out. It was almost 7 a.m. "You better go get some sleep," he said, kissing my cheek.

I remained a little longer, hugging my father, drinking in the familiar and very welcome scent of his Aramis cologne. "Well," I laughed, "this is normal bedtime for you, huh, Pop?"

"Exactly," he smiled. "I'm gonna do a little cooking, some chicken, and some tomatoes and peppers."

I rose from the sofa to leave. "Thanks, Pop."

"No, Trace, thank you. I feel a lot better, don't you?"

I said, "Yeah. I really, really do." I walked up to our room on the second floor of the suite. Dad called after me: "Trace Face. One more thing. Give me your phone number!"

I beamed all over. He'd never known my number. Never asked for it. Never called before.

I went to my room with a smile, and immediately woke

Julie. I gave her a hug, thanked her for prodding me and told her everything that happened.

Around 8 a.m., I fell across my bed and stared at the ceiling with a big, crazy smile. I hugged myself. So this is what it feels like to have a father. Pretty cool!

—1996

SAMMY DAVIS, JR.,
AND THE RAT PACK

○

Certainly those who live on the margin of society—the Upper Bohemians, whose manners soon become the style for the culture—seek frantically to find different ways of emphasizing their non-conformity. In Hollywood, where Pickfair society in the twenties counterfeited a European monarchy (and whose homes crossed Louis XIV with Barnum & Bailey), "non-conformity," according to *Life* magazine (in its jumbo Entertainment issue of December 22, 1958—readership twenty-five million), "is now the key to social importance and that Angry Middle-Aged man, Frank Sinatra, is its prophet and reigning social monarch." The Sinatra set, *Life* points out, deliberately mocks the old Hollywood taboos and is imitated by a host of other sets that eagerly want to be non-conformist as well. Significantly—a fact that *Life* failed to mention—the reigning social set and its leaders, Sinatra, Dean Martin, Sammy Davis, Jr., are all from minority groups and from the wrong side of the tracks. Sinatra and Martin are Italian, Davis a Negro. In earlier times in American life, a minority group, having bulled its way to the top, would usually ape the style and manners of the established status community. In Hollywood, the old status hierarchies have been fragmented, the new sets celebrate their triumph by jeering at the pompous ways of the old.

—Daniel Bell, "America as a Mass Society: A Critique,"
from *The End of Ideology*

No one would suggest that any of the Clan films were artistically important. But none of us was ashamed of them. They made a great deal of cash, and they still turn up in the annual *Variety* list of all-time money-makers. People took them for what they were—good, amusing entertainment. They picked up the fun we were having, and it was infectious.

—Sammy Davis, Jr., *Hollywood in a Suitcase*

This section is about Davis and the Rat Pack. The most well-regarded of the three books about the Rat Pack excerpted here is also the earliest: Richard Gehman's *Sinatra and His Rat Pack* was published in 1961 when the Pack was in its heyday. Both Shawn Levy's *Rat Pack Confidential* and Lawrence J. Quirk and William Schoell's *The Rat Pack: The Hey-Hey Days of Frank and the Boys* were published in 1998 with the very different tone of the passage of an era. The excerpts from all three books deal with the arrival of Davis as a member of the Pack. The brief excerpt from J. Randy Taraborrelli's *Sinatra: Behind the Legend* gives an account of the racial jokes that Davis endured when performing with the Rat Pack. The excerpt from James Spada's 1991 biography of Peter Lawford deals with the making of *Salt and Pepper*, which Lawford and Davis produced. Davis appeared in more movies with Lawford—*Ocean's Eleven, Sergeants 3, A Man Called Adam, Pepe, Salt and Pepper,* and *One More Time*—than with either Sinatra or Martin. Finally, James Wolcott's "When They Were Kings," which appeared in *Vanity Fair* in May 1997, gives a cultural and historical overview of the significance of the Rat Pack and male rebellion in post–World War II American society.

"SAM,"

from *Sinatra and His Rat Pack,* by **Richard Gehman**

Groucho Marx said of him, "He's better than Al Jolson—all Jolson could do was sing." Milton Berle once called him "the greatest entertainer in the world." Last year, his income from nightclub appearances, radio, television and films amounted to more than $1,200,000. His name is Sammy Davis, Jr. He is a nervous, complicated man who is just approaching the peak of his vast talent. And he is a Negro. All the members of The Rat Pack, with the possible exception of Peter Lawford, have known poverty, hunger and suffering, and some have known prejudice, but nobody else is black. Some believe that this is what drives Sammy Davis, Jr.

A hideous old American dogma used to hold that Negroes do nothing but eat watermelon, laugh and tapdance; they have a natural sense of rhythm, the dogma said, and they just like to sing and clown around and play horns all the time. It occurred to me, the time I interviewed Davis, that that sorry expression of a frame of mind that still imprisons so many of my fellow citizens was never more sadly exposed for its essential falsity. Davis' arrestingly brilliant ability to entertain may come from some instincts with which he was born or which he acquired soon afterward, but it is far more likely that the wildly acrobatic work he does onstage, and his tireless activity offstage, are due to factors he cannot control, emotional wounds slashed into him by the abovementioned bigots. It is not *because* he is a Negro; it is because of what being a Negro can do to a sensitive human being.

Davis is the way he is because he must do something to keep the fear concealed, I remember thinking during that brief session; or because he is trying to show as dramatically as possible that he should not be judged by the color of his skin. This, of course, has caused him further pain, and the pain has spurred him into further excesses of behavior, and they in turn—an endless cycle— have brought more accusations and more disapproval.

The most commonly heard opinion of Davis from unthink-

ing outsiders is the one most frequently applied to Harry Belafonte, the singer. "He hates being a Negro," people say, as
though there was something illogical about that here in the
home of the free. Using this thesis, vicious jokes have been fab-
ricated about him, and not always by Southerners—often, indeed, by comedians who loudly protest their lack of prejudice.
Why should the two men not hate being Negroes when they are
reminded on every side that being one in the United States is
still tantamount to being a second-class citizen! Belafonte could
not find an apartment in midtown Manhattan because of the
color of his skin. Davis has been the protagonist in so many
cruel stories that perhaps only his talent, acting as a valve for
what must seethe inside him, has kept him from violence. The
valve has become sputteringly uncontrollable. It has become a
defensive reflex. He became a Jew when he felt that he could
find some peace in that faith, but he could not keep from saying, in public, what I heard him say in Miami at the Summit
Meeting: "I happen to be the greatest Jewish Mau-Mau dancer
of all time." Or, on another occasion: "They kept me out of the
St. Patrick's Day Parade for *two* reasons."

Those remarks are more defiant than defensive, perhaps;
their irony is less pathetic than pugnacious. Perhaps, too,
Davis' marriage last year to May Britt, the Swedish actress,
who is as white as a girl can be, also was a challenge to those
elements in society who are still behaving as though Lincoln
never lived. The prejudiced ones are not all white. There are
Negroes who hate, or feel contempt for, other Negroes.

The story goes that one night Davis pulled his sports car up
in front of Lindy's, the famous New York restaurant, leaped
out in a cashmere sport jacket and tight-fitting pants, and ran
inside, a couple of cameras swinging from straps around his
neck. Two Negro musicians, acquaintances of his, were standing in front.

"Hiya, Sam," one said.

Davis did not hear the man; he went by without speaking.

The man turned to his companion and said in disgust,
"How white can you get?"

The story may be as unfounded as all the rest of the Sammy Davis, Jr., jokes, such as the one in which a woman says, "Nigger!" and he looks up in alarm and says, "Where? *Where?*" I print these two, which are mild compared to the others, regretfully, but I feel I must set them down to show what Davis, who wants nothing more than to be disliked for himself alone, must go through every day of his life.

At last year's Democratic National Convention, when Davis was introduced on the platform along with other stars, some jeers were heard. Later, Davis said, "It would be very easy for me to say the Southern delegates booed. You know as well as I do why they booed, but I ain't gonna say." He was referring to his forthcoming marriage. A reporter said that he was near tears as he left the platform.

Later that week, at the Lotus Club, in Washington, D. C., he was picketed, booed and insulted by fourteen members of a lunatic group, George Lincoln Rockwell's American Nazi Party. Rockwell himself, that paranoid, led the picketers, all of whom wore brown shirts and swastikas. One led a black dog which bore a sign, "I'm black, too, Sammy, but I'm not a Jew." Later, Davis said, "In London where I was booed by a similar group, and for the same reason, I told the English that it could never happen here, in the U. S. But I was wrong, I guess." And to his audience in the club, after his performance, he said, "They're a bunch of idiots. They don't bug me and I hope they don't bug you. And I'd like to thank you as I've never thanked an audience before. What could have been a disastrous night has become one I shall never forget because of your kindness." In London, while he was appearing at a club, pickets had carried signs that said *Sammy Go Back to the Trees.* They belonged to the Fascist group led by Sir Oswald Mosley.

Miss Britt also felt the sting of disapproval. Soon after the impending marriage was announced, Twentieth Century-Fox announced that it would not be picking up its option on her services as an actress. A studio spokesman piously declared that it was not because she was marrying Davis. "It's no secret," he said, "that her picture, *The Blue Angel*, was unsuccessful at the box office. We don't believe we have any future work that would suit her." He added that she had turned down several parts that were offered her, and said, "She is a pretty determined dame." Most people felt it was the studio that was determined. To have gone on making pictures with May Britt could have exposed all the rest of the company's films to mass picketing in certain areas. The company's action aroused such an outcry from other stars, the late Buddy Adler denied that Miss Britt's contract was being terminated. She has not made a picture since, however.

This was Miss Britt's first exposure to the blind mindlessness that has been tearing at her husband all his life. Davis went into the Army when he was seventeen. He and another youth were the only two Negroes in a company of seventy-odd. One day as he was standing in a line, a white man grabbed him by the shirt and pulled him out of line.

"What'd you do that for?" Davis asked.

"Niggers go to the rear," the man said.

Davis swung his toilet-articles kit, caught the man in the mouth, and knocked him down. Lying on the ground, the man looked up and said, "You're still a nigger."

Up to that time, Davis told W. Thornton Martin of *The Saturday Evening Post*, his reaction always had been to strike back, as violently as possible. As he looked at the man on the ground, still hating him, he came to an important decision: "I decided that the only way to fight was with what intelligence and talent God has given me."

Davis is the most religious member of The Clan. A few years ago, after an automobile accident in which he lost an eye, he met a rabbi in Las Vegas who began giving him some pamphlets and books to read. Soon afterward he began taking instruction, and eventually he became a Jew. "I found the faith gave me something I'd been missing—peace of mind—so I converted."

It was a difficult move. It took courage. Davis knew that

people might well think he was not serious, or that others would wonder why he was adding to his troubles as a Negro by taking on the burden of a second minority. He did not hesitate. He felt that his life had been spared in the accident, and that he had to make the gesture of dedicating himself to God. To his delight, just before his marriage, May Britt also adopted the faith. She did it without urging from him.

Friends say that Davis is a changed man since his marriage. He is quieter and calmer—except when he is onstage. Then he is perhaps the most athletic entertainer alive. It is exhausting to watch him as he sings, dances, tumbles, plays the drums and trumpet, does imitations, clowns with the orchestra and reduces his tiny tailored suits—they look as though they were made for him at the Lilliputian Bazaar—to sopping, clinging rags.

"I work to get the people on my side," Davis often says. He told Martin, "The other night there was a guy sitting ringside, looking at me with sheer, naked hatred in his face. I gave my whole show something extra because I wanted to get him, and finally I did. I heard him turn to his friends and say, 'I don't care what anybody says, this guy's O.K.' That's the only way I can fight."

Sinatra and Davis met in 1940. Davis had been doing an imitation of Sinatra as part of his act, and Sinatra was amused by it. In 1947 Sinatra put him into his bill at the Capitol Theater in New York, and they were close friends from then on, except for a brief period in which Davis incurred the wrath of The Leader.

Talking to Jack Eigen in the winter of 1959, Davis said, "Talent is not an excuse for bad manners. I love Frank, but there are many things he does that there are no excuses for . . ." Word at once came to him that Sinatra was furious. Sinatra is said to have got hold of a tape of the program. He took action promptly. He had previously had the screenplay of *Never So Few* rewritten so that there would be a part for Davis. He ordered the Negro part written out and hired Steve McQueen instead. Earl Wilson wrote, "T'was reported that Sammy was ready to hurl himself prostrate on the stage to ask Frank's forgiveness." Later Sinatra did relent, and since then Davis has seemed determined never to fall from favor again. He uses only the most glowing terms when he speaks of The Leader.

On March 25, 1959, while Davis was appearing at the Copacabana in Manhattan, I saw him in his suite in the Hotel New Yorker. He fidgeted constantly, moving from chair to chair, leaping to the huge sofa and squatting there on his haunches; he was like an excitable nuthatch. When I asked Davis about Sinatra's reactions to his Chicago comments, he said he could not discuss the incident. Presently I asked him what it was about Sinatra that caused him and other members of The Clan to be so slavish in their adoration. He glanced over his shoulder and said, "Why, because Frank is a very, very, very, great man." He looked puzzled, as though wondering what on earth would have made me ask that question.

At that time Davis was in the middle of a schedule that was, for him, routine. He was finishing up an eighteen-day engagement at the Copacabana, after which he would go to Kansas City for one night, then to Hollywood for one night, then to open at The Sands in Las Vegas. After the latter engagement, which lasted two weeks, he opened at the Moulin Rouge in Hollywood, went to Australia for two weeks, and returned east for another tour.

"How do you stand it?" I asked him during our interview. Again he looked puzzled. "Why, I've been doing this all my life," he said. He added that he had been working since the age of three. By the time he had gone into the Army, he said, he had put fourteen years in show business behind him.

Born in Harlem, on December 8, 1925, Davis comes from a family of entertainers. His father, mother and uncle all were professionals, and his first appearance came at the age of three in Columbus, Ohio, in the family act. At five, the Gerry Society, which enforced child-labor laws, put a temporary halt to his career by yanking him off the stage while he was appearing in

New York, but his father later solved that by passing him off as a midget, making him pretend to smoke a cigar. Until he was eleven he trouped with his uncle, Will Mastin, in a tabloid musical comedy that played all over the country. In 1936, Mastin broke up that act and he, Davis, Sr., and the boy went out on the road as the Will Mastin Trio, featuring Sammy Davis, Jr. Some weeks they split only thirty dollars between them. The father no longer works with Davis—a heart attack retired him in 1959—and the uncle has become his personal manager, but Sammy still cuts his earnings three ways, after he has paid his taxes and the eleven people he keeps on his payroll.

The Army claimed him in 1943. He wanted to get into the Air Corps but ran against the color-line. Negroes with less than two years of college were not admitted into the Corps. He had had less than two years in school. An athletic heart, which was not serious enough to keep him out of the service, nevertheless kept him from being sent overseas, and eventually he went into Special Services, producing and performing in camp shows. During this period he gradually became aware that singing and dancing were not his only talents. He began developing his impersonations. When he finally was discharged he went back to his father and uncle and reformed the old act. The two older men stepped into the background.

Sinatra gave the Trio the first big break by hiring them for his Capitol Theater engagement. Jack Benny also helped; they toured the west coast with him in 1951. Herman Hover, owner of Ciro's in Hollywood, brought them to open a show that starred Janis Paige, and before the latter quite knew what was happening, the show was stolen away from her. From then on, they got top billing everywhere they went.

"After twenty-three years," Thomas B. Morgan wrote in *Esquire*, "Davis had become an overnight sensation."

Soon after the Ciro's engagement, he was the most wanted entertainer in the entire field. Steve Allen used him on his Sunday night TV show; a Broadway musical, *Mr. Wonderful*, virtually a one-man operation, was assembled to show off his talents. The reviews were not especially good, but Davis kept the show running for a year. That was in 1956. He had lost his eye in 1954: while driving from San Bernardino to Hollywood at eight in the morning, he hit another car that pulled out of a driveway. His head slammed into the steering wheel. He even made a joke of that; when he first began wearing an eye patch, he would close his nightclub act by saying, "I've got to go and pose for a Hathaway shirt ad."

Meanwhile, he was becoming a sensation in another way. Women naturally were attracted to him because of his immense vitality, and it was perhaps inevitable that some of them would be white. Among them was Kim Novak. She and Davis were seen together frequently until their companionship came to the attention of the late Harry Cohn, head of Columbia Pictures, who held Miss Novak's contract. According to rumors that still circulate, Cohn told Miss Novak that she had to stop seeing Davis. She refused, the story goes. Then, the accepted version says, Cohn called in Davis and told him he must stop seeing Miss Novak. He too refused. The two young people continued to meet occasionally.

On January 10, 1958, Davis married Loray White, a singer, in Las Vegas, in a ceremony that came as a surprise to his friends. More ugly rumors circulated widely, so widely that many people accepted them as truth. Davis finally decided to make a statement about them, to get the actual truth on the record, but he did not do it until after it was reported, on April 25, that he and Miss White were separating after less than three months of marriage. He then gave an interview to Dick Williams, entertainment editor of the *Los Angeles Mirror-News*. Williams wrote, "Sammy Davis, Jr., swears those rumors that a Hollywood big wheel forced him to marry Singer Loray White under threat of a working over by hoods are completely untrue.

"Backstage at the Hollywood Center Theatre, where he is starring in *The Desperate Hours*, Sammy confided that marrying Loray was strictly his own idea. 'Nobody asked or suggested that I marry anybody. Nobody threatened me.' "

Williams then quoted Davis as follows:

"After we were married she started spending money like crazy. In seven weeks she ran up bills of $27,000. She ran up $4,200 in bills for shoes alone at Wilshire stores. The grocery bill for one week was $600. She spent $6,000 in two weeks at the shops at The Sands . . .

"My business manager blew up. He told me it had to stop. I couldn't come close to affording it.

"So we split up. But don't make Loray the heavy. She just wasn't used to that kind of living. Her mother told me, 'Sammy, you're too good to my daughter.' "

In November of the following year, Davis announced that he was in love with Joan Stuart, a twenty-one-year-old Toronto dancer. Miss Stuart is white. Her father told a newspaperman, "My wife and I disapprove wholeheartedly." Davis said in Hollywood, "I have never met Joan's parents, nor have they given me the opportunity to speak to them on the telephone. Joan is over twenty-one and knows her own mind. I love her very much and we want to get married. I don't want to hurt her family any more than I would hurt mine. I hope I can meet her folks and prove to them I am not the goblin of our times or an ogre." Later he changed his mind about Miss Stuart. On April 4 he announced that the engagement was off.

When Davis began going around with May Britt, there were more rumors. It was said that her studio was trying to break them up. This time he resisted all outside pressure. They were married in Hollywood on November 13, 1960, in a Jewish ceremony held in Davis' home. Sinatra was best man. At first Davis would not kiss his bride for newspaper photographers. "There are enough haters in the world already who are waiting for that shot," he said. Moments later, he did kiss her.

The wedding brought Davis more criticism, but he had expected it. He told Mike Wallace, the TV reporter, "I've seen mixed marriages work, and I'm sure ours will work, too. After all, we didn't just meet and then get married two weeks later. We went together for a year, and in that time we explored all the problems."

Sinatra said to a friend at the wedding, "We're all behind Sam—if ever a guy deserved happiness, he does." The Leader had spoken; whatever he faces in the future, Sammy Davis, Jr., at least knows that his fellow Rat Packers are all his staunch supporters.

Curiously enough, he is not bitter over the comments of the bigots. "Look," he said to a friend not long ago, "I've got a wife I'm in love with, we're expecting a baby—we know there'll be problems with him as he's growing up, but we're prepared to help him get through them. I've got my work. My career's never gone better. At last I've got everything I've wanted all my life. I'm just too busy to hate back."

—*1961*

"SONNY BOY,"
from *Rat Pack Confidential*, by Shawn Levy

For someone who would take orders, Frank could always count on Sammy.

Sammy Davis, Jr., was the kind of guy about whom God seemed not to have been able to make up his mind. On the face of things, by his own reckoning, he had more strikes against him than you could count—he was short, maimed, ugly, black, Jewish, gaudy, uneducated. But he could do *anything*: song, dance, pantomime, impressions, jokes, and even, in a manner of speaking, drama. He overcame so much that his merely being there among them was an epochal triumph: He was the Jackie Robinson of showbiz.

And yet when he saw himself in a mirror he was disgusted: "I gotta get *bigger*," he'd implore himself. "I gotta get *better*."

He was so used to being excluded that he was willing to kill himself with work to be let in. He'd suffer all manner of indignities: Frank's clumsy racial jokes; years of Jim Crow treatment in theaters, hotels, and restaurants; the nigger-baiting of high-rolling southerners in Vegas casinos; a patently bogus marriage to a black dancer intended to quiet journalists about his taste for white girls; the explicit disdain of mobsters and other bosses. But he kept at it, convinced that sheer will and talent would stop the world saying no.

Who was he trying to impress? His mother, a showgirl, was a cipher in his life, a ghost whose approval he never seems to have missed; his father, a small-time song-and-dance man, he eclipsed when still a boy. All the know-it-alls, naysayers, and bigots who'd ever discouraged him he'd silenced with sheer talent, guts, and drive. The gods themselves nodded with pleasure upon him: "This kid's the greatest entertainer," declared Groucho Marx at Hollywood's Jewish mecca of leisure, the Hillcrest Country Club, one afternoon, "and this goes for you, too, Jolson" (to which Jolie merely responded with a smile). He was not only the first black man through the door but one of the all-time greats, regardless of origin.

Yet he felt hollow: All the money and fame and sex and sycophants in the world still couldn't squelch the nagging inner sense that he was a *nothing*—and that if he could only rouse a little more out of himself, he could finally be a *something*. He sang that he was "133 pounds of confidence," that he was "Gonna Build a Mountain," that he had "a lot of livin' to do," and he sounded like he meant it. But each garish boast gave off a vibe of whistling past a graveyard; in his heart of hearts, he could never vanquish the sense that all the work he'd done to get so far could be snuffed out by a mere wave of Fate's lordly white hand.

Sammy was the baby of the Rat Pack, born four days before Frank's tenth birthday, and that banal fact—more than race, size, taste, line of work, personal habits, common friends, political leanings, money, sex, or power—was the single governing factor in their relationship. Frank was always the big brother allowing the kid, Sammy, to hang out with the older guys; Sammy was always the precocious little brat tugging feverishly at his idol's sleeve. Neither had actual siblings, but they filled those roles for each other: Frank needed to be the patron as much as Sammy needed to be patronized. Everything about their mutual solicitude, affection, and trust, every aspect of their difference and of their symbiosis, lay in germ form in the simple age difference between them.

Uniquely among his peers in Frank's circle, Sammy was a showbiz brat. His mom, Puerto Rican–born Elvera "Baby" Sanchez, was so committed to her career as a chorus girl that she worked until two weeks before her child arrived; as soon as she was able to return to the stage, she left the kid with relatives in Brooklyn and hit the road along with Sammy, Sr., who was the lead male dancer in Will Mastin's vaudeville act.

After that, there was barely a whiff of Elvera in her son's life. She and Big Sam split for good not long after their son was born, which might have made Sammy's story another "deprived baby beats the world to win his mama's love" yarn but for the fact that Big Sam and Mastin, with the approval of Sammy's extremely protective grandma, Rosa Davis, took the boy on the road with them from the time he was three and provided him with as big and loving a family as most children ever have. Chorus girls, singers, comics, and musicians were his society; dressing rooms, boardinghouses, and buses his playgrounds. He never attended so much as a day of kindergarten in his life—Big Sam and Mastin hid him from child welfare authorities by gluing whiskers on him and billing him as a midget—but he was steeped in a showbiz curriculum virtually from birth.

In later years, Sammy looked back on his tender introduction to showbiz as an idyll, but it was a terrifically difficult era. The Chitlin Circuit, as the route of black vaudeville and burlesque houses was known, never paid what the white theaters did; moreover, Sammy broke in when all forms of live entertainment were taking a hit from talking movies, radio, and recorded music. Scuttling back and forth between sporadic, low-paying jobs, Big Sam and Mastin frequently went without food so that their little protégé might not go hungry—and even then his supper might consist of a mustard sandwich and a glass of water. With grim regularity, they all returned to Harlem to sit waiting for new offers of work, which became even less steady with the advent of the Depression.

This was hell for Mastin, by all accounts a decent, intelligent, gifted man who'd risen to a position of respect within the narrow world of black showbiz. Although he never crossed over to broad white appeal, Mastin was a success, able to keep dozens of people on the road with him throughout the twenties. When he had to dissolve his traveling show to a two-man act featuring just himself and Big Sam, he surely felt as though he'd shrunk in the world; trouper that he was, though, he never let on, least of all to Sammy, that there was anything small about the small time.

And Sammy would've noticed if he had, because he was watching. He spent his early years studying acts from the wings, then imitating what he'd seen for the backstage entertainment of his makeshift family. He was a natural, and Mastin and Big Sam quickly realized it would give the show a lift if they put the little ham onstage. They slathered him in blackface and sat him in a prima donna's lap while she sang "Sonny Boy," the Al Jolson hit; mugging and mimicking during her sober reading of the song, Sammy brought down the house.

In time, he would master little comic bits, dance steps, vocal impressions, and songs of his own, and his skills grew along with his exposure. From special billing—"Will Mastin's Gang featuring Little Sammy"—he became a full-fledged part of the act, the Will Mastin Trio, with all three sharing equally in the profits. They were flash dancers: Cat-quick and athletic, they could do time steps together or improvise wild solos, all energy, all arms, legs, and deferential smiles; for six or eight minutes a night, they could wring an audience limp with their sheer gutty bravado.

It was as a member of the trio that Sammy found himself in Detroit in the dog days of 1941, a substitute opening act for the Tommy Dorsey band. As he wandered backstage marveling at the size of Dorsey's operation, Sammy was offered a handshake by a skinny white guy in his twenties: "Hiya. My name's Frank. I sing with Dorsey."

"That might sound like nothing much," Sammy recalled later, "but the average top vocalist in those days wouldn't give the time of day to a Negro supporting act." And Frank did more: For the next few nights, until the regular opening act returned, he would sit with Sammy in his dressing room shooting the breeze, talking about the show life. The kid couldn't believe his luck.

But if meeting Sinatra was a glimpse of a raceless Eden, the next few years were a crushing racist hell. Sammy was drafted into an army that was a cesspool of bigotry. He felt it the moment he arrived in Cheyenne, Wyoming, for basic training.

"Excuse me, buddy," he asked a white private he came across while trying to find his way around. "Can you tell me where 202 is?"

"Two buildings down. And I'm not your buddy, you black bastard!"

It was a slap in the face, but it was only the beginning. For two years, Sammy was denigrated, demeaned, and, truly, tortured. He was segregated by a corporal who created a no-man's-land between his bed and those of white soldiers. His expensive chronograph watch (a going-away gift from Mastin and Big Sam) was ground into useless pieces under a bigot's boot. He was nearly tricked into drinking a bottle of urine offered to him as a conciliatory beer; his tormentors reacted to his refusal to imbibe it by pouring it on him. He was lured to an out-of-the-way building and held against his will while "Coon" and "I'm a Nigger" were inscribed on his face and chest with white paint.

And there were the beatings. "I had been drafted into the army to fight," he remembered, "and I did." He was goaded frequently into using his fists as a means of settling the score with the pigs who abused him, breaking his nose twice, scoring his knuckles with cuts.

Only when he was asked by an officer to take part in a show

for the troops could he lift his spirit above the dreadful situation. At first, he didn't want to expose himself on a stage and entertain the very people who'd been mistreating him, but he couldn't resist the temptation to perform. George M. Cohan, Jr., was also stationed in Cheyenne and convinced Sammy to help him create a touring production that would visit a number of military installations. Sammy threw himself into the work with a kind of violence, seeking release, vindication, and even revenge by being the best song-and-dance man anyone had ever seen.

"My talent was the weapon," he recalled, "the power, the way for me to fight." For the last eight months of his service time, the show was continually on the road, far from his most virulent antagonists. It kept him sane, maybe even alive.

But when he got out, his eyes having been opened to his situation as a black man with grand aspirations in America, he found himself increasingly crushed by the gap between his ambitions and his opportunities. He was befriended by Mickey Rooney, who, though still one of the hottest stars in Hollywood, was unable to get him movie work. He winced at the ebonic clichés employed by performers on the Chitlin Circuit. In reaction, he adopted a stage manner so patently artificial that he sounded, in his own words, like "a colored Laurence Olivier." Even the tone-deaf Jerry Lewis was to encourage him to forgo his "with your kind permission we would now like to indulge" routine, but Sammy only did so after, typically, listening for several self-lacerating hours to tape recordings of his own inflated persiflage. And he reacted with despair and self-loathing whenever he was confronted with the insidious—and frequently overt—limits placed upon him in the Jim Crow era.

Nowhere were these barriers more painfully imposed than in Las Vegas, where the Will Mastin Trio debuted in 1944. Vegas was still a cowboy town, "the Mississippi of the West," as blacks unfortunate enough to live there called it. The black population, whose members swelled the ranks of janitors, porters, and maids at the emerging hotel-casinos on the Los Angeles Highway (which had yet to be christened the Strip), was restricted to living, eating, shopping, and gambling in a downtrodden district known as Westside—a Tobacco Road of unpaved streets bereft of even wooden sidewalks, lined by shacks that lacked fire service, telephones, and, in many cases, electricity and indoor plumbing.

Sammy ought to have been used to segregation. The trio arrived in Vegas not long after a stint in Spokane, where they were forced, for lack of a black rooming house, to sleep in their dressing room. But Vegas galled him more than anything he'd experienced before, in part because of the appalling contrast between the glamour of the Last Frontier hotel and the shack in which he was forced to spend all of his offstage time, and in part because the gaiety and glitz of the casino—which he wasn't allowed to walk through or even *see*—had an almost visceral allure for him.

As in the past, the only time he ever felt lifted out of himself and his miserable situation was onstage—"for 20 minutes, twice a night, our skin had no color." As in the past, he fought off his frustrations and the indignities of racism with ferocious performances—"I was vibrating with energy and I couldn't wait to get on the stage. I worked with the strength of 10 men." But never, as he dreamed might happen, did a casino manager or owner grow so enamored of his performance that he broke the color line by offering him a drink and a chance to try his luck at the tables.

And so it went. He forced himself higher and higher in the ranks of showbiz, garnering accolades, cutting records, standing out a bit more from Big Sam and Mastin with each performance, getting paid a little better with each gig. At the same time, he was hustled by cops to the backs of movie theaters, snubbed at the doors of the Copacabana and Lindy's, barred even from men's rooms in some of the theaters he packed with paying customers. If he grew to hate himself in some twisted fashion, he could hardly be blamed.

But repeatedly he found in his corner that skinny guy he'd met in Detroit. When Sammy was in the army, Frank had become a monster star, and when he was discharged and caught up with Mastin and Big Sam in Los Angeles, he made his way over to NBC studios in Hollywood, resplendent in his dress uniform, to watch Sinatra perform his weekly stint on *Your Hit Parade*. After the show, he waited out back with the bobby-soxers and autograph hounds and sheepishly offered Sinatra a piece of paper to sign.

"Didn't you work with your old man and another guy?" Frank asked, and he invited him to the next few shows, letting Sammy drink in rehearsals and backstage ambiance until another gig dragged the Mastin Trio back onto the road.

Two years later, Frank insisted that Sidney Piermont, manager of New York's Capitol Theater, book the Mastins as his opening act at $1,250 a week—a sum that staggered Mastin and Big Sam. Sinatra never told Sammy that he was behind the act's being hired—Piermont had wanted the Nicholas Brothers and then gagged at the price Sinatra wanted to pay Mastin—but in every other respect he treated Sammy like a peer throughout the engagement. They parted bosom pals: "Remember," Frank told Sammy as he left for his next booking—and this was his most profound gesture of friendship—"if anybody hits you, let me know."

But in the early fifties, no one, it seemed, wanted to hit Sammy. He was the quickest-rising star in nightclubs and theaters, particularly among the New York and L.A. cognoscenti. In 1951, the Will Mastin Trio opened at Ciro's, the hot Sunset Strip nightclub. The room was packed with Hollywood royalty, and Sammy and Company couldn't do enough. Dancing, singing, little comic bits, everything was a hit, nothing more so than Sammy's impersonations of such white stars as Jimmy Cagney, Cary Grant, and Humphrey Bogart. The same good fortune followed at an engagement at the Copacabana, the dream club of Sammy's youth, some months later. He was on the map to stay.

There was nevertheless a feeling of vertigo to it all. Although all the right people came to his shows, although he was welcome in the homes of Hollywood's crown royalty, he sensed a distance between himself and the fellow to whom all this good fortune fell, an inner gap separating the real man from the personality he'd become. He became famous for his tight pants, his extravagant spending, his largesse, his energy. But he'd also become infamous, in the tabloid press, as a consort—often only rumored—of white actresses, and the black press could be cutting in their comments about his seeming disregard for his race.

He was calculating and savvy enough to know that all publicity was good publicity—he was thrilled that his name made for hot ink—but he was wounded by the unfairness at the root of it. His race excluded him from a number of opportunities, so he created his own success; his success lifted him out of his race and made him a star simply because of his sheer talent; yet his talent could never entirely erase his race and, in fact, made him more visible as a black man and thus more open to injustice and prejudice. He walked a perilous line between one self, the black man who could be snubbed at the doors of exclusive New York nightclubs, and another self, the showbiz whirligig whom everybody wanted a piece of. He couldn't avoid being "Sammy Davis, Jr.," even when "Sammy Davis, Jr.," was the butt of jokes, gossip, and irrational hate.

Success, money, career offers, work—all this kept the doubts at bay for some of the time, but he was still profoundly susceptible to anxiety about his hold on his life. He would read reviews and compare them to previous notices from the same critics; he would call up clubs he was playing and ask, his voice disguised, if it was still possible to get a table for that evening's performance, collapsing in secret gratitude at the news that his shows were sold out. He was such a lost, addled soul that he began seeking answers in, of all places, Judaism, the religion of so many of the showbiz uncles who'd taken him so readily under their wings. He knew he could never escape who he was, but he kept searching for ways to somehow, maybe, evolve out of it.

Little by little, barriers fell as to the sheer force of his talent.

In 1954, the Mastin Trio was invited not only to play the Frontier but to stay there, to eat, gamble, and socialize among the white customers and make a whopping $7,500 a week besides. Sammy would have to commute back and forth to L.A., where he was doing some record work, but it was a dream gig and they leapt at it. You simply couldn't do any better than that.

Which was why it was so tragic, the car crash. Driving his Cadillac convertible to Los Angeles late on the night of November 19, 1954, listening to his own hit record "Hey There" on the radio, Sammy crossed into oncoming traffic in order to avoid a car that was making a U-turn right there in front of him on the highway. In the ensuing collision, his head hit the steering wheel. A stylized cone of chrome sticking out of the center of it like a battering ram put out his left eye.

His thoughts upon seeing his own mangled face in a piece of broken mirror as rescuers came to fetch him? "They're going to hate me again."

He was rushed to a hospital near Palm Springs, and Hollywood rushed to his side. Tony Curtis and Janet Leigh waited on him as he was in surgery; Frank visited constantly, as did a steady parade of showbiz lights; Jeff Chandler took the stage in his stead in Las Vegas—and nobody complained.

And when he came back, at Ciro's, dancing and singing and gagging with maybe even more energy than before, not to mention a rakish eye patch, the world clapped its hands raw and cried with affection for him. The accident turned out to be the thing that put him over the top; he could do it all, even beat death. It was like Frank dying on-screen in *From Here to Eternity*: It made him forever more.

An entire Broadway show, *Mr. Wonderful*, was built around him. There was a rags-to-riches story to it, and Chita Rivera and Jack Carter had parts, but the point of it was Sammy's nightclub-style performance in the second act, a partially scripted, partially free-form extravaganza of the sort that Al Jolson used to deliver when he was still in the legitimate theater. Mastin and Big Sam were on the stage with him, but it was

Sammy's name on the marquee. He did benefits, TV spots, radio appearances; he partied every night in restaurants and clubs and later in his hotel suite; he became a notorious tomcat on the prowl.

Soon enough, he was so big that the movies came calling. He played Sportin' Life in Otto Preminger's *Porgy and Bess*, and, in a great legends-of-Hollywood yarn, stunned producer Samuel Goldwyn into silence by declaring that he refused to work on Yom Kippur. "Directors I can fight," Goldwyn lamented. "Fires on the set I can fight. Writers, even actors I can fight. But a Jewish colored fellow? This I can't fight!"

A Jewish colored fellow: a whirling dervish: an up-and-coming superstar: just as he'd always dreamed.

—*1998*

"SAMMY,"

**from *The Rat Pack: The Hey-Hey Days of Frank and the Boys*,
by Lawrence J. Quirk and William Schoell**

Dean Martin was an eight-year-old playing in Steubenville and Jerry Lewis not even a twinkle in his father's eye when Sammy Davis, Jr., was born in Harlem in 1925. His father was a dancer in a vaudeville troupe headed by a friend named Will Mastin. Sammy's mother had left his father and gone off with another vaudeville group, so his father took him along with him when he went out on the road. When Sammy was three and bookings—and food—became scarce, his grandmother Rose told her son, Sammy's father, that he had better send the boy home to live with her. Sammy, Sr., hated the idea of being separated from his son and namesake, so he decided to grit his teeth, leave show biz, and get a normal job, although he was heartbroken at the thought of it.

After a few weeks of looking for show business jobs in New York and finding nothing, Sammy, Sr., tried to steel himself to get something similar to what he'd done before becoming a vaudevillian, driving a taxi or washing dishes, but he couldn't bring himself to do it. One afternoon he saw his small son dancing with Grandma Rose—whom Sammy, Jr., always called "Mama"—and recognized that the kid had absorbed some of his talent. When Will Mastin asked Sammy, Sr., to come back out on the road with him he eagerly agreed and decided to take his boy along with him. In between gigs they'd go back to Mama Rose.

In New York Rose hid Sammy, Jr., who was now five and eligible for school, from the truant officers, but she insisted her son get a tutor for the boy when they were traveling to some misbegotten town or another. Sammy, Sr., and Will had included the child in their act: they hired two other dancers and billed the fivesome as "Four and a Half." They were on the bill in a theater in Michigan when a lady do-gooder marched backstage and raised hell with the manager. According to her Sammy, Sr., and Will were practically child abusers, forcing such a small boy to dance and pretending he was having fun when he was obviously just being exploited. The result was that the manager let the act go and for several days the boy, his father, and "Uncle Will" went hungry, sleeping in train terminals and making tomato soup out of hot water and catsup. The temperature outside was minus 32 degrees. It wasn't the aforementioned do-gooder who rescued them but another woman who saw their plight, took them home with her, and fed them.

Eventually the group got more bookings and life looked a lot brighter, except for the times when Sammy's father drank too much, ranted at everyone, and created tension. There were also more do-gooders in the guise of the Geary Society, who enforced a law that said no one under the age of sixteen could appear on the stage. Not even disguising little Sammy as "Silent Sam, the Dancing Midget" could keep the Society off their backs. The result of this was that Mama Rose was granted custody of the boy. She would allow her son to take the child with him on the road but only if he followed strict orders. If Sammy, Jr., hadn't been so desperate to go—show business was already in his blood—she probably would have forbade it altogether.

When Sammy was seven his father took him out to Brooklyn, where Warner Bros. maintained a film studio. He auditioned for a singing and dancing role in an Ethel Waters two-reeler, *Rufus Jones for President*, and won the title role. He followed this up with another small role in a picture starring Lita Grey and her son, Charlie Chaplin, Jr. Lita wanted to adopt Sammy and take him out to Hollywood with her—she could see that vaudeville was on its last legs—but Mama Rose would have none of it. As far as she was concerned, her grandson was as much her "baby" as his father was.

Will and the two Sammy's continued their theatrical wanderings, only now their official billing was "Will Mastin's Gang, Featuring Little Sammy." The three of them always dressed exactly alike: spats, vest, cane, and so on. In a restaurant in Missouri little Sammy got his first taste of racism when a white waiter at a restaurant counter told the trio that "niggers" had to sit on the other side of the room. People in show business, the white folks they met on the road, had generally been friendly and open-minded. Occasionally, when they'd been refused service or a room in a particular inn, Big Sammy had told his son that it was because they were show people. Now he had to tell his son that as far as some people were concerned, their skin color made them different, something to be feared and even hated. It troubled Sammy, Jr., that there were individuals who would dislike him when they didn't even know him.

As the years proceeded, the Will Mastin Gang crisscrossed the country, slipped back and forth across the border into Canada, went hither and fro, piling up bookings, making money, getting somewhere if never quite where they wanted to be. They were stars, but only on a third-rate vaudeville circuit. At least the days they had money outnumbered the days when they were broke, which was different from the way it used to be. No one could deny that having little Sammy in the act was what made all the difference, although there would come a time when his partners would deny all that and more.

Sammy was fifteen and the trio was playing Detroit when

there occurred the first, if hardly momentous, meeting between Sammy and future fellow Rat Packer Frank Sinatra. The Will Mastin group was on the same bill as Tommy Dorsey— Dorsey's usual opening act was apparently stranded somewhere or other—and guess who was Dorsey's vocalist? Frank came over to Mastin and his gang backstage and introduced himself. Sammy had heard of Frank—who had yet to make a movie and hadn't quite started to cause feminine hearts to flutter—and had heard him sing on Dorsey's records, but neither of them had any idea that someday they'd become very close friends.

During World War II Sammy was inducted into the Army, where he encountered more prejudice of a particularly vicious kind than he ever had before. The corporal in his unit put him and another black soldier in one corner of the barracks and pushed the cots six feet away from the nearest ones, when all the other cots were only divided by two feet. When the sergeant saw what had been done, he insisted that the "Negro" cots be moved and be made uniform with the others. Then there was one soldier named Jennings who influenced a whole group of his friends to pick on Sammy: pretending to be friendly they handed him a glass of beer which was actually urine, and later tricked him to an isolated barracks where they drenched him with white paint and wrote "coon" on his forehead. They called him "nigger" and "ugly pygmy." Sammy got many a black eye in fights with these charmers whenever he could.

On the other hand, many of the white soldiers had no problem with Sammy and left him alone. The aforementioned sergeant, who was also white, was always friendly and sympathetic to Sammy. He lent him books from his library and encouraged him to read. Learning of his vaudeville background, he convinced him to appear in shows at the Service Club, although Sammy was afraid of how the soldiers might react. "How can you run out and smile at people who despise you?" he asked. An "athletic" heart condition kept him from going overseas, and he had never received any training for something of practical use to the Army. To his amazement and delight his dancing seemed to win over—or at least "neutralize," as he put it—many of the soldiers in the audience. He began to think of his talent as power, a weapon he could use to make sure he was acknowledged. A determination for this "pygmy" to succeed in spite of all the odds, in spite of whatever hatred his enemies could muster, was born in him. It was this determination that turned Sammy into a veritable giant.

Sammy had his second, slightly more momentous meeting with Frank Sinatra when he got out of the Army. By this time Sinatra had become a gigantic star, a singing sensation, the guy who drove all the gals gaga. Sammy, who was back with what was now called the Will Mastin Trio, was doing a gig in Los Angeles when he heard Frank singing live on the radio show "Your Hit Parade." He decided to go to the NBC studios where "Your Hit Parade" originated and sit in the audience. Sammy couldn't stop thinking of how they'd once shared a stage in Detroit when Sinatra was nobody. Now he was a star, and the Will Mastin Trio were still, for all intents and purposes, nobodies.

After the show Sammy went around to the stage door with around five hundred screaming fans and waited for their idol to appear. Finally Sinatra stepped out and the crowd went wild. Considering the influence Frank was to have on the life and career of Sammy Davis, Jr., it is interesting to note how Davis describes this moment in his autobiography: "God, he looked like a star. He wasn't much older than a lot of us, but he was so calm, like we were all silly kids and he was a man, sure of himself, completely in control."

When it came Sammy's turn to get an autograph, Frank thought he looked familiar. Sammy reminded him that they had been on the same bill in Detroit about five years previously. Frank recalled that Sammy had done an act with his father and another man. Then he told him he'd leave a ticket for him if he wanted to see another show sometime the following week. Sammy went to the show and got word that Frank wanted to see him in his dressing room, where he found him holding court with a dozen show biz insiders. "He had the aura of a king about him," Sammy remembered. Before he said good-bye, Frank told him he could come around and watch a rehearsal sometime.

Meanwhile, things weren't going so great for the Will Mastin Trio. They were booked for another tour and would be working steadily for several months, but comparing their lot to Frank's, Sammy knew it was another dead end on the third-rate circuit. When this was over, however, the Trio got booked at the El Rancho in the new happening spot of Las Vegas, Nevada. Arriving at the fabulous hotel with its huge band and modern (for the period) technology, Sammy was impressed and felt like his group was finally moving a little closer to the big time. He knew, however, that it was the same old story in certain regards when he found out that they would not be allowed to use rooms in the hotel or enter the casino while they were working there. Instead they were escorted to the impoverished Negro section of town, where they would have to rent rooms. A colored woman—the terms "black" and "African-American" weren't in vogue at this time—charged them twice what it would cost at El Rancho for three rooms in a comparative shack. Sammy's father was disgusted that one of their own would do that to them, but they had no choice but to agree to the terms if they were to keep the gig. It was in Vegas that Sammy began perfecting some of his soon-to-be-famous impersonations of everyone from Stepin Fetchit to Jimmy Cagney.

From then on things began looking up. For one thing, the Trio moved upward to the infinitely more prestigious RKO circuit, which ensured them bookings at much better places—and at higher fees—than they had been doing previously. Mickey Rooney was putting together a post-war stage show and decided to have the Will Mastin Trio open the bill. Sammy was impressed with Mickey's down-to-earth, gracious attitude when he first met him at the Copley Plaza Hotel in Boston. And their senses of humor were a good match. Looking Sammy over, Mickey said, "Damn, I never find anybody who's shorter than me. Everybody's taller—even you. And you're a midget!"

Mickey was the first Hollywood personality to befriend Sammy and try his best to enhance his career. Rooney tried to get Sammy a role as a fighter in his film *Killer McCoy*, a remake of *The Crowd Roars*, but the studio went with another actor. One Christmas Eve when Mickey's show was playing Cleveland, a gatecrasher came into their post-theater party shouting about "niggers" and Rooney hauled off and belted him. "It took four of us to pull him off," Sammy said.

Some time later Sammy was watching a show at the Strand Theatre when he noticed something about the Negro acts on the bill. They all spoke that certain "colored" dialect (what today we might call "ebonics") on stage even if the performers did not speak that way off-stage. And the performers never directly addressed or really communicated in any way with the audience. It was as if they felt they hadn't any right to, as if they were expected to shuffle and speak bad grammar because they were colored.

Sammy made up his mind that that was not going to be the case with the Will Mastin Trio. Or at least, that was not going to be the case as far as he was concerned. His father and Will were older, set in their ways, too accepting of the colored man's place in the world (or comparative lack of it) to change now, but he was younger, sterner, more determined to have everything white men had, everything Sinatra had. His talent was his power, and his talent was undeniable.

Then a dream came true. Neither Will nor Sammy, Sr., had ever imagined the day would come when they'd play one of the first-class circuit theaters in New York City, but through the intervention of another show business figure who had never forgotten Sammy, they were about to become the opening act at the Capitol Theater. Three weeks at $1,250 per week, a sum that had been unheard of when the act first began.

Their benefactor? Frank Sinatra.

"Frank took me completely under his wing," Davis wrote in his autobiography. "He didn't just say, 'Well, you're working and that's fine.' He had our names up out front, he was wonderful to my family, and he had me to his dressing room between almost every show. If I was there at dinner time, he'd take me out to eat with him."

Many people have wondered how come Sammy Davis spent so much time seeking Frank Sinatra's approval, emulating him, agonizing whenever Frank got mad at him, loving him, and obsessing over him to such a degree. Why did he—as many of Frank's friends did—put up with so much crap? The answer is that Frank Sinatra was a true friend when Sammy needed one. Frank stuck up for him, went to bat for him, gave his career the boost that it needed to push him into the majors—and in a time period that is very different today, a politically incorrect era when no white man had to go out of his way for a black one.

The head of Loew's Booking, Sidney Piermont, told Sammy that not only did Sinatra insist on having the Trio in the show—Piermont felt they were still comparative unknowns and didn't want to risk it—he demanded the $1,250 for them, too. Frank had never let on how big a role he had played in getting them hired.

It was also Sinatra who suggested that Sammy do some singing of his own. He heard Davis do an impression of him, and of several other singers and thought his own voice was good enough to do a straight number or two. Later on Frank thought Sammy might have picked up a little too much by listening to him and suggested he develop his own style.

From New York the Trio traveled to Los Angeles, where they appeared at the famous Slapsy Maxie's nightclub, and then went on to the even more famous Ciro's, the top of the lot. The headliner at Ciro's was supposed to be Janis Paige, but audience reaction to the Trio, especially Sammy, was so strong, that the blonde didn't have a chance. It was in her contract that the opening act only perform for so many minutes and could only take two bows, but the audience kept asking for more. Not only did they take four bows, Sammy gave an encore, his impression of "a colored Jerry Lewis." Janis Paige cooled her heels in the wings, her fury mounting, and shot out looks that could kill as the three men finally vacated the stage. The unexpected feedback got her off her game and she was off-key and rattled throughout the set; everyone in the audience kept talking about the opening act. From then on she decided that she would go on first and the Trio could bring up the rear in what was actually the coveted headliner spot.

It was around this time that Sammy first met Dean Martin's then-partner, Jerry Lewis, who was to become a close friend. Jerry gave Sammy some good advice, too. It was one thing for Sammy not to speak in a so-called colored dialect, but his grammar and speech were impeccable—by any standards. It made him sound "high-falutin'," as if he were condescending to his audience. The average white person didn't speak that well, let alone a black one. Jerry argued that if Sammy wanted to appeal to the widest possible audience, he had to be "a little less grand." Sammy admitted that he did sound "like a colored Laurence Olivier." It was understandable that he had rejected the Negro-speak, but he had gone too far to the other extreme. Worse yet, it sounded phony. Jerry also suggested that he screw up once in a while, that the occasional mishap would only endear him to the audience. Lastly, he said that it came off as if his father and Will were his servants, the way he spoke to them and had them hand him his props on stage. Davis absorbed this excellent critique and made some changes, although throughout most of his career he continued with the somewhat pretentious "with your kind permission I'd now like to sing" patter.

There was something else that troubled Sammy, but that he could do nothing about: his appearance. It wasn't so much his height that bothered him. Mickey Rooney had certainly proven that you didn't need to be tall to make it to the top, and he'd given out enough black eyes in the Army and elsewhere to know size didn't always matter. But one critic, in a positive review of his act, referred to him as "ugly looking." Sammy recalled the time when he was around ten years old or so when a little colored girl drew a picture of him making him appear grotesque and underlined the word "ugly" at the bottom of it.

True, the lower half of Sammy's face did pull to the side

when he sang or talked, creating distortion in his face, but aside from that he was rather handsome. He had gotten used to his face. He looked at it in the mirror and decided he'd be so damned busy on that stage that no one would ever notice what he looked like anyhow.

But then something happened that for quite a while took his mind off merely whether he was pretty or not. During an appearance at the New Frontier in Las Vegas in 1954, he was involved in a severe car accident and lost an eye. Although he learned to compensate and discovered he could see more with one good eye than he ever imagined, his equilibrium was affected and while convalescing he entertained fears that he might fall on his face when attempting to dance. Sinatra visited him at the hospital, causing a near-riot among the nurses, and gave him a pep talk. He told him he looked dynamic in his black eyepatch, and for a while Sammy toyed with the idea of leaving it on for good as a trademark.

One of the major early triumphs for the Will Mastin Trio was being hired to sing and dance for the crowd at the world-famous Copacabana club in New York. Sammy would never forget the night he and drummer Buddy Rich had gone to the Copa to see Frank Sinatra. The minute the doorman saw Sammy's black face, Rich was told his reservation had been "misplaced."

When Sinatra found out about it, he called Sammy personally and invited him to his show. He laid down the law with the management and the reservations clerk and told them all how very unhappy he would be if his friend wasn't admitted. Sammy was understandably apprehensive but on the chosen night he was admitted without incident. Furthermore, he discovered that Frank had invited several of his friends to sit with Sammy at his table so he wouldn't feel isolated in the audience. Now he and Will and his father were headliners at the same club that had once refused to seat him.

That was why Sammy was devastated when one night at the height of his glory he saw Frank Sinatra walking dejectedly down Broadway, virtually unrecognized by passersby who'd once screamed at the sight of him. This was at the point when Sinatra's career had hit the toilet. Sammy ran after him and tried to get his attention, but got the feeling that his friend would rather not be seen by anyone, that he'd rather not know anyone had witnessed his humiliation: Frank Sinatra, once the idol of millions, walking down Broadway unmolested. . . .

While Sinatra plummeted, Sammy went higher and higher. First he tackled television, becoming a frequent guest star on Eddie Cantor's show. After his first appearance, his representatives at the William Morris office were flooded with hate mail. In a panic the sponsors told Cantor that they might pull him off the air if anything like it happened again. Cantor's response was to tell his sponsors to go to hell and let him deal with the public. He hired Sammy for all three of the remaining shows of the season. Not for the first time Sammy realized that many people of the Jewish faith, who'd been persecuted themselves, refused to go along with other whites who discriminated against black people.

Sammy and the rest of the Trio had done vaudeville, the greatest nightclubs, radio, television, and Sammy had even been in films. The only field left to conquer was the Great White Way. It was only a matter of time before Sammy was signed to do a Broadway show. The show was *Mr. Wonderful*.

In its original concept, the musical would have been ahead of its time. Sammy was to play an entertainer much like himself, only he goes to Paris where he figures there will be less racial prejudice to deal with. The conflict comes when he meets up with an old friend who urges him to come back to New York, to try and make it in his own country no matter how much more difficult the odds.

But in out-of-town tryouts the critics responded well to everything but the message of racial equality, or at least to the fact that they felt the message was delivered with little subtlety. Sammy felt it was important for the musical to say something; the backers argued that what good would having a message do if there was no audience to deliver it to? The public was coming chiefly to be entertained and that was it.

By the time *Mr. Wonderful* got to Broadway most of the juice had been taken out of it. Sammy's character had never gone to Paris; instead he was a big shot in a small pond, a small town somewhere in the good ol' U.S.A. The conflict was still supposed to be whether or not he would leave the small success he had in Nowheresburg and try to make it in New York City, only Sammy argued that there really wasn't any "conflict" anymore. Why wouldn't the fellow want to try for major success in the Big Apple? "Instead of a story about a sophisticated, sensitive guy who doesn't want to live with prejudice," he said, "Charley Welch has become a schnook who doesn't have the guts to try for success."

In spite of this—or perhaps because of it—*Mr. Wonderful* became a big hit. One would imagine that by now Sammy had moved on to become a solo, but the Will Mastin Trio was still part of the billing, even appearing on the marquee of the musical. (Will and Sammy, Sr., had small parts in the show.) The producers argued that if Sammy truly wanted to go legit, he couldn't just recreate his nightclub act on the Broadway stage; it was time to jettison his father and Will. Underneath Sammy knew that they were right. He was the draw of the act and always had been—but he couldn't be disloyal to the two men who'd helped him enter show biz and who'd meant so much to him over the years. Afraid that they'd eventually be shunted to the side, Sammy, Sr., and Will (especially the latter) got Sammy to agree to a contract that everything would be split three ways in virtual perpetuity even if only Sammy were hired for a particular gig. This deplorable situation continued even after the two older men retired.

Each evening after the show, Sammy would have parties at his apartment. Attendance was mandatory. No matter how tired they were or even if they had dates or other things to do, fellow cast members such as Chita Rivera were told to be there; Sammy wouldn't take no for an answer. A night owl, Sammy would want to stay up until dawn and insisted everyone else keep him company. If someone left before the sun came up, citing fatigue or an early appointment, he would sulk and whine. He turned the *Mr. Wonderful* cast and hangers-on into an entourage who had to do what he wanted them to do: play Monopoly (a passion of Sammy's), quote Shakespeare, trade gossip, drink. Years later Sammy would admit that he'd turned these people into virtual prisoners.

Another favorite pastime of his was to hit the clubs, often dragging along with him Chita and the others whether they wanted to go or not. He'd found that not every chic Manhattan nightspot had a color barrier, and if they did, he often was the first to break it. He palled around with the owner of Danny's Hideaway, who wanted him to think of the place as his second home. He ate cheesecake at Lindy's with Milton Berle, another Jew who was all for blacks getting their piece of the pie. He debated whether or not to go ahead with his plans and meet some friends at Longchamps, expecting that certain look from the maitre'd, but when he screwed up his courage and walked inside his friends took him to their table and there was no problem. When he requested that he and a buddy move to another booth—there were chorus girls at their table and he, after all, was a star—he was only half-joking.

Sammy had been instrumental in getting the casinos to change their policies about barring admittance to blacks. He would not perform anywhere where blacks were banned, so casinos or clubs that discriminated never got his services no matter how much money they offered him. As he became a bigger and bigger draw, the recalcitrant markets recognized that it just wasn't good business to keep blacks out if it meant Sammy Davis, Jr., wouldn't perform for them. It was largely because of his efforts, his refusing to accept the status quo, that blacks were eventually admitted into casinos and into many of the tony downtown clubs.

Still, there were holdouts. One of these was the famous El Morocco, perhaps the snootiest Manhattan nightclub of all.

One night at his apartment where he was, as usual, holding court, his friends begged him to let them all go out on the town somewhere. El Morocco was suggested. But when one person phoned the club and asked for a reservation for Sammy, there was hemming and hawing until they were bluntly told that Sammy and his party had better go elsewhere. Ironically, music from *Mr. Wonderful* was being played that very moment by the orchestra in the background. Yet the star of the show himself would not be permitted to enter the establishment.

From then on El Morocco became a symbol to Sammy, a symbol that he had come this far but not far enough. In truth it had as much to do with ego—how dare they think that a Broadway star wasn't good enough for them?—as with Sammy's constant drive for racial equality. It didn't occur to him that he was seeking the approval of people who judged others by their clothing and pedigree, how much money they made, which block they lived on, snobs who treated other, "lesser" white people like dirt—did he really expect equal treatment for a black man from such as these? Still, his star status had gained him entree into many a place and situation that the average black (and many whites) would not have been privy to, and he was determined that El Morocco would acknowledge his place in the world or else.

While many of Sammy's friends understood his obsession with the club, others, white and black, were tired of the way Sammy always made an issue of his race, tired of the way he would always foist himself—and them—upon Upper East Side people and places where, instead of being able to relax and have some fun, they had to brace themselves for a slight or insult and Sammy's outraged reaction to same. To them, Sammy was courting the favor of frivolous, bigoted, shallow people— people to whom appearance was everything—when he could just as easily have gone bar-hopping in Greenwich Village, where the bohemians didn't care if you were white or black or even what sex you slept with after the bars closed. It became less and less about equality and more and more about living his stereotypical definition of La Dolce Vita. Just as Sammy had never considered if it would really be so great to allow blacks into—let's face it—crooked casinos where they could have their hard-earned money ripped off along with white folk, he never wondered if acceptance at El Morocco should be his true criterion for success.

None of this, of course, changes the fact that El Morocco's policy was outrageous, and one can't help admiring the bantamweight Sammy for taking on this snooty Goliath as he did—if the whole business hadn't backfired. On the night *Mr. Wonderful* finally closed and a cast party was held, he left the soiree before it had hardly begun and insisted that a white couple he was good friends with go with him to El Morocco. As the couple had been to the club on many previous occasions, they were admitted—with Sammy in tow—but they were given a table in what is known in the restaurant business as "Siberia": the declasse section of the club reserved for tourists and other commoners. So instead of partying with his friends, fellow cast members, and other well-wishers at an establishment that welcomed his patronage, instead of celebrating the long run of his hit Broadway show and saying good-bye to people he'd worked with for months, he sat and stewed at El Morocco until he could take the deliberate slight no more and insisted he and the couple leave.

One Wednesday morning this man with an understandable if occasionally self-destructive chip on his shoulder picked up a newspaper and read the headline HUMPHREY BOGART DIES.

Sammy had been very fond of and grateful to Bogart. He liked his wife, Lauren Bacall. His first thought was to call Frank. He knew how much Frank idolized Bogey. But Frank Sinatra wasn't taking any calls. He was too distraught—and more—to talk.

—*1998*

EXCERPT FROM
Sinatra: Behind the Legend,
by J. Randy Taraborrelli

Only once—to anyone's memory, anyway—did the shenanigans get out of hand onstage, and that was the night Joey Bishop walked off. Frank and Dean, in an improvisational routine, started calling each other "dag." Even though Frank had used the phrase "dag" for years as a short version of "dago" when he was bonding with fellow Italian Americans, Joey—who had recently been lauded for his defense of Italian Americans on *The Jack Paar Show*—became offended and left. Later, when Frank asked him why he had done that, Joey said, "Hey, Frank, you ever think about how you're gonna feel when you leave the stage and somebody calls you a dag. You're not gonna like it, and if you argue about it, the other guy's gonna say. 'Hey, what's your problem? I heard you say it yourself onstage.' I don't know how to act out there when you start that stuff. Am I supposed to think it's camaraderie? I'm sorry, but I can't stand on that stage when you're doing dago jokes." Frank agreed, and neither he nor the rest of the fellows used the word onstage again.

"If you tell Frank something and you're right," said Joey Bishop, "then you were home free. The key to our relationship was trust. He trusted me. We all trusted each other."

It can be said, though, that the fellows didn't always offer Sammy Davis the same consideration when it came to ethnic concerns. Historically, most people who have written about the Rat Pack, including Nancy Sinatra, make note of the cracks about Davis's color and how, while "a little rough," they were acceptable "because of what they knew was in their hearts." In retrospect, much of it does not seem funny.

For instance, all of the fellows wore white robes with their names stitched in back for their daily steam-room ritual. One day, Sammy went into the steam-room and couldn't find his robe. When he asked about the missing garment, he was informed by the attendant that Frank had ordered a new one for him. Then the attendant reached under a counter and presented Sammy with a brown robe, along with brown towels and brown soap. "Mr. Sinatra said you can no longer use the white towel or the white soap," said the attendant solemnly. Then Frank and his buddies came from behind a curtain, and everyone laughed at Sammy's reaction.

Or, while onstage and with the lights low, Frank would say to Sammy, "You better keep smiling, Sammy, so we can see where you are."

When Sammy did his Sinatra impression of "All the Way," Frank would say, "He's just, excuse the expression, a carbon copy."

Or, during some other shows, Dean would pick up Sammy and say, "I want to thank the NAACP for this wonderful trophy." (Joey Bishop explained, "When I wrote that bit, it was supposed to be 'I want to thank the B'nai B'rith for this award,' referring to the fact that Sammy had recently converted to Judaism. But Dean couldn't remember the words B'nai B'rith. He blew it every night until he finally changed it to NAACP.")

Later, Dean said to Sammy, "I'll dance wit ya, I'll sing wit ya, I'll swim wit ya, I'll cut the lawn wit ya, I'll go to bar mitzvahs wit ya. But don't touch me." (Sammy, stomping his feet hysterically, would practically roll on the floor while laughing at these jokes.)

Sinatra's dedication to racial equality went back years, all the way to his Hoboken childhood, when he himself felt the sting of prejudice because of his own ethnicity. People still remember that when Sinatra first began singing "Ol' Man River" back in the forties, he was careful to replace the line "Darkies all work on the Mississippi" with "Here we all work on the Mississippi." (After he made that lyrical change, most other performers followed suit whenever they sang the Kern-Hammerstein song in concert.)

In years to come, Sinatra opened up many doors for Sammy Davis, especially in Las Vegas, where he demanded that Sammy be allowed to perform in certain hotels and be paid what other stars were paid. But did that give him and his Caucasian friends the right to joke about Sammy's race? Indeed, Sinatra historians have always been baffled by his, and the other Rat Packers', seemingly complete disregard for the ideal of racial tolerance during their shows in the early sixties.

As Sammy himself once put it, "For the times, yeah, the jokes were offensive. But, man, look at the company I was keeping. I had to put up with it. I loved those guys, and I know they loved me. But, yeah, it wasn't right. I didn't like it a lot of the time. Sometimes I had to wonder, Are these cats for real or what? I had to bite my tongue a lot."

—1997

EXCERPT FROM
Peter Lawford: The Man Who Kept the Secrets,
by James Spada

In October 1967, Peter and Sammy Davis roared through the streets of London's Soho on matching minibikes, dodging traffic and waving to gawking onlookers. Sammy's license plate read "SALT 1"; Peter's read "PEPPER 1." They were on their way to Alvaro's, a trendy discotheque on King's Road in Chelsea, and the club was having to turn away dozens of neck craners every week once the word got out that Lawford and Davis were regulars.

The pair were in London to star in *Salt and Pepper*, a James Bond takeoff developed by Peter for Chrislaw, and they set the English capital on its ear. "Swinging London" was the epicenter of the "youth-quake" that was radically transforming the world's tastes in fashion and popular music. Peter and Sammy were much taken by all the experimentation with drugs, sexual freedom, and personal style. "It's stimulating, frightening, fun," Sammy told a reporter.

It was ironic that Peter and Sammy—old enough at forty-

three and forty-one to be the parents of most of the "revolutionaries"—had become such a media rage. As one journalist
noted, "Every newspaper from the *Sunday Times* to the *Daily
Sketch* has come out with details of *Salt and Pepper*. . . . The
entertainment columns of the daily press and feature pages of
the color magazines are having a scoop day."

The excitement was created largely by the formidable repu-
tations of the pair as former Rat Pack swingers and by Peter's
aura as the former brother-in-law of a martyred U.S. president.
But there was another reason why Peter's presence caused a
stir—as Graham Stark, one of *Salt and Pepper*'s British costars,
recalled: "I always rather held the boy in esteem. He was a
young Englishman who had gone to Hollywood, and anyone at
MGM was a star to us. We grew up on Judy Garland, anything
by Arthur Freed—and Lawford was involved. He actually
kissed June Allyson on-screen—I could have killed him!"

At Alvaro's—where the two went every Saturday for
lunch—Peter and Sammy were surrounded by some of the
would-be hippest young people in London, who hung on their
every word and treated them as entertainment icons. Before
long the two men had co-opted the mod look for themselves.
They wore their hair long, grew pork-chop sideburns (Peter's
were gray), and donned Nehru jackets, bell-bottoms, and love
beads. Peter had slimmed down again and wore blue jeans with
a patch on the back that read, "Get your shit together." Peter
and Sammy thought it all made them look more youthful and
"with it," and many of their London admirers agreed. Others
thought they were making fools of themselves.

Just as Peter and Sammy had adopted the self-conscious hipness of the Rat Pack, they now embraced the sixties mod style
wholesale, complete with swinging parties, flower-child jargon,
and experimentation with LSD and marijuana. Peter considered
marijuana a godsend, a way to get high without drinking and
further damaging his liver. Earlier, he had been adamantly opposed to any kind of drug use and had lectured Molly Dunne
about its evils. "I was smoking marijuana long before Peter

was," she recalled. "He didn't want me to smoke in the beach house. He'd say, 'Don't you smoke that stuff in here. Go outside!' And then he becomes this drug addict!"

Graham Stark went to some wild parties thrown by Peter and Sammy. "Sammy took up residence at the Mayfair in the Maharajah's suite and we were all invited up there at various times," Stark recalled. "There was a lot of action, girls falling out of cupboards. And why not? They were both big film stars and all those little darlings just loved them."

The "free love" aspects of the mod scene appealed mightily to Peter. Among the many pretty young women who "fell out of the cupboards" was one who belonged to Sammy. "Sammy had found this beautiful little model, a white girl," Milt Ebbins recalled. "He fell in love with her, and they were living together while they were filming *Salt and Pepper*. Peter stole her away. Sammy came to me and said, 'That fucker, I'll never talk to him again.' I asked Peter, 'What did you do?' And Peter replied nonchalantly, 'I stole his girl.' "

Peter and Sammy patched it up, and in between all the swinging, there was a movie to make. The idea for the film had come to Peter after a friend had referred to him as "salt" and Sammy as "pepper." He decided to turn it around and commissioned a script in which he would play Chris Pepper and Sammy would be Charlie Salt, a couple of nightclub owners in London who get involved in Bondlike intrigue, replete with comic bobbies, a car with a machine gun for an exhaust pipe, and all the requisite chases. Milt Ebbins got the go-ahead from United Artists executives for Chrislaw to produce the project after Michael Pertwee wrote a script they liked. Ebbins was named the film's producer, his first such assignment, and Sammy and Peter were named executive producers.

It was a difficult baptism for Ebbins. With a relatively small budget, he had hoped to film the London street scenes in Soho. But the congestion caused by sightseers prompted London police to ban the shooting and forced him to reconstruct Soho on the back lot at Shepperton Studios in Boreham at a cost of sixty thousand pounds ($144,000).

Ebbins was soon confronted with another, more serious problem. "Peter was the world's worst businessman," he recalled. "He always made decisions based on his emotions. He hired people because he liked them, not because they were necessarily right for the project." When it came time to hire a director for *Salt and Pepper*, Peter wanted Richard Donner, who at that point had directed only one minor film and some episodic television. Peter and Sammy had appeared in a *Wild, Wild West* episode Donner had directed, and Peter liked him.

Ebbins was skeptical, but when Peter insisted he agreed to hire Donner. "He's an incredibly successful director now," Ebbins recalled. "He's made *Superman, Lethal Weapon*—but in 1967 he wasn't ready. When the UA executives saw Donner's cut, they decided to reedit the film without his input. It cost us fifty thousand dollars to fix it."

According to Donner, the fault was not his. "I had a bad time on that film," he recalled. "Sammy and Peter were very undisciplined and there was a lot of cutting up. We'd have an eight o'clock call and they'd show up at noon, hung over from whatever it was they had ingested the night before. It was terrible for me, and I had no way of controlling them because they were the producers. What was I going to do, fire them?"

Donner quickly discovered that when Peter and Sammy did show up they usually didn't have much of an idea of what was in the script for the day's shooting. Instead, they would improvise conversations, do bits of business that had little to do with the plot. Donner decided to let them go off on as many tangents as they wanted. "I figured when I cut the picture I could just take all that extraneous stuff out. But then they fired me two weeks after we finished shooting. I was so angry at Peter at that point that if I'd found him it would have made the papers."

Despite everything, Donner and Peter remained friendly and later went into business together, with a group of other partners, in The Factory, an exclusive, trendy discotheque in West Hollywood. "There was a bit of hero worship in my feelings for Peter," Donner recalled. "The women just flocked to him. It was unbelievable. I always wanted to be a pilot fish to Peter's shark—you know, the little fish that hangs on to the shark and eats up anything that falls out of its mouth? Peter had so many gorgeous girls around him I was content with his overflow. I did very well through him."

Critical reaction was mixed when *Salt and Pepper* was released in September 1968. Most reviewers thought the film a waste of Sammy's talents, and the Los Angeles *Herald-Examiner* was hard on Peter for never seeming "quite sure as to whether he is supposed to be James Bond, Mr. Lucky or Peter Lawford." *Variety* summed things up by noting, "This is not a picture for thinking audiences."

—1991

"WHEN THEY WERE KINGS,"
by James Wolcott, *Vanity Fair*

"I present our hoodlum singer . . ."

With these words of mock homage, an astonishingly young and lanky Johnny Carson introduces Frank Sinatra to the stage of the Kiel Opera House in St. Louis, Missouri. The year is 1965; the event, billed as a "Frank Sinatra Spectacular" and broadcast on closed circuit to theaters across the country, is a benefit for Father Dismas Clark's Half-Way House for ex-cons. Sinatra said, "Be there," and they were there—Dean Martin, Sammy Davis, Jr., Trini Lopez, Kaye Stevens, and an amalgamation of two different bands, including members of the Count Basie Orchestra, conducted by a lean cat named Quincy Jones. Joey Bishop was listed on the original program, but had to bow out when he "slipped a disk backing out of Frank's presence," according to Carson, his replacement, who was only three years into his tenure as host of *The Tonight Show*. A recently discovered kinescope of this bash—under the new title, *The Rat Pack Captured*—will be screened this month at the Museum of Television & Radio in New York and at the Los Angeles branch, and will also be broadcast later this year on "Nick at Nite"'s cable channel. The edited 90-minute version of the benefit—featuring Frank, Dino, Sammy, and Johnny—represents the only known full-length video of the Rat Pack in performance. (A two-volume compact disc exists of the Rat Pack performing at the Villa Venice club in Chicago in 1962—a gig they were strong-armed into doing by the mobster Sam Giancana.) The Rat Pack kinescope, found in a closet at the Dismas House, is more than a historical curio. It has the glamorous wham of a championship prizefight. It's an opportunity to catch three of America's greatest showmen in their tigerish prime (with Carson along for the ride), before they became total legends and turned into leather.

There's Dean Martin with his sleepy power, like a leopard in a smoking jacket, finishing his few songs with the words "I'd like to do some more for ya, but I'm lucky I remembered these." There's Sammy Davis, Jr., a gleaming revolver of a man, belting out a maudlin Anthony Newley torch song as if he means it, goofing around with "I've Got You Under My Skin" ("it's a little lumpy, but you're under my skin"), demonstrating the latest go-go dances (the monkey, the jerk, the frug, the mashed potato), and, in a final tour de force, doing quick carbon copies of Billy Eckstine, Nat King Cole, Frankie Laine, Mel Tormé, Tony Bennett, and Dean himself. And then there's Sinatra, confident, not the Adam's apple on a stick he was or the barrel-chested belter he would become, cruising inside the luxury-limousine sound of the Count Basie band, not so much singing the up-tempo numbers ("Fly Me to the Moon," "You Make Me Feel So Young") as riding them home, his rabbit jabs providing the punctuation to his cagey phrasing and eased-off vowels. Frank Sinatra has been called great for so long that it's easy to forget how great he is. Praise becomes platitude. At one point, alluding to Sammy's set, he says that the song he's about to perform makes for "a slight duplication here, but I don't think you'll mind too much," launching into his own rendition of "I've Got You Under My Skin," which he contours and tattoos as if romancing for the first time. Dean amuses, Sammy is mahvelous, but only Sinatra, with his Manhattan-skyline voice, conjures a mood and a spell.

After Sinatra's set comes the usual Rat Pack foolery, some at Dean's expense ("The only reason he's got a good tan, he found a bar with a skylight"), but with Sammy as the primary butt. The racial ribbing, though not as crass or persistent as the kidding on the Villa Venice CD, conveys the edginess of the civil rights era. Sammy mentions something about getting Martin Luther King, Jr.'s, permission to appear. Dean lifts Sammy in his arms and says, "I'd like to thank the N.A.A.C.P. for this wonderful trophy." Sammy, who had converted to Judaism, is hailed as the only Jewish Muslim: Irving X. What's interesting about the last segment, aside from the forced joviality of the racial horseplay, is Carson's surfacing irritation as the buffoonery (deliberately bad imitations of Jimmy Cagney, etc.) drags on too long. He feels extraneous on the stage, checking his watch and saying he has to catch a plane, and although he is not nearly the star at that point that Frank, Dino, or Sammy is, he isn't grateful to play stooge to the gods. We see in his broomstick posture and sentry eyes the isolated power that Carson would become. The show ends with all four wailing away at "The Birth of the Blues," with Dean taking a brilliantly timed pratfall just as he wings into his verse.

The excitement that this kinescope has sparked testifies to the unfading legend of the Rat Pack and their streamlined influence on male bravado, which can be observed in everything from the resurgence of "bachelor pad" music and the cocktail hour to the nostalgia for the Vegas of yore in movies like *Casino* and *Bugsy*, when the city still swung and the red lobbies weren't clogged with Mr. and Mrs. Big Butt America pushing strollers between the slots. The Rat Pack is the Mount Rushmore of men having fun. The designer Mossimo Giannulli keeps a large photograph of the Rat Pack in his Laguna Beach home, like an eternal flame. "These guys are my idols," he told *InStyle* magazine. "They just cruised. They had this great group of people, love and friendship." The fact that the press keeps trying to manufacture fresh new Rat Packs—the acting Brat Pack of Judd Nelson, Ally Sheedy, Andrew McCarthy, Molly Ringwald, and Rob Lowe; the literary Brat Pack of Jay McInerney, Bret Easton Ellis, and Tama Janowitz—indicates the constant itch for a group energy, a moving amoeba of excitement, a scene.

The term "Rat Pack" originally designated not Sinatra and his flying wedge but an informal Hollywood social set revolving around Humphrey Bogart and his pals. Nathaniel Benchley designed the letterhead of the group's stationery, which bore the loyalty oath coined by Bogart, "Never rat on a rat." Sinatra, who idolized Bogart, was a member in good standing, along with Judy Garland and agent Irving "Swifty" Lazar. After Bogart's death in 1957, Sinatra, with his natural charisma and inability to be alone (see Gay Talese's classic study in *Esquire* in 1966, "Frank Sinatra Has a Cold"), filled the social void and then some with his own Rat Pack, also known as the Clan—names Sinatra disavowed as inaccurate and uncouth. "There is no such thing as a clan or pack," he explained. "It's just a bunch of millionaires with common interests who get together to have a little fun." The members of this floating bacchanal included Martin (with whom Sinatra co-starred in *Some Came Running*), Joey Bishop, Sammy Davis, Jr., and Peter Lawford, classy dames like Angie Dickinson and Shirley MacLaine, and supporting players like Sammy Cahn, Cesar Romero, Don Rickles, Milton Berle, and the director Lewis Milestone.

It never hit me until now that the Rat Pack formed during the same period that the Beats rolled onto the scene—Jack Kerouac, Allen Ginsberg, William Burroughs, and all those other spontaneous bopsters. (Kerouac's *On the Road* was published in 1957, the year Bogart's Rat Pack gave way to Sinatra's.) At first the two outfits couldn't seem more bizarro-worlds apart, the Rat Packers showing the money in their sharkskin suits and slick grooming, the Beats bumming around in fleapit pads from Monterey to Morocco on the path to Buddha-hood. Yet both were a reaction to the suburban conformism of work-home-family in the Eisenhower era. The Rat Pack, like the Beats, disdained middle-class moderation in their pursuit of freewheeling kicks. ("This [cigarette] ain't got no printin' on it at all," Dean Martin muses in the Rat Pack video.) Like the Beats and their fictional alter egos, the Rat Pack were always in motion, nocturnal creatures partying in a perpetual Now. And like the Beats, the Rat Pack had their own special hipster lingo to winnow out the squares from the truly anointed, a code that sounds like something cooked up by Steve Allen in a jazzy frame of mind. Kitty Kelley provides a glossary in her 1986 biography of Sinatra, *His Way*: women were "broads," "bird" equaled penis (as in "How's your bird?"), "a little hey-hey" meant a good time, "clyde" was an all-purpose noun, and death was "the big casino."

> Nice, France, August 11 (A.P.)—The second wave of Frank Sinatra's Hollywood clan hit the Riviera beaches as cane-twirling Sammy Davis, Jr., danced down the ramp of a jet airliner.
> "I would have been here earlier, daddy-ohs, but the hotel clerk in London forgot to wake me," Davis told waiting reporters and photographers.
> —*New York Post*, August 11, 1961

Personal hygiene aside, where the Rat Pack and the Beats parted company was in their attitudes toward power in all its seductive guises. To the Beats—self-educated in the prophecies of William Blake and Eastern notions of nonattachment—the Pentagon, Madison Avenue, and Hollywood were all manifestations of Moloch. "Hollywood will rot on the windmills of Eternity / Hollywood whose movies stick in the throat of God,"

Allen Ginsberg declared. (And this was before Pauly Shore.) While the Beats were content to woo nodding fields of young minds, the Rat Pack enjoyed the view from the penthouse suite, where sex and money were plugged into the same socket. With Sinatra as their king, their Pope, *il padrone*, the Rat Pack were a royal court, granting and receiving favor. Seas of gawkers parted in hushed wonder when they crossed the lobby of Las Vegas's Sands Hotel, the casino which is the Xanadu of Rat Pack lore. The Sands was where they did their most famous engagements (the double live album *Sinatra at the Sands*, available on CD, preserves the brassy ebullience), drawing the high rollers and their minked molls. Nick Tosches sets the scene in his 1992 Dean Martin biography, *Dino*:

> It was not just the dirty-rich *giovanostri* and *padroni* who were drawn to them, to their glamour, to the appeal of darkness made respectable. The world was full, it seemed, of would-be wops and woplings who lived vicariously through them, to whom the imitation of cool took on the religiosity of the Renaissance ideal of *imitatio Christi*. The very songs that Sinatra and Dean sang, the very images they projected, inspired lavish squandering among the countless men who would be them. It was the Jew-roll around the prick that rendered them ithyphallic godkins, simulacra of the great ones, in their own eyes and in the eyes of the teased-hair lobster-slurping *Bimbo sapiens* they sought to impress.

Not exactly how I would phrase it, but, hey, man, to each his own bird!

The ranks of Rat Pack wannabes weren't restricted to swarthy men and wives in lobster bibs. Elvis Presley's "Memphis Mafia" was a high-cholesterol Rat Pack. Heavy swingers in their own fields wanted to tap into the electricity. John F. Kennedy was fascinated by Sinatra's chick action. It was at the Sands where

J.F.K., following a Sinatra performance, was introduced by him at a friendly mixer afterward ("blowjobs on the house"—Tosches) to Judith Campbell, whom Sinatra later hooked up with Sam Giancana, thus giving the Mob a direct mouth into the White House. It was Sinatra who triangulated Hollywood, Washington, and the Mafia. The Rat Pack sang "The Star-Spangled Banner" at the Democratic convention that year. Sinatra attended Kennedy's inauguration in top hat, cape, and swallow-tailed coat. Then it all went black. The president, fearful of bad publicity, skipped a visit to Sinatra's Palm Springs spread to stay at Bing Crosby's instead, a snub that infuriated Sinatra. Marilyn Monroe, rumored to have been having an affair with Robert Kennedy, tried to commit suicide at Sinatra's Cal-Neva Lodge in Nevada, a favorite hangout of Giancana's, and succeeded a few days later in Los Angeles. Sinatra, the Kennedys, Monroe, the Mob—for a few short years, it was a dizzying round of musical beds. Perhaps no book captures the dangerous golden-nooky pop-myth glamour of the period better than Norman Mailer's *An American Dream*, which begins with a reverie about double-dating with J.F.K. and ends with a drive to Las Vegas, where the narrator phones his dead sweetheart in Heaven, who tells him that Marilyn says hello. It's an honorary Rat Pack novel.

In the first flush of Camelot, before Marilyn Monroe overdosed, Giancana tried to arrange a hit on Castro, and J.F.K. was assassinated, Sinatra and pals shot a caper movie for his production company that stands as the definitive photo album of the Rat Pack phenomenon, *Ocean's Eleven*. Other Rat Pack films would follow, such as *Robin and the 7 Hoods*, but this is the one with the *essence de rat*. Shot in 1960, *Ocean's Eleven* was directed by Lewis Milestone, who had earned his distinction with *All Quiet on the Western Front* and *A Walk in the Sun* before setting aside his taste and dignity to baby-sit these overgrown delinquents. At night the Rat Pack would perform at the Sands and make major hey-hey until dawn, catnap, then slouch before the camera. They look like sirloin in the atomic light of day, while Angie Dickinson, reciting her lines off a blank slate in her mind as Sinatra's long-suffering wife, is pure custard. The guys play military buddies who meet to plan the great heist of all time, knocking out a power line in Las Vegas and hitting the casino vaults during the blackout confusion. (In an enlightened piece of casting, Sammy drives a garbage truck.)

Incidental dialogue reflects the Kennedy euphoria—and its cynical opportunism. Standing around in the game room with pool cues and cigarettes, the gang swaps *Playboy* fantasies about what they'd do with a big score. Sinatra suggests buying out the Miss Universe pageant, "and just sit around and talk to the girls, one by one. Find out how things are in Sweden." Why buy what you could get for free? asks Peter Lawford, who had married into the Kennedy clan. The key, he says, is "turning money into power. . . . Think I'll buy me some votes and go into politics." "*I'm* the one that's going into politics," Dino ripostes. His platform? asks Sammy. "Repeal the 14th and the 20th Amendment, take the vote away from the women and make slaves out of them." "Hey, will it cost much?" Frank asks. "Oh no, we've got the price controls—no inflation on slaves." Lawford, vainly trying to steer them back to the big picture, reiterates that politics is the real racket. "Pay off your own party, settle for an appointment. . . . Hey, fellas, do you have any idea how much money a man can steal if he was something like commissioner of Indian affairs? That's what I'll be, commissioner of Indian affairs!" "That you'll never be," Dean says, " 'cause I'm gonna be secretary of the interior, and *I* won't appoint you." It's a disjointed scene, but the message is clear: money equals power equals male prerogative. Then they quit trading philosophy and gather around the pool table to plan their low-tech, low-I.Q. operation.

Like Elvis Presley's *Viva Las Vegas, Ocean's Eleven* is one of those dumbbell diversions that have achieved a permanent splotch in the rec room of pop culture. It's a real 60s guy fa-

vorite, like *Rio Bravo, The Great Escape,* and (my own inde-
fensible must-see) *Hatari!* Its cult status has little to do with
quality, more to do with a high kitsch quotient that sticks like
chewing gum in the *Mad* magazine of the mind. The schlock
highlights include the blaring and much-imitated musical score
by Nelson Riddle; Sinatra receiving a backrub in his orange
mohair sweater; Dino, backed by a jazz combo (dig those crazy
goatees), singing "Ain't That a Kick in the Head" to a trio of
cloned-sheep fans; and Richard Conte asking, as his doctor
studies his X-ray, "Is it the big casino?" A perfectionist in the
recording studio, Sinatra didn't believe in undue strain on the
movie set, breezing through as few takes as possible. After
Conte buys the big casino, suffering a heart attack as he crosses
the street, other members of the gang gather on the street to
share the news. Heads nod. Without bothering to change expression, Sinatra then exits the scene as if heading for a sandwich, and Lawford remarks, "He's taking it hard." Not so
you'd notice! What rescues the movie from utter plywood is its
comic anticlimax, when the scheme runs aground and the
money literally goes up in smoke, and the Rat Packers file out
of Conte's chapel service across the screen like a lost patrol—
past the Sands marquee bearing their names. Their walks have
singular style, adding up to an absurdist coda.

Years later, *Ocean's Eleven* inspired one of the classic movie
parodies, *SCTV*'s "Maudlin's 11," in which the *SCTV* regulars
trade finger-snapping slang with one another ("Absoposi-
tively," "Bingo, dingo!") as they plan a heist with such vocal
enthusiasm ("Oh, *yeah!*" "Cool, man, cool!") that everybody
in Vegas knows the score. In a takeoff on the *Ocean's Eleven*
strip-club scene, the acerbic Bill Needle (Dave Thomas) belts
out the theme from *Exodus,* acknowledging the crowd's flat response with a surly "Thank you for that great round of indif-
ference," kissing off his stripper wife with the words "You're
just nothing but a bringdown anyway!" What the *SCTV* parody exuberantly nails is the gee-whiz juvenile giddiness under-
lying the Rat Pack swagger and camaraderie. Their jive is not

the genuine laid-back hip of jazz, but the loud tones and threads of lounge lizards trying to pass as jazzy. Most of the Rat Pack humor is corny, retrograde. The Rat Pack mystique is not about being innately cool; it's about wanting to be cool so much you give each other contact highs. "Oh, *yeah*!" It's white soul, without the soul.

The fascination with the Rat Pack expresses a longing for an everyday masculine style that's cool and crisp, without being James Bond swanky. The Rat Pack video was shot in 1965, before the hippie insurgence feminized men, fluffing their hair and softening the sharp cut of their wardrobes into more flowing lines. Even the slouchier postures of the Rat Packers (like Dean's modified John Wayne roll) carry more purposeful thrust than the nudist-colony droop of male hippies. When unabashed masculinity returned to pop culture, it did so with a vengeance, pumped up on steroids and so thickened that its meat-men (Conan the Barbarian, Rambo) could barely speak, or, conversely, ranted like a neighborhood bully (Andrew Dice Clay). Rat Pack male-bonding infiltrates such revisionist guy pictures as *Good-Fellas* (a rotting-carcass Rat Pack) and *The Usual Suspects* (the twist being that the soulful gang leader is played for a fool by the Joey Bishop mascot, portrayed by Kevin Spacey). Quentin Tarantino's stuff has a perverse Rat Pack streak. But if the spirit is there, the look is wanting. A lot of the younger male stars, even when they dress keen, have junkie-dank skin and sticky, unwashed hair that would have made Sinatra in his prime drag them through a car wash to straighten out their clyde.

The razor-blade flair of the Rat Pack style gleams best in a time bubble or a deliberately retro fashion spread. It complements the overall style of the Kennedy-kaboom 60s; it jibes with the design and decor—tail fins, stand-up bars, African masks, breezeways, Mondrian rectangles, and curvilinear signs. The ladies in this bachelor paradise sported cocktail dresses and bouffants with enough hair spray to stop a bullet; when these walking powder puffs made small talk or indulged in dry laughter, they turned up their wrists just so. That's all Audrey Hepburn now. The natty extravagance of the Rat Pack look clashes with shopping-mall functionalism—fern bars, family minivans, video rentals, and computer monitors casting gray death rays. Clubs have lost most of their dressy cachet; they've become day-care centers for night owls. (Only in the last few years have cocktails and cigars made a self-conscious comeback.)

The comedy of trying to emulate a rich Rat Pack attitude in the downwardly mobile 90s is what animates *Swingers*, a modest cult hit written by and starring Jon Favreau. The movie, funny but acrid (burnt around the edges), has also spawned a spin-off book, a *Swingers* manual. Favreau plays Mike, a shlub strictly from Loserville who mopes over an old girlfriend and gets nowhere fast as an actor in Hollywood. He also M.C.'s at a comedy club on open-mike night. His best bud, Trent (Vince Vaughn), is his pep coach in cool. "You are so money and you don't even know it," Trent tells him again and again. (Vaughn based his characterization on the Rat Pack jargon he used to make up to amuse his actor-friends.) To get Mike out of his funk, Trent suggests they go to Vegas. "Vegas, baby, Vegas!" Grabbing the first cocktail waitress they meet, Trent spins her around and introduces her to Mike: "I want you to remember this face here. This is the guy behind the guy behind the guy." Their cover story doesn't translate into clout. They don't rule the blackjack table or command the hospitality suite, but end up in a trailer at dawn with the cocktail waitress and her friend; sex for both couples proves a non-event. It's clear that, for all their front, Mike and Trent are a couple of doobie-doobie-don'ts. They have jangly personas but little genuine personality, which may be the point of the film.

Back in L.A., Trent and Mike don't hold court in a conversation pit, as in *Ocean's Eleven*, but play video games and cruise dumpy bars looking for "babies" and "bunnies." Having gotten one bunny's number, Mike leaves so many annoying messages that she finally picks up the phone and says, "Don't ever call me again." Mike and Trent want to be finger-snapping free with the ladies, but they lack the hard peanut shell of a Frank or a Dean—they're too sincere and eager to "communicate." Whereas Sinatra described himself as an "18-karat manic-depressive," these guys are passive-aggressive, finky rather than outrageous and flamboyant. Their fear, hostility, and fur trapper's approach to women come out in pissy little gestures, such as Trent's tearing up the phone number of a woman he's just met, Mike's persistent phone calls and snide references to "skanks" (like he's some bonus). As with most passive-aggressives, it's hard to gauge how much of their behavior is intentionally obnoxious and how much is self-centered cluelessness—a not knowing any better. Compared to manic-depressives, with their mighty mood swings, passive-aggressives operate out of a very tight but ambiguous pocket. The true godfather of these swingers is not Sinatra, but David Letterman, smoking a big cigar behind his deflector shield of nervous, impervious irony.

It could be argued that *The Rat Pack Captured* and the backhanded homage of *Swingers* augur a last hurrah. After all, Dean Martin, Sammy Davis, Jr., and Peter Lawford are dead; Frank Sinatra has been ailing so long that public radio ran a premature obituary on him in February, which featured an extract from Michael Ventura's novel, *The Death of Frank Sinatra*, and a plea not to flog us with "My Way" over the final credits of his life. The Sands Hotel was demolished last year, to clear ground for a megaresort. The Vegas the Sands typified is itself extinct, the former sin capital emasculated and deloused by theme parks and chain restaurants ("that Pirate of the Caribbean horseshit," as Trent says in *Swingers*). In time the Rat Pack may be as forgotten as the Ritz Brothers.

But I doubt it. For baby-boomers, the biggest chunk of the population, the Kennedy years will always exert a dark, sexy undertow, in part because the deaths of Marilyn Monroe and J.F.K. still appear mysterious, intertwined. The 60s still seem young, dashing. They say you can't live in the past, but of course you can; that's practically all pop culture does now, is live in the past. The past is a permanent tape loop constantly being sampled and updated to create a new montage. Through the miracle of editing, Fred Astaire now dances with a vacuum cleaner. John Wayne sells beer. We're all Zeligs now. "Let me swing forevermore," Sinatra sings in "Fly Me to the Moon." For better or worse, you got your wish, daddy-o.

—May 1997

PROFILES AND
THE PRESS

○

Most of what I read about us after the opening indicated that the people liked the relationship between my father, Will, and me: the two vaudevillians who knew the business backwards and the kid they'd taught it to. They liked the contrast between the old show business and the new. Maybe they also understood our feelings for the business, maybe they caught our desperation to make good—there's no way of knowing all the things which contributed to create the image of us that they liked. Little by little we had changed our clothes, our jokes, our manner—everything. Whatever we were on the stage had evolved through the years until on opening night at Ciro's the combination of circumstances was finally right and it all fell in place, like when the three cherries on a slot machine all come up at once. —Sammy Davis, Jr., *Yes I Can*

I have read a lot, but I am not well read. I have traveled a great deal without being worldly. I have had almost every kind of human experience, yet in middle age I've just become adjusted to myself. I am very proud indeed of the varied talents God bestowed on me, yet I have always been keenly aware of my limitations. So, in such brilliant and gracious company as the John Hustons, John O'Haras, and Humphrey Bogarts of this world, I had to fall back on my other abilities. To hold my own with such a distinctive set of characters and personalities, it was necessary to extend my role as entertainer. I tried hard to be amusing, good company, erudite and knowledgeable about the things I knew about . . . There was a lot of me in those days that could have been picked on and exploited by a man with the abrasive perception of Bogey. He never tried.
—Sammy Davis, Jr., *Hollywood in a Suitcase*

I'm being isolated from my own people. I'm an outcast. Obviously I'm not white, but now it's gotten so the colored people don't want me, either. It's like I'm the man without a country. —Sammy Davis, Jr., *Yes I Can*

Davis's relationship with the press, especially the black and tabloid press, was sometimes stormy. His interracial sex life and marriage made him a target for the Hollywood tabloids during the 1950s and 1960s. This highly sensationalized aspect of his life also made him a target for the black press, which sometimes accused him of being an Uncle Tom. But some of his staunchest supporters wrote for the black press, too, and many black journalists admired his talent and fame, if not his politics and sex life. Also, the black press reported Davis's benefits and donations to black causes much more thoroughly than the white press, although the benefits he gave for nonracial causes were often publicized in the mainstream press. The fact that Davis remained a personality for the black press throughout his entire life (*Jet* devoted an entire issue to him—June 4, 1990— when he died), shows that, despite the tensions he had with blacks, he maintained a black audience throughout his career and that blacks felt he was important, one of their most accomplished persons who had done well in the face of great odds in the white world. This section is a compilation of press pieces about Davis that appeared in both the black and the white press over his career. Also included are a number of long features on Davis from some of the leading magazines of the day. In the 1960s and early 1970s, especially, Davis was an object of great interest to the press and publicity mills of America. Some of this coverage is laudatory. In other pieces, he is criticized, even dismissed, as imitative, a middle-of-the road performer of ordinary ability, a kind of loathsome white cultural toady. This view prevails particularly among the more intellectual writers here—Albert Goldman, Donald Bogle, Gary Giddins, Margo Jefferson, and Hilton Als.

This section begins with a feature on Davis that appeared in the September 1955 issue of *Playboy*, "The Sammy Davis Story" by Eric Franklin, where the energetic dancer is touted as a rising star whose life has all the elements of a Hollywood biopic.

Next is a cover story from *Down Beat* entitled "This Is the Year for Sammy Davis" (September 21, 1955), where Davis discusses how he developed his taste for jazz. Incidentally, he mentions his sister in this piece. Little is known about her directly through Davis. He never discusses his relationship with his sister in any of the books he wrote. According to this article, his sister introduced him to jazz, or at least to Dizzy Gillespie. It is also interesting to note that Davis largely learned about jazz while in the army, where he learned to read books, perform solo, and face the racism that pervaded American society outside the subculture of traveling performers.

What follows is a series of articles about Davis written by columnists Evelyn Cunningham, probably the most powerful black columnist of her day, and George E. Pitts, all appearing in *The Pittsburgh Courier*, one of the most widely read black newspapers in the country. Two of Cunningham's pieces are mentioned in *Yes I Can*: her open letter of February 2, 1957, and Davis's response, which she incorporated as her column of the following week. The third column is a supportive piece she wrote about Davis in 1963. Pitts was always very supportive of Davis, constantly endorsing him as the greatest entertainer of the day. His column is from October 11, 1958, detailing a day on the set of a *General Electric Theater* drama that Davis was filming; the second piece by Pitts, which appeared in June 1960, is entitled "The Readers Write About Sammy Davis, Jr."; Pitts then wrote "Sammy Davis, Jr., Sounds Off" in February 1961. A column by George F. Brown, a more in-depth piece entitled "Inside Sammy Davis, Jr.," appeared on March 3, 1962.

The next series of pieces deal with Davis, Louis Armstrong, and the Little Rock racial crisis of 1957, all of which appeared in *The Pittsburgh Courier*. The first piece is dated October 12, 1957, presenting Davis's response to Armstrong's statements about the tension over school desegregation in Little Rock. Davis was surprisingly negative about Armstrong's statements, surprising especially in the light of the almost universally positive reception Armstrong received from the black press and the black community generally for his remarks. Davis himself, in the coming weeks, was to be severely criticized for his position. Examples of the positive black response to Armstrong's remarks are two pieces by Evelyn Cunningham in June and September 1957.

Two articles appeared in *The Pittsburgh Courier* in 1960 about Davis and May Britt, the first in August, where Davis talks about his impending marriage to Britt, among other things; and the second, in November, is an account of the wedding itself.

The final piece from *The Pittsburgh Courier*, dated August 6, 1966, is a feature on Davis's film *A Man Called Adam*, which was of major importance to the black community at the time of its release because so few dramatic vehicles for blacks were being made then.

A series of short pieces follows from the August 1959 issue of *Dance Magazine* (Davis on tap dancing) and the December 24, 1960, issue of *Melody Maker* (jazz critic Leonard Feather on Davis's interracial marriage).

Several pieces from tabloid magazines are included here to give some sense of how Davis was covered in that popular medium. Most of the coverage Davis received in these magazines involved his relationships with white women, the most sensational topic of the day that would make a black man interesting to the people who read these magazines, mostly women. Five are from *Confidential*, one of the leading scandal sheets, including the infamous Ava Gardner piece from 1955. The February 1959 issue of the *National Police Gazette*'s article, "Sammy Davis, Jr.'s, Phony Romances with White Stars," takes a different approach from *Confidential*'s, suggesting that Davis was so publicity hungry that he engineered photo ops to give the impression that he was dating white women who had no interest in him. In this article, Kim Novak, as she has always done publicly, denied any sexual interest in Davis with a bit of reverse psychology, expressing fear that many would consider her racist for denying an affair with a black man. Considering the public's reaction to Davis's marriage to May Britt the following year, this reasoning hardly seems convincing, and the safer route for any white star at the time, who wanted to continue to be a star, would be to deny any such connection with a black man. In *Yes I Can*, Davis said, tactfully but unambiguously, that he had an affair with Novak and most Hollywood insiders at the time confirm this. Finally, there are three articles from fanzines, two from *Movie Mirror* (November 1964 and February 1967), the first about how Davis's black friends responded to Davis's marriage to May Britt and the second about Davis's uneasy relationship with Sinatra; and one article from *Motion Picture* (September 1960) about the upcoming Britt-Davis marriage.

In this section I have also included selections from Davis's FBI file, including material relating to the investigations of two racist, extortionate letters that Davis received, one in 1962 and the other in 1974, as well as material related to Davis's civil rights and social reform activities. Although these files have been, in some cases, heavily censored by the FBI, they still show the extent of Davis's involvement, not only with the mainstream civil rights movement of the 1960s but also with the peace movement and the black power movement. Also included in these files is a memo regarding Davis's 1963 claim that he had been kidnapped in the late 1950s by Chicago gangsters and warned to discontinue his alleged romance with Kim Novak.

What follows are several lengthy features on Davis covering

a span of ten years, from the late 1950s to the mid-1970s. Here one can see how Davis himself changed and how mainstream opinion changed about him—from largely glowing admiration in "What Makes Sammy Run" (Esquire, 1959), "Sammy Davis," a feature in *Life* magazine, which ran on November 13, 1964, and *The Saturday Evening Post* feature, "Don't Call Him Junior Anymore," which appeared on February 13, 1965, both centered on Davis's starring role in *Golden Boy*—to the post–Nixon endorsement piece: "Sammy Davis, Jr., Has Bought the Bus" (*The New York Times Magazine*, October 15, 1974). This piece takes a far more ambivalent view of Davis, seeing him as a more complex, more contradictory, more confused, and even more desperate man than the earlier laudatory features tended to present. To be sure, Davis's endorsement of Nixon had cost him points and standing with the mainstream liberal press, but Davis, by the mid-1970s, was no longer the wonder boy of American performance arts. He was middle-aged, he was establishment, he was Las Vegas, and he was becoming a parody of himself. On the opposite ends of the spectrum are pieces by Albert Goldman from *The New York Review of Books* (January 20, 1966) and Bruce Jay Friedman from *The New Yorker* (April 8, 1974). Goldman is scathing in his criticism of Davis, occasioned as a review of *Yes I Can*, in unmasking him as an artificial black performer, a fraud endorsed by a white philistine mainstream that has little understanding or appreciation of real black cultural expression or talent. Friedman's humorous piece about helping Davis take a vacation is a defense, ironic at times, but still a defense, indicating that by the mid-1970s Davis was actually in need of one because criticizing him had become de rigueur.

Despite being probably one of the most famous black Jews in the world, Davis was written about very little in the Jewish press. "Sammy Davis Seeks Black-Jewish Unity" is taken from the *St. Louis Jewish Light* (September 17, 1969). In it, Davis discusses black-Jewish relations at a time when they were very troubled.

The next four pieces—an evaluation of *A Man Called Adam*

from Donald Bogle's *Toms, Coons, Mulattoes, Mammies, and Bucks*, probably the most popular of all historical accounts of blacks in American cinema (originally published in 1973); Gary Giddins's review of a *Sammy and Company*'s episode on jazz (*The Village Voice*, June 2, 1975); Margo Jefferson's piece on the Ultimate Reunion tour that appeared in *Vogue* (September 1988); and Hilton Als's review of *Why Me?* that appeared in the *Voice Literary Supplement* (August 1989)—are all quite negative. It is interesting that blacks wrote three of the four pieces. Davis had never been the darling of the black literary or intellectual set, as these pieces show, and was abhorred by the intellectual left, both black and white. By this point, these writers had taken the parodic Davis as a straw man. It is odd that none of them chose to look more deeply at Davis's complex, dense self-construction, even if they found it personally distasteful, to ask how and why such a construction could exist— as they would have done, say, with Miles Davis, no matter how much of a sellout they might have thought him to be for the music of his electric period or how terrible his personality (and he was a far more unpleasant man than Sammy Davis at his worst and could just as easily be accused of artistic fraud), or with any number of other black artists or entertainers. What is interesting about these features on Sammy Davis is not that he is criticized but that he merits absolutely no respect whatsoever, an attitude that I cannot imagine any of these critics taking with virtually any other black artist of any note. Why Davis is so despised is far more interesting than the fact that he is. These pieces say something about the cultural contention over artistic reputation. Who gets to be called a genius? Who is exposed as a fraud?

Davis's death was a major news story across the United States and around the world. Included here are *The New York Times*'s obituary and the editorial that it ran praising him.

Finally, this section closes with two features on Davis from *Nevada* magazine, one from November/December 1981 and the other from September/October 1990, both tributes. It seemed fitting to end this section with journalism from a magazine that represents the state where Davis shaped so much of his career and where his career shaped so much of one of that state's major industries.

"THE SAMMY DAVIS STORY,"
by Eric Franklin, *Playboy*

There is no doubt that the single, most spectacular personality to emerge on the show business scene this year is a little guy named Sammy Davis, Jr.

Sammy sings, and he does imitations, and he dances, he plays a number of musical instruments and he acts well enough to have a Broadway producer talking about building a play around him. In addition to these many talents, he's an especially likable guy, who possesses showmanship, wit, charm and a black eyepatch. The last item is important and we'll get to it later.

The story of Sammy Davis, Jr., would make a perfect super-colossal film musical. Though the man himself is a refreshingly original performer, his life reads like the script for a typical Hollywood heart-tugger, to be played in Supercolor and CinemaScope, with Stereophonic sound, of course.

The picture begins with his birth, backstage, in a dressing room of the old Hippodrome Theatre in New York. His father, Sam Davis, Sr., and his uncle, Will Mastin, are a well-known act on the vaudeville circuits. For two whole years, little Sammy just loafs around and absorbs the show world atmosphere. But this soft life is not for him. At age two, he gets into the act, mimicking the adult performers in those little take-offs that showfolk call "impressions."

The paying customers are definitely impressed.

Perhaps the idea of a two-year-old toddler wowing the audience may bend your credulity a bit, but it's true nonetheless. And at four he auditioned for a role in an Ethel Waters movie.

Nothing very remarkable about that. What's remarkable is, he got the part. And later on, when he began to show dancing ability, who offered to give him lessons?

How's this for a scene? Sam, Sr., speaks: "Son, there's a man here wants to show you a few things about dancing." "Is he a dancer himself, Daddy?" "Yes, son, he's a mighty fine dancer." "What's his name?" "Robinson," says the man, "but you can call me Bill."

MONTAGE: *Robinson and Sammy. Robinson doing his famous trademarks and Sammy picking them up, bit by bit: the trigger-like turns of heel and toe, the lightning thrust of arms and legs, the rapid twist and turn of the body, the thrill-packed finale and the burst-of-glory ending.* INSERT SHOT: *A page of the* New York Post. *Earl Wilson's column. Sammy's photo. A phrase of Wilson's fills the screen: ". . . his feet remind one of liquid rhythm."* CUT.

Here's where The Sammy Davis Story really starts moving. He's a grown man now. Along the way his nose has been flattened, so he looks like a little bantam-weight fighter. We see him performing at various night clubs around the country (let's have some railroad-track footage in here). He's singing, say, *Because of You.* After a few bars in his own voice, the barrel-chested tones of Vaughn Monroe roll out of him. Then, in rapid succession, we hear deft facsimiles of the Frankie Laine hysteria, the Billy Eckstine lushness, the Tony Bennett desperation, the Nat Cole gentleness, the Mel Tormé fuzz. The audience applauds, but Sammy isn't finished yet. Now he's talking the lyrics in the style of a familiar actor: "Because of you, you dirty rat . . . my romance . . . my romance had its start, yes it did . . ." It's Cagney: the crowd roars. Then Sammy gives them Jimmy Stewart, Cary Grant, Lionel Barrymore, Edward G. Robinson, Jerry Lewis . . .

Someplace, we'll have to splice in shots of Sammy beating the drums, Sammy slapping a bull fiddle. Sammy pounding out boogie-woogie on a Steinway . . .

And now we're ready for the tragedy. It's November, 1954,

and Sammy's been signed to record the title tune for a film called *Six Bridges to Cross*. He climbs in his car and heads for Hollywood. It's a long, lonely drive on the road at night. Maybe Sammy switches on the radio to hear a little music. He smiles, starts to sing along with it. He's feeling great—sitting on top of the world. But the camera knows better: it sees the ominous headlights approaching at high speed from the opposite direction. There's a screech of brakes, a close-up of Sammy's startled face, and the radio song does a fast segue into dissonance.

We'll need a hospital sequence: doctors talking in low voices, loved ones in tears, snatches of phrases like ". . . may not pull through . . ." and ". . . even if he does, his left eye . . ."

And now it's time to film the sensational final scene. The set is built to resemble the floor of Ciro's, a very swank Hollywood night club. The place is packed. There's a charged-air feeling of expectancy among the crowd. And *what* a crowd! Celebrities all—famous stars of the entertainment world! The camera dollies over them and we spot beauties like Ava Gardner, Dorothy Dandridge, Betty Hutton, Gloria DeHaven. And a few others that seem familiar . . . why, isn't that Humphrey Bogart? And Judy Garland? There's Dick Powell and June Allyson . . . Jack Benny . . . Jeff Chandler . . . Janet Leigh and Tony Curtis . . . and look (lot of middle-aged women will see this film, we've got to please everybody), there's Liberace.

The m.c. is making an announcement, but we're too far away to catch the words. The band strikes up a fanfare and a little man strides out onto the floor. Even before the spot hits him, we know it's Sammy. He's alive. His left eye is gone and across his face is a black pirate patch, but all the rest of the self-assured, socko Sammy is there.

What a moment. All those people, all those stars and celebrities—what do they do? Why, they rise to their feet and give this little guy a *ten minute* ovation! We can't use all of it, of course—too long—so we cut to the performance. "I'd love to gain complete control of you, and handle even the heart and soul of you . . ." Sammy pours out the liquid lyrics of Cole Porter's *All of You*. It's one of his fastest selling records. Now he's singing *My Funny Valentine*. That's in his album: it's over the hundred thousand mark. Now he's belting out a wonderful burlesque of Billy Daniel's *Black Magic* and Billy is in the audience, laughing and applauding with the rest. "Meanwhile, back at the ranch . . ."

Our camera leaves him here, in the spotlight where he belongs. We move up and back till the spot is just a bit of light in the center of the giant Supercolor, CinemaScope screen, and the Stereophonic sound swells to a finish.

End of movie. Intermission for purposes of popcorn and reflection.

The accident came just as Sammy was beginning to really catch on. It could have been a setback—perhaps a big one. Instead, it has helped boost him to a fame he never knew before. This little guy is a great entertainer, but it was the Sammy spunk that made a great many people notice him for the first time.

"So long now," says Sammy, adjusting his patch. "Have to go pose for a Hathaway ad."

You've got to like a guy like that.

—September 1955

"THIS IS THE YEAR FOR SAMMY DAVIS,"
Down Beat

One afternoon a couple of months ago, Gerry Mulligan, Chet Baker, and Russ Freeman went uptown to the Apollo Theater in New York to catch the show and pay their respects to the headliner.

Later that day it was Marilyn Monroe, Joe DiMaggio, and Harold Arlen who squeezed through the narrow door into the crowded room backstage at the Apollo for the same reason.

Along with several thousand others, this renowned threesome had just finished cheering the last show of the night by Sammy Davis, Jr.

Sammy broke through the backstage chaos to greet them. They told him what he has been hearing from both the famous and the rest of us throughout the country for many months: "You were great!"

But Sammy is in no danger of dozing into complacency under this continuous blanket of praise. He retains a drive and a fierce determination to keep topping his last performance that are unique even in the endlessly self-challenging land of show business.

There was the time, for example, earlier this year when Sammy agreed to appear at the Charlie Parker memorial concert in Carnegie Hall despite the fact that he was on a rigorous schedule at the Copacabana that same night.

Rushing over to Carnegie Hall between shows, Sammy intended to make only a brief appearance onstage, but the audience kept clamoring for more, and Sammy, as usual, kept knocking himself out.

Finally, followed by the largest storm of applause of the night up to that point, Sammy ran off stage and into the wings where he exclaimed breathlessly to no one in particular, "Now—let's see somebody top that!"

And nobody has topped Sammy since, for this is Sammy Davis' year. This is the year of his big break-through into full-voiced success as a leading recording star. And come this fall, this also will be his first year as the star of a Broadway show. There will be films to follow. Sammy has already signed for two with his friend, Frank Sinatra, who has an independent production company.

Though 1955 represents a record harvest, Davis certainly had been far from an unknown during the last several seasons. As the featured performer of the Will Mastin Trio (supported by his uncle, and his father, Sammy Davis, Sr.), the junior Davis had become the center of one of the most acclaimed acts in recent night club history.

He played—and continues to play—all the country's leading rooms again and again with no sign of audience satiation.

But this year Sammy Davis, Jr., has become a familiar name to many millions more chiefly as the result of his series of Decca hits.

He also has a long-term, best-selling album on the label, *Starring Sammy Davis, Jr.*, with others to follow. Then, too, there have been an increasing number of television guest shots on programs like Ed Sullivan's, and there's little doubt that by the end of the year, Sammy will have convincingly parlayed his multiple talents into a prosperous Broadway run as the star of *Mr. Wonderful.*

In the new musical, Sammy not only will act, but also will run through his chromatic scale of specialties that could outfit a whole variety troupe. Aside from singing, Sammy is a skilled dancer, an often incredibly exact impressionist, an exuberant drummer, a raconteur of sharply improvised wit, and in all, a full-ranged personality of commanding and always entertaining presence.

He is also an articulate, well read, and perceptive observer of many fields outside of his own branch of show business.

He is further a man of determined principle—as in his attitude toward TV and his role in it. Negroes have been seen from time to time in TV guest shots, but as Ella Fitzgerald has pointed out, no Negro yet—no matter how talented—has been given a TV series of his or her own.

"TV will open up eventually," said Sammy, "but first there'll have to be a pivot man somewhere, a man who'll open it up and prove it can be successful with a series of his own. It seemed for a time a couple of years ago that I might be the pivot man at ABC-TV, but their ideas didn't coincide with mine.

"One thing is sure," Davis spoke with feeling, "I will never do anything on TV that has a tinge of Uncle Tom. No series is worth that, I never forget that I play the Apollo once a year, and I have to be able to walk down the street here and know that I haven't done anything to be ashamed of or that has made others ashamed of me."

He then switched the talk to music and brought out several new LPs, among them a set by the Hi-Lo's and albums by Gerry Mulligan and Count Basie.

"I travel with hundreds of LPs," Sammy explained, "wherever I go. And a lot of them are jazz. I'm very proud of my jazz collection. Actually, it's mainly since I was in the army in 1943–45 that I began to listen to jazz. Before the army, I didn't know anything much about it. My sister helped, too. I remember she bought me one of the first Dizzy Gillespie records on Guild."

Sammy now speaks knowledgeably of jazz and keeps aware of its progress and of newcomers in the field. He, too, has his favorites, among them the Count Basie band ("the swingingest band in the world") and Woody Herman.

"Woody," Davis observed with emphasis, "has given more opportunity to more people to do what they want to do in music, and thereby, he has advanced jazz a great deal.

"There are only a couple of bands like Woody and Basie," he continued, "that can get real excitement going in person. And Kenton, I remember hearing him in California for the first time. He really excited me!

"He looked like electricity, dressed up in a suit, tie, and hair. When he spread out his hands at the end of *Birth of the Blues*, you'd think electricity was coming out of his fingers. There, by the way, is where I picked up the hand spread on that number. Stan, too, is another man who has always given new talent a chance to expand.

"As for the major jazz influences," Sammy went on, "there was Bird, of course. What can you say about that man? I have so many of his records.

"You know, to me, there is a sadness about jazz. Certain people have it when they play. Chet Baker has it, for example. And Bird had it even when he was swinging on fast numbers. I think a painter might picture Bird in the form of a clown—with a sad mouth. Dizzy used to have this quality of sadness at the beginning. Like on that Discovery album with strings—Dizzy's passage after the vocal in *Swing Low Sweet Chariot*."

Davis talked further about jazz, moving on to what he doesn't like, namely the "overcool guys."

"As soon as anyone forgets the audience that pays him," Sammy said, "he's on a wrong kick. You can't turn your back on the audience. Sure, I get disgusted with a heckler at times, but there are hundreds more in the audience who have come to see me. You owe them something. Or if you don't feel you do, then don't make live appearances. Just make records.

"I remember Stan Getz at Birdland one night," Sammy said, shaking his head. "He was playing to his drummer—with his back to the audience. On the other hand, what I dig about Chet Baker is that when he finishes a number, he bows, and points to the other men in the band. Speaking of Chet, I think he's got a great voice—a kind of combination of Mel Tormé and Matt Dennis."

A relatively new singer who he also strongly praises is Carmen McRae. They recently recorded several duets for Decca, and Sammy describes her as "just fantastic." In fact, said Sammy, "if good singing comes back, Carmen has got to be the biggest star that ever happened. She sings so great."

—*September 21, 1955*

"OPEN LETTER TO SAMMY DAVIS, JR.,"
by Evelyn Cunningham, *The Pittsburgh Courier*

Dearest Sammy: Right off hand, I can't think of anything I dislike about you. Not only are you one of the greatest entertainers in the world, but from what I hear, and what I see, you also seem to be one of the nicest. In a way, I'm as proud of you as I am of Ralph Bunche, Thurgood Marshall and the rest of the guys who'll be written about in history books.

So when you invited me to your press party, I was real tickled to get a chance to meet you. I didn't expect that you and I would get to be boons on sight or that you would even remember my name after we'd met. All I wanted was the kicks of being in close quarters with you and maybe getting a small idea of what makes you tick. You see, I'm a 14-carat fan of yours.

Anyway, I got the most awful sinking of the stomach when I got to the party and saw at a glance that it was a press party for people on the colored papers. My stomach turned over again when I suddenly realized that it had been a long, long time since I'd been to this type of all-colored press party in New York. Seems they kind of went out with ankle-strap shoes.

But I'm crazy about you. So after my stomach got righted, I made mental excuses. I said to myself: He's got something special to say to us that's exclusively for us. Or something really big is coming because this doesn't make sense.

Nothing came. You were charming, gracious and entertaining. You hopped from guest to guest and you went to the trouble of engaging in small talk with us. But you weren't happy. Neither were we. Every now and then I got the feeling that you were embarrassed, that you didn't think that the party was such a good idea after all.

And then you made a short talk. You said, with great sincerity, that you were deeply appreciative of the Negro press and the Negro patrons who had helped keep "Mr. Wonderful" running on Broadway so long. You intimated that despite the negative reviews of the show when it opened, Negroes were in a large measure responsible for making it a hit. For this, thanks.

But Sammy, wouldn't it have been a gasser if you had said the same thing at a press party to which you had invited people from both the daily and weekly papers? It wouldn't have offended the daily boys. In fact, I've got an idea they would have respected you even more.

Don't get me wrong. I don't want you running down to Montgomery and jumping on buses or yelling and screaming about your civil rights. But in many, many quarters, integration is fashionable and chic. And you have access to these quarters. In short, I don't think the press party was necessary. But I love you anyway.

Love and kisses, E.C.

P.S.—Ain't it rough being cullud? There's always something!

—February 2, 1957

"CUNNINGHAM SPANKED BY S. DAVIS, JR.,"
by Evelyn Cunningham, *The Pittsburgh Courier*

Sammy Davis, Jr., as articulate as he is talented, has taken this lady to task for an open letter written to him last week concerning a party he threw for the Negro press.

In a lengthy letter, which unfortunately cannot be reprinted in full, he says this writer "reminds me of the little girl who is unhappy unless she's busy making others unhappy by stirring up imagined grievances."

"Like the little boy who shared his prized toy with a friend only to have it smashed to pieces in front of his face, I was hurt when I read your open letter to me. I have always admired you as a writer and since it has not been my pleasure to be in your company, other than on formal working occasions, I looked forward to your being my guest. So, I am sorry that the absence of the white press marred your fun."

He writes that he was "surprised that my gesture of friendliness was so misconstrued as to reap the wrath of a few."

". . . In my association with both segments of the Fourth Estate, I have yet to hear any comment or objections from anyone attending a press party to which the Negro press had not been invited and you are, of course, aware that the situation exists whereupon the Negro press is ignored when there are gratuities or niceties to be extended. It seems to me that with the space you have and the ability you have shown, you could utilize it better by fighting the things that make it necessary for there to be a white and a Negro press. I feel that as a member of the free press you could wage a better battle for integration by devoting your aims to and for the public rather than using your privilege to express personal grievances."

Then he points out that this column would serve better to point out, for instance, that a Negro navigator took part in the recent jet flight around the world.

"... In short, Miss Cunningham, the party was necessary to me because it was my way of saying thank you for the many nice things you have said about me and for the support that the Negro press and public had given my current Broadway show. Thanks for letting the public know that I did appreciate that support. It was my pleasure to enjoy your company and I am indeed sorry that the feeling was not mutual.

"P.S.—And, Miss Cunningham, I don't find it rough being colored. Sincerely yours,

"Sammy Davis, Jr."

And that's what Sammy thinks.

—*February 9, 1957*

WEEKLY COLUMN,
by Evelyn Cunningham, *The Pittsburgh Courier*

If you have never seen Sammy Davis, Jr., perform in a night club, it is next to impossible to believe what you hear about him. You don't accept the claims that he is the "greatest entertainer in the world."

You may admit that he is versatile, that he does a number of things well, but unless you've seen him on a night club floor, you don't buy anybody's assertion that he does everything better than other entertainers.

So much has been written and said about Sammy Davis, Jr.—about both his professional and personal life—that it seems there's nothing left to be said.

But there's so much more—so very much more. You see, this little fellow is one of those rare human beings who grow and grow every day. His mind is agile, more agile than his feet, his wit or his way with a song. He has learned to adjust, to cope with, to place any bitterness that may spring up, in its proper perspective.

Davis just wound up a three-week engagement in New York's Copacabana. With the newspaper strike going on, it was still his most successful date at that famed spot. He was due to fly to Germany for two days of recording, then back to the U.S. and Las Vegas.

To repeat what has been said thousands of times, Sammy was sensational at the Copa. When you felt that he had given as much as it is possible for any entertainer to give, he still gave more. At one point he said, "I love what I'm doing! I dig it!" And you knew it was absolutely true.

For some time now, Sammy has been fooling around with racial quips and jokes, involving all kinds of races. He seems to get a big kick out of kidding Jewish people and Negroes. Not once has he slipped beyond the bounds of good taste and discretion. He has simply been funny and if you are Jewish or Negro you have gotten a special kind of joy at laughing at yourself.

Some time ago, I told Sammy that I liked the racial patter he was doing, and I added facetiously, "You're really getting emancipated." It was my way of saying that I was happy he wasn't falling into that Negroid trap of being overly sensitive about everything racial.

Anyway, during Sammy's closing night performance at the Copa, I had occasion to say to myself, "Wow! This man is about as emancipated as a man can get!" For he did something I never thought I'd see. Along with his usual impressions of well-known personalities, he did some rather obscure and little-known people. And then he did Stepin Fetchit, Mantan Moreland and Willie Best.

Well, most people (Negroes, at any rate) know these old-time comedians. A lot more have seen them on old television movies. But for the most part, they are entertainers that the "new" Negro is trying to escape from and reject. Fetchit, Moreland and Best have been relegated to a past that many are ashamed of.

Sammy knows all this. But he has a warm respect for these fellows and he knows that without them, there could hardly have been any Dick Gregorys, Nipsey Russells and Sammy Davises.

He said that to the audience. He told them how much he loved to watch them in the old movies and how really funny they were. And in the telling of his feelings, he conveyed, without actually saying so, that the three were great comedians, not great Negro comedians and not typical Negroes.

He did it beautifully. And there was not one Negro in the audience who felt any resentment. Then Sammy did the impressions. They were great.

I love the social significance of the experience. But then, I'm prejudiced. I love Sammy.

—January 26, 1963

"BEHIND THE SCENES WITH SAMMY DAVIS, JR.,"
by George E. Pitts, *The Pittsburgh Courier*

That Sammy Davis, Jr., is a versatile performer goes unquestioned. But, when time came to rehearse for his first TV dramatic role (GE Theater last Sunday) producers speculated as to what could happen to Davis. Many actors, veterans among them, are a bit nervous when working on a tight, three-day shooting schedule. Some of them ask that the set be closed to outside visitors. With Davis the sound stage was loaded with people—people sitting, standing, leaning against and hanging onto almost every conceivable object. Adding to the general confusion were about 20 children working in the show with Sammy. They clustered about him, hanging onto his sleeves and trousers. They climbed all over him as they clamored for attention. Sammy permitted everyone who desired to do so to remain right on the set. As an actor he is "very good," according to director John Brahm. Sammy impressed as a quick study—learned his lines quickly—and managed them faultlessly during the takes. In one emotion-packed scene Davis was supposed to break down and cry—a tough assignment even for a seasoned actor, especially before such a large audience. As Brahm prepared to shoot, the crowded stage became so silent you could almost hear the silence. A few of Sammy's close friends crossed their fingers, as one admitted later, that Sammy would get through the difficult scene without too much trouble. And he did just that! When the director quietly said, "Cut," breaking the silence, the stage exploded with a sudden roar of applause. The crew—doing a rare thing—joined in the applause—their highest possible compliment to an actor. That's why you saw such a fine performance by the little guy on the General Electric Theater last Sunday night. Afterwards Sammy said that regardless of what success he finds as a dramatic actor, he will never give up his night club act. "Sure I'd like to do three or four of these things a year," he said. "Who wouldn't? They're fun and a challenge, but it sure isn't like playing a club. There's where I do something, it may be a song, a joke, a dance, or just a bit of business, but when I do it, regardless of what it is, I get an immediate reaction from the audience. I get a terrific kick out of their reactions. Knowing if you're good enough, you can make people laugh and feel happy is a wonderful feeling. With a show like this (TV) I may not know what people think of me for a long time."

—*October 11, 1958*

"THE READERS WRITE ABOUT
SAMMY DAVIS, JR.,"
by George E. Pitts, *The Pittsburgh Courier*

Letters, mostly from Negroes and largely Negro women, have come into the office either protesting or asking what we think of the fact that Sammy Davis, Jr., is always making headlines with white women. More specifically, the letters point to the recent incident in London in which a rabble-rousing group hurled heated racial epithets at Davis for openly courting his next intended, blonde May Britt.

Mrs. Eve Thomkins of Brooklyn, stated: "It's good for him, why doesn't he stay in his own race?"

From Atlanta, a Mrs. Taliafero, who identified herself as a Negro, wrote: "The demonstration serves him [Davis] right. It seems that all of our most eligible Negro men [we assume she refers to those earning boatloads of dough] run to white women as soon as they get to the top. Look at Harry Belafonte, Herb Jeffries and all the rest [what rest, lady?] they all married white women."

In Davis' defense (if it can be called that) Mrs. Joseph Morton of Philadelphia wrote: "So what if he does marry a white woman? I feel that it's his own business and hers. I can't stand a Negro who objects to an interracial marriage. After all, isn't ours a fight for integration? If we can't accept an interracial marriage, we certainly are not ready for all the benefits of being accepted as first-class citizens. These idiots in England who called Mr. Davis names probably aren't worth bothering about. If I were him I would forget about them, marry whomever I chose and let them keep on calling names."

And the letters continued. One of the most interesting was from a male Negro, John Mason of Indianapolis: "I don't dig all those white people giving Sammy Davis hell for courting a white woman. It should be their own business. It seems that they always raise cain when a Negro man gets ready to marry a white woman, but little or nothing is said when a white man marries a Negro woman. Look at how little was said when Pearl Bailey married a white man; Lena Horne married one too. Look at Diahann Carroll, Mattiwida Dobbs, Eartha Kitt. I didn't see any demonstrations at all. I say more power to Sammy Davis, Jr., and good luck on his marriage, whoever it is."

—*June 25, 1960*

"SAMMY DAVIS, JR., SOUNDS OFF,"
by George E. Pitts, *The Pittsburgh Courier*

Some hippie once wrote, "Nothing can follow Sammy Davis, Jr., except World War III." This well-meaning critic didn't know what he was talking about. World War III would be a piker trying to outdo this swinging cat. He does everything humanly or inhumanly possible onstage, everything short of eating up the floorboards. At Pittsburgh's Town House, last week (despite icy roads and hazardous snow drifts) he drew out the crowds. He sang, mimicked, danced, played drums, trumpet, piano, ad-libbed and cracked jokes. Davis did the almost incredible feat of staying on stage two hours and 15 minutes— and held the audience in the palm of his hand.

In a hotel room interview, Sammy chatted at will about everything, from his beautiful wife, TV and movies to his personal convictions. "I've found my wife everything I've ever longed for, and I'm so tickled that we are expecting a baby in August," he elaborated.

Sammy, admittedly upset by all the furore over his marriage to May Britt, said he just wants to be left alone in his private life. He said bigots and crackpots have been on his back and still write crank letters by the dozen. Even his friend, Frank Sinatra, has been a hate target, because of their association, Davis said. "Frank had to hire two secretaries to dispose of the hate letters he received, because we're friends. The letters to Frank usually start out, 'Dear N———r Lover'," he revealed.

"But through it all I've grown stronger—learning to ride with the punches. Naturally all this hurts, but I've had to learn to live with this kind of pressure all my life, and if you can't live with something you believe in—life's not worth living."

What's he done about it all?

"I don't want to shoot anybody—[he's an expert gunman, bigots] so to protect myself, I've hired a private bodyguard to keep these haters away from me."

Why is he so swingin'?

"I sorta developed the mike-in-hand, hip-shakin' dance swingin' routine while singing, because of this kisser of mine. I used to get on stage and wonder how I could possibly hold an audience, singing beautiful songs, with this bashed in face of mine. So I began doing all sorts of things to hold attention. I'm not beautiful, you know!"

About Bobby Darin?

"I call him the white Sammy Davis, Jr., now."

To his Negro pianist?

"If you don't learn some manners, I'll get all my fellow Jews against you."

To his white guitarist?

"I know you're a member of the White Citizens Council, but I hired you because you're a damn good guitarist."

To the Southerners in the audience?

"Chuckle if you like, but you ain't gettin' me down to Mississippi. Come to think of it, don't know if I'll try Sweden either."

About George Pitts?

"You dirty raaaat!"

Davis also revealed that he had just completed two days in a strenuous recording session as the first artist signing on with the new Frank Sinatra record company. "It's a gas," he said. "A real constructive thing. Frank is letting each artist buy stock in the company—a sort of share the profits deal, real crazy."

Negro comics?

"Badly managed . . . badly managed, but Nipsey Russell and George Kirby are two of the greatest."

Davis also expressed strong admiration for the Rev. Martin Luther King, Jr., for whom he recently participated in a gigantic benefit at New York's Carnegie Hall. "I consider that one of the most magnificent things I've ever done—and I had a good time doing it."

Davis greatly admires the work of Ray Charles. "A genius if ever I saw one. He does everything beautifully. He has that universal appeal—not confined to any one audience. Appeals to them all. If you don't dig Ray Charles, you're just plain crazy."

Do I dig Ray Charles? Certainly—and Sammy Davis, Jr., too!

—February 18, 1961

"INSIDE SAMMY DAVIS, JR.,"
by George F. Brown, *The Pittsburgh Courier*

"Certain members of the fourth estate call it a clan," Sammy Davis, Jr., said with a sly, pixieish smile, "but it isn't really. We're just a group of clean, wholesome, ordinary guys who meet once a year to take over the world."

That's the way Sammy parries questions about the Clan, notably Frank Sinatra and Peter Lawford. Others in good standing (or leaning) in the Clan are Dean Martin, comedian Joey Bishop and actress Shirley MacLaine. All talented people constantly in the blaze of public attention.

Like the others in the Clan, Sammy has long ago grown weary of defending or explaining his friends to "Clydes." (Note to squares: "Clyde" means a square.) Like most famous people, Sammy is often misquoted and misunderstood by those who believe all the gossip they read and hear.

The public image of Sammy Davis, Jr., a singularly talented individual, is often in sharp contrast to the private Sammy Davis, Jr. He is deeply serious and introspective and shy and a bit sensitive around strangers, but around intimates he glows with warmth and his generosity is legendary. He has a quick intelligence that catalogues people very quickly. He has a great store of gags around friends and his energy is boundless.

In a radio interview he parried all sorts of questions from how he was doing at the Copacabana to how was his wife. Later someone asked him about Peter Lawford. "Peter Lawford," he smiled, "why he's Big Daddy's brother-in-law!" That cooled it. For those who came in late or just returned from Tibet, Peter Lawford is President John F. Kennedy's brother-in-law by dint of being married to the President's sister.

Another fan asked him about Frank Sinatra and he answered with the crack he reserves for predominantly white audiences: "Sinatra? Sure, he's the leader," he said, "but he's your leader. My leader is Martin Luther King."

Another famous member of the Clan, Dean Martin, teamed with Sinatra last year to lure a top collection of stars to a benefit for integration leader Martin Luther King. The way these stars performed for four solid hours it was believed that they must have been paid. But Sinatra, Martin, Davis and all the other greats displayed their wares gratis.

Perhaps $20 million worth of talent is not going to work that hard for nothing unless they have great esteem for Sammy and the cause he believes in. In a wild and frantic series of skits, Sinatra, Martin and Davis almost wrecked staid Carnegie Hall and the packed house loved it. The Clan did it for Sammy, nothing more.

Still rumors persisted that the Clan had cooled on Sammy since he married actress May Britt, a Swedish bon bon. This, too, isn't true. The stars have commitments all over the country and seldom can get together except in Hollywood.

Now the mob is asking if Sinatra's marriage to dancer Juliet Prowse will break up the Clan. Said Sammy: "That scene has been overdone." That closes the subject.

Sammy is a dedicated family man now and at the drop of a

hint he will whip out scores of pictures of his daughter Tracey just like any other guy on Main St., USA.

"I've never been happier," he said in all seriousness. "I never knew how great it could be to have a home and family. For a long time I used to be awfully lonesome, no matter how many people were around or how many people I knew. It's quite a difference to have someone of your own to go home to and whom you can share everything."

He is totally wrapped up in his daughter Tracey. "I want her to grow up in a world where she won't be aware of color. I know things won't always be like I want them for her, but my wife and I hope to minimize and not anticipate all the problems she might have to face because of her mixed parentage."

That is a tipoff on the fact that Sammy is a thoughtful and articulate young man and not always the public image of a frivolous entertainer who made too much money too soon.

During his New York stand Sammy electrified the columnists by saying that he and May (pronounced "My" and not May) want five babies.

Wrote Dave Hepburn in the New York Amsterdam News: "He wants five kids . . . Now five children for a factory worker or the mailman, or somebody in a nine-to-five job is all right. But how can a busy performer and an equally busy wife find time?"

"You see, both of us love kids," Sammy said, "and we feel that a big family is a stable family."

There is a play on words in that statement, but Sammy is sincere when he says he wants a big family. Fact is, they are expecting another baby. When Sammy and May are on the road Tracey stays with a nurse in their home in swanky Beverly Hills, Calif.

No question about it. Sammy stays busy with his night club chores and sandwiches in appearances in such shows as The Rifleman, Dick Powell Show and Hennessy.

Sammy has plans for his own television show. "I've got a series in mind—something like a modern in-America 'Casablanca' with me and a partner running a place and getting into all kinds of trouble. The partner would be of the Peter Lawford type. I'd like to do the series so that I can have more time at home with my wife and daughter."

Unlike a number of other famous Negro performers Sammy does not look down on his own people and he is gracious to the Negro press, because he has seen the unbecoming conduct of other stars in this matter.

Sammy has his feet on the ground and he does not feel that his earning power has insulated him against the race problem, as witness his benefit for Martin Luther King. He still does benefits for worthy causes and really works.

He and Sinatra are still great friends. He is happy with his wife and child and his career never looked brighter.

Sammy has it made but he is not resting on his laurels; he is looking ahead. He has matured and his career is dedicated to the future of his family.

That's the true inside of Sammy Davis, Jr.

—*March 3, 1962*

"SAMMY DAVIS, JR., SAYS SATCHMO NO SPOKESMAN,"
The Pittsburgh Courier

Louis Armstrong is a paradox whose stature as "a spokesman" for the Negro is being challenged by Sammy Davis, Jr., Broadway and night club star.

Davis was speaking of Satchmo's recent statements to the effect that the United States should clean house in places like Little Rock and other points south before asking entertainers like himself to go on overseas tours as goodwill ambassadors.

"You cannot voice an opinion about a situation which is basically discrimination, integration, etc.," Davis said, "and then go out and appear before segregated audiences . . . which Louis Armstrong has done for many years."

Armstrong's manager, agent Joe Glaser, told the New York Post there would be no reply from Louis.

"You can't get hold of Louis; he's on the road," Glaser said. "He doesn't want to talk about Sammy Davis, Jr. If Sammy Davis, Jr., wants to talk about Louis Armstrong and get some publicity, let him.

"But Louis is not interested in getting into any argument with him. Who cares about Sammy Davis, Jr.?"

Asked whether he had appeared before segregated audiences, Davis said: "Yes, before I became a headliner. I had no choice. It was a financial situation where if you wanted to eat you had to perform before segregated audiences.

"As soon as I got to the point where I could demand any kind of salary and my name became where people wanted to see me, I decided then and there—this was a few years ago— that I would not ever perform where my people could not come to see me."

Davis continued: "It's a thing naturally very close to me. I'm just so damned mad."

Davis said he told Canadian reporters that he agreed with Armstrong when Louis attacked the Eisenhower Administration on the Little Rock situation, but not with his choice of words.

Davis praised Armstrong as an entertainer and expressed hope that the jazz man would live up to the words he had said to the press.

"Louis Armstrong has always been regarded—let me be as kind as I possibly can; I think Louis Armstrong first of all is a great talent—great, as much as I hate the wordage, a great credit to his race, but he has also been regarded by his race as a man who . . . well . . ."

Davis was interrupted, but reflected:

"Louis, as you know, less than a year ago, did a song which had a very objectionable word in it in our day and time. And when they went to him and said, 'Why did you release this record with this word in it?' why Louis said, 'Well, man, it's just this song and I sing it this way.' However, the song was made by white performers and they had the word taken out." Davis said he referred to the lyrics of "Mississippi Mud," which read, "Darkies beat their feet in the Mississippi mud." He said the white performers sang it, "People beat their feet . . ."

"So all of a sudden," Davis said, "when he becomes, to quote his own manager: 'He [Armstrong] is a champion of his people,' I must in all honesty read the statement and chuckle to myself, unless he has done a complete reversal. And if he has, I must then say why didn't it happen ten years ago?"

Finally Davis said:

"For years Louis Armstrong has been important in the newspapers. They have always been ready to give space if he had anything to say that really was important, and he never has. Now this happens. I don't think it's honest. If it is, why didn't he say it two years ago? He doesn't need a segregated audience."

—October 12, 1957

"LOUIS' CRITICS SHOULD JUMP IN LAKE,"
by Evelyn Cunningham, *The Pittsburgh Courier*

Some people think Louis Armstrong is a "controversial figure." They question his on-stage chatter. They don't go for his kind of showmanship. They don't like the fact that so many white people literally worship him. They hold to a theory that a white-world idolation of a Negro artist is the kiss of death.

To each his own. Me, I think all this kind of Louis Armstrong propaganda is for the birds.

Here's a man in his 60's who has probably contributed more to the development of pure jazz than anyone else in the world. What the heck more do you want? You want he should also be a Bunche, a King, a Belafonte, a Robinson?

Horn blowers and all other kinds of musicians have been saying for the last few decades that Louis Armstrong is their inspiration, their teacher, their idol. Dozens of the finest trumpeters aspire to emulate the great Armstrong. Many have conceded that no one can or ever will be able to do with a trumpet what Armstrong can.

In Africa, Australia, Europe, they dig Satchmo. Not especially because he's colored, but mainly because he's bringing them pure, unadulterated jazz, a truly American form of music. Personally, I'm happy as all get-out that a colored guy is the one best equipped to carry this message.

Sure, Louis is different from our current crop of entertainers like Sammy Davis, Jr., Harry Belafonte, Eartha Kitt, Lena Horne and the others. These folk are younger, more sophisticated and came through an entirely different era. But they are certainly no more talented than Louis Armstrong. Nor are they any more artistically dedicated. Nor are they any more articulate.

That's another thing. Some people don't like the way Louis Armstrong talks. They don't like the shades of the old Southland. So Louis should talk like a proper Bostonian when his whole background and heritage are in the South? With his horn he is articulate as anyone in the world. And when he talks, he has a real gift of communicating profound knowledge in one brief phrase. Not many people can do this.

So what do you want out of Louis Armstrong? Blood?

—*June 8, 1957*

"GIVE 'SATCHMO' THE SPINGARN MEDAL,"
by Evelyn Cunningham, *The Pittsburgh Courier*

Well, everybody's been saying that things would come to a head sooner or later. Nobody—but nobody—figured Louis Armstrong would do the trick.

Roy Wilkins, Jackie Robinson, Lester Granger, and all the leadingest of the race leaders have said their piece. They have echoed the sentiments of the blacks throughout the nation. But nothing has shook. Oh yea, there have been conferences, assurances, and promises. But nothing has really shook.

But ole Satchmo—one of the most maligned of all Negro entertainers—has shook up everybody. As his wife Lucille says—and she probably knows him better than anyone in the world—"Louis' talk is strictly 1920, and New Orleans style. So when he says something, he leaves no margin for error as to what he means."

So when Louis said the State Department is wasting time sending him to Russia, because "what am I going to say when they ask me about Little Rock?" there's no way he can be misunderstood.

Mrs. Armstrong said she had gotten a wire from her husband shortly after his statements had hit every corner of the world. The wire indicated that of all the people in the world he was most concerned about what her feelings in the matter were. She said she promptly wrote him a long letter, telling him of her great pride in him. She insists he is the "world's greatest diplomat. You have no idea the questions they ask him and how beautifully he fluffs them off."

Armstrong's manager and long-time friend, Joe Glaser, thought Louis' stand was "wonderful. Now the people who've been calling him an Uncle Tom can see that he's a real, real man. I'm with him all the way. When the President invited Faubus to confer with him, I was astounded, bewildered and sick. All Louis did was voice the sentiment of all of us."

Meanwhile, Armstrong's strong protests have been seconded by Jackie Robinson, Lena Horne and Eartha Kitt, to name a few of the famous ones. But more importantly, he's getting a hurray from hordes of nameless, faceless people who've been waiting a long time to hear some say what Louis did.

All of this must be terribly confusing to many whites who have thought that Louis was their "boy" and wasn't like the rest of "those radical Negroes."

So maybe the NAACP should give Armstrong the Spingarn Medal. No kidding!

—*September 28, 1957*

"SAMMY DAVIS, JR., TALKS OF POLITICS AND MAY BRITT,"
by Jonathan White, *The Pittsburgh Courier*

Sammy Davis, Jr., as versatile a conversationalist as he is an entertainer, really touched all bases, as he entertained members of the press in his suite in the Elmwood Motel, a few steps away from the scene of his current record breaking appearance at Al Siegal's Elmwood Casino, in Windsor, Ont.

Sammy talked about international and national politics, his coming marriage, the race question, his finances, photography, May Britt, his itinerary for the coming months, his wedding in October, religion, his current affair, his visit to South America, May Britt . . . and oh so many other things.

About his wedding plans, Sammy definitely assured the

press that he will be married in October and his current plans point to a small wedding at his home in Los Angeles. Although he has not decided on who will perform the ceremonies, he has already had several preliminary discussions with Rabbi Nussbaum, who may officiate. He also revealed that his bride's parents would be there along with some of his personal friends.

"It won't be a mammoth affair, I assure you," Sammy stated, "but I've a lot of friends who I am sure will want to attend when I set the definite date."

Sammy informed that following his appearance at the Elmwood Casino, which to date has been a "real gasser," he will go to London to do a one man show. He called the London audiences "the greatest."

"You know they don't applaud you until the end of the show," Sammy explained. "You work hard and they sit there . . . you know they are digging you but no applause, they just enjoy you quietly . . . and then you are engulfed in a wave of applause. This boy is really something."

By the same token, Sammy was most critical of the South Americans. "Man you can have those cats. Sure, the way they approach this color question is something to behold. They really give you the greatest feeling . . . but man after that you can have São Paulo, and Rio and all the senoritas down there. I just don't dig that jazz they put down. Even the folks who can speak English refuse to do so. Boy, they are really something."

On politics Sammy admits he is all for Kennedy. He feels he will make a great President. "I have had the pleasure of knowing John personally and have met with him as a social equal on several occasions. I think his ideas are tremendous and it will be the greatest thing for this country if he puts them into effect."

Asked if he would stump for Kennedy, Sammy said he

would if called upon. "But if I feel that my appearance on John's behalf would cost him a single vote I would remain silent. I admire the man just that much and would do all in my power to help him even if I were called upon to make a great personal sacrifice."

Asked about his future plans, Sammy admitted that he plans to direct most of his efforts in the area of television and the motion pictures. He is more than pleased with his recent television efforts, particularly his appearance in his first dramatic try as "The Patsy" for United States Steel and his appearance with "The Leader," Frank Sinatra. "It is most gratifying that the audience reaction has been so warm and wonderful to me in this medium," Sammy said.

He also admitted that he had a lot of fun when he appeared with Sinatra and gang in "Ocean's Eleven," the current film which was premiered in Las Vegas this week.

Needless to say, where Sinatra was concerned Sammy had nothing but the most to say.

And then the little man with the great big talent embarked on his favorite subject . . . May Britt.

—*August 13, 1960*

"A 'PRECIOUS MOMENT IN MY LIFE,' SAYS SAMMY,"
by Chester L. Washington, *The Pittsburgh Courier*

While entertainment experts here were speculating on what effect—if any—the marriage of Sammy Davis, Jr., and the blond Swedish actress would have on their careers, the buzzing was still going the rounds about the "closed" Jewish wedding rites held high up in the Hollywood hills.

Sammy himself explained why he had barred the press from the actual double-ring ceremony. "I thought that part of the sacred moment should be ours."

However, his buddy, Frankie Sinatra, stood by him as scheduled, as Sammy's best man.

Actor Peter Lawford, Miss Britt's parents—who flew here from Stockholm for the wedding—Sammy's mother and father and his stepmother and a photographer-friend were among the few attending the rites. The photog took exclusive pictures as a wedding present, Sammy announced.

Actually, a sudden case of intestinal virus—which the actress attributed to a shrimp meal—almost caused Miss Britt to miss her own wedding.

The illness had her and Dan Cupid virtually hanging on the ropes, but she went through with the ceremony despite this because, she was "anxious to marry Sammy."

She did, however, miss the wedding reception in the palatial Beverly Hilton Hotel's Nordic Room, but Sammy appeared to convey her regrets.

Wedding Setting Lavish

Immediately after the ceremony, Sammy cordially invited a small battalion of newsmen and photographers, including your correspondent, into his plush Hollywood hillside home at 8850 Evanview Drive.

The picturesque bower of white chrysanthemums, where the traditional Jewish marriage rites had been performed by Rabbi William Kramer, was still standing.

Mrs. George Rhodes, the wife of Sammy's musical arranger, was the matron of honor.

Bride Wore Beige

The blonde bride wore beige—a form-fitting figured dress of silk and satin, topped by an exquisitely jeweled tiara and a tulle veil.

The slippers too were of matching soft tan. Her corsage was made of white roses and blending lilies of the valley.

Sammy admitted he was "nervous" at the rites, but added: "She was the most beautiful bride I ever saw."

Miss Britt told newsmen Sammy had given her a Cadillac as a wedding present and that she had given him a Corvette.

Thanks Newsmen

Sammy told newsmen he wanted to "thank the American people" for accepting him and his wife "just as two human beings." He said that Miss Britt had adopted the Jewish religion without being asked to do so by him. "I think having the same religion is more important in our case . . . because it is a close form of communication . . . on a spiritual level," Sammy said.

Meanwhile Sammy's friendly Hollywood Hills neighbors were celebrating the occasion by blasting recordings of Davis' "Happy to Make Your Acquaintance" and Sinatra's "Making Whoopee" from their homes on the hillside.

Sammy said the wedding was "the most precious moment in his life."

After the ceremony, May's father and Sammy's dad, Sammy Davis, Sr., with their arms around each other's shoulders, drove to a road leading down into Hollywood's glittering sea of bright lights, chatting and smiling as if they were sitting on top of the world.

—November 26, 1960

"SAMMY DAVIS' NEW MOVIE TO BE RELEASED SOON,"
The Pittsburgh Courier

"There is nothing, outside of a cyclotron, that can perform with the limitless vigor of Sammy Davis, Jr." wrote a well-known commentator in a national magazine.

And he was not exaggerating. The frenetic entertainer stars in Broadway shows, works on regular television shows and hosts TV specials, wrote a best-selling autobiography, has hit records and albums on the market, makes constant appearances at charity benefits, holds a multi-million dollar contract with a Las Vegas nightclub as a performer and heads Sammy Davis Enterprises, a business complex resting largely on his own talents as a performing artist.

In addition to all these mind-reeling activities, Davis last winter starred in a new motion picture, Joseph E. Levine's "A Man Called Adam," which is due to open locally in late summer.

The Embassy Pictures release is the first project of Davis' Trace-Mark Production, an independent motion picture production company whose name stems from Davis' two children, Tracey and Mark. The firm is headed by James Waters, Davis' former business manager, who, with Ike Jones serve as the producers of the film. Joseph E. Levine serves as executive producer.

According to all reports, "A Man Called Adam" is the first major American film production concerned primarily with Negro life since "A Raisin in the Sun" four years ago.

Davis portrays Adam Johnson, a famed jazz musician with profound personal and professional problems. Although these problems stem from the accidental death of his wife some years before, many of them find expression in the delicate area of Negro-white relationships, and in the continual anguish attendant upon any celebrated Negro personality existing "in white America."

Entirely shot in New York, "A Man Called Adam" offered many seldom-found opportunities for Negro actors, who appear in both major and smaller roles in the film.

For example, for the first time in his long and illustrious career, Louis Armstrong is given the chance to portray on the screen an honestly conceived dramatic character. After years of being seen on the screen less as an actor than as a picturesque entertainer, Armstrong is cast as Willie "Sweet Daddy" Ferguson in "A Man Called Adam," an aging musician who comes out of retirement in an effort to make a comeback.

Preview audiences report that Armstrong does a real down-to-earth job of acting.

Young Cicely Tyson, one of the most promising Negro actresses on the Broadway stage, has the leading feminine role in the movie. She portrays the role of Claudia, an idealistic college girl and civil-rights worker who becomes involved in the affairs of Adam.

Another new Negro talent who makes an important step in his career in "A Man Called Adam," is Ossie Davis, who plays Nelson, a jazz composer and arranger. The author of the play "Purlie Victorious," Ossie recently has important film roles in "The Cardinal" and "The Hill."

Three important white stars, all of them good friends of Sammy Davis, appear with this impressive Negro cast. Frank Sinatra, Jr., portrays a young protege of Adam. Mel Tormé is guest starred as Vincent, himself, and Peter Lawford appears in the special guest role of Manny, Adam's manager.

"We tried to show jazz musicians as they really are," explains Ike Jones. Jones, the first Negro to produce a feature motion picture in this country, was associated with the late Nat "King" Cole, and brought the screenplay of "A Man Called Adam," an original by Les Pine and Tina Rome, to the Davis organization. "This was a project that Nat had wanted to do but never got a chance to work on," he says. "Since it is a story of a Negro jazz musician it seemed a natural for Sammy to undertake."

Jones and Pine spent more than six months in actual research among jazz musicians—living with them, traveling with them, listening to their talk. "Most pictures of jazz players are cliché-ridden. I cannot recall a single one that dealt with these people in other than in a stereotyped fashion," Jones says.

"We try to be authentic in our language," he continues. "Traveling in buses for a series of one-nighters is a hard life, and in our picture the men do not suddenly break out in a gay theme song of joys of the road as they journey from one job to another."

Some of the finest jazz music ever heard on screen is featured in the film. Davis' trumpet playing was dubbed by Nat Adderly, one of the country's leading jazzmen. Louis Armstrong naturally plays his own music, and jazz buffs will immediately recognize, in smaller roles, the talents of Bill Berry, Gene Carlett, Tyree Glenn, Buster Bailey, Billy Kyle, Danny Barcelona, Junior Mance and Kai Winding.

Leo Penn, director of "A Man Called Adam," worked with a fully-integrated production crew on the film. "But," says production manager Steve Brody, "Our crew was selected on the basis of skill, not race."

—August 6, 1966

"THE NAME DROPPER,"
by Donald Duncan, *Dance Magazine*

We've found a new guest critic for tap dancing, an ardent champion of that art form named Sammy Davis, Jr. How could anyone improve upon his "review" of the tap dancing prowess of his old friend Gene Kelly? Says Sammy, "*Man*, that boy can sure lay down some iron!"

When Davis was in NYC for the premiere of *Porgy and Bess* we drew him out on the subject of dancing. That day his natural ebullience had a slight nervous edge. As yet he hadn't seen the picture, and he was worried about the impression his portrayal of Sportin' Life would make on his "date"—his mother. (P.S.: She loved it.)

We began by asking Sammy where he had learned to dance. "To be honest," he replied, "I don't remember. As a kid I picked it up—from my folks and from others in show business. I guess I'm still picking it up. A few years ago there was a lot more around to see—and to steal from."

Sammy's uncle, Will Mastin, was very close to the late great Bill Robinson, and "Bojangles" coached young Sammy in a few time steps. "I can't remember them now, but one thing he taught me I'll never forget. It's that you've got to keep it *simple*. All the time the people have to understand what you're talking about—even if you're talking with your feet."

In *Porgy,* "It Ain't Necessarily So" had some choreographic problems. The number was pre-set by Hermes Pan, but Davis couldn't make it work for himself and asked to bring in his own choreographer, Hal Loman. ("We think, act and dance as one.") Pan understood; after all, he has often done special work for stars like Astaire in shows choreographed by someone else.

Davis has high praise for the dance people who have appeared on bills with him on the cabaret circuit, citing as a top example Augie & Margo. "It's really exciting to see an act that *tight*," he said.

The accolade of which Sammy is proudest came from Ulanova, who saw his show at the Moulin Rouge in Hollywood. Backstage, after he had apologized for his kind of hoofing, he was told by the ballerina, "You can dance with me *any* time!"

—August 1959

"THE AGONY OF SAMMY DAVIS,"
by Leonard Feather, *Melody Maker*

The whole story of Sammy Davis, Jr., and his troubles has not been told. Behind the headlines about his marriage to May Britt lies a pathetic story of humiliation and suffering, of race-hatred and terror, few details of which have been made known to the public.

Sammy's troubles were first widely publicised when a bunch of Oswald Mosley Fascists tried to start a riot in London.

A similar scene occurred only a month ago in Los Angeles, when American Nazi youths, wearing swastika arm-bands, were arrested after picketing a theatre where he was appearing.

But those are just the surface aspects of the agony Davis has had to endure. Matters have now reached a stage at which policemen and private detectives have to guard him every minute.

In San Francisco, in Las Vegas, wherever he appears, nobody knows when the next anonymous telephone call will threaten to bomb the night club, or to bomb the home in which his bride is recuperating from an illness.

Many Americans claim to be without prejudice. Very few, though, have dared to take a positive stand in the Davis affair—they are afraid to become involved in something they feel is too inflammatory.

Luckily there are men like Frank Sinatra, Sammy's best man, who doesn't care what anyone says and is firmly loyal in his friendship.

The presence at the wedding of the sister and brother-in-law (Mr. and Mrs. Peter Lawford) of President-elect Kennedy was an indication that some important people in an influential position refuse to be intimidated.

Freedom

Nevertheless, even the knowledge that they have these good friends cannot give peace of mind to Mr. and Mrs. Davis.

Ironically, it is not until they get away from Sammy's native land that they will be able to feel an air of comparative freedom. Perhaps in Paris or Stockholm—though not in London, where he is scheduled to go back to work next April—Sammy may find a relaxation from the atmosphere of hostility that makes it difficult for him and his wife to have a single moment of untroubled calm.

Meanwhile, even when she is well enough to return to work, May Britt will find that every door in the Hollywood studios is closed to her.

The brave men who produce this nation's movie and television shows are afraid to give her any kind of a job now that she has dared to marry the man she loves.

Miss Britt, interviewed recently on a television programme, answered questions about her situation with great frankness. She is fully aware of the price she has had to pay in terms of her career.

Fortunately, she has enough strength of character to know

that there are more important values in life than the dollar sign.

And, luckily, Mr. Davis's own talents are so tremendous and so completely irreplaceable that there seems to be no immediate danger to his career. In fact, Sammy just took on a new assignment.

Famous

Starting in January he will have his own radio programme every night on KRHM, an important radio station in Los Angeles.

One of his first guests, in a series of three interviews, will be Frank Sinatra. Sammy will chat with the famous, play records (he has a tremendous collection of jazz LPs), and talk about music and show business.

—December 24, 1960

"WHAT MAKES AVA GARDNER RUN FOR SAMMY DAVIS, JR.?,"
by Horton Streete, *Confidential*

Having shown up barefoot over Europe and half of Latin-America, luscious Ava Gardner even topped herself last month when she popped up on the cover of a national Negro magazine with an article, under her personal byline, titled "Sammy Sends Me."

On the inside, Ava declared herself at the top of her handsome lungs.

"Don't ask me why," she gurgled, "I just know that Sammy Davis, Jr., just sends me, as a performer."

It would be highly inappropriate to ask the lovely lady why. But a question more in order would be: How do you mean, "as a performer?" Because the evidence is that Sammy sends Ava, period.

Nor is he the first bronze boyfriend to rate high in the Gardner date book, as you will soon discover. For now, let's see how far Sammy sends her.

There is, for instance, a windswept night last fall when the telephone tinkled softly in Ava's 16th-floor suite at New York's elegant Drake Hotel. When the spiciest dish on the silver screen answered it, she got a message she couldn't resist.

"I'm calling for Sammy," said a rich, deep baritone. "He wants you to come uptown and have some kicks."

The sultry Miss Gardner needed no further identification, or a road map. She reacted as though she'd been given orders for a command performance. Throwing a mink wrap around her million-dollar shoulders, she darted out into the night and headed straight for Harlem, the home of happy feet.

She Made an Unscheduled "Guest Appearance"

She was bound for the famed Apollo Theater, headquarters for the world's top colored entertainers, where Sammy was closing a record-breaking week featuring his songs, dances and comic routines. The last show turned out to be the best when, to the pop-eyed amazement of a howling, cheering crowd that packed the theater to the rafters, Ava came slinking into the spotlight for an unscheduled "guest appearance."

Hand in hand with Sammy, she "goofed it up" for a few minutes, then the pair pranced off into the wings and, after a couple of curtain calls, strolled out of the place for a date more sensational than anything advertised on the theater's marquee.

Slowly, Sammy and Ava elbowed their way through the dense crowds swarming around them. Even those who didn't immediately recognize Hollywood's "Queen of Sex" needed no glasses to determine that Davis had on his arm a choice item of "ofay," Harlem's slang term for a white chick.

In a desperate effort to escape the mob at their heels, the pair ducked quickly into the Shalimar, one of the plushiest upholstered cellars on uptown Seventh Avenue. Moving to a table, Ava and Sammy ordered up a few rounds of Scotch and milk, currently her favorite drink because, as Ava likes to explain to friends, it's wise to get your vitamins with your tippling.

"They Really Impressed Each Other"

Apparently the milk lost out that particular night. "Just a couple more rounds and Ava would have been plastered," said a bartender. "Her eyes were beginning to glaze after the second drink."

It was the first time Gardner had met Sammy on his home grounds but far from their first game. It would seem Sammy had begun "sending" as far back as early 1952, when he played a series of Hollywood nightclub engagements.

The Gardner gamin was busy charming Frank Sinatra at the time; in fact, it was Frank who introduced her to Davis. But Ava isn't the type to let chores of the moment interfere with her recognizing a fascinating new male. A mutual friend present at their first meeting said, "They really impressed each other." Sammy used the jive talk Ava was to adopt later in describing their mutual reaction.

"We just dug each other, that's all," he said.

But it wasn't until Ava's marriage to Frank went on the rocks that she and Sammy really began to sizzle. They were seen often together in Hollywood, Las Vegas and New York. And they were purring on all 12 cylinders by the time she returned from last summer's shoeless tour of South America.

It was in Rio de Janeiro, incidentally, that Ava paused long enough to test that old charge that "Latins Are Lousy Lovers," and apparently found it so.

Less than an hour after she made a hasty exit from the sedate Gloria Hotel (at the management's request, according to a spokesman for the hotel), Ava checked into the snappier Copacabana Palace and had the entertainers put on a special four a.m. show, just for her.

Ava Was Anti-Latin but Pro-Sammy

A young Brazilian singer, Carlos Augusto, beguiled the boiled Miss Gardner with such songs as "Bahia" and "The Black-gold Ballad." When the one-party show broke up well after dawn, he was invited to her beige-and-green 10th-floor suite, where he, Ava and a press agent nipped up more giggle soup.

Carlos got large ideas when Miss Gardner retired to her bedchamber to change into something comfortable. He still walks around Rio in a daze, describing the chiffon dream who came back out for a nightcap. "I almost couldn't breathe," he said. "My temples were pounding!"

Much of what followed must be veiled in censorship. The climax can be revealed, however. Ava vanished in a mist of rum and Carlos found himself with—the press agent.

By the time she flew back to New York, the anti-Latin Ava was very much pro-Sammy. She visited him only once at the Apollo Theater, but they used to play return engagements at each other's hotels.

Bellhops at the Warwick Hotel are still prattling about her sassy trips to Davis' quarters in suite 2409. And a pal who dropped in at Ava's diggings in the Drake remarked, "They were the chummiest."

But dark-skinned gents have been proving their powerful fascination for Ava for years. Another example was when she became entranced with the mambo and even more engrossed with Perez Prado, the mustached little Cuban who claims to have invented the weird tempo.

Not long ago, when Prado played the Oasis, a black-and-tan night spot on Hollywood's Western Avenue, ringsiders were goggle-eyed to note Ava in constant attendance. This time it was she who was "sending"—messages backstage to Prado. Between shots of Prado's wild music, she visited with him off the bandstand and the results must have been gratifying as Miss Gardner now does a wicked mambo.

Before all this, Ava had a bosom-heaving crush on Herb Jeffries which had even blase Hollywood mumbling in its cock-tails. Back in the late forties, the copper-skinned crooner from Detroit was strictly a nickel-and-dime-warbler. Things changed dramatically when Ava's green eyes started smiling at him a few years ago.

She ran across him during one of her off-beat excursions and promptly named herself his sponsor. Ava's plugs with influ-ential friends started zooming Herb to the top and his salary for singing in gin mills soared from $250 to $750 and $1,000 in the plushier spots. The handsome colored crooner also won a series of screen tests and was set for movie roles as a Mexican troubador.

It was a cozy arrangement with "manager" and "client" never far from each other's sight. In fact, the management of one Hollywood sauce factory, "The Red Feather," courteously asked Miss Gardner to stay the hell out of their joint, as she was monopolizing their main attraction, to the annoyance of other customers who apparently also wanted their moments with the muscular singer.

This problem never became acute because it was about that time that Jeffries had the poor grace to switch his attention to another Hollywood doll, Ronnie Quillan, who much later dis-tinguished herself by trying to carve crooner Billy Daniels away from his face because he wouldn't quit two-timing her with other white women.

It must have been Ronnie's luck to be deviled by runaround sweeties all her life, because she married Herb, years before the Daniels incident, and ran herself ragged trying to keep Herb out of strange boudoirs—strange to *her*, that is.

There was one occasion when her temper was worn thin af-ter a search for Jeffries wound up in an apartment on Holly-wood's South Raymond Street. Herb was there, all right. So, it turned out, was Ava Gardner.

Not the least of her other coffee-toned knights was an even more striking music-maker, Dizzy Gillespie. Ava liked him, his bop tunes and beret so much that she used to join him on the bandstand when "the Diz" spent a riotous season at Billy Berg's, one of Hollywood's cooler establishments for "hepcats."

Diz intoxicated Ava to the point where she went out and bought herself a beret and a pair of huge, horn-rimmed glasses to match his "reet" costume. She was no musician, but didn't waste her other talents while on the bandstand. Between numbers she used to cavort with Dizzy in an act which many of Berg's customers swore was more entrancing than the tunes.

Dizzy ranked her company "the most" and used to tell his Negro friends that Ava was the "greatest ofay" he'd ever known. No one has ever asked Ava whether she enjoys such distinctions. On the record, though, she seems to be collecting them. As the lady herself says, they really "send" her.

—March 1955

"SHH! HAVE YOU HEARD THE LATEST ABOUT SAMMY DAVIS, JR.?,"
by Matt Williams, *Confidential*

From Sunset and Vine to Broadway, the whispers go round and round about that engaging little bronze guy who used to wear a black patch over his left eye, Sammy Davis, Jr.

"Heard what he's up to *now?*" one curvy starlet will ask another. If the second shakes her head, she's in for an ear-tickling half hour of spicy chitchat, all adding up to the fact that Sammy's a sensation these days—in more places than on the stage.

Not so long ago the gossip columns snapped and crackled with items about his friendship with that globetrotting glamour girl, Ava Gardner. There were even published photos showing Sammy and Ava as a cozy twosome.

It was hard for some of Hollywood's top Don Juans to understand it all.

Public Not Aware of All Sammy's Conquests

Sammy's no collar ad. His nose wanders down his face uncertainly and he has a lantern jaw that makes him look like he's always on the verge of picking a fight.

Instead, he's picking off movieland's snappiest sirens. By no means all of these cozy conquests reach the public print. For instance, with the recent release of the Allied Artists picture, "Phenix City Story," wolves from the Atlantic to the Pacific sat up to take notice of its curvy star, Meg Myles. Watching her wriggle in and out of scenes and hearing her sing the film's sexy theme, "Phenix City Blues," they one and all wanted to know where this bosomy babe had been hiding.

They'll get the answer—which was carefully deleted from Meg's booming press build-up—right here. It's too good a secret to bury.

The lowdown is that, when she wasn't on camera, the fully-packed Miss Myles was steaming it up with Sammy at the Sunset Colonial Hotel on Hollywood's famed Sunset Strip. What's more, their undercover blaze flared up within hours of first setting eyes on each other.

It all began on a nippy night in October, 1954, when Meg went out on the town with an old friend, Duke Mitchell, who had gained a degree of local fame singing in a now defunct nightery called the Tablehoppers. After a few refreshments, the ill-fated Mitchell suggested they adjourn to Sammy's suite in the Colonial, explaining he'd introduce Meg to his pal, Sammy Davis, who was a camera bug and would take her picture.

He did, too! Reels of 'em. For, in spite of the cuties crowding his date book, Sammy had to admit he had seldom seen a pigeon like Meg. An admiring glance, traveling upward, revealed shapely gams, leading to 36-inch hips, and a positively fabulous 42-inch bust!

It was Sammy's happy fate to learn a few hours later exactly how the curves got stacked that way, and the process deserves description for babes who want to billow in the right places.

When dressing to make the boys' eyes bulge, Meg starts with what's called a "Merry Widow" corselette, a satin and lace contraption which stretches from just under the bust to just above the hips and is tightened in the back till a doll has a waist like a wasp. Over this, Meg slips a Playtex girdle to slim her hips and help the corselette hoist her spectacular superstructure. A bra that never quite seems up to its responsibility finishes the basic construction.

Here's News for the Duke

Sammy couldn't know all this at first glance, of course, but what did meet his eyes had him clicking his camera shutter like a Geiger counter. Nor was that all. As the evening wore on, he turned the focusing over to Mitchell while he hopped nimbly in place for a few shots of himself with Meg. Before he'd finished, he'd snapped up more than the Myles likeness. In fact, Mitchell eventually was to find himself moaning the blues, while Sammy and Meg made livelier music.

As a matter of fact, although it may be news to him, Duke got knocked out of the picture that first night of the photographic free-for-all. If he wondered why Meg broke up the snapshot and guzzling session to insist that he take her home, he'd have sizzled had he bothered to follow her after she left him.

Home for Few Minutes—Then Back with Sammy

The Myles minx continued on to her own apartment at 1830 North Whitley Avenue but got a telephone call just 15 minutes later. It was Sammy, asking whether Meg might not like to return to his place for a late, late show. She only had to say yes once and that Davis boy was in his long, black Cadillac convertible, racing to get her. Meg got back to her own den about noon the next day.

Whatever Sammy's got, it was good enough for Meg. In the

next few weeks she often failed to show up at her own place the whole night long. Perhaps she feared getting out of a warm nest and going home, but at any rate, residents and employees of the Colonial got used to spotting Meg arriving at Sammy's suite at one or two a.m. and slipping out hours later—in broad daylight—to whistle down a cruising cab.

What startled them and made identification unavoidable was that busty Meg often wore men's clothing for her getaway. And there's no man's shirt ever made which could adequately camouflage Miss Mmmmyles!

Not that Sammy and Meg confined all their activities to his cozy hideaway. Occasionally, they'd sashay out on the town for late, late dinners at such spots as the Hamburger Hamlet, where the two would moon at each other over cheeseburgers, medium rare. Meg was so wild about that Davis boy that she chose him to help her celebrate her birthday, November 13, 1954, and it was launched at the same ground beef palace. The festivities continued at a pace fast enough to age a wench 10 instead of one year.

Something happened, though, that blew their happy time higher than a kite. All that's known is that daredevil Davis had Meg as his off-screen guest on his last appearance on the Colgate Comedy hour just before his near-tragic auto accident. Although it cost Sammy his left eye, he bounced out of the hospital his old vivacious self, except for one person—Miss Meg.

Meg meandered over to her favorite playgrounds in the Colonial on the first November night in 1954 when Sammy was released from the hospital. As usual, it was an all-night get-together but—for Sammy, at least—the thrill was gone. As was her custom, Meg slipped out shortly after dawn, to discover later it had been her last cut-up with Sammy. Although she buzzed him on the phone continually, Davis made it crystal clear he was off to new conquests.

Don't get us wrong. Little Miss Myles isn't the type to sit and brood and it didn't take her long to spin up a few new romances (such as her spicy interlude with actor Ralph Meeker).

She wasn't even beyond going back to an old flame. Teaming up with the much-abused Duke Mitchell, the pair formed a warbling act and opened at a new gin parlor, the Tabletoppers (not to be confused with the old Tablehoppers).

She had a style—a sexy, throbbing quality to her voice— which not only captivated the late-hour guzzlers but won her the screen test that got her the role in "Phenix City." And there were those who knew the old Meg—B. S., meaning before Sammy—who said she seemed to have improved miraculously.

They can't figure it out. Do you suppose some of those nights with Sammy really *were* spent on singing lessons?

—*March 1956*

"WHO BROKE UP THEIR ROMANCE?,"
by Hy Steirman, *Confidential*

This is the tragic love story of the century.

In the playwright's world, Romeo and Juliet united in death when their parents wouldn't let them wed.

But in real life—the king gives up his throne for the woman he loves—and travels around the world with a 25 million dollar bank account.

In our case—Sammy Davis couldn't give up the Negro race. Kim Novak couldn't give up the white race. They didn't have 25 million dollars to soothe the hurt of what friends and business associates keep telling them.

The tragedy of this story is they were born 100 years too soon.

Sammy and Kim had met several times, but when Kim brought some friends to see him perform at the Chez Paree in Chicago, she became his greatest fan. This was about a year ago. They dated a couple of times, the blonde (sometimes purple-haired) love Goddess of millions of movie fans, and, as Sammy describes himself, "a one-eyed, flat-nosed ugly like me."

Of course there was the fact that Sammy is colored and Kim is white. But in showbusiness there is no such thing as a color line among the entertainers themselves. A man or woman stands or falls on his or her talents.

Sammy happens to be America's greatest all around entertainer. Kim happens to be the Number 1 woman Box Office draw at the movies.

What do they have in common besides talent? Kim is the main support of her family. So is Sammy. Both still live with their families and have very strong family ties.

Before their dating turned to love, both realized that if they continued to see each other in Hollywood, they would have to be prudent about it. Hollywood is a very small town. They couldn't go to a restaurant together like Chasen's or the Brown Derby. They could only go to the small intimate parties to which both of them had been invited.

Even so the gossip started.

The columnists had a field day even though the pair had never been seen together "openly." They began to ride Sammy and Kim.

It didn't hurt Sammy.

It hurt Kim.

Hollywood is not only a small town—it's a provincial village. It was all right when they went to parties, but as soon as a few columnists began to twist the knife, people in Hollywood took the cue. People would walk out of a room if Kim entered it. Friends would avoid calling. She was being frozen out of Hollywood where she was the reigning Queen.

The dilemma of what to do.

Quit movies and marry Sammy?

Don't quit movies and forget him?

Her first consideration was her family. She had no "big" money other than her salary and she is the main support of her family.

Her decision was to go ahead with the marriage. Every day brought more obstacles. People were becoming more cruel.

The pressure was beginning to mount to an unbelievable crescendo.

Sammy received pressure from his friends, too. Frank Sinatra, one of his closest buddies, called and said, "Sammy, you're making a serious mistake."

It is reliably reported that Sammy lost his temper at Frankie telling him, "You're a hell of a one to talk. You invented mistakes. You get away with 'murder' and people love it. If I tried a tenth of what you do—they'd hang me in the morning."

Nevertheless, Sammy and Sinatra are still friends.

The greater pressures came from Columbia Studios, where Kim reigns, and the William Morris Agency who manages Kim.

It was Harry Cohn, the volatile head of Columbia and a good friend of Sammy's who took Sammy aside. "Do you realize this girl is a $20 million dollar property to me? Have a fling if you must—but don't get married."

Not long afterwards Cohn died of a heart attack. It is rumored around Columbia that several executives still needle Kim with words to the effect that this romance killed Harry Cohn.

The death of Cohn had a sobering effect.

They didn't want to take his advice and just have an affair and skip marriage. They wanted marriage.

A thousand stories and rumors were now flying around Hollywood and New York—none of them true. Every time a blonde-haired girl applauded Sammy at a night club, it was reported in the columns that Kim was at ringside.

It got to the point that Sammy would avoid being introduced to fellows who escorted blondes, just so people wouldn't get the wrong idea.

If anything, Sammy is a determined young man. He is no skirt chaser (despite what some magazines have said in the past). He has a strong sense of pride in his race, so much so that to date he has refused to play before a segregated audience.

These qualities have endeared him to many people in Hollywood. His closest friend, and the one who counts the most in his life, Jerry Lewis, made no comment on the Sammy-Kim affair. Jerry told him it was a decision only he could make.

Sammy was so disturbed he was ready to hop on a tramp steamer to Hong Kong and give up show business. Kim was ready to do the same for him.

But responsibilities, the studios and the William Morris Agency finally won out. Pressure broke up the romance. That and the fact that each one must continue to work and support their separate families.

Whenever Kim was questioned about Sammy she became confused.

First she said she knew him.

Then she said she didn't.

Then she said she loved him.

Then she said she didn't. From Kim's standpoint—it was utter chaos.

All Sammy said was they were friends.

They haven't dated since May.

This fact did not still the rumor mills. The gossip faucet would not dry up.

A dramatic decision had to be made.

Sammy made it.

He married a colored girl. After telling the press about it on a Tuesday, he tied the knot on a Thursday.

Did this stop the gossip?

It did not!

Again a rumor flew around the country with lightning speed that two thugs flew out to Las Vegas where Sammy was playing. They were reported to have said to Sammy:

"You have one eye—do you want to try for none? If you don't—marry a colored girl in three days or else . . . !"

Sammy denies this emphatically!

Those close to Sammy swear it is not true.

Even Sammy's personal backers told him that he could do whatever he pleased—they would stand behind him.

The decision to break off—the decision not to see her again

and the decision to get married—all these were Sammy's own. The situation demanded action. He took it.

Has it helped any?

No. Both are miserable. Both go to great lengths not to meet at parties or in restaurants or at the studio.

This despite the fact that Sammy's mother and father and family like Kim, for she enthralled them when she visited them this year.

This, despite the fact that Kim's family likes Sammy, for he spent some time with them at the farm when he was in Chicago, and Kim's sister took the only photograph ever made of the two of them together. Sammy made sure it would never be printed—for he burned all the negatives.

Thus here are all the elements of a play that perhaps only an Arthur Miller could write with truth, with insight and with passion.

—*December 1958*

"WILL HOLLYWOOD BLACKBALL SAMMY DAVIS AND MAY BRITT?,"
by Hy Steirman, *Confidential*

By the time you read this, Sammy Davis, Jr., will be or will be about to be married to May Britt.

This might not be particularly startling information except for these facts: Davis has been called by Jerry Lewis, "the greatest entertainer of our time." May Britt is a highly successful young movie star.

Davis is a Negro American; May Britt is white and Swedish. He is a convert to Judaism; she is Protestant.

Mix these ingredients all together and you have, in America, a brew explosive enough to make the A-bomb look like a firecracker. While Frank Sinatra has commented that it's "nobody's damn business who Sammy wants to marry—except Sammy's," there are strong areas of prejudice in this country which may not let Sammy and May (pronounced My) lead their own lives.

Aware of this, May says, "We are quite aware that, loving each other and getting married, we shall have difficult problems to solve and many obstacles to overcome . . . It is possible we may happen to find hotels where we are not allowed to stay as husband and wife. There may be some states in America where we will not be received in the families. There may be public places where we will be obliged to part due to the different colors of our skins.

"Well, let it be so. We will avoid staying at these hotels and places, and not visiting these 'friends' will not be a great sacrifice to either of us."

It is apparent that both Sammy and May have worked hard and long at exploring the difficulties they will face. Commented Sammy to a friend: "I am not exactly handsome. I'm a Negro and a Jew and now I'm getting married. Any newly-married couple expects to face problems.

"I have my friends in Hollywood as I have in New York, Cleveland, Detroit and Chicago. These friends are the people you care about. You're concerned with what your friends and family think.

"You can't worry about the guy across the street or the fellow around the corner who's going to make trouble. You have to live your own life."

Just how do their friends feel about the wedding, bound to be the most controversial in the last two decades of show business? "My family is in full accord," says Sammy. "So are all my friends. Not one guy has said, 'Gee, you better think about this twice.' "

The brilliant entertainer was positive when asked what the leader of the Clan, Frank Sinatra, thought about it. "Frankie's best man, that's what he thinks about it."

Forgotten, of course, was the attempted interference by Frankie when Sammy and Kim Novak were thinking of getting married several years ago. It led to the blow-up that kept the two devoted friends apart for over a year. Sammy ended up not marrying Kim. How much of this was due to Frankie's powerful influence and how much of it was due to pressure from the super-sensitive Hollywood moguls no one is certain to this day.

One thing is sure—Sammy was caught in a maelstrom of prejudice during the Kim Novak affair. Not only was Sinatra upset, but the late Harry Cohn, head of Columbia pictures, called in Sammy and said, "Do you realize this girl is a $20 million property to me? Have a fling if you must—but don't get married."

Not long afterwards Cohn died of a heart attack. Some bitter executives state that it was tension caused by this romance that killed Cohn.

Additional pressures were put on Sammy by the William Morris Agency which manages Kim.

Another strong influence was a conversation between Sammy and Frankie which went something like this:

"Sammy, you're making a serious mistake."

The volatile and usually even-tempered Sammy was said to have exploded with, "You're a hell of a one to talk. You invented mistakes. You get away with murder and people love it. If I tried a tenth of what you do—they'd hang me in the morning."

Another story that made the rounds had gangsters visiting Sammy and telling him, "You have one eye—do you want to try for none?" Sammy has denied this but the story still makes the rounds to this day.

Perhaps the worst blow of all to the Sammy Davis–Kim Novak affair was Hollywood society. The couple could not go to the parties they had formerly attended. Although they were never seen in public together, every time Sammy spoke to a girl, columnists like Dorothy Kilgallen "itemed" the story. It got to the point where Sammy and Kim got "together" only by telephone and letter.

Hollywood had damned that romance!

Has the glittering city, which boasts that its show-business has no color lines, suddenly grown up? Will it accept the fact a young couple is getting married—or will the usual neurotic circus come to town? No one can be sure.

But the minute it was publicly announced that Sammy and May were engaged to be married, a studio official at 20th Century-Fox issued a statement that set the tone of treatment May could expect in Sammy's Hollywood. May Britt's contract won't be renewed when the option is due, said the official this past June. "It's no secret that her picture, *The Blue Angel*, was unsuccessful at the box office. We don't believe that we have any future work that would suit her."

Asked if the engagement to Sammy Davis had anything to do with the decision, the spokesman said no. However, one reporter said the man grimaced as he said it. The statement was made one week after the engagement announcement.

When the sound of the first shot died down, the screams of dismay could be heard round the world. Sammy's and May's friends rallied round the flag and let loose a barrage against 20th Century. This prompted Buddy Adler, late production chief, to issue the following statement. "May Britt is under long term contract to 20th Century-Fox and there is no factual basis for any story that the studio is terminating her contract."

No one is denying that 20th Century is taking a long hard look at the facts. While May admits that she still gets her weekly check, she is not quite sure just what her studio will do after the honeymoon is over.

Says May, "When I marry Sammy my films will not be shown in many states and towns. On that account I may be prevented from working. Should this happen, I will return to work in Europe where these race discriminations do not exist or are not so deeply felt."

Prejudice may not be as deep in some parts of Europe, but it certainly exists. When Sammy was in London on a personal appearance tour, after the announcement of his engagement, he was confronted by a group of demonstrators from Sir Oswald Mosley's British Fascist Union Movement. They were shouting, "Go home, nigger. Sammy back to the trees. Boycott the Sammy Davis show. We have no need for half-castes here."

Waving banners and growing ugly, about thirty of the demonstrators clashed with stagehands and police. After it was over a very sad Sammy remarked, "I never expected anything like this. I just cannot understand it.

"This is little London, England, not the nigger-hating South. I cannot get over it. This is 1960, not 150 years ago. If they start like this they will be lynching people in 20 years' time."

Newspapers showed their shame editorially. It was summed up by Cassandra, columnist for the 5 million circulation *Daily Mirror*, who wrote:

"Dear Sammy Davis.

"I don't know you. You don't know me. I have never seen your show and I assume you have never seen mine. All I know is what I read in the papers.

"But this is just to tell you that the beastly racial abuse to which you were subjected had nothing to do with what English people think and feel.

"I, and maybe I can speak for a few others (say 51,680,000 minus 100 of the population), feel revolted, angry and ashamed at what happened."

But the demonstration is the kind of wound you can't patch with a Band-aid. As the announcement of the engagement was made in England, Sammy and May had yet to learn how the U.S.A. felt about it. A self-assured Sammy commented, "I'm positive they're not small-minded enough to try to badger a guy into not marrying the girl he loves."

First hurdle for the engaged couple was New York. On the streets Sammy found he was being greeted with, "Hi, Sammy. Congratulations; she must be a wonderful girl."

Judging from the "guys on the streets" and the mail Sammy received, his own private poll indicated that 85% of the people were in favor of his marriage. Others were cautionary, telling him to make sure first. "About 2% of my mail has been the no-signature, hate letters," he said.

Still, there were, and are, predictions that the marriage won't work—not because of the bride and groom—but because of the glass house they live in.

Not only are the studio heads alarmed and May and Sammy concerned, despite the nonchalance and "who cares" attitude, but there have been several concrete examples that show how some people feel. Strangely enough one occurred at the Democratic national convention. There was a faint booing when Sammy Davis showed up with Frank Sinatra and Peter Lawford (Jack Kennedy's brother-in-law).

In Washington, D.C., George Lincoln Rockwell (see December, 1960, issue of *Confidential: America's Two-bit Hitler*) staged a demonstration against Davis. Rockwell's pro-Nazi group is the closest thing this country has to the English Mosley group.

A realistic May and Sammy have considered the fact that her career is in great jeopardy. As May points out privately, "It is true that I am fond of my work, but it is also true I would give it up for Sammy's love. I love him more than anything else in the world.

"I have never in my life known any prejudice. Why should I have to think about it now? After all, where I grew up in Sweden, we have no anti-Semitism."

May's father and Sammy are fast friends, so at least family and friends are rooting for him. Her father, Sammy and May herself are all for having lots of children. "I don't care if the kids are black, white or polka dot," says Sammy.

"For Sammy there are no barriers," says May, "but I am aware that this marriage is a crisis in my life. There are going to be race problems. Things may be tough at times.

"But whatever should happen to us, Sammy will make no scenes about insults offered. He is a quiet, peace-loving man who likes people.

"He is so honest, so open, so completely without phoniness, dynamic and full of life. And he needs loving as much as I do. Lots of it, and lots of children."

Comments Sammy, "Truthfully, I've had no panic signs yet. . . . I'm happy to tell you there's no problem and I just know there won't be."

Despite these brave words Sammy has confessed that "if the people of America want me to go to Europe to live because I'm going to marry May Britt, I'll do it.

"But I've got a flash for you. I just know that they don't feel that way. I'm positive they're not small-minded enough to badger a guy into not marrying the girl he loves."

A great American philosopher and President, Abraham Lincoln, once said, "America has faith in those who have faith in her."

Abe must have been right, for Sammy has been signed to do four TV shows, he has three movie scripts from which to choose and he's already booked ahead at the Buffalo Town Casino in Windsor, at the Las Vegas Sands, Lake Tahoe, San Francisco and the New York Copa.

While it becomes apparent that Sammy has too much talent to be blackballed, May has yet to be offered a movie or TV role in Hollywood since the engagement announcement. Only time can prove what Hollywood really thinks. Even if the party invitations don't come in, Sammy's friends are behind him because the Clan approves the marriage. Thus with Peter Lawford, Tony Curtis, Joey Bishop, Dean Martin and Jerry Lewis on his side, along with the king, Sinatra, Sammy Davis and May Britt could possibly end up with the happiest marriage in Hollywood—which would be a novelty in that town.

—*January 1961*

"ARE WHITE STARS SWITCHING TO NEGROES?,"
by Aaron Putnam, *Confidential*

"*Would you be happy if your blonde, blue-eyed daughter came home with a buck nigger and said she wanted to marry him?*"

This question shocked millions of radio listeners recently

when it was asked on an interview program of the British Broadcasting Corp. The speaker was Sir Gerald Nabarro, Member of Parliament.

His comment was an obvious reference to Sammy Davis, Jr., who had just arrived in London with his blonde, blue-eyed wife and their coffee-and-cream colored daughter.

Sammy ignored Sir Gerald's blast. His only reply was: "The word 'nigger' is rotten and stinks to high Heaven."

Then he told the British press that he planned to live in England with his family because "here in England there is freedom."

Subsequently, he received more than 100 threats of violence from British bigots. There was so much "freedom" that he hired two husky bodyguards to protect him and his Swedish spouse, May Britt.

Then he had trouble finding a suitable home. He heard that actor John Mills, father of teen-age star Hayley Mills, wanted to sell his country estate outside London. Davis offered to buy it, but Mills turned him down. Other estate owners also refused to sell their properties to Davis.

But the only surprising thing about Sammy's reception was his crack about England's freedom from racial prejudice. He should have known better. On a previous visit to London, demonstrators picketed his hotel and the nightclub where he was appearing.

"Go home, nigger," they shouted. "Sammy, go back to the trees."

Deeply hurt and close to tears, Sammy and May held a press conference at the time.

"I never expected anything like this," Sammy said. "This is London, England, not the nigger-hating South. I just cannot understand it."

Yet nothing like that ever happened to him in America. No pickets jeered him in New York, Hollywood or Miami. He never felt it necessary to hire bodyguards.

But the prejudice was there just the same. Sammy Davis found it out.

"It's impossible to hope to be accepted as an equal in any town if you are colored," Sammy once said. But he has learned it's even more impossible if you are colored and your wife is white.

When Hollywood was told that May Britt, the beautiful, blonde star, slated to become the second Marlene Dietrich, was to marry Sammy Davis, Hollywood turned against them. Strangely enough, so did Harlem.

It wasn't the first time a white movie star had switched her romantic interest from white men to colored men. But this particular switch was the most explosive—because they got married.

Many white movie stars (male and female) had crossed the color line and dated or even had love affairs—but very few ended in marriage. An interracial marriage seems to end the career of one, sometimes of both partners. In the case of Sammy Davis and May Britt, May's movie career was extinguished the minute she said, "I do," to Sammy Davis.

Sammy's preference for white girls has made him one of the most controversial men in *Show Biz*. His singing, dancing and acting talents were matched by his talent for getting involved with white women.

The former talents were what attracted Ava Gardner to the one-eyed Negro entertainer. She liked him so much she once wrote an article about him for a Negro magazine. The article, bearing Ava Gardner's byline, was titled "Sammy Sends Me."

It is legend in Harlem that after catching his act at the Apollo Theater, Ava accompanied him to a nearby nightspot for a round of hand-holding and elbow-bending.

When word of this got around, the columnists began speculating on a big romance. The South was horrified.

Luscious Lana Turner also adored Sammy. When he played a top Hollywood night club, she always arrived alone for the last show and stayed that way until Davis joined her after his act.

Another of his ardent admirers was super-sexy starlet Meg Myles, famed for her 42-inch frontage. And there were others—screen stars and starlets, Las Vegas chorines, even a blonde elevator operator who got a lift out of Sammy. He was, in effect, a one-man integration specialist for white stars.

Biggest explosion to rock Hollywood occurred when Kim Novak switched to Sammy Davis. This was the torrid romance of the century.

Sammy once told pals he couldn't understand how Kim could fall for "a one-eyed, flat-nosed ugly like me." But she did.

They tried to keep their romance secret, confining their dates to private parties and quiet evenings at home in L.A. and Chicago. But Hollywood columnists learned what was going on and started honing their sharpest knives.

Pressure from friends and studio executives began building up to the explosion point, Frank Sinatra, an old pal of both Sammy and Kim, warned Sammy to go easy.

"You're making a terrible mistake," he said.

"You're a hell of a one to talk," Sammy replied. "You invented mistakes. You get away with 'murder.' If I tried a tenth of what you do, they'd hang me."

There was a widely-circulated report that two strong-arm goons collared Sammy outside a Las Vegas night club and threatened: "You now have one eye. Would you like to try for none? That's what'll happen if you don't leave Novak alone."

The late Harry Cohn, Columbia Pictures president and the man who made Kim a star, finally called Sammy on the carpet and stormed: "Do you realize you're fooling around with a $20 million piece of property?

"Have a fling if you must," he added. "But don't get married!"

Soon after this meeting, Cohn died of a heart attack. Some Columbia executives believe the Novak-Davis romance contributed to his fatal seizure.

In the sobering spotlight of publicity, Kim and Sammy decided to stop dating. Then Sammy announced his surprise marriage to Loray White, a beautiful sepia singer. Whether or not this merger was arranged by Columbia Pictures, as some Hollywood insiders claim, it lasted only three months.

Davis then began pursuing May Britt, a long-legged, blue-eyed Swede whose resemblance to Kim was more than coincidental.

May, who starred in a remake of the old Marlene Dietrich hit, *Blue Angel*, was being groomed to be a new Screenland sexsation. But her Hollywood career ended when she married Sammy. His movie work also fell off, although his nightclub popularity didn't suffer.

An unwritten law in Hollywood is that interracial romance is okay, so long as it's kept quiet, but interracial marriage is taboo.

Top Negro stars such as Lena Horne, Dorothy Dandridge, Eartha Kitt and Harry Belafonte have married outside their race. But no top Box Office white star has married a Negro, despite the current trend to integrated romance.

Hollywood was shaken to its tinsel foundations last year by rumors that its two *Most Valuable Players* had formed their own exclusive sports club. These sizzling reports concerned the friendship between Doris Day, Hollywood's vestal virgin, and Maury Wills, base-stealing shortstop of the Los Angeles Dodgers baseball team.

Maury was voted the National League's Most Valuable Player of 1962. And Doris, the world's biggest box-office attraction, has long been Movieland's M.V.P.

Doris has always been a sports fan, so no one was particularly surprised when she rented a season box next to the Dodgers' dugout. And at first no one realized she was rooting for the fleet-footed Negro shortstop more than his teammates.

"Sight-to-see at Dodgers Stadium when the Dodgers play," reported Walter Winchell, "is Doris Day (she never sits down at the games) rooting hard. She occupies the field box next to the Dodgers' dugout. So she can greet the players every evening with a blown kiss, etc. . . . ."

Long about mid-season last year, other fans began noticing that DD was blowing one player more kisses than the rest. But this seemed only natural, since Maury Wills was then heading for a new record.

In the process, Hollywood gossips say, the base burglar also stole his favorite fan's heart. The rumors gathered momentum at the end of the season when it was reported that Doris and her husband, composer-producer Marty Melcher, were nearing the end of their marriage.

"One of the 10 most famous females in show business can't convince her best friends that her interest in a ballplayer is strictly professional," commented Hearst columnist Dorothy Kilgallen. "She isn't having much luck convincing her husband, either . . ."

"The whole thing is absurd," Melcher said of the rumors. "I love my wife. She's a wonderful girl."

Then he packed his bags and moved out of their $250,000 Beverly Hills home. Doris also avoided the press, but by this time newspaper headlines informed the world that the separation rumors were true.

The movie moguls were stunned. They had spent millions molding Doris into the image of America's "girl next door." Her publicity buildup made fans forget she was at least 40, had been married three times and had a 21-year-old son.

Her father, divorced from her mother, married a Negro a few years ago. The Hollywood rajahs feared Doris might follow his example unless they took drastic steps to prevent such a merger.

Every major studio has an interest in her career, for Doris makes movies for them all and almost all her films are big moneymakers. So the pressures applied to DD and Maury must have been enormous.

In desperation, MGM press agents tried to create a new love interest that might be more acceptable to DD fans. They came up with ruggedly handsome Stephen Boyd, her leading man in *Jumbo*. Studio flacks informed columnists that Steve, not Maury, was the new knight for Day.

New York columnist Earl Wilson dutifully reported: "Girl-Next-Door Doris Day's new heart interest isn't a baseball player, but her somewhat younger leading man, Stephen Boyd."

But Steve refused to be a smoke-screen. As soon as *Jumbo*

was finished, he flew back to England. Reporters mobbed the British actor at London Airport and demanded to know if it was true he planned to wed Doris.

"I'm flabbergasted," he replied. "It's so false and ridiculous I have no words."

Despite the many column items and rumors, the consensus in Hollywood is that Doris Day and Maury do have a common interest—religion (Christian Science), and this interest should not be construed as a romance or even a flirtation. "Can't a white woman talk with a Negro without being accused of a love affair," commented one writer. "She is definitely not switching to Negroes."

One colored fighter was never seen in public with a white woman, but his boudoir services were in such great demand that *three* Hollywood Love Goddesses shared him—and all three seemed sublimely happy with this arrangement.

An Oscar-winning actress once supported a Negro folk singer for over a year. When she realized he didn't want to work she switched back to white men.

A famous Negro singer, married to a gorgeous girl of his own race, pays the rent of a blonde, Las Vegas dancer. She stopped dating other men, even though he could only be with her one or two weekends a month.

One of Hollywood's top actors, a much-married man with a wife and several children, once kept two mistresses in the same apartment. One was white, the other colored. He admits, "I'm not prejudiced."

During his first two marriages, José Ferrer became an expert on integrated amour.

His first wife was Uta Hagen, who recently won the Antoinette Perry Award for the year's best performance as an actress in the Broadway stage show, *Who's Afraid of Virginia Woolf?*

It was a wolf of a different color that broke up the Ferrer-Hagen togetherness. Specifically, a black-and-Red wolf named Paul Robeson.

Back in 1946, José and Uta did *Othello* with the Negro actor-singer in the leading role. As the show traveled around the country, the Ferrers refused to stay in any hotel that would not rent a room to Robeson. The three became very close.

Uta and Robeson, in fact, became even closer than the *Othello* script called for. After playing scorching love scenes on stage each night, they went right on playing long after the curtain came down.

Returning unexpectedly to his Detroit hotel suite one evening, José caught Desdemonda and the Moor in the midst of an off-stage undress rehearsal that definitely was not in the original script.

Ferrer was highly indignant to find his wife engaging in such un-American activities with an avowed Communist. So the road show was terminated abruptly. The Ferrers returned to New York and set up housekeeping in separate quarters.

While working on his Broadway production of *Cyrano de Bergerac*, José hired private detectives to spy on Uta. They began a round-the-clock watch on her new home, a four-story brownstone on Manhattan's elegant East Side.

One night shortly before Christmas of 1946, the private eyes saw Robeson enter the brownstone. They phoned Ferrer and he came hotfooting over to lead a two a.m. raid on his wife's domicile.

Bursting into her digs, the raiders gathered enough evidence to win José an alimony-free divorce. It was the best Christmas present he ever had.

After his divorce, José married Phyliss Hill, a shapely starlet who played a small role in the Broadway production of *Cyrano*. They separated a few years later, for the usual Hollywood reasons, and he set off for Europe to make *Moulin Rouge*.

During a stopover in London, he bumped into an old pal, sepia singer Pearl Bailey. They promptly got integrated.

José and Pearl became such a torrid twosome that London gossipests predicted she would become the third Mrs. Ferrer.

But Pearl had other plans. She suddenly married Louis Bellson, a white drummer formerly employed in Duke Ellington's band. Gallantly, José threw a party for Pearl and her skin-thumper. Then he dutifully kissed the bride and light-heartedly went his way.

Mixed marriages, rare among actors and actresses, are commonplace on the musical side of Show Business. Almost every popular Negro singer attracts admirers outside his race. If there seems to be a trend, in the past decade, for white stars to date Negroes, the reverse is also true. Negro stars are switching to whites.

Harlem-born Harry Belafonte, for example, has received proposals and propositions from thousands of white women. His name has been linked romantically to such Hollywood beauties as actress Joan Fontaine and sexpot Tina Louise.

Harry and Joan were the stars of *Island in the Sun*, first American movie to deal with a love affair between a Negro and a white woman. Though the screen romance never got beyond the hand-holding stage, this was more than enough to stir up the bigots, segregationists, Ku Klux Klan and Black Muslims.

Belafonte couldn't understand what all the shouting was about.

For nine years, Harry was married to Frances Marguerite Byrd, a beautiful, light-skinned Negro who is both a practicing psychiatrist and fashion model.

A week after they were divorced in 1957, he married Julie Robinson, only white member of the Katherine Dunham dance troupe.

Whether Belafonte's second marriage hurt his career is debatable. He still earns more than $1 million a year.

No one ever called Lena Horne "controversial." She has been married to white musician Lennie Hayden for 15 years without a hint of criticism or scandal.

Lena has a son and daughter from a previous marriage. Her lovely daughter, Gail, is the steady date of director Sidney Lumet, estranged husband of heiress Gloria Vanderbilt. But their marriage plans have been frustrated by Gloria's refusal to give Lumet a divorce.

Before she married William McDonald, wealthy Los Angeles real estate dealer, sexotic singer Eartha Kitt was pursued by some of the world's most notorious wolves. Her passionate playmates included the late Aly Khan, Orson Welles, the Marquess of Milford-Haven, Porfirio Rubirosa, and Arthur Loew, Jr., heir to the Loew theater millions.

A Negro newspaperman once asked Eartha why she never dated men of her own race (after she selected her ten favorite men, all white, for a Negro publication).

"When I'm on stage," she retorted, "I belong to the public. When I'm offstage, I reserve the right to select my own friends."

Eartha teamed up with Orson Welles in Paris to co-star in his production of *Faust*. The portly actor escorted her around the Paris bistros, but the jealousy bug bit him when he learned he wasn't her only date.

Then Orson, in turn, bit Eartha.

While they were playing a tender love scene in front of the cameras, he chewed her luscious lower lip so hard it bled. Later, Eartha told reporters that when she asked Welles why he behaved in such an ungentlemanly fashion, he merely muttered something about women being no damn good.

Some observers thought Welles was just *'orsin'* around. Or maybe he was hungry. But a more logical explanation is that he was piqued by the huge emerald ring that had suddenly appeared on Eartha's fingers.

Orson thought the emerald was a gift from his rival of the moment, Prince Aly Khan. Actually, it was presented to Eartha by Aly's father, the late Aga Khan, who always had an eye for ambulating artworks.

When it came to meeting millionaires, Eartha was a *Do-It-Yourself Kitt*. Some of the richest men on earth contributed to her collection of baubles, bangles and beaux.

Society columnist Cholly Knickerbocker once wrote:

"Eartha Kitt's current romance would end in marriage if she and her adorer were just Miss Nobody and Mr. Anybody. But he's the son of a famous tycoon who would disown him if the story reached the headlines."

The guy was the playboy heir of one of the world's greatest banking families. He was willing to risk his father's wrath to marry Eartha, but she dropped him for another millionaire.

Her romance with Arthur Loew, Jr., also seemed to be headed for the altar. Then he suddenly switched his affections to Debbie Minardos, beautiful widow of Tyrone Power. Their marriage hit Eartha hard.

"After she broke up with Arthur and even after he married," a friend says, "Eartha kept a picture of him in her bedroom for a long time."

A real racial storm in a teapot was brewed by the one and only Tempest Storm.

So far as her Hollywood neighbors were concerned, the statuesque stripper lived up to her stage name when she wed Negro singer Herb Jeffries. Tempest gambled her million-dollar career on the mixed mating. And though she still is America's favorite peeler, she lost both the marriage and her chance of becoming a movie star.

Dixie devotees of the G-string art were particularly incensed by her inter-racial merger, for this peeling belle was born and bred in Florida.

She first met Herb at a party in her Beverly Hills mansion. Like the *Man Who Came to Dinner*, he returned for seconds and then stayed on and on. Personal friends and professional co-workers advised her she was heading for trouble, but she ignored the Storm warnings.

When Herb popped the question, Tempest answered "Yes." Before they could be married, however, there were a few technical problems to overcome. One of these was that Jeffries already had a legal spouse.

His white wife, Betty, was a former Rose Bowl princess. She

agreed to get a divorce. Then she suddenly suffered a nervous breakdown and had to be confined to a hospital.

Herb's divorce finally came through and he wed the superbly-stacked stripper in San Francisco City Hall.

Though Hollywood frowned on the Storm-Jeffries mating, their nightclub careers grew bigger than ever. As a husband-and-wife act, they were a smash hit.

Herb's earnings began to approximate his take back in the days when he was the toast of Paris and Hollywood—before his career took a sudden dive. His new popularity also brought him many new fans, mostly young, white and female.

The babes apparently succeeded where bigotry failed. Fed up with watching predatory dolls stalk her handsome hubby, flame-haired Tempest booted Jeffries out of their Beverly Hills lovenest and filed for divorce, three years after the wedding.

Like Jeffries, Billy Daniels is a part-Negro singer who could pass for white. He too has been married to three white women. His first wife killed herself; the other two divorced him.

"The feeling we had for each other was trampled to death by other women," said second wife Martha Braun, a fashion model and society beauty. "There were dozens of them— blondes, brunettes and redheads; chorus cuties and society belles; married and single; beautiful, homely and in-between.

"And all of them were white!"

Singer-actress Dorothy Dandridge has worked in many nightclubs where, as she puts it, "Negroes were not permitted to socialize." But that didn't prevent well-heeled wolves from wanting to socialize with her.

In affairs of the heart, she ignores the so-called color line. Her first husband was Negro dancer Harold Nicholas. The second was white Jack Denison, Hollywood restaurant owner. Both marriages ended in divorce.

A few years ago, Dorothy was courted by dashing, debonair Curt Jurgens, Germany's multimillionaire actor. He wanted to marry her, but a Hollywood blackball broke up their romance.

On his return to Europe, Jurgens told the press:

"I could have braved the American prejudice toward people of color and led a happy life with the one I loved—in Europe. But Dorothy's life and career are in America. She could not resign herself to give them up. These links were stronger than her love for me."

After the Jurgens affair, Dotty's career went into a tailspin. She remained a nightclub headliner, but the movie roles that had made her the world's most famous Negro actress suddenly stopped. Early this year, a few months after she divorced Denison, Dorothy filed a bankruptcy petition.

Though she earned more than $100,000 the past two years, she was broke.

Walter Winchell quoted her as saying: "No matter how well balanced a woman may be, too much sex and sin—even if it is only play acting—is dangerous."

No matter what other faults he has, no one could ever accuse Marlon Brando of racial prejudice. His taste is truly universal and has included such exotic dishes as chocolate bon-bons, Chinese fortune cookies, Mexican tamales and American cheesecake.

His first wife, Anna Kashfi, was a Welsh rarebit who was raised in India. Second spouse Movita is a sultry Mexican spitfire. Between marriages, he romanced such sexy starlets as France Nuyen (Chinese-French), Rita Moreno (Puerto Rican) and Barbara Luna (Hungarian-Filipino).

He has dated Negroes, Polynesians, Orientals, Caucasians and mixtures of all four. Harlem cuties, slant-eyed Saigon sexpots, Australian beauties, Tahitian temptresses and Continental charmers are all in his little black books.

Marlon could be setting the pace for Hollywood stars of the future. For he realizes that Cupid is color blind.

As one psychiatrist put it, "Many people are fascinated by miscegenation, the crossing of the races. The big breakthrough in thinking came after World War II when thousands of GI's, stationed in Japan during their courting years (the early 20's), dated and married Japanese girls.

"Today, the emergence of African nations has given greater status to the Negro.

"Of course some men and women are so guilt-ridden by anti-Negro feelings that the pendulum swings in the opposite direction. To prove they are *not* prejudiced, they date and some even marry men and women of other races. The more of it there is, the more commonplace it becomes. I wouldn't say Hollywood stars are switching in this direction, they are simply ahead of the rest of the nation in dropping racial barriers."

—*September 1963*

"SAMMY DAVIS, JR.'S, PHONY ROMANCES WITH WHITE STARS,"
by George Roberts, *National Police Gazette*

It was a small, private gathering, so the story goes, just Marilyn Monroe, her escort, photographer Milton Green and singer Mel Tormé. The table was small, the Hollywood night club jam packed and the press photographer was having trouble fitting the threesome into the picture. "Ready . . . say cheese," the cameraman said. "Hold it," came a frenzied shout. It was the nightclub's headliner, singer Sammy Davis, Jr.

With a smile, a shove, and a push, Sammy made the trio into a cramped quartet.

That was a few years ago, but Sammy hasn't changed!

It's been said that Sammy Davis, Jr., can smell the odor of a flashbulb before it's popped!

"He's a lens lover," a movie official told the *Police Gazette*. "He isn't at all camera-shy, especially when a film actress is ready to say 'cheese' for the birdie."

The multi-talented Negro entertainer manages to thrust his face into many photos being taken of filmland's famous stars. And when all is said and done, there's Sammy, on page one with the most glamourous of Hollywood's guys and dolls.

For example, take the time in 1954, when Frank Sinatra and

Kim Novak were making the film, "The Man with the Golden Arm." Wherever Frankie goes—Sammy is sure to follow. Sinatra is a big name, big names cluster around the crooner from Hoboken, and big names are the big game that Sammy Davis, Jr., likes.

Between takes, in Sinatra's dressing room, Sammy was questioning Frankie about the newest Hollywood chick, Kim Novak. Now Sammy is not at all bashful about asking someone for a favor. One thing led to another and Sinatra, a guy who couldn't care less, introduced the Negro entertainer to the honey-haired movie queen.

Kim Novak was very polite to her co-star's buddy; Sammy out-gushed himself in trying to make Kim aware of his charms. A ten minute chat, that was all, or so thought Kim Novak. How wrong she was.

For the next two weeks the night-clubbing Kim had a constant shadow. Wherever Kim and her perennial escort, Mac Krim, real-estate broker, went, there was Sammy hopping over to their table to "have just one drink." But if the photographers came over to take Miss Novak's picture . . . *No, he wouldn't mind getting in this one . . .*

Louella and Hedda picked up the story. The scandal magazines sent out their writers, who, without one shred of evidence, printed the story of the alleged lovers; Negro singer and white movie-star. Miss Novak was as helpless as the owner of a sick puppy.

"No!" cried Kim Novak to the besieging reporters. "It's not even worth a comment."

But when Sammy Davis, Jr., faced the newspapermen it was a different story. It wasn't what he said that kept the tongues wagging, rather it was what he didn't say, and how he didn't say it. A leer, a carefree grin; a "well you know how it is, boys, some guys got it and some guys ain't," type of attitude. The members of the press are sharp. They knew what Sammy was implying . . . and they wrote it just that way.

A few months ago, a scandal sheet kept the fires burning by

writing a story filled with innuendoes about the romance, a romance, by the way, that never was.

With this in mind, the editors of the *Police Gazette* interviewed Kim at a fashionable hotel in New York. Her plush suite overlooked Central Park, it afforded a magnificent view to anyone who could peel his eyes off the lovely film beauty.

Explodes Romance Myth

In a soft, almost husky voice, Miss Novak said to us:

"This is the first time I denied this to anyone."

"Why is that?" we asked.

"Because I was afraid," she said, "that the public would get the impression that I'm against a person because of his color.

"But the fact is," she continued, "that the rumors were and are malicious. They tried to infer things that never happened."

"Did you ever date Sammy?"

"I have never even been alone with Sammy, no less date him. That's the truth," she said. "You know," she continued, "I'm worried."

"Why are you worried, Miss Novak?"

"Because," her blue eyes blazing, "you can't express yourself in matters of this kind without getting into trouble."

We assured her that the *Police Gazette* would print only what she said.

"It's a great tragedy," she continued, "when the gossip-mongers spread such stories about Sammy and me. I never even had any interest in him. I used to see him at parties or nite-clubs. But I always had another date," she explained.

"Exactly how do you feel about Sammy?" we asked.

"He's a great entertainer and we're friends. Please," she begged, "don't make it sound like I don't care to be linked with a Negro. That's not true."

"Are you in love, Miss Novak?"

"No," she answered. "I have never been in love with anyone. If I were I'd be married. I dated Mac Krim for a long time. I like him very, very much. But I don't feel that I love him."

That was that! Miss Novak had exploded the Sammy Davis, Jr., myth.

A Ring for Eartha Kitt

One of the most amusing incidents concerning Sammy, happened during his chase after sultry Negro singer, Eartha Kitt.

He came to her one evening, a 7-carat diamond ring in hand. "For you," he said.

"But, Sammy," Eartha answered, "we're not engaged."

"Maybe we will be later . . . just wear it as a friendship ring."

A few days later, Sammy Davis, Jr., announced his engagement to Miss Kitt. She sent back the ring and gave a flat denial to the newspapers.

"He's a very nice boy," Eartha said. "I like him but he's very mixed-up."

About that time movie-hero Jeff Chandler, got a watch from Sammy. It was inscribed: "To Jeff—thanks for the shoulder."

"I don't remember the incident," explained Mr. Chandler, "or which girl it was he cried to me about. And he probably doesn't remember either."

Frank Sinatra who was still living with Ava Gardner, introduced Sammy to her four years ago.

"Hi," said Ava.

And Sammy started day-dreaming.

The Sinatra-Gardner duet became a solo, each of them going their independent ways, Sinatra to royalty and Ava to bullfighters.

Ava came to New York on a publicity jaunt. Sammy called her and asked if she would appear on stage with him at the Apollo Theater. She assented, and with her New York squire, disk jockey Bill Williams, Ava posed for the photographers with Sammy.

Sammy had a field day: He put his arms around her shoulders, the flashbulbs exploded; he held hands with her, the flashbulbs exploded; he rested his cheek against hers, the flashbulbs exploded.

Ava's studio bosses squirmed in their chairs. Ava had done Sammy a favor. It was over, she thought. She was wrong.

The Negro performer called her up a few days later: "You can do me a terrific favor, Ava," Sammy began. "I've got a chance to make the cover of "Our World" magazine, but I've got to get a big name performer to be in the picture with me. Huh?"

What Sammy had neglected to tell Ava was that he had tried to get Italian beauty Gina Lollobrigida, but she refused.

Bill Williams explained why Ava had accepted: "Ava is one of the sweetest gals you can meet. She'll help anyone out."

The story eventually appeared in the December issue of "Our World," under the title "Sammy Sends Me." Soon other magazines used stories suggesting that there was more than just a professional interest and routine friendship between Ava and Sammy. The articles in fact said little and proved less. But overnight, Ava's friendship with Sammy became an infection point for gossip. Ava's reputation had been hurt. Sammy did little to relieve the pressure exerted on Ava.

Ava Gardner's Story

Bill Williams said: "To have such a twisted story come out about the kid is disgusting. There's no truth to the inferences they tried to write into their stories. It's a shame that a girl like Ava, who tries to be so regular and help everybody, has to get the dirty end of the stick."

Ava Gardner was finally forced to make a public statement: "It was a completely innocent thing. I've known Sammy for a few years and it wasn't that kind of relationship in the beginning, nor will it be that way."

But Sammy kept on making headlines with white girls. Meg Myles star of the "Phenix City Story" was linked with Sammy. Meg was going with a Caucasian friend of the Negro singer. Sammy didn't bother to deny the story. Meg Myles was not a big enough star to fight the gossip and her career has suffered considerably.

When asked why he is seldom seen with Negro girls, Sammy said: "The colored girls who would be right for me, I never meet. I never get invited to the home of anybody who has an eligible daughter. I walk a road that is very lonesome."

But Sammy didn't stay lonesome very long. He found and escorted some delectable colored girlfriends. First he went with Harlem models, Ruth King and Toni Harris. Then the papers talked of the forthcoming marriage between Sammy and sepiasongstress, Dorothy Dandridge. A girl, inexplicably called China Doll, walked for a few brief moments hand in hand with Sammy. He became engaged to the windy-city beauty, Claudia King. But the romance wilted.

Sammy's Marriage Failed

At last, on January 10, 1958, Sammy Davis, Jr., married a singer, Loray White, at the Sands Hotel in Las Vegas. Miss White had just received a Mexican annulment from her former husband, Frank Gallo.

Harry Belafonte served as best man. One face was notable by its absence, Frank Sinatra's.

The marriage lasted three months. The whispered cause of the estrangement and ultimate divorce . . . the missing guest Frank Sinatra.

It seems that Frank Sinatra was playing at the Sands in Las Vegas. Sammy wanted to see his friend, Frankie. He wanted to fly to Vegas and he wanted to fly alone.

"It's just ridiculous," said Sammy, "she knows the feeling I have for Frankie."

"I told her to put my stuff in cases and I'd move over to my grandmother's house.

"There is no divorce in sight," Sammy insisted, "but as for the future, as much as I do care, I couldn't care less."

But his wife did get a divorce. And now that Sammy is back

on the prowl he'll probably get more publicity from romances that he never enjoyed. All the girls that ever knew him, say simply: "He's a nice guy." But as a lover, poor Sammy Davis, Jr., is a very funny guy.

—February 1959

"WHY SAMMY'S NEGRO FRIENDS WANT HIM TO LEAVE MAY!,"
Movie Mirror

A young man . . . a Negro, walking past a poster on a building in New York, looked up and read the words announcing Sammy's appearance in the Broadway play, *Golden Boy*. He turned to his companion and said, "That's what happens when they get rich. They all move away from their people and marry white folks." His friend, a trumpet player who has played with all the top bands and fills in when a recording studio in New York needs extra musicians answered: "I've been around Sammy, man, and if you think he's forgotten his people, you're out of your skull. Sammy Davis didn't wash off his black skin in his fancy Hollywood swimming pool. And what about the kid he and his white wife adopted? He wasn't a white kid. He was a Negro." The first man, the one who accused Sammy of running out on the Negro people, answered: "Just the same. If he weren't a millionaire, do you think he'd have gotten himself a beautiful white wife?"

This story was told to us by the musician. "I don't understand it," he said. "It's discrimination, just the same as what went on when a lot of white people threatened Sammy and Miss Britt before they got married. But, if they do get divorced, a lot of folks I know, black folks, are going to be pretty happy about it. There's a lot of resentment about colored entertainers marrying out of their race. Like Harry Belafonte and Lena Horne, Eartha Kitt, even Marian Anderson, and Billy Daniels and Pearl Bailey. Folks say: 'What's the matter with them? Are they too good for their own people, now?' Like I say, I don't understand it but it's there."

If they do get divorced . . . Was it true about Sammy and May? Four years of marriage. The birth of a daughter and the adoption of a son. The brave stand the couple took in the face of so much criticism. Was the marriage going to end, and if it was, would it end on that most ironic note of all . . . cheered on to its dissolution by the voices of Sammy Davis' own people . . .

The rumors of a break-up in the marriage of Sammy Davis and May Britt are not new ones. Almost from the beginning, the union of an American Negro and a blonde freckled-faced beauty from Sweden was cast into the shadows . . . shadows that forecast imminent divorce everytime the couple was separated for even the briefest moments of time. When Sammy would travel to location for a film, leaving May behind with their two children, the gossip columnists predicted trouble. The current whispers, however, seem to be riding on the strongest tidal wave of dissension ever. Sammy, busy in New York with rehearsals for his Broadway play, *Golden Boy*, countered the first hints of trouble by sending for May last spring. She joined him and their good friends, Richard Burton and Elizabeth Taylor, at a closed circuit telecast on behalf of the National Association for the Advancement of Colored People. She was also present at several parties with Davis and the Burtons, and voiced her pleasure at the news that Sammy would sign up for a role with Liz and Dick in their newest film, *The Sandpiper*. But, her flight back to the Coast left the gossip columnists wondering why, if Sammy was going to be on Broadway for at least a year, she didn't take an apartment in New York to be with him.

Surprisingly, a good deal of the detractors were not white people, although Sammy and May were subjected to agonies by too many brutal and disgusting demonstrations that were carried on by white critics as far away as London when they first married. Surprisingly, many Negroes, it was recalled, had advised the couple not to marry, and many others, today, confide that they would not be against the possibility of a divorce between Sammy and May.

A lot of them quote author James Baldwin's comment to white people: "I don't want to marry your sister . . . I just want you to get off my back." One pretty chorus girl, a Negro, said: "I now get calls to dance in Broadway shows. In a mixed group. Once I had to cross my fingers and hope for a colored revue, or wait for an opening in a floor show in a nightclub in a colored neighborhood. Now I can dance on Broadway with girls from all over the country. But it's still tough. I don't even go out with these girls after the show because I don't want to have a columnist writing up that I'm with a white fellow, even if he's only a friend of a girl I work with. Right away I'll start getting calls from my family. They'll tell me not to get stuck up and not to forget who and what I am. I feel sorry for Mr. Davis. I know what he must be thinking and going through. But, I understand how my family feels, too."

Militant voices amongst several Negro groups have been stressing the separation of the races. All upheavals . . . all social changes . . . are accompanied by extremes of every degree. The civil rights issue has been clouded over by so many varying shades of dissension. As a result, if Sammy and May are currently going through a marital disturbance, the very fact that they are an interracial couple is bound to cause comment from both black and white who will be quick to point out . . . "I told you so."

This will not be the first time Sammy's personal life has been attacked by critics using a racial angle. After Sammy was divorced from his first wife, a Negro dancer, Loray White, he was engaged to a strikingly lovely, blonde Canadian girl, Joan Stuart. Joan, who has been called a lookalike for Kim Novak, admitted that her own family very strongly opposed the match. Her mother frankly said: "It's disgusting." Nevertheless Joan and Sammy went ahead and planned a wedding. Then, Sammy announced that they had broken their engagement. "We know that our marriage would invite hostility. We were aware of the tall mountains we'd have to climb and the cross we'd have to bear. I didn't care. I'd love Joan if she were white, green, yellow or polka-dot, but other things entered the picture . . ." Even then, in 1960, there were rumors that Sammy was advised by people very close to him that "it wouldn't work and you'll only be hurting the girl more than yourself." However, shortly after his break-up with Joan, Sammy married May Britt. At the ceremony, he refused, at first, to kiss his new wife in front of the photographers. "There are enough haters in the world already who are waiting for that shot." Later, he relented. When May's father, Mr. Hugo Wilkins, was asked how he felt about his new son-in-law, the tall, sturdy Swede answered: "He is a wonderful person. I'm happy that my daughter has married him." A rabbi united Sammy and May in a traditional Jewish ceremony. A wine glass, wrapped in a napkin, was placed on the floor. Sammy crushed the glass, thus recalling, as all Jewish bridegrooms do, in the midst of his own personal happiness, the history of unhappiness of the Jewish people since the destruction of the second Temple two thousand years ago. The fact that Sammy Davis had converted to Judaism (as had May, who had been born a Lutheran) was recalled by every newspaper that covered the story of the wedding. In reading these accounts, Sammy may have remembered what other Negroes said when he became a Jew. "The charge made against me is that I want to be white. That accusation hurts. I have been accused of being Anti-Negro," Sammy said. His voice broke. He seemed almost about to cry. "The rules which are set up by Negroes and whites against a Negro in the spotlight are so strenuous they're impossible to live up to . . . Anyway, the most prejudiced people in the world are the oppressed. They have no other way to fight back, so they fight prejudice with prejudice . . . I have to watch myself more closely than any progressive man of the white race . . . The most frustrating thing about being a Negro performer is that you live with a tug of war going on to decide who your friends are going to be. I don't want to be a martyr. I know I'm a Negro. I've never forgotten it.

How can I, when I look in the mirror every morning. But, I'm ready to fight for my right to pick my own friends. And my religion is my business."

As for his alleged marriage troubles now, whatever the reasons the gossip columnists feel are strong enough to break him and May up, they are not racial ones. Both of these people have long ago proved themselves in their fight against bigotry and hate. May, in her gentle, quiet way, has fought a battle from the very moment she decided to marry Sammy. She bore a child knowing all the time she carried little Tracey, that so many people waited for the baby's birth with cruel commentary . . . "just to see what color it would be." She and Sammy waited for it with faith because this child was the fruit of their marriage and their love for each other.

Sammy has been a fighter ever since he was a child himself. "Momma," he once cried, his bloody head resting against his mother's breast; his lips battered from a cruel beating he had just gotten from two other boys. "Momma. Why did they hit me?" She led him to a mirror and pointed. The little boy understood. "I'll fight back," he vowed, "in the best way I know how." And he fought back. He fought for his right to dignity. "I refused to be just a hoofer, sleeping in bus stations between jobs. I wanted to communicate with my audience . . . to tell them . . . 'look . . . I'm a man!' " But can Sammy fight against his own people . . . the people who also remember when they looked into a mirror once and realized they were living in a white man's world, but somehow, they would have to live *in it*, and try to live *with it*.

"It doesn't surprise me," another entertainer said. She had been married to a white man; had had a child and then divorced her husband. "Marriage is tough enough if you're the same color. I wish I had married a man of my own race. My husband was a good man; a gentle man, but I hated to see that look in his eyes when people stared at me after he introduced me. He was so hurt."

In discussing the rapidly changing attitudes of people, Lena

Horne described a trip she took to speak to a rally. "I was scared to death," she said, "not of the white people in the South, but of the Negroes.

"Frankly, I was afraid they might reject me. After all, who am I to go to Jackson, Mississippi, to give these people any of my worldly wisdom? These people are living the battle every minute of their lives. I would be grateful if they (the Negroes) didn't throw eggs. They didn't throw eggs. They were kind. But if that rally had been in New York they would have thrown eggs." Miss Horne indicated that several members of her race had already told her in essence, "what do you know about anything we live with? You are married to a white man; you live in a swanky house; *you live in a white world*."

In talking with many of these people, Sammy's words come back . . . "My own people have accused me of wanting to be white . . ." His marriage to May must have justified that opinion in the minds of Sammy's accusers. Now, with the marriage rumored to be in trouble, one might understand why those who want the couple to separate are making their feelings known. If only Sammy Davis could meet them all, face to face, and repeat what he has said before: "I've never forgotten I'm a Negro . . . I have never forgotten what it was like to be a Negro growing up, nor a Negro trying to make it in the world. And, I never did nor ever will forget my people. But, I must lead my life the way I have to."

—*November 1964*

"WHY SINATRA KEEPS MIA AWAY FROM SAMMY DAVIS, JR.,"
by Tad Dean, *Movie Mirror*

It's no secret that Sammy Davis has not been a visitor to the home of Mr. and Mrs. Francis Albert Sinatra. Mia, Frank's lovely bride, has yet to play hostess to Sammy or to his lovely blonde wife, May Britt.

As a matter of fact, it's no secret that Frank has deliberately taken steps to keep Mia away from Sammy now and it would appear that the talented entertainer is the only member of the Clan . . . or ex-member, if you prefer, who never kissed the bride.

There are two reasons for this snub. The first is based on an old story; the second on a twist of fate that intruded just when Frank and Sammy, according to several insiders, were about to forgive and forget the past and give their old friendship still another try.

Let us take you back a little in time so that you will get the older picture clear in your mind and then you might understand why the first ice crystals formed in what was once a warm and close relationship.

Sammy Davis, Jr., was doing his usual routine, belting "Birth of the Blues" to an appreciative dinner show audience in the Copa Room of the Sands Hotel in Las Vegas. In the same hotel's casino rolling the dice was Frank Sinatra.

Once it had been a ritual that whenever Frank was in town and a member of his Clan was performing, he would never miss jumping on stage to kibitz. The audiences loved it, especially when Frank was backed by his lieutenants—Dean Martin, Joey Bishop, and Sammy. But now, whether by secret ballot or the Leader's command, the Clan dropped Davis from its rolls.

Prior to Sammy's opening of a five-week stint in the spring, Frank called a meeting of the Summit nightly in the Copa Room. It was almost like ye olde days with Martin holding a glass in his hand and Sinatra and Bishop ribbing him about his drinking. They were billed as "Dean Martin and his friends, Frank and Joey." Sammy was conspicuously absent. He used to be on the first team when the group was originally formed in 1960 at the time that the Clan invaded Las Vegas on location for "Ocean's Eleven."

For a full month it was Standing Room Only for their nightly antics. The 1966 Summit Act was booked in the hotel for three weeks. Financially they clicked to a new attendance record in the plush show room. Reportedly, all three collected $75,000 each for their nocturnal frolics.

But, the multi-talents of Sammy Davis, Jr., were missing. Without him the trio had to carry the entire load for 85 minutes on stage. Martin was introduced first, but since he supposedly couldn't be located, Frank took over for about 10 minutes of Sinatra. Dino was finally "discovered" and joined the two on stage for a bull session around a cart of booze. Joe, clad in a waiter's uniform, mixed the drinks.

Sammy's demise from Sinatra's favor is still mysterious. Once previously he had his membership revoked. According to Davis it was a big misunderstanding. While appearing at the Fontainbleau in Miami Beach he was interviewed by a local reporter. A few of the quotes attributed to Sammy were highly uncomplimentary to Frank. Sammy criticized the Leader for some of his extra-curricular activities in the wine, women and song department.

Within twenty-four hours after the story broke, the fireworks ignited on both coasts creating a disturbance which unnerved several people.

In Hollywood, Frank was raging. In Miami, Sammy was frantically trying to get Sinatra on the telephone. Frank's associates know all too vividly that when he's annoyed at someone it takes a small miracle to appease him. Sammy, for months, was unable to explain. Frank just didn't want to listen. Finally, one of the other Clan members, reportedly Bishop, acted as peacemaker. He persuaded Frank to hear what Davis had to say.

What he said basically was this:

"Sure I had the interview, but I didn't say all of those things. Some of the quotes I did say were taken out of context. If I did anything wrong, I apologize."

Frank had a change of heart. He reportedly put his arm around Sammy's shoulder when they held their arranged meeting in a Hollywood restaurant. Frank then extended his other arm to Sammy and called off the misunderstanding with a warm handshake.

Sammy was reinstated in the Clan with full privileges. But the scars never quite healed. Today Frank and Sammy are cool again.

In a way, Sammy himself drifted away from Frank's "In" group. His many show business activities and his move to New York for "Golden Boy" left him little time to be available for fun and games with the boys.

Marriage to May Britt had changed Sammy, too. Previously he admitted that he had drifted into a life that included too much drinking at times and he found it hard to stay away from the gambling tables. Reportedly his losses once nearly sent him to bankruptcy court.

"I want to be a family man," he said when he took May as his bride. "We plan to have many babies."

With the exception of Dean Martin, it's rather difficult to be a good Clan member and practice the family plan.

Then, Frank himself took on a more domestic cast after his marriage to Mia. Those who like to think of themselves as insiders in Frank's life predicted that very soon the Sinatras and the Davises would be swapping dinner invitations and Frank would welcome Sammy back into his good graces with pretty Mia ready to sweeten the reconciliation with one of her radiant smiles.

Unfortunately this reunion will have to be postponed for quite a bit longer. Sammy is currently making a hectic tour all over the country—doing nite club stints and charity work so that his packed schedule cancels out any hope for seeing friends.

When the time finally comes, the friendship that was once something Sammy could boast about with pride and affection may be his to boast of again. At that time, everyone hopes Mia will finally meet the man her husband once loved as a brother . . . and perhaps still does.

—February 1967

"WHY THEY MUST MARRY,"
by Gordon White, *Motion Picture*

While the world watches, May Britt and Sammy Davis, Jr., go ahead with their plans to marry. There is no doubt of it: they are about to become the most controversial husband and wife in the history of Hollywood.

Already, their plans to marry have aroused the sympathy, rage, understanding, respect and contempt of a world half-startled by their courage, half-dismayed at their madness.

Is their love the ultimate folly? Can their relationship ever be accepted—or will the world punish them with social banishment?

No one knows how this strangest of strange love stories will end. Indeed, it is almost as difficult to say how it began.

Ten years ago, Sammy Davis, Jr., was a struggling unknown, bursting with talent, seething for his big break.

I sat with him on one of those days in the offices of a Vine Street music publisher Sammy visited frequently to learn of new songs, new shows and new names in the entertainment world he loves so much. He was dressed in wash-weary jeans, well-worn but well-polished black shoes, a plaid sport shirt and a smile.

I will never forget the words to a song which he sang softly to himself.

"*Fools rush in and here I am, very glad to be unhappy . . .*" went the lyric. Another part of the song said, "*. . . but for someone you adore, it's a pleasure to be sad.*"

It is remarkable how prophetic those words were.

Sammy got his break. Today, he is "one of the few great acts in show business." Tough, show-hardened critics compete with superlatives in their reviews of his performances. Nightclub-goers swamp the bistros wherever he appears. But the most graphic and extravagant compliment ever paid to an entertainer was that of his good friend Frank Sinatra, who called Sammy "the heart and soul of show business."

In 1954, following an auto accident, Sammy learned that Fate had "called a second strike on me." He lost an eye in the auto crash.

"The first strike," he continued, "was being born a Negro and having to bear, as all Negroes must, the agony of racial prejudice. Now, I have to live with half my sight."

But Sammy snapped back with verve and bounce. He earned and enjoyed respect and admiration rarely accorded a Negro entertainer. His friends, Frank Sinatra, Dean Martin, Peter Lawford and other top names in entertainment welcomed him to their midst, and he was officially declared "one of the clan."

However, shortly after, Sammy became involved with one of the best-known blonde actresses in films. She and Sammy denied there was anything "between" them, that they were just good friends.

At the height of all the speculation, Sammy, on very short warning, married an attractive Negro singer, Loray White.

Gossip insisted that his marriage to Loray (a divorcée with a young son), was an "arrangement" and had been performed only to relieve the torrid gossip that Sammy was having a wild affair with an important white actress.

Sammy and Loray heatedly denied the rumor, but a few months later, they announced their intentions to divorce.

One close friend of the couple said, "Sammy worked a business deal with Loray to provide her with a weekly expense allowance of $250 if she would marry him. She agreed because she thought it would be good publicity for her career."

Another insider claims that anonymous phone calls, allegedly at the behest of a movie executive, threatened to have Sammy killed if he did not stop seeing the "important" actress.

"That was not at all the reason for the failure of our marriage," Sammy said later. "Loray and I didn't get along from the very beginning. We made a mistake. When we began yelling at each other too frequently, we decided to call it quits."

Loray insisted that she had not married Sammy to "take the heat off an affair he was having with an actress," nor had it been a loveless marriage. She said she still loved Sammy.

No one in Hollywood believed, however, that Sammy and Loray had ever been more than just friends.

Last November, Sammy announced that he was engaged to the beautiful, blonde Canadian dancer, 21-year-old Joan Stuart.

But two months later, at a private Hollywood party, it happened.

"I was just there," says Sammy. "Just like I go to lots of parties. I know what goes on in the minds of some people. I am a Negro, perhaps the only Negro at a party. Will I, as they say, keep my place? They were waiting. But at this party, my whole life changed in an instant. As a Negro, I know there is an understood, but unspoken, rule that I must not even look at a girl whose skin is not my color.

"That's the way it was. I was in the midst of the struggle again—trying to make them understand, without begging, that I was a human being; that although I knew they could tear my heart out if they chose, I trusted them; that because I was a Negro I was not a freak, but a man with all the yearning for love and happiness they had.

"And right in the middle of all that, May walked in. I looked at her and she looked at me. Something happened inside and I cried out, in my mind, 'Oh, God! Don't do this to me!'

"But it happened. It clicked between us and a door in my heart opened to a room I had never known before. It was filled with love and happiness for me. And I couldn't stay out. And somehow I knew that for May it was the same thing.

"I knew, too, that if May and I were ever going to be together we would both pass close to hell. And May knew it, too."

At 24, Maybritt Wilkens is one of the most strikingly beautiful women in Hollywood. Born in Stockholm, her early ambition was to be a photographer. She studied and, at 17, went to work in a model agency as a photo-retoucher. Italian movie producer Carlo Ponti visited the office, took one look at May and ignored the models' photos in the filing cabinets.

In Italy, during the next few years, May made 11 movies. She was seen in *War and Peace*, then brought to the U.S. by Buddy Adler, head of 20th Century-Fox. Soon, she was starring in *The Hunters*, *The Young Lions* with Marlon Brando, and *The Blue Angel*.

In 1958, May married Ed Gregson, the son of a wealthy Los Angeles stockbroker. The marriage failed and May sued for divorce in September, 1959.

Four months later, she walked into a room and looked at Sammy Davis, Jr.

"After that," said May, "I don't think I remember much else, except that I was terribly in love. I think in my heart I knew what was ahead, but it didn't matter. Nothing matters now except the happiness and peace we want in our life, together."

In April, Sammy reported that his engagement to Joan Stuart was off and had been off for some time because her parents had objected to him on racial and religious grounds.

In June, after frequent meetings with Sammy's parents and May's, the couple announced in London that they would marry after September 28, the date May's divorce from Gregson becomes final.

But the peace that Sammy and May seek so desperately may be difficult to attain.

Hardly had the reports of their intended marriage been made public than a hurricane of criticism began brewing. Noisy placard-bearers demonstrated in picket lines outside London's Pigalle Theater night club where Sammy appeared. "*Sammy Davis*," said the signs, "*go home.*"

But it is the stinging anonymous gossip, especially in Hollywood, that is hurting Sammy and May the most.

"Sammy always said he'd never marry a girl of his own race," says a one-time friend of the entertainer. "All his life he has been on the search for the white goddess who will relieve him of the torment he suffers as a Negro. Sammy will deny it, but I believe that it was always his intention, a dream so vital to him, that he would die without it. Sammy has often said that he cannot understand why he should not have the social right to marry a white girl. He does not seem to comprehend that no one quarrels with his right, only his wisdom."

There is also considerable anxiety among both May's and Sammy's friends because of the emotional complications that can develop between the man and the woman of a mixed marriage. In many ways, the intimate relationship that will come between Sammy and May will be similar to other marriages. In other ways, it will not.

Strangely enough, there is the feeling that whatever scorn, ridicule or embarrassment they may bear will do little to harm the marriage. They expect it and are prepared to face it.

Rather, it is the situations that might arise between them in private that could do the greatest damage to the union.

No intelligent human being can completely ignore that his skin is a different color from others. Intelligent persons consider the difference and take a stand.

May has decided that though she is of the white race, her love for a Negro is above any deep-seated racial loyalty. It simply does not matter to her that Sammy is colored. All that matters is that she loves him.

But intelligent persons also understand that there is no such thing as a perfect personality. Anger, joy, hate, sadness and love are emotions all adults experience, regardless of color. Yet, what might be a normal easy-to-mend spat between a husband and wife, could, for May and Sammy, prove disastrous.

May is a vibrant, sensitive and beautiful woman. Her love for Sammy shows that.

Still, one particular ugly word uttered by May in a moment of fury or petulance could kill her happiness—and Sammy's.

In the movie, *Island in the Sun*, Harry Belafonte and Joan

Fontaine fall in love. They have intimate and somewhat clandestine meetings among wind-kissed hills. It is a strange, but idyllic, love affair. Yet, in the end, they part.

Belafonte tells Joan that, as her husband, he could not endure the agony of waiting for, of thinking about, the instant in their marriage that would tear his heart out—when she, in the spasm of a quarrel would look at him with contempt and call him "Nigger!" something she would regret.

But Sammy says he and May cannot let society run their lives.

"We will be criticized," says Sammy, "but we will not be denied our rights as human beings. This is why I *must* marry May."

Is it true? Does Sammy feel that only by conquering a "blonde goddess" can he acquire the stature he yearns for—that of a "human being"? If not, why have all his involvements been with blonde girls?

By falling in love with May and announcing their marriage, has Sammy really shown great courage?

One Hollywood actress, who knew May in Rome, says:

"From a woman's point of view, it is May who will in the end face the greater test of courage. Sammy's desire for a white wife is understandable. But he will be able to continue as a performer.

"May has everything to lose. As far as her studio is concerned, her career is finished, even if they don't marry. Her option has been or will be dropped. That seems to be a certainty from what I hear."

But consider the courage of a girl who is willing to chance such an unlikely marriage. Bravely and openly she chooses to run the gamut of ridicule, scorn, contempt, humiliation heaped on humiliation, insults, the loss of friends, offensive humor, everything a woman tries to avoid because these are the things that hurt her most.

Until now, May has lived in the convenient movie world of make-believe. Scripts directed her young emotions. Even in her marriage, the simple, legal handiness of divorce was a refuge.

But as the fiancée of Sammy Davis, Jr., May must marry him or admit to an admonishing world that she has made a mistake that ruined her life. Failure to go through with it now would be inferred by the world that the romance was a gaudy bid for publicity on both their parts.

They have professed their love for each other and stated they would have children—even if, as Sammy has said, "our kids turn out to be polka dotted."

With regards to the children they plan to have, one Los Angeles minister denounced this intention as "a plan of ultimate selfishness. Neither of them is considering the feelings of those children."

An older woman, once close to May, says:

"It is very simple. Any woman can understand it. May loves Sammy. But her love is tempered with that strange quality which I can only call the irresistibility to misery that is so attractive to some women. It's the kind of thing that draws some women to soap operas and love stories soaked in anguish and passion. It is a very real need for a woman like May to lift her marriage above the ordinary, to give it a great purpose, a deep meaning, a kind of brave significance.

"If you agree with May and Sammy, you call it courage. If you don't, you call it madness. I call it love."

Some time ago, after her divorce from Gregson but before she met Sammy, May reportedly told a girl friend that the failure of her first marriage taught her one thing.

"A woman cannot love a man," said May, "just because he is attractive or charming or rich or a great lover. She must have a deeper reason than that. She must give something of herself. Not just her heart. That is easy to give. Some women give it only because they know they can get it back. Nor just her passions. A woman is by nature, full of passion; it simmers within her always.

"No. It is from the deep, untouchable depths of her that she must give. Some of her spirit, a great part of her soul, her being as a woman which she may treasure in her heart of hearts. That is what I shall give."

Sammy Davis and May Britt want only to exchange their love.

The trials and tribulations ahead do not matter. No matter what the world thinks, May has found the man she loves. In her own way, with her own hopes, she has waited for him high on the hill of her dreams.

For Sammy Davis, Jr., the search is over. All that is left is to reach her now where she tarries, smiling, beckoning openly for him to come and take her.

And he will go to her and fight for her and protect her and love her and worship her.

Is this courage or madness?

Sammy and May will find out soon enough!

—September 1960

SAMMY DAVIS, JR.'S, FBI FILE

To: SAC, New York (9-3298)

From: Director, FBI (9-38936)

UNSUB; AKA, T. A. N.;

SAMMY DAVIS, JR.—VICTIM

EXTORTION—RACIAL MATTER

OO: BA

Re New York airtel dated 12/14/62 with enclosures.

In view of the nature of the letter addressed to victim, the Bureau feels this should have been handled as an Extortion—Racial Matter. Therefore, investigation should be conducted and results reported in accordance with existing instructions concerning extortion cases growing out of Racial Matters.

New York will immediately submit appropriate copies of a

letterhead memorandum suitable for dissemination, inasmuch as the original complaint was received by the New York Office. Set out details of the racial aspect in this letterhead memorandum.

Los Angeles will expedite investigation requested in referenced airtel and submit results to Baltimore in order that Baltimore may incorporate the information in a closing report as soon as possible.

Baltimore include in their report results of examination by the Laboratory of the items submitted by referenced New York airtel.

NOTE:

By airtel dated 12/14/62, New York submitted a threatening letter which had been directed to victim fr. Baltimore, Maryland, on 12/7/62. The contents contained language which would indicate this should have been handled as an Extortion—Racial Matter. New York, Baltimore and Los Angeles are being instructed to so handle. New York is to immediately submit a letterhead memorandum containing the racial aspects of the case.

The envelope containing the letter was addressed SAM DAVIS, JR., Stanton Theater, 516 N. Howard St., Baltimore, Md. and was postmarked "Baltimore, Md. Dec. 7, 5:30 p.m., 1962." The letter is quoted as follows: "You black common low down hore monger S.O.B. bastard were going to get you we tried to get you in London also that low down common white trash you shack up with also that mongrel breed kid so watch your step nigger before you leave the city signed T.A.N. we do not wont niggers to lower our white race."
Result of examination:

Q1 and Q2 were searched through the appropriate sections of the Anonymous Letter File but no identification was effected.

TO: Mr. Belmont DATE: 12-27-63
FROM: A. Rosen
SUBJECT: UNSUBS;
SAMMY DAVIS, JR.
ALLEGED KIDNAPING

This is to advise that the Chicago Courier, a Chicago, Illinois, newspaper on 12-21-63 carried an article alleging that Sammy Davis, Jr., the well-known entertainer and associate of Frank Sinatra, Sr., was kidnaped in Las Vegas several years ago by a pair of tough Chicago gangsters. According to this article, Davis was released when told by his kidnapers to "forget about any plans you have to wed movie actress Kim Novak." The article went on to state that this incident was just disclosed a few days ago following the kidnaping of Frank Sinatra, Jr.

The article states that this incident was known by a few of Sammy Davis, Jr.'s, close associates but that Davis did not discuss it at the time. The article alleges that Broadway Columnist Frank Farrell leaked this item a few days ago and that it was not known what action Federal authorities might take in regard to this matter. It is reported that this kidnaping was arranged by certain people in show business as a "friendly kidnaping" to convince Davis not to marry Kim Novak. The article concluded by alleging that a "death note" was left in Davis' dressing room at a benefit show in Santa Monica, California, within the past week.

No information was located in Bureau files concerning the above-mentioned kidnaping or the recent "death note." This story may well be an attempt by Davis to obtain publicity similar to that afforded the Sinatras in the recent kidnaping of Frank Sinatra, Jr.

<u>ACTION RECOMMENDED</u>:

1. In view of the publicity afforded this matter and the likelihood of press inquiry, it is recommended that we interview Sammy Davis, Jr., to determine if this alleged kidnaping or the "death note" recently received by him constitutes a Federal violation. If approved, attached is a teletype instructing our Los Angeles Office to conduct this interview.

2. This teletype also instructs Los Angeles and Las Vegas to submit any information those Offices may have received concerning this matter.

Memorandum to Mr. Belmont
RE: UNSUBS;
      SAMMY DAVIS, JR.
      ALLEGED KIDNAPING
Addendum (AHB: [initials censored]), 12/27/63:
      I do not think we should interview Sammy Davis, Jr., based on information in the Chicago Courier, alleging Davis was kidnaped "several years ago," nor concerning the alleged death note left in his dressing room last week. If there is any substance to either of these allegations, Davis had a responsibility to notify the FBI or other appropriate authorities.
                                                A. H. Belmont
      The "Los Angeles Times" issue of 11/17/61 contained an article captioned "Entertainers Plan Disarmament Rally" which disclosed that Sammy Davis, Jr., would participate in a demonstration for disarmament which was organized by a group of Hollywood entertainers and writers under the name HELP-Help Establish Lasting Peace. The group planned to hold a rally in front of the Hollywood Palladium in connection with President Kennedy's visit there.*

*President's Visit to Los Angeles, Cal., 11/18/61 (62-107429).

"The Worker" issue of 11/21/61, contained an article captioned "Kennedy Says Ultras' Actions Peril Nation" which reviewed an address given by President Kennedy at a Democratic Party dinner in Los Angeles, Cal., on Saturday.* The article disclosed that over two thousand pickets were in the area of the Palladium, the site of the President's address. The sponsors of the picket line included celebrated movie stars, such as Sammy Davis, Jr., who were sponsors of the peace workers organization known as HELP-Help Establish Lasting Peace.

*11/18/61

The following references contain information concerning Sammy Davis, Jr., in connection with the rally for freedom in support of the Birmingham, Ala., movement which was held on 5/26/63, at Wrigley Field, Los Angeles, Cal., under the sponsorship of the NAACP. Sammy Davis, Jr., made an announcement concerning the offering that was taken. Davis was reported to have pledged $20,000, which was said to represent one week's earnings in Las Vegas, Nevada.

By airtel dated 7/19/63, Los Angeles Office furnished a two-page resolution captioned "The Time Is Now" which was published in the "Hollywood Reporter," issue of 7/17/63. The resolution carried the names of 153 writers, actors, producers and directors and called for the entire industry to join in the crusade against discrimination. The name of Sammy Davis, Jr., appeared on the resolution.

Detroit letter dated 7/18/63 made reference to Bureau letter dated 7/1/63 which requested information concerning the association of [name censored] with Sammy Davis, Jr.

The references set out hereafter appear in the file captioned "March on Washington" and contain information concerning Sammy Davis, Jr., in connection with the March which was scheduled to be held on 8/28/63. The references disclosed that [remainder of report censored].

The "Los Angeles Sentinel" issue of 10/1/64, identified "Stars for Freedom" as a non-profit organization of outstanding personalities in motion pictures, the arts, science, and public affairs.

———

The following references in the file captioned "American Nazi Party" (ANP) contain information concerning demonstrations planned by the ANP against Sammy Davis, Jr. On 7/12/60, George Lincoln Rockwell, Organizer and Commander of the ANP, led a group of individuals in picketing The New Lotus, 727 14th Street, NW, Washington, D.C., where Davis had opened an engagement. Davis had reportedly commented during a demonstration at a performance in England, that such an incident could not happen in the US and the ANP intended to prove that it could happen. The ANP planned a demonstration on 7/19/60 at the Black Saddle Restaurant while Davis was being interviewed by radio personality Steve Allison. It was learned, however, that Davis would not appear in order to avoid a disturbance.

Newark letter, dated 2/24/64, made reference to Milwaukee letter to Bureau dated 1/31/64, with lead for Newark to ascertain whether Sammy Davis, Jr., had been in contact with Martin Luther King.

Washington Capital News Service release dated 2/23/64, disclosed that the NAACP announced that comedian Steve Allen and singers Lena Horne and Sammy Davis, Jr., would be co-chairmen of a special civil rights television program to be aired nation-wide on 5/14/64.

The following references contain information regarding Sammy Davis, Jr., in connection with his plans to join the March on Montgomery, Ala., from Selma, in protest of voter discrimination. Initially, Davis was scheduled to begin the march from Selma on 3/21/65. The references later indicated that he would arrive from Atlanta on 3/24/65 and join other entertainers at the conclusion of the march at Montgomery.

The "New York Herald Tribune" issue of 4/5/65, carried an article captioned " 'Answer to Selma' Benefit Raises Record $150,000," which reviewed the benefit held at the Majestic Theater, NYC, on 4/4/65. The article related that approximately sixty Broadway performers appeared in the benefit which began with Sammy Davis, Jr., introducing Mayor Wagner. The beneficiaries of the performance included the Voter Education Program of the Southern Christian Leadership Conference and CORE.

It was noted that as of 8/25/65, "Golden Boy," a musical comedy starring Sammy Davis, Jr., was billed at the Majestic Theater, 245 West 44th Street, NYC.

[Name censored] advised that on 11/13/65, [name censored] and Martin Luther King, Jr., discussed the financial status of the SCLC and a means by which additional funds could be obtained. King indicated that he wanted a benefit to be held at Madison Square Garden in NYC, and that he would contact Sammy Davis, Jr., in the hope that Davis could obtain performers such as Richard Burton and [name censored]. (Locality not given.)

[File censored] Jackson, Miss., on 6/25–26/66. The references disclosed that Davis was requested by the SCLC to secure movie and entertainment personalities for the entertainment program for the conclusion of the march. Davis was reportedly engaged in personal appearances in Las Vegas at the time, and it was not determined if Davis had definitely committed himself.

On the evening of 6/25/66, Sammy Davis, Jr., was present to entertain the marchers at Tougaloo College near Jackson, Miss.

In addition to Davis, the entertainers included [names censored].

The following references in the file captioned "Communist Infiltration of the SCLC" contain information concerning Sammy Davis, Jr. During January 1964, a contribution of $16,900 was made to the SCLC by a group of individuals in California through Davis. In February 1964, Davis was identified as Vice President and Treasurer of the Will Master Trio. The references disclosed that from March 1965 to December 1966, Davis was to arrange and/or perform for benefits to raise funds for the SCLC or Martin Luther King, Jr., President of the SCLC.

On 10/15/67, an SA of the FBI attended a benefit performance for the SCLC which was held at the Oakland, Cal., Coliseum. Sammy Davis, Jr., provided the opening remarks and stated that all races must learn to live together in a peaceful manner. Vocal performances were given by Davis, [name censored] and Joan Baez and a brief address was given by Dr. Martin Luther King. Following her performance, Joan Baez stated that when Sammy Davis, Jr., made his planned trip to Vietnam in the near future (no further details), she hoped that he would ask all the US soldiers there to come home.

On 5/2/68 [name censored] advised that one [censored] informed [name censored] that he [censored] had recently spoken with Sammy Davis, Jr., who was in Chicago with the production "Golden Boy," and that Davis was going to give "us" (the SCLC) his May 20th proceeds.

The following references in the file captioned "Poor People's Campaign" (PPC) contain information concerning the activities of Sammy Davis, Jr., in connection with the Campaign. The references disclosed that the SCLC was endeavoring to secure the services of Davis and other popular entertainers for a PPC program planned for 5/9/68 in Atlanta, Ga. Davis reportedly appeared at Resurrection City, the Campaign site near the Lincoln Memorial, Washington, D.C., on approximately 5/21/68 and presented a check for the amount of $17,800 to the Rev. Ralph Abernathy for the PPC. The check represented the proceeds of a benefit performance of "Golden Boy" given by Davis in Chicago, Ill.

On 9/18/70, [name censored] furnished information concerning a motion picture which was being filmed for the Black Panther Party (BPP) by [name censored], Chicago, Ill., motion picture producer. Informant stated that [name censored] had indicated that he had obtained the funds to complete the film from Sammy Davis, Jr., who was reportedly very sympathetic toward the BPP as he had been very impressed with the film concerning one Fred, believed to be Fred Hampton, former Deputy Chairman, Illinois BPP, deceased. [Name censored] reportedly stated that Sammy Davis was to contact United Artists to request assistance in the preparation and nation-wide distribution of the film. Informant stated that [name censored] mentioned that [name censored], probably [name censored], another Chicago, Ill., film producer, would travel to New York some time during the week of 9/21/70, to obtain the money from Sammy Davis.

The results of a name check on captioned individual, who you advised was born on December 8, 1925, at New York, New York, and who currently resides in Beverly Hills, California, were furnished the White House on February 3, 1972. Since that time, our files reveal the following information which may relate to him.

The March 7, 1972, issue of "The Daily World," a communist publication, reported that an all-star show had raised $38,000 for the Angela Davis defense fund. It noted that Sammy Davis, Jr., told the crowd of 6,500 that he wears a "Free Angela" button because he shares "her blackness."

Our files further reveal that on the same occasion, Mr. Davis noted that while he does not necessarily share the political convictions of Angela Davis, he supports her because she is a black woman. This benefit was sponsored by the Southern California District Communist Party, although this sponsorship was not publicly indicated.

In May, 1972, we learned that the Italian American Civil Rights League (IACRL) was actively advertising a fund raising "night of entertainment" scheduled for June 4, 1972, at the Madison Square Garden center. Sammy Davis, Jr., and Jimmy Durante were billed as headliners for this event. The IACRL was formed in May of 1970 with several members of the organized crime element as its officers. The League was an outgrowth of several demonstrations directed against the FBI Office in New York City between April and June, 1970, which demonstrations were originated and arranged by Joe Colombo, Sr., identified as a leader of an organized crime element in New York City, who was shot and gravely wounded at an IACRL-sponsored rally on June 28, 1971.

NOTE: Per request of Alexander P. Butterfield, Deputy Assistant to the President.

TO: DIRECTOR, FBI
               (ATTN: FBI LABORATORY)
FROM: SAC, LAS VEGAS (9-456) (P)
SUBJECT: UNSB, aka
               "The General"
               "Der Fuhrer";
               SAMMY DAVIS, JR.—VICTIM
               EXTORTION
               OO: Las Vegas

Enclosed for the Laboratory are the following:

A threatening letter dated 1/19/74, received by SAMMY DAVIS, JR., on 1/29/74, at Reno, Nevada. The letter was written on the reverse side of a billing invoice from the Monterrey Pharmacy, 12901 Riverside Drive, Sherman Oaks, California, to [censored] California, dated 10/31/71.

One U.S. Postal Service postal free envelope which contained the above letter.

One small card bearing the name Institute for Family Neurosis Research. The card also bears the handprinting on front and back sides, [censored].

One memographed sheet dated 12/4/73, signed by "DER FUHRER."

One Xerox copy of enclosure number four. This is being submitted inasmuch as the contents of this sheet, due to its length, is not being set out verbatum in this airtel and is being submitted for the Supervisor's Desk at the Bureau.

Enclosed for the Los Angeles Division is one Xerox set of the above items.

For the information of Los Angeles, [name censored], another well-known entertainer, received a similar threatening letter in Las Vegas, and it is believed the UNSUB is the same in both cases.

The letter handwritten in ink reads as follows:

"1/19/74

"From: U.S. Armed Forces

"To: Sammy David, [*sic*] Jr.

"You are on a death list. The police cannot help you."

"If you wish to stay alive, go to the L.A. (SFV) Nike Missle Base for instructions."

"The General"

The letter was written on the reverse side of a billing invoice dated 10/31/71, from the Monterrey Pharmacy, 12901 Riverside Drive, Sherman Oaks, California, and is addressed to [censored], California.

The above letter was contained in a red and white U.S. Postal Service postage free envelope. A return mailing label glued on the front of the envelope bore the handprinted name "Sammy Davis, Jr., Harrah's, Reno, Nevada." No postmarks were noted on the envelope.

Also found inside the envelope was a small card bearing the name "Institute for Family Neurosis Research." Beneath this appears the handprinted name [censored]. The other side of the card bears the handprinting "KGIL, (213) 894-9191."

Reportedly KGIL is a radio station located in San Fernando (Los Angeles County), California, and [name censored] is a disc jockey affiliated with this station.

Another item contained in the envelope was a memographed sheet dated 12/4/73, bearing numerous well-known names and accusations. The bottom of the sheet lists the name of the editor as [name censored] and the sheet is signed by "Der Fuhrer."

On 1/31/74, this case was discussed with AUSA E. PIERRE GEZELIN at Reno, Nevada. GEZELIN was of the opinion that this matter constituted a violation of the Federal extortion statute.

Also on 1/31/74, SAMMY DAVIS, JR., was interviewed by SAS of the FBI and acknowledged receipt of the above items. DAVIS, however, was unable to furnish any information concerning the identity of the sender. He was of the opinion that the person who prepared the letter and other items was a "nut."

"SAMMY DAVIS,"

Life

His role in *Golden Boy*, based on Clifford Odets' famous play, demands everything Sammy Davis can give it—and it leaves him physically and emotionally spent. He sings 10 songs, does four dances, has to turn from comedy to a delicate love scene. After the grueling prize-fight scene, he has a mental crack-up which sends him off stage in near-hysterics.

Even for so versatile an actor, this is a brilliant bravura performance, and without it *Golden Boy* would bog down in soap opera. Sammy gets paid more than any Broadway star in history—a total of about $10,000 a week plus fringe benefits. He's worth it.

It was not the pay, however, that drew Sammy into *Golden Boy*—he has made much more in nightclubs. It was the chance to show off all his talents and act a serious part. Distinguished actors have played *Golden Boy*—Luther Adler was in the original 1937 production, William Holden in the movie, John Garfield in a Broadway revival. Four years ago, Hillard Elkins had the idea of making it into a musical and changing the plot—which Clifford Odets agreed to do. The original hero was an Italian boy who wanted to play the violin but allowed himself to be seduced into boxing for a quick buck. The musical would make him a Negro—a Harlem youth hungry for knowledge, yearning to escape the slums.

There are parallels between this and Sammy's life. Born in Harlem, Sammy was put on the stage by his father when he was 3 and never went to school a day in his life. He did not learn to write his name until he was 12. Show business was a hard, harsh life for him—but it did lift him out of Harlem.

Golden Boy encountered incessant trouble. Odets died before he could finish his re-do and four other writers tried to make something of it. After rehearsing for 12 weeks, and only a month before the New York opening, William Gibson, author of *The Miracle Worker*, completely overhauled the play. The first director was fired after Sammy had tried to punch him and threatened to quit five times.

The only thing that has remained constant throughout is the prize fight. All the punches in it are carefully planned. Yet the two go about it with such ferocity that at least once a week a real cruncher lands on target. Sammy says he has been "knocked silly" half a dozen times. "Fortunately, I'm supposed to be punchy in the last scene, and the show ends only five minutes after the fight."

When Sammy married May Britt in 1960, there was a round of jokes from the comedians and a good deal of honest doubt among their close friends. Sammy had been married once before to a Negro dancer named Loray White—"it lasted about 20 minutes," says Sammy. He became one of the more notorious members of the Hollywood Clan, a heavy drinker and gambler, eager to be seen in public with beautiful actresses. "My life was rotten," Sammy says now in retrospect.

He knew that if he married May Britt, a white actress, it would be out-of-bounds to most people. "I didn't do it to change anybody's mind," says Sammy. "If they want to hate, let them." When he proposed, Sammy warned May. "I told her, how rough it was going to be. I painted, and you'll pardon the expression, as *black* a picture as I possibly could. But May said she loved me." Sammy and May announced their engagement in London, where he was appearing in a club. "Right away the hate boys started in," said Sammy. "What a thrill it is to come out of a nightclub filled with people paying to see you perform, and then to see the English Nazis with swastika armbands picketing."

Hate mail began to flow in. "I really expected to lose some of my club dates," says Sammy. "I was putting my career on the chopping block. It even occurred to me that I might never work again."

The Davises stayed married and the shock of seeing them together wore off. "People accept us now," says Sammy, "even my own people—and they hadn't before I married May. There was a wall between me and my soul brothers. I couldn't even go up to Harlem, the chill was so bad. Some of the things I was doing was making it tough on all of them. The cats on the corner, they're the real barometer. They used to say, 'Hey, ease up on us, baby.' But when I married May, they realized it was legit and true."

Sammy still has to answer for the marriage, sometimes with

bitterness. He tells of a man who came up to him and asked what Sammy thought of mixed marriages, "I pointed to my little daughter," Sammy says. "I told him, 'That's what I think of mixed marriages. God gave mine the most beautiful child He ever put on this earth. But some people,' I said, 'will still call her a nigger.' "

Frank Sinatra once told Sammy Davis, "You smoke so much and drink so much and work so much that one day you're gonna open your mouth and dust is going to come out. Slow down." Sammy can't. He probably plays more benefits than any other man in show business. He did 10 rallies for President Johnson and Bobby Kennedy in October alone, when *Golden Boy* was in crisis. "Sammy has that young-in-heart attitude," Sinatra says, "but he's getting close to 40. He goes to the refrigerator for a snack, opens the door, and when that light hits him, he does 45 minutes of his act." Sammy can rarely get to sleep before dawn. He smokes three packs of cigarets a day, and during rehearsals carried around a silver mug of bourbon and Coke. He rarely goes out to dinner without half a dozen cast members and he picks up the check.

Despite his enormous Broadway income (which includes percentages of gross and net receipts plus an expense allowance), he gets to keep only one third of it. The rest goes to his father and uncle, Will Mastin, under an old contract which expires in 1965.

He only slows down on Friday night before the show, when he and May hold Jewish services in their home. Sammy, born a Catholic, converted to Judaism after his car crash in 1954, in which he broke his nose and lost one eye. "I needed some answers about religion and about me. I found them in Judaism. As a Negro, I felt emotionally tied to it. Both Negroes and Jews are minority groups and we've both had our problems. Every Jew I've met has a dignity and a strength. Judaism gives me something to hold on to."

—*November 13, 1964*

"A FIVE-MONTH ORDEAL, WITH A WHOLE CAREER AT STAKE,"
by Thomas Thompson, *Life*

Three days before *Golden Boy* opened in New York, Sammy Davis vanished. The disappearance did not become known until 2:30 on a bleak, rainy Saturday afternoon, by which time the Majestic Theater was jammed to the rafters for a preview performance. Finally, it was 20 minutes past curtain time and it seemed that Sammy had really cut and that a $600,000 show was about to die. The show's producer, a young, ambitious former actor's agent named Hillard Elkins, ordered the curtain raised, walked out to face the impatient mob, and in an unsteady voice told them:

"Due to the pressures of rehearsal, Mr. Davis will not be able to appear. We are canceling the afternoon's performance. You can either get your money back or . . ." His words were drowned out in a groan heard clear across 44th Street.

Sammy didn't show up for the Saturday night performance either. By that time Elkins, who had been flooding the city with desperate phone calls, had had time for one hasty runthrough with the understudy. Trying to salvage some of that day's $20,000 box office, Elkins sent the understudy on for the evening performance, but as soon as the announcement was made, three fourths of the house—most of whom had paid $9.60 apiece just to see Sammy—promptly got in line at the exchange window.

Where was the star? Sammy Davis, who wanted desperately to be as famous on Broadway as he was in Las Vegas, and for whom *Golden Boy* had become a personal crusade, had awakened that morning with an aching body, his head woozy from one of the most grueling pre-opening ordeals any performer ever endured. For four months *Golden Boy* had been on the road from Philadelphia to Boston to Detroit to New York, and both star and show had been beaten and ripped and clawed apart so many times that nobody knew what was right anymore. The preview performances in New York had not gone well, and in these last hours before opening, drastic changes were still being made.

Everything had come to a head for Sammy on that rainy morning, and he made a decision. He told his wife that he had to get away.

"I'm gonna flip, honey," he said. "I'm gonna run through a wall if I have to go down to that theater today and do two shows and rehearse tomorrow and open Tuesday night. I can't do it. Let me be alone today."

He walked out of his newly rented town house on 93rd St., just off Fifth Avenue, got into the $27,000 silver Rolls-Royce that is the flagship of his personal fleet of cars, and drove to a friend's apartment. There he fell into bed and tried to sleep, shutting his eyes but not his mind to the furies that loomed on Tuesday night.

For Sammy was much more than the star of *Golden Boy*. He *was* Golden Boy. In its agony on the road, he had given so much of himself to repair it, dredged up so much of his own being and infused it into the story, that it was impossible to divorce the man from the role. If the show were rapped on Broadway, it would—he felt—indict his whole life. And Sammy could not take that.

"I'm doing this show for only two people," he had told a friend a few days earlier, "Walter Kerr [of the New York *Herald Tribune*] and Howard Taubman [of the New York *Times*]. If they knock me, I'll be destroyed." The friend pointed out to Sammy that this was patently absurd, that he could go back to Vegas anytime and make $30,000 a week, or to Hollywood, or to the open arms of any nightclub proprietor in the world. Sammy shook his head slowly. "You don't understand," he had said. "This is more. This is truth. I've got to succeed!"

Finally Sammy dropped off, sleeping through the preview matinee that afternoon and well into the night. As soon as he awoke, he turned on television and tried to escape *Golden Boy* by watching an ancient movie. He read from the Warren Re-

port, and then, at 4 o'clock in the morning, he called his producer, who by this time was far worse off than Sammy: "I've
never done this before in my professional life, Hilly. But I'll
make it up to you on opening night."

"Maybe we'd better delay once again," said the producer.
"Give us time to freeze the show."

"No," Sammy said quickly. "Put off that opening one more
day and I'm out. Sue me. Do whatever you want. I'll buy out.
I'll write you a check for $600,000 tonight, or if you wait until
tomorrow, I'll get you the cash. But we're not postponing,
baby. We're gonna do it."

As much as Sammy Davis really feared the judgment of the
critics, he could not wait any longer to hear what they had to
say. *Golden Boy* was the opportunity he had been waiting for
all his life, a chance to be in a musical drama that would startle
and provoke and hurt as much as the original Clifford Odets
play had in 1937.

When *Golden Boy* began its out-of-town trials in Philadelphia
in June this year, it was suddenly obvious to Sammy that none
of what he wanted to accomplish was happening. The local
critics were kind to his performance and to the stunning sets
and to the music, but they dismissed the story. Somehow the
starkness of the drama seemed to be written with a pen dipped
in soapsuds. Sammy was alarmed.

When the production moved to Boston in August it still
lacked sting, and it took another clobbering. The town's most
influential critic, Elliot Norton, called the story "soap opera"
and, more painful, said Sammy was a lousy actor. Sammy cut
out the review, circled it in red and pasted it up on his dressing
room mirror to read every night before going on.

At Elkins' request, playwright William Gibson came up to
watch the show, said the *Golden Boy* book needed a complete
factory overhaul, and agreed to act as play doctor, bringing in a
new director, Arthur Penn.

In three weeks Gibson, with Sammy's advice and counsel, wrote a brand-new show. The company moved to Detroit in the blazing heat of August, rehearsed and opened the show in four days. Since the local newspapers there were on strike there were no reviews, but the audiences were clearly moved. Some women wept at the play's final scenes. But Penn and Gibson and Davis could see that the show still was not right, that the changes so far were just a beginning.

Sammy threw more and more of himself into the writing and production. Often when he was finished on stage he would work over music and lyrics with the show's two composers. Sometimes he would sit with Gibson in the quiet hours between midnight and dawn and explain what it is like to be black and live in Harlem and stand in Central Park to see the lights downtown, sparkling and seemingly forever out of reach.

Sammy himself wrote one of the most moving lines in the show. It comes toward the end when he and the white heroine, played by Paula Wayne, finally admit to each other that they are in love. Sammy holds up his hands and asks her, "What color? What color are these?" While the girl searches for an answer, Sammy spins and replies joyously, "No color! No color at all!" It was a scene from his own life, something he had once said to May.

Sometimes it alarmed the star to see how much of himself was going into *Golden Boy*. He told a friend one night: "I'm scared. It's so close. It's me." Even so, when Gibson offered him a new line of dialogue, Sammy rejected it quickly. "My boy wouldn't say that," said Sammy. "I know him. I've lived his life."

As the tension built up through countless new versions and exhaustion began to overtake all concerned, Sammy felt compelled to act as confessor, benefactor, reassurer and clown to the entire cast. His jokes were corny but they cut through the tension:

"Man, if there's one thing I'm not, it's two-faced, 'cause if I was, I'd be wearin' the other one."

Or, "One white fellow looks at me, and I say, 'Yes sir.' They all look alike to me."

Or, "People always pick on me 'cause I look like a banjo."

Or, "Two places I know I ain't popular—Egypt and Mississippi."

Despite all his efforts, when the show moved to New York everything it had gained in Detroit seemed to vanish. Four additional weeks of previews were scheduled but the disasters mounted. The sound system was not working properly, and during the play's most poignant moments the audience would cry out, "Louder! Can't hear you!" This angered Sammy, as did the faint applause at the end, hardly enough to give them a curtain call. He stormed into the producer's office and yelled, "Either we close down and fix everything and stop giving previews until we're ready, or we close down permanently! Dig?" Elkins dug, and spent another small fortune installing one of the most elaborate sound systems ever conceived for a Broadway show.

Tinkering continued. Scenes were rewritten and rewritten and rewritten 10 times more. In the last week before the opening, Sammy was thrown two new numbers, a difficult song and solo dance. On Friday, he learned that other major changes were going in over the weekend. On Saturday, unable to take any more, he did his disappearing act.

The next day, Sunday afternoon, Sammy reappeared at the theater, plunged willingly into rehearsal of a new ending for the first act and worked until well past midnight. Monday was another ordeal—a new lyric shoved in here, a string of new lines, a dance rehearsal that dragged on all afternoon, a final preview performance that night, and expressions of stark panic on every face.

Sammy promised to rest Tuesday, opening day, but he didn't. Instead he attended a luncheon of the National Conference of Christians and Jews and accepted their Brotherhood Award. He then went to the theater and rehearsed all afternoon, straining a voice that was already crippled by nerves and overuse. He quit about 6 and ordered spaghetti sent to his dressing room, watched Huntley and Brinkley ("My only contact with reality," he says. "Whatever I'm doing, I stop to watch these guys").

By this time he was nearly crowded out of his dressing room. Dozens of floral offerings and more than 500 telegrams were pouring in—from "Larry and Joan"—whom Sammy proudly identified as Sir Laurence Olivier and his wife, from California Governor Pat Brown, from Bobby Kennedy, from most of the greats of show business.

But the one Sammy wanted to see most of all was not there. He anxiously ripped open every wire and read the name, but there was none signed "Frank Sinatra." It was difficult for Sammy to conceal his hurt.

"Maybe Frank didn't send one on purpose," Sammy said. "Maybe he wanted to make me mad and provoke me into a better performance."

But that excuse didn't help. Sinatra has been Sammy's personal idol, the Big Talent—and Sinatra had warned him not to risk so much on Broadway. Sinatra had said, in effect, "You don't need New York. Why expose yourself to the critics?" Sinatra himself—handsome and powerful and white—had never risked his career on Broadway. But Sammy would.

Then it was curtain time. A thousand other thoughts fought for his attention. "Maybe we haven't got it," Sammy wondered. "So many chi-chi people have been coming in and saying, 'That line's a little too much,' and we'd take it out. So maybe we haven't got anything left. . . ."

His entrance applause was not the ovation he had expected. It was merely a polite "welcome." His first song went badly. His voice was so nearly gone that he had to wear a microphone. But from that moment on he reached down inside himself and poured everything he could into his performance, using his voice, selling it, phrasing it, making an audience forget there was gravel in it. His dancing? Sammy hoofed all over the stage doing everything from softshoe to acrobatic ballet. But his acting was his trump card and he flung it down proudly, performing with a sting and power he himself had long covered up with wisecracks. His performance ended to a wild ovation.

But, in those few long hours after the final curtain, fear still gnawed at Sammy. Until the reviews were in, the applause didn't matter. He sat in his dressing room amid the flowers and the still-arriving telegrams, and waited. The first inkling came on the radio at 11 p.m. The critic said the show was a smash, "as exciting as *Porgy and Bess*." Sammy was elated, but nobody ever bought a ticket after hearing a radio review. Then came another radio critic who lambasted the show, faulting it for bringing in the race issue. "The race issue!" Sammy exploded. "With me in it, what did they expect? The Chinese issue?"

He slipped into a tux and walked across the street to Sardi's, where the crowded restaurant stood as one and applauded him. He accepted their congratulations woodenly, finally pushed his way out and drove to Danny's Hideaway on the east side of Manhattan where 700 invited guests were eating ravioli and corned beef and drinking the producer's Scotch. Sammy was trancelike, a prisoner waiting for the jury to come in. Finally he was called to the telephone and told that Kerr's review was in. "He hates it, huh?" said Sammy. "Read it to me." The Davis face screwed up in fear, then began to melt—slowly, then rapidly—and finally exploded into a bright howl of happiness. Kerr, with reservations, gave the show an enthusiastic review. Taubman followed with an even better one. Five of the six newspaper critics liked *Golden Boy* and studded their reviews with "money quotes"—the kind that look great on billboards and in newspaper ads. All six reviews hailed Sammy Davis as a star of the first magnitude.

"They're raves!" Sammy yelled, dancing around and hugging everybody. "I'm ten feet tall! I'm a Broadway star! We've got a hit, we've very definitely got a hit!" And since Sammy was laughing and yelling, everybody was laughing and yelling, and since Sammy was crying, everybody was crying. And after a long time, and a drive uptown to a quieter pub where he could read and memorize the reviews, Sammy grew morose again.

Somebody asked him about Sinatra.

"I've never been more hurt in my life," he said. "But who needs Sinatra?"

At last Sammy was sure. He doesn't need Sinatra, anymore.

—*November 13, 1964*

"SAMMY DAVIS:
DON'T CALL HIM JUNIOR ANYMORE,"
by Trevor Armbruster, *The Saturday Evening Post*

Inside dressing room "A" at New York's Majestic Theater, he sits and waits for the curtain. He has dabbed makeup powder on his cheeks, smoothed his hair with grease and placed a narrow strip of bandage over his right eye. He has donned khaki pants, white sneakers and a bright orange jersey which conceals the microphone taped to his chest. Now he turns to face a mirror framed by 30 lights—a scrawny, one-eyed, broken-nosed Negro with a jutting jaw. "Five minutes," echoes the call from the stage director's desk. "Five minutes, please."

He has been in the dressing room for more than an hour. He left his brownstone town house on East 93rd Street just before seven o'clock and drove downtown in his gray Rolls-Royce with his chauffeur riding in the back.

At the theater a waiter brought steaming pots of soul-food to the dressing room—pigs' knuckles and neckbones and tails and feet and rice and black-eyed peas. For a moment he seemed embarrassed, but he recovered quickly. "Baby," he grinned, "I just eat this stuff on the nights that I'm colored. Wait till you see what I eat on the nights that I'm Jewish."

He finished his dinner and slumped down on a couch. The television set blared noisily. A babble of voices mounted in the hallway outside, but he slept until 8:15. Then his valet, a balding, sad-eyed, quietly efficient man named Murphy Bennett, nudged him and said it was time to dress.

Three years ago, when Richard Burton played in *Camelot* at the Majestic, this dressing room belonged to him and he called it his pub. Now the *décor* is different. Pasted on the walls are the 218 cables and telegrams that flowed in on opening night—from Bobby Kennedy, Peter Lawford, Nathan Leopold, Jack Benny and California Gov. Edmund G. (Pat) Brown. Interspersed among them are photographs of Queen Elizabeth, John F. Kennedy, Audrey Hepburn and a weeping Mrs. Medgar Evers. "You can kill a man," the caption reads, "but you can't kill an idea."

". . . to your places." The stage manager's call nips at his reverie. Out front the curtain is rising, and through a dressing-room speaker he can hear the staccato gymnasium sounds that take the place of an overture. Now the sounds become a rhythm, an acoustical tattoo, as fighters spar, skip rope and pummel leather punching bags. A young production aide is standing at the doorway. "Are you ready?" he asks. "Baby," says Sammy Davis, bounding out of the dressing room, "I was born ready."

In the original version of Clifford Odets's play, *Golden Boy*, the protagonist was an Italian youth torn between a promising career as a violinist and the more immediate rewards of the prize ring. As a straight dramatic role, the part—played first by Luther Adler on Broadway in 1937, then by William Holden in the movie version two years later and finally by John Garfield in a 1952 stage revival—was demanding enough. But now, in the context of a musical, the part is tougher than ever.

As Joe Wellington, a bitter, ambitious youth struggling to escape his Harlem ghetto and find success through violence in the distant, diamond-studded world downtown, Sammy Davis is taxed as never before. He must remain on stage for 105 of the production's 125 minutes; he must dance four numbers and sing 10 songs. He must also act. He must make the audience understand—if not sympathize with—the frustrations of a basically unsympathetic character. And he must establish the integrity of his love for a white woman to such a degree that the audience is not repulsed by their affair.

Golden Boy is a potpourri of brilliance and imperfection. But there are few imperfections in Davis's performance. He *dominates* that stage, and now the smart money people are saying the show will have a long, successful run.

Sammy Davis had yearned to win acclaim as a legitimate actor. He staked his reputation on succeeding in this show. He sacrificed an estimated $800,000 in earnings to accept the part, and he poured all his energies and talents into five grueling months of tryouts and rehearsals. "It's been a long, uphill climb," he says. "Don't let anyone ever tell you different."

On the surface, the most surprising thing is that he even bothered to make that climb. For at 38 this versatile performer—Milton Berle once called him "the greatest entertainer in the world"—had seemingly conquered every conceivable challenge in his field.

As a dancer, mimic and comedian he had drawn standing-room-only crowds consistently throughout the world. He had been the only American entertainer ever invited to play two consecutive command performances by the Queen of England. As a singer he had made 32 albums; in 1963 alone his records sold more than one million copies. As a television star he was the first Negro to break the color barrier in a dramatic show. As a movie actor he had appeared in 10 films. And then he had been on Broadway before—as the star of a 1956 musical called *Mr. Wonderful,* which ran for more than a year.

Since 1957 Davis had received—and rejected—more than a dozen offers to return to Broadway. His close friend, Frank Sinatra, cautioned him against another stage appearance; so did his managers. They pointed out he could earn $1.5 million a year simply by staying where he was. The weight of logic seemed to be on their side. Why, then, did he gamble on *Golden Boy?*

"After *Mr. Wonderful,*" he says, "I was pretty leery about

the theater. I said the only thing I'd come back for was something I believed in greatly. Well, baby, this is it. It shocks, not just to be shocking, but only to be honest." Then, too, he had been living on the road nine months a year for more years than he could remember. A Broadway appearance would allow him to spend more time at home with his wife, May Britt, and their two children, Mark and Tracey.

Yet probably the single most compelling factor behind his decision to accept the part was a compulsive desire to prove that he could excel as an actor. Few people accepted him as one, and the rejection stung. "Sammy doesn't want people to think of him as The Nightclub Entertainer anymore," explains his valet, Murphy Bennett. "He wants people to look at him and say, 'There goes Sammy Davis, The Actor.' "

The image Davis projects today is not quite so clear-cut. In public he sometimes appears overly aggressive, irritatingly sure of himself. Yet in private he often seems lonely, plagued by self-doubts and easily hurt. His personality is, in fact, a study in contradictions.

He reads voraciously, speaks articulately on subjects ranging from poetry to the trouble in Vietnam. He believes in flying saucers with a fierce intensity ("I've seen 'em, baby"), and he fancies himself an amateur James Bond. ("In London, I had the same chamois-cloth gun holster under my arm. I learned to drink like Bond, and I even started taking cold showers. Only I couldn't stand the cold water.")

He has dropped the Jr. from his name and insists today on being treated with the respect due an entertainer who has Made it Big. He loves making money, and he spends it wildly on records (6,000 albums) and clothes (600 pairs of shoes, 200 suits) and gadgets ("They ain't gonna put out a gimmick in the world that I ain't gonna have; they're too much fun") and cars (a Rolls-Royce, a Corvette Sting Ray, a Lincoln Continental, a Buick station wagon, a Ford Mustang and a custom-made Cadillac with a built-in bar and two telephones). He also gives time and money unflinchingly to charity.

Hillard Elkins is a man who knows something about the Davis drive. Elkins has been an actor and an actor manager, and now he is *Golden Boy* producer. He is only 35, but he has risen to the top very quickly.

"Ten years ago," Elkins begins, "Sammy's goal was simply to make more money than any other Negro entertainer. He did that. Now his goal is to be the best in anything he does. He knew he'd reached the zenith in nightclubs. Where could he go to grow. Nowhere. So he accepted a challenge that most performers will not accept." Adds *Golden Boy* director Arthur Penn: "The man is almost presumptuous. He has a vision of excellence that by virtue of his education and background he simply has no right to have. But he has it nonetheless."

Davis's education and background did leave something to be desired. Born at 140th Street and 8th Avenue in Harlem, he spent his first birthday in a crib backstage at the old Hippodrome. His father, mother and adopted uncle, Will Mastin, were vaudeville troupers.

At four he made his movie debut in a Warner Brothers comedy called *Rufus Jones for President*. At five he learned to sing professionally, but while his talent may have delighted audiences, it angered the authorities, who yanked him offstage for violating child-labor laws. Determined to keep the act together, Mastin stuck a fat cigar between his teeth and introduced him as a 45-year-old dancing midget. He never spent a day in school.

In 1943, at the age of 17, he joined the Army. Eventually transferred into Special Services, Davis wrote, directed and produced camp shows and sharpened his talents as a singer, dancer and mimic. Upon his discharge he rejoined his father and uncle in the Will Mastin Trio and began to play a succession of one-night gigs in third-rate theaters.

In 1951 Jack Benny helped them get a booking at Ciro's in Hollywood. The manager offered $500 a week; they wanted $550. Finally their agent promised to pay the first week's difference from his own pocket. They signed the contract and, within two weeks, shared top billing. Their income tripled.

"After the war," Davis once told an *Esquire* reporter, "I'd been hungry and mad. You couldn't work certain hotels because of the Negro bit. Certain headliners refused to go on with us because we stole the show. I was *so* hungry. I was trying to do everything. I could do 50 impersonations. Play the drums. Play the trumpet. Play the bass fiddle. Play the piano. Dance. Sing. Tell jokes. Well, then we made it. After that night in Ciro's, every day for the next three years I had a new chick. Wine, women and song. It's the old story of the guy who doesn't have it and then he gets it. He fluffs friends. He does a hundred things wrong. He knows he's doing wrong, see, but he can't stop.

"I bought 12 suits at a time, $175 a whack. I bought tailor-made shirts, cars—fast ones. I bought gold cigarette cases for everybody. All my life I wanted to buy something in a store and not ask how much. I had credit everywhere. Between 1951 and 1954 I must have blown $150,000."

Such extravagance failed to harm Davis's growing popularity. He made guest appearances on *The Steve Allen Show* and the Colgate *Comedy Hour*. He made a pilot television film for ABC called *Three's Company*, which remained on the shelf for lack of a sponsor. And—with the trio—he played the nightclub circuit: New York, Chicago, Hollywood, Miami, Las Vegas.

Davis worked relentlessly on developing other talents. He became enamored of photography and submitted a batch of pictures to a national magazine. He used the name David Sampels. Only after the pictures were accepted did he reveal who David Sampels was. "I had to find out if I was any good," he says.

"Then he decided to learn how to play the vibes," comedian Karl Barrie remembers. "He didn't just take it on one level. He mastered it. So many performers will take a thing halfway and stop when they get applause. Sammy has to satisfy himself."

Yet Davis was desperately unhappy. His hopes were accelerating faster than his ability to realize them. He felt imprisoned by the color of his skin. He sensed, correctly, that no amount of financial success would ever enable him to overcome that. "I was tempted, man, to go abroad, to get outta here." Then he rejected that idea. "It was swinging all right in London and Paris," he says, "but none of the Negro artists there were actually creating anything. I suddenly realized that I never saw a single happy expatriate."

Davis has always had a unique, almost masochistic talent for adding handicaps to the ones he acquired at birth. In November, 1954, he suffered one that almost ended his career—an auto accident that resulted in the loss of his left eye. "I spent three, four days in total darkness," he recalls. "I began thinking about my faults. That's when I began to change."

Soon after leaving the hospital he added another handicap. "I was trying to find a religion that would say something to me and talk about *my* needs," he says. "I met a rabbi at a benefit in Las Vegas and got interested in Judaism. It gave me something I'd been missing—peace of mind. So I converted. For a long time I was reluctant to go into a synagogue. I was afraid people would think I was trying to pull something. I may joke about it, but it's not something I take lightly."

The loss of an eye and his religious conversion seemed only to enhance his stage appeal. His income soared. Soon he found new ways to spend it. He bought an interest in a Hollywood nightclub called the Moulin Rouge. He became a partner in a restaurant operation. He gambled heavily and aroused the interest of the Internal Revenue Service, which claimed that he and his father owed the Government $56,000. "I'm not one of the great businessmen of all times," he says. "At least, I wasn't then. I had no setup for it. My business manager, Jim Waters, and my lawyers started to take over a few years ago, and I'm afraid they succeeded in straightening me out."

In 1960 Davis added a third significant handicap—one that few of his friends thought he could ever overcome. For years his romantic affiliations had spiced the gossip columns. He dated Kim Novak (their relationship reportedly came to a crashing halt only when Columbia Pictures president Harry

Cohn asked Davis, "You're blind in one eye. Would you like to try for two?"). He married Negro dancer Loray White (they separated three months later and eventually were divorced). He became engaged briefly in 1959 to a blond Canadian named Joan Stuart. Then he met Swedish actress May Britt.

"I invited her to a barbecue," Davis recalls, "and she brought a date. And she didn't sit at my table—she sat at another table. And she didn't sit facing me—she sat with her back to me. And I figured I'd fight it to the bitter end."

On November 13, 1960, in the living room of Davis's Hollywood home, Rabbi William M. Kramer pronounced the couple man and wife.

"We used to get 15 to 25 hate letters every day," Davis recalls. "You just don't believe people can be that low." Until last year the couple retained bodyguards for their protection.

"Sammy explained the way it could be, before we married," May says, "and everything happened just the way he said it would. But I loved the man then, and I still love him. Besides, people are getting used to us now. You get to the point where you almost relax and then, wham, it hits you. But so far the kids have not been affected. At three and four, they lead a pretty sheltered life. And Sammy is a marvelous husband. Much more than I expected. I would have settled for less."

As a Negro married to a white woman, Davis is asked endless questions about interracial marriages. They bore him and sometimes make him angry. "All I can say is that my marriage works," he snaps.

Curiously, Davis had won acceptance as an entertainer prior to 1960 in almost every corner of the globe—except in Harlem. There he was criticized unjustly for being "anti-Negro."

"Sammy's career just threw him into another element," explains George Rhodes, his musical conductor. "But those cats uptown—they figured he was trying to be something he wasn't, that he didn't want to be around his own people. They didn't realize you have to be downtown to get your head above the water."

The situation changed when Davis began getting involved in the struggle for equal rights. "Seven years ago," he says, "I couldn't have cared less. But now I care. In the past few years I've read about Negro history until the good eye gets sore. I've done benefits. The march on Washington. The reason I want to fight now is my two kids. I want to be able to look at them and say, 'It's going to be better.' "

As he became increasingly committed to "the cause," Davis sought entertainment vehicles which could further it. The opportunity materialized in an unexpected quarter.

"It was around October, 1961," recalls producer Hillard Elkins. "I was in London, and I heard Sammy was appearing at the Prince of Wales Theater. So I caught the midnight show. He started doing this number. He was wearing blue jeans and an old T-shirt and all of a sudden I said to myself, 'That's Golden Boy.'

"We got together the next day and I said, 'Sammy, I've got the greatest idea of the century. You've gotta do *Golden Boy*. It's the story of a young Negro breaking out of the ghetto and—well, it's *your* show.' He couldn't promise anything, but he said he'd think it over. And then around Christmas he called and said, 'Swing, baby.' "

Elkins swung. He purchased the rights to *Golden Boy* and persuaded Odets to try to rewrite his drama as a musical. In March, 1963, he signed Davis to a contract—and established a Broadway precedent. He agreed to pay Davis 10 percent of the weekly box-office gross, 15 percent of the production's profits and a fat expense account. The total is approximately $10,000 per week—the highest figure ever earned by a star on Broadway.

Rehearsals began at New York's Ethel Barrymore Theater last May. "We're going to Philadelphia to break in the show, Boston to have some fun and Detroit for the race riots," Elkins joked. But from the beginning, almost nothing happened according to plan.

Odets had submitted two drafts before his death in August,

1963. Both missed their mark. A series of "play doctors" then tackled the problem with no conspicuous success. No one seemed able to raise the story above the level of mediocrity.

Golden Boy opened at Philadelphia's Shubert Theater on June 26. Reviews were mixed. Critics were kind to Davis but found the script unconvincing. Five weeks later the show moved to Boston. The book had been revised and tightened. "But I felt we were still in a lot of trouble," Elkins recalls.

Critics agreed: *Golden Boy* was deep in crisis. Less than eight weeks remained before its scheduled Broadway opening. Director Peter Coe had to be fired. Producer Elkins had exhausted his supply of rewrite men. Davis was disconsolate. Everything he had wanted so badly to achieve seemed to be eluding his grasp.

"Sammy's biggest difficulty," said playwright William Gibson, who had been called in to rescue the script, "was the lack of material. He was trying to establish the whole entertainment value of the show in the songs. He knew there was nothing else except the songs. And he was overacting."

On August 25, *Golden Boy* opened at Detroit's Fisher Theater. Critics panned it again. For nearly two weeks, ever since Gibson had finished rewriting the script, the cast had played one show at night and rehearsed a totally different show during the day. Davis poured himself into the effort, dredging up emotions and experiences from his own past to help Gibson understand the meaning of Negro frustration, but he was physically and emotionally exhausted. One final effort remained.

"We called it 'Operation Transfer,' " producer Elkins says. "We closed the old show on a Saturday night, rehearsed around the clock and opened the brand-new show on Monday night." Adds Davis, "It was the hardest time I've ever gone through in my life."

Audience response to the new effort was hearteningly encouraging. "For the first time in months, we felt that we were on the right track," Elkins remembered. Yet much remained to be done.

In mid-September the show moved on to New York. Elkins postponed its opening date three weeks. The cast was exhausted; Davis begged for a day off. He didn't get it. The show was still in serious trouble, and everyone knew it. Music and lyrics still sounded strangely out of place. Whole scenes seemed disjointed. Characters lacked motivation. In Philadelphia and Boston, Davis played the part of a Negro musician who turned to the prize ring. In Detroit he dropped the musician's identity and became a premed student. The character still strained credulity.

Then Gibson had an idea. Why not make him simply a bitter young Negro, a boy whose tremendous ambitions lead eventually to his self-destruction? Revisions continued. On Friday—four days before the opening curtain—Davis learned that other changes would be added over the weekend. "That Friday night was the only time he was ever obstreperous about acting," Penn recalls. "He couldn't absorb what I was saying. He had worked himself to the end of his resources, and he couldn't do more."

The next day Davis disappeared. Five minutes before the curtain rose on a preview performance, May Davis called Elkins and said she didn't know where her husband was. Elkins canceled the matinee. He put on the show that night with able understudy Lamont Washington in the title role. Seventy percent of the audience walked out in disappointment. Desperately Elkins tried to locate his star.

At four o'clock on Sunday morning Davis called the producer. "Welcome home, Penrod," Elkins said, trying to appear blasé. "If you want to open Tuesday, we'd better rehearse today."

"I'll be there," Davis said. He was.

"I never ran away from anything before in my life," Davis says. "But if I hadn't run on Saturday, there would have been nothing, absolutely nothing. That Saturday didn't come out of fear, or thinking, 'Oh, God, what are the critics going to say?' I'd been promised a day off and I never got it. I know my voice.

Three doctors all said the same thing. 'Rest, or you'll never be able to sing on opening night.' "

The weather on opening night was dismal. A bone-chilling drizzle fell on the city, adding to the mood of general pessimism. The curtain rose early, just after seven o'clock, and it was obvious almost immediately that something was wrong. Davis's voice was harsh and gravelly; he was spitting out his lines instead of letting them flow from inner conviction. His first song was disappointing. An uneasy feeling swept over the audience.

Suddenly, toward the middle of Act 1, he recovered. The songs flowed smoother and he was understating emotions— doing at last what Penn and Gibson had told him so many times to do. He maneuvered through the difficult kissing scene with Paula Wayne without a mishap. He handled the tricky father-son confrontation in the second act with feeling and skill. Then the show was over. Waves of applause brought him back on stage three times. Yet as he walked to the dressing room, he still seemed mired in a quicksand of self-doubt. "My voice was in rotten shape," he said.

He waited until the crowds had left his dressing room, slipped on a tuxedo and went, finally, to the opening-night party at a restaurant across town to await the reviews. Tension rose. Finally someone yelled that Walter Kerr's review (in the *Herald Tribune*) was in. "He hates it, huh?" Davis asked.

But Kerr didn't hate anything. "Mr. Davis," he wrote, "is not so much at the top of his form as he is on top of a brand-new situation, licking it hands down. . . . The performance is there and it is serious, expert, affecting." Someone else said Howard Taubman of *The Times* was giving the show a rave.

The atmosphere of tension dissolved into wild frivolity. "I didn't think we were gonna get the *Times* and the *Trib*." Davis beamed. "It's a hit. A great big hit. I feel ten feet tall."

Every night for the next several weeks his dressing room was crowded with celebrities. One evening, clad in a blue terry-cloth robe, Davis lounged on the floor, sipping from a golden mug containing bourbon and Coke.

"You won't believe this," he remarked, "but right now do you know that Dean Martin and Jerry Lewis are at Vegas at the Sands? Gambling? Drinking? They're not legit, though."

Someone in the room said, "Well, Sam, looks like you're pretty busy."

"Man," Davis replied. "They got me workin' like they think I'm colored or sumpin'. Damn."

He stayed in the dressing room for half an hour, and the knot of admirers slowly disentangled. He changed into a brown-checked suit, grabbed his coat, sprang down the steps and burst into a cluster of fans waiting by the stagedoor entrance.

"Don't you ever get tired of signing autographs?" someone asked. "No, baby," Davis replied, scrawling his name with a spiderweb flourish. "I've waited twenty years for this and I ain't gonna give up now."

He finished and started walking down the corridor to the street, his black cane tapping a cadence on the asphalt. Chauffeur Herb Seeger was waiting with the Rolls-Royce. "Hey," someone shouted. "There goes Sammy Davis." Davis whirled and waved. "How ya doin', my man?" he asked. Then he stepped into the car and was gone.

—*February 13, 1965*

"WHAT MAKES SAMMY, JR., RUN?,"
by Thomas B. Morgan, *Esquire*

In a typical ten-day period recently, Sammy Davis, Jr., had this schedule: the final week of an eighteen-day engagement at the Copacabana (sixteen performances interspersed with general frolicking, a record date, television and radio interviews, and two visits with Cye Martin, his tailor); a one-night stand in Kansas City to receive an Americanism award from the Ameri-

can Legion; one night at home in Hollywood; and the opening
night of a two-week date in Las Vegas at the Sands Hotel, the
management of which has a contract with him for the next four
years, eight weeks a year, at $25,000 per week. The schedule
could have been extended. The day after closing in Vegas,
Davis was due for three weeks in Hollywood at the Moulin
Rouge, another nightclub with which he has a five-year million-
dollar deal, followed by two weeks in Australia, followed by an
Eastern tour. Photographer Burt Glinn and I, however, arbitrar-
ily pursued Davis through that ten-day period. Since this short,
skinny, one-eyed, broken-nosed, umber-colored singer-dancer-
musician-actor-mimic may be, as Milton Berle has said, "the
greatest entertainer in the world," and may even be, as
Groucho Marx has decided, "better than Al Jolson, who could
only sing," we wanted to find out what we could, naturally,
about what makes Sammy, Jr., run.

Like most men, Davis lives a life of quiet desperation. The
only differences are that he has little privacy to live it in and
that on the average of twice a night, thirty weeks a year, he
must stand in a spotlight, and be Sammy Davis, Jr.—cosmic,
sentimental, bursting with energy, and immensely talented—no
matter how he feels inside. If he were an average performer, the
challenge might not be so great.

"But you see," says Davis, "what I do is different. Most Negro performers work in a cubicle. They walk on, entertain, and
sing twelve songs before they say good evening. They never
make any personal contact with the audience. Long time ago, I
knew I could only make it if I broke through this wall. I was
convinced that a Negro boy could do comedy—you know the
kind I mean. Not the yassuh, nossuh thing. I decided I could
make it as a person, like Jolson or Danny Kaye made it. Well,
to do that, you have to be honest with an audience. You got to
have antennae and feel what they want. And you have to try to
keep your personal feelings from interfering with your communication."

The Davis act has a basic structure—songs, impersonations,

dancing, laced together with comic patter or sentimental chit-chat. The structure never changes, yet every performance is different.

"The patter between songs," says Davis, "is something that can't be planned. You can't write it if you're going to be honest. I can vary the act at any minute with a signal to Morty Stevens, my conductor. I snap my fingers a certain way and he knows we are going to go into *Let's Face the Music*. I tap my foot just so, and it's going to be *Old Black Magic*. If you're honest, you can feel the right way to get to them every time. Otherwise, Dullsville, Ohio. I don't mean all good shows are alike, either. You've got three kinds of shows—a routine show, a fun show, and a performance show. The fun show is lots of tumult and laughs. The performance show is the one, like opening night, where you belt it all the way. What I do works because I am trying to be honest.

"You take most of the material in my act: aside from the songs, I don't do any bits that I didn't contribute to. I have a choreographer—Hal Loman—but we work out the dances together. Nothing fancy about my dancing. I like to make clear sounds with the taps. Bojangles—that's Bill Robinson, who taught me a lot—he used to say, 'Make it so the people can understand it.' That's what I try to do.

"Sometimes the impersonations get in the way. They blur your image with the people and you die as a performer without a distinction of your own. I used to do a song called *Why Can't I Be Me?* That's the story of most of my life. Every guy wants to sound like himself. But I keep the impersonations in the act because the audience wants them. They're like a frame. The audience says, gee, that's his best stuff, what's he going to give us next?

"The big thing is understanding the songs and projecting them honestly. When I sing *I Got Plenty o' Nuttin'*, I think about a guy who is happy with his life. Doesn't make any difference how *I* feel. I think how *he* feels. When you have that, daddy, you don't need any tricks. All I want is they should like me—say this is a nice guy. Just let them give me one thing— applause—and I'm happy."

Nightclub audiences do curious things when Davis is on- stage. For one, they are prone to give him standing ovations. For another, they tend to gasp out telling comments—telling about themselves as well as the performer. Early in his act, Davis comes on wearing a grey porkpie hat, black suit, black shirt, white tie, with a trench coat flung over his shoulder, a cig- arette in one hand and a glass of whiskey-colored water in the other. He blows smoke into the microphone, sips the drink, and says, "My name is Frank Sinatra, I sing songs, and we got a few we'd like to lay on ya." Davis puts the drink on the piano, throws the trench coat on the floor, and begins *The Lady Is a Tramp*. The audience always applauds wildly and somebody is certain to cry out: "My God, he even looks like Sinatra," or words to that effect. A broken-nosed Negro does not look much like Sinatra, even though the latter is no work of art him- self, but the illusion of Davis' voice and visage and movements, plus the complete rapport which has been established between entertainer and entertainees, produces a kind of Sinatrian hallu- cination.

For the full sixty minutes of his act, Davis sustains this kind of communication. It could be defined as an atmosphere of col- orlessness in which he not only makes the audience forget that he is a Negro, but also makes it forget that it is white. This is why one of his closing bits has a special irony that is all Davis. He is sitting on a stool in a circle of light. He has, it seems, al- most sung himself out in an effort to entertain. His coat and tie are off. He takes a few deep breaths and suddenly he brightens. "What do you say?" he asks. "Let's all get in a cab and go up to my place!" For one goofy moment, nobody laughs. Here is the source of his power and also the reason for his private des- peration. In the spotlight, he and they are colorless. In the real world, he is a colored man who has made it and yet can never make it all the way. When the applause finally comes, it is deaf- ening. The performance drives to a rocking, exploding, belting finish, and Davis is gone. As someone once said, "The only thing that could follow that act is World War Three."

Thus driving and thus driven, Sammy Davis made $1,200,000 last year—over half from nightclubs and the rest from records, TV, and movies. When you say it slowly, it sounds like a lot of money, but his net is considerably less. Besides taxes (he's in the ninety percent bracket), he has eleven people on his payroll: valet, secretary, conductor-arranger, drummer, guitarist, office manager, typists (for answering fan mail), and various assistants; his overhead is $3,500 a week. His agent takes ten percent. And even though his father retired from the act in 1959, because of a heart attack, and his uncle, Will Mastin, moved over from dance manager to manager in 1958, he still splits what is left equally with them, and presents the act to the public as the Will Mastin Trio featuring Sammy Davis, Jr.

The three-way split of the profits is unique in show business. Davis believes he must spend on the "millionaire" level, yet the contract with father and uncle provides him with a mere thirty-three percent, of which still another ten percent goes to a group of Chicago investors.

Davis has not saved much money nor has he put his earnings to work for him with any conspicuous success. He owns a piece of an unspectacular restaurant in Hollywood and has an interest in a line of sports shirts ("Creations by Sammy Davis, Jr.") and a hand grip for cameras. He put money into some TV and movie properties. But mostly the money goes for living well, if not too wisely. It would be surprising if it went any other way.

Davis was born in Harlem, December 8, 1925. His mother, father, and uncle were all in show business. He went onstage before he was three in a theatre in Columbus, Ohio. He did a talking act with Uncle Will when he was three and a half. He appeared in a movie, *Rufus Jones for President*, made at Warner Brothers' Long Island studios, at age four. The next year, in the midst of singing *I'll Be Glad When You're Dead*,

You Rascal You at the Republic Theatre in Manhattan, he was pulled off the stage by a member of the Gerry Society, which enforced child-labor laws in those days. Until he was eleven, he trouped with his uncle's fifteen-person vaudeville act. When the authorities became suspicious, his father put cork on his face, stuck a cigar in his mouth, and passed him off as a dancing midget. In 1936, the vaudeville act was disbanded and the Will Mastin Trio, a straight dancing act, was born. They danced in beer gardens and theatres all over the East, making as little as $30 a week (for the trio) and spending part of the time on relief. Davis' education consisted of less than two years in school and a few lessons from a now-and-then tutor.

In 1943, Davis was drafted into the Army. He passed the Air Corps cadet tests, but Negroes with less than two years of college training were not being accepted. He was transferred to the Infantry, in which he took basic training in one of the earliest integrated units. Three times he was rejected for overseas duty because of an athletic heart. Toward the end of the war, he was transferred again, to Special Services. In camp shows, he developed as a singer and mimic. "What was more important," says Davis, "I met a sergeant by the name of Bill Williams who gave me about fifty books to read. He's really the guy who educated me."

After the war, with Davis' songs and impersonations added to the act, the trio's luck improved. They traveled six months with Mickey Rooney, who encouraged Davis to develop all of his talents instead of concentrating on just one. Frank Sinatra, whom Davis had first met in 1940, got them three weeks on his bill at the Capitol on Broadway in 1947. In spite of favorable reviews, nothing happened. They toured the West Coast with Jack Benny, through whose help they were booked into Ciro's, Hollywood, in 1951. Herman Hover, the owner of Ciro's, offered them $300 a week to open a show starring Janis Paige. The trio held out for $350. Finally, Arthur Silber, their agent, put up $50 of his own for the first week, and the contract was signed. The act caught fire. By the second week, the Will

Mastin Trio was costarred with the headliner. They moved on to a date at the Chez Paree in Chicago at $1,250 a week and were not headed again.

After twenty-three years, Davis had become an overnight sensation. In the eight years that followed, the trio went round and round on the nightclub circuit—New York, Miami, Chicago, Las Vegas, and Hollywood. Davis made eleven record albums for Decca Records. He took intermittent turns as a guest performer on TV—notably *The Comedy Hour* and *The Steve Allen Show*. He appeared in *Mr. Wonderful* on Broadway—a mediocre show that ran for a year because it was cheaper for Davis' growing audience to see him in a theatre than in a nightclub. In Hollywood, he made *Anna Lucasta* and the spectacular *Porgy and Bess*. The money poured in.

"After that night in Ciro's," Davis recalls, "every day for three years I had a new chick—wine, women, and song. After the war, I'd been hungry and mad, baby. You couldn't work certain hotels because of the Negro bit. Certain headliners refused to go on with us because we stole the show. I was so hungry. I was trying to do everything. We used to do an hour-and-forty-minute show. I could do fifty impersonations. Play the drums. Play the trumpet. Play the bass fiddle. Play the piano. Dance. Sing. Tell jokes.

"Well, then we made it. It's the old story of the guy who doesn't have it and then gets it. He fluffs friends. He does a hundred things wrong. He *knows* he's doing wrong, see, but he can't stop.

"I bought twelve suits at a time—$175 a whack. I bought tailor-made shirts, cars—fast ones. Once I bought twenty-one pairs of shoes from Lefcourt in New York. All my life, I wanted to buy something in a store and not ask how much. I lost all sense of value. I had credit everywhere and just signed my name. Between 1951 and 1954, I must have blown $150,000. My head got *so big*. I wanted to pick up every check and pay every tip. The first time I was booked into the Copa in New York, I bought a pack of cigarettes and left the girl change from a twenty-dollar bill. I wanted to do that because once I went in there as a nobody and they put me on the side. I bought a Cadillac El Dorado. I bought gold cigarette cases for everybody. I remembered when, for Christmas presents, my dad and uncle and I used to exchange a carton of cigarettes. Every day was like Christmas. I got snotty. Everybody I saw it was, 'Hello, chickee. Love ya, baby. See you later.'

"It takes a terribly long time to learn how to be a success in show business. People flatter you all the time. You are on all the time. And if you're a Negro, you find yourself using your fame to make it socially. Let's face it. The biggest deals with the big moguls are made in a social way, around the pool, that sort of thing. If you're not there, well, you're not *there*. So I used to think the greatest thing in the world was to be invited to a movie star's house.

"Things got bad. One night in Vegas, I lost $39,000 playing blackjack. That's how bad it was. There's nobody who's got that much money to lose.

"I feel I've been changing. If a man doesn't change, he isn't one to swing with. But his friends stick by him while he's changing.

"November 19, 1954, I'm driving along with a buddy at eight in the morning near San Bernardino on the way to Hollywood. It was a beautiful, typical, happy California morning. A car pulled out of a blind drive and I hit it going fifty-five or sixty. The steering wheel hit me in the face. I got the car stopped and ran over to see if the lady in the other car was all right. She was, until she looked at me. She turned green. Then I felt my left eye. They took me to the hospital and Dr. Owen O'Connor and Dr. Frederick Hull removed the eye. If they hadn't done that, I might have gone blind in a month. I spent three, four days in total darkness. I began thinking about my faults. I was sure God had saved my life. That's when I began to change.

"I met a rabbi at a Jewish benefit in Las Vegas and got interested in Judaism. I found the faith gave me something I'd been missing—peace of mind—so I converted. When I am home, in Hollywood, I try to attend services whenever I can. For a long time, I was reluctant to go into a synagogue. I was afraid people would think I was trying to pull something. While we were working on *Porgy and Bess*, Sam Goldwyn thought I was kidding when I said I wanted to be excused for the High Holy Days. Then he had to believe me when I said I would take off anyway.

"I admit the Jewish thing has been a bit of a problem. It couldn't have been more of a problem if I'd have had my eyes fixed and become Japanese. But I think everyone has to find God his own way. Sometimes it takes something like the loss of an eye to get you thinking about it. Life is very confused and you need something. I accept the Jewish idea of God. As I see it, the difference is that the Christian religion preaches love thy neighbor and the Jewish religion preaches justice. I think justice is the big thing we need."

Davis has not been without a sense of humor about his religious conversion. During his nightclub act he is likely to say, "I could have starred in *The Defiant Ones*, but I lost the part when they found out I was Jewish," or "The Irish kept me out of the St. Patrick's Day Parade for *two* reasons." On the *Porgy and Bess* set he looked accusingly at German-speaking director Otto Preminger and said: "You made lampshades out of my people." But the justice he seeks, of course, is the most elusive of human ideals. Instead, there is irony, which Sammy Davis runs from and into almost every day of his life.

During his stay in New York last spring, Davis' dressing room was a small, seedy, two-room suite on the third floor of the Hotel Fourteen, which adjoins the Copacabana. One night after his late show, the average crowd of thirty people was milling in the twelve-by-fifteen-foot living room. Among them were Sidney Poitier, the actor, and Archie Moore, the fighter; Fran Warren, the singer, and Althea Gibson, the tennis star; three plainclothes cops ("just friends"), and a Mrs. Goldman and her daughter ("We're fans!") from Queens, Long Island,

and twenty-or-so other people who were helping themselves to the liquor, watching TV, and fooling around with the expensive portable stereo rig on the mantel—yakking and puffing as though none of the satires on show biz had over been written.

Davis was in the bedroom, wearing a white terry-cloth robe with a torn pocket and drinking bourbon-and-Coke from a sterling-silver goblet, which a friend had given him. With him were his valet, Murphy Bennett; his secretary, Dave Landfield, who looks a little like Rip Torn and is an aspiring actor; and a man from Hollywood, one Abby Greshler, who seemed proudest of the fact that he originally brought Dean Martin and Jerry Lewis together as a team. Greshler was there to organize a movie vehicle for Davis based on Joey Adam's novel, *The Curtain Never Falls*, about a Broadway-Hollywood star and heel. As usual, Davis was conducting his business in a fishbowl. He has no secrets from his valet, his secretary, or from almost anyone else. In exchange, his employees are deeply attached to him. A guest once said to his valet: "Tell you what, Murphy, I'll kill Sammy, and you come work for me." Bennett replied: "If Sammy dies, I'll just have to go with him."

Davis was passionately convinced that *The Curtain Never Falls* with himself in the lead would be an important step forward for all Negro actors and entertainers.

"So the hero in the book is Jewish," he said. "We make him a Negro. It works, motivation and everything. Look, I want to make it as a movie actor. I always wanted to act, but what chance was there? I remember when the reviews came out for *Mr. Wonderful*—everyone was crying about the beating we took and I was walking on air because Brooks Atkinson said I was a believable actor. Atkinson said that. Or you take *Porgy and Bess*. Now I simply *had* to play Sportin' Life. I mean, he was me. I worked to get that part. My friends—Frank and all the rest—worked to get it for me. So one night after Sam Goldwyn saw me perform, he called me into his office and pointed his finger. 'You,' he said, 'you are Sportin' Life.' Let me tell you, I mean, playing that part was the gasser of my life."

"Well, this'll be great, too," said Greshler.

"The way I see it, Abby, the movie positively can't preach. It's got to show it. Here's this hero. He knows there are only three ways a colored cat can make it: as a fighter, ballplayer, or entertainer. He's got to make it, see? I remember one time a guy asked me, 'How far you going to make it, Sammy?' and I said, 'I've got an agent, some material, and talent.' So the guy says, 'Yes, but you're colored.' And I said, 'I can beat all this.' Now this is what the hero in the movie wants. Only he's ready to renounce everything he is to make it. He's a character who's ashamed of his father, see? That's the way we'll do it. People have to believe it's honest."

"They will, Sammy, they will," said Greshler.

Davis and Greshler shook hands, resealing their contract, which would never be more formal than that until the money talk began in Hollywood. Davis turned and walked into the living room to join his guests. In the crowd, he looked smaller than he seems onstage. He is about five foot six and weighs only a hundred and twenty-five pounds. His hair, combed flat, is neither brown nor black, but somewhere in between. It is next to impossible to determine which eye is the blind one. He has a U-shaped scar across the bridge of his nose, which was broken in the 1954 accident. His face is thin, the jaw slightly underslung. As Bob Sylvester once said, he looks as though he had been hit in the face with a shovel.

Davis spied Sidney Poitier, who is husky and tall and reminds you of an unspoiled Belafonte who can also act.

"Sidney!" cried Davis. "I'm glad to see you, baby!"

Sidney Poitier embraced him, lifting him off his feet. The room, which had been shaking with noise, became quiet, except for some shooting on the TV, and Tony Bennett lisping on the stereo.

"Everybody's got to see it, baby," said Davis, turning to a clot of people on his blind side. "I mean, you have to see Sidney in *Raisin*. Only the end—a definite gas!"

Now Davis embraced Poitier, then backed away, bending

over, shoulders hunched, hands dangling in a precise imitation of Poitier in *A Raisin in the Sun*, crying: "I'm thirty-five and what am I—I'm *nothing!*"

A girl laughed, "Oh, you're something, Sam, and you're only thirty-three," and everyone laughed with her.

"She's got to die," said Davis, pinching her cheek. "If she makes one more remark, death!"

The crowd began to thin out after a while. Poitier and Moore and many of the people that no one knew departed. Davis paused to say good-bye as each one left. At the door, he did a short bit with a girl who asked him how he was getting along with the head doctor. Davis has had some psychoanalysis, but he is rarely in Hollywood long enough to accomplish much.

"Well, I've had a little, baby," said Davis. "I'm still sick, but I understand it now, see what I mean? I told the doc I didn't want to understand myself, I just wanted to be better. So he says, what you got, a cold or something—what better?"

Then Davis kissed her cheek and sent her on her way. A hard core of a dozen cordial-to-very-close friends remained. Dave Landfield, the secretary, strapped on one of the two gun belts hanging in the closet and practiced his fast draw.

"Not that way, Dave! Dave—God, I could draw faster with a pencil and paper," Davis said. "Get the thumb on the hammer, man, and do it all in one motion."

Over his bathrobe, Davis buckled on a gun belt holstering a single-action Colt .45 six-shooter. He tied the holster things above his knee. He drew the gun, twirled it three times over his trigger finger, and brought it down smartly into the holster. He drew again, very fast, cocking and dry-firing in a split second. Then he twirled the gun vertically, horizontally, over and back into the holster. (In Hollywood, Davis has a collection of thirty Western guns and, next to Mel Tormé, he is the fastest nonprofessional draw in town. Once I saw him hold a bottle at waist level, *throw* the bottle to the floor, and draw, cock, and shoot before it hit the carpet. "I love things Western," he says. "Morty, Dave, Arthur Silber, and I go to Phoenix and dress up in the tailor-made jeans and the tailor-made shirts, the cowboy hats, .45's on our hips and Winchesters in the saddle holsters. We ride out like cowboys and talk about the south forty, tip the hat back with the thumb, and chew on filter cigarettes.") Davis demonstrated the fast draw a few more times.

"You dig, baby?" asked Davis.

Landfield nodded and Davis retired to the bedroom to dress. As he hung up his gun belt, he said to me: "I'm crazy to make a Western. Can you imagine a colored Western—they'll never do it! But if they do, it'll be the first time they let the Indians win!"

From the Hotel Fourteen, Davis and the hard core of friends rode three cabs to the Hotel New Yorker. Davis was living there in the penthouse. (Going up in the elevator, I remembered a story I had once heard about Bert Williams, a great Negro song-and-dance man of twenty-five years ago. When Williams played New York, he also rented a penthouse at a midtown hotel. The only difference was that his lease required him to enter and leave the hotel by the service elevator. One night, Eddie Cantor was riding up with Williams and asked him if it bothered him using the service elevator. "Mr. Cantor," Williams said, "the only thing that bothers me is applause." A great deal of progress has been made since then, I thought, but there was still a strong trace of Williams in Sammy Davis, Jr.) Parties of varying intensity were held every night at the penthouse during Davis' eighteen-day engagement at the Copacabana and this night was no exception. When Davis arrived, three Copa girls, a former owner of the Chez Paree in Chicago, Davis' lawyer, another one of Davis' assistants named John Hopkins, and comedian Jack Carter and his date were waiting. Hopkins and Murphy Bennett tended bar. Landfield sent out for hamburgers and Davis turned up the stereo. The hamburgers arrived and talking stopped as the guests leaped to the feast. In a twinkling, the hamburgers were gone. Everyone got one, even the pretty girl reclining on the floor underneath an oak bench—everyone, that is, except Davis.

"It's a definite steal," he said, cheerfully, but for an instant he looked as though he would have liked a hamburger.

The party broke well after dawn. Only a few bitter-enders remained when Davis' father and stepmother came in from their room down the hall. They had flown to New York from Hollywood, where they live with Sammy, Jr., for a vacation and to see him at the Copacabana.

"How's my baby?" asked Sam, Sr., and kissed Sam, Jr.

"I'm fine, Dad."

Davis stepped back to examine his father. The older man is taller and heavier and the family resemblance is faint. He wore a new suit.

"You're getting fat, Dad," said Davis.

"I'm going to get fat as I want to."

"Well, then, get into your old clothes. Nothing looks worse than a fat man in a Continental suit."

"See what kind of a boy I have," said Sam, Sr., and the two men embraced, laughing.

To me, Sam, Sr., said: "We have a fine house out there. We all live in it together—the wife and me, Sam's two sisters, grandmother, and Sammy. A fine house, yes! Believe me, it's a kick for a man who was born on West Thirty-ninth Street."

(Sam, Jr., was proud of the house, too. It had been built by Judy Garland on the side of one of the Hollywood hills, just up the road from where Davis' friend, James Dean, used to live. Davis had bought the house a few years ago for a reported $75,000. Built on three levels, it provided an apartment for Davis' grandmother and more-or-less private quarters for the family of Sam, Sr. The upper floor—living room, bedroom, terrace and guest room—was Davis' domain, furnished with white rugs, mostly black furniture, and gigantic lamps. The terrace overlooked the inevitable swimming pool. The most unusual piece of furniture was Davis' bed, which was twice the size of the average double bed; otherwise, the house was ordinary-California-expensive without being lavish.)

"It is a fine house," Davis said. "It means a lot to me. Someday, I'd like to arrange things so I can spend some time there."

Davis finally went to bed that morning at eight. He was up at noon in high spirits. After lunch at P. J. Clarke's with Dorothy Kilgallen, the columnist, he walked crosstown. Everywhere he went, people on the street spoke to him, a bus driver pulled over to the curb to shake his hand, and teen-agers chased him for his autograph. A few days earlier he had been taking such a stroll on Seventh Avenue and had obliged a middle-aged lady with his signature. A crowd had formed and had followed him to the door of a haberdashery. From inside, he had seen a hundred noses pressed to the window. The crowd had grown, tying up traffic on the street. At last, an irate police sergeant had forced his way into the shop.

"Mr. Davis," the policeman had said, "you got a crowd outside."

"I didn't bring them," Davis had said.

"I'll call some more cops for you."

"No, I'll get out all right."

"How can you stand it?"

"I worked twenty years for this, sergeant. I can wait."

Now as he walked, Davis enjoyed the waves and glances of passersby again. "This sort of thing started a couple of years ago," he said to me. "All of a sudden, it was there. People knew *me*. Then I was sure I'd made it." His high spirits lasted through a sloppy recording session at Decca studios late in the afternoon. He was not in good voice and, besides, the songs were not right for him. When Dave Landfield, the secretary, asked him, "What next?" Davis said: "Well, Dave, baby, it's a definite leave from here in two-oh minutes, maybe even one-five, followed by a definite cab, which will speed me to Danny's Hide-a-Way for a little din-din. Then it will be another cab-ola to the Hotel Fourteen, that is, one-four. After that, chickee, it is a definite lay-down with closed eyes and Morpheus dropping little things in them for about forty winks, until I awake again, as myself—like refreshed—ready to go on. I mean, baby, is that clear?"

Davis laughed. When he is very happy, indeed, his talk often becomes a combination of hip, show biz, jazz, and, of course, English. It is in-group lingo of the kind he shares with his Hollywood friends—Frank Sinatra, Dean Martin, Peter Lawford, Eddie Fisher, and Tony Curtis—who are members of a determinedly informal organization known as "the clan."

In about one-five, Davis said to me, "Let's split," which meant *leave*, and we rode a definite cab to Danny's Hide-a-Way, a midtown restaurant in which Davis frequently dined. He ate his one big meal of the day with gusto. At seven, I followed him to the hat-check counter where he retrieved his derby, cape, and umbrella. A teen-age girl asked for his autograph. Davis signed a postcard for her.

"Thank you, Sammy," she said.

"You're welcome," he said, walking toward the door.

A heavy-set blond man, waiting to get to the hat-check room, said: "That's very nice, but why don't you do that in the *street*—"

A car was waiting for Davis. He stood inconclusively on the sidewalk. He looked through the window into Danny's trying to spot the man. Then he got into the car. By the time he arrived at the Hotel Fourteen, he was deeply hurt and enraged.

"What a Jackson!" he said.

"What's a Jackson?" I asked.

"A Jackson is some guy who calls a Negro 'Jackson' or 'Bo,' " he explained. "I'd like ten seconds with that rat!"

What can happen to Davis at any time, no matter how high he is flying, had happened.

Davis' early show was, in many subtle ways, below par. His timing was off. He did not kid with the audience. The beat of his songs was slower. It was not a happy show. Afterward, he returned to the dressing room, changed into the terry-cloth robe, and lay on the couch. Mike Silver, the drummer who travels with him, sat in a chair with his sticks in his hands, watching TV. Murphy Bennett straightened the bedroom. Davis was almost as alone as he ever is.

"I've never, never tried to be anything but what I am," he said. "I am a Negro. I'm not ashamed. The Negro people can mark a cat lousy for that and they won't go to see him perform. Well, we have Negroes here every night. If you go hear a Negro and see some Negroes in the audience, then you know how they stand. They'll ignore a guy who's marked lousy, see? So, I've never been the kind of guy who was ashamed. See, it's a matter of dignity. That's what makes something like that Jackson so tough on you. One time I went on in San Francisco and a guy down in the front row says to another guy, 'I didn't know he was a nigger,' and walked out. It's tough to play against that. In the Army, the first time anybody called me a bad name, I cried—the tears! I had spent all my life with my dad and uncle. I was loved. I was Charlie-protected. But now, this is the thing that is always just around the corner. It's like you can't get into El Morocco because you're colored. See?"

Davis' second show that night was better than the first, but he still seemed chilled. About four a.m., accompanied by fifteen men and women, he went to a West Side nightclub. Legally, it was closing time, but the bartender gathered up bottles, mix, ice, and glasses and carried the makings into a large back room. Cecil Young and three fourths of a Canadian jazz quartet were having a last drink before calling it a night. Like the patrons, the fourth member of the quartet—the bass fiddler—had already gone home. Seeing Davis, Cecil Young began telephoning around to find another fiddle player. When the man arrived, sleepy-eyed, the jam session began. Davis, Young, the Canadians, and the new man played wildly and wonderfully for ninety minutes. Davis sat in on drums, blew the trumpet, and sang scat with Cecil Young. When it was over, the hurt was out of his system.

During a break, Cecil Young had said to me: "Jazz isn't polite, son. Jazz is, pardon the expression, screw you. If you don't like it, well, that's all. But if you do like it, then I like you, dig?

With jazz, you thumb your nose when they don't like you. You get the message out, daddy."

Davis picked up the check for his friends and the group moved over to his penthouse for the sunrise.

A few days later, Davis landed in Las Vegas after overnight stops in Kansas City and Hollywood. Murphy Bennett had arrived a day ahead of him and had set up the suite at the Sands Hotel which would be Davis' home for the next two weeks. The stereo was rigged and 250 records (from Davis' collection of 20,000) were stacked neatly in the bedroom. There was fresh ice in the ice bucket and the silver goblet had been polished. After the rehearsal and a steam bath, Davis settled on a couch in the living room to relax until it was time to dress for the opening.

Jack Entratter, manager of the Sands, telephoned to report that five hundred reservations had been turned down for the dinner show. A friend called to tell Davis that his wife, Loray White Davis, was in Las Vegas divorcing him. Davis had been married in 1958 and had separated from his wife in less than three months. During the separation, a settlement had been made, but this was the first Davis had heard of the Nevada divorce proceedings. He shrugged. It was all over long ago. Another friend called to give him the latest on the romance of his friend Eddie Fisher who, with Elizabeth Taylor, was exciting Las Vegas and the world at that time.

Davis sighed. "Vegas I like," he said. "I feel like I've come home. You know I've performed in this town like twenty-nine times. We used to come in here before we were anything and when there were only a couple of hotels. The Sands I like. I was offered $37,500 a week to go into another hotel, but I turned it down. Very low pressure here. Easy. You're not fighting the knives and forks. It builds, but the pace is slower. You're running all the time, and then it's nice to come down to the Vegas pace."

Davis called to Landfield, the secretary.

"Hey, baby, call up Keely [Smith] and Louis [Prima] and tell them we'll be over after our show tonight. And find out what the Count [Basie] is doing. We'll swing with him tonight. And chicks. Chicks, we need. Ah, it's like a vacation. You can tumult all night, sleep all day, get a little sun—sun, I need—play a little blackjack. Oh, fine!" And he lay back on the couch, running.

—October 1973

"SAMMY DAVIS, JR., HAS BOUGHT THE BUS,"
by James Conaway, *The New York Times Magazine*

A shaft of light cuts through the gloom of the Las Vegas Hilton's Ballroom Internationale, striking a slight figure in a blue plaid suit standing just below the stage. An enamel American flag gleams in his lapel, a heavy gold peace medallion hangs from his neck; his right hand, resplendent with precious stones and their settings, is raised in a victory salute. As the applause mounts, the hand contracts into a black fist, then drops, a gesture so brief as to pass almost unnoticed.

Sammy Davis, Jr., has just been introduced by Elvis Presley, the Hilton's main attraction, and a friend who gave Sammy the massive star sapphire he wears. Sammy likes to tell that story— "Elvis said it was the biggest black star he had seen, and that he wanted to give it to the biggest black star he knew"—and later he will tell the story, upstairs in Elvis's private "superstar" suite. Sammy has taken the night off from his own show at the Sands to party with his third wife, Altovise, a handsome black dancer who was once a member of Sammy's troupe, and with Donald Rumsfeld, President Nixon's aide and director of the Cost of Living Council, who is staying at the Davises' with his wife, Joyce.

Tonight is the finale of the Rumsfelds' Western swing that took them from the Republican National Convention in Miami to Los Angeles, to attend the Republican-sponsored party there for prominent entertainers, and then to Las Vegas, to lounge around Sammy's private pool and play a little tennis. They are young and appealing, more in the hale tradition of college seniors winding up a successful summer vacation than in the role of Nixon's unofficial ambassadors to Beverly Hills.

Elvis plays to Sammy's table, striking poses in his white satin jump suit unzipped to reveal a wedge of bare chest, tossing Altovise a scarf, offering them asides in the middle of his oldies ("It's so hot here in Heartbreak Hotel"). Several times Sammy cries, "Yeahhhhh," for him an ecumenical response that may signify anything from joy to exasperation. He says of Elvis's performance, "It's a put-on," but adds, "He does it himself. That's what's so gorgeous about the man."

After the show, Sammy is accosted by well-wishers—"I just want to shake your hand, Mister Davis," "Thank you for being you," "You're so *cute*, Sammy"—all of them personable, and all but one of them white. He responds with humility, signs several menus with a special gold pen, takes the face of an eager young matron in his hands and kisses her on the cheek.

Upstairs, Elvis's friends and assorted votaries gather in the superstar bar, to wait for Elvis to emerge from his dressing room. They all have mid-South drawls and gold pendants that dangle from their necks, wrought into the letters TCB, which stand for Take Care of Business—Elvis's organizational credo.

Charlie Hodge, a guitarist, calls out, "Hey Sammy, we saw you on television with the President," and Sonny West, Elvis's bodyguard, says, in apparent seriousness, "We met the President, too, Sammy. We went with Elvis when he gave Agnew that present. You know, the gold inlaid Magnum with ivory handles."

Elvis steps from his dressing room. He wears a silver necklace and a jacket in the style of the American Revolutionary Army; his shiny black hair just touches the red suede collar. He carries a bottle of mineral water in one hand, and in the other a bottle of cough syrup, which he sets aside to shake hands with Sammy.

"I want ya'll to see my new ring," Elvis says, and Sammy, Altovise, the Rumsfelds and half a dozen others bend over Elvis's splayed, jeweled hand.

"Now this here's a star ruby. You see plenty of star sapphires, but you don't see many star rubies. We need some light."

A flashlight is produced, the beam focused on the ruby.

Sammy cries, "You've just ruined my good eye," and staggers away, hand clamped to his face.

Elvis says, "We need more light. Get a spot."

While the spotlight is being sought, Elvis shows Sammy his turquoise bracelet set in Mexican silver. His valet appears with a pair of white trousers draped over one arm, which is decorated with more turquoises. Sammy says that he would like to have a pair made for himself, and Elvis tells him, "I give ya my permission."

Sammy leaves Elvis to the Rumsfelds and returns to the bar to entertain the good ole boys, to show them his star sapphire and his computer wrist watch, and to tell them about his upcoming voyage to Europe, when he will have to charter a 10-passenger helicopter just to fly himself, Altovise and their luggage from John F. Kennedy Airport to the deck of the Queen Elizabeth 2.

The Sands's black Cadillac is waiting at the front door of the Hilton, and Sammy and his guests say good-by to Elvis. Outside the superstar suite, Sammy pauses in the corridor to do an impersonation of Elvis on stage, mimicking Elvis's catatonic stance and what Donald Rumsfeld calls his "weird" smile. The impersonation is successful; Joyce Rumsfeld takes him by the shoulders, shakes him playfully, asks, "What are we going to do with you, Sammy?"

"Well," he says, "you're stuck with me for the next four years."

It's the "new" Sammy Davis, Jr. His friends speak of a new-found peace of mind, of the fact that he "has gotten his head together at last," and even that he "is realizing the Sammy Davis destiny." That destiny entails playing a lot of golf at the Las Vegas Country Club and drinking pitcherfuls of Pimm's Cup, thick with fresh strawberries and sliced cucumbers; it is proprietary. Sammy himself speaks of "running the corner, not standing around on it," of "buying the bus, not fighting for a position on it," and of "working within the System, because the System won't let you fight it."

Sobriety also appears to be part of the destiny. He used to drink as much as two bottles of bourbon a day, until he collapsed a year ago with nervous exhaustion and a misaligned liver ("I looked at my liver on the electric scanner in the hospital. It was the shape of the state of Texas"). That was the end of a decade of highly-publicized indulgence during which he went through an unreckonable amount of Jack Daniel's and was most readily identified with the band of professional *bon vivants* that included his old friend Frank Sinatra, Dean Martin and Peter Lawford. They made a film together, "Ocean's Eleven," and Sammy recalls "drinking Salty Dogs—gin and grapefruit juice—at 8 in the morning, just to get the blood flowing . . . I drank so much my left eye would start to close, and they'd have to stop filming."

Girls and drugs were part of that period: "Today when I meet guys in my own corporate structure and they tell me about some girl they had at a party, I tell them about the way I used to have *three* . . . I went on acid trips, smoked pot. But when I came down from some trip I was still black. It was a period I had to go through to appreciate what I have now. There's nothing left to do—I've done it all and even invented a few things. Now I have what every cat really wants—the homey thing of sitting around having coffee with your old lady."

Billy Rowe, Sammy's press agent and a successful black businessman, says, "Sammy has been all over the landscape. Most great blacks—Joe Louis, Satchmo—they move in a straight line toward what they want. But Sammy didn't know what he wanted. He's been through many life cycles. He went through a militant period, wearing—what do you call them?—

denims. He survived the Rat Pack. He knows now that the two most important things in America are the dollar and the ballot."

Sammy has just become the first black ever to own a piece of Las Vegas's Strip, after paying $720,000 for an 8 per cent interest in the Tropicana. When he first came to town with his father and Will Mastin to perform in 1944, they were paid only $350 a week, and could not get a room anywhere except in the predominantly black section north of town. Now the Tropicana is being augmented with a new superstar suite just to accommodate Sammy and his entourage, and he will be paid $100,000 a week to occupy it and perform. This year he expects to gross more than $3-million. N.B.C. has given him a contract for a television series due to begin next year (tentatively entitled "Beat the Devil," about a man who can do no evil); he plans to star in two films, one about a black small-town lawyer who defends a white man charged with raping a black girl, one about the first black jockey to win the Kentucky Derby.

1972 is also the year in which Sammy Davis, Jr., hugged the President of the United States, in view of millions of his fellow Americans. Sammy was performing at a rock concert in Miami's Memorial Stadium when he was visited on stage by Richard Nixon, fresh from his renomination at the Republican National Convention. Nixon spoke of the American dream that "will not truly come true until every person in this country has a chance to see it come true in their own lives," as, he said, he and Sammy had done. And Nixon told the young Republican audience, "You aren't going to buy Sammy Davis, Jr., by inviting him to the White House. You're going to buy him by doing something for America."

I met Sammy Davis, Jr., approximately one week after his figurative and literal embrace of Nixon, when he was under attack for this, for accepting a special jet to fly him to Miami, for his apparent inconsistency. In the past, Sammy was an ardent supporter of John and Robert Kennedy; recently, he endorsed

Bobby Seale for mayor of Oakland. The meeting wasn't easy to arrange. Sammy has never liked the press—white or black—distrusts and has contempt for most reporters. ("This guy from Newsweek walked into my dressing room and said, 'Now I've got to ask you these questions about your income tax.' He drank a whole snifter full of brandy. Have you ever watched somebody come apart? They had to take him back to the hotel and put him to bed.") He eventually said, "People write so many lies about me. Write the truth, man. Just write what you feel," which was characteristic of a man who equates emotion and reality and is impatient with too much analysis. He stood in the study of his sprawling ranch-style apartment, located in the Sands's Aqueduct Turf Club and crowded with a pool table, recording equipment and cases of tapes packed for the trip to Europe, and he spoke of his endorsement of Nixon with what seemed to be barely controlled rage.

"You've got to deal with realities. JFK and Bobby Kennedy were great men, but they ain't here! Now Nixon made me some promises—don't ask me what promises, because I won't tell you. Promises can change. But Nixon has increased appropriations to black colleges, he's done away with the quota system. I dig Nixon because he doesn't do any front-running. He doesn't want publicity because he knows he'll get ripped. There's an honesty about the man I love."

Reaction to Sammy's endorsement of Nixon was widespread shock, sometimes tempered by understanding. Julian Bond, the black state legislator from Georgia, terms the endorsement "unbelievable, an irrational act. He's a great entertainer, but that doesn't mean he knows anything about politics." Charles Evers, Mayor of Fayette, Mississippi, and a friend of Sammy's, admits he was surprised, but adds, "Anytime a black man does something different, we jump all over him . . . Sammy did what he thought was right. He shouldn't be criticized for hugging the President. Sammy is a warm emotional person—he would have hugged anybody." Shirley Chisholm says, with some irony, "Sammy has the right to make his own decision. Everybody wants a winner—that's the name of the game in American politics."

Most black leaders around the country were reluctant to talk about the endorsement. Newark Mayor Kenneth Gibson flatly refused to comment, but a member of his administration said, "The feeling in the barber shops and pool halls here is that Sammy was just an inch away from kissing Nixon's tail."

Speculation about why Sammy decided to back Nixon is widespread, and based mostly upon the assumption that his endorsement will mean a significant number of black votes for the incumbent (Shirley Chisholm says, "Black people don't vote in blocs anymore. They make their own decisions now, and most of them are going to stay home on Election Day"). Sammy has been accused of embracing Nixon because he wanted a high political appointment (Sammy does speak longingly of a post at the United Nations); he has been accused of seeking impunity from alleged income tax evasion. But the real reason seems to be much simpler.

Home was once a tenement on the corner of 140th Street and Amsterdam Avenue in Harlem, since demolished. His parents were both vaudeville dancers who separated shortly after his birth in 1925; Sammy was raised by his grandmother, Mrs. Rosa B. Davis, a stalwart woman known to him as "Mama," who managed to keep him from school and the truant officers. She could not prevent his father from taking Sammy on a road trip when he was only 3, along with his father's friend, Will Mastin, later described as Sammy's "uncle." Sammy appeared first at the Pitheon Theater in Pittsburgh, on that trip, where he sat on the lap of the team's "prima donna" and did Al Jolson–type imitations of her, while she sang "Sonny Boy." He has been traveling and performing ever since.

Harlem remained his home. "Life was different then," Sammy recalls, "fights were different. People didn't get killed, there was no drug problem. A caper was to steal fruit from the corner stand. A cop would catch me by the shirt, and say, 'Do you want me to kick your butt, or do you want me to take you to your grandmother and let her kick your butt?' I'd start to cry, and he'd let me go . . ."

He was drafted, and in the Army he was exposed to real discrimination for the first time. He often fought with white recruits; once he was offered a bottle of urine, which he was told was beer. A black master sergeant taught him to read. He was discharged, and he and his father and Mastin formed the Will Mastin Trio and began their rise on the entertainment circuit until they were playing the better clubs in New York, Los Angeles and Las Vegas. They became well known for their dependability and for their fast and furious "flash" dancing.

Sammy began taking on more responsibility, altering the act to fit the times. He also began to do things his father insisted that he must not do: impersonating white actors like James Cagney, Edward G. Robinson, James Stewart, demanding rooms in segregated hotels in towns where they appeared, attempting—unsuccessfully—to be admitted to the Copacabana, El Morocco and Lindy's.

The rise of Sammy Davis, Jr., is carefully chronicled in his autobiography, "Yes I Can," written by Jane and Burt Boyar from Sammy's own taped accounts of his experiences. The book was published in 1965 and became a best seller; it is a vivid narrative of driving and consummated ambition, but often idealized. The child protagonist of "Yes I Can" is ingenious and uninhibited, has little in common with the "scared kid who slept with the covers over my head," as Sammy now recalls, was equally at ease off and on a stage (later in the book that line between metaphor and reality disappears).

The book is interesting in another way. It is supposedly Sammy's view of his own life, yet the narrator becomes guarded and stereotyped in direct proportion to the degree of his success. It is not necessarily a shallow view, but one in which he seeks to minimize his own anxieties. Thus, after Sammy finally gets a part in a Broadway production, which he thinks will add prestige to his career, he believes the show will fail but does a "bit" to hide his tears. He loses his left eye in a car crash in

1954, while the trio is earning a record $7,500 a week at the New Frontier in Las Vegas, and it seems that his career is finished. The doctor tells Sammy that he will have to wear a patch, and he responds, "Aha. Floyd Gibbons, eh?"

The accident proves to be the beginning of the big money, and general acceptance. With the encouragement of family and friends—particularly Frank Sinatra—the trio opens at Ciro's in Los Angeles, to the delight of an audience including "the Cary Grants, the Bogarts, the Edward G. Robinsons, the Spencer Tracys, Gary Coopers, Jimmy Cagneys, Dick Powells—standing and applauding. I saw tears rolling down June Allyson's cheeks." He begins to spend money lavishly, buying jewelry, clothes and cars; he associates with white women, though his father disapproves ("Dad always said I was going to get us all killed," Sammy says today with some bitterness). Once he returns to Harlem to escape the "tightrope" of success, but suspects that he is only "playing a corny scene from any one of a thousand old movies."

Midway through the book Sammy converts to Judaism (his mother was Catholic, but he was never confirmed). He has already been given a mezuzah by Eddie Cantor (though he equally cherishes a gold medal stamped with a St. Christopher on one side and a Star of David on the other), read many books on Judaism and talked with several rabbis; he decides, "I have always been a Jew in my thinking and my own undefined philosophies." Many people were shocked by the conversion. (Buddy Hackett says, "I don't know what the conversion did for Sammy, but it sure confused my mother.")

Some of his friends interpreted the conversion as "a step up the social ladder," and as "a form of rebellion against his background." And many people considered it a boost to his theatrical career. A considerable percentage of most nightclub audiences were Jewish, as were the majority of club owners where Sammy performed, as were the promoters. He was proposed by Milton Berle for membership in the Friars Club, an exclusive club of predominantly Jewish performers and en-

tertainers, where today Sammy retains the honorary title of
Bard.

Nipsey Russell, a comedian and an old friend of Sammy's—
he began to call Sammy "Samela" after his conversion—denies
that the conversion had any significant effect on his career.
"Sammy was already well-known, he would have made it to
the top no matter what. He has a notoriously fast take—he can
develop a line or a bit spontaneously, off the top of his head.
You almost never see him rehearse, and when he does rehearse,
those vibrations are always there. People like to watch Sammy,
regardless of what he does."

Much of "Yes I Can" is devoted to his agonizing and
abortive attempts to be admitted as a guest to prestigious clubs.
These barriers come down one by one (when he is served a
Coke in the Copa, a voluble racist has to be thrown out, and
Sammy plays "the scene of enjoying myself"); finally, in the
company of Jane and Burt Boyar, Sammy gains entrance to El
Morocco but realizes he still is faced with "the stone wall between acceptance and rejection"—because they are seated on
the wrong side of the room.

He begins to refer to himself as "Charley," a nickname bestowed upon him for obscure reasons by Sinatra. Sammy becomes "Charley Good Son" when speaking kindly of his father
to an audience, after his father leaves the act. To admirers he is
alternately "Charley Nice Star," "Charley Straight," "Charley
Modesty." He begins to drink heavily, entertains lavishly (and
often "pulled a fall-asleep" to get people out of his apartment),
is briefly married to a black chorus girl named Loray White in
1959.

He meets the Swedish actress May Britt, falls in love, and
decides to marry her because he is not "Charley Chameleon"
influenced by adverse publicity and sentiment, of which there
was a great deal. May calls Sammy "Sharley Brown." When
she asks him how much he loves her, he says, "Darling . . . ask
Elizabeth Barrett Browning." Sammy fears violence and therefore doesn't want to be seen in public with May; he also

"didn't dare just stay around the room with her because it would emphasize the fact that we were never going anywhere together." So he becomes the "Mad Social Director" sending guests and hors d'oeuvres to her room. (They were divorced in 1968, after having one daughter and adopting two sons. May gave the reason for the divorce as "no family life to speak of.")

Near the conclusion of "Yes I Can," Sammy bears little resemblance to a deprived kid from 140th Street and Amsterdam Avenue. He is one of the highest paid entertainers in America and a movie star; he is acquainted with many influential people. He owns a home in Beverly Hills, and his wife is about to have a baby.

Nevertheless, he sometimes gets "a creepy feeling that I personified the lonely star cliché."

Afternoon in Davis's sitting room, with cut glass bowls filled with packs of cigarettes, and three tiny poodles that drift like balls of fluff across deep orange pile. Sammy stands with his back to sliding glass doors and a suburban setting: the private pool, the Rolls safe in its slot, the couple in tennis whites strolling across manicured crab grass, racquets raised in the clear desert air. He wears tight trousers and brown suede shoes with raisers. His childlike body is incongruous with that fierce head, the smile armed with perfect teeth, the one bright eye belying its plastic counterpart.

He begins to dance, stiffly at first, then wildly, arms dangling, body arching forward like some antic gyroscope, heels perilously close to the glass. He sings raucously:

> Everybody take a look at me.
> I'm downhearted as I can be.
> I got the blues, we can't lose,
> 'Cause we got on our dancing shoes.

It is the first verse of the song with which the Will Mastin Trio opened their act, and Sammy's father has just bet that

Sammy doesn't remember the words. His father has driven up from his home in Beverly Hills to visit his son and to catch Sammy's show, where he will sit later at a specially prepared table, with a glass of Bristol Cream on the rocks, and snap his fingers and jerk his legs so violently that people around him have to move their chairs. His response to Sammy's performance is almost Pavlovian, and even now he has to control himself.

"I have to shake my head, says Sam Davis, Sr. "Sammy used to say he was going to be a star, and I didn't listen. Now he's the living end."

"It makes you humble," says Sammy, "remembering what went before."

He shuffles across the carpet, carrying a highball glass and a sweating pitcher filled with Pimm's Cup, which he sets decisively on the coffee table in the television room. His walk has a stiff, aged quality, totally at odds with the suppleness of his performance; the dancing was an interruption in his monologue about the inevitability of being black—"A black person never leaves the ghetto"—and forgotten now.

"I used to get so angry," he says. "I wanted to do a number for my people, but I got so bogged down in all those organizations. I'd end up asking the militants what good it did to shoot a fireman in the back, why we had to rip off our own kind . . . Now I'm being hassled by other blacks, I'm being called an Uncle Tom."

He feels that much of the press is overly-critical of his success, of the fact that he once imitated white stars and is now often associated with the white establishment, and of his failure to play a leading role in the civil-rights movement.

"I wish I had a goddamn film of me marching in Selma, in Tougaloo and Atlanta, just to prove it. Once Bull Connor came up to a car I was sitting in and just stared at me. It was like a bad movie . . . I didn't march up front because I wasn't one of the organizers. And I don't think performers should be leaders. Also, I was on the Klan's 10-Most-Wanted list. I couldn't stay for the rallies after the marches because I had to fly back someplace and perform. But I was there!"

During the last decade, he says, he has contributed substantially to the N.A.A.C.P., SNCC, CORE, Food for Black Children and the Urban League, as well as B'nai B'rith and Bonds for Israel. He has also performed free at many benefits.

"Some people say I should give all my money away. I'll give mine away when John Wayne gives his away. It's relative. If everybody agreed to do the same, I'd settle for 50 grand a year and expenses."

When Sammy laughs, his jaw performs a lateral starboard glide, the mended eyelid flutters; he will often cross a room just to touch the person with whom he is talking—a bit of sympathetic magic that never fails.

He adds, "There's nothing wrong with making a lot of money. If you're not going for the roses, you don't go."

He once told an interviewer on National Educational Television's "Black Journal," "Money don't make you free. Popularity don't make you free . . . I'm shackled with the same things that happened to the brother in Watts . . . Our real religion and the thing that connects us all is our blackness." When asked what he and Angela Davis have in common, he says, "I share her blackness." When he says, "A black is a black is a black," he seems to be affirming some divine order, rather than excoriating the arbitrary limitations of our society.

He has often spoken of the "religion" of blackness. For Sammy, the spiritual and the temporal are intimately involved. He denies that he is particularly superstitious (after the car accident in which he lost his eye, he gripped the combination Star of David and St. Christopher medal so hard it left a scar in the palm of his hand), then adds with real conviction, "If people aren't superstitious, why do they fear the Devil?"

Before his conversion to Judaism, he read a book about scientology that he considered "an awakening." More recently, he became interested in the occult and on a tour of Australia attended a black mass, where the sight of people drinking the blood of animals made him sick.

"I respect the people involved in the black arts—they aren't to be messed with. Shakespeare said there are more things in heaven and on earth than we suspect—all that jazz. Well, there's something in all of us that makes us want to turn the hourglass over. But there are also heavy tolls involved in Satanism. I walked away from it."

Sammy would like to direct a musical; he would like to produce and direct films about black families, "without a lot of sex, just everyday problems of black people. There's so much exploitive garbage in films about blacks today—like 'Shaft' and 'Sweetback.' " He would like to produce another book, not a sequel to "Yes I Can," but the *pensées* of a successful black man, dictated in tranquility. He would also like to have children with Altovise.

Conversation with Sammy swings between anticipation and anticlimax: He watches people closely, seems to be searching for something that he rarely finds. He is quick to find fault, quicker to make amends.

A poodle prepares to vomit on a shag rug. Sammy's press agent, Billy Rowe, just stares at it, saying, "Now don't get sick, dog. Don't get sick . . ."

Sammy says angrily, "Billy, what the hell are you standing there talking to a dog for?" But he has to laugh, and goes himself to get a towel.

His father admires a diamond ring left on the table. Sammy says, "That's an *old* ring, Dad."

"Diamonds don't wear out, son," his father says, but Sammy just shakes his head.

They discuss Sammy's new part-ownership of the Tropicana, and the fact that he is the first black man to buy into the Strip.

Mr. Davis belly laughs: "They're gonna be after you now."

"They ain't gonna be after s———!" says Sammy, and this time he doesn't laugh.

The room has slowly been filling with members of Sammy's retinue: George Rhodes, his conductor, Murphy Bennett, one of three personal secretaries who assist Sammy with almost everything, from the choice of jewel settings to hotel reservations. Sammy gets out of bed at approximately 1 P.M., and those afternoons not devoted to golf usually involve him in the logistics of a successful and highly mobile career. He also employs five dancing girls to open his show, five band members, a valet, a bodyguard, a cook, an advance man, two press agents and more. The luggage of his troupe totals almost 100 pieces.

Sammy has numerous friends and acquaintances who often drop by the apartment. One of his closest associates says, "All superstars like to have a lot of people around, but Sammy has more than most. Some of them are just ego-feeders, who want to share in his glory. Sammy never turns anybody down. He's actually nicer to his enemies than he is to his friends."

He seldom sees his old friends in show business, or the members of the defunct Rat Pack, including Sinatra. If the unresponsiveness of their press agents is any indication, those and other stars are reluctant to comment upon the phenomenon of Sammy Davis, Jr.

Supper is served at a long table, in view of the pool. A dozen people partake of spareribs, thick slices of roast pork, boiled cabbage, rice and potatoes; Sammy eats steak. A Vegas hairdresser and his attractive wife have joined the regular members; as they struggle to open a bottle of Bordeaux, she says, "Sammy, you have the cutest behind in show business."

The group is subject to the stresses of any big family. Altovise is a more solid presence than her husband: She moves through various social situations with an air of pleasant authority, she isn't limited to a purely supportive role (on her birthday, Sammy interrupted his show to pay tribute to her, only to discover that Altovise was upstairs in his dressing room, talking to friends). Conversation is animated and general; Sammy is treated more like a moody prodigal son than the head of the groaning board. When he tells Shirley Rhodes to sit on one side of the table and she ignores him and sits next to Altovise, he picks up his plate and stalks into the television room. A few people—Altovise, Shirley, Murphy—glance after him, are apparently reassured by the sight of only his head projecting above the coffee table, as he sits on the rug watching the color presentation of "Ponderosa."

After supper Sammy climbs into his private golf cart and drives to the Sands health club for a rubdown and a steam bath; between shows, he stays mostly inside his dressing room, while out in the superstar bar George Hamilton entertains the troops ("When this Administration is out, I'm going to tell the story about that number Sammy and Lawford pulled on me in London, with all those Secret Service men . . ."), which include Red Skelton and Danny Thomas.

"I can't get any better than I am now," Sammy says. "I've been up here too long. But I'm still afraid of tomorrow; I try not to take it for granted. The higher you get up the mountain, the longer the fall."

And then: "Dad always said I couldn't do the things I wanted to do. My whole thing in life has been to prove him wrong."

At the 1960 Democratic National Convention in Los Angeles, Sammy appeared on stage with other celebrities, and was booed by a small contingent of Southerners. The event so impressed him that he wept and didn't stay for the following ceremonies. According to Billy Rowe, a member of the Kennedy Administration subsequently asked if Sammy would like to serve the Government in some appointive capacity, and Rowe said he thought the offer should come directly from the President, which didn't happen. The same type of overture was made by the Johnson Administration, Rowe says, and again he unsuccessfully attempted to secure personal recognition of Sammy by the President.

In July, 1971, President Nixon invited Sammy to the White House and personally appointed him to the National Advisory Council on Economic Opportunity. Photographs of this and other obviously happy meetings with Nixon occupy prominent places on the wall of Sammy's dressing room. A year later, he was invited to attend the Republican National Convention in Miami and to sit in the President's box; Sammy and Altovise were roundly applauded when they entered the convention hall, and he was to prove the extent of his gratitude, and his unpredictability.

To write the truth about Sammy Davis, Jr., I must certainly write what I feel. As an entertainer, Sammy is phenomenal; as a man, he is warm and mostly guileless—chemistry that is antithetical to politics. He seeks stability in a life that has always been volatile, he hankers after a piece of America's heartland. But middle America as a state of mind can be elusive, and nowhere is this fact more apparent than along Las Vegas's Strip, where money is the sole determinant, hypocrisy is impossible and only children are grotesque. The existence of a superstar is by definition groundless, and here that splendid flight can be totally without interruption.

I must also write about Sammy's prime dicta: Get the roses, sit on the right side of the room, beat the Devil—whether by pulling the covers over one's head, or gripping a fistful of mezuzahs, St. Christopher medals, Stars of David and peace symbols. Most important, accomplish the above by doing what one must not do, even if it means astounding friends and fans by appearing on a stage where "the President was expected. Sweat was pouring off me, I was so excited. A million thoughts ran through my head. He came from the front, right through the crowd, and I said to myself, 'Oh, my God!' Nixon was bright, loose, he had a sense of humor. He used the words of John Kennedy and Martin Luther King, and I knew he was speaking from the heart, and not using the phrases of clever writers. He said you can't buy Sammy Davis, Jr., unless you do something for America. That's the first time a President of the United States ever said that about a performer."

—October 15, 1974

"COMICS," REVIEW OF *YES I CAN*,
by Albert Goldman, *The New York Review of Books*

Before he became the Dreyfus of the nightclubs, the comedian Lenny Bruce often officiated as Lord High Chancellor of show business. In a typical sketch, "The Tribunal," Bruce arraigns before an imaginary court the most famous entertainers in show business. He orders them to divulge the amount of their weekly earnings and then to demonstrate talents equal to such enormous salaries. The stars are all found guilty of fraud. Minor offenders are let off with light sentences. Frankie Laine's wig is burned; Sophie Tucker's sweat-stained gowns are confiscated. But when the court comes to the case of the man called "The World's Greatest Entertainer," Sammy Davis, Jr., the magistrate shows no mercy. "Mr. Junior" is explaining how he earns $40,000 a week mimicking Jerry Lewis ("Hey Dean, I gotta boo-boo") when the outraged judge breaks in. "Strip him of his Jewish star, his stocking cap, his religious statue of Elizabeth Taylor—30 years in Biloxi!"

Lenny Bruce's scornful caricature of Sammy Davis, Jr., is intended to epitomize dozens of famous performers whose success is wholly out of proportion to their talents and whose moral pretensions are absurd in view of their private lives. Davis is an especially inviting target because he commands one of the highest salaries in the night-club business for one of the most routine acts. His singing is nondescript, a mixture of the styles of at least half a dozen other performers, including his hero, Frank Sinatra, and Billy Eckstine, Billy Daniels, Tony Bennett, and Anthony Newley. His dancing combines familiar routines from vaudeville and musicals; his comedy derives from Jerry Lewis (as does his Catskill *tumler*'s stage presence); and even his "impressions," the strongest part of his act, are for the most part borrowed from a handful of relatively obscure Broadway comics. Only his versatility, his energy, his fanatical desire to please, are wholly Davis's own.

In another performer this all-inclusive embrace of the going thing might simply indicate a lack of talent, but in the case of Sammy Davis, Jr., it means something more. One notes, for example, that in all his work there is not a single expression of that racial identity (still potent in performers as different as Ray Charles and Dick Gregory) that has traditionally given the Negro entertainer his power. Thus Davis seems to be refusing the label "Negro entertainer"; he is taking his "color" from his professional milieu rather than from his ethnic origin. He might even be called the first "colorless" Negro performer; for like Diahann Carroll and Bill Cosby, later embodiments of the same idea, what Sammy Davis, Jr., offers his audience above everything else is the opportunity to "prove" that they can respond to a Negro without consciousness of his race.

Yet his prosperous middle-class audiences are torn by conflicting feelings about this highly successful Negro. For some of them Sammy Davis, Jr., is the butt of a considerable number of defamatory and obscene jokes, some turning on his physical defects, others on his conversion to Judaism, and still others on his marriage to a white woman. These jokes seem to suggest another, antagonistic side to the public's reaction to Davis: The little black boy, blind in one eye, has managed to sneak under the fence into the big white mansion.

This image of the maimed intruder—suitably glamorized—is the view that Sammy Davis, Jr., holds of himself. His autobiography, *Yes I Can*, is a testament to his relentless determination to become a star—one who could hurdle the barriers erected against Negroes. To achieve this goal, he learned to perform with virtuosity all the material his audiences had been accustomed to associate with famous white performers. Having achieved success, he crashed every gate that had once been closed against him. Yet the least valuable parts of *Yes I Can* are those in which Davis speaks of his life as a Negro. The forms of intolerance from which he especially suffers are not those that afflict most Negroes, nor even successful Negroes: They are the embarrassments of a Negro "star" bent on being just like his white colleagues. What he most often complains about is exclusion from supper clubs and hotels, crank letters, the difficulty of buying a house in fashionable white neighborhoods, and various social prohibitions, especially the taboo against sleeping with white women. Davis himself knows that these are not the real frontiers of the racial revolution. The most savage insults he suffered were not at El Morocco, but at basic training camp in the U.S. Army. But the Army was for Davis only an accidental collision with reality; in other respects, he has lived in the fantasy world of Show Biz—perhaps one of the few real sanctuaries in America for ethnic minorities.

Davis, the son of a vaudeville dancer and a chorus girl who abandoned her child to go back to the "line," was reared from birth in the insulated and tolerant world of show business, and probably this fact is more important than his being Negro. He had relatively little experience with racial prejudice until he entered the Army, and by that time his personality and ambitions were formed. Brought up in this limited world, Davis naturally aspired to be one of the most successful men in it. Always an idolator of the stars, a brash Broadway "hippie," constantly "on," constantly doing the "bits," he identified with white America—or that part of it "the Business" represents. Even his conversion to Judaism can be understood as an act of conformity to his professional world.

It is hardly surprising, therefore, that the best parts of *Yes I Can* should concern not the problems of the Negro, but the powers and perils of stage life. Like many men who suddenly rise to stardom after years of poverty and hardship, Davis lived recklessly, throwing his money around. But he was a lonely spectator of his own success. He became increasingly bitter and angry, drank and gambled heavily, and then began to fear that he had lost the mysterious power to "touch" his audience. He threw himself into marriage with a Negro show girl, hoping that this would stabilize his life and redeem his now soiled reputation (particularly with the hostile Negro press). But marriage only deepened his despair, and finally made him attempt suicide. The story ends on a Hollywood note. Davis miraculously recovers, marries the Swedish film star, May Britt, and in the final "fade" stands with moist eyes over the hospital bed of his wife and newborn child.

—January 20, 1966

"LET'S HEAR IT FOR A BEAUTIFUL GUY,"
by Bruce Jay Friedman, *The New Yorker*

Sammy Davis is trying to get a few months off for a complete rest.
—Earl Wilson, February 7, 1974

I have been trying to get a few months off for a complete rest, too, but I think it's more important that Sammy Davis get one. I feel that I can scrape along and manage somehow, but Sammy Davis always looks so strained and tired. The pressure on the guy must be enormous. It must have been a terrific blow to him when he switched his allegiance to Agnew and Nixon, only to have the whole thing blow up in his face. I was angry at him, incidentally, along with a lot of other fans of his, all of us feeling he had sold us down the river. But after I had thought it over and let my temper cool a bit, I changed my mind and actually found myself standing up for him, saying I would bet anything that Agnew and Nixon had made some secret promises to Sammy about easing the situation of blacks—ones that the public still doesn't know about. Otherwise, there was no way he would have thrown in his lot with that crowd. In any case, I would forgive the guy just about anything. How can I feel any other way when I think of the pleasure he's given me over the years, dancing and clowning around and wrenching those songs out of that wiry little body? Always giving his all, no matter what the composition of the audience. Those years of struggle with the Will Mastin Trio, and then finally making it, only to find marital strife staring him in the face. None of us will ever be able to calculate what it took out of him each time he had a falling-out with Frank. Is there any doubt who Dean and Joey sided with on those occasions? You can be sure Peter Lawford didn't run over to offer Sammy any solace. And does anyone ever stop to consider the spiritual torment he must have suffered when he made the switch to Judaism? I don't even want to talk about the eye. So, if anyone in the world does, he certainly deserves a few months off for a complete rest.

Somehow, I have the feeling that if I met Sammy, I could break through his agents and that entourage of his and convince him he ought to take off with me and get the complete rest he deserves. I don't want any ten per cent, I don't want any glory; I just feel I owe it to him. Sure he's got commitments, but once and for all he's got to stop and consider that it's one time around, and no one can keep up that pace of his forever.

The first thing I would do is get him out of Vegas. There is absolutely no way he can get a few months' rest in that sanatorium. I would get him away from Vegas, and I would certainly steer clear of Palm Springs. Imagine him riding down Bob Hope Drive and checking into a hotel in the Springs! For a rest? The second he walked into the lobby, it would all start. The chambermaids would ask him to do a chorus of "What Kind of Fool Am I," right in the lobby, and, knowing Sammy and his big heart, he would probably oblige. I think I would take him to my place in New York, a studio. We would have to eat in, because if I ever showed up with Sammy Davis at the Carlton Delicatessen, where I have my breakfast, the roof would fall in. The owner would ask him for an autographed picture to hang up next to Dustin Hoffman's, and those rich young East Side girls would go to town on him. If they ever saw me walk in with Sammy Davis, that would be the end of his complete rest. They would attack him like vultures, and Sammy would be hard put to turn his back on them, because they're not broads.

We would probably wind up ordering some delicatessen from the Stage, although I'm not so sure that's a good idea; the delivery boy would recognize him, and the next thing you know, Sammy would give him a C note, and word would get back to Alan King that Sammy had ducked into town. How would it look if he didn't drop over to the Stage and show himself? Next thing you know, the news would reach Jilly's, and if Frank was in town—well, you can imagine how much rest Sammy would get. I don't know if they're feuding these days, but you know perfectly well that, at minimum, Frank would send over a purebred Afghan. Even if they were feuding.

I think what we would probably do is lay low and order a lot of Chinese food. I have a hunch that Sammy can eat Chinese takeout food every night of the week. I know I can, and the Chinese takeout delivery guys are very discreet. So we would stay at my place. I'd give him the sleeping loft, and I'd throw some sheets on the couch downstairs for me. I would do that for Sammy to pay him back for all the joy he's given me down through the years. And I would resist the temptation to ask him to sing, even though I would flip out if he so much as started humming. Can you imagine him humming "The Candy Man"? *In my apartment?* Let's not even discuss it.

Another reason I would give him the sleeping loft is that there is no phone up there. I would try like the devil to keep him away from the phone, because I know the second he saw one he would start thinking about his commitments, and it would be impossible for the guy not to make at least one call to the Coast. So I'd just try to keep him comfortable for as long as possible, although pretty soon my friends would begin wondering what ever happened to me, and it would take all the willpower in the world not to let on that I had Sammy Davis in my loft and was giving him a complete rest.

I don't kid myself that I could keep Sammy Davis happy in my loft for a full couple of months. He would be lying on the bed, his frail muscular body looking lost in a pair of boxer shorts, and before long I would hear those fingers snapping, and I would know that the wiry little great entertainer was feeling penned up, and it would be inhuman to expect him to stay there any longer. I think that when I sensed that Sammy was straining at the leash, I would rent a car—a Ford LTD (that would be a switch for him, riding in a Middle American car)— and we would ride out to my sister and brother-in-law's place in Jersey. He would probably huddle down in the seat, but somehow I have the feeling that people in passing cars would spot him. We'd be lucky if they didn't crash into telephone poles. And if I know Sammy, whenever someone recognized him he wouldn't be able to resist taking off his shades and graciously blowing them a kiss.

The reason I would take Sammy to my sister and brother-in-law's house is not only that it's out of the way but also because they're simple people and would not hassle him—especially my brother-in-law. My sister would stand there with her hands on her hips, and when she saw me get out of the Ford with Sammy, she would cluck her tongue and say, "There goes my crazy brother again," but she would appear calm on the surface, even though she would be fainting dead away on the inside. She would say something like "Oh, my God, I didn't even clean the floors," but then Sammy would give her a big hug and a kiss, and I'm sure that he would make a call, and a few weeks later she would have a complete new dining-room set, the Baby Grand she always wanted, and a puppy.

She would put Sammy up in her son's room (he's away at graduate school), saying she wished she had something better, but he would say, "Honey, this is just perfect." And he would mean it, too, in a way, my nephew's bedroom being an interesting change from those $1,000-a-day suites at the Tropicana. My brother-in-law has a nice easygoing style and would be relaxing company for Sammy, except that Al does work in television and there would be a temptation on his part to talk about the time he did the "Don Rickles Show" and how different and sweet a guy Don is when you get him offstage. If I know Sammy, he would place a call to C.B.S.—with no urging from any of us—and see to it that Al got to work on his next special. If the network couldn't do a little thing like that for him, the hell with them, he would get himself another network. Sammy's that kind of guy.

One danger is that my sister, by this time, would be going out of her mind and wouldn't be able to resist asking Sammy if she could have a few neighbors over on a Saturday night. Let's face it, it would be the thrill of a lifetime for her. I would intercede right there, because it wouldn't be fair to the guy, but if I know Sammy he would tell her, "Honey, you go right ahead." She would have a mixed group over—Italians, an Irish couple, some Jews, about twelve people tops—and she would wind up having the evening catered, which of course would lead to a commotion when she tried to pay for the stuff. No way Sammy would let her do that. He would buy out the whole delicatessen, give the delivery guy a C note, and probably throw in an autographed glossy without being asked.

Everyone at the party would pretend to be casual, as if Sammy Davis wasn't there, but before long the Irish space salesman's wife (my sister's crazy friend, and what a flirt *she* is) would somehow manage to ask him to sing, and imagine Sammy saying no in a situation like that. Everyone would say just one song, but that bighearted son of a gun would wind up doing his entire repertoire, probably putting out every bit as much as he does when he opens at the Sands. He would do it all—"The Candy Man," "What Kind of Fool Am I," tap-dance, play the drums with chopsticks on an end table, do some riffs on my nephew's old trumpet, and work himself into exhaustion. The sweat would be pouring out of him, and he would top the whole thing off with "This Is My Life" ("and I don't give a damn"). Of course, his agents on the Coast would pass out cold if they ever got wind of the way he was putting out for twelve nobodies in Jersey. But as for Sammy, he never did know anything about halfway measures. He either works or he doesn't, and he would use every ounce of energy in that courageous little show-biz body of his to see to it that my sis-

ter's friends—that mixed group of Italians, Irish, and Jews—
had a night they'd never forget as long as they lived.

Of course, that would blow the two months of complete rest,
and I would have to get him out of Jersey fast. By that time,
frankly, I would be running out of options. Once in a while, I
pop down to Puerto Rico for a three- or four-day holiday, but,
let's face it, if I showed up in San Juan with Sammy, first thing
you know, we would be hounded by broads, catching the show
at the Flamboyan, and Dick Shawn would be asking Sammy to
hop up onstage and do a medley from "Mr. Wonderful." (He
was really something in that show, battling Jack Carter tooth
and nail, but too gracious to use his bigger name to advantage.)
    Another possibility would be to take Sammy out to see a
professor friend of mine who teaches modern lit. at San Francisco State and would be only too happy to take us in. That
would represent a complete change for Sammy, a college campus, but as soon as the school got wind he was around, I'll bet
you ten to one they would ask him to speak either to a film
class or the drama department or even a political-science group.
And he would wind up shocking them with his expertise on the
Founding Fathers and the philosophy behind the Bill of Rights.
The guy reads, and I'm not talking about "The Bette Davis
Story." Anyone who sells Sammy Davis short as an intellectual
is taking his life in his hands.
    In the end, Sammy and I would probably end up in Ver-
mont, where a financial-consultant friend of mine has a cabin
that he never uses. He always says to me, "It's there, for God's
sakes—use it." So I would take Sammy up there, away from it
all, but I wouldn't tell the financial consultant who I was taking, because the second he heard it was Sammy Davis he would
want to come along. Sammy and I would start out by going
into town for a week's worth of supplies at the general store,
and then we would hole up in the cabin. I'm not too good at
mechanical things, but we would be sort of roughing it, and

there wouldn't be much to do except chop some firewood, which I would take care of while Sammy was getting his complete rest.

I don't know how long we would last in Vermont. Frankly, I would worry after a while about being able to keep him entertained, even though he would be there for a complete rest. We could talk a little about Judaism, but, frankly, I would be skating on thin ice in that area, since I don't have the formal training he has or any real knowledge of theology. The Vermont woods would probably start us batting around theories about the mystery of existence, but to tell the truth, I'd be a little bit out of my depth in that department, too. He's had so much experience on panel shows, and I would just as soon not go one-on-one with him on that topic.

Let's not kid around, I would get tense after a while, and Sammy would feel it. He would be too good a guy to let on that he was bored, but pretty soon he would start snapping those fingers and batting out tunes on the back of an old *Saturday Evening Post* or something, and I think I would crack after a while and say, "Sammy, I tried my best to supply you with a couple of months of complete rest, but I'm running out of gas." He would tap me on the shoulder and say, "Don't worry about it, babe," and then, so as not to hurt my feelings, he would say he wanted to go into town to get some toothpaste. So he would drive in, with the eye and all, and I know damned well the first thing he would do is call his agents on the Coast and ask them to read him the "N.Y. to L.A." column of a few *Varieties*. Next thing you know, I would be driving him to the airport, knowing in my heart that I hadn't really succeeded. He would tell me that any time I got to the Coast or Vegas or the Springs, and I wanted anything, *anything*, just make sure to give him a ring. And the following week, I would receive a freezer and a video-tape machine and a puppy.

So I think I'm just not the man to get Sammy Davis the complete rest he needs so desperately. However, I certainly think someone should. How long can he keep driving that tortured little frame of his, pouring every ounce of his strength into the entertainment of Americans? I know, I know—there's Cambodia and Watergate, and, believe me, I haven't forgotten our own disadvantaged citizens. I know all that. But when you think of all the joy that man has spread through his night-club appearances, his albums, his autobiography, his video specials, and even his movies, which did not gross too well but were a lot better than people realized, and the things he's done not only for his friends but for a lot of causes the public doesn't know about—when you think of all that courageous little entertainer has given to this land of ours, and then you read that he's trying, repeat *trying*, to get a few months off for a complete rest and he can't, well, then, all I can say is that there's something basically rotten in the system.

—April 8, 1974

"SAMMY DAVIS SEEKS JEWISH-BLACK UNITY,"
St. Louis Jewish Light

Sammy Davis, Jr., American entertainer, and a convert to Judaism, said recently in Israel that he hopes to "transmit the spirit and the will of the Israelis to black men struggling for independence in America."

"I'm involved and committed to my own people at home, my black brothers and sisters, in our struggle for what the Israelis have been able to achieve—independence, unity, spirit, the will to survive," the singer told Mary Selman of the Jerusalem Post. "I hope to transmit that will to my people."

Davis, who was converted to Judaism in 1955, was in Tel Aviv for one day to give a benefit performance for Beit Halochem, a center for war invalids. In the afternoon, dressed informally in a jersey and khaki slacks, he visited wounded soldiers at Tel Hashomer Hospital, sang, danced, chatted, and when he was through with his performance, thanked them.

"It is a thrill for me to be accepted so warmly and so beautifully by you," he told the patients. "I hope to come back one day and to be able to stay much longer. Your hospitality, your courage, your warmth I will never forget for as long as I live."

Haym Topol flew in with Davis from London on Tuesday night, and accompanied him on his visit, translating, singing, and acting as a general liaison. "I don't think I've ever acted as a bodyguard before," he commented later.

The two performers took turns singing before a circle of patients gathered outside the hospital—Davis sang "Summertime" from "Porgy and Bess," and Topol sang the title song from his hit film, "Salah Shabati," accompanied by much clapping and "oomphs" from the audience.

When the pair visited individual patients, Davis was obviously moved, and at one point, asked to be taken to a private room to rest for a few minutes.

In an exclusive interview after the hospital visit, Davis explained his reasons for giving a benefit performance for the Israeli veterans:

"They fought a war; I'm against all war, all things that war brings—crippled children, wounded men, the disorder. I think if there weren't religious differences, I would do it for the other side as well."

But, he said, the reasons for a war make a great difference, and it was the reason for the Middle East war that brought him to Israel.

"I hope to bring my people the spirit of fighting a basic wrong, and knowing how to do it in the proper way; being proud of accomplishments and being proud of togetherness. Even if I were not a Jew, I would have to be proud of the fact that here you see a group of people who have a common bond. They are Israelis."

Davis denied that Negro anti-Semitism in America is as widespread as has been reported, but said that it does exist to a degree. "The oppressed pick on the oppressed," he commented with a sigh.

But, he said, Negro anti-Semitism is never directed against him. "As long as you've got that ticket, as long as you've got that bond," he said, pointing to his skin, "then your opinion is respected, and your right to choose your own way of life.

"I happen to be a black Jew," he added, "and the fact that so many Israelis are dark is very important to me. But I couldn't live here. With all the trouble that black Americans have, I can only help my people if I'm there, and that's where I got to be. Whatever it is, it's my country, and I must try to do everything I can—rightfully, constructively—to help my people to achieve a position in the country which is my birthright."

"I also love Israel," he concluded.

—*September 17, 1969*

"A MAN CALLED ADAM AND THE SON OF SUNSHINE SAMMY,"
from *Toms, Coons, Mulattoes, Mammies, and Bucks*,
by Donald Bogle

At the same time Preminger's rambunctiously absurd effort [*Hurry Sundown*] appeared, movie viewers were also presented with a psycho-drama, *A Man Called Adam* (1966). The film starred Sammy Davis, Jr., with Cicely Tyson, Peter Lawford, and Ossie Davis. Except for Tyson's sensitive and intelligent work as the ingenue, the acting and direction were pedestrian at best. In fact, the only saving grace of this tawdry film about a disturbed and difficult jazz musician wallowing in self-pity was that it unintentionally revealed the funkiness and confused, misplaced anger then felt on American street corners. The feature seemed to have a certain oppressive centered-in-the-ghetto air about it (perhaps because it was such an inexpensive film and because its producers shrewdly distributed it in ghetto areas), and certainly the idea of a jazz film itself appealed to black audiences. So, too, did the idea of a new black heel of an anti-hero. (This idea was later successfully picked up in 1971 with

Sweet Sweetback's Baadasssss Song and *Shaft*.) But the movie's great failing was what the producers had thought was its great asset: Sammy Davis, Jr. Had he been a better equipped actor, the character at least might have succeeded.

Throughout the late 1950s and early 1960s Sammy Davis, Jr., had had a spectacularly lackluster film career. He always received featured billing in movies. Because he had been an entertainer nearly all his life, beginning as a tot with his father in the Will Mastin Trio, the black press sentimentally gave him good coverage. Audiences had been conditioned to think of him as a show-business legend. Yet his actual film performances were far from outstanding. His first film of the 1950s, *The Benny Goodman Story*, was hardly memorable. In his next feature, *Anna Lucasta*, he and Eartha Kitt were billed as "the entertainment world's most electrifying pair." Yet there was little electricity to the coupling. As the hard-as-nails sailor boy friend Davis was miscast and totally unconvincing, clearly lacking the physical presence and personality for a lead role. Afterward there came his most publicized appearance, as the flashy, jive-ass nigger Sportin' Life in *Porgy and Bess*. Here he seemed more at home, but the Gershwin music was more interesting than the character. At times, too, Davis came across like a shrimp trying to act like a big fish. The secret to playing the coon Sportin' Life was to be rowdy and outrageous but to do it with the greatest of ease. Sammy Davis, Jr., seemed to be trying too hard.

In the features that dominated his career, the clan movies in which he costarred with Frank Sinatra, Dean Martin, and Peter Lawford, he alienated black movie patrons because he was too much the coon-pickaninny figure. On the surface the clan pictures were egalitarian affairs; underneath they rotted from white patronizing and hypocrisy. In *Ocean's Eleven* (1960), Davis portrayed the agreeable lackey sidekick. In an era in which token niggers were popping up in offices throughout America, he became the "showcase nigger" for the white stars. To maintain such a privileged position, Davis underwent much abuse in his films. At the conclusion of *Robin and the 7 Hoods*, when Davis, Dean Martin, and Frank Sinatra were all dressed as Santa Clauses, the racial joke of a ludicrous black Santa was at Davis's expense. In that same film it was apparent that Sinatra ordered him about as he never did the white actors. When he shouted for Davis to cut out the nonsense, it was no different from Will Rogers threatening to give Stepin Fetchit a kick in the pants in the 1930s (except that in the earlier pictures there was no pretense of equality).

In *Sergeants 3* (1962), in which he was actually cast as a diligently faithful coon servant, the movie tried prettifying the situation by making him a hero. But in Davis's work there was too much exaggeration, too much playing up to whitey for him to satisfy black audiences. He wanted desperately to please, and as he scampered about on his missions in the film he was curiously reminiscent of Harold Lloyd's little black sidekick Sunshine Sammy. With *A Man Called Adam* Sammy Davis, Jr., may have wanted to redeem himself. But he was dramatically unprepared for the role, and he failed terribly in the scenes in which he whined or broke down in pathos. Later he returned to his comic coon figures when he costarred with Peter Lawford in *Salt and Pepper* (1968) and its sequel *One More Time* (1970). As he portrayed Lawford's loyal man-Friday, Sammy Davis, Jr., was a regrettably embarrassing figure with little spunk or artistry.

—*1994*

"JAZZ ON TV: PLAY IT AGAIN, SAMMY!,"
by Gary Giddins, *The Village Voice*

Sammy Davis, Jr., is not for all tastes, certainly not for mine. Invariably described as an entertainer because he doesn't do any one thing especially well, except, at times, dancing—he is presently bringing his brand of hyperthyroid candor to an ABC variety/talk TV show on Sunday nights. He is not a man of moderation. Incapable of receiving a joke without assuring us that it killed him or at least made him fall on the floor, he can even react to Bob Hope's prehistoric witticisms (memorized and spun out like ticker tape) with a paroxysm of appreciation, his arms jangling like a marionette's, his body undulating all over the chair. He likes to say words like "dig" and "gig" and even "outasite" but he can't pronounce them without stretching his mouth with the effect of cradling them in quotation marks. I always get the feeling this is part of an effort to show (a) that he is still a soul brother even though he once expressed his patriotism by placing his ear to Richard Nixon's navel and (b) that he is still a hip soul brother even if he can't swing. His theme song is the odious "I Gotta Be Me," one of those songs designed to justify anything, like his pal's "My Way." For a sidekick, Sammy's got the obsequious William H. Williams, a real pro at hawking Alpo.

A couple of weeks ago, Davis did an all-jazz show. His guests were Count Basie, Dizzy Gillespie, Sarah Vaughan, and Billy Eckstine. And Bob Hope who opened the show and was gracious enough to leave before the entertainment started. To Davis's immense credit, there was a lot of music on the show and a relatively small percentage of jive. Eckstine and Vaughan sang two songs apiece, then collaborated on a duet. Basie played piano with the studio orchestra (never making it to the talk couch, wise man) and Gillespie performed with his quartet augmented by his prodigious disciple John Faddis.

Most of the talk was pretty harmless, if rarely provocative. Sarah had the best line. Sammy asked her how it felt to be a living legend (in jazz, if you've persevered for more than ten years, you're a legend). She responded: "Well, when I'm at home and all alone, I look in the mirror and I jump up and shout, 'Yeah! You're a living legend!' " Eckstine reminisced about raiding all the bands of the '40s to put together his seminal aggregation. Sammy explained that all the names B. dropped were legends. Sammy frequently offers helpful explanations to the "nice people"—that's how he refers to the folks in videoland (and don't think it didn't make me feel pretty guilty, not feeling so nice and all). Dizzy noted that European audiences were much hipper than American audiences.

The only offensive remarks came from Davis, and my interpretation of them may be off the wall. He twice referred to Gillespie as the jazz musician who spread the most international good will. This struck me as a gratuitous slur on Louis Armstrong, whom Davis began attacking in 1957 when Louis had the chutzpah to tell Ike to go to hell for not interfering in the Little Rock segregation battle. My interpretation seemed less distant from the wall when, a few minutes later, Sammy amended himself. "I'm not talking about that hot club jazz, but modern music." Oh. Albert Murray recently told me that killing your father is not a Negro story, that the young musician always reveres the older musician because the young musician is merely someone without experience. Dizzy certainly knows that, and took no time in delineating the Armstrong-Eldridge-Gillespie chronology of jazz. John Faddis certainly knows it (he was even playing an upturned horn). If Sammy doesn't know it, what does he think that "Jr." is all about?

The question of whether jazz is a continuing music—an evolving art—or one man's memories, is the real subject here. In the middle of the show, Davis seated himself at the piano, played a Basie cliché, and dedicated the show to "all the jazz players who never made it big but just kept on a playin." This sentimental little speech was by no means the incisive description of jazz that William B. predictably called it, but it was heartfelt and okay. Except . . . if Davis feels so strongly about the underappreciated jazzman, why in hell did he not bother even to identify some of the musicians on this very show—especially Faddis, who should at least have been acknowledged as one of the young players keeping the tradition going.

The point being: Sarah, at 51, was the youngest of his guests that evening. The talk was about the good old days, when B. had a band, when Sam sat in with Diz (now there's a jazz moment that never became legendary), and when the world was young. Sammy, clearly moved by his own eloquence, pointed out that the great thing about jazz is that it never dies. So why was there no one under 51 on a show dedicated to jazz? Why is there never anyone under 51 on shows dedicated to jazz? A couple of years ago, Timex did the last of its TV jazz spectaculars. You know the guests without my telling you: Duke, Basie, Ella, Diz. The youngster of the troupe was Brubeck, age 55. What I found offensively hypocritical and dangerous about the Davis program is that masquerading, as respect for an extraordinary legacy, was little more than a poisonous indulgence in nostalgia. Play it again, Sammy.

Three of the guests came up during the bop era, when they were considered rebels. Today they are roots. Why was there no representative of today's rebels, those who need and deserve the exposure and who are enriching the tradition in a way Sammy's emotionalism never could? Ultimately, why is jazz always celebrated on TV as yesterday's news? If you watch for jazz on the tube, the message is clear: jazz is old folks' music. Significantly, a lot of young players, jazz players, have picked up on the message and eschewed the name. If jazz has survived the social obloquy of the '60s, it has not muddled past economic barriers. For a decade, musicians have been learning what's in a name: to wit, if you dress up your music in the accoutrements of pop, you may get a shot at the big time via the rock culture (take it, Herbie and Chick, and let's not forget Charles Lloyd, a true blast from the past), because they aren't going to get bus fare from jazz tributes like Sammy Davis's.

There have been infrequent attempts to present jazz intelligently on the tube. The Jazz Repertory Company has been enlivening its concerts by showing snippets from the old kinescopes. CBS once did a show called *The Sound of Jazz*, on which Billie Holiday was confronted with the Holy Trinity of the tenor, Hawk, Pres, and Ben, and Mulligan and Guiffre were also present. For several years, public (remember when they used to call it educational?) TV presented superb broadcasts, first under the guidance of Ralph Gleason (there was a classic half hour of Coltrane), then Dan Morgenstern (he filmed

Hawkins's final appearance, perhaps the most moving footage ever taken of a great man's last stand). There were also some splendid Newport films on NET, and one remembers Fr. O'Connor's fine series on weekend afternoons on CBS. Yet the most remarkable jazz broadcast I can recall was a stunningly imaginative and varied tribute, several hours long, to Robert Kennedy. Whoever said we'd have to wait until another public figure was assassinated before that kind of program would be repeated was evidently right. (In Europe, jazz is on TV regularly.)

There is of course a technical problem in presenting any kind of music on TV. The sound is lousy. When Miles Davis appeared on Dick Cavett's show, the technicians couldn't figure out how to make the saxophone audible. The rock producers have solved this by employing simultaneous radio broadcasts. It must endlessly be inquired why these same producers approach jazz as timorously as eunuch suitors. It wasn't too long ago that B. B. King couldn't get past the "race" market. But after he made the breakthrough, he was seen playing uncompromising blues on Mike Douglas.

Jazz—all kinds of jazz—needs exposure in the media. We all want to see more of the experienced, established musicians; not only Sammy's line-up, but Erroll Garner, Roy Eldridge, Joe Turner, Dexter Gordon, Clark Terry's big band, Earl Hines, Jimmy Witherspoon, Anita O'Day, Lionel Hampton, Stan Getz, Benny Carter, and on and on. But if the Young Turks are excluded, then jazz has been effectively wrapped in a baggie and deposited in a time capsule. Only in jazz does every generation of innovators have to fight for a position in the tradition.

If Sammy Davis isn't going to have the balls to present a Freddie Hubbard, 38, much less a Hannibal Marvin Peterson, 27, who is? Not Carson, and forget the prime time. Only Joe Franklin regularly books jazz musicians (even Cecil Taylor, Sonny Rollins, and Roy Brooks) and, with all due respect, I don't think this makes for a satisfactory image of jazz. The music is alive and well right here in New York City; generation gaps to the contrary exist only in the eyes of the media. So next time Sammy Davis wants to deliver an encomium to all those faceless jazzmen who never made it but kept on trucking, let him present one or two on his show. If he doesn't know of any, he just has to send me a stamped, self-addressed envelope.

—*June 2, 1975*

"STRANGENESS IN THE NIGHT,"
by Margo Jefferson, *Vogue*

When Frank Sinatra, Sammy Davis, Jr., and Dean Martin announced that they would join forces for a national tour, it seemed as though the Rat Pack, that 1960s Las Vegas-meets-*Playboy* magazine version of on-the-road hipsters, was back in force. What a shining emblem of the days when life was a perpetual boys' night out if you were a grown man with money, fame, and power! Rat Packers drank and partied, traded ethnic slurs with gusto, and spoke their very own slang, a code in which all women (excepting Mother) were broads; death was "the big casino"; a good time was "a little hey hey," and a penis was a bird (as in "How's your bird, old man?").

Then, Dean Martin dropped out, owing to what the press called health problems; and the gossipmongers, everything from alcohol abuse to bad nerves. I felt bad for him, but hoped the result would be a better show. After all, Sinatra and Davis were the superior performers in their day. Sinatra the ultimate dream man—passionate and vulnerable; Davis the ultimate showman—the no-holds-barred vaudevillian who'd do anything to make you happy.

The truth is, their show, which toured the country last spring and hits the road again this month, combines the shabby spectacle of Rat Pack sensibilities at their worst with the sorry sight of talents thoroughly past their prime.

After all, do you really want to hear Sammy sing "The

Candy Man" again, or listen as he drops into dated soul dialect every few sentences to get a laugh? Do you want to hear Sinatra, who's rarely in good voice these days, bully and bluster his way through song after song? Why should you have to hear tired jokes about Radio City being the home of the world's biggest organ (the world's biggest bird, get it?) or watch Frank turn Sammy into a little blackamoor court jester—a ploy that anyone who's seen old Rat Pack movies like *Robin and the 7 Hoods* will remember.

First, Frank told us that Sammy drinks strawberry soda not because he's on the wagon, but because he hopes it'll change his skin color. Then, he let Sammy launch into a song beginning "I dreamed last night I got on the boat to heaven," only to break in after "I dreamed last night" and ad-lib "that he was white!" Sammy tried to counter with "I guess it wouldn't be too bad, but I wouldn't want to give up my sense of rhythm." Then, lest even that seem too insolent, he sang on to the line, "That's the moment I woke up, thank the Lord," and rushed over to Frank, crooning "Thank the Lord" on bent knee, eyes cast worshipfully downward.

"I'd like to propose a toast to you, your families, your children, and your grandchildren," Sinatra told the audience at one point. "May you all live to be a hundred. And may the last voice you hear be mine." But after what I saw and heard, I say unless that voice can be safely confined to an old record, don't risk it.

—September 1988

"BLACK NARCISSUS,"
REVIEW OF *WHY ME?*,
by Hilton Als, *Voice Literary Supplement*

Dear Sammy: At first I wasn't going to write this as a personal letter because personal letters are just that—personal. But then I thought, This has to be as much about me as it is about you

because that's how you want your readers to react. Because
what this book is about, man, is love. Totally. I know what
you're getting at here because I'm all about that myself—love.
So that made me think, Why not, *why not* write this as a personal open letter in response to your openness as revealed in
your second autobiography in however many years it is since
Yes I Can, your first, was published. *Yes I Can* was a pretty
long book, remember, and how much can one man *alone*, albeit
a superstar, have to say? I could never have that much to say
even though I, too, have been a man alone, have been there,
suffered and come back. And although I am not a superstar yet,
I am in a similarly exciting, dangerous, compelling, grateful,
amazed, personal, humble, exciting, personal, and incredibly
humble field—the writing thing. Writing is something that *really* brings you to your knees and makes you want to sing *The
Impossible Dream*, isn't it? It's a field that always requires my
personal best as well as yours, Sammy, and you give your all to
it in *Why Me?* because that's just the way you are, that's what
you do. And you know what makes you incredible just as you'll
know what makes me incredible after you read this because,
dig, I had the *guts* to lay this all on the line in a personal way. I
had the *chutzpah* to write yet another boring piece that con-
tributes to the general confusion of Negroes representing their
own Negroness and being personally critiqued by other Negroes in front of a largely white audience. I mean, who needs it.
Not you. Because what you have written here is Everynegro's
Autobiography. It is all of our stories rolled into one even
though many of us have not had the millions that you've had so
we could leave the country whenever things became personally
unbearable, or picked up a Swedish first wife, or made any of
those personally complicated gestures such as adopting Judaism
as our personal faith. I've often wondered if you did that so
that you would have some place, *somewhere* to dump the anxiety that many of us feel by identifying with the oppressed but
not necessarily your own oppressed. And did you think your
Judaism would then lead to some kind of—like crazy man!—

assimilation? Sammy, you bring new meaning to the idea of the signifying monkey. But dig, such personal heaviness is eclipsed for me, Sammy, by the beautiful and heavy, personal but open way certain other gestures in your personal and public lives have put you right up there as yet another empty symbol of achievement. Remember that deep hug on Nixon, Sam old boy? I mean man . . . And even though, as you explain so movingly in *Why Me?*, the mouth *bleeds*, superstardom as a goal can become a curse. And even though you have to know what it is you don't want once you have it and you don't want to be any more famous than you already are, which is kind of the book's *moral*—or one of them—then why write a book in the first place, the superstar auto(didact)biography being just a little more grist for the personal publicity mill? I'm telling you, Sam, all of this heaviness cooks on a low flame for a long time in the back of my mind (what's left of it) because it's all so funny I can't cry for laughing. (That last bit was a little Negroism, which your book is peppered with. Usually you put it into the mouth of your father, a song and dance man himself, kinda like a hipster Uncle Remus.)

But the fame thing was such a kick in the head, Sammy, because it acted as a beautiful chick does, in terms of the effect you wanted it to have on your personal life—to maybe make you believe that after all the tuxedoes and pinky rings and relaxed hair, somebody could really, really, personally *like* a boy who was more or less self-educated, had a glass eye and a flat nose and a weird way of twisting his mouth to the side when he sang. But isn't that the beauty of showbiz, Sammy? The illusion thing? I know just what you mean. Regardless of that weird dichotomy, Sammy, when it's beautiful it's *beautiful*.

—August 1989

"SAMMY DAVIS, JR., DIES AT 64; TOP SHOWMAN BROKE BARRIERS,"
by Peter B. Flint, *The New York Times*

Sammy Davis, Jr., a versatile and dynamic singer, dancer and actor who overcame extraordinary obstacles to become a leading American entertainer, died of throat cancer yesterday at his home in Los Angeles. He was 64 years old and had been in deteriorating health since his release from Cedar-Sinai Medical Center on March 13.

The showman was born in a Harlem tenement, grew up in vaudeville from the age of 3 and never went to school. His talents as a mime, comedian, trumpet player, drummer, pianist and vibraphonist as well as singer and dancer were shaped from his childhood and made him one of the nation's first black performers to gain mainstream acclaim.

With heavy jewelry around his neck and on his fingers, and clad in a snug jumpsuit or tuxedo, the short, slim showman with a broken nose, defiant jaw and big, crooked smile had a rakish charm that energized stages for decades. He sold out leading nightclubs and concert halls, won personal triumphs in such Broadway musicals as "Mr. Wonderful" (1956) and "Golden Boy" (1964), illumined movies and television and made scores of hit recordings with such signature songs as "What Kind of Fool Am I?," "Candy Man," "Mr. Bojangles" and "I've Gotta Be Me."

The triumphs were punctuated by sometimes ugly controversies—abuse and slurs by whites, particularly over his marriage to a white actress, May Britt; resentment by blacks over what they viewed as his white life style, and widespread skepticism over his mid-1950's conversion to Judaism.

Mr. Davis also endured major health setbacks. He lost his left eye in a near-fatal 1954 auto crash, had reconstructive hip surgery in 1985 that enabled him to dance again, and was told last year that he had throat cancer. He underwent eight weeks of radiation treatments for a carcinoma growing behind his vocal cords, until his doctors said the cancer was in remission. He had smoked heavily for many years.

The debilitating illness and treatment prompted 26 of his fellow entertainers to salute his courage and long-time efforts to lower racial barriers in a two-and-a-half-hour television tribute on Feb. 4. The frail but indomitable Mr. Davis, whose voice was only a husky whisper, did not speak, but he rose to do a brief soft-shoe step to a standing ovation.

Only a year earlier, he had announced his defeat of alcohol and cocaine. He completed a world tour with Frank Sinatra and Liza Minnelli (who filled in for an ailing Dean Martin) and publicized "Why Me?," a book on which he had collaborated with his friends Jane and Burt Boyar as a sequel to their best-selling 1965 Davis biography, "Yes I Can."

The 1989 book said that John F. Kennedy had asked Mr. Davis and Miss Britt not to participate in the 1961 Presidential inauguration, lest the sight of an interracial couple anger Southerners. Mr. Davis also recounted the racism that haunted his life, from bloody fights in the Army to being turned away from New York nightclubs.

"An Affinity" for Judaism

His conversion to Judaism, according to the book, arose from self-scrutiny during his convalescence from the 1954 car crash. His family was Baptist and until then he had thought little of religion, but he studied Judaism deeply, concluded "it teaches justice for everyone," and found "an affinity" between Jews and blacks, who have both "been oppressed for centuries."

The second biography also explored the breakup of his marriage to Miss Britt, who, in divorcing him in 1968, cited "no family life to speak of," and his neglect of their three children: a daughter, Tracey, and two adopted sons, Mark and Jeff. He had previously been married briefly to Loray White, a dancer. In 1970 he married Altovise Gore, also a dancer.

Mr. Davis admitted to compulsive carousing, reckless gambling and spending ($50 million over 20 years while earning $3 million a year) and excessive drinking and smoking.

With characteristic bravado, he once again hailed himself as a reformed man, boasting of sobriety with such ironies as "The hardest thing is waking up in the morning and realizing that's as good as you're going to feel all day."

Supported Humanitarian Causes

Yet there was a more private side to Mr. Davis. The entertainer eschewed publicity while taking part in civil rights marches and contributing generously to humanitarian causes. His many awards included induction into the Hall of Fame of the National Association for the Advancement of Colored People, honorary degrees from black colleges, and a Kennedy Center honor for career achievement.

A deep regret of the aging Mr. Davis was his support of Richard M. Nixon during the 1972 Presidential election campaign. He later renounced his backing, accusing Mr. Nixon of having made civil rights promises he did not keep. Looking back in 1987, Mr. Davis affirmed that if the Kennedy Center salute to his career did not soften his rancor over the inaugural racial rebuff by President Kennedy, "I don't know what does."

Sammy Davis, Jr., was born to Sammy Davis and the former Elvera Sanchez on Dec. 8, 1925, in a Harlem tenement at 140th Street and Eighth Avenue. He was brought up by his father's mother, Rosa Davis, while his parents, both vaudevillians, were on tour. In his third year, his mother left the act and also the family, and he joined the Orpheum circuit with his father and Will Mastin.

With typical zest, the youngster learned show business while his father got him occasional tutors to appease truant officers. As sound movies began to cripple vaudeville, the troupe shrank and eventually became "The Will Mastin Trio, featuring Sammy Davis, Jr."

Drafted at 18, he graduated from comic books after remedial reading lessons from a black sergeant while he battled racist taunts and insults from white G.I.'s, who repaid him several times by breaking his nose. Performing in Army camps around the country, he worked hard, he recalled, to reach the bigots, "neutralize them and make them acknowledge" him.

Some Lean Years for the Group

After the war, with vaudeville nearly dead, the Will Mastin Trio had several lean years struggling to break into variety theaters and cabarets around the country. Gradually, as Mr. Davis honed his talents, the act became his showcase, with his father and uncle providing tap and soft-shoe background.

The group, now "starring Sammy Davis, Jr.," began playing top variety houses and nightclubs, becoming headliners and repeatedly breaking box-office records, while he gained solo prominence with recordings and television appearances as a variety showman and actor.

On Broadway, Mr. Davis had many concert successes and starred in three musicals. One, in 1956, was the quasi-biographical "Mr. Wonderful," which drew from Brooks Atkinson, drama critic of The New York Times, the observation that the show "comes alive only when young Mr. Davis rocks and rolls, tap-dances or does imitations."

The other two musicals were an updated version of "Golden Boy" in 1964 and a 1978 revival of "Stop the World, I Want to Get Off."

Perhaps his most enduring movie role was Sportin' Life in "Porgy and Bess" (1959), a part that elicited high praise from Bosley Crowther, motion picture critic of The Times.

Mr. Crowther wrote that "in every respect he is the sharpest and most insinuating figure in the show."

He played an avuncular dancer in "Tap" (1989), his last movie role. His other films include "Ocean's Eleven" (1960), "Sergeants 3" (1962), "Johnny Cool" (1963) and "Robin and the 7 Hoods" (1964).

In addition to his wife, Altovise, his mother, his daughter, Tracey, and sons Mark and Jeff, Mr. Davis is survived by his son Manny; two sisters, Ramona James of Manhattan and Suzette Davis of Portland, Ore., and two grandchildren, Andrew and Sam Michael.

A funeral will be held tomorrow at 11 A.M. at Forest Lawn Memorial-Park in the Hollywood Hills, with burial at Forest Lawn Memorial-Park in Glendale.

—*May 17, 1990*

"A STAR, A SURVIVOR,"
editorial, *The New York Times*

A middle-aged man, on hearing recently that Sammy Davis, Jr., was near death, remarked, "I can't imagine a world without Sammy Davis in it." Many other Americans, even if they were no particular fans of the entertainer, probably feel the same way, and for humane as well as theatrical reasons.

Sammy Davis was a national celebrity for the four decades before his death yesterday. His marriages, friendships, politics, religion—all have been fodder for gossip columnists and magazines. He lent his name to a golf tournament. He was a faithful presence at charity dinners and telethons. He was, in short, a star, a durable fixture in the firmament of American life.

But there was more to Sammy Davis, Jr., than endurance. He was a tiny atomic bomb of a man who worked so hard and expended so much energy onstage that he left audiences awestruck. It was typical of him: he worked overtime to overcome racial discrimination, to recover from an auto accident in which he lost an eye, to reach the top in a business where short, unglamorous, one-eyed black men were not supposed to.

He was an incandescent figure. And the glow survives.

—*May 17, 1990*

"SAMMY!,"

by Ann Henderson, Nevada

One night at Harrah's Tahoe, Sammy Davis, Jr., stunned his audience. He stopped midway through his show and told the roomful of people that he was picking up the tab.

"I didn't feel I was giving them the kind of show I should give them," he explains. "I wasn't performing like I felt I should, so I said, 'You're all my guests.' It wasn't a grandstand play. It's what I believe. The man who pays his money to come see me deserves the best I got. If I give them the best show I can, it's up to them to like it or not. At least I know I've put the best foot forward, which is important to me."

The incident reveals a fundamental, life-long concern of Davis—individual dignity. He has had to work hard to win it. His race, his Jewish faith, his early reputation as a playboy, even his versatile talent often blocked his efforts. The story of his success in show business, of his freedom to perform on stage as his sense of artistry demanded, and of his opportunity to live as he wished is also a Nevada story, intimately involving the racial policies of the day, and the place of a black entertainer in the white casino world.

In 1945, when Davis was appearing at the El Rancho in Las Vegas with his uncle and father as the Will Mastin Trio, he was not allowed to do anything but perform. "Offstage we were colored again," he says. "I had to stay on the West Side. Black performers couldn't walk through the clubs. We had to go out the back way."

In his 1965 autobiography *Yes I Can* Davis wrote, "Night after night I had to pass [the front] door to get a cab. Once, between shows, I stood around the corner where nobody would see me, and waited for the door to open so I could catch the short burst of gaiety that escaped as people went in and came out . . . listening and wondering what it must be like to be able to just walk in anywhere."

But changes came, if slowly. By 1954 Nevada gaming was in

its adolescence and after 26 years in show business Davis found his career was on the move. He was one of the stars that gamblers were flocking to Las Vegas and Reno to watch. Breaking the long-standing rule against blacks, the Last Frontier in Las Vegas gave him a room while he was performing there. In Reno, Charlie Mapes and Bill Harrah also were humanizing show business.

"Charlie Mapes was crazy anyway," Davis says. "He didn't care what anybody said. And when I told him I wanted to play blackjack, he told me it was okay to play. Bill Harrah set the tone . . . treated performers as human beings. It was very much appreciated."

Davis credits black entertainers like Lena Horne and Billy Eckstine with helping to break down the barriers. "They were very important because of their demeanor," says Davis. "To hell with onstage—all colored guys can dance and sing, you know. But it was how they carried themselves offstage that counted.

"Lena came to Vegas as a motion picture star. One day her child went swimming in the hotel pool and they drained it. She handled it with dignity—just like it never happened—and then she just didn't play there for about two years."

During his 50 years in show business Davis has heard or seen vituperative expressions of bigotry from both whites and blacks. But in the face of prejudice and in poverty, Davis has tried to maintain his dignity, as has long been the tradition among black entertainers. "Bojangles," a song that has been Davis' trademark, captures that need for dignity, and he still cannot sing it without thinking of his forebears.

" 'Bojangles' has a lot of meaning for me because I go back to that period. There was a great mystique about the black entertainers of the late twenties and early thirties. They were minstrels in the traditional sense; wherever the coin of the realm was being passed around they would dance—whether it was on the corner, a little bar.

"I know at least 30 men who were Bojangles. [Tap dancer

Bill Robinson was the most famous.] They had frayed cuffs, but always had one good pressed suit, and they ironed their shirt on the lightbulb. They'd pass the hat, but always maintain their dignity."

White performers also helped greatly in breaking the color barriers. In the 1960s, Davis knew he was making history when he began to appear onstage as a member of the Rat Pack. The Pack was an alliance of Davis, Frank Sinatra, Dean Martin, Peter Lawford and Joey Bishop, and the Sands in Las Vegas was headquarters for their shenanigans.

"It was one of the most exciting periods in show business," says Davis. "They were filming 'Pepe' in Vegas and at the same time we were doing 'Ocean's Eleven,' and at night all five of us appeared at the Sands.

"And it was fun. We made it up—a lot of ad-libbing. Celebrities came to see the show because they knew it was one of those things that couldn't happen again. It was wild, and it could only happen in Nevada."

He starred with the Pack in movies like "Ocean's Eleven," "Sergeants 3" and "Robin and the 7 Hoods." He was accepted everywhere as a singing and dancing star. But in many ways, he was an exception—a successful black in a white industry.

"I was always under the impression that money and position would eliminate the walls of prejudice," he says now. "But the only thing success did was grease the way for me as an individual and did nothing to help the guy behind me.

"In Nevada there were still some rotten people who tried to stop it [equality] any way they could—the old school that was entrenched in gaming, who still believed that colored people brought you luck if you rubbed their heads."

Davis says he listened to his contemporaries who were concerned, like Sinatra and Jack Benny. "Frank said the first place we've got to change is our own joint [the Sands], and we had a ready ear in people like the owners, Jack Entratter and Carl Cohen."

There were many other understanding whites, he adds.

"Black people didn't create civil rights. White people and black people working together created it."

Today Davis can relax in the palatial Star Suite at Harrah's Tahoe, with its spectacular view of the Sierra, and reflect upon the changes he has seen. "As I look back on it, and I see this state—what it has grown into—the advancements are so marked. I think everyone who lives in Nevada should feel proud of what they've accomplished. It's go for the gold." So entrenched are the advancements, according to Davis, that they are no longer noticed. "The contribution to the state of Nevada that the black performer has made is taken for granted now because it is a reality."

As bigotry became less a problem for him, Davis discovered a new obstacle to his quest for individual dignity. Fans and critics stereotyped him.

His first movie roles alienated black movie patrons, according to film historian Donald Bogle. "In 'Ocean's Eleven,' " writes Bogle, "Davis portrayed the agreeable lackey sidekick. In an era in which token niggers were popping up in offices throughout America, he became the 'showcase nigger' for the white stars." But to Davis the roles were a chance to continue the fun and excitement of working with people he respected, and who respected him.

Even away from the movies, Davis' talents have burdened him. Dancer, singer, actor, comedian, player of umpteen instruments, impressionist—Davis became known as "Mr. Versatility." And 15 years ago an important part of his act was the fast draw, which came about because of his role as TV's first black cowboy. His appearance on the "Zane Grey Theater" caused a lot of talk. Viewers wondered what he could know about cowboying. In defense, Davis says he began to collect single action Colts and became gunslinger perfect on the draw. Some people still think of him only as one of show business' fastest guns.

The problem is that Davis doesn't want to be known as a fast draw specialist or a show business jack-of-all-trades. He prefers to be thought of as a serious artist, a creative performer who invests himself in his act. Consequently, he has changed his show over the years—less dancing, more concentration on perfecting and varying his singing. He does more of the standard challenging tunes and, of course, his hits. "I ain't got but four hits," he jokes, "so that rules out a medley." But no matter what song he sings, he seldom fails to win ovations and yells of "Bravo!" from an audience.

Recently, Davis has directed his energy toward an off-beat area of acting—soap operas. Not only did he become addicted to the soaps when he was hospitalized five years ago, but now he plays a character for two weeks a year on "One Life to Live." He believes that for the most part the acting on the soaps is better than it is on evening TV. "The subject matter is better too," he says. "They deal with subjects that they won't even touch in prime time." Davis claims the soaps challenge him to work on serious acting, but the controversial subjects are probably just as great an attraction to him.

The individual dignity and artistic freedom that he worked for he has now. But he realizes the achievement would not be sufficient if he were to forget the past. And so he hasn't forgotten. Referring to his tendency to chain-smoke and the troubles that it causes on public conveyances, Davis likes to quip, "Took me 20 years to get on the bus, and now I gotta worry about where I smoke."

—*November/December 1981*

"SO LONG, SAMMY,"
by Bill Willard, *Nevada*

It was in Coffee Dan's, one of Hollywood's memorable gathering spots for showpeople, that I first met Sammy Davis, Jr. Located at Sunset and Vine opposite the NBC Radio building, the place was a constant hum of deals over breakfast, lunch, dinner, and beyond midnight.

Mel Tormé called me over to his table. It was in the spring

of 1947, and I was busy writing, directing, and producing shows for Armed Forces Radio.

"Meet Sammy Davis, Jr.," Tormé grinned. "He wants to be on your 'Jubilee' show. He needs the work."

Sammy shot back, "We were on 'Jubilee' when Jimmy Lyons was producer. You're the one who needs the work."

It was an intriguing gathering, with Tormé, one day to be hyped nationally as "The Velvet Fog," a title he learned to hate, and the skinny 21-year-old tapdancer/impressionist/phenom. A few years later Davis would become one of the biggest stars to appear onstage in Las Vegas, Reno, and Tahoe, or anywhere else for that matter. When I first met him, he was part of a trio named for his uncle. By the time he died last May 16, he'd been titled Mr. Entertainment and Mr. Wonderful. You could say "Sammy" in most parts of the world, and people would know whom you were talking about.

On that day at Coffee Dan's, Davis looked small in stature, pencil thin. He dressed sharply and spoke articulately through a jutting jaw. He told us that his uncle, Will Mastin, and dad, Sam, Sr., enjoyed performing in Las Vegas at El Rancho Vegas, the first of such casino resorts on Highway 91 outside the city limits. The drawback to playing those dates, he grimaced, was the awful personal treatment. The three men were not permitted to stay on the hotel side or in the casino and had to take rooms on the west side of town where blacks were ghettoed. Las Vegas was earning its bad black image of "Mississippi of the West."

He described the other two resorts on Highway 91, renamed "The Strip" by Guy McAfee, boss of the year-old Golden Nugget downtown. They were the Last Frontier and the Flamingo, which, Sammy informed us, flopped on its Christmas Eve opening in 1946, and owner Ben "Bugsy" Siegel was attempting to restore the fortunes with another opening, hoping to calm the jitters of the mobster backers.

Sammy said their pay of $500 a week at El Rancho Vegas was certain to climb higher, and it did, as I noted when I moved to Las Vegas two years later. (One day in Coffee Dan's, I was made a radio-show offer I didn't refuse. After moving to Las Vegas in February 1949, the deal fell through. But, captivated by my new surroundings, I stayed, and within 18 months was a columnist for the *Las Vegas Sun*, reviewer for *Variety*, and married to a beautiful dancer.)

The Will Mastin Trio, Featuring Sammy Davis, Jr., now was very much in my sights. The trio appeared at the Flamingo in May 1951, third on the bill with Mickey Rooney and Frances Langford. Sammy & Co. had been lured away from El Rancho by Flamingo entertainment director Maxine Lewis, who upped the trio's salary to $550 a week. (El Rancho had offered Sammy $500 to appear as a single act minus his uncle and dad, but Sammy nixed that deal instantly.) Rooney later took the trio along on a nationwide tour, and the junket enlarged Sammy's horizons considerably.

By October 1952 the trio was earning $1,000 a week at the Flamingo. With hindsight, my review at the time predicted greater triumphs for Sammy: "The budding Davis, Jr., proves his ability on all counts, and should become a top star one of these days. Versatility is shown in his amazing legmania, but is heightened when he parades some accurate and, at times, slightly vitriolic mimicry."

Two years later, after his solid hit at Ciro's in Hollywood following an Oscar show, Sammy was featured prominently on the Last Frontier marquee above "Will Mastin Trio." I saw him often after I began a hilarious gig that lasted for five years as a straight-man/character in the Silver Slipper Stock Company, headed by one of the funniest of all time burlesque comedians, Hank Henry. We had Sammy night after night in the audience at the Silver Slipper. He, along with Frank Sinatra's entourage and Howard Hughes with his adoring females and aides, Hollywood stars, world celebrities, and show people, haunted our 2:30 a.m. shows with constant cheering, laughing attendance. Hank name-dropped shamelessly, and from time to time Sammy would pop up on our stage to take part in a sketch, maybe take the pie in the face or the squirt of seltzer on his crotch.

Sammy took off one night for Los Angeles by car after the midnight Last Frontier show, smashing up on the Cajon Pass outside of San Bernardino in Southern California, losing an eye in the accident. By now Sammy was an established Hollywood name, pal of Jeff Chandler and Tony Curtis (Sammy was en route to a get-together with them) and other stars.

He was back in the spotlight in 1955 when members of the famed Friars Club roasted Sammy at the Beverly Hilton, the first time the Friars had ever held such a function for a black performer, said the initial notice in *Daily Variety*.

The next year Jack Entratter of the Sands inked Sammy to a two-year contract, calling for 25 grand a week, the same he was pulling down at the New Frontier. Davis had always wanted to play the Copa Room at the Sands, chiefly because of his friendship with one of the nitery's other bosses, Frank Sinatra.

It must be mentioned that Entratter, major-domo of the Sands, was responsible for the great shows in the Copa Room through the '50s and midway through the '60s. During his chiefdom, the most publicized entertainment event in Las Vegas history took place when "The Summit," headed by Sinatra, with Sammy, Dean Martin, Peter Lawford, and Joey Bishop, took over the Copa Room on the night of January 20, 1960. Entratter also was instrumental in breaking down the strict color-racial barriers on the Strip by hotel guesting and honoring blacks in the casino.

That summit meeting of Sinatra's Clan, which some have called the Rat Pack, was prelude to their filming *Ocean's Eleven*, a fantastic yarn about a bunch of war vets heisting five Strip casinos. Sammy's part in the movie was to drive the garbage truck that picked up the loot.

There was the great party period in the '70s when Sammy once gave a wingding for the entire County of Clark, or at least 1,000 citizens at Caesars Palace. I had now begun to question

Sammy's performances in print. Take this *Variety* review—please!—from 1975:

"Sammy Davis, Jr., has now changed his act where the junior could well be changed to a senior. He has mellowed so much that his onetime supercharged kinetics have faded away into the distance. . . . Davis has reached and passed an earlier goal, that of being a unique voice, recognized instantly, just like The Man, his idol, Frank Sinatra."

Before he left for Broadway to star in "Stop the World, I Want to Get Off" in 1977, I went to his dressing room at Caesars Palace to tape some Sammy thoughts. I asked about his being set adrift after Howard Hughes bought the Sands and other Las Vegas hotels where he had worked for so many years.

"Well, let me put it this way," Sammy answered. "I've always felt the people I had to work with—I worked with Jack Entratter for 17, 18 years—I didn't care who owned the Sands, I really didn't care. And when Walter Kane took over after Jack passed away, there was a great void for me, but I became very friendly with Walter Kane, and he really became like a father to me.

"But Walter was locked in by a corporate structure that knew nothing and knows nothing about show business per se. And no matter what Walter Kane's recommendations, or the other people involved in theatrical background, you got a corporation of guys who sit there and say, 'He's going to make more in one week than I make in a year.' They've got to resent it." He added, however, "if you got the clout, you don't have to be a particular favorite of theirs.

"Forget all the ABC's like 'How many people does he bring in? Does he bring in gamblers?'

"It's getting a little colder in terms of those relationships that we used to foster, when everybody was making $20,000 a week and happy to make it, and Frank was making 25."

He recalled the first time the Will Mastin Trio got $25,000 at the New Frontier. "I was hysterical." Then they moved to the Sands. "When Jack Entratter said we'll pay you 30, I thought that was all the money in the world. But the town has grown, attitudes have grown. But the industry is still with the man who owns the performer, meaning the one who owns him psychologically."

By the '80s he had given up booze and wild parties, settled down with his wife, Altovise, and only had the noxious habit of smoking left to defeat. In his act during those years, hunched over and doing the Sammy shuffle complete with lighted cigarette, he told audiences that his doctor ordered him to give up all his vices. "I only got one of three left, that ain't bad," he would chuckle.

Approaching his 60th year and with most of his early hard-won entertaining reputation still intact, he was beset by a bum hip. It's tough to hoof with a bad hip. "The old hip just wore out over the years. Iron wears out, so I guess blood and bones can wear out, too," he told interviewer Pete Mikla of the *Las Vegas Review-Journal*. He restored some of his pedal instincts with a prosthetic joint installed in his pelvis and afterward could tap out his rhythmic messages in staccato form, but never like the old days and nights.

But boy, could he still talk. On November 12, 1986, Sammy came to UNLV to inaugurate the "Rap With the Artist" series begun by musicologist Arnold Shaw, who had established the Popular Music Research Center at the university. (As chair of the advisory committee, I was Shaw's chief lieutenant.)

The Judy Bayley Theatre on campus was packed. Sammy laid out his life in warm, open fashion to the audience. It was a beauty.

The last time I saw Sammy was some 42 years after our first salutations at Coffee Dan's. Musically speaking, the occasion was not a happy one. The musicians' union had called a press conference at the Sahara Hotel and urged Sammy, Jerry Lewis, Shecky Green, Tony Orlando, and Robert Goulet to help fight corporate types in the resort industry who were intent on replacing live music and musicians with tapes and synthesizers. It was a sticky matter for Sammy and Jerry, who were performing as a duo at Bally's.

Sammy arrived looking exceedingly thin with deep lines in his face, hollowed from his then-secret fight with throat cancer and other ailments.

Later he took the microphone and, as photographers snapped and TV cameramen rolled, Sammy got off with his wry humor, spoken with typical clipped inflection:

"We can't have this town, which was built on live entertainment, live music, go the other way. Don't let them do this thing to us." He paused, grinned, and shot his best line: "If there's no live music, no band, who'll play 'Melancholy Baby'?"

On a melancholy night last May, I watched the lights on the Strip dim and then go dark after the curtain fell on Sammy. Even that tribute might not have been exactly solid with the fleetest of all pop hoofers. He always wanted plenty of light, action, and real live music.

—September/October 1990

INTERVIEWS AND WRITINGS

I woke up feeling stiff, my whole body aching. And angry at myself. Why would anyone sleep on a couch when he's got a king-sized bed in the Star Suite at Harrah's? Bombed was why. Smashed. To not have to look at myself. It had been daylight when the party ended.

   I dragged myself to the bar and, ignoring the coffeepot, I poured a vodka and Coke. I pressed away a throb in my forehead and thought of a line in [James Baldwin's *Another Country*]: "Rufus, this shit is got to stop." I sighed, *Yeah Ruf, but not right now.*

—Sammy Davis, Jr., *Why Me?*

It was a strange time, the sixties, a strange feeling suddenly being "black." Yet overnight thirty million "colored people" and "Negroes" had become "blacks." It was difficult to think of myself as a "black" after all the years of hating "black bastard," "black motherfucker." Nobody ever got called "Negro bastard" or "colored motherfucker." It was always "black" and the word was nasty and hard. Only a few months earlier I'd heard someone say, "This black guy . . ." and was offended by it. I berated him: "I've never seen a person with black skin. I've seen people with brown skin, tan skin, but never black."

—Sammy Davis, Jr., *Why Me?*

Why do I run into the face of adversity when I could live in the comfort of my surroundings and my wealth and what have you? Why am I constantly in the midst of it when I don't have to be—when I could sit on the top of the hill, as they did years ago, and observe the battle? I really don't know why, man. When you get the flak, you wake up and say, "To hell with it," because you feel you can just give your money. That way I can keep my commitment and don't have to expose myself to it. But that isn't where it's at, because I know my people deserve better. They deserve better than a lot of intellectualizing. That [intellectualizing] don't mean nothing to the brother on the corner. He doesn't understand it and he wants something concrete that he can believe in.

—Sammy Davis, Jr., *Ebony*, March 1974

This section includes Davis's 1955 *Down Beat* Blindfold Test in which he showed himself highly astute about music and frankly critical of pieces that he doesn't like—a surprise to readers who know Davis as the infamous sycophant of his later TV appearances. (Steve Martin said that when he appeared on the *Tonight Show* in the early days of his career, Davis laughed so hard he fell off the sofa. Martin was deeply impressed until he discovered that Davis fell off the sofa laughing for every comedian.)

One of the first big interviews of Davis done for a major mainstream publication, "I Call on Sammy Davis, Jr.," appeared in *The Saturday Evening Post*, May 21, 1960, right after the filming of *Ocean's Eleven*. What is striking about this piece is that Davis's love life, so much an attraction for his public, is never brought up. Davis had just divorced his first wife, dancer Loray White, at the beginning of 1960; had broken off an engagement with Joan Stuart, a white woman, because her father did not approve the union; and was at the time of the publication of the piece engaged to May Britt, a Swedish actress. Perhaps the magazine's reticence is meant to make Davis acceptable to its middle-American audience. Here the reader is given more the mythology of the hard-driven, ultratalented Negro, self-conscious but not bitter, assimilated but not accommodating, an exciting discovery (not a fad), a true up-from-the-bottom showbiz story. The interview permits Davis to talk at length about his career, racial prejudice, and his new movie, *Porgy and Bess*, which opened toward the latter part of 1959.

In a short 1962 piece from *Melody Maker*, once again Davis discusses music, with some observations about Anthony Newley, whose songs Davis recorded several times in his career to great critical and commercial success.

Oriana Fallaci's interview with Davis focuses mostly on Davis's personal life, particularly his marriage to May Britt. This is from Fallaci's collection, *The Egotists*, published in 1968. She interviewed Davis in 1964.

Roy Newquist's interview focuses on Davis's professional opinions and judgments, once again revealing that Davis was a man of considerable depth in his evaluation of show business talent. This is from Newquist's collection of interviews entitled *Showcase*, published in 1966.

Davis's 1966 *Playboy* interview is the longest printed interview he ever gave and certainly the most searching and wide-ranging. It is largely autobiographical and self-reflective. It is remarkable how closely it echoes *Yes I Can*, which had just been published the year before, demonstrating that even though the book was ghost-written, it strongly captures Davis's voice.

Davis's 1971 interview from *Sepia* provides the reader with the opportunity to see how Davis expresses himself for a black audience.

There are two articles that Davis wrote about his friendship with Sinatra, probably one of the most famous and mythologized friendships between a black and a white performer in American show business history. The first is from an August 1956 issue of *Down Beat* and the second is from a 1971 issue of *Today's Health*.

Davis gave a revealing interview to *People Weekly* that appeared on August 28, 1978. The occasion was his return to Broadway, after an absence of nearly a dozen years, to perform in a revival of *Stop the World, I Want to Get Off*.

Finally, two pieces by Davis that appeared in *Ebony*: "Why I Became a Jew," February 1960, and "Is My Mixed Marriage Mixing Up My Kids?," October 1966. Two chapters from *Hol-*

lywood in a Suitcase are also included: the first deals with Davis's love of horror movies and the second is his trenchant assessment of blacks in film.

"SAMMY SPEAKS—HARSHLY, KINDLY,"
by Leonard Feather, *Down Beat*

A couple of years ago, when Sammy Davis, Jr., took his first *Blindfold Test*, he revealed a degree of perception rarely found among artists whose interests and activities have been polarized by the glittering magnet of Broadway show business.

This came as a surprise to some but not to those who had observed the hefty trunkfuls of jazz LPs without which Sammy never travels.

On a recent return to town he expressed keen interest in subjecting himself to another record reviewing session. As usual, he was given no information, either before or during the test, about the records played.

The Records

1. Pete Jolly. *Jolly Jumps In* (Victor). Jolly, accordion.

I don't know who it is, I don't know any of the people involved, but I think it's just adorable. I loved everything about it, including the wonderful humor. The accordionist swings . . . It's unbelievable!

And if I'm not mistaken, they don't have a piano. There's a couple of spots where you'd expect a piano to fill in, but it didn't. But the wonderful thing with the tambourine and the cute harmonics and everything—it's all just delightful, and I wish you'd tell me who it is so that I can buy it right away! I'd give it five stars.

2. George Wallington. *My Funny Valentine* (Norgran). Arr. Sonny Lawrence.

I think it's just a horrible record. I don't know who the

arranger was, but he should be lined up against a wall and taught harmonics and not to change a thing that's as beautifully written as *Funny Valentine*. How come he didn't like the chords that Richard Rodgers wrote?

In the first chorus, he changed the channel completely for the strings. This is an example of an arranger taking too big a liberty. And the pianist—I didn't like anything he did. I think it's just a horrible record. I think the company that put it out should be ashamed, and I give it absolutely no stars at all.

3. Clifford Brown–Max Roach. *Daahoud* (EmArcy). Harold Land, tenor; Richie Powell, piano.

I think that's Max and Clifford—I was convinced after the solo by Max, because he has a roll thing he does, with beats around the toms, and the snare, and back and forth. It's just a wonderful buoyant, bubbly record; I get the impression that when you play it you have to hold it down because it's liable to jump right off the turntable. It's beautiful.

All the solos are well constructed, and they really go; none of the guys seem to be fumbling for what to do. The pianist, the saxophonist, Clifford—everything he plays is so well constructed. Five stars.

4. Ella Fitzgerald. *A Satisfied Mind* (Decca). Camarata Ork.

Naturally it's Ella, and anything she does I'd have to give four or five stars to; the only thing that stops me from giving this five is the song, which I didn't care for too much. But the arrangement is good, and Ella is always great; I don't think there's anything I could say about her that hasn't been said before, and much better, so I'll just say she always gives a five-star performance but because of the song this is a four-star record.

5. Buddy Rich. *Sweets Opus No. 1* (Norgran). Harry Edison, trumpet.

That second trumpet solo sounded like it could have been Charlie Shavers. And the drummer has hands like Buddy. On the other hand, I'm not so sure that Buddy would have done the thing that the drummer did on the last part. But it has a loose feeling like one of those all-star sessions used to have. I'd give it three stars. No, on second thought, I'd give it four, because the guys were having a ball playing; at least it sounded that way.

6. Sammy Price. *Please Don't Talk About Me When I'm Gone* (Jazz tone). Vic Dickenson, trombone; Price, piano, vocal.

Ha! I'd have to give that four stars because it's a long time since I've heard a record that made me laugh like that. It's wonderful to hear a record that a guy gets that funny on. "I gotta go back and play the piano," he says—I've never heard anything on a record like that!

I don't know who the vocalist was, but, of course, I know Vic Dickenson. I love him. This particular song is one he made before, years ago, when he was with Eddie Heywood, remember? That was one of the finest things I ever heard. And this is a wonderful thing—I'll give it four stars, because of Vic, and the very humorous vocal.

7. Stan Kenton. *The Opener* (Capitol). Frank Rosolino, trombone; Bill Holman, comp.; Charlie Mariano, alto; Sam Noto, trumpet. Drummer not identified.

Sounded like a Frank Rosolino trombone solo. I'm not familiar with the band; possibly it's an all-star thing. I didn't like the composition, but I did like the solos. The thing that disturbed me about this was that the drummer had a sound—that ringing cymbal sound, like *shhhhhhhhh*, that goes all over whatever harmonics the band is playing. I'm a guy that likes a crisp cymbal sound.

The composition sounded like an imitation of something that Gerry Mulligan might write. I don't think it was Mulligan, though, because his would have been a little more definite in harmonics. For the soloists, though, this one is worth three stars.

Afterthoughts by Sammy

I'm very happy to see how jazz-conscious the big record companies have become in the past six months. They're giving opportunities to a lot of young guys who deserve a break. And, of course, to a lot of others who are not ready for it. I think Kenton has done a wonderful thing with the *Kenton Presents* series on Capitol.

I only hope that the companies don't let this become a trend to the point where they'll sign up anybody who can play a chorus of jazz. This should only be for the people who have a talent that needs proper showcasing.

The truly great things always stand up. The early Mulligans are just as exciting to listen to today as when they first came out. And Dizzy—despite all the clowning—when he puts that horn to his mouth, look out!

—*October 19, 1955*

"I CALL ON SAMMY DAVIS, JR.,"
by Pete Martin, *The Saturday Evening Post*

His bones are small. His hands and feet are tiny. He moves with catlike grace. As a result of an auto accident he has only one eye he can see with, and his face is mashed in, but Sammy Davis, Jr., talks with passionate sincerity. There is no chip on his shoulder, no belligerence in his voice.

I had seen him first while he was being interviewed as half of a Mike Wallace TV show. I'd been the other half. Davis had worn pointed, black-velvet dancing pumps. He had talked about the troubles a Negro entertainer encounters while plying his trade up and down this country.

Now I was talking to him face to face. The black-velvet pumps were gone, but the rest of him was still there—the passionate intensity, the absence of any complaining note in his voice. I had eleven pages of questions in my briefcase, but I asked him only two of the questions on those eleven pages. Words flow readily from Sammy Davis, and we discussed anything and everything which came to mind—including his problems as a Negro entertainer and the solace he finds in the Jewish religion.

"In my interviews," I explained, "I jump around; then I try to put things together in some kind of order when I finish."

"Jump anywhere you want," he told me.

"People are going to want to know why you adopted Judaism," I said.

"The word is 'converted,' " he said. "I was converted because of one fact. Inside of every man there is a need to try to reach God in his own way. My dad is a Baptist, my mother was a Catholic. Her maiden name was Sanchez. She came from Puerto Rico. I tried Catholicism, but while it's the answer for millions of people, it was no answer for me. Nor did I change to Judaism because any of my friends influenced me, although some people say, 'He's around Jews so much he wanted to be a Jew.' The thing I found in Judaism which appealed to me is that it teaches justice for everyone."

"Is that the important word in your religion?" I asked.

"It is to me," he said. "Also, there's an affinity between the Jew and the Negro because they've both been oppressed for centuries. Another thing, the writing and wisdom of the great Hebrew scholars fascinated me. Once I read a little of their writings I wanted more. I found myself thinking, *This is good, this is honest. Anything that's any good I've ever done in life has been based on honesty. The only times I've gotten into trouble were when I wasn't honest—when I tried to cop out on things and be gracious instead of honest.*"

"Is it hard to become a Jew?" I asked. "Do you have to do a lot of studying?"

"It's not a thing you take lightly," he said. "There are three degrees of Judaism: Orthodox, Conservative and Reform. But you can be Chinese and a Jew or a Negro and a Jew. There is a congregation of Orthodox Negroes in Harlem who have their own temple. I manage to make it to a temple once or twice a month myself, and when Yom Kippur comes around, I don't work. I fast, meditate and read from the Talmud."

"I've heard that when the movie *Porgy and Bess* was being filmed, you refused to work during Yom Kippur."

"That's right," Davis said. "I warned Mr. Goldwyn, who was producing the picture, three weeks before we went on location. I said, 'Mr. Goldwyn, we'll be on location at the height of the high holy days, and I don't work on the high holy days.' He thought I was joking. He laughed and gave me a pat on the head, but when Yom Kippur came closer—when it was only a week away—I said, 'Mr. Goldwyn, you don't think I'm serious, but I am a Jew and I don't work on Yom Kippur and there's nothing you can do about it.'

"He asked, 'You mean being a Jew isn't just a joke with you?' I said, 'No, sir.' He asked me to sit down and talk to him about it, and I must have convinced him that I was sincere, that it wasn't a fad with me, because he stopped production on a Monday. He told me, 'If you really believe—and I feel that you do—I'll hold up my production, although it will cost lots of money.' Nobody worked on that Monday because the whole scene that day had to do with me, and the overhead kept right on mounting."

"That's a lot of moola," I said.

"That was quite a gesture for Mr. Goldwyn to make," Davis said. "But that's the way he is. Once he scrapped half a million dollars' worth of film and started all over again because he didn't like the footage already shot.

"One of my favorite stories about Mr. Goldwyn," he went on, "has to do with the time he walked in on a picture Danny Kaye was doing which was supposed to have a very posh background. Mr. Goldwyn felt the drapes and said, 'Where did you get these drapes?' The property man said, 'We got them from our usual drape place.' Mr. Goldwyn shook his head. 'They don't feel like the script to me,' he said. 'The script calls for luxurious drapes, and these don't feel luxurious to me. Buy better drapes.' "

Changing the subject, I asked Davis for some advice about which words I should skip in conversation or in making talks because they might prove offensive to Negroes.

"I have to watch myself more closely than any progressive man of your race," he said. "You might not believe it, but I'm frequently accused of being anti-Negro."

"I've heard a lot of things about you," I said, "but not that. Who says that?"

"Both Negroes and whites," he told me. "The charge most frequently made against me is that I want to be white, and that accusation hurts."

"What's the basis for that accusation?" I asked.

"What's the basis of any accusation?" he said quietly, "Something which was done in innocence. Something you're ignorant of, but somebody else picks it up and makes a thing of it. You don't know how or why it started, because nobody ever comes to you and explains. You only hear it after it's been going for several months and rumor has hardened into assumed fact."

"Does anybody ever make charges like that about Harry Belafonte or Sidney Poitier?" I asked.

"I know Belafonte has been subjected to them," he said. "The rules which are set up by Negroes and whites against a Negro who's in the spotlight are so strenuous they're impossible to live up to. For example, if I hire anyone who isn't a Negro to work for me, I'm anti-Negro. I have twelve to fifteen people working in my office, in my home and on the road. Of the six people who travel with me on the road, five are colored, one is white. The white man, my musical conductor, has been with me for ten years. But I still get it thrown into my face that he is white, although he's the best man for the job."

"Isn't that a kind of reverse intolerance?" I asked him.

"Of course," Davis told me. "But it was more that way in the beginning than it is now. My Negro friends finally are beginning to accept my white conductor. Anyhow, the most prejudiced people in the world are the oppressed. They have no other way to fight back, so they fight prejudice with prejudice.

"The important thing to remember is that not all white people are members of the White Citizens Council and not all Negroes are members of the N.A.A.C.P. The most frustrating thing about being a Negro performer is the tug of war to decide who your associates are going to be. I have no desire to be a martyr. I know I'm a Negro. I've never forgotten it. How can I, when I look in the mirror every morning? But I'm ready to fight for my right to pick my own friends."

Davis thought about that for a moment, then added, "But as the years go along, some of the embarrassing and humiliating things I have to endure as a Negro entertainer have eased up because there are pioneers who have helped dilute the burden of prejudice. Belafonte put on the first television show ever done by a Negro. He got a good rating, but it was rough going. The point is, however, that because he did that first show, it is easier for other Negroes to do other television shows.

"Take Jackie Robinson in professional baseball. It was rough on Jackie. Nobody can tell me anything else. But because of Jackie and the insults he took, and the people who yelled at him and threw black cats out onto the playing field, it was easier for all the Negro ballplayers who came after him. Jackie made it that way because he was a gentleman, despite provocation. He just hit that ball a little harder and dug for those ground balls a little deeper. He didn't know it, but he was making it better for Willie Mays."

Having met Robinson and having heard him talk, I knew what Davis was talking about. Holding himself in check must have been almost impossibly hard for him; yet he'd done it.

"Jackie told me himself," Davis went on, "that the greatest day in his life was when he suddenly found out that he was no longer a Negro baseball player, but just a ballplayer. He could argue with the umpire and shake his fist at him, and while the people in the stands might boo and say, 'Get that bum off the field!' it wasn't racial. He told me the first time he was thrown out of a game he went into the locker room and jumped up and down and laughed and cried, because he had arrived. He was just like any other guy.

"When a reviewer wrote about Sidney Poitier, 'He is one of the most important actors of our time,' not 'the most important Negro actor of our time,' that made all the difference. But as for the entertainment world, I've got another flash for you. Every colored man can't sing and dance. Every colored man hasn't got rhythm. The same way that not every Negro is a Jackie Robinson or a Ralph Bunche."

"And not all white men are Doctor Oppenheimer or Dwight Eisenhower," I said.

"Right," he said. "Bill Robinson, the hoofer, made my end of the business a little easier. He opened a mental door for the rest of us. What infuriates me is the impatient people on both sides of the color spectrum. I can't hope to have equality until I'm ready to give equality to all other members of my race."

I asked him, "Did you ever have a chip on your shoulder?"

"I was born with one," he said with a suggestion of a smile. "My nose was broken twice in fights. I stopped that because physical fighting doesn't make it. The only thing that accomplishes is to give you the personal satisfaction of hitting somebody in the mouth. But you haven't convinced the individual you hit. I have a story to tell you, but I don't know whether you'll want to print it."

"Let's hear it," I said.

"O.K.," he told me. "When I went into the Army I was seventeen, going on eighteen. I had spent thirteen years in show business, all of them hand to mouth. My family was locked out of more hotels than ever let us in. You haven't lived until you've slept in a bus station in Eastport, Maine. And mind you, all during that period the other Negroes as a race didn't help me. They wouldn't book me. I also couldn't get booking in a white theater. So I was what you might call bitter.

"My first day in the Army I found myself in a unit composed of seventy white fellows and one other colored. The other colored boy was an appeaser. He always said yes, sir, and no, sir—not just to the officers but to the other enlisted men. I thought him an Uncle Tom, a role I never intended to play. I was standing in line in the washroom, waiting to get to the sink, when one of the white fellows grabbed me by the back of the T shirt and pulled me away. 'What's that for?' I asked, and he said, 'Where I come from, niggers stand in the back of the line, behind the white people.' I took the little bag in which I carried my toilet articles and I hit him in the mouth with it and knocked him down. I'll remember what happened next if I live to be a million. He looked up at me, wiped the blood from his mouth and said, 'But you're still a nigger.' From that moment I decided that the only way to fight was with what intelligence and talent God has given me. Sometimes it works.

"The other night there was a guy sitting ringside at the Copa, looking at me with sheer, naked hatred in his face. I gave my whole show something extra because I wanted to get him, and finally I did. I heard him turn to his friends and say, 'I don't care what anybody says, this guy's O.K.' That's the only way I can fight."

I wanted to know which of several kinds of audiences he liked most: a night-club audience, a motion-picture audience, the audience at a Broadway play or a musical-comedy audience. He said, "A night-club audience is something special. With those people you must be up on your toes every second. You have to be able to duck the punches they throw at you. You have to have a shifty attack to get through their defense. If they're sufficiently bagged and they're laughing at the dirty story being told by the big salesman who's picking up the tab, carrying the fight to them can be rugged.

"To keep from being trampled underfoot at such times, you have to be able to ad lib at a moment's notice. If you are the kind of performer who walks out on a stage and sings the same song or tells the same joke every time, you've had it. If some character yells at you, 'You stink, Davis!'—and that's one of the more mannerly remarks you encounter in my business—it would be easier to be a hoofer, for a dance routine can go on regardless of interruption. But I decided a long time ago I didn't want to be just a hoofer, because a hoofer has no communication with his audience other than the technical skill he's packed into his legs and feet. I like to establish an intimate relationship with an audience. A bullfighter must feel the same way about a bull. Either the bull dominates him and gores him, or he learns how to dominate the bull until he can turn his back on him and walk away without being afraid. To me, this is the most important thing a performer can do. If he's good, he establishes that kind of communication."

"How can I describe it?" I asked him.

"I don't know how," he told me. "But I'll put it this way—negatively. You can't do it by believing that an audience is composed exclusively of not very bright ten-year-old kids. Even if they act that way, they can spot a performance which has only a surface slickness—which is cheap, shoddy and phony underneath. Even if the slobs out front behave like adult delinquents and seem to be paying no attention to you while they beef to the waiter about the liquor, they're examining you like a microbe under a microscope. They're aware of you, and as far as they're concerned, you're naked, bare and exposed. For that reason you have to be totally honest with them or you're an idiot to try at all. This is particularly true now that that monster called television has made every ten-year old child a critic. Not only is he a critic but, thanks to the TV scandals and investigations, he thinks everything is a lot of hooey."

"Take canned laughter," I said. "No matter who uses it, you can't help feeling it was taped during an old Bob Hope show and is being used all over again."

Davis went on, "As I was saying, anyone's a critic now. He may not write a column of criticism, but he's Brooks Atkinson, he's John Crosby, he's *Variety*. That's the reason why a performer who cons himself into thinking that a night-club entertainer can be less than honest with his audience is stupid. That's why certain performers can no longer find employment. Their attitude tipped their audiences—'I'm doing you a favor by being here.' That kind of attitude doesn't last one booking.

"I'll go further than that," Davis added. "Being honest with an audience is more important than having talent. I've seen lots of guys who make me say to myself, 'I don't like the way he sings, and I'm not thrilled by the way he tells a joke, but he sells me the idea that he's having fun, so I like to go see him because he makes me have fun too.' Take Tony Bennett, for example. He's believable, and I love to watch Nat Cole work. He's so easy he makes whole audiences feel relaxed. But I can't stomach some performers in the night-club field because they take themselves too seriously, and when they do that they're not being honest. After all, none of us is in a night club doing *Long Day's Journey into Night* or *Sweet Bird of Youth*. A night-club performer is a guy who's out there to make people happy for an hour or two. That's the only message he has for his audience."

"I take it that you prefer a face-to-face appearance?" I asked.

"Right," he said. "In a movie you're trying to communicate with a camera, and a camera is a one-eyed beast whose guts are glass, cogwheels and wire. I've been in a movie. They tell me I was able to communicate in *Porgy and Bess* in spite of the camera getting between me and the audience, but I don't know how I did it. Movies are O.K. in their place, but they're also very quiet and very technical, and the electricity which runs them is A.C. or D.C. instead of being generated people to people.

"Even the legitimate actors on a Broadway stage are more concerned with communicating with each other than they are directly with an audience. It's against the ordinary rules for an actor to step forward and away from the rest of the cast and talk directly to the audience."

"Not unless he's in a Tennessee Williams play or a revival of *Strange Interlude*," I said.

"It's even true of a musical-comedy entertainer," Davis added, "unless the entertainer's name happens to be Ethel Merman. Merman is so great she just walks to the footlights and belts it out, regardless of the rest of the cast. Even Mary Martin was washing that man out of her hair for the other Navy nurses who were on the stage with her."

"How about Jolson?" I asked.

Davis snapped his fingers. "You've got me," he said. "Of course Jolson could do it too. He'd stop in the middle of a musical and say, 'I don't feel like messing with the rest of the plot. You all know what's going to happen anyhow. The boy is going to get the girl. So I'm going to sing some songs for you.' And the audience loved it."

"I've seen Danny Kaye do that too," I said.

"You wouldn't see Danny doing it in a legitimate show," Davis told me. "He'd string along with the plot. I know, because I saw Danny in *Lady in the Dark* and in *Let's Face It*. And while he was only great in both, he didn't take time out to hunker down between the footlights and have an intimate conversation with his audience. In both of those shows he was strictly a legitimate performer."

I said, "I can see that a performer like you or Danny has got to keep his act fluid when he's appearing in a one-man show or in a night club."

"Right," Davis said once more. "But I don't think Danny goes out of his way to do his whole show off the cuff the way he used to. I don't mean he can't ad lib if he wants to. I've seen him break up people who've worked with him for years in his shows. He'll do some little thing and he'll have them yukking hysterically. But there are planned breakups too. Every performer who ever told a joke has them."

"For example?" I asked.

His lips moved as if he were running over a list of things in his mind. He said, "I had a trumpet bit. I'd pretend to get my finger caught in one of its valves, and I'd say to my musical conductor, 'Morty, why don't they put a little Vaseline in these valves!' He'd laugh, and pretty soon the audience would laugh too. It wasn't much. It wasn't even funny, but it sounded spontaneous and unrehearsed. What spoiled it was that Morty and I got so sure of that laugh that we were doing the bit in a routine way. But to get back to my original point, night clubs keep you sharp. Movies are all right for an actor who likes that type of technique, but if you happen to be a go-go-go type, like me, they get you down until you can't stand them.

"I sat on the *Porgy and Bess* set for five solid months just going crazy, because I'm a 'let's do it now' type. I'm used to doing things right the first time I try. I don't like doing them five times or ten times, because screen actors have always done things that way. We had real pros, like Sidney Poitier and Pearl Bailey, in *Porgy and Bess*, and with talent like that it was murder having to do take after take of the same tiny bit of dialogue or action."

I said, "It must be like stopping a halfback who's headed for a touchdown and asking him to run through the play again."

"What bugs me," Davis said, "is you do a scene as long as five pages; it's very complicated, it's highly dramatic, you're trying to reach a certain pitch. You reach it, and you know it's good. The director yells, 'O.K., cut, print!' I've even seen peo- · ple applaud on a sound stage after the actors have done a scene, only to have the cameraman say, 'Sorry, we ran out of film,' or the soundman say, 'Oops, we didn't catch the last two words.' And you have to do the whole thing over again.

"It's the most maddening thing I've ever experienced," Davis went on. "I'm constantly assured that it's great discipline for an actor; that it makes him channel his talents and his emotions, whatever that means. Television is just the opposite."

"I was going to ask you," I said.

"I mean filmed television," Davis explained. "They seldom do even as many as three takes there. They haven't the time. You'd better be right first time around."

"You mean they're not comparable?" I asked. "I had thought that perhaps filming TV and movie making were much alike."

"They can't be because of the lack of time," Davis said. "You're putting a half-hour show on film; that means you've got to put thirty-eight pages of story in a can in three days, and you can only work from eight in the morning until six in the evening. I've done three dramatic TV shows. The first one was a *G.E. Theater* production, I also did a Zane Grey Western. That was a difficult one because it involved so much action, but it got a tremendous rating."

"I understand you've always wanted to do a Negro Western," I said.

"The story of the Negro in the West has never fully been told," he said. "In fact, it's never been told at all. Nobody knows about the Tenth Cavalry. They were referred to in the history books as the Buffalo Soldiers, but nobody knows that they were Negroes, and nobody knows that they were responsible for making peace with the Apaches."

"I'm a history buff myself," I said, "but I've never heard of Buffalo Soldiers."

Davis went on, "Anyhow, to backtrack, it became a big gag around Hollywood about Sammy Davis wanting to do a Western. People said, 'He's Jewish and he's colored. You'd think that would be enough, wouldn't you? But no, this character wants to be a cowboy too. Can you picture a Jewish colored cowboy?' However, when I told Dick Powell, who produces TV shows, about my ambition, he didn't think it was funny. He took it very seriously, and it was in response to a suggestion by Dick that Aaron Spelling, the writer-producer, called me one day and said, 'I think I've got an idea for you.' Then he told me about the Zane Grey Western. It was O.K., although it wasn't what I'd always wanted to do in a story sense. I haven't yet done the kind of Western I'd like to do."

I looked at him inquiringly, and he said, "It's very simple. I just want to do the kind of Western every other Western star does—riding horses, pulling a fast gun, the whole bit."

"Like Wyatt Earp or Jim Garner," I suggested.

"Like that," Davis told me.

"But to get back to the technical side of television," I said, "I don't see how you could get the feeling of communicating with the other actors or the public—or anything except the camera."

"You can't," he said. "All you can hope is that the guy who is sitting in his living room at home, watching his TV screen, will get some faint idea of what you're trying to say or do."

"What's the big difference between acting for television film and acting for motion pictures?" I asked him.

428   THE SAMMY DAVIS, JR., READER

"One screen is big, the other is small," Davis said. "You'll notice, a television shot rarely shows an actor from head to toe. Most of them are knee-up shots or waist-up shots. If you're involved in a fight scene, and the TV camera has got to go all the way, it goes; but ordinarily the emphasis is on the close-ups. That brings up something else. When you're doing close-ups for TV, your acting can be much broader than in a motion picture. If you raise an eyebrow on a wide screen in a theater, several feet of eyelash flutters upward, and the size of that simple action is unbelievable. Understanding such things makes a person a better performer."

"You also did a Broadway show," I said. "Why?"

"I wanted to find out if I could adjust to that medium too."

"I don't know what to ask you about that show," I said, "because I didn't see it."

"I can cover the whole thing in two sentences," Davis told me. "It was not received well by the critics. It was received beautifully by the public. In fact, it ran for eleven months, so you can see it was a success as far as the people were concerned. But we had only one good review out of seven. Thank God for a columnist named Barry Gray. He almost made a holy cause out of us. He asked why the other critics didn't at least mention the fact that the audience had a lot of fun. But apparently that wasn't important.

"The night we waited up to see our first reviews," Davis added, "you could imagine what kind of celebration party we had. It was like a blast celebrating the opening of a morgue."

"Or like being at a Tom Dewey party the night after Truman clobbered him," I said. "I went to one of those."

Davis continued, "The title of the show was *Mr. Wonderful*, and a lot of critics asked, 'Who does Sammy Davis think he is, calling himself Mr. Wonderful?' That was pretty ridiculous, because the role I played in the show was anything but wonderful, and I didn't think up the title. The story was about a kid who wore a leather jacket and long sideburns—a motorcycle-riding type who had nothing and never had had anything. He was working in Jersey as a night-club performer, and that's all he wanted to be. Then he met this down-and-out vaudevillian who could see that he had something special, so he gave him proper training. He kept him from making all the mistakes he'd been making, and soon the kid was a star."

Davis seemed to brood for a moment, then brightened. "The most wonderful thing happened during that show," he said. "Three weeks after we opened, a woman stood up in the audience during a matinee and announced, 'I don't care what the critics say, I love it.' And another fabulous thing happened. The show ran so long that most of the papers sent their critics around to re-review us."

"Did they change their minds?" I asked.

"It wasn't so much that they changed their minds," Davis explained, "but they did admit, reluctantly, that we must be a success. Brooks Atkinson said, 'The charm of *Mr. Wonderful* still escapes me, but it has lasted so long that it is now considered on the hit list.'

"All we were trying to do in that show," Davis continued, "was to provide an evening of relaxation—laughs, songs, music and dancing in abundance. We just wanted people to enjoy themselves." He paused, then concluded thoughtfully, "There were these two things about that Broadway experience, and both of them were important. We refused to admit that we were through because we had taken a licking, and we didn't try to pretend we were anything we weren't. If you can combine those two things, they will carry you through almost any situation."

—*May 21, 1960*

"I WON'T LOWER MY SIGHTS, SAYS SAMMY DAVIS,"
Melody Maker

What do I like, you say? Well, a lot of things. For one thing, I dig records, and I take gobs of them, maybe four hundred or five hundred, with me whenever I travel.

You know, a man who travels a lot has to take his pleasure with him. So I've got the records and a great little portable stereo phonograph rig.

I've also got all kinds of records, from the classics to country and western.

Country Music

Sure I've loved country music for a long time, since long before it was the big thing in popular music. I think Hank Williams and Kitty Wells are the greatest. What a great writer, that Hank Williams!

And Ray Charles . . . well, he's the boss, that's all. A fabulous performer. He's got the soul all right, and he did a wonderful good turn for country music, too.

I guess my first love must be performing or I wouldn't be in this business.

Doing "The Desperate Hours" has been a tremendous experience because it's one of my first serious drama flings. But I bet I'll be getting back to musicals.

New Musical

I'm scheduled now to do a new musical of "Golden Boy" at the end of 1963. You can tell from that how little time I've really got to myself. It's more than a year away and the plans are already being made.

In the meantime I'll be planning my Variety revue for England next spring. I'll be there for ten weeks and I'm especially looking forward to it. That's because I must say that I dig the British the most. Some of them are my close friends.

Take Tony Newley. I regard him as a good personal friend, and also as one of the outstanding talents of our time.

This guy is great, as a writer and a performer. Look at his score for "Stop the World." It's just the end.

I did four of the tunes from it in London. Actually I was the first guy to record "What Kind of Fool Am I?" last year in England. Now it's on the charts here.

Formula

I'm happy about that for Tony and myself. If anybody would have told me Sammy Davis will have a hit with that song or with any song on a record I'd have said, "What are you, some kind of nut?"

What else do I like? I guess I like record hits, like anybody else will admit if he's honest.

I'm sorry to say I can't sing country music. I just can't and that seems to be the formula today. But maybe the pendulum has swung around a little.

After all I do actually have a record on the charts now. How do you like that? So does Nat Cole with "Ramblin' Rose" and Tony Bennett with "San Francisco."

Let's put it this way. I'd love record hits so long as I never have to lower my sights on quality.

You know what I mean?

—September 15, 1962

"SAMMY DAVIS, JR.:
THE LUCK TO BE UGLY,"
from *The Egotists,* by Oriana Fallaci

The most talked about couple in America lived in a house in New York City, on Ninety-third Street East, halfway between the luxury of Park Avenue and the desolation of Harlem. A mile or so south and you find only whites, a mile or so north and you find only blacks: they lived in that limbo because she was white as white and he was black as black. They married, not caring that she was white and he black, and brought into the world a daughter who was neither white nor black and adopted a son. They went on loving each other, living together, cost what it might. It might have cost him his death at the hands of a criminal or a madman; it had already cost her the contempt of a lot of people. She was May Britt; he was Sammy Davis, Jr. The house was elegant; before it stood their Rolls-Royce; inside it there triumphed a happiness to us incomprehensible. May said, "It's four years now since I made a film, and I have no intention of returning to making films. Being an actress didn't matter to me, I became one by accident. It was all through Mario Soldati, who saw me in Stockholm. But it was only when I met Sammy that I realized that my real vocation was this, being a wife and mother. And what more can I want? When you see my husband, you'll understand that I can't want more: he's such a beautiful man, in every sense. He has a beautiful heart, beautiful courage, a beautiful intelligence. For me everything about him is beautiful, his smile, his expression, his face. Oh, you should see him with his short haircut, he looks like a boy! But he's no boy, he's a real man, a man who lives his life in reality, not waiting for kingdom come, and that's another reason why I like him, I love him, I'll always like him, I'll always love him." Together they were beautiful, what a pity they have parted.

Waiting for me, that November, in the big living room was May with Tracey, their coffee-colored daughter, and Mark, their adopted son, also Negro. "We love children. Whether the world approves or not, we intend to have lots of children, our own and adopted." After a while Sammy arrived, the ugliest man I'd ever seen. Perhaps being next to May, who is so beautiful, made him look even uglier, so small and skinny and twisted, with his huge nose flattened by punches, his mouth that opens wide like a pink oven, like the mouth of an ogre, his glass eye (he lost the sight of it in a motor accident many years ago) that always looks in the same direction while the other looks all around. But a very strange thing happened. As the minutes, the hours, passed, he grew steadily less ugly, until he almost wasn't ugly, and then he wasn't ugly at all, and then he was almost beautiful, and then beautiful: the paradox of May.

He was beautiful in his ingenuousness, his honesty, his opti-
mism, the youthful joy with which he showed me his rich man's
house, his hundred suits, his two hundred pairs of shoes, his
three hundred shirts, his dozens of cameras, gold cuff links,
gold watches, gold rings, gold cigarette holders, gold tie tacks,
the absurd and useless luxury that compensates for his hard
life, his youth spent washing dishes, cleaning out toilets, the hu-
miliations, the disappointed hopes. But his greatest compensation was the woman he had managed to marry, as in a fairy
tale, the tale of the princess and the toad. The princess falls in
love with the toad, and the toad turns into a gorgeous young
man, a miracle for which he pays dearly every day, for which he
will go on paying as long as he lives. So it's plain that he talked
of nothing else, that he was able to talk of nothing else, it was
an obsession. Actor, dancer, singer, convert to the Jewish faith,
friend of the Kennedys, star of movies, plays, and a musical,
Golden Boy, which was reaping success on Broadway, author
of a book entitled *Yes I Can*, he could have talked about a great
many things. And instead he talked only about one thing; he
was obsessed by it. About his compensation. About his fairy
tale. About his love for the blond white woman who was in
love with him. And it is the quality of that love that makes this
interview remain so fresh, so worthy of our continued attention.

ORIANA FALLACI: *On my way to your house, Mr. Davis, I had a
very disturbing thought. You have absolutely everything to
make you hated by the multitudes of mean-minded and stupid
people: you're a Negro, a Jew, married to a beautiful blond.
. . . Truly there's no other internationally famous person who
contrives to combine so many "sins" into one. And I concluded: goodness, this man must positively enjoy doing battle
with the world, irritating people, provoking them, defying
them. . . . But do you really enjoy it, Mr. Davis, or does it make
you unhappy?*

SAMMY DAVIS, JR.: I don't enjoy it in the least. I've no taste for quarreling. I'm not much of a quarreler, and a lot of years have passed since the day when, as a boy, I realized that you can't spend your life coming to blows with your neighbor. In any case, brawls don't get you anything except a broken nose and an ugly face. I don't want to fight anybody intentionally, on principle. I only want to lead my life according to those standards I believe to be right, and the "sins" that are combined in me aren't aimed at irritating, provoking, defying anyone. They arise out of reality, logic, out of being consistent. I'm a Negro, and that's a reality. I'm a convert to Judaism because in Judaism I found the religious faith I was looking for, the solution to a spiritual crisis that was troubling me, and so that was an act of logic. I married a beautiful blond because I loved her and she loved me, so that was simply being consistent. Nothing else. I never thought, "I'll be a convert to Judaism in order to annoy the Catholics, the Methodists, the Presbyterians, and the rest." I never said, "I want to marry a blond, beautiful white woman." All I ever said was, "I'll marry the woman I fall in love with, and she will bear my children." That's all. Chance or destiny willed it that the woman should be blond, beautiful, and white. Period.

Not period, seeing you don't enjoy it, you said so. Not period, seeing it precipitates and redoubles and trebles all the prejudices, the outrage, and the hostility. Not period, seeing . . .
. . . seeing it makes me unhappy. And it certainly does make me unhappy. I get hurt easily, and who wouldn't get hurt in my position? Wouldn't you? You can't even have the faintest idea; you can go wherever you want, you can, with your white skin. You can enter any place, you can, with your white skin. Nobody throws you out of a hotel because you're white. Nobody stops you from entering a restaurant because you're fair. Nobody! And it isn't very nice, believe me, to go into the El Morocco with your own wife and see people making faces, turning their backs on you. It isn't even logical. It's absurd! Why should they make faces, turn their backs on you? Because

you married a white woman, Sammy, obviously. And why shouldn't I have married a white woman? Because it's against the rules, obviously. What rules? *The* rules, Sammy. Rules? I've never gone by rules set by other people; I've always felt that they don't count for anything, rules, if your own conscience doesn't want to accept them. So don't tell me I can't play this piano because it's against the rules; don't tell me I can't have that Rolls-Royce because it's against the rules; don't tell me I can't marry a white woman because it's against the rules. If I love her, the white woman, if she loves me, if I can be a good husband to her and give her what she desires, why can't I marry her? Because it's never been done before, Sammy, obviously. Ah, yes? It's never been done? Then I'll do it. If the law of it's never-been-done were a valid logical, consistent law, the world wouldn't exist. Progress wouldn't exist. Houses, ships, the printed word, radio, cars, rockets wouldn't exist! Fellini's movies wouldn't exist, Ingmar Bergman's movies wouldn't exist, the window wouldn't exist, nothing would exist. Who made the first window? Assuredly someone who was told you can't because it's never-been-done. To which he replied: then I'll do it. And he did it. Not because he enjoyed doing battle with people, irritating, provoking them. Not to give offense. But because he was within his rights to try. Just as I was within my rights to leave Catholicism for Judaism, to marry May. . . .

Sacred rights, Mr. Davis, but I have a question to ask you—an unpleasant question, maybe, and a very serious one. When you married, you and May, didn't you think about the responsibility of bringing into the world children who would be neither black nor white? Weren't you at all scared at the thought of imposing too hard a life on your offspring? The world is what it is, Mr. Davis, society is as you know it. It isn't comfortable to be neither black nor white: rejected by the whites because you aren't white, by the Negroes because you aren't black. It presents terrible problems, not belonging to any particular race, finding oneself in the middle . . .
Problems? No offspring of woman's womb is without

problems. You, white and fair as you are, are you without problems? You think maybe you have fewer problems or substantially different problems from a Negro with crinkly hair? Let's have a look at them, these problems. Physical problems? The answer to that one is my daughter Tracey: a beautiful child, exquisitely made, wonderful. Mental problems? It's common knowledge that to mingle races does good, it's common knowledge that pure races always end up producing idiots. Aristocratic families, royal dynasties, have died out because as a result of being pure they bred idiots. This is a genetic law, not a personal point of view; it's true of plants, animals, human beings. And this leaves aside the fact that there's no such thing as a completely pure race; each of us has a drop of blood from some other race, a little drop of Jewish or Arab or Negro or Chinese blood, or whatever. Human, social problems? The world is improving. Believe Sammy, it's improving. Prejudices are growing fewer. What once even the imagination balked at is now beginning to be accepted in reality. Life for Tracey will be much easier than it has been for me, for my wife, for you, for today's adults. I am convinced that Tracey will have fewer problems being half white and half black than you, all white, and myself, all black, have had.

It's comforting and good too that you should be so optimistic, Mr. Davis. But are you sure you're not living in a world of hopes and dreams rather than of cruel realities?
Ah! I live in the most tangible reality, believe me. I know very well that I could be killed for the choice I've made, that anyone might take a shot at me: that's a reality too. But I'm an optimist, and I also know that those who'd like to shoot at me constitute a mad minority; the majority is composed of good folk, decent folk. If this weren't so, we'd still be living in caves and eating each other like fish, snakes. I'm optimistic, yes, and I have my own reasons for being so. I'm optimistic because when I met this woman, I said to myself no, she can't love me, there's no future in it, Sammy, don't even think about it, you're ugly,

you're black, you've only got one eye, you've got a broken nose, and she looks like a fairy. Come on, Sammy, come on! And then I discovered that she loved me, that there was a future in it even though I was black and ugly and had only one eye and a broken nose. I'm optimistic because everyone said, "All right, but even so you can't marry." But we did. I'm optimistic because they said, "All right, you've done it, but it can't last." But it is lasting, and it'll go on lasting. This doesn't mean I'm saying, "Go ahead, baby, marry a Negro yourself, bring a baby into the world who's neither white nor black." No, I'm only saying that I've done it and it worked for me. It showed I was right, and that makes me optimistic.

But you're in a privileged position, Mr. Davis. You're famous, you're popular, you're rich, surrounded by admirers. Like Duke Ellington, Louis Armstrong, Harry Belafonte, Sidney Poitier, you can do things other people can't. People will always more easily accept rebellion, affirmations of principle, audacities from someone who is someone. When all is said and done, yours isn't a typical case. In the El Morocco they might make faces, turn their backs on you, but the doors of the El Morocco are open to you.

I never open a door, I never let anyone open a door to me, unless I'm sure, confident, that the door will stay open for whoever follows me. I never enter a club that won't admit other Negroes. I never enter a restaurant that won't admit other Negroes. I never work in a theater or a movie that doesn't give work to other Negroes, because I can't forget that if I'm admitted, it's because others entered before me, because they opened those doors, one by one, little by little, so that I can open them a little wider. And so I must see to it that after me another will open them a little wider still, until they are flung wide open. In short, the fact that many doors are open to Sammy Davis, Jr., means that the same doors are open to others. James Baldwin would never have started writing books if Richard Wright hadn't written them before him. I would never have succeeded if other Negro actors and singers hadn't succeeded before me. A Negro, you see, whatever he's doing, a Negro never does it just for himself. He always does it both for himself and for the others of his race, even though he might not be aware of it. And I know, my wife knows, that by getting married we have contributed something. I know, she knows, that we have contributed something by bringing Tracey into the world, and we are proud of it. You see, look, take my musical comedy on Broadway, *Golden Boy*. I'm proud to be on Broadway, I feel ten feet tall. When I think of it, my goodness, I can feel both my eyes. Las Vegas, Hollywood, London, for me nothing was worth Broadway. But I know that being on Broadway doesn't help only me. It helps twenty Negro boys who are in the show along with the same number of white boys. It helps to stir the stagnant waters of a theater of which people ask only gay musicals that raise no problems. When on Broadway has there ever been seen such real integration? When on Broadway has there ever been shown the love story of a Negro and a white girl? *Golden Boy* wasn't that originally, either; it was the story of a Jew who from being a violinist becomes a boxer. Well, now it's the story of a Negro who from being a violinist becomes a boxer and loves a very fair white girl. And people come to see it, every night the theater is full, people are accepting it!

No, Mr. Davis, people come to see, but they don't accept it. People fill the theater for your sake, not for the love story of the Negro and the white girl. For weeks now there have been articles about the "inopportunity" of showing a love story between a Negro and a white girl. People leave the theater making faces, saying, "How about that, what a thing." I quarreled with a friend of mine over it, Mr. Davis, and . . .

Yes, I know. They're the same people who make faces and turn their backs when May and I go into the El Morocco: decent, democratic, maybe even cultured Americans. Americans who maintain they're totally in favor of the Civil Rights laws, ready to defend the theory but not to accept the reality, not to recognize that a Negro and a white girl can love each other, marry, bring children into the world. Americans who go lightheartedly to see Tennessee Williams plays, which in the name of art show the most degrading sides of our society, without batting an eyelid. It doesn't mean a thing. I'm sorry for them, sincerely, but it doesn't mean a thing; they're a minority. And even this minority must feel something when I cry to the woman I love: "What color, what color are my hands? No color! No color!" At the bottom of their hearts they themselves must also feel that love has no color, love is simply love. I added those lines myself; *Golden Boy* is me in a way. I know exactly what it means to be involved in a love story of that kind, to feel yourself stared at when you walk down the street, to feel humiliated, knowing that, however things go, you're going to get very hurt. And in any case the central problem of *Golden Boy* isn't that either; it's the problem of a man who, halfway between the worlds of the whites and the Negroes, feels at ease with neither the whites nor the Negroes and rejected by both whites and Negroes.

But that's the problem I meant when I spoke of the responsibility of bringing into the world children who are neither white nor Negro, Mr. Davis. It's the problem . . .
It's not my daughter Tracey's problem.

Isn't it your problem, either, Mr. Davis?
No. No. No. I know a lot of Negroes who can't manage to communicate either with Harlem people or with Park Avenue people, and they're rejected both by Harlem and Park Avenue. But I'm not one of them. They are misfits, and I am not a misfit. They don't get on with either whites or Negroes, while I get on with both whites and Negroes.

There's one thing I've heard said, Mr. Davis: that you prefer being with whites to being with Negroes. Your greatest friends and supporters—Frank Sinatra, Peter Lawford, Danny Kaye, Jack Benny—are white, after all, are they not?

And Sidney Poitier, Harry Belafonte, Duke Ellington are Negroes, are they not? And my great friends? Harry and Sidney
belong to my generation, we grew up together, we read books
together, together we chose the road we did. No, there's no
truth in the idea that more of my friends are whites than Negroes. The fact is that many of my friends are actors, and there
are more white actors than Negro actors, in the proportion of a
hundred to one, I'd say. Obviously I'm seen more with white
people than with Negroes. Obviously I am going to be talked
about, publicized, supported by a greater number of whites. So
what? I love the Negroes. God knows I love them!

*But do the Negroes love you, Mr. Davis? Especially since your
marriage to May, are you sure the Negroes love you? There's a
racism that's never spoken of, Mr. Davis, the racism that Negroes display toward whites or toward Negroes who marry
whites. Shall we talk about that, Mr. Davis? Because I haven't
quarreled only with . . .*
During the electoral campaign I was alongside Bob Kennedy. I
was fighting for him because I believed, I do believe, in him, because I was, I am, convinced that he will be a good senator and
as good for America as his brother was. Well then, Bobby's last
big rally was held in Harlem, the evening before the elections.
And I was there, together with May, to ask the Negroes to vote
for Bobby. Thousands and thousands of Negroes. And . . . well
. . . it's ridiculous, it's incredible even, but they applauded me
more than Bobby. Yes, the Negroes love me, and since my marriage to May they've loved me even more. Their racism . . . but
who denies it? Does a white skin maybe give exclusive rights to
hatred, contempt, error? Don't you understand that we Negroes have just as many idiot racists sick with fascism as you
whites have? As many full of the same fears, the same arrogance as the whites, the same lack of dignity and generosity?
Ah, those who belong to the Ku Klux Klan are neither better
nor worse than those who belong to the racist Negro Black
Muslim movement. They are both extremists, both disgusting,

and I reject the one as strongly as I do the other because I believe that the answer to the race issue does not lie in reciprocal hatred, reciprocal contempt. I do not believe the Negro race to be an inferior race, but nor do I believe it to be a superior race, a model race. Quite simply, it's a race like any other: with its geniuses and its imbeciles. God! These things have to be said! We're in 1964, we're no longer in 1925, when an actress would walk around with a leopard on a leash! It has to be said that not only love has no color, hatred and violence have no color either!

Neither more nor less, Mr. Davis. In fact, as I was going to say, I haven't quarreled only with a white friend over Golden Boy, *I've also quarreled with a Negro girl friend of mine. She also twisted her mouth into grimaces, and I asked her why. Wouldn't you marry a white man? And she replied: "No! No! No!"*

I know girls like that, too. One of them is in my company. A lovely Negro girl who's very intelligent and talented, she can't stand white men, white people, and she'd never marry a white man, she'd never even talk to a white woman. My wife is the only white woman who gets a word or a smile out of her. What should I say to her? She makes me angry and sad, but I console myself with the thought that Negroes of this kind are in the minority. Months ago when there were the Harlem riots, only two thousand Negroes joined in. And there are three million Negroes in Harlem. One mustn't judge the Negroes and the whites by the worst of them. It would be the same as judging Italians by the gangsters with Italian names. When I think about Italians, I don't think of the Al Capones, the Anastasias, the Johnny Dios, the Frank Castellos. I think of the good folk, the vast majority, who come to America in the hope of finding something—a good life, happiness—work hard to get it, and decently and honestly build their families and their fortunes. Or else . . . yes, or else it would be the same as judging the Jews by the grasping moneylenders who have Jewish names. When I think about Jews, I never think of the characters who lend money. I think of the millions of martyred victims of the pogroms, the millions killed in concentration camps, I think of the unhappy people whose religion I have embraced. Or else . . . yes, or else it would be the same as judging racism solely in an American context. When I think about the people who make faces and turn their backs on me, I don't think only of New York and the El Morocco; I think of London, Rome, Paris, Stockholm. Bigotry and prejudice aren't limited only to my country, to my people. My marriage to May had a bad reception elsewhere too: in Europe, in Italy. . . .

I don't think so, Mr. Davis, it's not so. In Italy you have been treated very decently. We Italians have many defects, but they do not include making faces at a Negro because he's a Negro. We're not racist.

Ah, no? I read more mean articles in the Italian press, after my marriage to May, than I don't know where. I even took proceedings against the weeklies. It isn't at all true to say that there's no racism in Italy. Try asking an Italian: "Would you marry a Negro? Would you let your daughter marry a Negro? Would you bring children into the world with a Negro? In short, would you do what Sammy Davis and May Britt have done?" Try it, and then tell me what they answer. Even the nicest, most cultured, most democratic people, even the people who cried out against Goldwater, would in the majority of cases react like your white friend and the Negro girl you know. They'd answer, "No! No! No!" In Italy, in Europe, you can go into any hotel you want, any restaurant you want, certainly, but the feelings that follow you when you walk down the street with your wife who is white are the same. At most, they respect you because you're a success. But this doesn't mean a thing when you deserve it. And I deserve it. Success didn't come to me by chance, I worked thirty-five years of my life to get it. I've washed dishes in kitchens, I've cleaned out toilets, I've emptied trash cans, and I started acting when I was four. When I was four years old, I used to act and sing with my parents. When I was six years old, I was engaged by some other people and left my parents' company, I never even went to school, because of it. I studied by correspondence course, or by reading books, and I sweated plenty, I still sweat plenty today, just as I used to, more than I used to, every night is my first night, every song is my first song, I deserve what I have, I deserve it down to the last drop, so why should people even want to deny this much to me?

Mr. Davis, one question. Do you count yourself a happy man? A lucky man and a happy man?
Of course I'm a happy man! The happiest you'll ever meet. Of course I'm a lucky man! The luckiest man you'll ever meet! What more can I ask than what I have? God has given me everything, everything: money, popularity, family. And he gave me this extraordinary wife, so good, so beautiful. And he not only granted that I should love her but also that she should love me, ugly as I am, with only one eye, and a broken nose, and small too, and black. How can I complain? I can't complain about anything, anything!

Not even about your broken nose, your one eye, your ugliness?
I know I'm dreadfully ugly, one of the ugliest men you could meet, but ugliness, like beauty, is something you must learn how to use. All my life I've resisted the temptation to be a little less ugly, to have my nose fixed, for example. My bone structure is good, my jaw line is good, my cheek bones are good, my body is well proportioned. Maybe, if I'd had my nose fixed, I'd have become almost passable. But what does being passable make you? It makes you mediocre: neither ugly nor handsome. Complete ugliness, utter ugliness, like mine, though, is almost attractive. Yes, yes, I'm convinced that a really ugly man, in the end, seems attractive. A man who is so-so you don't even stop and look at, much less follow. A man like me you see, you stop and look at him, you follow him to go on looking at him, to as-

sure yourself that he really is the ugliest thing you ever saw, and from looking at him so much you know what happens? What happens is that you find something attractive about him, and you like him. Isn't this what happened to May? As for my eye, ah, the optician did such an extremely fine job on it that you can't tell the false one from the real. I look more as if I have a squint than as if I'm blind in one eye. Look, my eyelid doesn't even droop, it stands up nice and straight, a masterpiece, and . . . you want to know something? I see much more now that I have only one eye than I used to see before, when I had both. With my one eye I've discovered a lot of things: Judaism, for example. With my one eye I found my wife and married her. With my one eye I have made her the mother of our children: me so black, her so white, me so ugly, her so beautiful. God, isn't she extraordinary, my beautiful wife? Look what a woman! Look! With one eye I got her, with one eye! And it doesn't matter to her at all that I only have one eye, not to her it doesn't.

—*November 1964*

"SAMMY DAVIS, JR.,"
from *Showcase,* by Roy Newquist

In the course of a casual conversation, just before his death, Ian Fleming paid what I consider to be the perfect tribute to Sammy Davis, Jr. We were talking about reincarnation when he said, "Next time I'd like to be born as Sammy Davis, Jr. He's the most incredibly gifted man I've ever seen—and to think of being able to take an audience and hold it and actually reshape it to make it *your* audience must be the most thrilling thing that can happen within *any* lifetime."

After seeing Mr. Davis in nightclubs, on television, and in *Golden Boy* I can only concur with Ian. But if there *is* such a thing as reincarnation, and we have a choice of identities, how many Sammy Davis, Jr.'s, will there be?

DAVIS: I was born in New York City, into a theatrical family. I was in show business by the time I was two years old. My interest, therefore, was something I inherited—I had no choice in the matter. Most kids have a choice of what they want to be—I guess you could call it a misery of choice. Not me. No chance to be bricklayer or dentist, dockworker or preacher—I guess I was meant for show business even before I was born.

Now, I'm not complaining. I am very pleased and happy about the association I have with show business, my whole life in the business, not because I am—in quotes—successful—but because it's great to perform. I was as happy when I was in the opening act at the Strand Theatre in New York or the Royal in Baltimore. Show business is a love affair, as far as I'm concerned, and I can't imagine doing anything else.

N. How were your talents—and they can only be called extraordinary—discovered?
DAVIS: They weren't discovered. Nobody discovered them, I never discovered them. They became a matter of awareness.

Actually, I don't think anyone has discovered them yet. I would like to think that whatever—again, in quotes—is a Sammy Davis—and every performer, every artist, would like to know—has not been touched yet. Let me put it this way: If I had to look back on my life and think, "Hey, I didn't grow any that year!" I'd be a very unhappy man because you can't survive without growing. I suppose it starts out as a point of view, and in a way it's a very commercial thing, but you must, in our country, progress. Grow, improve, develop.

The one thing about America as contrasted to any European country is the way we've got to make headway. The cats in Europe can stand still. Take Gerry Mulligan, who's sitting here with us: he could go to Europe right now and live for the rest of his life like a king, and he could live like a king based on what he did ten years ago. You dig? Because all the cats over there are blowing what they blew ten years ago. They don't progress. I've never seen it to fail that any expatriate, whether he's an artist in terms of being a writer or an artist as a musician or an actor, they go over there and stay and when they come back—man, they're ten years behind even if they've only been gone a year.

Our country motivates artists, it's a wheel that runs and runs fast. You don't know what's going to happen next week in America, who's going to be top dog. And just when you have it all figured out—just when you decide it's all Beatle-rama—up comes Louis Armstrong with "Hello, Dolly." Louis Armstrong never had a million-seller in his life, and all of a sudden he's top dog with "Hello, Dolly."

There's no telling. No predicting. Nothing for sure. You can't sell a big band—suddenly a big band starts to go. You can't sell jazz, they just won't dig it, and all of a sudden in one little town way out in left field jazz starts swinging. But you go to Paris and you see the cats they're blowing the same things that went on long, long ago.

Now, the same thing applies to our business—we can't stand still. Not for a minute. I don't want the audience to second-guess me—not ever. I don't care what I open up with, but I don't want them knowing beforehand. I can't afford to have them say, "Well, he sings and he dances, then does the impressions, and then he plays the drums." In Vegas, for a long while I didn't play any instrumental and I didn't dance. Then I cut out the impressions for three or four visits, and people would begin to ask for them. I keep switching.

Golden Boy surprised and bugged a lot of people. They said, "Why does he want to do a Broadway show?" I did it because I want to grow. Sure, the money is marvelous, but if I can't live with myself after I've made the money then the money is no good. I know, when I leave *Golden Boy*, that I'll be a better performer than I was when I went into it because of the exposure to fellow-actors, the regimentation, the sort of confinement that a Broadway show has upon an individual in terms of what he must do onstage. I'll be better, that's all.

The same goes with television. I did one special, and it came off great, and I was very happy about the reaction to it, but if I can't make the next show better—if I can't top it—then I don't want to do it. I want to get out of it, because if it isn't better I'm no good to anybody.

The cat that makes it in America, the cat that's talked about, the cat that survives, he can change the world around him because everybody wants to copy him. You dig? The Mulligan sound went around the world. Ever hear of a Japanese sound coming this way, or a German sound, or an English sound? Take Beatle-rama, the whole fantastic thing. It's a throw-out from us. The other day I was doing "Hullabaloo" and I said to somebody, "We've got guys in prison, guys who can't get a job, who can sing a hell of a lot better than these English cats." They come over here and do Negro music—they finally learned the blues. Or maybe they just learned to write the chords. We bounced it over there ten, twenty, thirty, forty years ago, and now we're getting it back.

N. *I'd like to ask you about* Golden Boy—*from the standpoint of your night-after-night performance. Do you vary, at all, or is the audience consistent in its reactions?*
DAVIS: The audience reaction changes every night, and I have to play the role according to my audience. Some nights, for instance, the love scene can be played in a very tender manner, the way you'd do it in a serial love story, and other nights it's got to be a blood-and-guts love story. But that's an actor's problem he has to work out. Therefore the night club experience pays off. In a night club you've got to size up your audience quickly—do they want to hear you sing, do they want jokes and gags? Do they just want to laugh or do they want the artist? Hell, you find out what they want and go the whole route.

This is paying off for me in terms of the theater. There's enough give in the performance to shift the emphasis, slow it up or play it fast.

But I love doing *Golden Boy*. It's a great show, it's tremendous exercise. I don't mean in terms of physical exercise but in terms of mental. Not to be second-guessed, as I mentioned before, giving them what they want and a little bit more. I want to learn.

Most of the trouble with most people in America who become successful is that they can really and truly get by on bullshit alone. They can survive on it. You know, you can live on a good record for months. You can live on any one thing for months if you pick and choose your spot. One good TV show can make some people last longer than they have a right to last. They milk it and get everything out of it they can without putting in a new nickel's worth. I know a singer who lives on one hit every five years—and every five years it's the same record in a different tempo. In between times he does nothing. But I'm trying to achieve another level, and another one after that.

Do you mind if we get back to discussing Richard Burton— the conversation we had before we started taping?

N. No. I said that I wished Burton had stayed with Shakespeare repertory a little longer because I thought he needed the discipline.
DAVIS: Well, you know of course, Olivier and O'Toole and Albert Finney and Paul Scofield—all the brilliant Shakespearean actors who epitomize the British classical actor—say that as a Shakespearean actor Richard played, without doubt, the definitive Hamlet of all time. I'm not talking about the exercise he did here in New York, because all that was was an exercise. In which he said, "I want to go and do it now as an exercise and have some fun with it," because he already had done the definitive Hamlet. Because of age he couldn't go on to the deeper, older Shakespearean roles, but he did so magnificently with all the Shakespearean roles he performed that I don't know what he could garner by staying in repertory for a few more years. To me the discipline Burton has—or the lack of discipline—is a marvelous thing because it adds excitement. It makes Burton what Olivier ain't. (I love Olivier, I relish everything he does;

he's a genius. Don't mistake me. If you had to worship something mortal here on earth I would go and bow twice a day to wherever Olivier was standing.) But Olivier, who is a technical genius, works from the outside in and has a magnificent quality for this. Consequently, in *Othello* the whole thing he manufactured—playing Othello as a combination of a Jamaican and American Negro—was incredible. All sensuality, all cliché—he grabbed every cliché he had ever been exposed to in terms of Negroes; everything he read or heard or knew, and everything he could borrow from every Negro actor who'd played *Othello* was in those scenes.

But when I think in terms of Burton I find more excitement, more fluidity. Actually, I think he's finally growing into a splendid motion picture actor. Magnificent, in fact. But I think that on the stage he has all of the things most of our guys lack and most of the things the British cats lack. Now, both O'Toole and Finney are buddies of mine—I know them and I know their work very well. Each is marvelous in an individual way. For instance, O'Toole was great in one big Shakespearean play in London; he was superlative. He came back and did *Hamlet* and it was a fiasco. It was like "forget it." Yet he'll go back again, maybe in ten or fifteen years, and he'll be brilliant at it. But the first time out that Burton did for an important audience and the important London critics he was classified as *the* definitive Hamlet.

So as I said I don't know what he'd garner by going back to repertory. He got the discipline, maybe we should call it the foundation, he needs, and from now on he should develop as Richard Burton. He has taste, he has selectivity, he has timbre, richness of voice. He certainly has the gait of Shakespeare—it rolls off his tongue so beautifully that the guy from Altoona who came to see *Hamlet* to see the guy who'd married Elizabeth Taylor stayed to see Burton the actor. I feel pretty strongly about this because I think Burton is unique. You can't compare him to anybody.

Before you came Gerry Mulligan and I were talking about

jazz and what it is today as opposed to what jazz was when we first met. I was struggling, then, and he was doing the things that meant something.

Gerry's a cat who's vastly underrated. He's an underrated musician, an underrated arranger. He took and polished and really made the whole form of music they later labeled "West Coast Jazz." It wasn't West Coast Jazz—it was Gerry Mulligan. The cool sound. Everybody cashed in on it, but he never did cash in on it because he was the guy who never varied from his original point of view.

So what you're saying is that you would have loved Richard Burton to have assumed and kept the same posture dramatically that Gerry assumed and kept musically. But Richard did give in to the commercial in terms of motion pictures. But he did not give in artistically because he's taken all his repertory training, and his definitive *Hamlet*, and gone to the top in another art form. In other words, he's going to do a lot more than another *Hamlet*.

Watered-down Burton—even tricky Burton—is a better actor than most other actors could be in three lifetimes.

N. I surrender. I'd like to get back to you, now: Could you state your objectives as an entertainer? (And I have to use the word "entertainer" because you're so many things—actor, singer, dancer, etc.)

DAVIS: I want only one thing, and don't let anybody ever kid you. If you've worked as hard as I've worked for what I've gotten today; if you've paid as many dues in thirty-five years as I've paid, in one business (and this is the only business I know); then you want everything that's coming to you.

By the same token, however, rather than lie back and wait for it to come, I want to work for it. When I signed that contract with a motion-picture studio to produce my films you'd better know that I have worked for that contract in every area there is to work in, and I'm entitled to the contract. When I get a contract with a network I have paid my dues and I have worked to get it, and they know that they're going to get, for their dollar, the best that I have to offer. I'll give it the best. No "Catch you later."

Whether these shows will be successful or not nobody knows, but if you give your best you can hold up your head and say, "Well, hell, man, I swung at the ball. I swung at it so hard I twisted around three or four times." But if you just let the ball go past you can't hold up your head.

Before we did *Golden Boy* people said, "It's a bomb, it will never open up." We came in—we all worked hard (not just me). Everybody worked, contributed, knocked themselves out. Now the same people come back and say, "Well, I knew you'd make it—you've got Sammy Davis and this and that and how can you fold." It's very easy, how you can fold. Frank Loesser just folded for a million dollars—*Pleasures and Palaces* died in Detroit. So what I want is everything that's coming to me as long as it really is coming to me.

N. How has the fact that you are a Negro affected your career?
DAVIS: It's helped me. Enormously. It helped me in the beginning by making me mad—mad that I was colored. I saw cats around me who couldn't shine my shoes, as far as talent was concerned, getting all the breaks. This doesn't make for happiness. Then one marvelous day I woke up and said, "What the hell are you bitching about? Being colored isn't stopping you. Nothing is stopping you. Work, learn—if you want to be as good as they are learn to be as good as they are. Learn the things Donald O'Connor learned. Learn how to dance, how to sing, how to act, how to play an instrument, how to work in motion pictures, how to work in television. You want to be that good, then be that good. Work at it."

Being a Negro gave me this as a starter—made me determined to be the best. So being a Negro really hasn't hurt me in my profession.

Tomorrow I should know whether or not I sign a deal with a major network for television. Well, it's been a long uphill climb, and how sweet it will be because when I meet the three big cats at eleven o'clock tomorrow morning, when they have the figures and everything, how sweet it will be to know that it's happening. That once I thought, "Hey, I made it, and I never thought I'd make it because I'm colored."

I don't know if this makes any sense to you, but if it doesn't I can't explain it. What I'm really saying in essence is that life is what you make it. Being white can be a burden, too—you dig? Would you want to go through what Gerry Mulligan went through? As a white jazz musician? With every colored cat putting him down, and all the publications coming out saying, "His music's synthetic, it isn't real jazz," and going through all the pros and cons and analytical drivel that didn't add.

This, when the only thing he knew was what he was playing, and he knew better than the dopesters that what he was playing was good.

White, black, it doesn't make much difference—not if you're really out to prove something, because anybody who's really trying to prove something has a rough time of it. But if you can swing, if you've got the rhythm which in essence is the key to life, nothing else matters.

—1966

ALEX HALEY INTERVIEWS
SAMMY DAVIS, JR.,
Playboy

Whether Sammy Davis, Jr., as so often billed, is really "the greatest entertainer in the world" may be open to debate, but even his critics would admit that no one has worked harder— nor overcome more hardships and handicaps—to earn that appellation. Literally a child of show business (his parents, Sammy and Elvera Davis, toured with a vaudeville troupe headed by Will Mastin, whom he called his uncle), Sammy made his stage debut at the age of one and became a full-time professional when he was three. He had no opportunity for formal schooling and was forced to scuffle for pin money with Mastin and his father during the Depression years. But the younger Davis proved a quick study as a song-and-dance man, and soon eclipsed his elders to become the star of their struggling little act in carnival side shows and those few small-town theaters and night clubs that would book Negro talent in that pre–civil rights era.

After an eight-month hitch in the Army's Special Services—a traumatic firsthand exposure to racial bigotry and brutality for the 18-year-old entertainer (his nose was broken twice in beatings administered by white GIs)—Sammy rejoined the Trio with redoubled determination to make the big time. It finally happened in 1951, when Sammy (still second-billed to Mastin) electrified audiences—and earned rave notices—during a triumphant first engagement at Ciro's in Hollywood. Suddenly in demand for solo recordings and movie roles (in "Anna Lucasta" and "Porgy and Bess"), and celebrated for his kinetic performance in the Broadway hit "Mr. Wonderful," Sammy found himself rich as well as famous almost overnight. Living his new part to the hilt, after "a lifetime of waiting and wanting," he plunged headlong into the maelstrom of Hollywood night life: punishing the bottle, plunging at the gaming tables, playing around with the chicks and tossing big money away with spectacular—and self-destructive—abandon. His income and his audiences continued to grow, but his performances began to suffer—along with his health—and Sammy was soon several hundred thousand dollars in debt. But his fortunes had not yet reached their lowest ebb: Late in 1954, while driving from Las Vegas to Hollywood for a recording date, he was seriously injured in the automobile accident that cost him his left eye. Although he was soon working again at Ciro's, and even joking about his misfortune, he was privately distraught and depressed, and one night tried unsuccessfully to drive his car off a cliff. His two brushes with death, however, shook him into a fateful decision: A few months later, seeking "a purpose bigger than myself," he converted to Judaism amid a storm of publicity assailing him for insincerity.

If Sammy was looking for peace of mind, he was not to find it yet. When the news leaked out that he was secretly dating Kim Novak late in 1957, despite warnings from Hollywood higher-ups, Sammy became a target for racist hate mail—undeterred even by his brief marriage to a Negro dancer—that reached flood proportions with the announcement of his engagement to Swedish actress May Britt in May of 1960. Defying a barrage of anonymous death threats, Sammy and May were married six months later, with friend Frank Sinatra as best man and fellow rat-pack chum Peter Lawford among the guests. May's movie career was over, but the marriage flourished and Sammy's own successes multiplied—along with his family (they now have three children, two of them adopted). In the years that followed, he continued to make movies ("Ocean's Eleven," "Threepenny Opera," "Robin and the 7 Hoods"), performed at more benefits than any other entertainer in history, simultaneously starred in a successful Broadway remake of Clifford Odets' "Golden Boy," and in his spare time, co-authored "Yes I Can," a painfully candid best-selling autobiography. Saturating television with specials and guest shots, he eventually earned his own weekly series, but low ratings and lukewarm reviews forced its cancellation early this year after 15 shows. Undaunted, Sammy went on to produce and star in his most recent film, "A Man Called Adam," but it, too, was indifferently received both by the critics and by the public. Not pausing long enough to regret his mistakes—and well enough established by now as a jack of all entertainment trades to withstand such setbacks without jeopardizing his success—Sammy set out last summer on a nationwide one-man concert tour; the crowds were S.R.O. in every city.

Playboy interviewer Alex Haley caught up with the peripatetic star during an engagement at the Forrest Theater in Philadelphia (shortly before Sammy was hospitalized in Chicago with hepatitis). Haley tells of his experience: "I had been trying to get his ear, and his confidence, for two weeks, dogging his tracks from city to city, trying to penetrate both his shell of reticence and the cordon of cronies and co-workers with whom he surrounds himself, waiting in vain for Sammy to alight anywhere long enough to buttonhole him for anything more than a wave and a greeting. Genuinely apologetic, he finally took me aside and vowed that somehow he'd *make* time for me in Philadelphia. He was as good as his word; but it was still an uphill battle.

"Late every afternoon during the four-day engagement, whenever Sammy woke up, his close friend and secretary Murphy Bennett would telephone me to join them in Sammy's lavish suite at the Hotel Warwick. There, for the next two or three hours, we would try to talk, swimming upstream against a steady tide of bellboys bearing telegrams and delivering packages—mostly gifts from fans, which were added to the vocational and avocational miscellany already overflowing the suite: books, tape recorders, scripts, contracts, cameras, record players, movie projectors and the wardrobe of 50 suits Sammy takes on the road. Adding a note of shrill urgency to the melee, the phone rang incessantly and without mercy. Most of the calls were fielded by Bennett, but a few Sammy had to take himself—among them, one from Vice-President Humphrey, inviting Sammy to Washington to discuss a possible Vietnam tour; and several from Mrs. Davis in New York, requesting advice on wallpaper and bathroom towels for the family's new apartment on Manhattan's East Side.

"Each evening at eight, Sammy left for the theater in his $25,000 limousine, custom-fitted with intercom, bar, stereo, television and telephone. His stocky chauffeur, an ex-Marine named Joe Grant, denied that he functioned as a bodyguard: 'Just call me Sammy's right-hand man.' Be that as it may, Joe's own karate-trained right hand can split a cinder block. The marquee at the Forrest Theater—where Sammy had won an amateur free-style dancing contest at the age of three—read, SAMMY DAVIS—THAT'S ALL. Inside, Sammy sang, danced, did his impressions and his pistol-twirling act, imitated the walking styles of current Western stars, and followed up with a pantomime and an uninhibited drunk routine. Then his dancers took the stage as Sammy quick-changed to finish the show as a wistful clown. The audience gave him a standing ovation. Back in the hubbub of his dressing room, he acted out impromptu ideas for improving the show, accompanying himself with fiercely mouthed sound effects. Then, after several hours, 20 or 30 people set off in taxicabs, following Sammy to one of his almost-nightly private screenings of unreleased feature films. Later, though this relentless round-the-clock schedule was obviously draining his strength (he had been rubbing more and more at his plastic left eye—a sure sign, according to Murphy, that the 39-year-old star was really exhausted), he would talk with me back at the hotel—this time without interruptions and distractions. Often as not, the light of dawn would find us still immersed in conversation. We began with a question about a subject that preoccupies his profilers and perplexes even his closest friends: What makes Sammy run?"

HALEY: *Sammy, you seem to be in a permanent state of exhaustion—and perpetual motion—trying to keep up with your nonstop schedule of commitments. What makes you drive yourself so relentlessly?*
DAVIS: If you want to be the best, baby, you've got to work harder than anybody else. I'm not in this business to be second-rate. If you've worked and waited for a lifetime, and finally your opportunity comes, do you swing at the ball or do you bunt? Well, I want to swing at it.

HALEY: *Some might feel that you're trying to swing five or six bats at once.*
DAVIS: So what if I am? I'm not trying to *hit* anybody with them. I'm not Sammy Glick, stepping on people, destroying people. Why should you be put down because you're ambi-

tious, because you want to succeed—so long as you're not hurting anybody? Jesus! Is it criminal to have drive?

HALEY: *Of course not. But why do you take on more commitments than you can fulfill?*
DAVIS: Well, nobody starts out to do three or four major things at once. You start to do one thing, and suddenly a chance comes to do another. You're handling these two all right, then suddenly here comes another thing you can't refuse, and so on. After a while, it gets out of hand.

HALEY: *During the run of* Golden Boy, *you ran yourself ragged doing free benefits between shows—more than any other performer ever has done in so short a time. Why?*
DAVIS: Well, I wasn't thinking about setting some record. People just *asked* me. This one, that one, people I knew, people who knew somebody I knew: "Sammy, baby, just a little half hour for us." Another one: "You can't let *us* down." I'd say, "Yeah, yeah, OK—when?"—even when I knew I shouldn't. The dates always sounded a while off. Word filtered around I'd try to help good causes, and the promises started piling up on me. Man, sometimes in one day I'd be doing two, three benefits, then the show that night. If I tried to beg off because I was beat, they'd say, "Sammy, this organization helps your people: You've *got* to make it! We'll send a limousine." I *had* limousines: what I needed was *sleep.* But if I said no, they'd hate me—and I saw some of that, too. So I'd sleep on the way over in the car; chauffeur would wake me up to walk in the door and do the benefit. I got so run-down I *looked* it. And you know what I'd hear then? "Sammy, you're too tired! You got to quit doing so many benefits—just this one more for *us.*" I knew something was going to give. I kept feeling it, different ways—warnings, you know. I kept saying to everybody, "Give me some time off. I've got to have some rest." But they never really listened, and I tried to keep going—until finally it happened. I collapsed and had to miss several shows. You can only do so much to your-

self, then your body acts to save itself. I learned my lesson. I'm not going to let myself get that overburdened no more. I'll still help, but within reason. Anxiety to help anybody I can is the particular bag I happen to swing in as a human being. But there must be 5,000 good causes: I learned I can't help *all* of them.

HALEY: *Your nervous collapse was only one of many problems—bad reviews, script changes, firings, frictions, accidents, injuries—that seemed to plague the run of* Golden Boy. *Has that experience soured you on the theater?*

DAVIS: No, I'm going to go back, and I'm going to *keep* going back until I learn it. Most people cannot understand, even to this day, why a guy who makes a million and a half or two million dollars a year would want to come back and do a Broadway show. Well, I can't say I need the theater to exist as a human being: but it's my *vitamins*. Legitimate theater is marvelous if you can find the right set of circumstances to work under. In *Golden Boy*, we just didn't have all the right circumstances. It became too hard to perform—physically and mentally. I got hurt too many times, and finally I got bored with it.

HALEY: *To judge by its low ratings and lukewarm reviews, your recent television series was even less successful than* Golden Boy. *Why do you think it didn't click?*

DAVIS: I've got no cop-out. It was nobody's fault but mine. I apologize especially for those first five shows. I'm being as honest as I know how to be. They were horrible. We never got over that bad beginning—even when we started to swing those last six or seven shows. But it was a ball to be on for the 16 weeks it ran.

HALEY: *Do you plan to try again with another series?*

DAVIS: Someday, sure. I don't know about this coming season, though. If NBC doesn't pick me up, I've been offered other parts—like CBS wants me to be the CBS eye.

HALEY: *That sounds like type-casting. Your latest film,* A Man Called Adam, *which you produced and starred in, didn't fare*

much better than your TV series, either critically or commercially. Were you satisfied with it?
DAVIS: Not completely, but I liked it. I think we said some things never said before in a picture. I don't think it's as strong, as powerful, as great a picture, as, say, *Champion* or *The Defiant Ones*, or any of the others with that kind of punch. But I think it's a good, entertaining picture, in its own way. And even if the critics didn't like it, I'm pleased that a lot of them, and other people, were pleasantly surprised by my performance in it. I never before had a chance to really *act* in a picture, and I tried to act my ass off in this one, pal. I really did.

HALEY: *It's often said that everything you do as a performer is characterized by what one critic has called "a fanatical desire for approval." Is there any truth to that?*
DAVIS: Maybe so. I know every time I walk on a stage, or do a television show, or act in a movie, I feel like the cat in the old West who walks into a saloon with the guns on his hips and says, "OK, who's the fastest gun here?" And the audience out there is the cat who stands up and says, "I am. Let's go outside. I'm going to take you." Every audience is like that. Every time I walk on, I'm thinking, "Oh, God, is this *it*? Is this the time I fail? Is this the time this other cat's going to be faster than me?" But if I win them over, see, it's another notch on my gun. I have said on stage, when I haven't been able to move them, "Look, you people, I ain't leaving this stage until I find something you all like." And after doing a full show, I have gone on as much as another hour and a half, until I won them. It's like you've got these marvelous paints, and you want to get on that canvas *exactly* this beautiful thing you've got pictured in your mind, but you just can't seem to get that sun *bright* enough. I know the audience will courteously applaud just because I'm singing loud, but that's not what I want. I got to have them *pulling* for me: I want them feeling, "Oh, God, if he doesn't make it, he might run off and cut his wrists." They want me to climb that mountain. And then, "Oh, God—he *made* it!" That's how I've got to make them feel.

It's a constant challenge, because there's no sure-fire act, no sure-fire performer. You can be the world's biggest star, and any night that stage can fall from under you. The way this business is going today, it's getting to the point where you're really only as good as your last performance. I have to fight myself to put that foot across that magic dividing line between backstage and on stage—because I can never be certain what's going to happen out there. Take this show I'm doing right now. Opening night, the audience liked the show all right, but I knew something was wrong. I just sat and sat and sat in my hotel suite after the show and tried to figure what to do. It wasn't till the third or fourth night that it finally clicked. Now it's right. I got them turned on.

HALEY: *Your night-club and theater audiences are predominantly white. Do you think there may be some element of race consciousness in your compulsion to win their approval?*
DAVIS: No question about it. I always go on stage anticipating what people out there may be feeling against me emotionally. I want to rob them of what they're sitting there thinking: *Negro.* With all the accompanying clichés. Ever since I recognized what prejudice is, I've tried to fight it away, and the only weapon I could use was my talent. Away back, when I was learning the business, I had no education, no power, no influence; entertaining was the only way I had to change prejudiced thinking. I could see it happen every time Will Mastin, my dad and I did our act. For as long as we were on stage, our skin had no color: the people were just seeing us as entertainers. We didn't become Negroes again until we stepped *off* the stage. Again in the Army, especially the Army, where I met the most concentrated bunch of haters I ever experienced: On that stage, for the eight months I was in Special Services, that spotlight erased my color. It made the hate leave their faces temporarily. It was as if my talent gave me a pass from their prejudice, if only temporarily. And when I spotted haters in the audiences, I tried to give extra-good performances. I had to *get* to them, to neutralize them, to make

them recognize me. It was in the Army that I got the conviction that I had to become a great enough entertainer that the hatred of prejudiced people couldn't touch me anymore. See?

HALEY: *You said "the most concentrated bunch of haters" you ever met was in the Army. Was their hatred directed at Negroes in general or at you in particular?*
DAVIS: We all got it, but being a performer and a little guy besides, I guess I was an especially tempting target.

HALEY: *For what? Verbal or physical abuse?*
DAVIS: I don't like talking about it—even thinking about it. It don't *bother* me; I don't mean that. I mean I don't want nobody thinking I'm whining about it. When it was *happening*, I didn't whine; I fought it. And now it's over; it's past.

HALEY: *Will you give us some idea of what you went through?*
DAVIS: I met some prejudiced cats—all right? I got pushed and banged around some, got my nose broken twice—all right? But the roughest part wasn't that: the *roughest* was the psychological. Like, you know, I'd been all my life in show business. I had never known one white agent, manager or anybody else in any of the acts my dad, Will Mastin and I had worked with who hadn't been friendly, see? I don't mean every time we met they hugged me; they didn't. My point is that until the Army, nobody white had ever just *looked* at me and *hated* me—and didn't even *know* me.

From the day I got into the basic-training center—it was Fort Francis E. Warren in Cheyenne, Wyoming—from the first *ten minutes*, I started hearing more "nigger" and seeing more sneers and hate looks than I'd ever known all my life. Walked inside the *gate*, asked a cat sitting on some barracks steps to show me how to get to where I had to go: "Excuse me, buddy, I'm a little lost—" Cat told me, "I'm not your buddy, you black bastard!" When I got assigned a barracks, cats in there—most of them from the South and Southwest—don't want to sleep *nowhere* next to me. And there was this one guy elected himself head of the haters. First move he made, he ground his boot heel down on the $150 chronometer watch my dad and Will had borrowed the money to give me as a present. I had treasured that watch. Man, they did all kinds of things, *sick* things. One time I remember, I had just done my first show there at the center, and I mean I had *entertained* them. Well, back in the barracks, suddenly they all acted friendly. Offered me this beer—but it *wasn't* beer, man, it was warm piss. Then a cat "accidentally" poured it on me. Well, I went for him, ready to kill. He was a big cat, and I didn't weigh but 115 pounds. He broke my nose the first punch, but, man, I fought him like a wildcat, and before he beat me unconscious, I broke *his* nose, too. From then on, nearly as long as I stayed there, maybe every other day I had some knockdown, drag-out fight, until I had scabs on my knuckles! Got my nose broken again. It got so everybody white I saw, I expected to hear "nigger." Somebody ask me if I want my coffee *black*, I was ready to fight.

HALEY: *Were all the white soldiers that anti-Negro?*
DAVIS: No, there was *good* cats there, too—don't get me wrong—at least some that didn't want to get involved, or who didn't hate Negroes that bad. And I had a sergeant who was one of the finest men I'll ever meet. Anyway, I met George M. Cohan, Jr., and we got an act going with this WAC captain in charge of us. Well, one time some cats from headquarters came and said the captain wanted to see me, and I went with them into a building where they said she was—but there were four other cats waiting instead. Pushed me into a latrine; some of them held me and the others beat me. They wrote "coon" in white paint across my forehead, and "I'm a nigger" across my chest. Then they ordered me to dance for them, "Dance, Sambo—fast!" Man, I fought to get at them, but they pinned me and punched me in the gut until it looked like I'd have to dance or die. Don't even like to think about it! *Sick* cats! I danced until I couldn't no more. Then—bam! In the gut again—and I had to dance some more, until finally they saw I

was ready to pass out. Then they poured turpentine over me, and told me the reason they'd given me "this little lesson": They'd been watching me "making eyes" at the white WAC captain. She was my *boss*, man, my commanding officer—and that's the way I treated her. Didn't make no difference. Anyway, they finally left me there. I was so sick, I just wanted to crawl into the latrine walls and die, man; I just lay down and cried.

That was when, for the first time in my life, I didn't want to go out and do my act—go out there and smile at people who despised me. But I made myself do it anyhow. I was fighting myself so hard to stay out there that the fighting made me do maybe one of the best shows I ever did in my life. And I'm glad it did, because I discovered something. I saw some of those faces out there grudgingly take on different expressions. I don't mean for a minute that anybody suddenly started loving me—I didn't want that from them anyway—but they *respected* me. It taught me that the way for me to fight, better than with my fists, was with my talent. For the next eight months, going across the country doing my act, I nearly *killed* myself every show trying to make them respect me. Maybe I still am.

HALEY: *Do you feel any bitterness toward whites because of your Army experiences?*
DAVIS: No, I can't harbor that, based on one very simple fact. If I'm going to look at you with a jaundiced eye because you're white, then how are you going to look at me? Am I going to try to hide my bigotry, hoping that you'll show your tolerance? It makes no sense. I don't know how I can ask to be regarded as a fellow man, as I wish to be, without myself extending that same respect to you. I've met too many decent white people to hold the prejudices of other whites against them—even in the Army. Like that sergeant I told you about. He's the one who got me started reading something besides comic books.

HALEY: *You were in your late teens then. Is it true, as some writers have claimed, that you could barely read and write, that you'd never even gone to kindergarten?*

DAVIS: Yeah, it's true. What's more, I'll be turning 40 this year, and I *still* haven't gone to kindergarten. Haven't spent a single day in school my whole life. I say that with mixed emotions. I'm very proud in one sense; I'm very ashamed in another. For instance, you know I'm always being asked for autographs. Say a girl tells me, "My name is Rosemari, with an 'i.' " Well, I don't know how to spell the names. I can't hardly write anything but my *own* name. It's a constant, daily embarrassment. It's even more of an embarrassment because of my articulate façade. People think, "Why, he's *got* to have education." But I can't even write! Nothing but chicken scratches! That I'm not proud of. I'm proud that I've pulled myself up by my own bootstraps, with the help of some people who cared enough; but I'm not proud of having no education. What little I do have started on the road, when Will Mastin and my dad found someone around the theaters to tutor me to read and write. We'd work between shows in the dressing room—when there *was* a dressing room—until it was time for me to go on for the next show. Then in the Army, like I told you, this sergeant took a liking to me and started me reading books. Things like *The Picture of Dorian Gray* by Oscar Wilde, and some of Carl Sandburg's books about Lincoln; books by Dickens, Poe, Twain; and a history of the U.S. I would read every minute of the day I had free, then in my bunk until taps, then in the latrine until after midnight. At the PX I bought a pocket dictionary, and I would look up words in places where nobody would see me, then I'd read the books over again.

Imagine somebody 18 years old, grown, discovering the thrills of *Robinson Crusoe* for the first time—reading that kids of 10 take for granted. And a showbiz kid is already 10 years up on the average cat, in street-knowledge terms. Like, man, I'd had my first serious affair at 14, and at 18 I still didn't know what a serious *book* was. That's a sad paradox. I remember so well the first book I ever read about my own people, and the effect it had on me. It did something to me. That was *Native Son*, by Richard Wright. Then, later, I read *Black Boy*. They made me feel something about being black that I had never really felt before. It made me uncomfortable, made me feel trapped in black, you know, in a white society that had created you the way it wanted, and still hated you.

But to get back to your question. People hearing me today don't think I have no education. I've worked hard—*hard*, man, to be able to give this impression. Blood, sweat and tears went into every combination of words that I use now. I've read, and I've remembered. I've listened and recorded in my mind. Now, I'd be confident anywhere I was asked to speak. But I still make mistakes that infuriate me, especially when I'm corrected. People *very* close to me do that sometimes. Like Burt and Jane Boyar, who did *Yes I Can* with me; to this day, one of them will say, when we're alone, "You're pronouncing this word wrong." It *infuriates* me—but I know they're right. Say, I'll get up and extemporaneously make a speech that would put Burt to shame if he tried it. It'll just come off the top of my knot; it'll roll—brrrrr—and I'll look at Burt triumphantly. Then later on, he'll get me somewhere away from people and say, "You pronounced two words wrong," and that little comedown really kills me, because I've struggled so hard, you know? It took me five years, I guess, to quit saying "Ladies and gennermen—" It just hurts when I'm told I was making a mistake, particularly by someone very close to me, even though I know he only wants to help me. And I *want* them to help me, but I'm torn between "Help me" and "Geez, I thought I was doing good."

HALEY: *A friend of yours told us it bothers you that without a day's education, you earn more than the nation's top dozen college presidents. Is that true?*
DAVIS: Yes and no. On the one hand, I feel guilty about making all the money that I do. It's like, say, I talk to a cat, a policeman, that's exposed all the time to crime and corruption, and he's just saved someone's life, and what does *he* make? You know? But then I think that if I draw the people in, and they're willing to pay the tab, then I'm entitled to it. It's a mixed-up feeling.

HALEY: *While we're on the subject, would you mind telling us just how much you earn?*

DAVIS: Well, it fluctuates. This year, two million dollars. I know that sounds like an awful lot, but you have to consider that just yesterday my accountant told me that to keep my books even— understand me, just to break *even*, in terms of salaries, spending money and household things, plus taxes—I've got to make $17,000 a week. After all, I'm in the 90-percent tax bracket. Next year, I'll make less, about a million and a half, because of the six months in London with *Golden Boy* there. You make a lot less on the stage than in night clubs as a top act.

HALEY: *How much of that two million did you earn as a performer?*

DAVIS: I'm not sure of the exact amount, but as you know, I got a couple of other things going for me, too. There's the royalties from my book, for one thing. And I'm now sincerely and honestly in the motion-picture business. *A Man Called Adam* is on the screens now, and I've bought future film properties, such as Irving Wallace's *The Man*, which Ossie Davis will star in. I've also got two music-publishing firms—rather, my musical director, George Rhodes, has one and I have one. And I've got a record company: It releases through Reprise Records, but it's my company. All of the masters come back to me. And I've got a personal-management company; they're all part of my overall enterprises.

If you count the household help, and the West Coast office, I've got about 30 people working for me. I don't really know what the weekly payroll amounts to, or what I average spending just myself a week, either. But I know I don't spend as much as I used to.

HALEY: *During the first few years after you made it big, you spent several million dollars on custom-made suits and shoes by the dozen, expensive jewelry, limousines, parties, chartered planes, and enough photographic and recording equipment to*

fill a small warehouse. Why? What were you trying to prove?
DAVIS: Listen, baby, you ever had a *mustard* sandwich? Just
mustard spread on bread—and then tried to dance on the nour-
ishment from that? Will Mastin, my dad and me, we used to
heat a can of pork and beans on the radiator, when they were
nice enough to *have* heat in the radiator, and split it three ways,
eating right from the can. There were times when for a meal we
had a Mr. Goodbar apiece. Or a grape soda. I remember our
filling our stomachs with nothing but water! I mean, I paid my
dues, baby; don't you ever overlook that, and anybody who
does can go jump in the lake! We got stranded more times than
I can count! Our beds were *benches* in drink-water train de-
pots. And once in the winter in Ohio, I remember, it was so bad
we went to the *jail* and asked the man to let us sleep in there. In
the Thirties, I remember, we lost the old $90 car we had, and
we had to join Hank Keane's carnival. Eight, nine shows a
day—and that bally, "Heyyy! Here they come! Three little
hoofers, hot from Harlem!" There was no dignities then. Nobody was trooping around saying "Let's have our rights." You
were alone out there—*every* Negro performer was. We danced
so hard our feet scarcely touched the floor; but we kept saying
inside, "It ain't gonna happen, ain't *never* gonna happen for
us." Jesus, man! We starved. About literally starved. If we got
two little one-nighters a week, we were lucky! Like all Negro
performers, though, we put on the best front we could. But the
insults. The indignities. You haven't *known* indignity until you
have to dance, and have people throw money at you, and you
take the money off the floor.

Anyway, we'd go wherever it was, and we'd work. And then
we'd go back to my grandmother's little railroad flat and sit
waiting for some call, frustrated to death, knowing all the entertainment we had in us to give to people. And I'd sit all day
waiting to tune in on Jack Eigen's celebrity interview program
from the Copacabana. He'd always say, "I'm at the Copa,
where are you?" And I'd holler at the radio, "I'm up here in my
goddamned hole in Harlem, that's where I am!" And mean-

while, my grandmother's on relief, and The Man is coming around, checking up. "I hear your son was working"—meaning my father. And she'd say, "But he didn't make anything." And he'd say, "Well, if he's working, you're not supposed to be on relief." That seemed to be the concept in those days—if you were on relief, you were just supposed to sit there, and not even *try* to work.

It was a frightening thing to think, "*Jesus*, I'm never going to live, live *big*! I'm never going to be able to walk in some place and buy something and not ask the price. Never!" Just work, kill myself working, and waiting, and praying. It was like that song from *Sweet Charity*: "There's got to be something better than this." You know the humiliation for a Negro to walk in a store? You got on your front, that one good suit. You got on your Sunday shoes, the ones you use on the stage—we always prided ourselves on being neat on the stage; you walk in the store, you say, "I'd like to get one of those shirts you've got there in the window." And the man says, "You know that shirt's seven ninety-five." And you want to say, "Then gimme the whole fuckin' store!" You know? Because you knew his thoughts: "Snap, bop, broke, Negro, no money—deadbeat." Man don't want your business! Negro ain't got no money to pay for it! Negro going to ask for credit. Man, you'd dream it in your mind whether that's what he thought or not. If he'd done the same thing to eight white customers, it didn't matter to you. You see what I mean? So suddenly it becomes a personal vendetta with this guy. One time I walked in, taking the last ten dollars I had, when I had nothing else to *eat* on, and the man tells me the price of the shirt and gives me the eye, and I said, "Well, then, give me *two* of them!" And I walked out with my little package, saying to myself, "Boy, I sure showed him!" Who the hell did I *show*? What the hell did I *prove*? Nothing! But, boy, what satisfaction! Except that now I didn't have nothing to eat.

Anyway, we worked, and we starved, and we kept hoping that somehow, someday, something would happen. Only it

seemed like it never would. You know? And then—suddenly—
pfoom! It starts to happen! And you're looking around, blink-
ing like you're staring at the sun. And all of a sudden it's *your*
world. You *run* into stores. You say, "Hey, man! Gimme twenty
of them! And eight of *them*! And a thousand of those!" Man—
you understand? You walk around with a thousand dollars in
your pocket. Like, that had been a *year's* salary! Nobody else
can *know* that goddamn thrill—nobody! To be able to give
a waitress a hundred-dollar tip. *Nobody* knows that thrill
who hasn't been at the bottom of the barrel—where, as the
joke goes, the rent was a dollar a month, and you was still
12 months in the 'rears—'cause you couldn't pay even *that*
rent! So when I spend money now, I guess it's because that's
how it was for so long, man. It was so hard, baby, I really
couldn't tell you.

HALEY: *A few minutes ago you said you don't spend as much
anymore as you used to. Yet you still have a reputation for extravagance. Is it unfounded?*
DAVIS: Not entirely. I still live way beyond my means; I know
that. By that I mean I'm living beyond the means that my ac-
countants would *like* me to live. The difference is now I have
the security of knowing my family is taken care of. My wife is
taken care of so that she's in good shape if anything happened
tomorrow, and so is the rest of my family. My children each
have million-dollar insurance policies on me, and money in the
bank besides that. And I'm paid up on my taxes. I've got my
enterprises and corporations set up—legitimately. I don't want
to try to gyp the Government out of a goddamned dime. Including back taxes, I was $300,000 in debt when I met May.
But you know something? I don't really have any regrets. I had
lived *good*, you can believe that! 'Cause when I did it, baby, I
did it. Cats see me come in a town today, cats who knew me
then, and say, "Here he comes! My man! My *main* man!" And
I tell them, "Cool it, baby, I'm not doing it anymore." The way
I feel about what I blew is that it's a whole lot better to be able

to say "I was there," instead of "I never was." You know? A young cat suddenly makes $20,000 a week, he doesn't know how to protect himself. He doesn't know how to move. He's vulnerable to anything, everything. But now I've been there. I've made the mistakes. I've had the love affairs; I've had the controversy. What happened was I met May, and suddenly all the rest of it ceased to be attractive.

HALEY: *But you said you still live beyond your means.*
DAVIS: Well, I'm not on any austerity kick. I've worked hard, baby, and I still want to enjoy the pleasures and the luxuries of life. *Nobody* enjoys luxuries more than I do. I've got a limousine that costs $25,000 with all the fixtures. I sit there, I press that button, a television comes up. Ain't no other pleasure in the *world* like that for me. Press another button: The tape recorder plays. The bar—fix me a drink. It's right there! That's my *pleasure*, man! Do you understand what I mean? I *enjoy* opening my closet door and saying, "Oh, what suit should I wear?" So I have 20 suits too many! So I have too many tape recorders! And too many cars! I ain't *hurting* nobody! I didn't take a gun and stick somebody up and beat them over the head. I didn't rape nobody's daughter to get it! So I've got a lot of gold lighters; who did I *hurt* to get them? So I bought some gold watches at Cartier's; it gives me *pleasure*, is all.

Now, I wouldn't do this if it meant my family wouldn't eat, or I'd promised someone money and couldn't come up with it. I ain't taking no dope. If a lens comes out for one of my cameras, I'll *buy* it, and I don't care *what* it costs. Everybody has his *shtick*, that he enjoys doing, to give him personal pleasure. Mine is luxury. I *love* luxury! If I could wear cashmere underwear, I'd wear it. I love having my underwear made. I love having suits made, sending to Hong Kong for special-made shoes. I'm not going to cop out with "I never had it as a kid," because very few people ever had it as a kid. My point is that it's my *pleasure*: I love it, and I earn it, and nobody gives it to me, and nobody works any harder for his than I work for mine. That goes for a riveter on a bridge, for a ditchdigger: don't *nobody* work no harder than me, no matter what he works at. I'm out there sweating blood. So if I feel like having me a little Rolls-Royce, I buy one.

I used to gamble in Vegas—lost more money than I could make. Once I was 40-odd thousand dollars in debt, gambling. Blackjack, craps, anything I could get my hands on. But I don't owe it anymore. Now, I can afford to lose $10,000 at the tables in a six-week engagement in Vegas. I can't afford no *more* than that. The difference is my accountants would like for me not to play at all. They don't realize that $10,000 gives me some sort of adrenaline, gives me whatever psychological answers make it possible for me to earn all that *other* money. See? Ain't nothing going to happen on that stage if I'm bugged mentally. I'd be in a hospital someplace.

HALEY: *Aside from the things you've mentioned, what do you spend your money on? Do you make any contributions to charity?*

DAVIS: Last year I gave to various charities better than $100,000, and this year I'm going to give more. A man don't just lay around and not contribute something to the society he lives in.

HALEY: *How much of that amount goes to civil rights groups?*

DAVIS: I don't know—maybe half or more. The rest goes to other causes, right across the board.

HALEY: *Apart from donations, what do you do for civil rights?*

DAVIS: I give my time—a lot of my time—to benefits, personal appearances and such, as a professional entertainer. You ain't going to find nobody in show business—except for Dick Gregory—giving more of his time to civil rights than I do.

HALEY: *How about Harry Belafonte and Sidney Poitier? Do you contribute more than they do to the cause?*

DAVIS: *Nobody* could contribute more than they do. I could never match them based on their commitment. But I'll match them based on mine. We're *all* doing whatever we can, however we can, within our abilities to do. I can go to sleep at night knowing I'm contributing all it's possible for *me* to do, consistent with maintaining my business, which is being out there on somebody's stage about 300 nights of the year.

HALEY: *Have you participated, like Gregory, Belafonte and Poitier, in many civil rights marches or demonstrations?*
DAVIS: Yeah, I do that, too. I flew to Jackson, Mississippi, and I flew to Selma. I don't like talking about it, though, because I don't go for this "Where were you? I didn't see you in the march!" That bag that a lot of civil rights people are in. Because there are plenty of other contributions as important as marching. Like if you're privileged to be a personality, there's the responsibility of what new image of the Negro do you project when you're reaching all them mass audiences in movie theaters and on national television, and those big live audiences like I play to. The way I see it, my Broadway show fails for me, the movies I make fail for me, if they aren't presenting Negroes in an image that ain't never been seen before—an image of dignity and self-respect. Every night I do my act, I like to think I change at least a few more white people's way of thinking about Negro people. So—I give my money; I give my time. And I'm out there beating at prejudice night after night. What more have I got that I can give?

HALEY: *Most people would say nothing more. But you didn't start participating actively in the civil rights movement until five or six years ago. Why not?*
DAVIS: During my years of driving myself to get somewhere in this business, and then in the kind of personal reactions I had to making it finally, I wasn't thinking about nothing but *making* it, and then having a ball; wasn't thinking about *nothing* else. I didn't give a damn about no race cause. I knew about the

problems, but I just didn't care. I didn't care about nobody but me. I can't tell you the truth no more honest than that.

But then different things started to happen. Some of them had to do with me; most of them didn't, until finally I called up Harry and Sidney. I go to them when I'm bugged about something. Harry has been my friend for many years. And Sidney, I named my son after him, Mark Sidney Davis. They talked to me, and so did Ossie Davis. I was confused and angry, and maybe a little guilty.

HALEY: *About what?*
DAVIS: Well, for a long time I had thought that money, fame, popularity, people asking for your autograph, that was what it was all about; but it was beginning to gnaw at me. It's like a cat that's balling every chick he can meet. Then one day he finds out, floating in this marvelous dreamworld, that having sex per se is not the be-all and end-all of existence. There comes a time when he wants something else, something *more*. And the fast cars, the fancy clothes, the money, the chicks, all that jazz, they're not enough anymore. It's fun and games; it's adult Monopoly. But it's not enough to justify your life, and any cat that thinks it is had better wise up before it's too late. Well, I finally did—but I didn't know where to turn. I wanted to commit myself, but I didn't know how or to what. So I talked to Harry and Sidney and Ossie, and finally I knew: I wanted to help my people. When I said to them, "OK, where do I start?" they embraced me, they were so happy. Ever since then, I've been trying to make up for what I didn't do in the past. And it's been a gas! This is a glorious time to be alive.

HALEY: *And to be a Negro?*
DAVIS: Right! That's something I never felt before, that none of us ever felt before: pride in our color and in our cause. Jesus, I'm proud to be black when I can see the moves that I make and that others are making, and the opportunities that are opening up to my people. To me, that's where pride comes

from—when it's possible for my people, like everybody else, to *accomplish* something. Ain't nobody going to feel much pride in being black as long as we let ourselves fall into all the cliché categories they use against us: "They don't want to help themselves, they just want to sit back, and whatever we hand out, they'll take." That shows no dignity, no purpose, no nothing. Why can't we all live in a society where it becomes every man's obligation, white or black, to extend his hand, to help—to do what we know in our hearts is the right thing? I'm proud to say that I'm Honorary Mayor of Harlem. I did a lot of work up there with HarYouAct [a Harlem civil rights youth group]. And the most recent thing, a marvelous position, very dear to me: I've been made the head of the life-membership department of the NAACP. It's not something you *are*; it's something you *do*. It's the first time the job ever was held by a performer.

HALEY: *Honorary Mayor or not, weren't you heckled out of the pulpit in the middle of a speech for HarYouAct in a Harlem church a few years ago?*
DAVIS: I was booed right out of the church—by black nationalist rabble-rousers shouting, "You're not for the black man!" "What about your white wife?" Well, I carry a gun, you know. They let me carry one in New York, the hardest state to get a gun permit in, because they realized that I get some kind of threat about every day of my life. I'm not a violent man, but *that* marvelous day, that *fun* afternoon, I never in my life felt so much like shooting someone. What's my *wife* got to do with it? *I* was there! *I'm* black!

HALEY: *Despite your commitment to civil rights, many Negroes seem to feel that you're trying to disavow your race and your responsibilities as a Negro by "mixing" in the white world. What's your reply?*
DAVIS: Baby, the best answer I can give you is the background of all this. Everything rotten about me that's said around, or that's been in the press, was started by a Negro photographer. You re-

member that picture of me and Ava Gardner that was in *Confidential*? I was playing the Apollo Theater in Harlem. Ava was in New York publicizing *The Barefoot Contessa*. She did me a favor to come up to the Apollo and let me introduce her. William B. Williams was escorting her, and a guy from United Artists. Well, the four of us had one quick drink after the show, then later on at her hotel suite, two photographers took a cover shot of Ava and me for *Our World* magazine, with me in a Santa Claus suit. Then, when I got out of the costume, one photographer shot some pictures of me and Ava together, with the United Artists guy standing right with us. I told the photographer to give me the film, but he said he'd develop it for me. I told him to be very careful, because in the wrong hands the shots could make trouble for Ava. I felt embarrassed even saying that to another Negro, knowing he'd understand. Well, next thing I knew, that picture came out on the cover of *Confidential*, the United Artists guy cropped out of it entirely; and it had the headline blurb, "What Makes Ava Gardner Run for Sammy Davis, Jr., cheek-to-cheeking it in her 16th floor suite at New York's Drake Hotel?" And in the story, the one quick drink the four of us had had together became, "Ava sat glassy-eyed through a gay tour of Harlem with Sammy"; and quotes Ava had made about my performance on the Apollo stage— "exciting, thrilling, masculine"—were slanted to make them sound like she meant in bed.

That's what really started my troubles, black and white, all over the country. Eating me up! I don't care what I did, it was wrong. That "Sammy Davis, Jr., thinks he's white" bit. I'd take out beautiful Negro girls, like an old friend of mine, Ruth King, a top model, and the columns would have something like "The Negro girl with Sammy was only a cover-up for the white woman who was *really* his date." You know? In fact, I sometimes use a line in my act that I got from what I used to really feel during that time. I say, "I buy *Ebony, Jet, The Pittsburgh Courier* and the *Chicago Defender* because I can't *wait* to find out what I'm doing."

One day I'll be proud when I can see my kids not having to bear a stigma for being the children of an interracial marriage, not having to struggle for the rights that every white American takes for granted, and that'll make it all worthwhile. But in the meantime, it's a pain in the ass sometimes to be Sammy Davis, Jr., because I just can't make a right move racewise. My mother was born in San Juan, you know; her name was Elvera Sanchez. So I'm Puerto Rican, Jewish, colored and married to a white woman. When I move into a neighborhood, people start running four ways at the same time. It defies explanation, what it's like. No matter what you do, no matter where you go, you ain't right, even with your own people. It used to be I'd go uptown to Harlem, and all I could feel around me was arms. I could take my wife; it'd be beautiful. It was just downtown I'd get the hissing sounds. Now, uptown, too. The color don't make no difference. Every day becomes a challenge, to keep yourself level, to keep yourself from becoming embittered. Mind you, I'm *proud* to be black, but I don't want my blackness to be a burden to me. I don't want to have to wake up every morning saying to myself, "What can I do today to prove to white people that I don't fit the racial stereotype? And at the same time, what can I do to prove to my black brothers and sisters that I'm black, and I love them, and I'll help any way I can?" This is what certain groups indicate they want to make you do. It's unfair.

HALEY: *Have you ever wished that you weren't a Negro?*
DAVIS: Well, not professionally, anyway. Earlier in my life—despite all the barriers—it proved advantageous to be a Negro, because they hadn't ever seen a Negro doing impressions of whites, and all that jazz. I've never wished, or felt, that I'd be making it better in show business if I were white. That's been written about me, but it's not true. On a personal level, though, maybe I really have at least subconsciously wished, like probably every other Negro, that there was *some* way I just wouldn't have to go *through* all of it, you know? Because it's all based

purely upon the pigmentation of your skin, or the way your hair is. You might be the next Nobel Prize winner, but it don't matter: "If you're black, get back." You'd just like to look like everybody else so that people wouldn't automatically start hating you a block away. White cat sees you walking down the street, maybe from across the street, and he never saw you before in his life, and he's not even close enough to distinguish anything about you except that you're not his color—and just for that, right there, snap, bop, bap, he *hates* you! That's the injustice of it, that's what makes you cry out inside, sometimes, "Damn, I wish I wasn't black!"

HALEY: *Some say that's why you wear your hair straight.*
DAVIS: Well, years ago that might have been so, but the only reason I leave it this way is because it's become part of my image. A show-business personality, if he's created a successful image of one kind or another, has to keep that image. Like, I don't want to see Cab Calloway with a crewcut: He's a great performer, but at this late date he'd look pretty silly with kinky hair, and so would I. Am I supposed to cut it short and let it grow in natural just to prove I'm proud to be black? Even if I did, the Negroes who don't like me would find something else to knock me for.

I don't care whatever move I make, some of my own people won't like it. Maybe they'll like me when I die. But I can't die like normal; I got to be shot by some sheriff in Mississippi. Like Dick Gregory got shot at Watts. Shoot me—*bam*! Then they'll say, "I guess he really *was* on our side." I don't understand it. I would voluntarily *die* to have my own people love me as much as they love some of those goddamn phonies they think are doing so much fighting for civil rights! To me, the obligation of being a Negro is to carry the banner of being proud to be a Negro and helping in the areas you can best help in. In terms of the civil rights fighting front, if we're all picketing at Selma, or wherever else the particular locale is this month, then who's left to help put Negroes into motion pictures? Who puts the Negro into mainstream television? I've put dozens of Negro cats to work! I'm not bragging, but that's got to be recognized, too. We're all in the same battle; I'm just fighting it on another front.

HALEY: *A moment ago, without naming any names, you referred to some civil rights leaders as "goddamn phonies." Would you care to tell us who they are?*
DAVIS: I'd rather not.

HALEY: *Well, do you number Martin Luther King among them?*
DAVIS: I would give him my good eye. That's what I think of Dr. King. He's one of the great men of our time. They should retire the Nobel Peace Prize with his name on it.

HALEY: *Despite his Peace Prize and his continuing dedication to nonviolence, Dr. King has been accused—most recently during last summer's Chicago riots—of fomenting violence. Do you think there's any substance in that charge?*
DAVIS: Those who make such charges don't seem to realize that the Negro public's abiding faith in Dr. King's unflinching commitment to nonviolence—in the face of a rising tide of white violence against him and other Negro marchers—is just about the only thing that's kept the lid from blowing off the racial pressure cooker. Without his counsel of patience and brotherhood, the nonviolent Negro revolt could easily escalate into a bloody revolution.

HALEY: *Among those advocating a revolutionary course are a number of racist groups dedicated to "getting Whitey" and sabotaging "the white power structure." How do you feel about their philosophy?*
DAVIS: They're living in a dreamworld. They think they're going to "get Whitey" and take over the country. Well, I got news for them: They ain't going to get nobody or take over nothing! 'Cause whenever they get ready, right there is going to be the

end of it. The Man will just open one eye and swat them like a gnat, and that will be that. They ain't made no razor *yet* that will stop an atomic bomb. You know what them cats should do that are so mad? Go down to Mississippi and kill them cats that killed them three civil rights workers. Everybody knows who did it. Find out who bombed that church in Alabama: Wipe them out. If you want to deal in justifiable violence, why kill the man who's trying to learn the right road to walk? Destroy the guy who has already proven to be your enemy. You know who it was that murdered Mrs. Liuzzo down in Alabama; they're out walking around. Go down there and wipe them out, you're so brave. When they bomb your church, bomb *their* church! 'Cause then that would prove, as it was proved in Africa, "Ten blacks may be killed for every white you kill, but you'll cause such an upheaval that every eye in the world will turn toward Africa. And the world will look and say, 'The sleeping giant is awakening.' "

HALEY: *Are you serious about bombing white churches? Would two wrongs make a right? What if innocent children were killed, as they were in the Negro church bombing?*
DAVIS: Of course, you're right. I don't mean literally bomb churches. I wouldn't literally bomb where even the most violent segregationists worship. Not for the segregationists as much as for the meaning of the institution. What I really mean is take care of the bombers themselves. I'm saying that if these extremist cats want to get Whitey, let them go take care of all those known murderers, the bombers and the others, who are walking around free because segregationist juries wouldn't convict.

HALEY: *If they haven't been convicted in a court of law, how can you be sure they're guilty?*
DAVIS: In practically every case I mentioned, the evidence was airtight: their guilt was established by the prosecution beyond a shadow of a doubt. The segregationist juries simply chose to ignore it.

HALEY: *Then you'd feel justified in taking the law into your own hands?*

DAVIS: Yes—just as long as the law permits whites to kill Negroes, or "white Negro" civil rights workers, and get away with it. I'm for any kind of protest—including retaliatory violence against known killers who get off—as long as Negroes are denied the full rights that any other American enjoys.

HALEY: *Wouldn't such acts of vengeance—even if the victims were guilty—set back the Negro cause by alienating millions of whites, as well as Negroes, who deplore* all *lawless violence?*

DAVIS: I imagine millions of whites *would* be alienated, the same way millions of Negroes were alienated when their church was bombed and their kids were blown to bits. I never will get out of my mind that famous *Time* cover showing that stained-glass face of Jesus shattered by the bomb that killed those little Negro girls sitting there in Sunday school hearing about peace on earth. That sticks in millions of Negroes' minds—same as that other famous picture printed around the world, of that Alabama white cop's heel on that Negro woman's neck. You see, baby, too many people don't want to face the terrible truth that violence *begets* violence. American Negroes have been on the receiving end of white violence for over 300 years; it would be a grievous error for anybody not to recognize that, if he wants to understand what's happening—and the consequences of doing nothing about it. Unless white society acts to end that violence by punishing those who commit it, Negroes may run out of patience and take care of the job themselves. And because violence begets more violence, it could spark a bloodbath in which the innocent on both sides would suffer along with the guilty. I'm not applauding it; I dread it. But I'm afraid that's what may happen if something isn't done—soon, and once and for all.

HALEY: *Are you predicting more riots like the one in Watts?*

DAVIS: I'm predicting riots that would make Watts look like a

Sunday-school picnic—unless we get to work fixing what *causes* them. And you won't do that by blaming everything, like the FBI does, on black revolutionaries and Communist troublemakers. They don't start the fire; they just fan the flames. Put them all in jail, you'll still have riots. But the fact that riots are unplanned don't mean they're nothing but isolated outbursts of spontaneous hooliganism. Riots are simply *violent* manifestations of what Martin Luther King is protesting *nonviolently*, of what every black man in America is protesting, one way or another: the fact that our race has wrongly been denied that which is enjoyed and taken for granted by every other American. Rioters are people who have no stake in their country, no stake in their city, no stake in their homes, no stake even in their own survival. How much worse could death be than what they have to live with—and for? They feel they have nothing to lose—and they're probably right.

HALEY: *Do you feel that enough is being done in Negro ghettos such as Watts, Harlem and Chicago's South Side to eliminate the conditions that breed riots?*
DAVIS: Baby, you got to be putting me on! They ain't even scratched the surface in any of those places. You know what always seems to happen after every riot? Immediately, committees are formed to find out why it happened, and they investigate, and they study, and finally they turn in a fat, reassuring report—full of all the standard sociological platitudes—recommending *further* study and investigation and urging "better understanding between the white and black communities." The concrete results, if any, are way-out things like a new pocket park just about big enough to pitch pennies in, a front-page rat-extermination drive in one block where a baby was last bitten, a ceremonial street-cleaning campaign presided over by the mayor, and if we're really lucky, maybe a biracial civilian review board empowered to investigate police brutality and "make recommendations" for reform and discipline. Is it any wonder, when the *next* summer rolls around, that there's an-

other riot? You can't bail out a sinking ship with a teaspoon.

You want to end riots? Fumigate their breeding grounds: Wipe out the black ghetto and the slums. It's a chain of cause and effect: Give the Negro the same chance whites have to get a decent education, so that he can qualify for a decent job, so that he can live in a decent home, so that he can lead a decent, self-respecting life—so that he can live in dignity as a human being, side by side with his white brothers.

HALEY: *Many whites, particularly in Northern suburbs adjoining newly integrated neighborhoods, regard the Negro drive for equality of opportunity as a threat to their homes and jobs. Do you think there's any justification for that feeling?*

DAVIS: Negroes don't want to take away nothing that belongs to white folks. White folks ain't giving up their own rights by giving the Negro his. There's enough human rights for *everybody*; don't need to fight over them. But you know, the real *gut* reason whites are afraid of us isn't a matter of job security and property values. It's because we're not the same *color*. Anything that's different they don't understand, and anything they don't understand they fear—and anything they fear they *hate*. Well, they're just going to have to get used to the idea of having us around as equal partners in this society. We share the same land, just as we share the same aspirations. We're stuck with each other, baby, so let's make the best of it. You accept our faults, we'll accept yours, and let bygones be bygones. 'Cause if we don't learn how to live together, we're sure as hell going to die together.

HALEY: *How do you mean?*

DAVIS: The Negro's destiny in America is America's destiny as a democracy. Malcolm X said it: "As the black man walks, so shall all men walk." Well, if the Negro falls, American democracy will fall, because all of the things it stands for will have been betrayed. But I don't think that's going to happen. It may sound hopelessly idealistic and unattainable, when you look

around at all of the worsening racial strife we're confronted
with today, but I honestly believe that the day is coming when
the Ku Klux Klan and the White Citizens Council will be relegated to the history books along with CORE and SNCC, when
there'll be cobwebs not only on racist hate literature but on
these NAACP life-membership cards that I try to get just about
everybody I meet to sign up for. I may not be here to see it happen—even if I live to be 80—but I think my kids will be around
to witness the birth of a truly color-blind society.

HALEY: *As you know, extremist groups such as the Black Muslims share the view of the K.K.K. that American whites and Negroes will never be able to live together in peace and should
therefore acknowledge the inevitability of racial separation.
How do you feel about it?*
DAVIS: I feel that the vast majority of Americans, white and
black, want to get along with one another, and they're willing
to do whatever they have to do to iron out their differences.
That's what this country is all about. I think all those cats who
don't believe in that, who don't think it'll work and don't want
to try, who preach racial hatred and want to separate black and
white, they should get the hell out of America and go to some
desert island and live among their own sick kind. We don't
need them.

It may sound hokey as hell, but I *love* my country. It's no
paradise, God knows—and it never will be, color-blind or
not—but it's *my* country, like the man said, right or wrong. If
you're outraged by its racial injustices—and you ought to be—
then fight to *do* something about them; don't be a defeatist and
a dropout. If you don't like its foreign policy, then *bitch* about
it as loud as you like, 'cause that's your privilege as a citizen;
but don't put down the country that *allows* you that right.

HALEY: *You sound like a patriot.*
DAVIS: Maybe so. I'm a nut, I guess. I love America. It's given
me opportunities that no other country in the world could've

given me. If I had to go and fight, and lose my good eye, or die for this country, I would. Because there's no country better. I've traveled the world, and there ain't no place God ever created like America. Even with all the troubles we've still got to solve, if a guy doesn't want to let me into a hotel here, if I make enough money, I can *buy* the joint.

HALEY: *As a major star, Sammy, you're not likely to be turned away by many hotels anymore, even in the South. In fact, you might be offered the red-carpet treatment at a hotel that refused patronage to other Negroes.*
DAVIS: If I was, I'd tell them what they could do with the carpet. It's not any big, banner-waving thing with me; I just don't want to stay anyplace my people can't, and I don't care if they roll out an *ermine* carpet.

HALEY: *Would you refuse, for the same reason, to perform in a white-only club?*
DAVIS: Absolutely. I'd never even consider it. Even when I was poor and hungry, I didn't do it.

HALEY: *In those early days with the Trio, were there many clubs that wouldn't book you because you were a Negro act?*
DAVIS: I lost count of them. For years I remember telling Will and my dad that eventually we'd be able to make our way into clubs that had never booked Negro talent, if only we got good enough and pushed hard enough. But they kept telling me, "You can't. White folks ain't gonna let you get but so far." I been hearing that all my life. But I kept insisting, "Yes, I can!"—say, there's a good title for a book—and I kept believing that somehow, someday we'd be able to break down the wall of prejudice that was blocking us. Well, we finally did; but the battle still isn't won, because there are big clubs today—two of the biggest right in Las Vegas—that *still* won't book no Negroes on the stage; don't even want to see your black face inside the night club, star or no. And there are other clubs that wouldn't touch me with a ten-foot pole if I wasn't having the

luck to be hot and swinging now and people weren't lining up
to see me.

HALEY: *On the whole, though, wouldn't you say that the opportunities open to the Negro performer today are considerably
wider than when you were starting out?*
DAVIS: Much wider, overall, and getting wider every year—in
clubs, movies, television, theater, everywhere. But we're still on
a trial basis, in terms of both the onstage and offstage attitude.
They're still watching us. I know certain clubs that will book
only Negroes who "behave themselves." That's such a *marvelous* line—"if they *behave* themselves." How about the
drunken, loudmouthed big-time Charlies in the audience? How
about *their* behavior? I'm not knocking them for it, as long as
they don't mess up my act. My point is that *we're* not allowed
the luxury of getting as drunk as others can, the luxury of being
as loud as others can get.

It wasn't long ago that you could make $20,000 a week in
Las Vegas, but you couldn't live in a hotel on the Strip. I
worked at one of them—packed in the people, could have
rented a whole floor of the hotel with what I was making—and
I wasn't allowed to go into the main room. You had to have
your dinner served in your dressing room; and if you got a
room to stay in, it was in the back. And you stayed there, you
cooled it—no relationship with any of the people. It's not quite
that bad anymore. But now there's kind of a gentleman's agreement going on. "Hey, baby, we love you, but do us a favor and
stay in your suite as much as you can between shows, OK? It's
nothing personal, you understand. It's the customers; we get a
lot of them from the South." It's never "us"; it's always
"them." At least they're *ashamed* of it now. That's some kind
of progress. But we still got a long way to go.

HALEY: *Do you think Negro entertainers have reached the point
where they can succeed—or fail—on the strength of their talent
alone?*
DAVIS: Yes—most of the time. Only we're expected to have

more than whites if we're going to make it—and I don't mean make it *big*; I mean just get by. Let's face it: Every Negro jazz group ain't Louis Jordan in his heyday; every Negro band's not Count Basie; every Negro singer ain't Nat Cole. We've got, proportionately, just as many bad bands and bad performers as the whites could ever boast of. Some of the saddest acts I've ever seen were colored—sad as McKinley's funeral, man. My point is that just as we've earned the right to be judged on our merits as entertainers, we've earned not only the right to stardom but the right to mediocrity, the right to be adequate, OK, unsensational—and still make a living in this business. At this point, though, Negro performers aren't allowed that luxury; if they're going to make the grade, they've got to have something going for them besides their good looks or their sex appeal.

HALEY: *Shouldn't they?*
DAVIS: Of course they should—but whites should have to meet the same requirements. And that brings up something else that bugs me about show business today. Young performers, black and white, are getting caught up in the overnight-star syndrome. Some electronically augmented rock-'n'-roll group makes it big with one hit record, and audiences go flocking to see them; yet they'll ignore 17 highly talented, maybe *more* talented performers who've been around for years refining their talent, getting better and better, turning out one great song after another—only nobody's listening! Somebody like Damita Jo. Marvelous! One of the best voices in the business. Well, one night I went to catch her singing, and you could have shot deer in the place! There's no justice in it.

The kids breaking in today have plenty of ambition, and some of them even have talent, but they don't want to pay their dues; they don't want to *earn* their success. They're not interested in becoming *pros*—just stars. And they don't seem to have whatever it is that turned *my* motor on. You know, the all-consuming, almost disastrous desire to make it. I remember going into penny arcades and dropping a quarter into those

Record Your Own Voice machines. I'd sing like Billy Eckstine, Louis Armstrong; I'd speak like Edward G. Robinson; I'd sing in my own voice; then I'd play the records over and over at home. And talk about *envy*: I'd go to the show at the Roxy and the Paramount, and all I could think about was, "Why ain't that *me* up there?" I'd go back home and dance before a mirror, copy a cat. And I wasn't afraid to ask for help. I'd go to Larry Storch and say, "Teach me how to do Jimmy Cagney, Cary Grant. I want to learn." And he taught me. Same with Mel Tormé, who taught me how to handle guns—which I've made a standard part of my act. Even when I had started making it, I was still asking, still listening, still watching, still learning, experimenting, accumulating, practicing, polishing. I learned, in time, something a lot of your young performers today don't appreciate, really—the importance of every single thing you do on that stage. Every gesture, every inflection, every tiny thing the audience sees, hears and senses about you makes a positive or a negative impression. Each one alone may seem insignificant, but cumulatively, they can make the difference between a good act and a great one.

HALEY: *Other than your father and Will Mastin, who would you say has contributed the most to your success as a performer?*
DAVIS: Frank Sinatra, Mickey Rooney and Jerry Lewis—in terms of guys who really went out of their way, who did tangible things, who stood up and were counted where it needed to be done.

HALEY: *You named Sinatra first. Why?*
DAVIS: It would embarrass Frank if I told even half of the reasons why. I first met him in 1941 when he was singing with Tommy Dorsey in Detroit, when he was in his 20s. He just walked over, matter-of-factly, to Will, my dad and me, and stuck out his hand and introduced himself. That might sound like nothing much, but the average top vocalist in those days

wouldn't give the time of day to a Negro supporting act. But every night, for the rest of that engagement, Frank would sit down on the dressing-room stairs with me, and we'd talk show business.

After that, every chance I could, I'd show up at his radio shows. He'd see me in the autograph line and invite me to his dressing room. I'm talking about when he was *big*, and I was a *nobody*. Then, months later, out of the blue, we were playing Portland when a wire came for us to open in the Capitol Theater in New York with the Frank Sinatra Show—and at $1,250 per week! For us then, that wasn't just great money—it was incredible. Later I found out that Frank had insisted the management find us and book us with him. Introducing us to the audience, he'd say, "We've got three swinging cats here. Keep your eye on the little one in the middle; he's my boy!" After that show, Frank heard me do my impressions in his dressing room and gave me hell that I hadn't used them in the show. And he insisted that I needed to sing straight, using my own voice. I took his advice—and it seems to have paid off pretty good.

I guess a dozen times over the next several years, every contact I had with Frank, he went out of his way to do something for me, to help me up. That's the kind of guy he is: a sweet, outgoing, bighearted soft touch who'll do anything—literally *anything*—to help a friend. I don't know how many times—and he wouldn't want it known if I did—he has quietly picked up the tab for some friend in the hospital, or some other tight spot. But you don't hear many of these stories, and that's part of the reason Frank's such a misunderstood man. You don't hear about the *real* Sinatra, the father and the friend; you only hear about the legendary Sinatra, the swinger, the idol, the king, with guys supposedly standing around biting their nails to please him. You don't hear about what a kind, gentle guy he is; you hear about how he's supposed to be so *rude* to people. I can say, honest to God, I've never seen him say or do anything rude to anybody. If there are people asking for his autograph—

and there always are—he signs, he's kind, he's courteous. Yet still he gets that bum rap. I've seen him order away guys trying to protect him from the autograph hounds and say, "Wait a minute, these are the people who make my career for me. Yes, of course, darling, it will be my pleasure." He ain't got to *take* no rudeness, though. He don't sit still for no stranger, drunk or not, coming up to him with a big "Hey, Frankie!" and a playful punch on the shoulder.

HALEY: *With Sinatra's help, you were just beginning to make it really big when you had the accident that cost you your eye. How did it happen?*

DAVIS: I was driving from Vegas to Los Angeles to do the sound track for *Six Bridges to Cross*. In Vegas, our act was playing the New Frontier—$7,500 a week, the most we'd ever made—and to celebrate, my dad and Will had just given me my first Cadillac convertible. Charley Head, my valet, was with me. He'd been driving, then I'd taken over. We were keeping her under 50 that first 500 miles, taking it easy: I wanted to break her in nice, you know? When I took over the wheel, I remember I turned on the radio, and I heard myself singing *Hey, There*. Talk about a gas feeling, man! Then up ahead after a while was this green car—women in it; I could see their hats. The driver was pulling left, then right, then she'd straddle the lanes. I didn't dig what was happening with her for sure, so I stayed to the far right. Then suddenly she started into this wide U-turn— and stopped broadside across both lanes. No room for me to go right. My only move was to try swinging around her into the oncoming lane. Started around, saw cars coming at me, hit my brakes, cut hard right—but I knew I couldn't stop in time to miss her. I cut for her rear fender, trying to miss a broadside where the passengers were. Then, this *crash*! Never will forget that sound; you don't know what it's like unless you've been in a car crash. I saw her car spinning around, and then my forehead hit the steering wheel.

Man, the *pain*! But I saw my hand moving, so I knew I was

still alive. Blood was running down my face. Charley was in the back seat moaning. I opened the door and got out to help him. I saw his jaw hanging all loose, blood running from his mouth. I had just gotten my arm around him, trying to help him out, when he looked up at my face, and he made this gargling sound. I reached up, feeling with my hand—and man, there was my eye, hanging by a string! I was trying to stuff it back in when I started sagging down, blacking out. I was on the ground praying. After all them hard years, our act was just starting to get somewhere. "God, please don't let me go blind. God, please don't take it all away now." And I heard a siren, and felt some movement; kept hearing the siren, and knew I was in an ambulance.

When I came to, I was in the hospital, and this doctor was standing beside my bed telling me very calmly that he'd removed my left eye. How do you take *that* news, baby? In that bed, my head wrapped up like a mummy, everything dark, I did a whole lot of thinking. I might have gone off the deep end if it hadn't been for that public. Stacks of letters! *Thousands* of them! So many flowers the florists ran out; couldn't even get them all in the hallway! The nurses were reading names off letters, and flowers, and Bibles, and all kinds of things—from everybody I ever knew in show business and out, and people I never heard of, white and black, all over America, even the deepest South. People sending me their prayers and best wishes. Man, that's one of the reasons you can't tell me the different races have to hate each other; I've seen too much of the *good* in people, white and black.

Then, finally, came the day when the doctor took off the bandages. When I saw that first gleam of light, baby, I was ready to jump up shouting! And then I saw the doctor and the nurse and my dad and Will Mastin all standing there at the foot of the bed, and I knew I wasn't finished. I had another chance.

HALEY: *Did you have much difficulty adjusting to monocular vision?*

DAVIS: It wasn't easy. For a while, right after the hospital, I'd reach for something and miss it by two, three inches. And the first time I tried dancing again, I kept kicking myself in the other leg and tripping. I knew I'd have to learn how to dance all over again. Wasn't nobody going to be saying, "He's *nearly* as good as before." I had to be *better*! But everything's pretty straight now. I'm still aware that I'm seeing with one eye; things look flatter to me than they do to you, and I've got a blind side that I have to keep aware of. But with this one eye, I see more now than you would if you closed one of your two good eyes. My field of vision has expanded to make up for the missing eye, like a wide-angle lens.

HALEY: *For a year or so after the accident, you wore a black eye patch. What made you decide to take it off?*
DAVIS: Humphrey Bogart convinced me to quit that. He asked me, "How long you gonna trade on that goddamn patch? How long are you gonna keep using it for a crutch? You want people calling you Sammy Davis or 'the kid with the eye patch'?" Well, you know, I'd had myself figured with a glamorous trademark, but what Bogart said kept on bugging me—especially knowing he was right—until one night in Vegas I took it off and threw the goddamn thing away. I don't need no pity, and I got nothing to hide.

HALEY: *It wasn't long after the accident that you converted to Judaism. Did one have anything to do with the other?*
DAVIS: In a strange way, yes. After one show I did with Eddie Cantor, he saw me looking at his mezuzah—that's a holy Hebrew charm for good luck, health and happiness—and he insisted on giving it to me. He told me that his religion had the basic belief that every man should have freedom to face God in his own way. Well, I wore that charm around my neck all the time from then on—until that day in my car, just before the accident, I missed it; I had left it in my hotel suite. If I had followed my impulse to go back and get it, I'd have both my eyes today—but I didn't.

Anyway, when the bandages were removed after my operation, I noticed a clear outline of the Star of David cut into the palm of my right hand. Then I remembered Tony Curtis and Janet Leigh walking alongside me as I was being wheeled to the operating room, and Janet pressing something into my hand, saying, "Hold tight, and pray, and everything will be all right." And I had clutched what she gave me so hard that it had cut into my flesh. It was kind of like a stigmata; it shook me.

Then one Christmas I read a history of the Jews, and it astonished me to see the affinity between Jews and the Negroes: their oppressions, their enslavements—despised, rejected, searching for a home, for equality and human dignity. For thousands of years, they had held onto their belief in themselves and in their right to a place in the sun. It got to me so much that I visited a rabbi, who gave me books to read. There were already a lot of Negroes converted to Judaism, but *my* talking about converting worried the rabbi, because it could so easily be taken by people as a publicity stunt. He insisted that I not rush into it just because I was filled up with what I'd read about Judaism. He told me that neither he nor anyone else could make me a Jew, that only I could do it.

Anyway, around this time, I was getting into deeper and deeper trouble—debts piling up into the hundreds of thousands; my performances weren't what they should have been, and all my high-lifing, until finally I tried suicide, as you know. I tried to race my car over a cliff, but right at the edge the drive shaft hit a rock and snapped, and the rear half of it jammed into the ground and held the car right there at the edge like an anchor. God had his arms around me. The hardest thinking session I've ever had was after that—until finally I said to God, as a Jew: "Here I am."

HALEY: *Do you observe all the rituals and holy days of your new faith?*
DAVIS: Well, in those orthodox terms, I couldn't rate myself the best Jew; but I'm certainly not the worst one, either. If it's pos-

sible, I'd say today I feel even more committed than when I converted. It took me a long time to really learn the truth about commitment, but finally I have, and it's one of the most beautiful things that ever happened to me.

HALEY: *It was only a few months after your much-publicized conversion that your name hit the headlines again, this time linking you romantically with Kim Novak. Were they true?*
DAVIS: Yeah, they were—but, ironically, not until *after* the first stories appeared about us, and maybe, in a sense, because of them. It all started so innocently. Tony Curtis asked me over to his house one night for a drink. He was having some people in. Kim Novak was there, and we were introduced. I doubt we exchanged 20 words. She was just one of the group. Well, the next day one of the columns carried an item: "Kim Novak's new sepia love interest will make her studio bosses turn lavender." I called Kim. She knew I'd had nothing to do with the item. She said, "Come on over and let's talk about it." She was cooking spaghetti and meatballs. I went over. She said her studio had called, wanting to know if she'd seen me, and when she said yes, they wanted to know how many times. When? Where? What was going on between us? It would have to stop! Well, like me, Kim just naturally rebelled against anybody making rules for her. And so we became conspirators, drawn together by defiance.

Well, from that point on, the press columns took it and ran. I mean, they made sure *everybody* found out about it—and they added a few trimmings of their own. Everybody I knew started advising me; and everybody *she* knew was telling her, "Don't wreck your career!" The scandal columns were running items that I'd been warned by Chicago gangsters if I ever saw "that blonde" again, both my legs would be broken and torn off at the knee. And the Negro press started riding me harder than ever. Stuff like: "Sammy Davis, Jr., once a pride to all Negroes, has become a never-ending source of embarrassment. Mr. Davis has never been particularly race-conscious, but his recent scandal displays him as inexcusably unconscious of his responsibility as a Negro." That kind of thing.

Meanwhile, I rented a beach house at Malibu so we could meet secretly, and I had a guy drive me there incognito, like in the spy stories. The press was so hot on it, we didn't know if they wouldn't have movie cameras hidden on the road, so I got to hiding on the car floor while we drove there. Well, one night down on that car floor, it hit me in the face: What the hell was I doing there, sneaking around in the middle of the night? I was just confirming what they were saying: "You're not good enough to be seen with a white woman." I got up off the floor, told the driver to turn around, and that was that—the end of it. I never saw her again. If only I'd known my heart troubles were just beginning.

HALEY: *You mean your first marriage?*
DAVIS: If you want to call it that.

HALEY: *Why didn't it work out?*
DAVIS: It was doomed from the start. You got to understand the shape I was in. Deep in debt, from all my high-lifing. Tax problems. Losing my eye. Then this Kim Novak thing down around my neck. For the first time in my life, I started drinking the hard stuff. I felt like a man being pulled down into quicksand, with mosquitoes buzzing around his head. I was taping my TV shows, and they were hollow. Then one night, after a show at the Sands, I got drunk in the lounge, then got in my car and drove over to the Silver Slipper. The show was letting out when I saw Loray White—a Negro girl, one of the dancers. Once we'd had a little thing going. We'd broken up when she couldn't play it for laughs. Well, I took another look at beautiful Loray, and the thought occurred to me that if I had a Negro wife, maybe the papers would get off my back. I was drunk, I proposed, and Loray accepted on the spot. It was unreal. Drunk, I pulled her up to the bandstand and I announced our engagement. The club's press agent brought a photogra-

pher. It was done. By morning, it was all over America. I wake up, my head's splitting, it's on the radio, front-paged in Vegas, long-distance calls from all over, telegrams pouring in. What had I done? But what could I *do?* All my career needed now— all Loray needed—was for me to back down.

Next time I saw her, she said, "You don't have to marry me, Sammy." "Yes, I do," I told her, and I explained why. She said OK. So we got married, and afterward there was a party in a West Side saloon. I drank like a fish. Finally we left in my car, a buddy of mine driving us. Well, something snapped inside me, and the next thing I know I've got my hands around Loray's neck trying to choke her—as if it was all her fault. When I realized what I was doing, I must have, like, gone into shock, 'cause my buddy had to carry me into the hotel, like a baby, up to the bridal suite. Loray was in hysterics; even *he* was crying. Man, it was a mess. Well, every paper in the country smelled it was phony, and all kinds of rumors started. I began to draw bigger crowds than ever—but for the wrong reasons. To the public, I wasn't a performer anymore; I was a geek, a side show. I was close to the bottom, professionally and emotionally. Well, of course, Loray and I got divorced. It's not a pretty story. I'm not proud of it.

HALEY: *Two years later you met May Britt in Hollywood, and three months after that you announced your engagement, precipitating a storm of protest and hate mail from whites and Negroes throughout the country. Did you expect that kind of reaction?*

DAVIS: Well, I didn't think it would win me any popularity contests, but I didn't expect such a flood of venom. As long as I've lived with prejudice, I'm incredulous every time it hits me in the face—and this time it just floored me. Threats. Obscenities. Ravings. I've never seen anything as sick, as vitriolic as some of the letters I received. Things like: "Dear Nigger Bastard, I see Frank Sinatra is going to be the best man at your abortion. Well, it's good to know the kind of people supporting Kennedy before it's too late." When I played the Geary Theater in San Francisco that month, there were threats to bomb it, and letters, including one with a bullet drawn on it and the heartwarming message: "Guess when I'm going to shoot you during your show?" Man, how would you like to perform, wondering which burst of audience applause will help to cover the sound of a gunshot? When I played the Lotus Club in Washington, the Nazis were picketing me—carrying signs like "Go back to the Congo, you kosher coon." And a black dog wearing a swastika, with a sign on his back, "I'm black, too, Sammy, but I'm not a Jew." It makes you ashamed that a country like America has to be tainted with people like these. But when I walked on stage in the club, the audience in a body stood up, calling to me, "The hell with 'em, Sammy. We're with you." The world is 98 percent filled with *nice* people, see? It's only the other two percent who are idiots.

HALEY: *As you know, there was a widespread feeling among both whites and Negroes that you were marrying May in order to gain status in white society.*
DAVIS: Yeah, I know. It's a sad commentary that so many people's minds would jump to that conclusion about me. Even if they think I'm low enough to do something like that, they should give me credit for not being stupid. If I had been thinking about improving my status in the white world, baby, the *last* thing I'd do is marry a white girl. Don't take no genius to figure that out. I stood to *lose* whatever status I had, not gain. I got a sneak preview of that right after we announced our engagement: Friends started dropping off rapidly, both hers and mine, and suddenly they were nowhere to be found—and we're not looking for them. That's why I feel bound by hoops of steel to those who proved tried and true when the chips were down, who were risking a lot themselves, in the convictions they exhibited. You know? Like Frank—standing up with me, being my best man. Pat Kennedy, coming to my party, and Peter Lawford, then the President's brother-in-law, and others that I

haven't mentioned. They *knew*, and they risked a lot to prove their friendship.

For the information of those who may not have been able to figure out yet why I *did* marry May—despite everything we knew we were letting ourselves in for—it was love, sweet love, baby. How corny can you get, right? Well, I didn't care whether she was white, black, blue, green or polka dot—I *loved* her. And, miracle of miracles, she loved *me*. It was as simple as that. Well, maybe not quite that simple, because I kept asking myself *why* I loved her; I had to know, because it had to be for the right reasons. Well, I mulled it over a lot, and finally I realized it was because May, as my wife, in just being the kind of human being she is, would help me to make a better human being of myself; and that's just the way it's turned out. I'm not a new man or anything, but gradually, and in some ways rapidly, I'm getting to be a better person. She understands my drives, my needs, my frustrations, and she bends to them. She has been patient enough to let me develop in my own time and in my own way. And our love has been deepened and broadened by the things that we've had to face and to fight together—and I don't mean just the special problems of an interracial marriage.

HALEY: *How have you faced the problem of adjusting your marriage to the demands of your work schedule? In the two weeks we've been following you around, you haven't had time even for a visit with your wife and children—except on the phone—let alone for a night at home. Certainly that's not a satisfactory arrangement.*
DAVIS: Of course not. Even though May joins me on the road during the longer engagements, we're not together nearly enough, and I don't spend as much time at home as I wish I could. But at this point I've got no choice—and this is another area of her understanding. After the debts I piled up before my marriage, this is the first year I've been on my own financially. She understands that I need about two more years of this kind of working before I can *afford* to stay home more.

HALEY: *You've already collapsed once because of the pace. How much longer do you think you can keep it up?*
DAVIS: God willing, as long as I have to. I was told two years ago in this very room that I'd never sing again, that there were nodes at the bottom of my throat, and three specialists were going to strip my vocal cords, they were in such terrible shape from overwork. But I stuck by my guns, and I'm still singing today. So I think I'll be able to hold out long enough to get where I want to go professionally.

HALEY: *Where do you want to go?*
DAVIS: I'd like to work my way up to the class of the Duke, or Durante; they're so well established it doesn't matter whether they've got a show on or a movie running. They're liked, they're accepted, they're respected. But when you've devoted as many years to show business as I have, you know that it could all evaporate overnight, no matter how big you are. Things are really swinging for me now, but I can't help thinking that I might wake up some morning and find myself out of vogue, kaput, the way Frank did when the bobby-sox craze died out. He made a comeback; but I might not be so lucky.

You know what else haunts me? The thought of dying before I finish what I have to do. Like a few weeks ago: I'm in a plane, and Murphy is sitting next to me, and things have been going tremendously, and suddenly this cold feeling comes over me and I say to Murphy, "I'm going to die, because things are going too well. I'm going to die and I'll never finish it." If I can legitimately make the mark that I want to make as a human being and a performer, I'll be willing to go then. But I'm still hungry. I need more time. I need at least another good ten years in the business to try and create what I want to create.

HALEY: *And what's that?*
DAVIS: I want *two* kinds of success: One, I want to build—for myself and my family—an organization of enterprises and investments such as has made millionaires of some of my close friends. Like Frank. And to make all my own decisions. Frank

don't let *nobody* tell him what to do. The other kind of success I want is as a human being. That don't have nothing to do with making money. Some friends I've got—visit their house, they ain't got this, ain't got that, have to borrow dishes, all that jazz, but I got to envy how successful they are as human beings. Before I die, I want to be able to know that I gave my full share of the blood, sweat and tears that millions of both white and black people have got to give to win freedom for their kids and mine. Whenever death comes, I'll consider my life's been full and fruitful if I can get these things accomplished.

HALEY: *One more question, Sammy: If you could choose an epitaph for yourself, how would it read?*
DAVIS: That's easy: "It's been a gas."

—*December 1966*

"THE MANY LIVES OF SAMMY DAVIS,"
by Bob Lucas, *Sepia*

"I ain't running for President of the United States. I ain't running for Black of the Month, or Colored of the Month or Nigger of the Month! I'm trying to help my people in the best way I know how, working under the conditions I can function with.

"I can't stand on the corner and be a radical, because when they need somebody who can get on the 'Tonight Show' for a cause—for Angela, or this one or that one, or for the cause of my people's dignity—then I've got to have that avenue open. There ain't that many of us, unfortunately, who can do it."

Sammy Davis was not on a soapbox, nor was he giving a performance. He was seated at the table, relaxing after a steak dinner and continuing a rap session that began a few days earlier on a motion picture set. To one who has interviewed the most phenomenal entertainer in show business many times in many different places, this particular conversation was remarkable in many ways.

For openers, his deep sincerity overshadowed the humorous

images he employed. As many educated people do, he often deliberately lapses into ungrammatical speech to emphasize the point he is making. Though he is largely self-taught, Sammy's normal pattern of speech is flawless, and his vast vocabulary reveals he is an omnivorous reader.

Sammy has never been known for his lack of confidence—he's often described as "cocky"—but at this point in his life he is so positive he's got it all together he makes no apologies for his beliefs. "I really don't care whether white, black, blue or gray understands them," he declared, "I understand them."

Exactly what those beliefs are was the purpose of our chat with Sammy, first on location during the filming of "The Trackers," an ABC-TV Movie of the Week, and later at his new home in Beverly Hills.

In a sense, he summed it all up in his attitude today in confrontation with life, his own and the world around him: "Money don't make you free. Popularity don't make you free. Sure I live in Beverly Hills, but I'm shackled by the same things that happened to the brother in Watts.

"It's like when a brother comes up to me and says, 'Man, you're a Jew.'

"I look at him and say, 'What's your religion?' and he says, 'I'm a Baptist,' or 'I don't have one,' or 'I'm a Muslim.'

"I say, 'Well, our religion is blackness.' Our real religion and the thing that connects us all is our blackness. The religion of blackness, that's it."

Sammy's single-minded approach to life these days comes after years of self-conflict and doubt, of seeking to find himself in a confusing world in which he, himself, led many lives—the entertainer, the civil rights champion, the black Jew, the Hollywood star, a member of "The Clan," the bon vivant, ad infinitum . . . a variety of roles as divergent as has been played by any movie actor.

"Some people think Sammy Davis has a God complex," wrote a New York newsman some years back, then added, "but this is absurd. On the seventh day, Davis works."

Watching Sammy has always been a problem. Everyone always wonders what he can do for an encore to top the fantastic performance he always gives. What can he possibly do next?

To find out, we cornered Sammy after he finished "The Trackers," which marks another high point in a fabulous career that has been jam-packed with peaks.

The television film is a western in which he stars along with Ernest Borgnine. Sammy and Aaron Spelling are co-producers of the film that will be aired this coming season, and Sammy thus becomes the first black producer of a motion picture for television. His delight at chalking up yet another "first" was clearly evident.

Our visit with Sammy was remarkable in other ways. He has sometimes been compared to the peripatetic hero of the Budd Schulberg novel, "What Makes Sammy Run?" That's why Hollywood skeptics scoffed at the recent announcement by the diminutive dynamo that he was slowing down.

But it is a fact that Sammy Davis is taking it easier these days, but not when he is on a stage performing, or plunging through a chilly lake for a movie sequence, or directing the operations of his multi-faceted Trace-Mark Production Company. However, his concert and night club appearances have been sharply curtailed; the movie producer's chair proved so comfortable and creatively satisfying, Sammy plans to occupy it more frequently.

He has moved from the plush Ambassador Hotel into the newly-furnished mansion he bought for his wife, Altovise. Home life seems to agree with the superstar who was almost literally born in a theatrical trunk 45 years ago.

Mrs. Davis, her long, shapely dancer's legs appearing even longer and shapelier in a pair of bright red hot pants, discussed the final touches to be made in decorating the house. Sammy leaned back and remarked how pleasant it was not to have to rush off somewhere, as in times past. He strolled from one wing of the house to the other, no trace of the old "let's get the show on the road!" urgency in his movements. He seemed to be

savoring his role as lord of the manor as he inspected the projection room at the rear of the huge sunken living room,
checked the saloon-sized bar, approved his wife's placement of
a Charles White drawing.

There are those who credit Mrs. Davis with helping Sammy
come to terms with himself, and of somehow getting him to
better channel the seemingly limitless amounts of energy he formerly squandered. To an outsider, they certainly appear to be a
perfectly matched pair. Her name is pronounced Alta-veese,
she's in her 20's, and she is obviously tuned to Sammy's moods
and geared to match any pace he sets. The Davises hold hands
in public, sometimes indulge in discreet smooching, and Sammy
still introduces Altovise as "my bride," although they were
married May 12, 1970.

His tour of inspection finished, Sammy settled down and we
mentioned the recent NET show, "Black Journal," on which he
appeared. "You said a lot of things on that show that surprised
some people."

"But you've seen me, listened to me over the years," Sammy
said. "It never varies. As I said on that show, I do jokes, but
somewhere along the line I've got to relate to what's really happening."

Sammy is the first to admit he had a long row to hoe and
heavy dues to pay before he arrived where he is today. Time
was, many headlines ago, when he was a charter member of the
Hollywood Clan, that ring-a-ding group of entertainers, whose
leader was Frank Sinatra. (Sinatra and Davis are still close.
When the Chairman of the Board announced he was quitting
show business not long ago, Sammy sent him a wire: "Since
you retired, I'm singing better!")

The Clan's "thing" was fun and games: their playground
ranged from Hollywood to Palm Springs and Las Vegas. But
eventually the members went their separate ways, turning their
backs on the casual pursuit of babes, booze and bellylaughs.

By the time Sammy arrived in New York, in the spring of 1964, to begin rehearsals for his Broadway musical, "Golden Boy," he was a new recruit in the civil rights movement. "A few years ago I couldn't have cared less," he admitted at the time, "but now I care." Davis has for years freely donated time, energy and funds to all manner of humanitarian causes. But he realized there was now a greater demand on him.

"The contribution you make is not in terms of how much money you give to the cause, but in terms of what commitment you make to it," he said of the civil rights movement.

At that time in New York a group of black actors, writers and creative artists was deeply involved in the black liberation movement, both intellectually and actively. Among them were actors Sidney Poitier and Harry Belafonte, novelist James Baldwin, and the husband-wife acting team, Ruby Dee and Ossie Davis, plus several less well-known artists. Before her untimely death, playwright Lorraine Hansberry was one of the most active and articulate members of this informal association.

A year later in his dressing room backstage at the Majestic Theater, where "Golden Boy" was playing, Sammy Davis confided to us, "I sat down with these guys—with Harry and Sidney, Ossie and Ruby—and I asked them, 'What can I do?' They told me frankly they didn't have all the answers, but at least they're doing something."

Sammy himself began to do something. On one occasion he canceled a performance of "Golden Boy" in order to participate in the Selma-Montgomery march. When one woman theater-goer wrote to the New York Times objecting to the cancellation, the newspaper printed Davis' reply, which said in part:

"If any visitors were upset over my missing a performance, I have not been made aware of it. If they were, then I leave them with one thought—humbly, what matter if a man gains all the world and loses his soul?"

Sammy discovered he had as much soul as any other black man, and over the years his commitment grew until he worked out the philosophy by which he lives. It is intensely personal, forged in the racism he suffered in the U.S. Army, reinforced by the discrimination he had to overcome as he climbed the ladder of success, and yet tempered by the help and kindness he received from people of all races.

The Sammy Davis of today refuses to be intimidated by the extremists who advocate violent tactics and call for a black-white confrontation. On "Black Journal," typically, he resorted to humor to make a serious point: "You know, there ain't no way that you can put four Cadillacs against a tank; two rusty razors, you know, against an M-1; and a flame thrower against a bottle of Coca-Cola with a rag in it!"

He said: "When it gets right down to the nitty gritty, it's like trying to compare the NAACP, for instance, with CORE, SNCC, SDS, or whatever. You still need somebody who can walk in and do the number and deal with the man—when I say, man, I'm not speaking about whitey. I'm talking about the system, and we cannot defeat the system. We can hope to tame the system, change the system, but beat the system—never!

"So you better have some people who can deal with the system. Instead of having isolated heroes, we'd better be looking forward to trying to find 15 more Julian Bonds, you know? We need this kind of approach, as well as the cat on the corner, because we're all fighting for the same thing. That's why I say I'm not running for Black of the Month. I hate them kind of cats who do that, because you're not doing it for that reason, but for the overall good.

"We put too much emphasis on why we're trying to do something. A Jew from Israel, an Israelite, does not ask an American Jew, 'Why did you give me two million dollars?' He takes the two million dollars and does his number with it. It's time for black people to realize that we all can't be Ralph Bunche, we all can't be Malcolm X . . . name the list all the way down.

"But as a unified people, we can say, 'You're contributing as a black writer, as a black actor, as a black this, a black that.'

We can ask, 'Where is his head? Is he doing something constructive toward the overall good?' Because if all of us are out
on the corner, there'll be nobody there in the political arena,
there'll be nobody fighting in the other arenas."

Undoubtedly, it was Sammy's comments on Angela Davis that
triggered the most reaction—pro and con. Producer Tony
Brown asked him on "Black Journal" about the "Free Angela"
button he was wearing. "I don't share her political beliefs, I
share her blackness," Davis replied, "and I share the injustice
to any black person.

"I think she needs support both financially and morally, and
I think that if a guy like myself wears a button, that's letting
somebody in that crowd I go around with know where my
head's at."

Sammy pointed out that although the situation has changed
since the early days of civil rights struggle, his attitude "hasn't
changed from being concerned enough to go to Mississippi to
fight for my people's rights.

"What has happened is that as a popular black performer, I
get on television and talk about Angela Davis and the injustice
to Angela, then I'll talk about Rap [Brown] or talk about this
one or that one, the people other black—and white—performers shy away from.

"Somehow, if after doing all that, going through those
changes, I have to defend my position to some cat on the corner
who thinks he's doing something—and maybe he is . . ." Davis
paused and shook his head in a gesture of futility.

Then he smiled. "But the true brothers, whether they be
bourgeois, militant or radical, come to me and I deal with them
on a one-to-one basis, and they make me feel as if I belong. Because they all say, 'Sam, we know where your head is. Do your
number the way you gotta do it, because you help us.' "

Sammy Davis summed it all up: "I have no desire to be anything but what I am. My desire revs up only in terms of what

my contribution is to be. I've got more black people working. I've got more writers going in . . . that's my bag. Also to champion a cause, so we can get on the air and intelligently discuss and reach people who are not well aware.

"You know, I don't need no cat on the corner to tell me, 'You ain't no better off than I am.' I know that! And as he goes, I go. What I gotta do is let a white cat sitting in Orange County know that. I got to let him know there's black unity in Watts—and it's not only Watts, it's a block to block thing.

"The money—that's the easiest part of it. To give your talent for a benefit, the easiest part of it. But the hard part is to go to work in an honest way with brothers who are trying to do something. Also, somebody's got to get the money from the liberal whites, those the extreme radicals won't accept money from.

"Now if I can be a clearing house for that . . . if a brother says, 'I got some black children I gotta feed. I need 10 thousand dollars,' I don't care where the money comes from so long as those black children are fed. But the brother ain't gonna go because of his beliefs, he feels he can't face it, can't rap honestly with the man with the money . . . well, I respect that.

"But I can do it. And have done it. And will continue to do it!"

—*August 1971*

"THE FRANK SINATRA I KNOW,"
by Sammy Davis, Jr., *Down Beat*

I first met Frank in the early '40s, about three months before he left Tommy Dorsey to go out as a single. The band was playing Detroit, and a unit called Tip, Tap, and Toe was to open with them, but the unit was hung up in Canada. So they put us in for three days on the same bill as the band.

My first impressions of him were that he was a very nice warm guy, but I was close to Buddy Rich then because I wanted to learn drums. One thing I do remember is that Frank had the lapels taken off one of his jackets because he couldn't afford a cardigan.

We next met in 1945. I'd just gotten out of the army. He was doing the *Old Gold* and *The Hit Parade* shows from Hollywood at the time. I stood for tickets in the servicemen's line with my uniform on. I went backstage. He came out the stage door, and they rushed him to a car, and I yelled, "Hi, Frank."

I went two weeks in a row, and one day I caught him going into a rehearsal and asked him to sign my book. "You've been here a couple of weeks," he said. Seeing my discharge emblem, he asked why I wore the uniform in line, and I told him it was because I couldn't get tickets otherwise. Frank turned to one of his men and said, "See that there are tickets there for Sam from now on."

My dad, uncle, and I were laying off around this time so I used to go to both of his shows every week. I came to be known as the kid who hung around Frank. Frank was an inquisitive guy if he liked you, and he'd do little considerate things like once at the beginning of a rehearsal asking me if I wanted some coffee. I said, "Yuh," shaking a little and with my palms sweating.

"You're in show business?" he asked.

"Yeah."

"You work with your uncle and father?" And he asked about our act and what we were doing.

I didn't see him for a year and when we met, he said he was going into the Capitol Theater. I told him it would be great for us to get that kind of date. He said "Yuh." Without our knowing it, he went on to pitch us to Sid Piermont, head of Loew's booking agency. Sidney didn't know who we were, and by this time, we'd left town. All he knew was that I was a kid named Sam with a father and an uncle. He finally found us through AGVA.

We were a $300-a-week act then. "We can save on the budget," Sid told Frank.

"No," said Sinatra, "give them $1,000."

"But we can get the Nicholas Brothers for that."

"No," said Frank, "I want the kid."

That was our first major break. At that time I was doing just a six-minute hoofing act. Frank had a Thanksgiving party at the Capitol where I got up and sang. He told me I had a good voice and should sing. "You sound too much like me, but you should sing," is what he said.

After that, we became very close. I used to go to his home in California, and he'd ask how my career was going. I'd see him about once in every six months. This was in the late '40s and early '50s. I was getting a hold in the business. Every time I saw him it was a real breath of spring. No matter which of his own troubles and problems he was involved with then, he always had time to talk to me about my career. He'd advise me what to do and whom to watch out for.

Frank next saw our act in 1952, the act with the impressions, etc., in it, and he flipped. "This is it," he said. "Now why don't you make records?"

"I have no style of my own," I said.

"Find one."

"Well, they tell me I sound too much like you."

"Well," said Frank, "that's not the worst thing in the world. You could sound like Dick Todd. But sing more of yourself and go for yourself. One day you'll get your future together."

Our friendship has progressed beautifully since then as we've become more and more close. After my accident, for example, he had me at his home in Palm Springs recuperating for two weeks. Our friendship now is at the point where we expect nothing of each other except the friendship itself. He's likely to call up in the middle of the night, as he did once, and claim to be the house detective.

Frank is also the man for whom I'm starting my film career. My first picture will be *The Jazz Train* for his own company. It'll start in the spring. The show has been a very popular one in England. Frank will play an army captain, and I'll be his buddy. Don Maguire, who directed Frank's *Johnny Concho*, will direct *The Jazz Train*, too.

Another film project Frank has asked me to do with him is *The Harold Arlen Story*, to be produced by Sol Siegel for MGM. The title probably will be changed to one of Arlen's hits. I'll be the guy, a college friend of Arlen, who first takes him to the Cotton Club in Harlem and introduces him to the blues and blues-influenced music. My role then calls for me to go to work at the Cotton Club as a sort of composite of Cab Calloway and Bill Robinson, and Arlen will be depicted as writing material for me.

About *The Jazz Train*, Sinatra got me a lot of loot for the film, plus 25 percent of the picture. He personally made the deal for me, and that's just another indication of his generosity.

Another sign of the kind of guy Frank is that he didn't send a wire on our Broadway opening night of *Mr. Wonderful*. Instead he had sent a wire from Spain on the night we had the run-through. And two days after the opening, he called me.

"How did it go?" he asked. "I didn't send an opening-night wire. I knew it was going to be great." Frank was disturbed at the way the critics had reacted, but he was glad I was going to stick with it. "If the people like it, you're in business," he said.

Frank is the type of man every guy from a truck driver to a Hollywood producer would be proud to call "my friend." And it's not because of his position. It would be the same thing if he were a cabbie. The man stands for everything that is good in a human being and like a human being, he makes mistakes. But he never really hurt anyone else, only himself. Sure, he's made a lot of mistakes. But there's only been one perfect being. Frank oughtn't to be condemned for having made mistakes.

I'm very proud to be considered a friend of this man. He has ways of doing things that are unbelievable. Like when *Confidential* came out with its story on me. Disneyland opened about the same time. I went to the Disneyland opening with Frank and his three kids. Millions of people saw it on television. That was his way of refuting *Confidential* without ever mentioning it.

Sinatra the singer: His is the essence of vocal style. This man has an innate quality of knowing what is good musically. I guess you can sum that up best by saying that he has musical integrity. If you remember, even in the Columbia days, Frank has always surrounded himself with guys whose musical tastes were great. Like Axel Stordahl. Even when he did a bad song, there was a particularly good quality in the presentation.

Frank is now in an enviable position—he can record whatever he wants, and he makes a lot of records. As for being influenced by him, as one guy said, "It's good sense to sound like Sinatra because he sounds better than any other singer."

Another thing about Frank is that you can listen to him all night, and he never tires your ears. That's why he's so successful an album seller.

I have a complete collection of Sinatra. On the coast when we get together, I take a Dorsey record from the '40s and contrast it with one of his current releases. Even then you can see the beginning of what he has now.

He's painstaking about his recordings. Nelson Riddle doesn't write a note that Frank doesn't eventually change one way or another. He'll do 20 takes if he feels it isn't the way he wants it. He'll stay all day to get *one* ready. There was a session for *Wee Small Hours*. It was 3 a.m., and he was still going over certain things, listening to the playback, and shaking his head, saying, "No."

He was there until dawn until he got what he wanted. He hears the smallest detail. It's not that he doesn't trust Riddle, but there are certain things he wants done his way. It was Frank, incidentally, who selected Nelson for his dates. Riddle had always been sort of a free-lance artist. Nelson started doing things for Nat Cole, and Frank heard them. That's the way I think it happened.

Frank very rarely discusses his own singing, but he's ready, willing, and able to tell you about other singers.

As for whether Frank is a jazz singer, he certainly has a feeling for jazz. Remember the swinging thing he did for Dorsey, *Oh, Look at Me Now* and all the others since? Look, if I were to be around Laurence Olivier and John Gielgud for 30 years, some Shakespearean knowledge would have to rub off on me if I were a good student and listener. Now Frank was with James and Dorsey in the years when they had bands that had jazz soloists and a jazz feel, and it would be impossible for a lot of that not to have rubbed off.

Buddy Rich, for example, was an influence. Of course, he was also a target once, too. Frank didn't like the way Buddy would beat the drums sometimes when he was singing. Once in Detroit Frank was singing *This Love of Mine*, and Buddy was talking in the back of the bandstand. "Sh-sh-sh," went Frank.

"What did he go 'sh' about?" asked Rich.

Dorsey said at this point, "Keep it quiet, Buddy."

So Rich paradiddled instead. Frank went into the wings and from there on to the back of the stand, and he knocked Buddy off the drums. But they're very good friends now, and it was Frank who financed Buddy's first band.

So to sum up Frank as a singer, I would say Frank has the musical integrity to do what he feels like doing, and he does it all so very well that he's the musical end.

—August 22, 1956

"SAMMY DAVIS, JR., STARS IN *STOP THE WORLD, I WANT TO GET OFF*—BUT HE DOESN'T,"
by Linda Witt, *People Weekly*

Why are you returning to Broadway?
I have learned to respect that street. Last time in 1964, during *Golden Boy*, I was trying to prove so many things simultaneously. I was doing movies and TV too. Nobody can do it all at once. It helped destroy my marriage to May. The boogeying and booze didn't help the marriage much either.

Is this time around different?
I don't feel like I did before—like an interloper. I'm no longer the swinger, the fun cat, the guy who's doing Broadway as a giggle. I saw *A Chorus Line* so often I was practically the mascot. None of the shows I saw was making as much money as I make in Vegas, but every time I went I said, "I got to get back to the theater."

Is there anything you haven't done you want to do?
Yeah. Get a high school diploma. I mean it. I never was inside a school, so I couldn't even drop out. I didn't learn to read until I was practically a teenager. A black [sic] sergeant named Williams in the Army took me aside and told me about the classics. Up till then I'd been reading comic books. He turned me on to *The Three Musketeers* and gave me a dictionary—and the world.

You were in the Army during World War II when it was segregated. Are you bitter?
The bile goes away, but I don't think the bitterness ever disappears entirely. You must remember that I had always lived in the close-knit world of show business. In the '30s and '40s there was enough prejudice just against show people. We hung together.

What was the Army like?
It was horrible and very, very frightening. I couldn't have a white buddy, and I'd always had white buddies. It was at least a year before I saw a black officer. You'd never see us black cats in those patriotic war movies, but, man, we was in the Army, we was fighting the war.

Did you get in any trouble?
I got my nose broken. Somebody said, "Hey, nigger, stand in the back of the chow line." That was the second time it was broken, out of maybe five times. It was a guy bigger than me,

babe. It wouldn't be a guy my size. There aren't many guys my size! But I knew how to fight. My dad and my friend Sugar Ray Robinson taught me. Everybody told me, "Just stay in your place. You can't change the world." But I kept saying, "I don't want to change the world. I'd just like to change my part of it."

What about after the war?
That was tough, too. In those days the colored acts were the last hired and the first fired. Thank God for people like Frank Sinatra and Mickey Rooney. They said, "Hey, don't cut that act."

How did you meet Sinatra?
Once, before I went into the Army, my dad, Will Mastin and I had been his opening act in Detroit. He was still the boy singer, part of the Pied Pipers with Tommy Dorsey. When I came out of the Army, I started going to the Hollywood Canteen, and one day Sinatra noticed me and asked, "What's your name again? Sammy? Well, I'm going to call you Charley." I asked why, and he said, " 'Cause Charley's easier to remember." In 1947, when he played the Capitol Theater in New York, Sinatra said, "Get that colored dance act, that colored kid who dances with his relatives." I don't know how they found us, but they did. When he'd introduce us, he'd say, "I want you to watch the little kid in the middle—he's going to be a star." Later he and Jack Benny and Danny Kaye went to bat for me to be Sportin' Life in *Porgy and Bess*. Frank almost literally adopted me—and from that came movies like *Ocean's Eleven* and *Sergeants 3*.

Was this the start of the Rat Pack?
Actually, Bogart started that name. In those days teens hung out in "rat packs," and Bogie said, "We're the rat pack of Beverly Hills." At a recent charity show, Dean Martin and Frank and I all walked out on a stage together and, man, it was magic. We still care about each other.

Because of the rumors about Sinatra and Vegas, some people link you to the Mafia. Are you personally close to gangsters?
Look, I'm no Goody Two-shoes. I wasn't born yesterday. I know those guys don't work for IBM. I've been up against Senate committees twice, and what I always say is, if a man is a friend of mine, he's a friend of mine. I'm at a point in my career where there's nothing they can offer me, so whether somebody is "one of the boys" or not is irrelevant.

What about the rumors that the Mob forced you to stop dating Kim Novak back in the 1950s?
Those rumors weren't true. The reason Kim and I broke up wasn't the gang—it was the era. Our relationship was just bringing too much anguish. If it had only been a sordid affair, if we'd hidden and jumped into some grubby hotel bed, it would have been okay. But for a black man and a white woman to be open about love was unacceptable.

Did that relationship make it easier for you to marry May Britt?
Yes, but we had our problems too. We were picketed and we really got it from the crazies. But Frank was the best man, and our friends stood by us. It's crazy. Ain't nobody in his right mind going to create a relationship on a whim just to raise eyebrows—even in 1978. It's still hard between a black and a white.

Are you happy with your image?
That's one reason I like being in a play—I find it difficult to live with "the image." Not that I don't like Sammy Davis, Jr., but it's nice to get onstage and not be him. To take off all the brassiness and jewelry for a while.

Why do you wear so much jewelry?
It's a giggle, or it was. Now it's just part of me. And it's caused some odd moments. One guy—kind of limp-wristed—came up and said, "Isn't it about time you came out of the closet?"

What was your reaction?
I wanted to say all the wrong things like, "Some of my best friends are . . ." The truth is I'm not a homosexual, but I'm not ashamed to say I had a homosexual experience. And it was like drugs, which I've tried too. You make a choice. I was in the Army. I was 17, and I was little. A friend once warned me, "Hey, Sammy, don't ever do anything that'd get you busted. Little cats don't make it past the front door in prison." I didn't know what he meant. I learned in the Army.

Do you regret hugging Richard Nixon at the 1972 Republican Convention?
If the situation were the same, I would be motivated to do it again. How can you regret what was an honest expression? I hugged him for saying, "You cannot buy Sammy Davis' support," but in many people's eyes I became the President's lackey.

How do you feel about Nixon today?
A mixture of sadness and still a lot of respect. I was for Richard Nixon, because I thought he could do some good things, and I think he did.

What are your current politics?
Still the same—the man, not the party. There's nobody I'm about to root for now. As for President Carter and human rights, what Andy Young has said about political prisoners in this country we've all known for years. I think maybe first Carter ought to take care of our human rights problems here at home—the blacks, the American Indians, the poor whites in the South.

What about your own opulent life-style?
My family was on relief until 1954, but now any man who doesn't want to live like me is crazy. It's not the excess—it's the pleasantries.

Are there times in your life you wish you could relive?
Emphatically no. I do wish I could wipe out some of the pain I caused good friends. But would I be where I am today if I hadn't gone through the drugs, the booze, the women?

Will you ever retire?
Do you mean el quitto mundo? No, but I gradually want to slow down. I'm not yet at a point where I feel I've got it made, and there are still some things I want to say as a performer. I still get *shpilkes*—Yiddish for bubbles in the stomach—and maybe that works for me. The fear that when I walk out on that stage tonight I might fall on my ass is what gives me that something extra I need.

Are you going to behave this time on Broadway?
I won't be at Studio 54 boogeying every night. But the night I close I'm going to have the biggest party in New York there. But, hey, what am I saying, wouldn't it be funny if that guy wouldn't let me in?

—August 28, 1978

"SPOOKS,"
from *Hollywood in a Suitcase,* by **Sammy Davis, Jr.**

On the night I saw my first movie we were playing somewhere in downtown Chicago. The Will Mastin Trio did four acts a day, and it was midwinter. As usual, the Chicago winds were howling across the lake. It was an old and eerie theater, very typical of the vaudeville of the period. Between acts Uncle and Dad could rely on three shots of whiskey to keep warm. I just had to keep moving.

I was the most pint-sized, wide-eyed kid you ever saw. I never did grow too much, but in those days my size added to the act because the people thought it was cute. Onstage I danced my feet off, so there was no trouble keeping warm. But between acts I had to hang around the theater, mainly in the dressing room, trying to amuse myself. I guess I was lonely enough sometimes, although, as usual when you try to think back, I can remember only the good times.

I can recall that night as if it were yesterday. It was early evening, and my dad was going out for a couple of hours. Probably for a drink, but he might have found a game someplace. Before he left, he gave me a warning, and I noted a mood of seriousness: "Now don't you let me catch you going downstairs to see these moving pictures things. You stay right here. They're for grownups, you hear me. If I catch you down there, I'll whip your hide."

Papa then gave me a wink and closed the door softly behind him. I sat for a few minutes in a state of some bewilderment. The concept of moving pictures was completely beyond my understanding. The only actual pictures I'd seen were in cheap comics Dad sometimes bought me. It seemed absurd, yet fascinating to me that pictures like that could "move."

When Papa told me I mustn't go near them, of course it fanned my curiosity. I began to feel a strange compulsion to disobey him. The old man could be awesome when he got angry, and he had a strong right arm. I'd known his wrath more than a few times, and some stinging lessons on my backside had taught me not to provoke him if I could help it. But I realized he'd be away for an hour or two, and I knew the theater inside out. I quickly planned a clandestine route down to the stage. I gave him a few minutes to get clear of the building and peeked out the dressing-room door. There were a couple of guys hanging around, but they wouldn't stop me. They had no reason. The fact that I was being bad gave me the old exciting feeling in the belly that only fear can bring.

I slipped down the backstairs, running my hand along the grimy walls, and through the seedy area where the props were kept. I kept in the shadows and dodged into the security of the heavy black curtains on the side of the stage. The film had started, and images were already flickering over a huge sheet temporarily placed right where my family and I had done our act. I was just five years old.

At first I was merely full of curiosity, and I clutched the curtain because I feared discovery. I'd already worked out an escape route back again, just in case, but I snuggled into the folds of the curtain, fairly sure I could remain unseen.

Because of what Dad had said, and because I knew it would have to be something special and new, I thought I was ready for anything. But I was not prepared for what did unfold.

There on the screen was a nightmare which kept me riveted to the spot for the next eighty-five minutes. I had chanced upon the original Bela Lugosi *Dracula* for my initiation into movieland, and it held me immediately with so much fear that I could not move. My spine tingled, and the muscles in the back of my neck started making my head shake. My mouth opened even wider than my eyes, and my body shook uncontrollably.

Every shadow and cobweb in that dusty, cold theater seemed to become part of the unfolding drama. Years before CinemaScope came along I knew what it was like to be surrounded, literally, by the screen. As doors creaked on celluloid, wind whistled through the backstage props. The fiendish fangs of that dreadful Count gleamed amid the hanging ropes and dark lights of my hitherto-innocent vaudeville life. I stayed to the end of the film only because I would have fainted if I had moved.

As the lights went up, I quickly scampered upstairs. Dad had not yet returned, but when he did a few minutes later he knew immediately I had disobeyed him. He took one look at his tiny son, cowed, trembling, eyes nearly popping out of his head, and guessed where I had been. I was in such a state of shock that he thought I had been punished enough. He roared with laughter and gave me a little hug. "That'll teach you," he said, and, still snickering, began to change for the next act. Soon after, Uncle Will came in and joined the frivolity. Dad told me he had forbidden me because when he saw the film, he'd been scared to death himself.

I had been on the road with the trio for two years already. That was half a century ago. Since then I've probably spent a third of my waking life watching movies. My father had been completely wrong about one thing. *Dracula* was no punishment. I reveled in the utter fascination of it all. The film had been the greatest single discovery of my youth, a youth filled with a thousand exciting memories.

Dracula played two or three times every day, and I watched all the performances until the end of our run. I soon knew every last action of that immortal spine chiller, and it hasn't stopped fascinating, terrifying, and thrilling me to this day. Now that I have built my own screening room it was among the first films I acquired for my collection, and every now and then I pull it out and run it again. The experience is an exercise in nostalgia, but it still gets the old spine tingling away.

My informal education on the road with Dad and Will was split almost evenly between what I could learn from fellow vaudeville performers and the gems I could pick up on the screen. Because, from the moment *Dracula* scared the pants off me, no express train could haul me away from the movies. Both asleep and awake I lived all their dreams and dramas. No one can change the history I learned from them, even though it might not be according to the facts. To me Robin Hood and Abe Lincoln were equally important to the development of mankind, for I believed everything I saw on film. I learned all my vocabulary from Clark Gable and Errol Flynn. In all my waking hours, when I was not onstage or eating I was hunting down another film to see.

John Huston was once asked how much truth there was in his westerns. He thought about it for a moment and said that whenever he was given a choice between fact and legend, he always went for the legend. So do I. I can see "real" life all around me, but when that projector starts whirring, I want to sink into that adventurous oblivion only movies can bring. It's the ultimate luxury.

Because of that first experience, I have always remained

faithful to Bela Lugosi's famous and definitive interpretation of the Dracula role. The film industry has done a lot since with Bram Stoker's Gothic tale of the Transylvanian vampire, some of it excellent and some of it embarrassingly dreadful. But every minute detail of the original is implanted firmly in my head.

When the time came for me to set out on my own and make it in Europe, I knew I would have to add several dimensions to both my act and my life-style. Europe beckoned like the sirens in *The Odyssey*. But unknown to my advisers, who saw only an expansion of my personal audience and financial market as an entertainer, I had many other motives for crossing the Atlantic. The prime one had been an obsession with me for several years. I had to go see the studios where they made all those Hammer horror productions which, for a decade, had become the natural successors to the Lugosi legend.

I was the ultimate sucker for Hammer Films. They were tailor-made for me, and I had seen every one many times before hitting the tarmac at London Airport. Just about the first thing I did was fix up a visit to the studios. I had been around such places as the MGM lot a few times, and I was expecting something similar. When the car stopped outside the Hammer building, I just didn't believe it. I thought it was the reception area. Christopher Lee and Peter Cushing ushered me in, and I suddenly realized this actually was it. I found Hammer had done all those films on one and a half stages and had to get out at midnight so that someone else could start shooting at dawn. The entire operation would have fit in an MGM parking lot.

I was enthralled as I saw one of the low-budget blockbusters being made. The whole thing was incredible. Hammer was making millions, but at the studio you would have thought they were producing a low-budget educational film. They would churn out a whole film in days, not only one version for the British market but two other versions for the rest of the world.

I watched as they shot a fairly sedate scene for Britain. The makeup man came along with a little brush and splashed red paint onto Christopher Lee's lapels. Then they shot the American version. The same guy came along and threw paint all over him.

They stopped for a minute, changed clothes, and got ready for the Far East version. This time whole tribes of special effects guys came on with buckets of red paint and sloshed it everywhere. You'd have thought they had shares in the tomato industry the way they used that ketchup.

Later I had lunch with Chris and Peter, and they found my incredulity amusing. I couldn't get over it and finally said, "Well, no wonder you make so many millions. You just don't spend a penny."

Both of them looked at each other and then back at me. "What do you mean, millions?" Chris asked.

"Your last movie made ten million dollars in America alone," I said. "You must be very rich young men."

They looked at each other again, and I could see Chris's upper lip quivering as it does when he smells blood. "Ten million?" he said, and it was his turn to be dumbfounded.

"Sure, what's your cut?"

Both of them started fidgeting, and Peter Cushing said, "I was paid fifty pounds a week, and I'm the established star. What about you, Chris?"

Chris said, "Forty-five pounds, and I thought it was marvelous to be able to pay the rent again."

Their entire vision had been confined to that tiny little island known as England. They had shot three versions, all in the working day, but once they had gone home, they had forgotten about the rest of the world. I was glad to put them right on the facts, although I realized I was upsetting them considerably.

I don't begrudge Hammer Films their "cheap-film" reputation at all. They worked under such idiotic conditions and produced such marvelous films they deserved all they got. Even today the first thing I do when I get to London is call up and get them to send over the latest films, and a few of my old favorites as well. They know I am their number one fan. After a while I got to know everyone at Hammer and started collecting bits of scenery, props, costumes, and even masks and fangs. Often, when they delivered them, the whole cast would turn up direct from the set complete with makeup and costumes. When they arrived at the May Fair Hotel in a fleet of taxis, they used to scare the hell out of everyone. It was always an excuse for an instant party.

Chris Lee became a special friend. Obviously, with my own great personal affinity with Count Dracula, he was one of the first people I wanted to meet when I got to Europe. But our friendship really blossomed when he moved permanently to Hollywood. He and his family are always coming over to our home. They are very special people. After watching every Hammer production a thousand times, I think I know Chris's face better than he does.

My wife, Altovise, is as scared at horror movies as I am, but she never gets the same enjoyment out of this fear. She simply will not sit through a spooky movie. This comes in handy if you want to get rid of your wife for a while, but in reality it means I rarely play horror films at home. One occasion she felt she had to sit down and put up with it was when I showed Chris Lee's second *Dracula* movie, *Dracula, Prince of Darkness*, during one of his many visits. Chris, of course, kept saying things like: "Oh, God, do we really have to put up with this? Is it really necessary?"

As the film started running, I could feel Altovise fidgeting, but the rest of us settled down to enjoy it, and after about fifteen minutes we were completely engrossed, although poor Chris kept muttering and groaning at certain scenes. At the point when the screen Dracula "dies" in the ice, he said, "Thank God it's nearly over." Hammer had run out of ideas for killing Christopher and had spent ages devising the ice-death sequence.

When the lights finally went up, we had forgotten Chris was in the room; it was quite an experience to find him sitting there. We got over it only when someone poured him a glass of red wine and pretended it was blood.

Chris, of course, has many times pounced at me from dark corners in his full Dracula regalia. At one point he had scared me so successfully so often I decided it was my turn to scare the daylights out of him.

I planned it meticulously. I went to my dentist and asked him to make me the "perfect" set of fangs, ones that were actually molded into my mouth. Cost was no object, and he spent a great deal of time making them absolutely "authentic." I had many dress rehearsals with various friends and probably put as much timing into the act as for any professional engagement. To rile Mr. Lee, the whole thing had to be perfect.

My chance finally came when he visited me in the penthouse at the May Fair Hotel. I got him to the bar and mixed him a Mexican Mary with tequila and lime juice. I said it was a specialty of mine and wanted his opinion. I was so enthusiastic about it that he was eager to taste it.

I made a great play of mixing the drink, so the act would grab his interest. As I handed him the glass, I guessed I would have two seconds to slip my fangs in. Then I put on my most horrendous glare and shoved my face right over the bar close to his just as he looked up, saying, "*Ummmmmmm* . . . rather nice."

It worked like an instant nightmare. Chris flew out of his chair screaming. He turned livid and yelled, "Sammy, don't ever do that to me again. I nearly died."

I have had a few standing ovations in my time, but scaring Dracula right out of his pants was probably my greatest single theatrical achievement.

Chris, who comes from a decent middle-class family full of colonels and bishops, drifted into acting almost by chance when a cousin suggested he try becoming a "Rank Starlet"—a bit player for the J. Arthur Rank organization. He made a living of sorts for ten years before Hammer offered him a part.

He specialized in dying because, years before, Peter Cushing had said to him, "Become a type and do it well. There's always employment for types." So Chris had become a "dying type." There was never anyone who could die the way he could.

Whenever a scriptwriter thought up an ingenious way for someone to die, the studio yelled, "Send for that Lee chap." Dying gave him a reasonable living, and he eventually caught the eye of Hammer, which was casting *The Creature*, a remake of the old Frankenstein immortalized by Boris Karloff. At first the critics were cool. They said, "Young Christopher Lee looks as if he has been in a road accident."

At one point the Creature got shot in the eye and Chris had to slap "blood," which he had hidden in his palm, right into his face. The screaming that followed was for real. Chris later told me he'd stuck the acrid blood—Hammer people called it Kensington Gore—right in his eye and thought he'd gone blind.

His pay for the film was $1,500. The total budget was $200,000. Chris was glad of the check at the time. So far the film has grossed $25 million and, in terms of cost versus profit, is the most successful British film ever made. Christopher Lee had finally been established as a "type."

Lugosi had originally played Dracula as a melodramatic but wily scoundrel. The first film version, which I had chanced upon in the Chicago theater in 1931, established the Count, along with Superman, Sherlock Holmes, and Tarzan, as one of the great folk heroes. Dracula has since caught the public imagination in more than 200 films in ten countries, and the original novel has never been out of print.

In 1943 Lon Chaney invented a tough, fleshy Count Dracula, and Boris Karloff introduced John Carradine as the most gentlemanly and debonair of counts in *The House of Frankenstein*.

But it was Chris Lee who brought the story back as a vogue when Hammer started making Dracula movies in 1957. His gentlemanly, yet evil and chaotic, sadoerotic character, who managed to be elegant and deadly at the same time, gave the Count a new breath of life. Chris always used to tell me, "Dracula had something for everyone. But what gave him his real potency was that no one could entirely discount the vampire belief."

None of the people in horror movies liked the word "horror." Lon Chaney, Boris Karloff, Vincent Price, and Christopher Lee all preferred to call it the Theater of the Fantastic.

One of the reasons Hammer was so successful in this kind of film was that it had a brilliant special effects man called Les Bowie. He was the real Dr. Frankenstein because he would create incredible monsters in ridiculously primitive conditions for next to nothing. Dozens of eerie scenes of castles and misty forests were, in fact, only Bowie's mat paintings. His genius dumbfounds any casual visitor from Hollywood. In *One Million Years B.C.*, for instance, he created the world in six days and nearly got fired for going $200 over the $2,000 budget. The whole thing was crazy. He used oatmeal for lava and an ordinary water faucet to represent a vast prehistoric deluge. Bowie even parted the Red Sea for just $150, using every trick in the book to save money.

Bowie was also around when Boris Karloff was riding high in the monster genre. Boris, one of the greatest, finally decided there was nothing more he could get out of the part, or add to it, so he just gave up. In many ways good monster movies were never the same without him. In those days, if you got no satisfaction out of the job, there was very little reason for continuing. Being a monster of any consequence was the most arduous part in the business. When Fredric March, for instance, made the original *Jekyll and Hyde*, the studios had none of the makeup techniques of today. His mouth was puffed out with padding, and his false teeth were clamped onto his gums. The makeup people stretched his eyes and stuffed unimaginable things up his nose. Sometimes they pushed acrid putty up there which burned and made his eyes water. Suffering horribly like this, Fred played one of his most incredible roles, managing to make the definitive Jekyll *and* the definitive Hyde.

Anyone in the horror-monster business had to get used to being dreadfully abused by the makeup and special effects men. Vincent Price was another who was no stranger to having his face caked and stuffed. We all automatically think of him in the chiller role because he did it so well, but in fact, only a fifth of Vincent's 100 films since 1938 have been horror movies. He coined the characters of the wicked, aristocratic cheat and the deceiving, often demented psychopathic killer. Yet audiences enjoyed a certain sympathy for him because he managed to combine a commanding physique with a mild, suave manner. It is the touch of sophistication, laced with sharp, even dark humor, in all his characters which has established him firmly in the public mind.

He is, in private life, one of the most civilized men in the world, with a cultural side to his personality that most fans don't see. He has a fascinating knowledge of a whole range of things, including food and wines. He is an excellent raconteur and a gifted writer, and his knowledge of art borders on genius. When he discovered I had not read his brilliant book, *I Know What I Like*, he kindly sent me a copy. He didn't know I had set up a red alert all over the town we were playing to try to find one. In fact, my search was so successful that I ended up with six.

Vincent came into his own in Hollywood when the American equivalent of Hammer, American International, began specializing in Edgar Allan Poe stories. Until then AIP had only done cheaply made, and often dreadful, monster films. Poe handed the studio a gold mine and quickly established Vincent as a household name. Horrible chillers and thrillers found a fantastic medium in celluloid. Clever directors devised all sorts of tricks and gimmicks to exploit a torrid tale. Visually movies could often outdo the original stories, frightening people in a grossly entertaining way. They were fun, but it was easy not to take them too seriously because they belonged to the world of fantasy. Nightmares perhaps, but as with dreams, people woke up from the spell as they left the movie house.

Alfred Hitchcock, on the other hand, used many of the same tricks to create dramatic fear and tension from real-life situations. When audiences left a Hitchcock movie, they would often translate those fears to the dark shadows cast across the streets where they lived. *North by Northwest* displayed several typical examples of his brilliant ingenuity. When the villains are tracking down Cary Grant, they chase him into an auction room. Grant gets out of a seemingly hopeless situation by bidding ridiculously and being thrown out by the police, who then protect him. Later the script calls for Cary to meet his killers. The cliché would have been a dark doorway with a single lamp, a cat mewing, and a lot of shadows. Hitchcock said, "I want bright daylight in the open country."

The audience is always given all the information in a Hitchcock film. Hitchcock lets you know all the answers; that adds to the suspense. In *North by Northwest* the audience knew Cary was in a spot, but no one could imagine where the trouble would come from.

A car rumbles up and a man gets out. He stands there for a moment and says, "That's funny."

"What is?"

"There's a crop-duster over there dusting a place where there are no crops."

We all knew suddenly where the trouble was coming from. That's the kind of moviemaking which adds up to genius, and Hitch has done it often. I can't remember the times I've had to keep the lights on and the radio playing all night because I'd just seen a Hitchcock movie.

Hitch is one of those directors who like to have every last detail on paper before they start shooting. He invented the whole windmill scene in *Foreign Correspondent*, for example, while sitting in a small office in Los Angeles. Hitch asked himself, "What have the Dutch got that we can use dramatically?" Color was not used freely in those days and he didn't think tulips were dramatic enough. So he came up with windmills and sat down and wrote in the whole sequence.

Hitchcock is also the world's greatest artist with double exposures and back projection. *The Birds* used lots of trick photography of one sort or another. In *Lifeboat* only one shot was taken outside the boat. The rest was all back projection. Hitchcock always maintained he could make a film about a man in a telephone booth. In *Rear Window* he almost achieved this, using the camera to pick up every detail.

Hitch was always having rows with David Selznick about what spies should be chasing. In fact, when, two years before the atom bomb, Hitchcock said they should be chasing uranium in *Notorious*, Selznick lost his cool and sold the whole package to RKO for $800,000 and half the profits. "What Selznick failed to realize," said Hitch, "is that *Notorious* was not about uranium at all. It was a love story. The public are never interested in what the spies are chasing. It could be anything. It is the people who are of real importance."

The film was probably the best Ingrid Bergman ever did for Hitch. Better even than *Spellbound*, for which she did her homework in a mental home. *Notorious* was her final film with Selznick and her last successful film for a decade.

Within Ben Hecht's incredible script framework the chemistry between Cary Grant and Ingrid really ignited and generated a whole sense of erotic tension. This hadn't happened since *Casablanca*, arguably the only finer film she ever made. *Notorious* had so many of those magic moments. The close-up, for instance, of Bergman's hands nervously clasping and unclasping the key to the all-important wine cellar; "the longest kiss in history," in which the two stars move into several different situations still kissing; superb, masterly cinema. As a real-life sidelight to all this on-screen tension, Hitchcock's amiable inquiries into exactly what plutonium really was, and his excellent grasp of the facts, led to a full, clandestine FBI investigation.

My own favorite Hitchcock movie is *Rope*, which, considering the all-time classics he made, is thought a strange choice by some people. But the film has all the ingredients for me. One of the first Hitchcock color films, made in 1948, with an all-star cast headed by James Stewart, the plot follows two college boys who unemotionally kill a boy for fun and delight in confusing the police. It was brilliantly constructed. The whole New York background was a model and took up more space than the set itself because the crew had to shoot it from every angle. They had clouds of spun glass floating around all the time. They numbered all the clouds on the back and just hung them around, changing the position on every reel. When they came to dub Farley Granger playing the piano, they found he had no idea how the instrument should be played and his hands were straying everywhere. After the film was in the can, they had to get one of the music guys at Warner's to study Farley's fingers and rewrite the music to fit the action.

I remember when Hitchcock's *Psycho* first came out, we were playing just outside Boston. We all went to the movies in the afternoon and the film had us spooked for the rest of the day. Even after the show, when we went to a show business hangout called the Waldorf, we were still dodging the shadows. Murphy Bennett, who was then my road manager, couldn't stop talking about the movie. Michael Silver, our drummer at that time, kept giggling at his fears. I didn't let on exactly how scared I had been myself. But I had done the show with my heart in my mouth.

When we got back to the hotel, we separated, and I didn't get to my room for a while. When I did, I immediately went into the bathroom, and I knew Michael Silver was hiding in there. He wore a very distinctive after-shave lotion, and the smell was so strong I could actually trace him to the shower. Even though I knew it was him, a shiver went down my spine. It is an accolade to Hitch's greatness that to this day I can't go into a bathroom without pulling the shower curtains back.

Showing an unnatural calmness, I turned on the tap and left the water running. I crept up to the curtain, and I was mad, with both fear and anger. I turned my glass eyeball around and put on my most menacing gaze. Then in one quick movement I pulled the curtain back and screamed a terrific roar. Michael was crouching down. He shot up in the air and jumped about three feet. His arms went up, and I thought his eyeballs would pop out. I cannot repeat the torrent of bad language which accompanied this in case any lady or child might pick up this book believing it worthy of family reading. But amid pants and groans he went through just about every Anglo-Saxon swearword ever invented. Plus a few more on top.

I gave him a large brandy to calm his nerves and had a few myself for the same reason. Even so, I slept with the light on and locked the doors.

After beating him at his own game, I thought I had heard the last of it, but Silver wanted to get even. The very next night, as I was coming out of the elevator, he was hiding on the side of my blind eye, and I thought I was alone in the corridor. A voice said, "Room for one more, guvnor?" It was Silver's turn to see me jump to almost my own height.

"OK, Michael," I screamed. "You got me that time. But this is war. I am going to scare you absolutely shitless. I mean it, Michael. From now on you ain't going to know where I am. But you're sure going to find out. This is it, Michael Silver. You'd better sew yourself into that skin because I'm gonna make you jump right out of it."

Michael started pleading: "No, no, no, Mr. D., don't do that. I didn't mean it, Sammy. Don't do it to me."

But I was angry. I told him, "You shouldn't play this *Psycho* game with me because I'm better at it than you. You've got a lesson to learn around here."

For days he went around turning on lights, locking doors, walking with other people, giving a wide berth to corners, going to bed early, and constantly looking over his shoulder. The rest of the gang thought this was a great laugh and reported his antics back to me. But I had patience. I was going to wait for this one, and I let it go for a full week. I treated him normally, and we went about the daily routine of putting on a show. He began to relax, as I knew he would eventually. I wanted to set this one up perfectly. I sent for the mummy's mask from the old Hammer productions which the guys had given me a year or so before. I smuggled it into the house while Silver was eating. Then I bided my time.

I spent an hour getting my act together. I pushed a pillow up the back of my shirt, arranged so that I looked a genuine hunchback. I had the mask fitted perfectly and the lighting in the hall fixed so that it would give the best effect. Then I went into action.

I had chosen this moment because I knew he had a chick in the room and he would be at his most vulnerable and defenseless. You don't go out to scare the hell out of someone who is expecting it. This was war, and he was going to lose his skin.

We all crept up to the room, and I got Murphy to stand on one side with me behind him. A few others were hiding down the corridor. Murphy knocked.

"Who is it?"

"Murphy."

"I'm busy right now, Murph. I got a lady in here."

"I gotta talk to you right now. It's important."

Silence. A little rustling. We knew he was getting into his robe.

"OK. Wait a minute."

He opened the door, and Murphy said, "I got to talk to you about tomorrow."

"I can't talk to you now. I got a robe on, and besides, my gal's getting cold."

Murphy was moving just a little away from the door so that Silver had nearly come into the corridor. As Murphy turned and moved off, with Silver's eyes right on him, I pounced.

It was one of those Superman leaps from nowhere right in front of him. The man became demented immediately. He went up against the wall, and he had real terror in his eyes. Then he backed into the room, still swearing profusely, and actually peed.

There were no hard feelings. Michael knew he had it coming to him. But he never did try one on me again. We called a truce and shook hands on the deal. Neither of us wanted to go around for the rest of our lives waiting for the next heart attack to come bursting out of the shadows.

I don't even like nice surprises. It's a golden rule with anyone who knows me that nothing should be sprung on me. I like to be prepared for all eventualities. Surprise eliminates preparation. Second—and I admit it freely—from the moment I saw that first *Dracula* I have been spooked. This made every horror and monster film, every Hitchcock, every murder mystery, every spooky movie, and every frightening drama, from the original *Jekyll and Hyde* through *Rosemary's Baby* to *Death on the Nile*, very special for me. I live it every time for what it is. It *scares* me, and I love it. But I don't translate that fear out of the magic of the movies into my everyday life. There're enough scary things to cope with without personal theatrics. I get frightened at all sorts of things without anyone's bothering to set them up. Altovise is the same. We can cope when we know what's going on. We don't mind when it's on celluloid, but there are too many people out there ready to get you without anyone making a game of it.

Altovise knows that when she's in the house, she has to make a noise as she's walking around, just so I know it's her. A couple of years ago I went into the bedroom and called her and wandered around, wondering where she was. Someone must have told her I was calling because she came looking.

By then I had examined most of the annex where we sleep, and the lights were down. Because I lost my eye in a car accident, I have only part vision, and we have very soft carpets in that area. When I suddenly did a half turn and she was there, it sent an immediate shiver down my spine. She had inadvertently crept up on me. She knows better now because I hit the roof. I was genuinely in a state of immediate and blind panic.

Altovise gets scared even faster than I do. All I have to do when she is in bed is drag my feet along our wooden floor. I make one step and drag the other foot up to it. That's all it takes to make her quake with fear. I come along the corridor, and she says, "Davis. I know that's you. Stop it, Sammy. I know who it is. Sammy, don't do it to me."

She knows it's me, but she's never quite sure. So we get: "Mr. Davis, if you don't show yourself, I'm going to cry."

And I know she means it. So I show myself, and we cuddle up, and that's one of the few times neither of us is scared of anything.

—1980

"BLACK CATS,"
from *Hollywood in a Suitcase,* by Sammy Davis, Jr.

Being an entertainer has taken me to the fringes and into most aspects of our American way of life. It is one of the side benefits of the job, and I always appreciate hobnobbing with so many people from such varied backgrounds. The political world, for instance, fascinates me because it has a certain potency which I find irresistible. In show business we are as good as our last show, but politics seems somehow to go on forever.

I like to be around the handful of sincere senators who have good heads on their shoulders. If they know what they are doing, they can be extremely impressive. Kissinger was a powerhouse with an aura about him which gave him a strange attraction. The four Presidents I have known impressed me deeply.

Nowadays I've cooled down politically. I used to be very frustrated, angry, and impatient about what was going on. I wanted things to change fast. Maybe I was an optimist. You can heal such sores as violence politically, but it's difficult to change intolerance and bigotry by Washington decrees. I didn't feel I should keep quiet about my ideals. I used to shoot off my mouth about all sorts of things, both privately to anyone who would listen and publicly on any platform I could find. These days I don't get involved with the great issues. It is time for some of the young ones to take over. My generation of blacks has moved mountains, although many times it didn't seem like it. We've broken down many taboos. Now it is up to the younger generation of all colors and creeds to build on the foundations we have laid.

I no longer get up on platforms, but that doesn't mean I haven't got definite views about most issues. I just don't spout my mouth off anymore. If someone asks me what I think, I tell him as intelligently and coherently as I can. But I've thrown the soapbox away. Without any more excuses or explanations, I'm back in the entertainment business.

In the early sixties, at the height of President Kennedy's influence, I took part in America's greatest march for black freedom which brought 200,000 people to the streets of Washington. It was a demonstration but, more than that, it was an exercise in solidarity which was not trying to push the President into anything but to back him in the types of reforms and changes he had in mind. We felt confident that for perhaps the first time, it was really worth putting ourselves on the line. The march came just about a hundred years after the Emancipation Proclamation, and Kennedy said, "These recent months . . . have seen the decisive recognition by a major part of our society that all our citizens are entitled to full membership in the national community." It was strange that a century after the proclamation itself, this kind of thing still needed to be said. But it did, and it was, and we were very happy to hear it.

Planeloads of stars came up. Charlton Heston was there, with Paul Newman, Burt Lancaster, Marlon Brando, Lena Horne, Sidney Poitier, Bobby Darin, and Robert Ryan. The celebrities issued their own statement, saying, "All forms of racial segregation are injurious to the arts of the nation." It seems obvious now, but then it was daring.

I had become involved in the whole Kennedy era because of various things, including Sinatra's influence, and it was one of the most confusing and dreadful days of my life when Jack Kennedy got that bullet. Naturally we canceled the show.

We also stopped the show when Dr. King was assassinated; it just blew my mind that such a brilliant man could be so cruelly wasted. When Robert Kennedy was shot, we were in London at the Palladium doing *Golden Boy*. I heard about it ~al hours before anyone else in England. The man who ran my head office in Los Angeles had been in touch with the Kennedy family, and they were holding up the news of his death until all the members of the family had been told. I tried to keep the secret, but by curtain time, I knew I couldn't go on. It was only the second night in London, and the management pleaded with me to try to do it. Then the cast came and told me their careers would suffer if I didn't. They knew what I was thinking, but because hoofers are born with "the show must go on" syndrome, I did the first half, and I had tears streaming down my face the whole time. I could hardly hit the pitch, and my feet felt like lead. Eventually, during the intermission, I told them I was through for the night. I felt helpless. I asked the audience to pray for the senator and told them, "For once in my life my heart is not in this theater. It is somewhere in America, where one of our last dreams has just been murdered." I got muted, respectful applause, and I just walked off. I know that audience had paid its money to be entertained. But I had been Kennedy's friend, and if I had been false to that friendship, my entertainment value would be nil. They understood that.

When I think back to that night, I remember how angry and hopeless everything seemed. The Kennedy brothers and King had, among them, held not only the beginnings of the end of the black problem in America but also what seemed the answer to most of the world's other problems as well. They had been cruelly murdered by the bigots in our society, and it seemed the shits always got away with it. The guys who were wearing the authentic white hats were gunned down. And it suddenly seemed as if they had all died for nothing. The gun laws haven't changed because of them. Kids can still buy mail-order rifles. Violence remains all over the place. Peace has gone out of fashion. If their deaths had meant something, it might have been possible to come to terms with them. But it looked as if the sickness had come full circle and the world had gone crazy. I had recently been in Robert's company every day during the New York campaign. I, and everyone else around him at the time, had a tremendous feeling that great things were about to happen. We had a vision of a wonderful America which would be marvelous for everyone to live in, regardless of color or creed. We had caught his enthusiasm and we were all going forward together. It may have been naïve, but at the time it seemed very real. The violence of the deaths of his brother and of Martin Luther King suddenly seemed diminished as we strode on to better things. The advances of the black man in American society seemed imminent. We were on the Kennedy bandwagon again, and it looked and felt good.

Then, suddenly, we were sitting in the dressing room and heard that the guy, and all his dreams, had been wasted, and everything was back to square one. For me, the bitterest message of all was that I felt that 80 percent of all Americans were behind that final bullet—not just the bigots but the huge percentage who never gave a damn what happened. In many ways they were just as responsible.

Politics in Hollywood was always very much a two-sided affair. You've got the liberals, and you've got the conservatives, and both of them are deeply and genuinely involved with what they are doing. The liberals continually put their careers on the line when they back unpopular causes. But they seem to be winning through. Nowadays there is a huge liberal influence spreading over most of the country, and much of it is coming out of Hollywood. It certainly wasn't always like that. In the old days, during the studio system, all politics was taboo.

There is no doubt there were a lot of communists in the arts during the twenties and thirties. This came to a head during the McCarthy witch-hunt era, which upset everyone. No one liked what McCarthy was doing, but at the same time there were a lot of people around who were trying to upset America when the country was down and bleeding.

In the past two decades even the right wing has realized that people with humanitarian or liberal views are not necessarily Reds. "Extremists" gradually became the norm because it was no longer considered extreme to have liberal views. Conserva-
tre not as rigidly right-wing as they were in the forties.

Both sides are swinging toward the middle. The typical Republican of today would have been considered a liberal before.

For me the two-party democratic system is dynamite because it continually gives us a chance to change our political viewpoints. I don't think it is at all wrong for celebrities to back political causes. We are thinking, taxpaying Americans with a say in the running of the country. By this I don't advocate using my every show as a platform, but I do say we should put ourselves firmly and personally behind our political convictions. This is a commitment we have to make individually to ourselves, whatever the cost. We own property, and our children go to school; some of us are still affected by discrimination, so we have to make a stand, and to some extent this has paid off.

Things change, even though they seem to take a long time. It's like the Chinese pebble which ends up in Malibu. It just keeps rippling along, century after century, but it gets there in the end, and when it arrives, you don't even notice it. I subsequently supported Richard Nixon because I believed he was going to do some good, both for my people and for the country in general. You must remember that when he got into office the second time, it was an absolute landslide. Most of the country was rooting for him in a big way. They tend to forget that now. In the history of American politics no other President received a greater vote of confidence from the electorate. The nation was promised a lot of things, and so was I, not only by the Nixon supporters but by the President himself. One of the projects Nixon promised me was that there would be a huge educational program in the ghettos. It was one of many pledges he made which I have no doubt were genuine at the time. Watergate came along and rewrote history, so we will never know.

I don't mind admitting I am still a little bewildered over the whole Nixon episode. I believed at the time I could still be a confirmed Democrat, yet vote for the guy because I thought then he could do the job better than anyone else around. I knew I had to get off the fence and commit myself. When we got down to the Republican Convention in Miami, I understood they were happy to have me along because I was both black and Jewish and in theory could get some of those votes going toward Nixon. But we didn't go along hat in hand to vote for the guy. We also wanted to demonstrate that the Republicans would treat blacks as true equals. That's why I kicked up a fuss when I found I wasn't given the facilities I normally have when I am on the road—a penthouse suite. Nothing new about that. I always have the penthouse suite. I wanted them to look after both me and my entourage as we always lived. They had to demonstrate that we blacks had equal status with anyone on the bandwagon, and to that extent we got what we wanted.

It is true that a lot of people in the black movement resented it when I hugged Nixon on a nationwide TV show. Some of them got nasty and voluble. The blacks stayed, mostly, lukewarm to Nixon, and very little I said changed their minds. But I had long talks with the guy face to face, and I must say, even now, he impressed me. He promised much more funding to black colleges and many new reforms. He had done away with the quota system, and generally speaking, the more he said, the more I believed in him. Watergate was still some time off when we were together in Miami. I did not check out all the political affiliations and relied only on what my heart dictated, as I always had. As I now know, that can sometimes lead you into trouble.

Hollywood was divided over the Nixon thing, at least before Watergate. Some guys, like Redford, had chips on their shoulders about Nixon, and Redford went all out to make *All the President's Men*. But he had come along in the wake of a great movement which had made political stands very popular in Hollywood. At one stage just about everyone campaigning for George McGovern was far better known than the guy himself. Some aspects of show business also rubbed off on the politicians. George Wallace, for instance, turned his rallies into revival meetings straight out of *Elmer Gantry*. The Kennedys loved nothing better than a star-studded Hollywood-style gala.

I think most stars were serious and conscientious about their electioneering. Paul Newman, for example, could support Eugene McCarthy but also take the Republican stand for Pete McCloskey because he thought the issues right. Paul, like me, had no party loyalties. He, and many other celebrities, thought of Washington as a whorehouse. If you've got to visit a whorehouse, you might as well try to find the best whore in the place. It was a cynical but widely held view.

Later, when Nixon had been discredited, many people started throwing the crap at me in a nasty way. They wagged their fingers and enjoyed pointing out how wrong I had been. The flak got so hot at one stage I think I was pretty close to a nervous breakdown. Murphy Bennett had to help me onto the stage one night, and I was very close to crying. It was a traumatic experience, but I finally won through. Time heals, eventually.

I got over it by reminding myself that my original motives, however wrong I have been proved, were honorable and seemed rational at the time. For a start, I believed Nixon was going to do something about Vietnam, and I was proved correct in that. Since I had been there myself and seen the conditions, I had sworn to myself that I would back anyone who felt he could pull America out of that bloodbath. Nixon had, in fact, cooperated fully and personally with my visit.

I didn't go to Vietnam because I believed in the war. I went because there were so many black soldiers there, and no one seemed to care about them. White entertainers were going over in droves. They were putting on good shows, but to the blacks, they belonged to the political system back home, and they were extremely disillusioned about it. There was nothing for the young black soldier to relate to.

I think we eventually succeeded, although it was quite a fight. When we got there, we put on the first show in Da Nang, and there were 18,000 black soldiers out front. I did the show as best I could but didn't realize the difficulties we had faced until I talked to some of the guys afterward. The cats told me that if I'd given them any kind of patriotic crap—or talked down to them—they'd have walked out en masse. They had it all planned. One condescending statement, and they'd have given me hell. They weren't in the mood for a preaching session. I must have said the right things because they stayed, and they came back to many other shows.

When we got to talking later on, they all wanted to know why I was there. The show itself became insignificant. Some of them liked it; some of them didn't—it was the issue that was important. What were my motives? They were highly suspicious. Was I after political kudos in Washington? Was I there for the publicity? Was I showing my fans what a patriotic guy I was? The questions came thick and fast, and I had to spend a long time warding them off. The mere act of telling them that I was there because of the black situation was not enough. Luckily I had the means to demonstrate my sincere feelings and motives. I had been warned that something like this might happen, and I had come prepared. It was the very reason why I had never been across with Bob Hope. I'd been on half a dozen special TV shows with the guy, and I love him dearly, but the Vietnam thing was a different matter. We stood on different political platforms, and we could never share the same stage on any real issue.

Patriotism was a fundamental part of the Second World War. But Vietnam was different. Anyone who went over there and said, "Hey, you guys, you're fighting for the great America," would be howled down with abuse. That little joke had lost its steam—even with the enlisted volunteers who went out to fight Pearl Harbor over again and thought they were jumping into a John Wayne movie. It didn't hold water anymore.

The "nonwhites" from all ethnic groups had the worst time of the war. They turned to drugs, and they were often troublemakers. But I don't blame them for that. They didn't want to go near Vietnam in the first place and couldn't find a reason for staying once they had got there. Nothing improved. The Vietcong hated them, but so did the Vietnamese. Their own white officers treated them like dirt. There was little thanks when they got home. Few black heroes ever got on television.

I caught the mood of disillusion on my very first day. I went out on a helicopter patrol, and we soon came across a massive area which had been totally devastated. Right in the middle, in its own seeming Garden of Eden, was a small plantation with a big white house sitting splendidly in the middle of it. It had been untouched by the war because it belonged to a Vietnamese who had influence. Later, while I was talking to the guys in the camp, they pointed out that the Vietcong was only a few hundred yards away. The area in between was owned by another local dignitary. They weren't allowed to cross it. Yet the Vietcong used the area for lightning raids whenever they felt like it. You simply can't ask a guy to put up with a situation like that for very long. I saw nothing but hell and frustration which had eventually turned into naked anger and bitterness. And when the black guys got bitter, they were yanked out and put into psychiatric wards. You only had to say, "What the hell am I doing here?" to be put on your ass. *Catch-22* had nothing on what really went on.

No war is nice, for heaven's sake, but I soon found Vietnam was something else entirely. Very few of the guys out there had any idea what they were getting killed for. What they soon did find out was the dreadful injustice of that kind of war. Most of the blacks didn't even hate the enemy. They saw the Vietnamese government they were defending as hopelessly corrupt—at the cost of American lives.

The average Vietnamese was no different. When I first got there, I was billeted in an officer's home, complete with housekeeper. She told me one day, "The French came and went. They couldn't handle it. Nor could the British. You Americans won't last long."

That's what the guys were fighting for, a spirit of helplessness pervading the whole scene.

Because of this, thousands of them turned to drugs. They got some kind of solace from them. They would lace their cigarettes with heroin, which they could buy openly, $5 for a little tube. The detoxification center grew and grew and became about the most disgusting and degrading place on earth. Many of the guys would rather have been on the front line than trapped in that place. It was meant to be a hospital, and some of the doctors knew they had a very large problem. But the guy who ran it, who immediately made me want to vomit, treated it as a prison. Guys going through withdrawal symptoms were trapped in tiny cells. The place was covered with barbed wire, the food was pure garbage, and guys with real medical problems were being treated like common criminals. It wasn't long before I had chosen the detoxification center as my special project. I decided I was going to give them hell back home.

When I originally planned my journey, I had a long series of talks with people at the United Nations. Over the years I had done many benefits for the UN children's program, and I knew most of the top officials by their first names. Before leaving I sat down with Kurt Waldheim, the secretary-general, and told him that I was going as an entertainer, primarily for the blacks, but that I wanted to do something more.

Waldheim and I had a very frank discussion about the possibilities. He quickly accepted my argument that I was not looking for medals or glory, and he began to explain areas where I might help. In fact, many of the people at the UN were trying to get conditions changed in Vietnam. They were seeking ways of exerting pressure to influence Washington. Waldheim made it plain that my influence would be "very welcome" in various directions. One of them was to talk to the blacks about drugs—not to spy on anyone, but to try to find out the extent of the problem. With this in mind he gave me a Dr. Jaffy as an adviser, and I immediately felt the project was worthwhile.

In the end we went as an official delegation. A member of Jaffy's Drug Abuse Center came along with me and a Nixon presidential aide. We met every day between shows to compare notes. Throughout the trip I went everywhere without any kind of fear, and I had a secretary trailing me, taking notes all the time. I talked to just about everyone I could find, and when I went into places where the white guys didn't like to go, I talked into a pocket tape recorder. At first the blacks were openly hostile. I was called everything by them. But I went on talking and listening, and gradually the word seemed to spread that I was for real. Soon the hostility ended, and we were able to talk face to face. The blacks took me into their confidence, and I shall never forget them. I had been taken apart piecemeal, and they gradually put me together again. For them, I had to go see things at their worst. If nothing else, I had a press conference to go to back home and TV shows to do. I wanted to tell the American people, as far as I could, what it was really all about.

When the tour came to an end, I had seen one hell of a lot of Vietnam. I also found that as an official delegation we had a strong voice on many, many subjects. We didn't exactly stop the war, when we got home, but we certainly made some changes. President Nixon put into immediate effect ten of the twenty proposals we had made. That was a start. The most vital one as far as I was concerned was that he changed the detoxification center immediately back into a hospital. Only a week later they pulled down the barbed wire, opened the place up, and flew in a professional medical team to deal with the situation. People who went over there later told me there wasn't a guard in sight. The drug problem began to be seen in Washington for what it really was—a dreadful symptom of a dreadful war.

When I think back now, I know we didn't change that much, but at least we put some wrappings around the cancer, and I had the chance, over a long period, of helping explain to the American people what the blacks really felt about the war. Because of that, I like to think I wasn't wasting my time. I hope I have never been wasting my time when I became concerned about a political issue, even if I have sometimes felt misguided. After all, the kind of racism that existed in Vietnam had always been reflected in Hollywood. It is another of the things that make me hot under the collar. I feel the same way about blacks in war movies as I do about Hollywood's interpretation of blacks in the West. I was curious as a child to find out why there weren't any black cowboys. I learned that as a people we had been "freed" by Lincoln, and I just wondered where the hell we had gone. There weren't many books on the subject in those days, and the movies ignored it. It wasn't until I found a book called *Negroes in the West* that I realized blacks had played such a significant part in the taming of the West. The book had five very worn pictures of black cowboys, and they began to fascinate me. Over the years I picked up little pieces of information until I had a fairly comprehensive knowledge of life for the black man in the nineteenth century. But picking up these little strands was very hard work.

The older I got, the more frustrated I became at the way movies pictured the early black movements. It was as if we hadn't existed. We were seen only as buffoons or humble servants. I am not opposed to the industry showing this side of black life because, God knows, in reality it was a very large slice of how we existed. But this attitude by no means tells the full story. OK, so there *was* the Mandingo syndrome, but give me something else to balance the picture.

The industry was so sensitive about keeping black issues out of the movies it wouldn't even tell the story of some of the early black heavies. I tried for years to play a gangster, but I was told, even by good friends, that it was far too controversial. If a black played in any film, he should have no significance as a person—good or bad.

I used to dream up all sorts of ideas which might help give black actors some work, but ideas are anyone's property in Hollywood until they actually become "properties"; even then there can be half a dozen versions going around at the same time. Everyone with an original idea in Hollywood eventually finds it has been stolen. I cannot remember all the times I've been sitting at the bar in my house, chatting away with all sorts of people—producers, directors, writers, even actors—and I've said I'd like to do something, or had an idea, and then forgotten about it. Months later I've been sitting watching TV and seen the identical idea come up. When the credits start rolling, you know who got moving on what you said. In Hollywood, even mediocre people can make a generous living by picking up ideas and selling them.

I could reel off several dozen ideas which legitimately originated from the bar at my house. For a long time, for instance, Rod Serling would be up there for an evening, and we'd gas away all night. He had a very creative mind, and we both loved dreaming up improbable situations for his *The Twilight Zone*. We would bounce things off one another, and it would be a lot of fun. Rod dedicated his last book to me as a gesture of our friendship.

One night I had a great idea about a bigoted white man who got a strange disease and woke up to find he was black. Rod was crazy about it, but the sponsors thought the subject was too sensitive and turned it down. The story went around to a lot of people, but soon I forgot about it. Imagine my surprise when I found everyone raving about the film *Watermelon Man* and saw my own idea on the screen, chapter and verse.

The making of a black *Dracula* was also almost certainly born in my house. My love for, and knowledge of, horror movies is well known. Putting the Count into the ghettos among the super-hip blacks had been a pet project of mine for years. I was always talking about it at the house. As it happens, I don't like claiming credit for the film which eventually came out. *Blacula* was such a waste of a good idea and was so embarrassingly bad I feel it must be done again properly.

Before the black exploitation movies came along, it was practically impossible to find a black in films who had a word to say for himself. In order for a black cat to fight a white man in any sense of the word, the white had to be seen on screen skinning pet poodles and screwing babies so that when the black guy tackled him, the audience wanted anyone to beat him, whoever he was.

Things have changed, and some say that blacks are now overexposed. I find it difficult to argue with that, though I am acutely aware of the dangers. I've seen good black actors driven to the grave because they couldn't find enough work. I can't really tell the guys who survived, "Don't be exploited," because they look at you and say, "I'm an actor, and I've a wife and baby to support. I'll do any work I can find." But many aspects of the present scene fill me with fear. Much as I love some of the guys around Hollywood today, I'm not going to start handing out medals. It's been a long, hard fight, and a lot of people have died along the way trying to make it so that today blacks can just walk into parts. Most of them have no idea of the blood which has been spilled over the years.

For a long time Europe put America to shame. Europeans were doing good pictures there with fully integrated casts more than twenty years ago. They didn't bother to argue about a black man's sexual prowess. They let him act like a human being, especially in France.

Blacks in America, even a few years ago, had to fight colossal battles to have their work accepted both in films and on TV. I can remember when a very sensitive writer wrote a part for the *General Electric Theater* on TV which he specifically asked me to play. It was a warm, noncontroversial story about a young kid who had attached himself to a black soldier. The story had nothing to do with the "black problem"; it was about basic human relations, and the soldier could have been any color. It was beautifully mounted and written, and at first the TV company gave the go-ahead.

However, when the sponsors saw it and realized it would be playing against Dinah Shore, they tried to pull out. We had a tremendous fight, and for a long time it seemed we were losing. We brought a hell of a lot of pressure to bear, mainly on artistic grounds, but the racial issue came into it. General Electric even threatened to pull out all its sponsorship on TV if the film went ahead. We fought on, and the company eventually relaxed a trifle. It gave us an ultimatum. If there was any controversial reaction which could be linked to it, it would then pull out. We went ahead.

We ended up with higher ratings than the competition and got rave reviews. I was nominated for an Emmy, and the *General Electric Theater* laughed all the way up the ratings.

I remember it now as a huge fight with fierce interplay between finance and politics—all to tell a simple, human story about a black soldier. For me the nomination was the prize because it made the whole fight worthwhile, but even that had its farcical side. As soon as the nomination came along, everyone started taking bows and claiming responsibility. GE said it was "an enlightened company putting out new forms of theater experience."

The immediate overreaction was typical and predictable. GE offered me half a dozen parts. It was buying up anything that came along which could be built around a black guy. The GE people didn't even read the scripts. They brazenly wanted to cash in on the success they claimed they had created. "Hey, look," they said, "the public bought it. We've made a buck. Let's go, Sammy." I saw them looking through scripts with white parts they could turn into black parts, and on that ludicrous note, I took my leave.

All this was long before *Shaft* came along and started the whole black exploitation boom. There was nothing at all wrong with that film except for the 10,000 lousy imitations which followed it. It was made in interesting circumstances. The backing company was predominantly black, using white business money. It started the film and, as often happens, ran out of funds halfway through. However, it had made enough of the film to persuade black East Coast businessmen to buy a share. MGM wouldn't put up cash but guaranteed it a release, which solved many problems. The final financing of the film became almost "street" business. Blacks decided to back it, and some cats were putting in $300 from their savings. Others were finding thousands. It was the only reason *Shaft* got finished. Luckily they've all made their money back dozens of times over.

At first the film seemed a poor choice. It had no established star, and the story was cornball. That kind of movie had been done a million times. But it had a look, a classiness, and an authenticity (as well as the Isaac Hayes score) which made it unique. As the original black gangster movie it will always enjoy a special status. But I occasionally regret what happened when the moviemakers woke up to find *Shaft* had been such a success. They had board meetings and said things like: "OK, they want to see blacks on the screen. Let's give 'em blacks on the screen—until they get sick of them."

To a certain extent this was excusable. The pressure had been building for years to force the industry into more black participation. Suddenly, after *Shaft*, it realized that black audiences had been starved for this kind of film. They had become, in fact, a significant financial power as an audience, and the companies decided to cash in on it. The black community got a big kick out of seeing one of their own playing James Bond with a flashy car and a beautiful doll on his arm. So the studios made films in which the black cat kills the head of the Mafia and all his henchmen and guns down a few crooked cops while he's at it. It was exciting because it was new. The audiences would leave the movie, saying, "We're getting even, baby."

Unfortunately, the novelty value of these films wore thin rather quickly. They had no substance and soon reached a saturation point. This is a great shame because, with less haste and more sense, black movies could have had a truly significant role to play. Now it too has been overdone to the point where it is a cliché, and the whole movement toward intelligent black movies was passed over.

Richard Pryor is one of the very few actors to have emerged in any significant sense from the black movement in Hollywood. He is also the first black actor to play the industry at its own game. Universal set him up in a multipicture deal and gave him an office-bungalow next to Telly Savalas. Big deal. The $2 million price tag didn't even buy exclusive rights, leaving him available to sign with Warner's for a four- to six-movie commitment. He still has properties in the pipeline with Paramount and Columbia. He had blown his career with NBC-TV by being too outrageous. Yet his divorce from the studio was the biggest laugh in town. Under the contract they paid him $2 million not to appear on TV for five years.

Yet this guy, who can act his balls off, just as a sideline to his fantastic business deals, has played it his own way all along. When he appeared at a gay rights benefit at the Hollywood Bowl, he was so annoyed by the arrangements made for the black artists that he told the audience of 17,000 to "kiss my happy, rich, black ass," leading the organizers to shrug and say, "When you hire Richard, you hire Richard."

When you hire Richard, you hire a guy who not only can fill theaters with such films as *Car Wash* and *Greased Lightning* but also has the talent to be co-scriptwriter on Mel Brooks's *Blazing Saddles*. There isn't anywhere in the world that cat can't go if he wants to. I love Richard Pryor to the point of obsession. He is a comedic genius who can also play a beautifully sincere piece in *Lady Sings the Blues*. The scene in which he breaks down was completely ad-libbed. Richard is a black experience within himself. He's got it mastered. The freedom with which he works within his own sphere is unique and brilliant. I just hope they don't jerk him off into impotency as they have so many black artists.

Richard is riding high, but even he is unaware of the fight that went on before he was able to become acceptable as a screen hero. Possibly Stepin Fetchit made it a bit easier for Richard Pryor. Before you saw Elizabeth Montgomery and O. J. Simpson making love together, you had to have *Guess Who's Coming to Dinner*. We have a tendency to forget quickly in Hollywood. Great strides have been made, but more often than not they were made up of tiny footsteps which pushed a little farther on each tread. It is no longer necessary to be a Willie Best. They could always leave Willie in a room with Paulette Goddard because he was around only to make people laugh. He was lazy, stupid, and ugly so it could never be even vaguely suggested that any white actress would find him attractive. Paulette would never have been left alone with Harry Belafonte, let alone Richard Pryor.

Much of the future is up to guys like Pryor. People in films owe me things, and I could make some more movies. But my scope is severely limited. Richard, on the other hand, is a hot property who can demand and get what he wants. He is in the lucky position to take a lot of people with him and explore much of the talent hanging around.

In recent years the big studios have started minorities programs to explore the talents of various ethnic groups, as well as blacks. The programs have faced many difficulties, not least of all rip-offs from the minority groups themselves. When the programs first started, the Black Panthers and several other militant groups tried to take them over for their propaganda value. The second problem was that some of the studios tried to exploit the talent they found. It was a way of buying it up cheap.

Despite these setbacks, many of the schemes have been successful. Universal, for instance, had a very positive attitude toward its program. It used to find individuals and artistic groups and use the UCLA film club as a nucleus to get people together from every walk of life. From this, talented groups emerged and not only provided university film clubs with a lot of material but got the films noticed where they mattered—by the industry itself. Small groups used the scheme as a springboard to try out their ideas. To this extent the programs have been very useful. America used to be almost completely without an experimental cinema, so there was a constant thirst for new ideas and concepts. The minorities programs have been virtually alone in filling the gap.

Generally, in the United States the healthiest aspect of the movie industry is the sheer amount of activity which is going on. There is always such scope. And because it is geared to profits, successes, when they do come, are phenomenal. I agree that Hollywood seems to be excessively cautious in its real creativity. It scores a huge success with *Star Wars*, and immediately imitations spring up. But then along comes *The Deer Hunter*, and the picture changes overnight.

In some ways, TV is making much bigger strides than the movie industry. Even Mary Tyler Moore covered highly sensitive issues on her show. *Roots* was the ideal TV vehicle and would never have made it as a movie. There is a great deal of activity on the creative side of television. Several black actors have gone into directing on TV. Ivan Dixon, for instance, one of the cast of *Hogan's Heroes*, became a *Kojak* director. Georg Stanford Brown, one of the cast of *The Rookies*, became a director on *Charlie's Angels*. They are among a dozen good black directors presently learning their craft. Many of the advances being made behind the scenes date back to the explosion of the equal opportunities movement in the sixties. The corporations hired many token blacks and found, to their surprise, there was a great deal of talent around. Tokenism became a recognition of talent, and black advancement in the industry came surprisingly quickly.

Some of it was born out of genuine goodwill by socially aware people who recognized the need to change. People like Shirley MacLaine went out of their way to find work for blacks. If she couldn't find a wardrobe lady, for instance, she would hire an out-of-work black actress and teach her the job. She would often call me up and say something was available, did I know of anyone who wanted a job? That wardrobe lady may not be acting, but she is employed in the business, and because of her training, she need never be out of work.

I have got jobs for dozens of other people on the fringes to keep them in contact with films. The director Hal Ashby, for instance, lived at my place for a while when he was working as third assistant in the cutting room. He made his way up to the huge success he is today—by learning his craft from the bottom. Black actors don't get the opportunities, so they take anything that turns up. And if they have the talent, sooner or later it wins through. That is why I am still relatively optimistic about the future.

I have never retired from being in the middle of the black issue, but nowadays I take it a little more easily. I don't give lectures anymore, and I don't go on TV and rant about my convictions. But no black can ever stop being aware of what is going on in America, and to that extent I still consider myself involved. I am one of the few black entertainers, for instance, who have made it their duty to find out the situation outside the United States. I like to keep abreast of aborigine problems in Australia, and I have always been involved with what is happening in Europe.

One of the first things I did when I got to London was meet with Michael X, and it became one of the great pluses of getting to that lovely city. My dear friendship with this man will probably never be understood by the British, who saw only evil in him. At the time Black Power was an almost unheard-of concept. Michael began to challenge not only the white attitude toward blacks but the black attitude toward whites. He gave blacks their first real self-awareness and made them fight for a new identity.

My interest in Michael X was not necessarily to endorse his views, but merely to find out what was happening to the black movement in London. I would often go up to his small apartment in Notting Hill, and we'd gas away the hours on every subject under the sun. Inevitably we'd get back to black militancy. But I never saw the dark side of Michael X. He was deeply disturbed, but intelligent with it. He had a wide range of views on any number of different subjects. His knowledge of films was comprehensive. He was penetratingly bright and always concerned. He wanted changes quickly. I didn't necessarily agree with all his ideas, but they were profound. He was never the black militant with me. It would have been totally alien for me to sit in a London slum talking about "killing Whitey." He never sprung it on me. Consequently in all my dealings with the man I was never aware of the fact that he was an ardent militant with a few very outrageous ideas.

Michael was a very persuasive man, and I instinctively knew

many of his arguments were right. He was almost a lone voice between the white and black communities, and I found he was desperate to unite the different black factions in London. I agreed to do a special benefit at the London Palladium with the intention of trying to get all the black communities in London under one roof. The theme was unification, and to the extent that every one of the black movements in London was represented, it worked.

His concept of self-awareness linked to a change in the status of blacks is something they have never achieved in England. If Michael X had been around longer, they might have got much closer by now. They are still ripping each other off, and I think England's black problem has probably only just started.

After meeting Michael, I was interviewed by BBC television and let it be known, gently, that I was thinking of giving up my so far moderate stand on civil rights in favor of the Black Power movement. I declared, "I am not a Negro—I'm a black man." It seems strangely subdued these days, but then it was considered a highly controversial statement. When I then accused the British of not understanding their own black problem, all hell broke loose. The papers printed miles of comment—some sensible, some abusive. One day I was called to the telephone at the Palladium, and a man said he would be in the theater that night with a gun and would murder me. For the rest of the trip I had a squad of Scotland Yard detectives trailing me wherever I went. It was necessary, but it was no fun.

Despite this, I managed to get involved with the black movement in Britain. Besides the Palladium show, we did six late-night cabarets at the Playboy Club and a charity concert at the Lyceum Ballroom in aid of the starving children in Biafra and Nigeria. We charged $25 a head, a very large sum then, and we packed them in.

I also handed over $12,500 of my own cash to the British Black Power movement. I made it clear I didn't want it spent on guns or any other direct militancy. Michael had taken me to many black communities and was trying to raise the cash for some kind of cultural center for blacks. They also needed a place where cats could talk to lawyers and welfare people when they got into trouble. I was happy to pay toward that. It was an important aspect of my long love affair with London, but by no means the only one. Before I was through with that city, I was able to acquaint myself with just about every aspect of its fascinating life.

—1980

APPENDIX

○

Marshall and Jean Stearns's famous study *Jazz Dance* (1968) describes some of the technical aspects of tap and flash dance and the history of how these various steps developed through the examination of a particular noted performer. In short, it provides the reader a useful glimpse into the world of black dance from which Davis emerged.

EXCERPT FROM
Jazz Dance: The Story of American Vernacular Dance,
by Marshall and Jean Stearns

"Mattie Olvera and me were great dancers from the waist down," says Frank Condos, speaking of the famous team of *King and King*, "but from the waist up we didn't have much personality—we were just two homely looking guys, and neither of us could be called a ladies' man." What *King and King* could do from the waist down, however, made them a legend among dancers: five-tap Wings.

To explain a five-tap Wing, it is important to note what is *not* happening. One leg (the legs alternate) is bent at the knee and raised up and back—out of the way. *This leg does nothing*—or something additional. With the other leg, the dancer jumps up in the air, and on the way up and down, *makes five clear and distinct sounds on the floor with his foot.* "It's no use jumping higher to gain more time to tap because then your foot won't reach the floor," says one old-timer, "and jumping lower gives you no time to tap at all—that jump has to be just right." And he might have added that the taps have to be in perfect rhythm.

Tap dancers employ a staggering assortment of steps, body movements, and combinations of both—and sometimes agree on the names for them. Some steps are strictly tap, others may or may not use taps, depending upon the skill and inclination of the dancer, and still others dispense with tap entirely.

During the teens, tap dancing was evolving away from the original concept of the Irish Jig—that is, movement from the waist down only—toward a more flexible style. Specifically, tap was assimilating body movements from vernacular dance, putting them together in new combinations, and inventing steps of its own—including air steps, which employed the upper half of the body, too.

The rhythms could and would become more complex and swinging, but before this took place, tap dancing began to utilize the entire body and open up more possibilities for expressiveness. With this expanding repertory, new categories of steps evolved that any respectable tapper was supposed to be able to execute.

Dancers often distinguish between two classifications: "jazz" and "flash" steps, and combine them into standard routines with special names. "Jazz" steps consist of body movement in which taps are not essential. Originating among the folk, and later in the eccentric dancing of tent-show comedians after the Civil War, these steps surfaced gradually, blending with Clog and tap in minstrelsy and vaudeville. Some of the more easily performed movements, like the Shimmy and Charleston, eventually became "social" dances and were performed in the ballroom. To many of them—including the

Charleston—taps were occasionally added. Many of the steps that tap dancers adopted, however, were too difficult for the ballroom and were called stage steps.

Versions of two jazz steps became a standard part of a tap dancer's repertory: Falling Off a Log, and Off to Buffalo. Off to Buffalo consists of a shuffle, with one foot crossing and re-crossing in front of the other as the dancer edges sideways, usually toward the exit. Falling Off a Log employs a similar and alternate crossing of the feet, plus a leaning pause before the performer moves into his next step. (Joe Frisco, who billed himself inaccurately as "The First Jazz Dancer," used Off to Buffalo as his trademark.)

"Flash" steps consist of acrobatic combinations with expanded leg and body movements. Again, with one exception, taps are not essential. Besides being impressive—and sometimes startling—they serve a definite function. "You have to open and close with something that catches the eye," says Pete Nugent. "With the music *fortissimo*, nobody can hear taps." Flash steps are primarily visual and tap dancers use them to close their acts.

Two flash steps, or more accurately, combinations of body movement, became a standard part of the tap dance repertory in the late teens and early twenties: Over the Top, and Through the Trenches. (Their titles, of course, came from World War I, when they became popular.) Unlike most blended movements from the vernacular, these steps are generally credited by other Negro dancers to Toots Davis, who was performing them as early as 1913 in *The Darktown Follies* at the Lafayette Theater. "They are fundamental," says Charles "Cholly" Atkins, "and when done with real punch can wear you out fast."

Over the Top consists of bending forward, springing up, and bringing each leg, in turn, around from the back and across the front of the other leg—a figure-eight pattern that had previously been performed flat-footed—giving the impression of elaborate and energetic self-tripping. The audience often applauds because the dancer does not fall on his face.

Through the Trenches consists of long backward slides on

the outside edge of the foot, alternating each leg, while the body is bent forward at the waist and the opposite arm flails the air. "It came from the old running step," says James Barton, "held down to one spot." All of these jazz and flash steps can be faked—or executed with consummate skill.

The most important step of all, the Wing, became a standard part of the tap-dancers' repertory at an early date, although it was not fully extended until the thirties. It is based on a paradox. Unlike most tap, it is an air step, and unlike most jazz and flash steps, taps are essential. Actually the Wing is a dynamic compromise, a transitional blend of vernacular body movements and taps, executed mainly in the air.

The Wing, with its combination of taps with an upward spring, holds two opposing impulses in balance, creating a dramatic fusion which can be thrilling. "The Wing has everything," says Cholly Atkins, "jazz, tap, and flash."

Aside from the Pigeon Wing, an early folk step taken over and expanded into a kind of foot-shaking by the minstrel dancers, the word *Wing* was used to describe a combination known as Buck and Wing—the general designation for tap dance (and almost anything else) at the turn of the century. Introduced on the New York stage in 1880 by James McIntyre, the Buck and Wing began to swing—unlike the Clog, which preceded it—and launched a new style of Negro-derived dancing. As it surfaced in those days, the Buck was close to a Time Step and the Wing was a simple hop with one foot flung out to the side.

Dancers began to develop the Wing around 1900. Old-timer Willie Glenn first noticed it in 1902 and did not think much of it. "Now King Rastus Brown, he didn't do any 'winging' or jumping around," he observes. "He stayed on the ground and tapped." Throughout the early teens, the Wing remained more of a tap step than an air step. "They called it Buck and Wing," says Charles "Honi" Coles, "but there was no elevation, no *real* Wing in it."

By the twenties, the three-tap Wing was becoming established: On the way out and up a dancer's foot made one tap or scrape, and on the way down, two more. The number of taps inserted became crucial. Yet some great dancers still ignored Wings. "Bill Robinson wasn't much of a Wing dancer," says Pete Nugent, "but he'd stick one in occasionally." Other dancers, like Frank Condos, however, practiced Wings incessantly.

A variety of Wings began to emerge in the thirties: the Pump (the "winging" foot goes up and down—in the back), the Pendulum (from front to back), the Saw, the Fly, Rolling, Stumbling, the Double Back, and so on. Many dancers worked up their own Wings and the variations in performance became endless. Few dancers, however, considered a five-tap Wing possible, and even fewer attempted it.

"Around 1922 when I was with the *Dan Fitch Minstrels*," says Frank Condos, "an old-time singer asked me if I had ever seen a five-tap Wing and showed me his idea of how it could be done—that put me on the track." Condos was sixteen years old at the time and had already run away from home with his partner, Mateo Olvera. By the mid-1920's they were famous as the team of *King and King*. "Condos and Olvera sounded terrible," says Condos, who was born in Greece and brought to the United States when he was a year old, "so we changed it to *King and King*, which sounded good in Greek, too."

Condos was the spark-plug of the team. His father owned the Standard Restaurant opposite the Standard Theater in Philadelphia, where many Negro acts were booked, and as a freshman in high school, Condos worked in the restaurant after class, carrying meals to the performers, who soon became his idols. His father wanted him to be a lawyer, but young Frank watched the dancers and was fascinated. He saw some of the best. As a teen-ager he studied *Covan and Ruffin*, Eddie Rector, Jack Wiggins, *Buck and Bubbles*, and a team that gave him the idea for an act of his own, *The Three Eddies* (Chick Horsey was the outstanding Wing dancer in this group). "The best dancers," says Condos flatly, "were colored."

With boundless energy and determination, Condos began to practice upstairs in his bedroom while his father worried downstairs in the restaurant. "I went for those three-tap Wings and I said to myself, I'm going to try to do this step even better." One day, while practicing, he jumped too high and hurt his knee. "I told my father I slipped on the ice." Condos learned the hard way. "I practiced all the time, night and day, and I danced very, very hard. It just about wore me out."

By 1925 Condos and Olvera found a job in Chicago. "In those days," says Condos, "all you had to do was work up a soft-shoe routine and top it with a challenge dance—competing with each other—and you were in business. If you were any good, one circuit would hire you away from another and pay you more." *King and King* earned a reputation for sheer speed and energy and were soon referred to as "the fastest legs in the business."

Working everlastingly on the Wing, they began to execute it on the ball of the foot while throwing the foot up and out five or six inches (a mere three-inch "lift" had been considered sensational), and they added a mat of wooden strips, which helped on rough floors and accentuated the taps. In time they worked up their five-tap Wing, in which one foot scraped out and up and—in the process of coming back down—made four additional and distinct taps. "There wasn't many teams copying Mattie and me," says Condos, "because we did those Wings faster than anybody else. We had shoes with steel plates, and you could always hear our taps."

Timing is the crucial problem in any Wing, and with the five-tap Wing, timing the spring upward is excruciatingly difficult. "The hardest part after you've jumped up—with a tap—is getting those four taps on the way down," says Condos, "and *then going up into another Wing right away.*" The upper part of the body must be elevated before the feet begin to move or the result is a flat Wing, and the split second it takes to fling out a foot with one tap and bring it back with four more must be calculated precisely. "Those five taps come so fast—ta-ta-ta-ta-ta—it sounds like a machine gun," says Condos.

Condos's admiration for other dancers is unbounded, and his estimate of his own abilities, modest. Nor is he under any illusions about the act's limitations: "We got pooped out. Other guys would be fresh after sixteen bars. We were exhausted trying to give our act more flash." Condos is convinced that if they could have talked like Bill Robinson or sung like John Bubbles, they would have been a much bigger hit and lasted far longer. On the other hand Negro dancers are unanimous in their praise of Condos. "He had legs of iron," says Pete Nugent. "I've seen him do the impossible—a five-tap Wing without a mat *from a low crouch.*"

At first *King and King* wore black trousers and white shirts with long puffed sleeves in the early Eddie Rector style, but they soon switched to business suits, which made them look more prepossessing. Their usual act consisted of a soft-shoe to "Tea for Two," a clog to "Three O'Clock in the Morning," and their specialty—a challenge dance—to a fast-tempo "June Night." "We nearly killed ourselves trying to out-dance each other," says Condos, "and at the end of the act, my heart would be pounding like a trip-hammer."

When *Artists and Models* opened at the Winter Garden on November 15, 1927, *King and King* were the featured dancers. "We did mostly Wings," says Condos. The New York critics seemed to have no comprehension of the kind of dancing they were witnessing. Gilbert Gabriel in the *American* called them "soft-shoers," Robert Coleman in the *Mirror* described them as "buck and winging," and Burns Mantle in the *News* made an extra effort, calling them "tap dancers, or step dancers, or high-schooled ankle-twisters of some particular classification"—and then gave up. *Variety* reached a new high in poverty-stricken jargon by labeling them "tap steppers."

At least all the critics agreed that *King and King* were great. Referring to them inaccurately in the *Times* as "clog dancers," Alexander Woollcott documented the nature and extent of their impact on the audience: "Then a team named King and King (one of whom looks like a Chinese Sam Harris and each of whom shakes a mean foot) danced such clogs . . . as brought down the Winter Garden and spilled so much applause into the next scene that a prima donna, all squared off to sing some fearful ballad, was in no end of a pet." Dancers themselves simply refer to *King and King* as "the greatest of all Wing teams."

As the years passed, the act inevitably slowed down. "In the early days the audience loved it when you repeated a hard step three times in eight bars, and they would applaud as we piled on the Wings," says Condos, "but later dancers began to consider it corny—no matter how difficult the step was—so we changed to three or four difficult steps every eight bars, and that made it tough for us to show off our specialty."

In 1929 Condos and Olvera split up their act. Olvera started a trio with his brothers, billed as *King, King, and King* (who got rave reviews in *Broadway Nights* the same year and were lampooned hilariously by Ray Bolger shortly thereafter), while Frank Condos added his younger brother Nick and changed the billing to *The Condos Brothers*. "We took out some of the hard dancing which was wearing us down," says Frank, "and used just one tough step at the end of each chorus." Young Nick soon learned to do a five-tap Wing on either foot, too.

The Condos Brothers danced in *Earl Carroll's Vanities* in 1932. "At the audition for Earl Carroll," says Condos, "we did our soft-shoe number, and he started to walk out when our agent said 'Wait, they have another number,' and we hurried into our Wings. Carroll yelled with surprise and said, 'Why didn't you show me this right away?' " In the *Vanities* their act consisted mostly of Wings with a mixture of other flash steps.

Later in 1932 they toured Europe, where they met with mixed reactions: The English loved them and the French seemed puzzled. "We were booked into the London Palladium for two weeks and stayed two years," says Frank, "and then we went to Paris and it was weird—they liked eccentric and body movements, but they just didn't understand tap at all." *The Condos Brothers* stopped doing the Wings with complicated taps, at which they were unequalled, and substituted simpler flash steps.

For about eight years Frank and Nick danced as *The Condos Brothers*. Then the youngest brother, Steve, took Frank's place. Frank worked for a while as a single, appearing twice at the Music Hall in Radio City before retiring in 1937 to become a dance director. Since 1952 he has worked as a welder in a shipyard.

King and King employed the standard steps—both jazz and flash—in the tap repertory, building up routines with various combinations. "Sure, we did Falling Off a Log, and Off to Buffalo," says Condos, "but we worked them in early. Towards the end of the act we used Through the Trenches and sometimes combined Over the Top with Wings—a Wing on the right foot, left foot in back, and then Over the Top—but Wings were our specialty."

Speaking of routines, Sammy Dyer, who choreographed floor shows at the Club DeLisa on Chicago's South Side during the forties, observes: "In my experience four steps are basic: Falling Off a Log, Off to Buffalo, Over the Top, and Through the Trenches—you can put together anything you need from combinations of these four steps." Dyer is thinking of routines he created for his well-drilled group of chorus girls, known as *The Dyerettes*, and has assembled the lowest non-tap denominator.

Chorus girls could not always be expected to execute flash steps with great skill. They had their standard routine called The B. S. Chorus (some chorines thought it stood for "Boy Scout"), which combined the clichés of tap and non-tap and could be performed as a background for any soloist—with varying vigor. The B. S. Chorus is called a "chorus" because it lasts for the duration of a standard thirty-two-bar tune such as "Tea for Two." It is a "routine" because the thirty-two bars are divided into four parts of eight bars apiece, with each part devoted to a different step.

Thus the B. S. Chorus consists of eight bars of the Time Step, eight bars of the Cross Step (a step to the side with one leg crossing the other), eight bars of the Buck and Wing (employing the simplest of hops with little or no tapping), and four bars each of Over the Top and Through the Trenches, reduced to an easy pantomine. With a little luck and competent chorus girls, this often coincides—as it should—with the end of one thirty-two-bar chorus of the tune.

The average chorus line, with such notable exceptions as *The Dyerettes* and the Cotton Club girls, offered a pretty limp version of the real thing. Each of these steps (except Through the Trenches) can be performed with taps, and the performer who puts in taps quite justifiably feels superior, since he or she is executing a far more complicated maneuver. The acid test, therefore, is the number and quality of inserted taps, since like any other dance step, the B. S. Chorus can be a thing of beauty or a mess.

Not that there were no fine women tap dancers. If they were good, however, they usually performed alone, as soloists. Before 1920 and for at least fifteen years, Alice Whitman was tops. "She had clean, clear taps, something like Bill Robinson's," says Pete Nugent. Dancer Rufus Greenlee thinks that Etta Gross, one of the early women tap dancers, was as good as Alice Whitman.

As a youngster, Mae Barnes, who did the Charleston in the second road company of *Shuffle Along*, was an excellent tap dancer before she turned to singing. "In those early days," she insists, "a few of us chorus girls knew more flashy steps than the dance directors or choreographers."

Other women tap dancers—among many—were greatly admired: old-timers Katie Carter and Muriel Ringold; Lavinia Mack featured in *Runnin' Wild*; Cora LaRedd who danced in Cotton Club shows; Maud Mills, the sister of Florence Mills, nicknamed "Hardfoot Maud" because she hit the deck with such force; and later, Louise Madison of Philadelphia, who could cut a five-tap Wing like a man. On Broadway and especially in Hollywood, a series of white tap dancers had the chance to attain far greater fame: Ruby Keeler, Eleanore Whitney, Dixie Dunbar, Ann Miller, and Eleanor Powell—perhaps the best.

A second slightly more complicated combination of tap and body movements, known as the Shim Sham, became a standard routine in show business around 1931. (A third, called the Dip, is not as well known). The Shim Sham's origin is disputed: Both Willie Bryant and Leonard Reed, who were working together at the time, say that they had a comedy dance, "an old-man shuffle to a fast 'Goofus' rhythm," which they presented at the Lafayette Theater. An act named *The Three Little Words* saw it, slowed it down, and presented it at Connie's Inn as the Shim Sham. "We worked it out," says Leonard Reed, "and they got credit for introducing it."

On the other hand, flash-dancer Joe Jones, one of *The Three Little Words*, says he helped invent the routine during a rehearsal: "I had been practicing something like a Time Step and we just changed it a little." Actually, there is every reason to believe that Bryant, Reed, *The Three Little Words*—and other dancers—all helped to create this routine, since it contains elements of various older steps.

In any event it became popular in 1931 when *The Three Little Words* were dancing at Connie's Inn in Harlem. "We'd close the show at Connie's doing the Shim Sham and inviting everybody to get aboard," says Joe Jones, "and the whole club would join us, including the waiters. For awhile people were doing the Shim Sham up and down Seventh Avenue all night long."

The Shim Sham consists of one-chorus routine to a thirty-two-bar tune, with eight bars each of the Double Shuffle, the Cross Over, the Tack Annie (an up-and-back shuffle), and Falling Off a Log. Conceived as a tap routine, the Shim Sham became so popular that it evolved into a quasi-ballroom dance without taps—the movements can easily be faked—and survives to this day in the finale of television and other shows when the cast lines up to wave goodbye. Even Milton Berle, for example, can do a dilapidated version of it, but a good dancer prides himself on putting the taps back into it.

In 1933 Willie Bryant took over Lucky Millinder's old band

at a salary of $45 a week—the sidemen got less—and opened at the Lafayette Theater. Teddy Wilson, Benny Carter, Ben Webster, and Cozy Cole were in the band. "I taught all the musicians to do the Shim Sham," says Bryant, "and it was a big hit. It was the first time a band brought musicians off the stand to do a dance routine." Shortly thereafter Jimmie Lunceford's band staged a similar show.

Today, Wings, along with many lesser steps and the routines that evolved from them, are a lost art. "Some dance instructor worked out directions for doing my five-tap Wing," says Frank Condos wonderingly, "but I never heard of anyone learning it that way." Condos established no new tradition—a dancer might equal but he could go no further along those lines—while the demand for such dancing was swallowed up by the fast-growing popularity and prestige of ballet and modern dance. "Taps today certainly aren't what they used to be," says Condos. "Now they have what I call move-around dancing, with lots of ballet and no punch."

Gene Kelly is more specific: "Dancing is a man's business, altogether," he said in an interview, "but women have taken it over."

—1968

INDEX